SENSOR NETWORKS
FOR SMART HOSPITALS

SENSOR NETWORKS FOR SMART HOSPITALS

Edited by

TUAN ANH NGUYEN

Institute for Tropical Technology, Vietnam Academy of Science and Technology, Hanoi, Vietnam

ELSEVIER

Elsevier
Radarweg 29, PO Box 211, 1000 AE Amsterdam, Netherlands
125 London Wall, London EC2Y 5AS, United Kingdom
50 Hampshire Street, 5th Floor, Cambridge, MA 02139, United States

ISBN: 978-0-443-36370-2

For Information on all Elsevier publications
visit our website at https://www.elsevier.com/books-and-journals

Publisher: Mara Conner
Acquisitions Editor: Craig Smith
Editorial Project Manager: Ashi Jain
Production Project Manager: Prem Kumar Kaliamoorthi
Cover Designer: Vicky Pearson Esser

Typeset by MPS Limited, Chennai, India

Contents

6. Medical sensor network, blockchain and digital twin as the backbones of a connected ecosystem of smart hospitals

Xavier Fernando and George Lăzăroiu

7. Digital twins and medical sensor network to analyze start-up delay in smart infusion pump

J.V. Alamelu and Mythili Asaithambi

8. Healthcare data management using blockchain-enabled sensor networks

Ammar Odeh

9. Sensor networks and blockchain platforms for the future healthcare

Quazi Mamun

10. Digital twin and sensor networks for healthcare monitoring frameworks

Amirhossein Danesh, Shaker El-Sappagh and Tamer Abuhmed

11. Wireless body area network for e-health application

Kamal Das and Soumen Moulik

12. Anonymity preserving security protocol for wireless body area networks: towards the secure remote patient healthcare monitoring

Vincent Omollo Nyangaresi

13. Wireless sensor networks for smart healthcare

Venkata Krishna Reddy M, Premkumar Chithaluru, Manoj Kumar and Pallati Narsimhulu

14. Wireless body area networks for healthcare in smart hospital

Daniel Godfrey and Ki-Il Kim

15. Internet of medical things for accurate and sustainable medical decision making in heart disease management

Philippe Ea, Osman Salem and Ahmed Mehaoua

16. Blockchain and smart contracts for wearable health sensing

Jose Cedeño (Ricardo), Carlos Sánchez-Torres (Eduardo) and Jesus Favela

17. Blockchain technology for health insurance

Anupam Tiwari

18. Blockchain for security and privacy in the smart healthcare

Hamed Taherdoost

19. Sensors and security considerations for emergency vehicles

Mohan Vandabona, Vithushan Gnanaraj, Malindu Attygala, Danish Kumar and Alireza Jolfaei

20. Swarm intelligence for Cancer Care 4.0/5.0

R. Gunasundari and Rose Mary Mathew

21. Exploring human-based digital twins in healthcare: a scoping review

Nilmini Wickramasinghe and Nalika Ulapane

22. Cloud security for smart sensor network

Satyavathi Divadari

23. Applications of fog computing for smart sensor network

Mostafa Haghi Kashani and Sepideh Bazzaz Abkenar

24. Quantum computing for smart healthcare

Padmapriya Velupillai Meikandan, Paramita Basak Upama, Masud Rabbani, Md Martuza Ahamad and Sheikh Iqbal Ahamed

25. Knowledge graph-based reasoning in medical healthcare scenarios for IoT applications

Jialong Liu, Zhiwu Liang, Chong Mu, Lizong Zhang and Anthony S. Atkins

26. MedSync: blockchain-driven electronic health record on cloud

C.M. Nalayini, Shruthi Arunkumar and K.S. Jaishree

List of contributors

Sepideh Bazzaz Abkenar Department of Computer Engineering, Science and Research Branch, Islamic Azad University, Tehran, Iran

Tamer Abuhmed College of Computing and Informatics, Sungkyunkwan University, Suwon, South Korea

Md Martuza Ahamad Ubicomp Lab, Department of Computer Science, Marquette University, Milwaukee, Wisconsin, United States

Sheikh Iqbal Ahamed Ubicomp Lab, Department of Computer Science, Marquette University, Milwaukee, Wisconsin, United States

J.V. Alamelu M S Ramaiah Institute of Technology, Bangalore, Karnataka, India

Pedram Amiri Andi Faculty of Dentistry, Tehran Medical Sciences, Islamic Azad University, Tehran, Iran

Pendar Argani Faculty of Dentistry, Tehran Medical Sciences, Islamic Azad University, Tehran, Iran

Shruthi Arunkumar Department of Information Technology, Velammal Engineering College, Surapet, Chennai, Tamil Nadu, India

Mythili Asaithambi School of Electronics Engineering, Vellore Institute of Technology, Vellore, Tamil Nadu, India

Anthony S. Atkins School of Digital, Technology, Innovation and Business (DTIB), Staffordshire University, Stoke on Trent, Staffordshire, United Kingdom

Malindu Attygala College of Science and Engineering, Flinders University, Tonsley, SA, Australia

John Batani Faculty of Engineering and Technology, Botho University, Maseru, Lesotho

Juan V. Capella Institute of Information and Communication Technologies (ITACA), Polytechnic University of Valencia, Valencia, Spain

Jose Cedeño (Ricardo) Department of Computer Science, Center for Scientific Research and Higher Education of Ensenada, Baja California, Mexico

Premkumar Chithaluru Department of Computer Science and Engineering, Chaitanya Bharathi Institute of Technology (Autonomous), Hyderabad, Telangana, India; Department of Information Technology, Mahatma Gandhi Institute of Technology, Hyderabad, Telangana, India

Amirhossein Danesh College of Computing and Informatics, Sungkyunkwan University, Suwon, South Korea

Kamal Das SRM University-AP, Mangalagiri, Andhra Pradesh, India

Satyavathi Divadari People's Education Society University, Bangalore, Karnataka, India

Philippe Ea Center Borelli UMR 9010, Université Paris Cité, Paris, France

Shaker El-Sappagh College of Computing and Informatics, Sungkyunkwan University, Suwon, South Korea; Faculty of Computer Science and Engineering, Galala University, Suez, Egypt

Jesus Favela Department of Computer Science, Center for Scientific Research and Higher Education of Ensenada, Baja California, Mexico

Xavier Fernando Toronto Metropolitan University, Toronto, ON, Canada

Alireza Ghodsi Faculty of Dentistry, Tehran Medical Sciences, Islamic Azad University, Tehran, Iran

Vithushan Gnanaraj College of Science and Engineering, Flinders University, Tonsley, SA, Australia

Daniel Godfrey Department of Computer Science and Engineering, Chungnam National University, Daejeon, Republic of Korea

R. Gunasundari Department of Computer Applications, Karpagam Academy of Higher Education, Coimbatore, Tamil Nadu, India

Mostafa Haghi Kashani Department of Computer Engineering, Shahr-e-Qods Branch, Islamic Azad University, Tehran, Iran

Hossein Hassani Research Institute of Energy Management and Planning (RIEMP), University of Tehran, Tehran, Iran

K.S. Jaishree Department of Information Technology, Velammal Engineering College, Surapet, Chennai, Tamil Nadu, India

Alireza Jolfaei College of Science and Engineering, Flinders University, Tonsley, SA, Australia

Ki-Il Kim Department of Computer Science and Engineering, Chungnam National University, Daejeon, Republic of Korea

Murat Koca Faculty of Engineering, Department of Computer Engineering, Van Yuzuncu Yil University, Kampus, Tusba, Van, Turkey

Danish Kumar College of Science and Engineering, Flinders University, Tonsley, SA, Australia

Manoj Kumar School of Computer Science, FEIS, University of Wollongong in Dubai, Dubai, United Arab Emirates; MEU Research Unit, Middle East University, Amman, Jordan

Bao Le School of Computer Science, Duy Tan University, Da Nang, Vietnam

Chung Van Le School of Computer Science, Duy Tan University, Da Nang, Vietnam

Zhiwu Liang Shenzhen Institute for Advanced Study, University of Electronic Science and Technology of China, Shenzhen, Guangdong, P.R. China

Jialong Liu Shenzhen Institute for Advanced Study, University of Electronic Science and Technology of China, Shenzhen, Guangdong, P.R. China

George Lăzăroiu Toronto Metropolitan University, Toronto, ON, Canada; Curtin University, Perth, WA, Australia; Cardiff Metropolitan University, Cardiff, United Kingdom; Spiru Haret University, Bucharest, Romania

Steve MacFeely World Health Organization (WHO), Geneva, Switzerland

Quazi Mamun School of Computing, Mathematics and Engineering, Faculty of Business, Justice and Behavioural Sciences Charles Sturt University, NSW, Australia

Rose Mary Mathew Department of Computer Applications, Federal Institute of Science and Technology, Ernakulam, Kerala, India

Elliot Mbunge Department of Computer Science, Faculty of Science and Engineering, University of Eswatini (Formerly Swaziland), Manzini, Eswatini

Ahmed Mehaoua Center Borelli UMR 9010, Université Paris Cité, Paris, France

Padmapriya Velupillai Meikandan Ubicomp Lab, Department of Computer Science, Marquette University, Milwaukee, Wisconsin, United States

Soumen Moulik NIT Meghalaya, Bijni Complex, Shillong, Meghalaya, India

Chong Mu School of Information and Software Engineering, University of Electronic Science and Technology of China, Chengdu, Sichuan, P.R. China

C.M. Nalayini Department of Information Technology, Velammal Engineering College, Surapet, Chennai, Tamil Nadu, India

Pallati Narsimhulu Department of Computer Engineering and Technology, Chaitanya Bharathi Institute of Technology, Hyderabad, Telangana, India

Ihab Nassra Institute of Information and Communication Technologies (ITACA), Polytechnic University of Valencia, Valencia, Spain

Anand Nayyar School of Computer Science, Duy Tan University, Da Nang, Vietnam

Nhu Gia Nguyen School of Computer Science, Duy Tan University, Da Nang, Vietnam

Kimia Norouzi Faculty of Dentistry, Tehran Medical Sciences, Islamic Azad University, Tehran, Iran

Vincent Omollo Nyangaresi Department of Computer Science & Software Engineering, Jaramogi Oginga Odinga University of Science and Technology, Bondo, Kenya; Department of Applied Electronics, Saveetha School of Engineering, SIMATS Deemed University, Chennai, Tamil Nadu, India

Ammar Odeh Department of Computer Science, King Hussein School of Computing Sciences, Princess Sumaya University for Technology, Amman, Jordan

Anna Paleczek Biomarkers Analysis LAB, Institute of Electronics, AGH University of Science and Technology, Krakow, Poland

Vikram Puri School of Computer Science, Duy Tan University, Da Nang, Vietnam

Masud Rabbani Ubicomp Lab, Department of Computer Science, Marquette University, Milwaukee, Wisconsin, United States

Venkata Krishna Reddy M Department of Computer Science and Engineering, Chaitanya Bharathi Institute of Technology (Autonomous), Hyderabad, Telangana, India

Artur Rydosz Biomarkers Analysis LAB, Institute of Electronics, AGH University of Science and Technology, Krakow, Poland; Advanced Diagnostic Equipment Sp z o.o., Krakow, Poland

Osman Salem Center Borelli UMR 9010, Université Paris Cité, Paris, France

Carlos Sánchez-Torres (Eduardo) Department of Computer Science, Center for Scientific Research and Higher Education of Ensenada, Baja California, Mexico

Bhupinder Singh Sharda School of Law, Sharda University, Greater Noida, India

Hamed Taherdoost Department of Arts, Communications and Social Sciences, University Canada West, Vancouver, BC, Canada; Research and Development Department, Hamta Business Corporation, Vancouver, BC, Canada; Q Minded|Quark Minded Technology Inc., Vancouver, BC, Canada; GUS Institute, Global University Systems, London, United Kingdom

Anupam Tiwari Institution of Electronics and Telecommunication Engineers, New Delhi, India

Nalika Ulapane La Trobe University, Bundoora, VIC, Australia

Paramita Basak Upama Ubicomp Lab, Department of Computer Science, Marquette University, Milwaukee, Wisconsin, United States

Mohan Vandabona College of Science and Engineering, Flinders University, Tonsley, SA, Australia

Nilmini Wickramasinghe La Trobe University, Bundoora, VIC, Australia

Lizong Zhang School of Computer Science and Engineering, University of Electronic Science and Technology of China, Chengdu, Sichuan, P.R. China

About the editor

Tuan Anh Nguyen is a Senior Principal Research Scientist at the Institute for Tropical Technology, Vietnam Academy of Science and Technology, Hanoi, Vietnam. He received a BS in physics from Hanoi University in 1992, a BS in economics from Hanoi National Economics University in 1997, and a PhD in chemistry from the Paris Diderot University, France, in 2003. He was a Visiting Scientist at Seoul National University, South Korea, in 2004, and the University of Wollongong, Australia, in 2005. He then worked as a Postdoctoral Research Associate and Research Scientist at Montana State University, USA, during 2006–09. In 2012 he was appointed as the Head of the Microanalysis Department at the Institute for Tropical Technology. His research areas of interest include smart sensors, smart networks, smart hospitals, smart cities, and advanced nanomaterials. He has edited more than 69 books for Elsevier publications, 12 books for CRC Press, and 1 book for Springer. He is the Editor-in-Chief of *Kenkyu Journal of Nanotechnology & Nanoscience*.

Foreword

The book addresses the important and current topic of smart sensors, which offer advantages over traditional sensing elements because they include an embedded digital motion processor, are self-powered, present lower power consumption, high sensitivity, a lower concentration of analytes, and a smaller interaction distance between the object and sensor. Nanosensors also possess several important features, including high sensitivity, stability, robust response, portability, real-time detection, and selectivity. With respect to biomedical applications, smart biosensors present the potential to be integrated with self-powered bioimplantable systems, bioimplantable medical devices, wearable sensors for biomedical applications, sensor bioelectronics, and micro- and nanoelectromechanical systems.

Nanotechnology, which enables the development of devices at scales ranging from one to a few hundred nanometers, is a multidisciplinary area with the prospect of making people's lives simpler and safer while mitigating the impact of the technology on the environment. The interconnectivity of nano-networks and current communication networks demands the development of new network architectures and new communication paradigms to address the posed technical challenges. This book surveys the state of the art in nanosensor technology and networks as applied to the important field of smart hospitals.

Considering the support of artificial intelligence (AI), blockchain and digital twin technologies, sensor systems are becoming smarter and more secure, allowing, for example, the possibility of multiple digital patient check-ins. For smart healthcare applications, the combinations of intelligent wireless medical sensor networks, smart device implants, blockchain technology, and digital twins can provide information not only to monitor and manage patient clinical data in smart hospitals but also to improve connectivity and secure data sharing to deliver better patient experiences, using AI and streamline workflows, in addition to reducing costs.

Therefore this book explores how intelligent sensors and their networks can be used in smart hospitals and the challenges that are posed to the introduction of recent and innovative technologies.

30 chapters of this book cover a wide range of topics, including the wireless sensor networks, wireless body area network, medical sensor network, internet of medical things, blockchain technology, digital twins, fog/cloud/quantum computing, artificial intelligence, health data security and privacy. This book serves as a valuable reference for students, academic researchers, and professional engineers/scientists working in the field of computer science, electrical and computer engineering, electronics, sensors networks, healthcare... I commend it to you.

Marcelo Sampaio de Alencar
*Department of Electrical Engineering,
Federal University of Campina Grande (UFCG),
Campina Grande, Paraíba, Brazil;
Department of Communications Engineering,
Federal University of Rio Grande do Norte,
Natal, Rio Grande do Norte, Brazil*

From digital to smart hospitals: past, present and the future

Elliot Mbunge[1] and John Batani[2]

[1]Department of Computer Science, Faculty of Science and Engineering, University of Eswatini (Formerly Swaziland), Manzini, Eswatini [2]Faculty of Engineering and Technology, Botho University, Maseru, Lesotho

1.1 Introduction

Advanced digital innovations continuously bring digital transformation in healthcare systems globally, especially in the provision of healthcare services. Digital innovations that incorporate advanced technologies including artificial intelligence (AI), the Internet of Things (IoT) (Zhang et al., 2018), fifth generation (5G)/6G technology (Kumar et al., 2020), deep learning, the Internet of Medical Things, intelligent sensor networks (Rodrigues et al., 2019), machine learning, natural language processing and smart health applications present unprecedented opportunities to move towards smart hospitals. Such innovations inevitably support the development and deployment of predictive, preventive, modeling, participatory, diagnostic, and personalized intelligent tools to improve access to care remotely and most importantly, optimize healthcare management systems and support data-driven decision-making.

The concept of "smart hospital" is an emerging research area that involves the digitization of healthcare systems by utilizing intelligent digital health innovations and advanced technologies (Uslu et al., 2020) to connect smart digital devices and smart applications to collect, process and analyze health data. Health data captured through smart medical digital devices can be utilized to facilitate remote patient monitoring (Hassan et al., 2019), diagnosis of patients, making follow-ups and also predicting the health status of patients. Smart hospitals have the potential to support smart health and P4-medicine (preventive, participatory, predictive, and personalized) (Holzinger et al., 2015) and to effectively utilize hospital resources through connected intelligent digital health innovations (Zhang et al., 2018). This can further support prediction, early patient screening, diagnosis, disease

Sensor Networks for Smart Hospitals
DOI: https://doi.org/10.1016/B978-0-443-36370-2.00002-5

detection, surveillance, and monitoring of patients with chronic conditions. Policymakers, health workers and patients can tremendously benefit from smart hospitals by digitalizing their hospital operations which can subsequently reduce human errors, streamline workflows, and improve quality of care as well as the overall healthcare outcomes.

Despite the tremendous opportunities posed by the concept of smart hospitals, there is a dearth of literature on smart hospitals. Therefore, this chapter seeks to address this gap by explaining the concept of smart hospitals; digital technologies for enabling smart hospitals; barriers influencing the adoption of smart hospitals and finally, presents recommendations for effective adoption of smart hospitals.

1.2 Concept of smart hospital

The concept of smart hospitals emanated from the concept of digital hospitals. The idea of digital hospitals was crafted in the early 2000s, to capture, store and process health data using health information systems (Rajaei et al., 2024). The idea was to transfer patient files to electronic health records or move from paper-based systems (Serbanati, 2020). The increased demands to reduce cost while improving health outcomes and effective healthcare service delivery consequently led to the replacement of the "digital" with "smart" (Rasoulian-Kasrineh et al., 2021). The idea of developing smart hospitals was then introduced to create and optimize operational processes along with designing and using novel technologies and equipment. Smart hospital is an emerging concept which has not been precisely defined (Rajaei et al., 2024) and no policies or guidelines have been crafted yet to guide the implementation and rolling out of smart hospitals (Kwon et al., 2022). However, studies by Rajaei et al. (2024), Holzinger et al. (2015), and Sánchez et al. (2008) considered smart hospital as a highly interactive environment that is saturated with heterogeneous computing devices that use big data and context-aware computing. Also, Hu et al. (2022) highlighted that smart hospitals involve the use of optimized and automated processes built in an interactive environment that uses advanced technologies.

Several studies have been focusing on the smart building aspects of the hospital, including distributed sensors and networks to enable the automation of processes, be it professional workflows or patient position monitoring and transferring inside the establishment. Thus, a smart hospital can be defined as a healthcare facility that utilizes advanced technologies and innovative solutions to enhance patient care (Kaldoudi, 2024), improve operational efficiency, and optimize resource management. Smart hospitals leverage cutting-edge technologies such as AI, 5G technology (Kumar et al., 2020), data analytics, blockchain, IoT (Leng et al., 2020), machine learning, wearable technologies, telehealth and telemedicine to optimize, automate healthcare processes (Jian et al., 2022) and most importantly create a connected and intelligent healthcare environment.

1.3 Literature overview

The study applied the preferred reporting items for systematic reviews and meta-analysis (PRISMA) model to guide extensive literature searches and extraction of relevant papers. The authors conducted a comprehensive search for relevant articles by utilizing various electronic databases. These databases include CINAHL with full-text, Embase, IEEE, Springer, Taylor and Francis, Scopus, PubMed, MEDLINE and ScienceDirect. The search was guided by the following search terms: (TITLE-ABS-KEY ("smart hospitals") OR TITLE-ABS-KEY ("digital hospitals") OR TITLE-ABS-KEY ("intelligent hospitals"). Authors screened retrieved papers and selected papers written in English or with English translation, peer-reviewed papers and papers with smart hospital information. A total of 363 documents were retrieved and selected for this study. Among the selected documents, the majority (44.4%) were journal articles followed by conference proceedings (38%), and book chapters (7.2%) as shown in Fig. 1.1.

The concept of smart hospitals is still evolving with a dearth of literature, and its implementation can vary in different countries as well as in health settings based on healthcare needs and available resources. However, the existing literature shows that India, the United States of America, China, South Korea and Canada are among the topmost countries with more literature on smart hospitals as shown in Fig. 1.2.

1.4 Advanced technologies for smart hospitals

The study further analyzed the selected papers to understand the technologies that can be implemented in smart hospitals, their respective functions, and the adoption barriers. The subsequent sections present these findings.

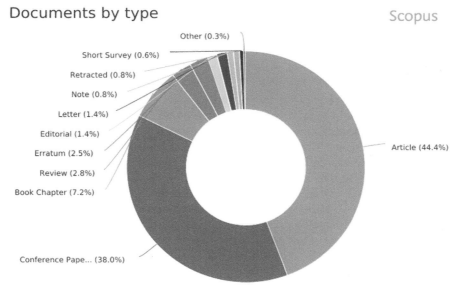

FIGURE 1.1   Retrieved documents type.

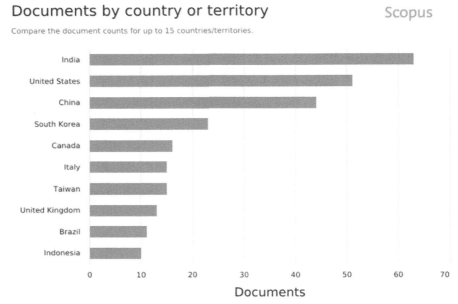

Documents by country or territory   Scopus
Compare the document counts for up to 15 countries/territories.

FIGURE 1.2   Topmost countries.

1.4.1 Smart hospitals enabling digital technologies

IoT and sensors, AI, telehealth and telemedicine, wearable technologies, electronic tags, mobile healthcare and applications, robotics, Blockchain, cloud computing, radio frequency identification (RFID) technology, deep learning and machine learning are among the enabling technologies facilitating smart hospitals as shown in Fig. 1.3. The functions of these technologies are explained in the following subsections.

1.4.1.1 Internet of Things and sensors

The IoT and sensors have gained increasing usage in healthcare, connecting medical devices and sharing patient data over the Internet (Mbunge, Muchemwa, *et al.*, 2021). Through IoT, smart hospitals tend to benefit in the form of real-time, ubiquitous and remote patient monitoring (Batani, 2022) by using sensors and wearable devices. Moreover, IoT and sensors facilitate real-time in-patient monitoring through their integration with related technologies like the cognitive internet of medical things (Istepanian et al., 2011), wearable IoT (Singh et al., 2020), Internet of Nano things (Istepanian et al., 2011; Mbunge, Muchemwa, et al., 2021), and AI (Mohanta et al., 2019). Internet of Nano Things (IoT) is the interconnection of nanoscale devices to communication networks to conduct tasks like sensing, actuation, and transmission through electromagnetic radiations (Mbunge, Muchemwa, et al., 2021; Pramanik et al., 2020). Thus, IoT and sensors, as well as their various variations, enable smart hospitals by supporting the integration of smart medical devices, data collection and sharing of patient data to provide personalized healthcare through context-aware and data-driven smart health systems. IoT and sensors

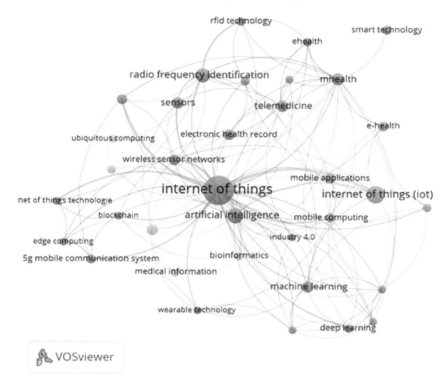

FIGURE 1.3   Smart hospitals enabling digital technologies.

facilitate remote and continuous monitoring of patients by collecting important patient data, such as body temperature, oxygen saturation and heart rate, which would be used to make smart healthcare decisions and provide patient-specific treatment, treatment adherence monitoring, effective diagnosis, smart rehabilitation and early and accurate diagnoses (Aceto et al., 2020; Mbunge, Muchemwa, et al., 2021). It is noteworthy that IoT works with other technologies, such as AI and big data analytics, to provide useful analysis and interpretation of collected data.

1.4.1.2 Artificial intelligence

AI is a multidisciplinary field that focuses on making machines smart, such that they can do tasks that are normally considered as requiring intelligence to perform them, such as image recognition, natural language processing and pattern identification. There are various sub-fields of AI, such as machine learning, deep learning, computer vision and natural language processing. AI's usefulness to healthcare professionals appreciates its role in enhancing their efficiency and optimizing patient care plans (Kamruzzaman, 2020). Combined with other technologies, such as IoT and robotics, AI can provide automation in a smart hospital (Mbunge, Muchemwa, et al., 2021), through sensor-based AI-embedded devices (Mohanta et al., 2019). Powerful AI algorithms help analyze huge data collected by sensors and IoT to facilitate data-driven patient care (Tian et al., 2019). Research has shown that AI outperforms human doctors in diagnosing certain diseases and conditions, such as cancer, and interpreting imaging data (Dhar & Ranganathan, 2015; Polat & Güneş, 2008). In a smart hospital, AI can play a critical role in various tasks, such as accurate and automated disease diagnosis, detection and prediction, smart medicinal drug development and discovery, emotive sensor-based AI smart devices' development (Mbunge et al., 2022), and development of context-aware patient care systems.

1.4.1.3 Robotics

Robotics play a huge enabling role in smart hospitals as they facilitate automation of various tasks, minimizing the need for human intervention and involvement, thus, facilitating the transformation of digital hospitals into smart hospitals. Integrating robots in smart hospitals transforms hospitals into contemporary entities that enhance patient care. For instance, robots and drones can be used to deliver medical supplies to in-patients, especially to those suffering from highly infectious diseases, as minimizing physical contact would reduce healthcare professionals' exposure to such infections (Zeng et al., 2020). Moreover, autonomous robots can perform repetitive tasks (Firouzi et al., 2021), allowing healthcare professionals to concentrate on other duties. Robotics technology, through such robots as telerobots, collaborative (Tavakoli, 2020), autonomous (Seidita et al., 2021), social and wearable robots (Khan et al., 2021), can substantially enhance healthcare service delivery in a smart hospital setup by carrying out surgical operations, developing vaccines and detecting and diagnosing diseases (Mbunge, Muchemwa, et al., 2021). However, the existing robots in healthcare lack emotive recognition, calling for significant enhancements if robotics technology is to deliver personalized and pervasive patient care in smart hospitals (Mbunge, Muchemwa, et al., 2021).

1.4.1.4 Blockchain

Security and privacy of patient data are critical to the success of any digital health interventions (Batani & Maharaj, 2023). With lots of data generated and collected in a smart hospital environment, there is a need to ensure the data are secured and patient privacy is upheld. Blockchain, a technology with soaring popularity in the financial industry, provides secure data storage and transmission in a manner that ensures nonrepudiation and immutability (Agbo et al., 2019; Ahir et al., 2020). Blockchain is an append-only data structure that allows for the storage of an ever-growing list of transactions (Mbunge, Muchemwa, et al., 2021) in what are called blocks (Ahir et al., 2020). Replication of data across several entities in blockchain ensures nonrepudiation, while immutability is achievable through the impossibility of computationally modifying and manipulating executed transactions. Thus, in a smart hospital setup, adopting blockchain would ensure effective and secure transmission and storage of health information and patient data. Blockchain has already been implemented in digital health environments to facilitate secure patient data storage and transmission by enhancing digital access rules (Gordon & Catalini, 2018), and securing patient identity and privacy, among others. Implementing blockchain in a smart hospital could foster scalability and patient-driven semantic interoperability by establishing robust application programming interface connections spanning several electronic and smart health technologies (Mbunge, Muchemwa, et al., 2021).

1.4.1.5 Cloud computing

As more and more data are collected through IoT and sensors in a smart hospital environment, there is a need to efficiently utilize the available computer hardware resources and allow access to analytics even though less computationally powerful gadgets. Cloud computing is a model that allows computer system resources to be delivered over the Internet and remote servers (Singh et al., 2021) in a pay-as-you-go mode. Due to hardware virtualization, cloud computing helps store, process, manage and analyze patients' data at low data storage costs but increases efficiency, providing faster and more flexible data access methods (Mbunge, Muchemwa, et al., 2021). By pooling computer resources together, cloud computing enables the creation of powerful virtual machines that can run computationally intensive AI models to provide smart care.

1.4.1.6 Drone technology

Smart hospitals require increased automation by using autonomous machines like drones and robots, which have revolutionized healthcare. Drones, for instance, can be used to enforce adherence and compliance with movements restrictions (Khan et al., 2021) while robots can be used to deliver medication to in-patients (Mbunge, Muchemwa, et al., 2021), deliver food and blood samples, undertake surveillance, advance health awareness initiatives and disinfect contaminated surfaces (Restás et al., 2021; Zeng et al., 2020).

1.4.1.7 5G/6G technology

Wireless communication among various devices in a smart hospital is indispensable as various applications and devices need to interact, sharing data and responses. Global networks capable of providing high transmission speeds, such as 5G/6G, play a crucial role in ensuring that the communication network does not bottleneck data transfer speeds, facilitating near real-time device communication and data transfer, ensuring timely feedback and actions. With high interconnectedness and heavy reliance on digital systems, smart hospitals need dependable and high-performance networks to facilitate reliable and faster data transmission. For instance, some digital health systems in a smart hospital could be meant to monitor patients with chronic conditions and some in the intensive care unit, where any changes in physiological parameter readings would need urgent attention in a real-time manner. For instance, smart hospital automation by integrating technologies like robots, AI, smart devices and cloud computing, needs high-speed and secure networks with ultra-low latency. 5G technology is increasingly becoming of paramount significance since it provides high data transmission speeds and longer and wider coverage (Siriwardhana et al., 2021).

1.4.1.8 Telehealth and telemedicine

Through telemedicine and telehealth, smart hospitals can provide cost-effective care, health support and surveillance, awareness and education, and knowledge and research (Albarrak et al., 2021; Bashshur et al., 2020; Batani, 2022). Health education and awareness are crucial to any public health intervention as prevention is better than cure. Adopting telemedicine in smart hospitals facilitates health research, patient outreach and supports the efficient provision of numerous health services, lowers operational costs and facilitates continued patient care even in cases where physical distancing has to be maintained, such as during the coronavirus disease 2019 (COVID-19) period (Mbunge, Akinnuwesi, et al., 2021). However, using telemedicine and telehealth requires reliable internet access (Gilbert et al., 2020), and it can deny equitable access to health services by those in areas with poor or no internet access, thus perpetuating the digital divide (Batani, 2022) as some patients may not have the requisite infrastructure (Dodoo et al., 2021). Ubiquitous computing, ambient intelligence and context-aware computing are among the technologies associated with smart hospitals to provide pervasive healthcare (Vecchia et al., 2012).

1.4.2 Application of emerging technologies in smart hospitals

Smart hospital technologies facilitate and expedite the adoption of smart health and smart healthcare services as some hospitals embrace smart digital health innovations to provide access to remote care (Hassan et al., 2019) and enhance operational efficiency, and disease diagnosis (Rajaei et al., 2024), detection, support virtual consultations, treatment and automation of processes. Automation remains an essential defining feature of smart hospitals, however, its scope has expanded to encompass multiple functions including tracking and managing patient health data (Kumar et al., 2020). In the past, smart hospitals primarily focused on automating administrative workflows to enhance productivity, minimize errors, and address workforce shortages (Kaldoudi, 2024). However, recent technological advancements have allowed automation to extend to essential medical activities such as diagnostic imaging, disease forecasting and prediction, patient monitoring, precise surgical procedures, patient care, prevention, patient monitoring, rehabilitation, and automation of processes to improve efficiency, as shown in Fig. 1.4. Smart hospitals present tremendous opportunities to improve patient outcomes, enhance patient experience, increase efficiency and productivity as well as reduce healthcare costs, effective resource mobilization and utilization. Thus, smart hospitals strive to provide personalized and remote patient care by utilizing advanced technologies and data-driven approaches, while adapting to the evolving needs of patients and healthcare providers.

1.4.3 Towards smart hospitals: adoption barriers

1.4.3.1 Context-aware computing

Context-aware medical systems are a crucial component of smart hospitals due to their ability to use implicit situational information to enhance conversations (Abowd et al., 1999). Context-aware computing refers to a computer application's ability to use situational and environmental information to respond to users' needs (Abowd et al., 1999; Zon et al., 2023). Understanding context requires determining the five Ws (why, what, when, where, who) at the minimum (Abowd & Mynatt, 2000). Thus, a context-aware computer application provides users with relevant information and/or services based on the context (Abowd et al., 1999). Context awareness is critical in a smart hospital setup as context-aware digital health systems can change their behavior in useful ways (Zon et al., 2023). Providing users with services or information based on context implies the smartness of a computer application or system and is critical in a smart hospital setup. For instance, in a

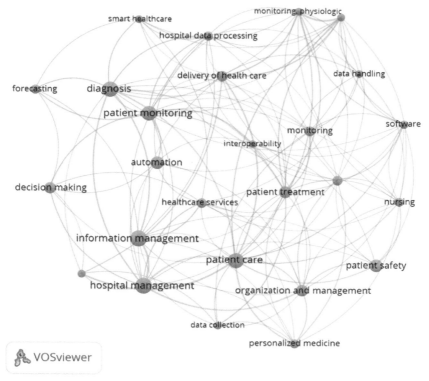

FIGURE 1.4 Application of emerging technologies in smart hospitals.

remote health monitoring system, health data can often be difficult to differentiate between benign (unlikely to be harmful) and dangerous if the context is excluded (Zon et al., 2023). For instance, a high heart rate could be a cause for worry (for instance, if the patient is sleeping, this may be deemed dangerous) or it may simply be that the patient being monitored is exercising; hence, the context is crucial in determining the course of action. Smart hospitals should automatically provide patients' smart devices with appropriate information and guidance about their tasks, locations and processes (Kim et al., 2012). Thus, applications developed for smart hospitals must be context-aware, such that they possess the ability to go beyond simple monitoring of a patient's physiological data and meaningfully interpret them. Failure to develop context-aware digital health systems can hinder the adoption of smart hospitals as medical systems could fail to make correct decisions due to their failure to determine user context from sensor data (Zon et al., 2023). The need for context-aware medical systems keeps increasing with the burgeoning of wearable sensors (Majumder et al., 2017, 2018).

1.4.3.2 Cognitive computing

Though smart wearable devices play a significant role in smart hospitals, they lack the cognition to monitor patients' emotions, particularly those with posttraumatic stress disorder (Mbunge, Muchemwa, et al., 2021). With various smart devices collecting data in a smart hospital environment, the cognitive ability of such devices would involve data collection from the environment, sensor-based interaction with human beings and appropriate and coherent reactions to human-like behavior. Designing such cognitive and emotion-capable AI-based health systems is normally bio-inspired and highly modular, and often takes a hybrid nature that infuses emotion modeling and high-level reasoning (Chakriswaran et al., 2019). Sensor-based cognitive AI health systems can revolutionize the healthcare landscape by enhancing patient care in numerous ways, such as mental health monitoring applications capable of listening to phone calls and analyzing speakers' voices to detect signs of anxiety, depression, stress and mood changes, smart wearable devices capable of analyzing patients' behavior (Mbunge, Muchemwa, et al., 2021). Thus, lack of cognition and emotion in smart digital health applications hinders the adoption of and full realization of the benefits of smart hospitals. It is therefore imperative that smart health applications in smart hospitals possess cognition, requiring redesigning some of the existing systems. Also, existence of several but heterogeneous and incompatible digital health tools, affecting the integration of the various digital tools (Rajaei et al., 2024) and interoperability (Mbunge, Muchemwa, et al., 2021).

1.4.3.3 *Lack of guiding policy and framework*

Health is a highly regulated domain and any innovations in it are subject to strict guidelines, monitoring and regulations. Regulatory frameworks and policies on electronic health innovations must enforce security and patient privacy (Mbunge, Muchemwa, et al., 2021), quality and safety of electronic health devices and applications (Digital Technologies: Shaping the future of primary care, 2018; Mahomed, 2018). However, these regulations and policies often lag, resulting in them being updated or enacted in response to those technological advancements, hence, the policy developments are mainly reactive as opposed to proactive (Batani & Maharaj, 2022; Digital Technologies: Shaping the future of primary care, 2018; Gaobotse et al., 2022). Oftentimes, policymakers fail to keep up with the pace of technological advancements (Meskó et al., 2017). Smart hospitals are powered by various digital and innovative solutions and would require continuous innovations to keep revolutionizing patient care through data-driven and evidence-based strategies. However, the reactionary nature of policymakers and lack of international World Health Organization (WHO)-approved frameworks to guide the integration of electronic health innovations hamper the migration towards smart hospitals as they are highly powered by technology, yet the lack of such regulatory frameworks delays the adoption and utilization of smart health interventions (Ernst et al., 2021).

1.4.3.4 *Cybersecurity issues*

IoT interconnected wearable medical devices and smart applications collect, process and analyze huge amounts of sensitive health data and automate processes. Such devices may have security vulnerabilities that can be exploited through cyberattacks and subsequently violate the privacy, integrity, and security of smart hospitals. The risk of data breaches compromises patient privacy and confidentiality.

1.4.3.5 Lack of funding and experts

Developing intelligent digital tools and implementing them requires huge financial commitment and experts in AI, robotics, and other emerging technologies (Rajaei et al., 2024). However, such skills critical skills are scarce in many developed and developing countries which hinders effective implementation of smart hospitals. Lack of digital infrastructure and resources (financial and skills) are among the critical barriers influencing the adoption of smart hospitals.

1.4.4 Recommendations

Governments, health ministries and the WHO should develop comprehensive and proactive regulatory frameworks and policies that facilitate and quicken the adoption and emergence of smart hospitals. This could be done by establishing national and international committees responsible for developing, updating and reviewing digital health regulatory frameworks, and these committees should include digital health researchers to provide insights on the newest smart health-related innovations that might require a review of the existing policies to ensure their adoption and utilization. International collaborations among these committees and with international health organizations, such as WHO, would help create standardized frameworks, policies and guidelines for implementing digital health innovations.

Digital health innovators and researchers should foster context-aware computing by investing in research and development to enhance context-aware computing in smart health applications to facilitate interpretation and response to patients' needs based on situational and environmental contexts. Thus, there is a need to promote the development of context-aware digital health systems capable of accurately determining patients' contexts from sensor data.

While there has been a proliferation of numerous digital health tools, systems and applications, they might not be suitable for use as-is in smart hospitals due to most of them lacking cognitive computing capabilities. Hence, there is a need to prioritize the redesigning of existing smart health applications and encourage the development of smart devices to incorporate the cognitive capabilities that are crucial to health systems ideal for smart hospitals.

Strengthen cybersecurity measures by implementing robust security protocols in smart health applications for smart hospitals. Additionally, interconnected smart devices used in smart hospitals must be regularly updated and patched for vulnerabilities to prevent possible cyberattacks. Healthcare professionals must also be trained on an ongoing basis on cybersecurity best practices to ensure that sensitive health data are protected.

To reduce the effects of the digital divide and a sluggish pace in smart hospital adoption, there is a need to address the funding and expertise gaps by encouraging public−private partnerships to attract investments and expertise from both the healthcare and technology sectors.

There is a need to promote interoperability and integration by developing guidelines and frameworks to enhance the seamless integration of diverse digital technologies within smart hospital environments. Regulators and funders should encourage collaboration among technology providers to create interoperable solutions that enhance the overall efficiency of smart hospitals.

1.5 Conclusion

Smart hospitals hold immense and unmatched potential in revolutionizing healthcare through smart health digital innovations. Various smart hospital facilitating technologies exist, such as AI, robotics, cloud computing, wearable devices and IoT, which help provide personalized, ubiquitous, data-driven and cost-effective healthcare. However, several adoption challenges, such as lack of context-aware computing and outdated regulatory frameworks. Overcoming the identified adoption barriers requires addressing them, such as developing context-aware digital health systems with cognitive ability, establishing guiding policies that are always up-to-date, enhancing cybersecurity measures and ensuring sufficient funding and expertise. As such, the authors presented recommendations to foster effective implementation and utilization of smart hospitals, ultimately improving health outcomes.

References

Abowd, G. D., Dey, A. K., Brown, P. J., Davies, N., Smith, M., & Steggles, P. (1999). Towards a better understanding of context and context-awareness. *Lecture Notes in Computer Science (including subseries Lecture Notes in Artificial Intelligence and Lecture Notes in Bioinformatics)*, 1707(1), 304–307. Available from http://springerlink. com/content/0302-9743/copyright/2005/.

Abowd, G. D., & Mynatt, E. D. (2000). Charting past, present, and future research in ubiquitous computing. *ACM Transactions on Computer-Human Interaction*, 7(1). Available from https://doi.org/10.1145/344949.344988.

Aceto, G., Persico, V., & Pescapé, A. (2020). Industry 4.0 and health: Internet of Things, big data, and cloud computing for healthcare 4.0. *Journal of Industrial Information Integration*, 18, 100129. Available from https://doi. org/10.1016/j.jii.2020.100129.

Agbo, C. C., Mahmoud, Q. H., & Eklund, J. M. (2019). Blockchain technology in healthcare: A systematic review. *Healthcare (Switzerland)*, 7(2). Available from https://doi.org/10.3390/healthcare7020056, https://www.mdpi. com/2227-9032/7/2/56/pdf.

Ahir, S., Telavane, D., & Thomas, R. (2020). The impact of artificial intelligence, blockchain, big data and evolving technologies in Coronavirus disease-2019 (COVID-19) curtailment. In *Proceedings—International conference on smart electronics and communication, ICOSEC 2020* (pp. 113, 120). Available from https://doi.org/10.1109/ ICOSEC49089.2020.9215294, http://ieeexplore.ieee.org/xpl/mostRecentIssue.jsp?punumber = 9210168.

Albarrak, A. I., Mohammed, R., Almarshoud, N., Almujalli, L., Aljaeed, R., Altuwaijiri, S., & Albohairy, T. (2021). Assessment of physician's knowledge, perception and willingness of telemedicine in Riyadh region, Saudi Arabia. *Journal of Infection and Public Health*, 14(1). Available from https://doi.org/10.1016/j.jiph.2019.04.006, http://www.elsevier.com/wps/find/journaldescription.cws_home/716388/descriptio.

Bashshur, R., Doarn, C. R., Frenk, J. M., Kvedar, J. C., & Woolliscroft, J. O. (2020). Telemedicine and the COVID-19 pandemic, lessons for the future. *Telemedicine and e-Health*, 26(5). Available from https://doi.org/10.1089/ tmj.2020.29040.rb, http://www.liebertpub.com/publication.aspx?pub_id = 54.

Batani, J. (2022). Reducing under-five mortality in makonde district's public healthcare. In *Institutions: An exploratory investigation into the potential role of emerging technologies*.

Batani, J., & Maharaj, M. S. (2022). Towards data-driven models for diverging emerging technologies for maternal, neonatal and child health services in Sub-Saharan Africa: a systematic review. *Global Health Journal*, 6(4). Available from https://doi.org/10.1016/j.glohj.2022.11.003, https://www.sciencedirect.com/journal/global-health-journal.

Batani, J., & Maharaj, M. S. (2023). Emerging technologies' role in reducing under-five mortality in a low-resource setting: Challenges and perceived opportunities by public health workers in Makonde District, Zimbabwe. *Journal of Child Health Care*. Available from https://doi.org/10.1177/13674935231189790, https://journals.sagepub.com/home/CHC.

Chakriswaran, P., Vincent, D. R., Srinivasan, K., Sharma, V., Chang, C. Y., & Reina, D. G. (2019). Emotion AI-driven sentiment analysis: A survey, future research directions, and open issues. *Applied Sciences (Switzerland)*, *9*(24). Available from https://doi.org/10.3390/app9245462, https://res.mdpi.com/d_attachment/applsci/applsci-09-05462/article_deploy/applsci-09-05462-v2.pdf.

Dhar, J., & Ranganathan, A. (2015). Machine learning capabilities in medical diagnosis applications: computational results for hepatitis disease. *International Journal of Biomedical Engineering and Technology*, *17*(4), 330. Available from https://doi.org/10.1504/IJBET.2015.069398.

Digital Technologies: Shaping the future of primary care. (2018).

Dodoo, J. E., Al-Samarraie, H., & Alzahrani, A. I. (2021). Telemedicine use in Sub-Saharan Africa: Barriers and policy recommendations for Covid-19 and beyond. *International Journal of Medical Informatics*, *151*. Available from https://doi.org/10.1016/j.ijmedinf.2021.104467, http://www.elsevier.com/inca/publications/store/5/0/6/0/4/0/.

Ernst, M., Richards, R. G., & Windolf, M. (2021). Smart implants in fracture care — Only buzzword or real opportunity? *Injury*, *52*, S101. Available from https://doi.org/10.1016/j.injury.2020.09.026, http://www.elsevier.com/locate/injury.

Firouzi, F., Farahani, B., Daneshmand, M., Grise, K., Song, J., Saracco, R., Wang, L. L., Lo, K., Angelov, P., Soares, E., Loh, P. S., Talebpour, Z., Moradi, R., Goodarzi, M., Ashraf, H., Talebpour, M., Talebpour, A., Romeo, L., Das, R., . . . Luo, A. (2021). Harnessing the power of smart and connected health to tackle COVID-19: IoT, AI, robotics, and blockchain for a better world. *IEEE Internet of Things Journal*, *8*(16). Available from https://doi.org/10.1109/JIOT.2021.3073904, http://ieeexplore.ieee.org/servlet/opac?punumber = 6488907.

Gaobotse, G., Mbunge, E., Batani, J., & Muchemwa, B. (2022). The future of smart implants towards personalized and pervasive healthcare in Sub-Saharan Africa: Opportunities, barriers and policy recommendations. *Sensors International*, *3*, 100173. Available from https://doi.org/10.1016/j.sintl.2022.100173.

Gilbert, A. W., Billany, J. C. T., Adam, R., Martin, L., Tobin, R., Bagdai, S., Galvin, N., Farr, I., Allain, A., Davies, L., & Bateson, J. (2020). Rapid implementation of virtual clinics due to COVID-19: Report and early evaluation of a quality improvement initiative. *BMJ Open Quality*, *9*(2), e000985. Available from https://doi.org/10.1136/bmjoq-2020-000985.

Gordon, W. J., & Catalini, C. (2018). Blockchain technology for healthcare: Facilitating the transition to patient-driven interoperability. *Computational and Structural Biotechnology Journal*, *16*. Available from https://doi.org/10.1016/j.csbj.2018.06.003, http://www.csbj.org.

Hassan, M. K., El Desouky, A. I., Elghamrawy, S. M., & Sarhan, A. M. (2019). Big Data challenges and opportunities in healthcare informatics and smart hospitals. *Lecture Notes in Intelligent Transportation and Infrastructure*, *1404*. Available from https://doi.org/10.1007/978-3-030-01560-2_1, http://www.springer.com/series/15991.

Holzinger, A., Röcker, C., & Ziefle, M. (2015). From smart health to smart hospitals, Springer Verlag, Austria*Lecture Notes in ComputerScience (including subseries Lecture Notes in Artificial Intelligence and Lecture Notes in Bioinformatics)*, *8700*. Available from https://doi.org/10.1007/978-3-319-16226-3_1, http://springerlink.com/content/0302-9743/copyright/2005/.

Hu, H., Su, J., & Ma, J. (2022). Editorial: Smart hospital innovation: Technology, service, and policy. *Frontiers in Public Health*, *10*. Available from https://doi.org/10.3389/fpubh.2022.845577, http://journal.frontiersin.org/journal/public-health/section/public-health-education-and-promotion#archive.

Istepanian, R. S. H., Hu, S., Philip, N. Y., & Sungoor, A. (2011). The potential of Internet of m-health Things m-IoT for non-invasive glucose level sensing. In *Proceedings of the annual international conference of the IEEE engineering in medicine and biology society, EMBS* (pp. 5264—5266). Available from https://doi.org/10.1109/IEMBS.2011.6091302.

Jian, W. S., Wang, J. Y., Rahmanti, A. R., Chien, S. C., Hsu, C. K., Chien, C. H., Li, Y. C., Chen, C. Y., Chin, Y. P., & Huang, C. L. (2022). Voice-based control system for smart hospital wards: A pilot study of patient acceptance. *BMC Health Services Research*, *22*(1). Available from https://doi.org/10.1186/s12913-022-07668-1, http://www.biomedcentral.com/bmchealthservres/.

Kaldoudi, E. (2024). Smart hospital: The future of healthcare. *Computational and Structural Biotechnology Journal*, *24*. Available from https://doi.org/10.1016/j.csbj.2023.12.011, https://www.sciencedirect.com/science/journal/20010370.

Kamruzzaman, M. M. (2020). Architecture of smart health care system using artificial intelligence. In *IEEE International Conference on Multimedia and Expo Workshops, ICMEW 2020*. Institute of Electrical and Electronics

Engineers Inc., Saudi Arabia. Available from https://doi.org/10.1109/ICMEW46912.2020.9106026, http://ieeexplore.ieee.org/xpl/mostRecentIssue.jsp?punumber = 9099356.

Khan, H., Kushwah, K. K., Singh, S., Urkude, H., Maurya, M. R., & Sadasivuni, K. K. (2021). Smart technologies driven approaches to tackle COVID-19 pandemic: A review. 3 Biotech, 11(2). Available from https://doi.org/10.1007/s13205-020-02581-y, https://www.springer.com/journal/13205.

Kim, E., Yoo, S., Hee, H., Park, H., Kim, G., & Ha, S. (2012). Patient satisfaction in a context-aware hospital guidance system. Studies in Health Technology and Informatics, 180, 1177–1179. Available from https://doi.org/10.3233/978-1-61499-101-4-1177, http://www.iospress.nl/bookserie/studies-in-health-technology-and-informatics/.

Kumar, A., Albreem, M. A., Gupta, M., Alsharif, M. H., & Kim, S. (2020). Future 5G network based smart hospitals: Hybrid detection technique for latency improvement. IEEE Access, 8. Available from https://doi.org/10.1109/ACCESS.2020.3017625, http://ieeexplore.ieee.org/xpl/RecentIssue.jsp?punumber = 6287639.

Kwon, H., An, S., Lee, H. Y., Cha, W. C., Kim, S., Cho, M., & Kong, H. J. (2022). Review of smart hospital services in real healthcare environments. Healthcare Informatics Research, 28(1). Available from https://doi.org/10.4258/hir.2022.28.1.3, http://www.e-hir.org/.

Leng, J., Lin, Z., & Wang, P. (2020). Poster abstract: An implementation of an internet of things system for smart hospitals. In Proceedings - 5th ACM/IEEE conference on internet of things design and implementation, IoTDI 2020 (pp. 254–255). Available from https://doi.org/10.1109/IoTDI49375.2020.00034, http://ieeexplore.ieee.org/xpl/mostRecentIssue.jsp?punumber = 9093722.

Mahomed, S. (2018). Healthcare, artificial intelligence and the Fourth Industrial Revolution: Ethical, social and legal considerations. South African Journal of Bioethics and Law, 11(2), 93. Available from https://doi.org/10.7196/sajbl.2018.v11i2.00664.

Majumder, S., Chen, L., Marinov, O., Chen, C. H., Mondal, T., & Deen, M. J. (2018). Noncontact wearable wireless ECG systems for long-term monitoring. IEEE Reviews in Biomedical Engineering, 11. Available from https://doi.org/10.1109/rbme.2018.2840336.

Majumder, S., Mondal, T., & Deen, M. (2017). Wearable sensors for remote health monitoring. Sensors, 17(1), 130. Available from https://doi.org/10.3390/s17010130.

Mbunge, E., Jiyane, S., & Muchemwa, B. (2022). Towards emotive sensory Web in virtual health care: Trends, technologies, challenges and ethical issues. Sensors International, 3, 100134. Available from https://doi.org/10.1016/j.sintl.2021.100134.

Mbunge, E., Akinnuwesi, B., Fashoto, S. G., Metfula, A. S., & Mashwama, P. (2021). A critical review of emerging technologies for tackling COVID-19 pandemic. Human Behavior and Emerging Technologies, 3(1). Available from https://doi.org/10.1002/hbe2.237, onlinelibrary.wiley.com/journal/25781863.

Mbunge, E., Muchemwa, B., Jiyane, S., & Batani, J. (2021). Sensors and healthcare 5.0: Transformative shift in virtual care through emerging digital health technologies. Global Health Journal, 5(4). Available from https://doi.org/10.1016/j.glohj.2021.11.008, https://www.sciencedirect.com/journal/global-health-journal.

Meskó, B., Drobni, Z., Bényei, É., Gergely, B., & Győrffy, Z. (2017). Digital health is a cultural transformation of traditional healthcare. mHealth, 3. Available from https://doi.org/10.21037/mhealth.2017.08.07.

Mohanta, B., Das, P., & Patnaik, S. (2019). Healthcare 5.0: A paradigm shift in digital healthcare system using artificial intelligence, IOT and 5G communication. In Proceedings - 2019 International Conference on Applied Machine Learning, ICAML 2019 (pp. 191–196). Available from https://doi.org/10.1109/ICAML48257.2019.00044, http://ieeexplore.ieee.org/xpl/mostRecentIssue.jsp?punumber = 8967488.

Polat, K., & Güneş, S. (2008). Principles component analysis, fuzzy weighting pre-processing and artificial immune recognition system based diagnostic system for diagnosis of lung cancer. Expert Systems with Applications, 34(1). Available from https://doi.org/10.1016/j.eswa.2006.09.001.

Pramanik, P. K. D., Solanki, A., Debnath, A., Nayyar, A., El-Sappagh, S., & Kwak, K. S. (2020). Advancing modern healthcare with nanotechnology, nanobiosensors, and internet of nano things: Taxonomies, applications, architecture, and challenges. IEEE Access, 8. Available from https://doi.org/10.1109/ACCESS.2020.2984269, http://ieeexplore.ieee.org/xpl/RecentIssue.jsp?punumber = 6287639.

Rajaei, O., Khayami, S. R., & Rezaei, M. S. (2024). Smart hospital definition: Academic and industrial perspective. International Journal of Medical Informatics, 182. Available from https://doi.org/10.1016/j.ijmedinf.2023.105304, https://www.sciencedirect.com/science/journal/13865056.

Rasoulian-Kasrineh, M., Sharifzadeh, N., & Tabatabaei, S. M. (2021). *Smart hospitals around the world: A systematic review.* Research Square, Iran. Available from https://doi.org/10.21203/rs.3.rs-258174/v1, https://www.researchsquare.com/browse.

Restás, Á., Szalkai, I., & Óvári, G. (2021). Drone application for spraying disinfection liquid fighting against the COVID-19 pandemic—Examining drone-related parameters influencing effectiveness. *Drones, 5*(3), 58. Available from https://doi.org/10.3390/drones5030058.

Rodrigues, L., Endo, P. T., & Silva, F. A. (2019). Stochastic model for evaluating smart hospitals performance. In *Proceedings—2019 IEEE Latin-American Conference on Communications, LATINCOM 2019.* Institute of Electrical and Electronics Engineers Inc., Brazil. Available from https://doi.org/10.1109/LATINCOM48065.2019.8937944; http://ieeexplore.ieee.org/xpl/mostRecentIssue.jsp?punumber = 8930892.

Sánchez, D., Tentori, M., & Favela, J. (2008). Activity recognition for the smart hospital. *IEEE Intelligent Systems, 23*(2). Available from https://doi.org/10.1109/MIS.2008.18.

Seidita, V., Lanza, F., Pipitone, A., & Chella, A. (2021). Robots as intelligent assistants to face COVID-19 pandemic. *Briefings in Bioinformatics, 22*(2). Available from https://doi.org/10.1093/bib/bbaa361, http://bib.oxfordjournals.org.

Serbanati, L. D. (2020). Health digital state and smart EHR systems. *Informatics in Medicine Unlocked, 21.* Available from https://doi.org/10.1016/j.imu.2020.100494, https://www.sciencedirect.com/science/journal/23529148.

Singh, R. P., Haleem, A., Javaid, M., Kataria, R., & Singhal, S. (2021). Cloud computing in solving problems of COVID-19 pandemic. *Journal of Industrial Integration and Management, 6*(2). Available from https://doi.org/10.1142/S2424862221500044, http://www.worldscientific.com/jiim.

Singh, R. P., Javaid, M., Haleem, A., & Suman, R. (2020). Internet of things (IoT) applications to fight against COVID-19 pandemic. *Diabetes and Metabolic Syndrome: Clinical Research and Reviews, 14*(4). Available from https://doi.org/10.1016/j.dsx.2020.04.041, http://www.journals.elsevier.com/diabetes-and-metabolic-syndrome-clinical-research-and-reviews/.

Siriwardhana, Y., Gür, G., Ylianttila, M., & Liyanage, M. (2021). The role of 5G for digital healthcare against COVID-19 pandemic: Opportunities and challenges. *ICT Express, 7*(2). Available from https://doi.org/10.1016/j.icte.2020.10.002, https://www.journals.elsevier.com/ict-express/.

Tavakoli, M. (2020). Smart wearable technologies, and autonomous intelligent systems for healthcare during the COVID-19 pandemic: An analysis of the state of the art and future vision. *Advanced Intelligent Systems, 2.* Available from https://doi.org/10.1002/AISY.2020000712020.

Tian, S., Yang, W., Grange, J. M. L., Wang, P., Huang, W., & Ye, Z. (2019). Smart healthcare: Making medical care more intelligent. *Journal of Global Health, 3*(3). Available from https://doi.org/10.1016/j.glohj.2019.07.001, http://jogh.org/current.htm.

Uslu, B. Ç., Okay, E., & Dursun, E. (2020). Analysis of factors affecting IoT-based smart hospital design. *Journal of Cloud Computing, 9*(1). Available from https://doi.org/10.1186/s13677-020-00215-5, http://www.journalofcloudcomputing.com/.

Vecchia, G. D., Gallo, L., Esposito, M., & Coronato, A. (2012). An infrastructure for smart hospitals. *Multimedia Tools and Applications, 59*(1). Available from https://doi.org/10.1007/s11042-010-0695-8.

Zeng, Z., Chen, P. J., & Lew, A. A. (2020). From high-touch to high-tech: COVID-19 drives robotics adoption. *RTourism Geographies, 22*(3). Available from https://doi.org/10.1080/14616688.2020.1762118, http://www.tandf.co.uk/journals/titles/14616688/asp.

Zhang, H., Li, J., Wen, B., Xun, Y., & Liu, J. (2018). Connecting intelligent things in smart hospitals using NB-IoT. *IEEE Internet of Things Journal, 5*(3). Available from https://doi.org/10.1109/JIOT.2018.2792423, http://ieeexplore.ieee.org/servlet/opac?punumber = 6488907.

Zon, M., Ganesh, G., Deen, M. J., & Fang, Q. (2023). Context-aware medical systems within healthcare environments: A systematic scoping review to identify subdomains and significant medical contexts. *International Journal of Environmental Research and Public Health, 20*(14). Available from https://doi.org/10.3390/ijerph20146399, http://www.mdpi.com/journal/ijerph.

Transforming healthcare through advanced sensing technologies

Bhupinder Singh[1] and Anand Nayyar[2]

[1]Sharda School of Law, Sharda University, Greater Noida, India [2]School of Computer Science, Duy Tan University, Da Nang, Vietnam

2.1 Introduction

The healthcare institution is a facility that provides specialized medical treatment, staffed by professional physicians, surgeons, nurses and allied health practitioners. Historically, such institutions were often managed by religious orders or volunteers but in contemporary times, they operate as highly technological corporations. The integration of Information and Communication Technology into the healthcare sector has been a significant area of research over the past two decades.

There are many applications that were previously unthinkable in the context of Smart healthcare now possible because of the development of nanoscale sensors. The focus is on smart healthcare which is a key component of the idea of a smart city. Although the introduction of nanosensing devices is expected to bring about substantial breakthroughs in personal healthcare, each nanosensor has limited processing power and storage capacity. Any application involving healthcare becomes dependent on the development of a nanosensor network. It first examines the nanosensor network communication paradigms in this chapter. It explores a range of smart healthcare applications, including body area networks, implanted medical devices for injury or malfunction, smart medicine delivery, and the Internet of Nano Things. It addresses the difficulties of implementing nanosensor networks in biological applications (Han et al., 2020).

Smart hospital systems encompass functions such as sensing, actuation and control to represent, analyze situations, and make decisions based on available data in a predictive or adaptive manner, thereby executing intelligent actions. Healthcare systems in general are the organizational structures involving people, institutions, and resources dedicated to delivering healthcare services to address the health needs of specific populations. The evolving landscape of healthcare, marked by technological advancements, has led to a swift

Sensor Networks for Smart Hospitals
DOI: https://doi.org/10.1016/B978-0-443-36370-2.00003-7

transformation in our perception of healthcare delivery. The existing Hospital Information Systems face several challenges that impede automation, including issues such as fixed information points and inflexible networking modes. The purpose of this paper is to present a thorough analysis of the state, difficulties and potential applications of sensors and nano-sensor networks in smart hospitals. Through an exploration of the various uses and consequences of these technologies, the study adds to the expanding corpus of information that guides the development of healthcare in the digital era (Agoulmine et al., 2012).

2.1.1 Objectives of the chapter

The smart hospital system is an original and comprehensive software solution designed to cater to the automation needs of virtually every hospital or medical institution, spanning activities from patient visits and operations to pathology testing. Fig. 2.1 shows the objectives of this Chapter. This chapter aims to:

- Provide a detailed overview of the sensors employed within a smart hospital system.
- Explore the healthcare facilities that face the challenge of achieving more with fewer resources.

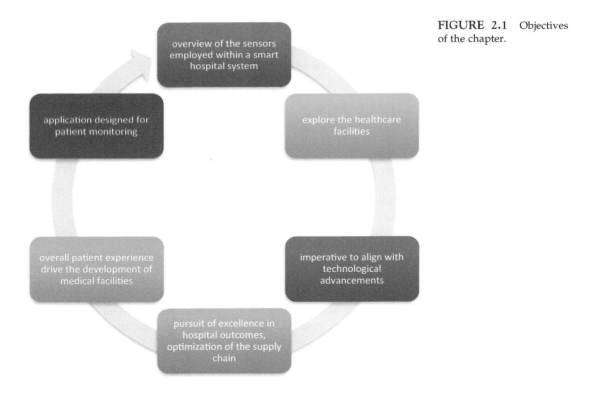

FIGURE 2.1   Objectives of the chapter.

- Study the imperative to align with technological advancements and meet evolving patient expectations.
- Pursuit of excellence in hospital outcomes, and optimization of the medicines supply chain.
- Enhancement of the overall patient experience drives the development of medical facilities capable of addressing current and future healthcare demands.
- Discusses the application designed for patient monitoring and outlines various methods for analysis and modeling within the smart hospital system.

2.1.2 Overview of smart hospitals and the increasing role of sensors and wearable

The development of information systems within the boundaries of smart hospitals and the academic discipline of information systems studies systems that are directly associated with information. It includes all of the linked hardware and software networks that people and organizations use to gather, filter, process, create and distribute data. Hospitals and other care facilities are building their pervasive healthcare systems with wireless sensor networks at their core. The purpose of this system is to wirelessly transfer vital signs, including body temperature and ECG from several patients to a network coordinator node. Under the direct supervision of medical professionals and skilled hospital employees, this central node functions. The system uses a mesh topology to create and maintain a network that includes a large number of mobile nodes and increases network lifetime. This system also uses a link-quality-based, energy-aware version of a source routing protocol.

There are several possibilities and problems associated with the emergence of mobile digital health. In order to provide creative healthcare solutions, digital healthcare must include modern technology through sensors. When used in conjunction with wearable technology and other platforms, smart sensors are essential for collecting health-related data, tracking the development of pathologies and assessing the effectiveness of therapies. The rapid, affordable and noninvasive diagnosis is made possible by digital healthcare where sensors are used in robotic surgery and for the online monitoring of vital signs while receiving treatment. The goal of the Sensor of Medical Things idea is to improve the quality of medical care while lowering costs and guaranteeing prompt response by integrating clinical systems, wearable medical devices and linked sensors (Dorj et al., 2017).

2.1.3 Definition and significance of nanosensor networks in healthcare

The Internet of Things (IoT), machine learning, augmented reality (AR), medical sensors, artificial intelligence (AI), big data, and big data are all used in healthcare to transform the industry. By connecting patients, medical equipment, clinics, hospitals, medical suppliers, and other healthcare-related entities, smart healthcare creates an intelligent health network. Biosensor networks and body chemical sensors are the backbone of healthcare, collecting a wide range of patient-provided medical data (Rani, 2022). Sensors provide the essential framework for healthcare by making it easier to identify unprocessed data and gather information. The sensor architecture presented in this work combines chemical and biosensors to detect and transmit physiological parameters from human bodies. Healthcare practitioners can monitor patients' vital signs and various medical issues with the use of these measured data (Ahirwar & Khan, 2022).

As instruments for identifying and tracking physical properties at the nanoscale, such as temperature, chemical species, and nanoparticles, nanosensors have become popular. These tiny instruments can monitor physical quantities and translate them into signals that can be detected and analyzed. Nanosensors are used in many different fields, including disease detection, medicine, pollution management, and process monitoring in manufacturing and transportation. In the field of medicine, nanosensors can measure a variety of physical properties such as- volume, concentration, movement speed, gravitational forces, electric and magnetic forces, pressure, temperature and more. They can also precisely identify cells at the molecular level for targeted drug delivery and monitor particular locations within the body (Han et al., 2020).

2.1.4 Relevance and scope of the chapter

Improving patient flow is the way to improve healthcare services since it may have a favorable effect on resource usage and service quality. The integration of a smart environment holds promise for augmenting people's experiences in physical settings, including hospitals. By implementing efficient scheduling guidelines and allocating healthcare resources in accordance with an optimum capacity plan, a smart healthcare environment has the potential to enhance patient flow (Sarkar & Misra, 2016).

The development of nanosensors is essential to the advancement of nanotechnology research. The need to identify and quantify chemical and physical characteristics at the molecular level, especially for the detection of poisons, pollutants and other analytes, is what is driving the increased interest in these instruments (Rizwan et al., 2018). This chapter examines the fundamental ideas behind nanosensors as well as ideas behind atomic force microscopy and atomic force spectroscopy in relation to the creation of nanosensors and nanobiosensors. The topic of sensors and nanosensors in smart hospitals, patient monitoring, applications and healthcare delivery is covered in detail with an emphasis on theoretical ideas, benefits and limitations and main uses (Datta, 2016).

2.1.5 Structure of the chapter

This chapter comprehensively explores the various dimensions of the sensors and nanosensor networks for smart hospitals: transforming healthcare through advanced sensing technologies. Section 2.2 elaborates on the sensors in smart hospital networks: significance and types. Section 2.3 expresses the nanosensor networks: foundations and applications. Section 2.4 discusses the sensors and nanosensors: applications in patient monitoring. Section 2.5 specifies the enhancing diagnostics and imaging. Section 2.6 stresses the challenges: concerns in implementation and viable solution: sensors and biosensors. Section 2.7 highlights the future prospects and emerging trends. Section 2.8 lays down the case studies. Finally, Section 2.9 conclude the chapter with remarks (Fig. 2.2).

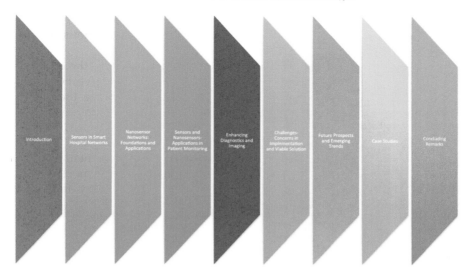

FIGURE 2.2   Structure of the chapter.

2.2 Sensors in smart hospital networks: significance and types

The using of preestablished rules to solve an issue analysis and modeling approaches allow for the description of the systems development in smart hospitals (Pramanik et al., 2020). The modern scientific methodology known as the analysis system, or system approach, looks at the constituent parts of complicated systems as interdependent, mutually dependent parts. Systemic analysis is a methodology whose breadth goes beyond the automation of concepts; it arranges data to maximize actions. The system approach's main objective is to make any complicated system simpler so that once its hardware configuration and dynamic structure are understood a model that enables effective intervention may be created. The competent method development team should include people with extensive modeling language and methodology knowledge. There are several approaches to system modeling that concentrate on decisions, organization, functions and resources (Nazari, 2020).

The use of sensor technologies in medicine is propelling tremendous advancements. Compared to earlier norms, this integration has resulted in patients living longer lives, having better quality of life, and having quicker access to critical therapies. Using sensors makes automation easier, which is why hospitals are adopting automated systems to control the temperature in operating rooms and other areas of the hospital. This is a recent development. The automation ensures that conditions are precisely calibrated to be maintained at ideal levels while reducing the possibility of human errors (Shahbaaz Singh Sahi & Kaushik, 2022). Fig. 2.3 shows the various types and applications of sensors and nanosensors.

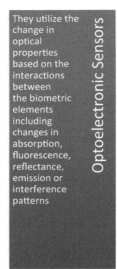
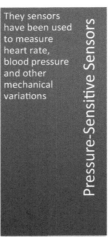
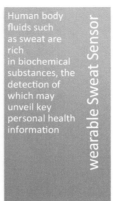

FIGURE 2.3 Types and use/application of sensors and nanosensors.

2.2.1 Monitoring sensors: wearables, biosensors and physiological sensors

The operating rooms are some of the most controlled facilities in the world and if certain standards are not met, patients might be in danger of contracting viruses from the air. The surgery site infections can be significantly impacted by the heating, ventilation and air conditioning systems. In response, operating theater conditions are precisely and automatically controlled through the use of sensors. The numerous environmental data points, including temperature, humidity, pressure and air particle concentrations are collected via connected sensors. The regulation-compliant safety conditions are guaranteed by real-time monitoring enabled by these insights (Oukhatar et al., 2021).

By utilizing semiconductor and flexible electronics packaging technologies, biomedical sensors provide an intriguing possibility to constantly and nonintrusively detect human physiologic parameters in real-time. These sensors include developments in neural sensing platforms based on microelectromechanical, biological and chemical sensing, electrocardiogram (ECG), electromyogram, and electroencephalogram (EEG). In the healthcare industry, biological, and chemical sensors are becoming more and more regarded as affordable substitutes for expensive analytical tools, especially when they satisfy specificity and selectivity requirements (Ramasamy et al., 2017).

Because of the low cost, ease of use, and portability of electrochemical transducers, commercial hand-held sensors for measuring metabolites and electrolytes, such as Roche Diagnostics' ACCU-CHEK, Abbott's iSTAT, and Sports Resource Group's Lactate Scout, have been developed. However, real-time monitoring in sports medicine is hampered by their reliance on blood samples. The major breakthrough has been made with the introduction of wearable biosensors, which allow analytes from eccrine sweat to be measured in order to assess mental and physical performance in athletes. Wearable sensor application to measure analytes from eccrine sweat and saliva that affect athletic performance. It also explores the use of these tools to evaluate athletes' stress levels and mental acuity using biomarkers from eccrine sweat, galvanic skin reaction and heart rate variability (Paliwal & Bunglowala, 2021).

2.2.2 Imaging sensors: X-ray, magnetic resonance imaging and computed tomography scanners for diagnostics

Medical practitioners can evaluate and assist in the diagnosis of a variety of medical disorders by using medical scanners, which provide visual representations of the human body. This procedure makes it easier to create individualized treatment programs for patients. Medical imaging is also used to monitor people for any long-term health problems that may develop; this function is frequently included into regular health screening programs. Radiologists now have the capacity to use a variety of medical imaging scanners to record minute details of the human body, thanks to the original discovery of X-rays. These modalities include ultrasound, positron emission tomography, magnetic resonance imaging, computed tomography and other methods (He & Eastburn, 2022).

2.2.3 Location-based sensors: asset tracking and patient flow optimization

Stretchable and flexible biosensors provide better signal accuracy and patient comfort while sensing physiological signals and performing biomolecular analyses, both of which are essential for the diagnosis, treatment, and management of diseases. Their superior mechanical qualities, along with their lightweight and soft nature, allow for efficient coupling with the skin-device interface while maintaining skin safety (Ali & Abu-Elkheir, 2015). This results in versatile and intelligent real-time sensing. The basic sensing concepts of biosensor systems and their uses are examined in this overview. It also talks about the future developments and possible uses of these biosensors. Wearable biosensors that are flexible have the potential to facilitate ongoing, long-term health monitoring in clinical contexts as well as ordinary healthcare activities (Pirmagomedov et al., 2016).

The technology of location tracking utilizes an interconnected network of IoT devices, including wearables, sensors, and beacons, to precisely monitor and track the location of patients and equipment within healthcare facilities. The digital transformation in healthcare brings several benefits, and here are some examples as:

2.2.3.1 Patient flow optimization

IoT location tracking enables the monitoring of patient flow within healthcare facilities, including waiting times, bottlenecks, and crowded areas. This data can be utilized to streamline processes, enhance efficiency, and improve the overall patient experience (Mujawar et al., 2020).

2.2.3.2 Staff tracking

IoT location tracking helps monitor the location and movements of healthcare staff within a facility. This information aids in optimizing staff allocation, improving response times, and ensuring compliance with safety protocols (Omanović-Mikličanin et al., 2015).

2.2.3.3 *Emergency response*

IoT location tracking facilitates the quick location and dispatch of emergency responders during medical emergencies within a healthcare facility. This leads to reduced response times and improved patient outcomes (Udoh et al., 2023).

2.2.3.4 *Asset management*

Location tracking technology is valuable for monitoring the location and status of expensive medical equipment, ensuring their availability when needed. This minimizes the time spent searching for equipment and enhances inventory management (Chelliah, Wei, et al., 2021).

2.2.3.5 *Elderly care*

IoT location tracking can be applied to monitor the location and movements of elderly patients in their homes or care facilities. This provides reassurance to caregivers and family members, particularly for individuals with conditions like dementia or mobility issues (Topel & Al-Turjman, 2019).

2.3 Nanosensor networks: foundations and applications

The term "e-healthcare" is also used interchangeably to refer to digital healthcare which is a subset of healthcare that uses internet technologies. This method makes it easier for users to get current medical datasets and clinical data. Its scope includes offering hospitals, physicians, and patients individualized healthcare services. A more personalized healthcare system is on the horizon because of the widespread use of wearable technologies, cellphones, sensor-enabled gadgets, and smart cloud storage. With the ability to gather a variety of health-related data, sensors allow for ongoing patient monitoring, which is especially helpful for those who are treating long-term conditions (Dinesh Kumar, 2013).

The selectivity of nanosensors depends on the characteristics of their recognition components, and they show specificity in the detection of different analytes. A single nanosensor is intended to detect a single kind of analyte. Also, multiplex nanosensors may identify many analytes at once (Materon et al., 2021). These unique features draw attention to the selectivity and specificity of nanosensor aspects that are dictated by their components of recognition. The design of nanosensors has made use of a variety of recognition components, including enzymes, aptamers, antibodies and specific functional proteins. Aptamers and antibodies are the most often used recognition components in nanosensor creation among them (Kumar & Kumari, n.d.). The body's chemical sensors and biosensor networks are critical platforms for obtaining healthcare data, and they are necessary for identifying bio and medical data that is required for Healthcare. Sensors and nanosensor systems sample, detect and transmit physiological measures from human bodies using a variety of chemicals and biosensors. In order to determine the composition and concentration of bodily fluids such as pH, $Ca+$, and glucose, chemical sensors are widely used (Gaobotse et al., 2022).

Sweat, tears and saliva are examples of bodily fluids that may be noninvasively sampled which gives wearable electronics substantial new possibilities. The human skin's outermost layer, known as the stratum corneum, may be collected without harming it. To reduce the danger of harm and illness, sensors based on the analysis of these bodily fluids provide increased user-friendliness (Vivekananthan et al., 2022). Wearable sensors that don't require invasive procedures have made it possible to use them for a wide range of purposes such as: (1) identifying biochemical biomarkers for the diagnosis and follow-up of conditions like diabetes, cystic fibrosis, dermatitis and peripheral blood vessel disease; (2) tracking physiological signals like heart rate and activity levels; and (3) integrating with human machine integrations to help people with speech and mobility impairments (Ramasamy & Varadana, 2016).

2.3.1 Definition and characteristics of nanosensors

Nanosensors which consist of an analyte, sensor, transducer which transforms energy into a different form and detector are able to measure at the single-molecule level. Nanosensors typically work by observing electrical changes in the materials that make up the sensor (Pradhan et al., 2023). From the solution, the analyte diffuses to the sensor surface, where it responds effectively and selectively. The transducer surface's physicochemical characteristics are changed by this contact, which causes a shift in its optical or electrical characteristics. This modification is then converted into an electrical signal, which is subsequently identified (Tang et al., 2018).

The promise of wearable medical technology is becoming more and more clear particularly in light of point-of-care testing improvements. Nanobiosensors based on chips and paper have been created to facilitate quick diagnosis of infectious disorders. Point-of-care testing makes sure that analytes are quickly found in close proximity to patients, which improves illness diagnosis, tracking, and treatment (Manogaran et al., 2021). Wearable nanosensors have the potential to provide dynamic, noninvasive measurements of biochemical markers in biofluids such as tears, sweat, saliva, and interstitial fluids, thereby providing continuous, real-time physiological information. Sensors are receiving a lot more attention now that smartphones and other mobile devices are commonplace. Because wearable monitoring technologies allow for continuous, real-time biomarker monitoring, they have the potential to provide light on the dynamic biochemical processes occurring in biofluids (Hassanalieragh et al., 2015).

2.3.2 Nanosensor networks for real-time hospitals and health monitoring

Everybody's life is impacted by healthcare which is deeply entwined with information technology and has made several innovations that have substantially improved health. The key element of this framework is the idea of supervision and monitoring (Khan et al., 2020). The word "monitoring" refers to the hierarchical structure that maximizes the smart hospital system's functioning and guarantees security (Suma, 2021). In order to find abnormalities without changing the system directly, monitoring is used. It acts as a tool to improve the work performance of human operators in this particular setting. Vital sign-taking and constant monitoring are very important while caring for hospitalized critically ill patients. In its most basic form, surveillance is the observation of actions, behaviors, or other elements, with a focus on data and ongoing attention (Jenkins, 2022).

Healthcare institutions use screening programs like enhanced positron emission mammography to find diseases like breast cancer. Of all the imaging modalities, ultrasound is one of the most commonly used methods to examine the kidneys, liver, muscles, joints and other body parts. Medical imaging is essential in today's healthcare for the assessment of various heart problems using cardiac imaging. This real-time tracking can provide insightful data on health and well-being. This makes it easier to diagnose diseases in their early stages, which enables quick medical judgments and early treatment commencement (Malik & Kumar, 2022). The next-generation point-of-care testing has been made possible by the development of several prospective point-of-care devices in recent years. Significant advancements in networking and wireless communication technologies have made it possible to envisage and create cutting-edge healthcare services. Multiplexed biosensing, microfluidic sampling, and transport systems have all been successfully integrated. To improve wearability and convenience of use, these components have been downsized and coupled with flexible materials (Byerly, 2019).

2.3.3 Nanotechnology applications in diagnostics and drug delivery

The use of unique characteristics present in materials at the nanoscale is known as nanotechnology (Kumar, Khan, et al., 2022). Nanotechnology is widely used in many different sectors and helps create smarter and more efficient products. It is known as "nanomedicine" when used in the context of healthcare and medicine (Han, 2023). Nanomedicine has demonstrated efficacy in treating common ailments including cancer and cardiovascular disease. Nanotechnology uses the unique properties of materials that fall between 1 and 100 nm in size to create or alter novel items, whereas nanoscience studies these properties (Dash, 2019). Nanomaterials which show distinctive optical, electrical and/or magnetic characteristics at the nanoscale and find uses in electronics, medicine and other sectors, are made possible by manipulating structures at the atomic size. Because of their large surface area to volume ratio and adherence to quantum mechanics rather than the traditional rules of physics and chemistry, nanomaterials are unique. So, nanotechnology is the engineering of usable products and functional systems at the molecular or atomic level (Goethals, 2019).

Nanotechnologies have a broad impact on almost every industry and facet of society, providing better-designed, safer, cleaner, more intelligent, and long-lasting goods for areas including agriculture, everyday living, medical, and communications. There are two types of nanomaterials that are added to common items (Banerjee et al., 2020). First, by utilizing their special qualities, nanomaterials may be added to or incorporated into already-existing goods to improve overall performance. Alternatively, by taking use of their unique properties, nanomaterials like nanoparticles and nanocrystals may be used directly to produce cutting-edge electronics. The future of many different industrial sectors will be significantly impacted by the potential benefits of nanomaterials (Chen, 2017).

2.4 Sensors and nanosensors: applications in patient monitoring

The hospitals must have a patient monitoring program each patient is monitored by means of an analog device that measures vital signs including blood pressure, heart rate and temperature. The software records these characteristics in a database by methodically reading them at intervals that are unique to each patient (Barnes & Zvarikova, 2021). Safe parameter limits are established for individual patients. For example, the acceptable temperature range for Patient X is between 36.5 and 37.5 degrees. An alarm is transmitted to the nursing station in the event that safety restrictions are broken or an analog equipment malfunctions (Desai & Shende, 2021).

The physical appointments, in-person visits, manual examinations and treatments involving a great deal of human interaction are all crucial components of traditional healthcare methods (Albalawi & Joshi, 2018). Using medical sensors, AI, big data, the IoT, machine learning and AR to transform healthcare through technology-driven applications and procedures, Healthcare 4.0 takes its cues. By linking patients, medical equipment, clinics, hospitals, medical suppliers and other healthcare elements, Healthcare creates a smart health network and decisions about medical treatment and care are increasingly being made inside this intelligent network with little to no human input (Hurley & Popescu, 2021; Singh et al., 2022).

2.4.1 Continuous vital sign monitoring using wearable sensors

Originally able to identify typical physical signals like temperature these wearable biosensors have developed to focus on more specialized biochemical indicators, including blood glucose for diabetes monitoring (Tsang et al., 2018). These sensors also have the ability to deliver real-time digital data that can be conveniently captured by smartphones or tablets, creating revolutionary opportunities for digitalized, customized treatment (Goel et al., 2021).

2.4.2 Remote patient monitoring and telehealth applications

The capacity to remotely monitor particular elements of a patient's health from the comfort of their own home is one of the reasons telehealth is becoming more and more popular. With this technique, which is called remote patient monitoring, medical professionals may manage both acute and chronic illnesses (Kumar, Khan, Latif, et al., 2022). It also lessens the danger of infection and saves travel-related expenditures for patients. The supplement to telehealth is remote patient monitoring which is especially helpful for patients who need continuous monitoring of certain medical problems or who have difficulty traveling. For those who do not have easy access to healthcare services, it works well to prevent health concerns (Huang et al., 2021).

Remote patient monitoring can be used to track a variety of symptoms and disorders, including asthma, chronic obstructive lung disease, high blood pressure, diabetes, weight changes, cardiac issues, and sleep apnea. Common equipment such as blood glucose meters, blood pressure monitors, weight scales and pulse oximeters are among the devices used for monitoring. Patients may require training on equipment such as fetal monitors, breathing apparatuses, apnea monitors, heart monitors, and specific monitoring for dementia and Parkinson's disease for more complex illnesses (Malik et al., 2021). The capacity to monitor and avoid major consequences in remote places, together with developments in medical technology and improved patient and provider knowledge of telehealth are some of the reasons driving the growing acceptance of remote patient monitoring. This pattern corresponds with the telehealth services rising acceptance and ease of use (Chandan et al., 2019).

2.4.3 Smart beds and mattresses for pressure ulcer prevention

Pressure ulcers typically form over bony prominences due to pressure alone or in combination with shear stress and/or friction. Immobilization and malnourishment are additional contributing factors. There are certain groups are particularly prone to developing PUs, including bedridden patients, individuals confined to wheelchairs, frail elderly individuals with limited mobility as well as those with conditions such as diabetes, poor nutrition, and chronic blood-flow diseases (Kumar, Hong, et al., 2022). Smart hospital beds are an essential component of patient rooms in many types of healthcare institutions, including features that improve staff productivity and ease patient movement. In order to provide more accurate patient care, manufacturing businesses have combined state-of-the-art technology with medical needs, developing beds with creative uses (Kavre et al., 2019).

The manufacturers currently provide wireless smart beds that are fitted with a gadget that is connected to the nursing staff directly (Abraham, 2016). With the help of this connection, nurses may keep a careful eye on the patient's health, vital signs, and overall well-being from a distance in accordance with the patient's planned rounds (Zhu et al., 2019). The hospital workloads are considerably reduced by smart beds, which have remote sensors and monitoring systems built in. Their arrival signifies a qualitative improvement in smart hospital operating procedures (Bhatt et al., 2017).

2.5 Enhancing diagnostics and imaging

The human body exhibits a range of dynamic physiological signals that are indicative of ongoing internal activities, making it a complex biological system (Dimitrov, 2016). Healthcare can advance significantly through the detection and assessment of biochemical and biophysical signals in real-time using integrated body sensors (Javaid & Khan, 2021). Long-term real-time patient health monitoring is made difficult by the fact that most clinical monitoring systems in use today rely on unwieldy, heavy equipment, particularly in outpatient settings (Mukati et al., 2023). There are recent advancements in wearable skin-integrated sensors have shown promising results in the continuous detection and diagnosis of physiological conditions (West, 2016). These sensors are lightweight, flexible and portable for enhancing diagnostics and imaging (Tien, 2017).

In our quickly changing digital age, the nexus of biomedical engineering and technology innovation has produced innovative technologies that allow accurate and simple measurement of physiological parameters (Zhang, 2022). Digital health technologies have emerged as a result of the reduction in the size of diagnostic tools that were able to continuously monitor vital signs as ECG and biomarkers (Jagadeeswari et al., 2018). These technologies include wearable and wireless technologies, lab-on-a-chip sensors, portable imaging devices, and smartphone-connected devices (Rejeb et al., 2023). Innovative nanosensors, or nanoscale devices that assess physical characteristics and translate these signals into information that can be analyzed have also been brought about by this progress (Aceto et al., 2020). The range of detecting modalities that these sensors cover, including piezoelectric, electrochemical, electromagnetic, and mechanoacoustic, is exciting since it means that they may be used for real-time, continuous, and affordable patient monitoring (Asif-Ur-Rahman et al., 2019). This talk acknowledges that nanosensors will soon be used in clinical settings (Metcalf et al., 2016). It covers the body of research on nanosensors, tackles important issues about the evidence for broad device use, and attempts to provide a framework for these developments (Kang et al., 2018). This framework takes into account a number of variables, such as the principles of technical and biomedical engineering, methods for validating novel sensors, and the conversion of continuous waveform data for analysis at the individual level (Manogaran et al., 2017).

2.5.1 Integration of sensors in laboratory equipment for efficient diagnostics

The integration of the sensors and IoT with smart healthcare technologies in laboratory equipment for efficient diagnostics is for patient safety (Singh, 2023). IoT is in essence a network that links physical objects, automobiles, home appliances, and other things (Zhan, 2021). For the purpose of connecting and exchanging data, these devices are integrated with electronics, software, sensors, actuators and connections (Qi et al., 2017). Because of this connectivity, there are chances to integrate the real world more directly into computer-based systems which can improve efficiency, provide financial benefits, and require less labor from humans (Firouzi et al., 2018).

2.6 Challenges: concerns in implementation and viable solution: sensors and biosensors

The global problem facing the healthcare sector is to successfully manage costs while improving the quality of services (Al Hayani & Ilhan, 2020). The achieving of superior healthcare management standards is essential to providing higher-quality medical treatment (Singh, 2022). This entails making prompt judgments based on informatics analysis, smart data analysis, the IoT, AI, and quick diagnostics (Gupta et al., 2016; Rahmani et al., 2018). A health service system using wearable and implantable technology, AI, the IoT and mobile Internet is what is meant by smart and intelligent healthcare (Wang et al., 2020). This system links people, resources, and healthcare-related organizations while dynamically accessing information. It also intelligently controls and reacts to the demands of the medical ecosystem (He, 2023). The informed decision-making is aided by smart healthcare which promotes communication among all parties involved in the healthcare industry and guarantees that participants receive the services they require (Noah & Ndangili, 2022). Fig. 2.4 presents the challenges and concerns of using sensors and sensor networks in smart hospitals.

Healthcare and smart hospitals have seen a transformation because of the sensors and nanosensors (Asorey-Cacheda et al., 2023). Healthcare providers may improve patient care, maximize operational efficiency and streamline processes by implementing sensors and nanosensors and technology (Uddin et al., 2021). The use of location tracking technology which enables the real-time monitoring of patients' movements within hospital facilities is a noteworthy application of sensors in healthcare (Mbunge et al., 2021). Sensors and biosensor technologies have the potential to revolutionize healthcare by improving patient safety, streamlining workflows and increasing operational effectiveness. It is impossible to exaggerate how crucial it is to protect patient data's confidentiality and privacy (Varadan et al., 2011).

Strict adherence to data privacy laws and strong cyber-security measures are necessary as healthcare systems become more digitally integrated (Canovas-Carrasco et al., 2020). It is crucial to protect patient data from breaches and make sure that laws like HIPAA are followed (Javaid et al., 2021; Jin et al., 2020). There are security challenges and concerns regarding the implementation of sensors and biosensors in the healthcare industry but taking care of these then it protects the privacy and data (Javaid et al., 2022). The following security guidelines need to be kept in mind (Fig. 2.5).

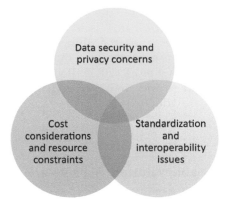

FIGURE 2.4 Challenges and concerns of using sensors and sensor networks in smart hospitals.

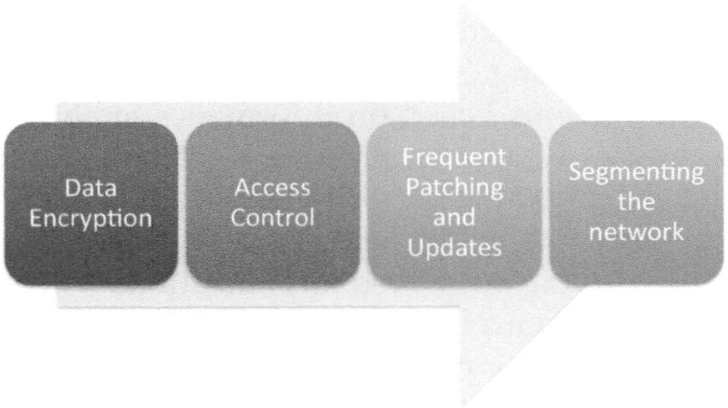

FIGURE 2.5 Security guidelines: viable solutions.

2.6.1 Data encryption

All data sent between IoT devices needs to be encrypted in order to guarantee secrecy and thwart unwanted access (Rolfe, 2010).

2.6.2 Access control

Tight restrictions on access should be put in place to prevent unwanted access to the data generated by IoT devices. This calls for the efficient management of user rights and the implementation of strong authentication procedures (Jabeen, Jabeen, et al., 2023).

2.6.3 Frequent patching and updates

To fix vulnerabilities and fend off possible cyber-attacks, it's critical to regularly update IoT devices with the most recent security updates (Yang et al., 2020).

2.6.4 Segmenting the network

With separating IoT devices from vital healthcare systems and putting segmentation into place, you may reduce the risk of security breaches and lessen the effect of compromised devices (Adam & Dhahi, 2022).

2.7 Future prospects and emerging trends

Smartphone apps and commercially accessible wrist-worn gadgets, such as the Apple Watch are becoming more and more common for tracking physical activity in real-time and provide a wealth of information on healthy habits in daily life (Varadan et al., 2008). The Food and Drug Administration approved the Apple Watch Series 4, the first wristwatch with pressure sensor-based single-lead ECG recording (Saylan et al., 2022). All ECG data was immediately sent by this wristwatch to the linked iPhone (Saylan et al., 2022). The big data analysis advances will influence digital health in the future by paving the way for the integration of machine learning-based studies with wearable health systems (Al-Rawahi et al., 2018).

The field of AI, automation and healthcare is seeing a paradigm change from hospital-centered to patient-centered and from disease-focused to health-focused methods as a result of unmet requirements in preventative medicine and advances in information and computer technology (Angelov et al., 2019; Khazaei et al., 2023). Over the past ten years, advances in nanosensor technology, wireless communication, robotics, automation, AI and IoT platforms have driven an exponential rise in the field of remote healthcare monitoring (Jung et al., 2016). So, reaching high healthcare management standards is essential to improving the quality of healthcare (Yang & Webster, 2011). This entails taking prompt action based on informatics analysis, smart data analysis and quick diagnoses (Wang, 2019).

2.7.1 Advancements in sensor technologies and their impact on healthcare

The signal fidelity for wearable sensors is important because machine learning and big data analytical approaches rely largely on high-quality data for algorithm training and analysis (Haroun et al., 2021). The effective amalgamation of these technologies holds promise for facilitating patient-focused chronic illness care, diminishing the necessity for recurrent clinician consultations and providing tailored on-demand therapies (Akyildiz et al., 2020). As an efficient and economical diagnostic tool for early illness detection, smart nanosensors are starting to emerge (Prabhu, 2021).

These nanosensors are able to identify biomarkers or analytes in minuscule quantities such as sweat, tears, saliva, and blood (Chelliah, Khan, et al., 2021; Das & Farihah, 2019). Indicators of healthy biological activities, pathological processes, or reactions to treatment treatments that may be tested objectively are called biomarkers (Naranjo-Hernández et al., 2020). The field of flexible electronics and nanomaterial science has brought to the creation of wearable biophysical nanosensors that are able to track bodily movements, human activity, and electrophysiological signals like the ECG and EEG (Olatinwo et al., 2019). Wearable biochemical nanosensors are being developed for the noninvasive measurement of molecular-level biofluid indicators such as metabolites and electrolytes (Solanki & Nayak, 2020).

2.8 Case studies and success stories: positive outcomes and improvements in patient care

Biosensors are being used more and more for continuous health monitoring. The vital function of blood oxygen monitors which are frequently located in hospitals and patient's homes is to identify changes in blood oxygen levels (Pretis et al., 2022). Quick medical attention is required in order to prevent brain damage and to identify a severe decline in oxygen levels (Ayaz, 2018). Patients requiring emergency, critical or newborn care, as well as those with heart and lung issues and anesthesia can all benefit greatly from these monitors (Ayaz, 2018). The variety of biosensors make it possible to continuously monitor vital health indicators including heart rate, blood pressure and blood sugar levels for the treatment of diabetes. Continuous monitoring offers significant insights into an individual's health condition and enables prompt interventions or modifications to treatment regimens as necessary (Sagar et al., 2021).

Step counters and physical activity monitors are becoming essential tools for encouraging people to start and maintain healthy behaviors (Jabeen et al., 2021). These gadgets have also made it possible to take part in health studies (Karatas et al., n.d.). More sophisticated biosensors that measure biological, chemical and physical health markers are now being developed by researchers. The increasing range of biosensors that scientists, physicians and the general public employ (Fu et al., 2016). These biosensors perform a variety of tasks including facilitating ongoing health status monitoring and accelerating test findings for timely interventions. They make use of a variety of processes including electrical currents, chemical attraction, light-detection systems and tiny wireless sensing technologies (Fouad et al., 2020). The mercury thermometer, one of the first biosensor technologies in medicine has developed to employ safer temperature-sensitive sensors to measure body temperature changes. The home pregnancy test is another popular biosensor that is a trustworthy substitute. It uses color-changing strips to identify pregnant hormones in urine (Gulec, 2023).

When a patient has a sore throat, clinicians frequently utilize the fast strep test, a biosensor, to swiftly check for the presence of streptococci bacteria. With a 95% accuracy rate, this test provides answers in a matter of minutes, enabling the start of therapy right away (Muthukaruppankaruppiah et al., 2023). The researchers want to provide fast diagnostics for illnesses such as hepatitis C, HIV and influenza in areas with limited access to public healthcare. Modern biosensor technology may now be integrated with wireless signaling and smartphone cameras to make health checks more portable and reasonably priced (Tall Jabeen et al., 2023).

2.9 Concluding remarks

Nanosensors play a crucial role in detecting antibodies, antigens, or nucleic acids in samples such as saliva, sputum, and blood, utilizing colorimetric, fluorescent, or electrochemical detection approaches. These nanosensors offer various advantages, including affordability, sensitivity, specificity, user-friendliness, rapid and robust performance, equipment-free operation, and easy delivery to end-users. Wearable devices like activity trackers and smartwatches provide unique insights into health and well-being. These cutting-edge technologies provide a plethora of creative approaches to mobile digital health and hold great promise for further investigation. These solutions are more viable and efficient when AI is applied. Digital healthcare benefits from the use of sensors from the standpoints of physicians, hospitals, and patients. These include lower costs, better treatment results, quicker illness detection, proactive treatment methods, and better medication and equipment management all of which eventually help to lower the number of errors made in healthcare procedures. In order to improve patient comfort, skin safety and signal accuracy, sensors with mechanical flexibility and stretchability that mimic human skin for mechanical compatibility show outstanding adherence to skin curvatures and body motions.

Although wearable technology has advanced quickly in recent years as many reviews have emphasized the usefulness of contemporary wearable chemical and physical sensors and their research progress, it still doesn't fully understand how wearable technology can completely change personalized health management. The key component of smart healthcare systems is their ability to provide insightful information on a service that was previously unavailable. Thus, a review of smart health systems and related sensors is done in this chapter. The sensors, nanosensors and system modeling become important because it makes it possible to represent the information flows between the different parts of a smart healthcare system and the range of parameters that are used when building models. This emphasizes how important it is to have a systemic approach.

References

Abraham, S. C. (2016). Internet of Things (IoT) with cloud computing and machine-to-machine (M2M) communication. *International journal of Emerging Trends in Science and Technology*. Available from https://doi.org/10.18535/ijetst/v3i09.13.

Aceto, G., Persico, V., & Pescapé, A. (2020). Industry 4.0 and health: Internet of Things, big data, and cloud computing for healthcare 4.0. *Journal of Industrial Information Integration, 18*100129. Available from https://doi.org/10.1016/j.jii.2020.100129.

Adam, T., & Dhahi, T. S. (2022). Nanosensors: Recent perspectives on attainments and future promise of downstream applications. *Process Biochemistry, 117*. Available from https://doi.org/10.1016/j.procbio.2022.03.024, http://www.elsevier.com/inca/publications/store/4/2/2/8/5/7.

Agoulmine, N., Kim, K., Kim, S., Rim, T., Lee, J. S., & Meyyappan, M. (2012). Enabling communication and cooperation in bio-nanosensor networks: Toward innovative healthcare solutions. *IEEE Wireless Communications, 19* (5). Available from https://doi.org/10.1109/MWC.2012.6339471.

Ahirwar, R., & Khan, N. (2022). Smart wireless nanosensor systems for human healthcare. Informa UK Limited. Available from 10.1201/9781003093534-15.

Akyildiz, I. F., Ghovanloo, M., Guler, U., Ozkaya-Ahmadov, T., Sarioglu, A. F., & Unluturk, B. D. (2020). PANACEA: An internet of bio-nanothings application for early detection and mitigation of infectious diseases. *IEEE Access, 8*. Available from https://doi.org/10.1109/ACCESS.2020.3012139, http://ieeexplore.ieee.org/xpl/RecentIssue.jsp?punumber = 6287639.

Al Hayani, B., & Ilhan, H. (2020). Image transmission over decode and forward based cooperative wireless multimedia sensor networks for rayleigh fading channels in medical Internet of Things (MIoT) for remote healthcare and health communication monitoring. *Journal of Medical Imaging and Health Informatics, 10*(1). Available from https://doi.org/10.1166/jmihi.2020.2691.

Albalawi, U., & Joshi, S. (2018). Secure and trusted telemedicine in Internet of Things IoT. In *IEEE world forum on internet of things, WF-IoT 2018 - Proceedings* (pp. 30–34). Institute of Electrical and Electronics Engineers Inc. Saudi Arabia. Available from https://doi.org/10.1109/WF-IoT.2018.8355206, http://ieeexplore.ieee.org/xpl/mostRecentIssue.jsp?punumber = 8353083 9781467399449.

Ali, N. A., & Abu-Elkheir, M. (2015). Internet of nano-things healthcare applications: Requirements, opportunities, and challenges. In *IEEE 11th international conference on wireless and mobile computing, networking and communications, WiMob 2015*. Institute of Electrical and Electronics Engineers Inc. United Arab Emirates. Available from https://doi.org/10.1109/WiMOB.2015.7347934, 9781467377010 914.

Al-Rawahi, M.N., Sharma, T., & Palanisamy, P. (2018). Internet of nanothings: Challenges & opportunities. In *Proceedings of Majan international conference: Promoting entrepreneurship and technological skills: National needs, global trends, MIC 2018* (pp. 1–5). Institute of Electrical and Electronics Engineers Inc., Oman. Available from https://doi.org/10.1109/MINTC.2018.8363165, http://ieeexplore.ieee.org/xpl/mostRecentIssue.jsp?punumber = 8360185 9781538637616.

Angelov, G. V., Nikolakov, D. P., Ruskova, I. N., Gieva, E. E., & Spasova, M. L. (2019). Healthcare sensing and monitoring. *Lecture notes in computer science (including subseries lecture notes in artificial intelligence and lecture notes in bioinformatics)*. (11369). Bulgaria: Springer Verlag. Available from https://www.springer.com/series/558, 10.1007/978-3-030-10752-9_10.

Asif-Ur-Rahman, M., Afsana, F., Mahmud, M., Shamim Kaiser, M., Ahmed, M. R., Kaiwartya, O., & James-Taylor, A. (2019). Toward a heterogeneous mist, fog, and cloud-based framework for the internet of healthcare things. *IEEE Internet of Things Journal, 6*(3). Available from https://doi.org/10.1109/JIOT.2018.2876088, http://ieeexplore.ieee.org/servlet/opac?punumber = 6488907.

Asorey-Cacheda, R., Correia, L. M., Garcia-Pardo, C., Wojcik, K., Turbic, K., & Kulakowski, P. (2023). Bridging nano and body area networks: A full architecture for cardiovascular health applications. *IEEE Internet of Things Journal, 10*(5). Available from https://doi.org/10.1109/JIOT.2022.3215884, http://ieeexplore.ieee.org/servlet/opac?punumber = 6488907.

Ayaz, M., et al. (2018). Wireless sensor's civil applications, prototypes, and future integration possibilities: A review. *IEEE Sensors Journal, 18*(1), 4–30. Available from https://doi.org/10.1109/JSEN.2017.2766364.

Banerjee, A., Chakraborty, C., & Rathi, M. (2020). Medical imaging, artificial intelligence, internet of things, wearable devices in terahertz healthcare technologies terahertz biomedical and healthcare technologies: Materials to devices. Singapore: Elsevier. Available from https://doi.org/10.1016/B978-0-12-818556-8.00008-2, https://www.sciencedirect.com/book/9780128185568.

Barnes, R., & Zvarikova, K. (2021). Artificial intelligence-enabled wearable medical devices, clinical and diagnostic decision support systems, and Internet of Things-based healthcare applications in COVID-19 prevention, screening, and treatment. *American Journal of Medical Research*, *8*(2), 2021.

Bhatt, C., Dey, N., & Ashour (2017). *Internet of Things and big data technologies for next generation healthcare.*

Byerly, K. (2019). Real-time big data processing and wearable Internet of medical things sensor devices for health monitoring. *American Journal of Medical Research.*, *6*(2), 2019.

Canovas-Carrasco, S., Asorey-Cacheda, R., Garcia-Sanchez, A. J., Garcia-Haro, J., Wojcik, K., & Kulakowski, P. (2020). Understanding the applicability of terahertz flow-guided nano-networks for medical applications. *IEEE Access*, *8*. Available from https://doi.org/10.1109/ACCESS.2020.3041187, http://ieeexplore.ieee.org/xpl/RecentIssue.jsp?punumber = 6287639.

Chandan, R. K., Singh, A. K., Patel, S., Swain, D. M., Tuteja, N., & Jha, G. (2019). Silencing of tomato CTR1 provides enhanced tolerance against tomato leaf curl virus infection. *Plant Signaling and Behavior*, *14*(3). Available from https://doi.org/10.1080/15592324.2019.1565595, http://www.tandfonline.com/loi/kpsb20.

Chelliah, R., Khan, I., Wei, S., Madar, I. H., Sultan, G., Daliri, E. B. M., Swamidoss, C., & Oh, D. H. (2021). Intelligent packaging systems: Food quality and intelligent medicine box based on nano-sensors nanotechnology in the life sciences. South Korea: Springer Science and Business Media B.V. Available from https://doi.org/10.1007/978-3-030-84262-8_19, springer.com/series/15921.

Chelliah, R., Wei, S., Daliri, E. B. M., Rubab, M., Elahi, F., Yeon, S. J., Jo, K. H., Yan, P., Liu, S., & Oh, D. H. (2021). Development of nanosensors based intelligent packaging systems: Food quality and medicine. *Nanomaterials*, *11*(6). Available from https://doi.org/10.3390/nano11061515, https://www.mdpi.com/2079-4991/11/6/1515/pdf.

Chen, E. T. (2017). *The Internet of Things*. IGI Global. Available from https://doi.org/10.4018/978-1-5225-2104-4.ch009.

Das, P., & Farihah, R. (2019). *Fundamental application of Internet of Nano Things* (Doctoral dissertation), 2019.

Dash, D. (2019). Internet of Things (IoT): The new paradigm of HRM and skill development in the Fourth Industrial Revolution. *IUP Journal of Information Technology* (4), 2019.

Datta, S. P. A. (2016). Future healthcare: Bioinformatics, nano-sensors, and emerging innovations. *Nanosensors: Theory and applications in industry, healthcare and defense.*

Desai, D., & Shende, P. (2021). Integration of Internet of Things with quantum dots: A state-of-the-art of medicine. *Current Pharmaceutical Design*, *27*(17). Available from https://doi.org/10.2174/1381612827666210222113740.

Dimitrov, D. V. (2016). Medical internet of things and big data in healthcare. *Healthcare Informatics Research*, *22*(3). Available from https://doi.org/10.4258/hir.2016.22.3.156, http://pdf.medrang.co.kr/Hir/2016/022/Hir022-03-02.pdf.

Dinesh Kumar, K. (2013). Human health monitoring mobile phone application by using the wireless nanosensor based embedded system. In *International conference on information communication and embedded systems, ICICES 2013* (pp. 889–892). India. Available from https://doi.org/10.1109/ICICES.2013.6508277.

Dorj, U. O., Lee, M., Choi, J. Y., Lee, Y. K., & Jeong, G. (2017). The intelligent healthcare data management system using nanosensors. *Journal of Sensors*, *2017*. Available from https://doi.org/10.1155/2017/7483075, http://www.hindawi.com/journals/js/biblio.html.

Firouzi, F., Rahmani, A. M., Mankodiya, K., Badaroglu, M., Merrett, G. V., Wong, P., & Farahani, B. (2018). Internet-of-Things and big data for smarter healthcare: From device to architecture, applications and analytics. *Future Generation Computer Systems*, *78*. Available from https://doi.org/10.1016/j.future.2017.09.016.

Fouad, H., Hashem, M., & Youssef, A. E. (2020). Retracted article: A nano-biosensors model with optimized bio-cyber communication system based on Internet of Bio-Nano Things for thrombosis prediction. *Journal of Nanoparticle Research*, *22*(7). Available from https://doi.org/10.1007/s11051-020-04905-8.

Fu, Q., Wu, Z., Xu, F., Li, X., Yao, C., Xu, M., Sheng, L., Yu, S., & Tang, Y. (2016). A portable smart phone-based plasmonic nanosensor readout platform that measures transmitted light intensities of nanosubstrates using an ambient light sensor. *Lab on a Chip*, *16*(10). Available from https://doi.org/10.1039/C6LC00083E.

Gaobotse, G., Mbunge, E., Batani, J., & Muchemwa, B. (2022). Non-invasive smart implants in healthcare: Redefining healthcare services delivery through sensors and emerging digital health technologies. *Sensors International*, *3*100156. Available from https://doi.org/10.1016/j.sintl.2022.100156.

Goel, S. S., Goel, A., Kumar, M., & Moltó, G. (2021). A review of Internet of Things: Qualifying technologies and boundless horizon. *Journal of Reliable Intelligent Environments*, *7*(1). Available from https://doi.org/10.1007/s40860-020-00127-w, springer.com/computer/hardware/journal/40860.

Goethals, I. (2019). Real-time and remote health monitoring Internet of Things-based systems: Digital therapeutics, wearable and implantable medical devices, and body sensor networks. *American Journal of Medical Research*, *6*(2), 2019.

Gulec, O. (2023). Distributed routing and self-balancing algorithm for Medical IoNT. *Simulation Modelling Practice and Theory*, 129102833. Available from https://doi.org/10.1016/j.simpat.2023.102833.

Gupta, P., Agrawal, D., Chhabra, J., & Dhir, P. K. (2016). IoT based smart healthcare kit. In *International conference on computational techniques in information and communication technologies, ICCTICT 2016 - Proceedings* (pp. 237–242). Institute of Electrical and Electronics Engineers Inc., India. https://doi.org/10.1109/ICCTICT.2016.7514585, 9781509000821.

Han, B., Tomer, V. K., Nguyen, T. A., Farmani, A., & Singh, P. K. (2020). Nanosensors for smart cities. China: Elsevier. Available from https://doi.org/10.1016/C2018-0-04422-9, https://www.sciencedirect.com/book/9780128198704.

Han, X. (2023). A novel assimilated navigation model based on advanced optical systems (AOS), internet of things (IoT) and artificial intelligence (AI). *Optical and Quantum Electronics*, 55(7). Available from https://doi.org/10.1007/s11082-023-04947-x.

Haroun, A., Le, X., Gao, S., Dong, B., He, T., Zhang, Z., Wen, F., Xu, S., & Lee, C. (2021). Progress in micro/nano sensors and nanoenergy for future AIoT-based smart home applications. *Nano Express*, 2(2)022005. Available from https://doi.org/10.1088/2632-959x/abf3d4.

Hassanalieragh, M., Page, A., Soyata, T., Sharma, G., Aktas, M., Mateos, G., Kantarci, B., & Andreescu, S. (2015). Health monitoring and management using Internet-of-Things (IoT) sensing with cloud-based processing: Opportunities and challenges proceedings. In *2015 IEEE international conference on services computing, SCC 2015* (pp. 285–292). Institute of Electrical and Electronics Engineers Inc., United States. Available from https://doi.org/10.1109/SCC.2015.47, 9781467372817.

L. He, (2023).

He, L., & Eastburn, M. (2022). Smart nanosensor networks for body injury detection. In *Proceedings - 2022 IEEE international conference on smart internet of things, SmartIoT 2022* (pp. 15–19). Institute of Electrical and Electronics Engineers Inc. United States. Available from https://doi.org/10.1109/SmartIoT55134.2022.00012, http://ieeexplore.ieee.org/xpl/mostRecentIssue.jsp?punumber = 9874440, 9781665479523.

Huang, J., Wu, X., Huang, W., Wu, X., & Wang, S. (2021). Internet of things in health management systems: A review. *International Journal of Communication Systems*, 34(4). Available from https://doi.org/10.1002/dac.4683.

Hurley, D., & Popescu, G. H. (2021). Medical big data and wearable internet of things healthcare systems in remotely monitoring and caring for confirmed or suspected COVID-19 patients. *American Journal of Medical Research*, 8(2), 2021.

Jabeen, T., Ashraf, H., & Ullah, A. (2021). A survey on healthcare data security in wireless body area networks. *Journal of Ambient Intelligence and Humanized Computing*, 12(10). Available from https://doi.org/10.1007/s12652-020-02728-y.

Jabeen, T., Jabeen, I., Ashraf, H., Ullah, A., Jhanjhi, N. Z., Ghoniem, R. M., & Ray, S. K. (2023). Smart wireless sensor technology for healthcare monitoring system using cognitive radio networks. *Sensors*, 23(13). Available from https://doi.org/10.3390/s23136104, http://www.mdpi.com/journal/sensors.

Jabeen, T., et al. (2023). An intelligent healthcare system using IoT in wireless sensor network. *Sensors*, 23(11). Available from https://doi.org/10.3390/s23115055.

Jagadeeswari, V., Subramaniyaswamy, V., Logesh, R., & Vijayakumar, V. (2018). A study on medical Internet of Things and big data in personalized healthcare system. *Health Information Science and Systems*, 6(1). Available from https://doi.org/10.1007/s13755-018-0049-x.

Javaid, M., & Khan, I. H. (2021). Internet of Things (IoT) enabled healthcare helps to take the challenges of COVID-19 Pandemic. *Journal of Oral Biology and Craniofacial Research*, 11(2). Available from https://doi.org/10.1016/j.jobcr.2021.01.015, http://www.journals.elsevier.com/journal-of-oral-biology-and-craniofacial-research/.

Javaid, S., Wu, Z., Hamid, Z., Zeadally, S., & Fahim, H. (2021). Temperature-aware routing protocol for Intrabody Nanonetworks. *Journal of Network and Computer Applications*, 183-184103057. Available from https://doi.org/10.1016/j.jnca.2021.103057.

Javaid, S., Zeadally, S., Fahim, H., & He, B. (2022). Medical sensors and their integration in wireless body area networks for pervasive healthcare delivery: A review. *IEEE Sensors Journal*, 22(5). Available from https://doi.org/10.1109/jsen.2022.3141064.

Jenkins, T. (2022). Wearable medical sensor devices, machine and deep learning algorithms, and internet of things-based healthcare systems in COVID-19 patient screening, diagnosis, monitoring, and treatment. *American Journal of Medical Research*, 9(1), 2022.

Jin, H., Yu, J., Lin, S., Gao, S., Yang, H., Haick, H., Hua, C., Deng, S., Yang, T., Liu, Y., Shen, W., Zhang, X., Zhang, X., Shan, S., Ren, T., Wang, L., Cheung, W., Kam, W., Miao, J., . . . Cui, D. (2020). Nanosensor-based flexible electronic assisted with light fidelity communicating technology for volatolomics-based telemedicine. *ACS Nano, 14*(11). Available from https://doi.org/10.1021/acsnano.0c06137.

Jung, S.-H., Kim, J. S., Lee, W. S., Oh, S. J., Ahn, J.-S., Yang, D.-H., Kim, Y.-K., Kim, H.-J., & Lee, J.-J. (2016). Prognostic value of the inverse platelet to lymphocyte ratio (iPLR) in patients with multiple myeloma who were treated up front with a novel agent-containing regimen. *Annals of Hematology, 95*(1). Available from https://doi.org/10.1007/s00277-015-2521-x.

Kang, M., Park, E., Cho, B. H., & Lee, K. S. (2018). Recent patient health monitoring platforms incorporating Internet of Things-enabled smart devices. *International Neurourology Journal, 22*, S76. Available from https://doi.org/10.5213/inj.1836144.072, http://einj.org/articles/archive.php.

Karatas, M. et al. (n.d.) Big data for healthcare industry 4.0: Applications, challenges and future perspectives. *Expert Systems with Applications*.

Kavre, M., Gadekar, A., & Gadhade, Y. (2019). Internet of Things (IoT): A survey. In *IEEE Pune section international conference, PuneCon 2019*. Institute of Electrical and Electronics Engineers Inc., India. Available from https://doi.org/10.1109/PuneCon46936.2019.9105831, http://ieeexplore.ieee.org/xpl/mostRecentIssue.jsp?punumber = 9102215, 9781728119243.

Khan, T., Civas, M., Cetinkaya, O., Abbasi, N. A., & Akan, O. B. (2020). *Nanosensor networks for smart health care*. In *Nanosensors for smart cities*, (pp. 387–403). Turkey: Elsevier. Available from https://doi.org/10.1016/B978-0-12-819870-4.00022-0.

Khazaei, M., Hosseini, M. S., Haghighi, A. M., & Misaghi, M. (2023). Nanosensors and their applications in early diagnosis of cancer. *Sensing and Bio-Sensing Research, 41*. Available from https://doi.org/10.1016/j.sbsr.2023.100569, https://www.journals.elsevier.com/sensing-and-bio-sensing-research/.

Kumar, P. M., Hong, C. S., Afghah, F., Manogaran, G., Yu, K., Hua, Q., & Gao, J. (2022). Clouds proportionate medical data stream analytics for internet of things-based healthcare systems. *IEEE Journal of Biomedical and Health Informatics, 26*(3). Available from https://doi.org/10.1109/JBHI.2021.3106387, http://ieeexplore.ieee.org/xpl/RecentIssue.jsp?punumber = 6221020.

Kumar, P. M., Khan, L. U., & Hong, C. S. (2022). Affirmative fusion process for improving wearable sensor data availability in artificial intelligence of medical things. *IEEE Sensors Journal*. Available from https://doi.org/10.1109/JSEN.2022.3153410, http://ieeexplore.ieee.org/xpl/RecentIssue.jsp?punumber = 7361.

Kumar, P. M., Khan., Latif, U., & Hong, C. S. (2022). Notice of violation of IEEE publication principles: Affirmative fusion process for improving wearable sensor data availability in artificial intelligence of medical things. *IEEE Sensors Journal*, 1. Available from https://doi.org/10.1109/jsen.2022.3153410, −1.

Kumar, S., & Kumari, P. (n.d.). Flexible nano smart sensors. *Nanosensors for smart manufacturing*.

Malik, A., & Kumar, A. (2022). *Assimilation of blockchain with Internet of Things (IoT) with possible issues and solutions for better connectivity and proper security* (pp. 187–207). Springer Science and Business Media LLC. Available from https://doi.org/10.1007/978-3-030-99329-0_13.

Malik, P. K., Sharma, R., Singh, R., Gehlot, A., Satapathy, S. C., Alnumay, W. S., Pelusi, D., Ghosh, U., & Nayak, J. (2021). Industrial internet of things and its applications in industry 4.0: State of the art. *Computer Communications, 166*. Available from https://doi.org/10.1016/j.comcom.2020.11.016, http://www.journals.elsevier.com/computer-communications/.

Manogaran, G., Alazab, M., Song, H., & Kumar, N. (2021). CDP-UA: Cognitive data processing method wearable sensor data uncertainty analysis in the internet of things assisted smart medical healthcare systems. *IEEE Journal of Biomedical and Health Informatics, 25*(10). Available from https://doi.org/10.1109/jbhi.2021.3051288.

Manogaran, G., Thota, C., Lopez, D., Vijayakumar, V., Abbas, K. M., & Sundarsekar, R. (2017). Big data knowledge system in healthcare. *Studies in Big Data, 23*. Available from https://doi.org/10.1007/978-3-319-49736-5_7, springer.com/series/11970.

Materon, E. M., Gómez, F. R., Joshi, N., Dalmaschio, C. J., Carrilho, E., & Oliveira, O. N. (2021). Smart materials for electrochemical flexible nanosensors: Advances and applications Nanosensors for Smart Manufacturing. Brazil: Elsevier. Available from https://doi.org/10.1016/B978-0-12-823358-0.00018-6, https://www.elsevier.com/books/nanosensors-for-smart-manufacturing/thomas/978-0-12-823358-0.

Mbunge, E., Muchemwa, B., Jiyane, S. 'esihle, & Batani, J. (2021). Sensors and healthcare 5.0: transformative shift in virtual care through emerging digital health technologies. *Global Health Journal*, *5*(4). Available from https://doi.org/10.1016/j.glohj.2021.11.008.

Metcalf, D., Milliard, S. T. J., Gomez, M., & Schwartz, M. (2016). Wearables and the Internet of Things for health: Wearable, interconnected devices promise more efficient and comprehensive health care. *IEEE Pulse*, *7*(5). Available from https://doi.org/10.1109/MPUL.2016.2592260.

Mujawar, M. A., Gohel, H., Bhardwaj, S. K., Srinivasan, S., Hickman, N., & Kaushik, A. (2020). Nano-enabled bio-sensing systems for intelligent healthcare: Towards COVID-19 management. *Materials Today Chemistry*, *17*100306. Available from https://doi.org/10.1016/j.mtchem.2020.100306.

Mukati, N., Namdev, N., Dilip, R., Hemalatha, N., Dhiman, V., & Sahu, B. (2023). Healthcare assistance to COVID-19 patient using Internet of Things (IoT) enabled technologies. *Materials Today: Proceedings*, *80*. Available from https://doi.org/10.1016/j.matpr.2021.07.379.

Muthukaruppankaruppiah, S., Nagalingam, S. R., Murugasen, P., & Nandaamarnath, R. (2023). Human fatty liver monitoring using nano sensor and IoMT. *Intelligent Automation and Soft Computing*, *35*(2). Available from https://doi.org/10.32604/iasc.2023.029598, https://www.techscience.com/iasc/v35n2/48926/pdf.

Naranjo-Hernández, D., Reina-Tosina, J., & Roa, L. M. (2020). Special issue "body sensors networks for e-health applications.". *Sensors*, *20*(14), 3944. Available from https://doi.org/10.3390/s20143944.

Nazari, A. (2020). Nanosensors for smart cities: An introduction. Nanosensors for smart cities. Iran: Elsevier. Available from https://doi.org/10.1016/B978-0-12-819870-4.00001-3, https://www.sciencedirect.com/book/9780128198704.

Noah, N. M., & Ndangili, P. M. (2022). Nanosensor arrays. *Nanosensors for Futuristic Smart and Intelligent Healthcare Systems*.

Olatinwo, D. D., Abu-Mahfouz, A., & Hancke, G. (2019). A survey on LPWAN technologies in WBAN for remote health-care monitoring. *Sensors*, *19*(23), 5268. Available from https://doi.org/10.3390/s19235268.

Omanović-Miklčanin, E., Maksimović, M., & Vujović, V. (2015). The future of healthcare: Nanomedicine and internet of nano things. *Folia Medica Facultatis Medicinae Universitatis Saraeviensis*, *50*(1), 2015.

Oukhatar, A., Bakhouya, M., & Ouadghiri, D. E. (2021). Electromagnetic-based wireless nano-sensors network: Architectures and applications. *Journal of Communications*, *16*(1). Available from https://doi.org/10.12720/jcm.16.1.8-19, http://www.jocm.us/uploadfile/2020/1218/20201218055937793.pdf.

Paliwal, G., & Bunglowala, A. (2021). Nanosensor and actuator technologies for wearable mobile patient monitoring systems: A review. In *Proceedings in mathematics and statistics* (pp. 83–95). Springer, India. Available from https://doi.org/10.1007/978-981-15-9708-4_7, http://www.springer.com/series/10533 , 21941017342.

Pirmagomedov, R., Hudoev, I., & Shangina, D. (2016). Simulation of medical sensor nanonetwork applications traffic. *Russian Federation Communications in Computer and Information Science*, *678*. Available from https://doi.org/10.1007/978-3-319-51917-3_38, http://www.springer.com/series/7899.

Prabhu, R. S. et al. (2021). *Internet of Nanothings (IoNT)—A concise review of its healthcare applications and future scope in pandemics*.

Pradhan, M. R., Mago, B., & Ateeq, K. (2023). A classification-based sensor data processing method for the internet of things assimilated wearable sensor technology. *Cluster Computing*, *26*(1). Available from https://doi.org/10.1007/s10586-022-03605-3, https://www.springer.com/journal/10586.

Pramanik, P. K. D., Solanki, A., Debnath, A., Nayyar, A., El-Sappagh, S., & Kwak, K. S. (2020). Advancing modern healthcare with nanotechnology, nanobiosensors, and Internet of Nano Things: Taxonomies, applications, architecture, and challenges. *IEEE Access*, *8*. Available from https://doi.org/10.1109/ACCESS.2020.2984269, http://ieeexplore.ieee.org/xpl/RecentIssue.jsp?punumber = 6287639.

Pretis, Gils, & Forsberg, M. M. (2022) A smart hospital-driven approach to precision pharmacovigilance. *Trends in Pharmacological Sciences*.

Qi, J., Yang, P., Min, G., Amft, O., Dong, F., & Xu, L. (2017). Advanced internet of things for personalised healthcare systems: A survey. *Pervasive and Mobile Computing*, *41*. Available from https://doi.org/10.1016/j.pmcj.2017.06.018.

Rahmani, A. M., Gia, T. N., Negash, B., Anzanpour, A., Azimi, I., Jiang, M., & Liljeberg, P. (2018). Exploiting smart e-Health gateways at the edge of healthcare Internet-of-Things: A fog computing approach. *Future Generation Computer Systems*, *78*. Available from https://doi.org/10.1016/j.future.2017.02.014.

Ramasamy, M., Kumar, P. S., & Varadan, V. K. (2017). Wearable nanosensor systems and their applications in healthcare. In *Proceedings of SPIE - The International Society for Optical Engineering*, *10167*, SPIE, United States. Available from https://doi.org/10.1117/12.2264812, http://spie.org/x1848.xml.

Ramasamy, M., & Varadana, V. K. (2016) Wireless nanosensor system for diagnosis of sleep disorders. In *Proceedings of SPIE - The international society for optical engineering*. SPIE, United States. Available from https://doi.org/10.1117/12.2219621, http://spie.org/x1848.xml.

Rani, P. (2022). Nanosensors and their potential role in Internet of Medical Things. Informa UK Limited. Available from https://doi.org/10.1201/9781003093534-16.

Rejeb, A., Rejeb, K., Treiblmaier, H., Appolloni, A., Alghamdi, S., Alhasawi, Y., & Iranmanesh, M. (2023). The Internet of Things (IoT) in healthcare: Taking stock and moving forward. *Internet of Things*, 22100721. Available from https://doi.org/10.1016/j.iot.2023.100721.

Rizwan, A., Zoha, A., Zhang, R., Ahmad, W., Arshad, K., Abu Ali, N., Alomainy, A., Imran, M. A., & Abbasi, Q. H. (2018). A review on the role of nano-communication in future healthcare systems: A big data analytics perspective. *IEEE Access*, 6. Available from https://doi.org/10.1109/ACCESS.2018.2859340, http://ieeexplore.ieee.org/xpl/RecentIssue.jsp?punumber = 6287639.

Rolfe, P. (2010). Impact of micro and nano sensors in biomedical measurement. *Key Engineering Materials*, 437. Available from https://doi.org/10.4028/http://www.scientific.net/kem.437.299.

Sagar, A. K., Banda, L., Sahana, S., Singh, K., & Singh, B. K. (2021). Optimizing quality of service for sensor enabled Internet of healthcare systems. *Neuroscience Informatics*, 1(3)100010. Available from https://doi.org/10.1016/j.neuri.2021.100010.

Sarkar, S., & Misra, S. (2016). From micro to nano: The evolution of wireless sensor-based health care. *IEEE Pulse*, 7(1). Available from https://doi.org/10.1109/MPUL.2015.2498498.

Saylan, Y., Akgönüllü, S., Özgür, E., & Denizli, A. (2022). Nanosensors for smartphone-enabled sensing devices. *Nanotechnology-based smart remote sensing networks for disaster prevention*. Turkey: Elsevier. Available from https://doi.org/10.1016/B978-0-323-91166-5.00003-3, https://www.sciencedirect.com/book/9780323911665.

Shahbaaz Singh Sahi, K., & Kaushik, S. (2022). Smart nanosensors for healthcare monitoring and disease detection using AIoT framework. Informa UK Limited. Available from https://doi.org/10.1201/9781003093534-19.

Singh, B. (2022). COVID-19 pandemic and public healthcare: Endless downward spiral or solution via rapid legal and health services implementation with patient monitoring program. *Justice and Law Bulletin.*, 1(1), 2022.

Singh, B. (2023). Blockchain technology in renovating healthcare: Legal and future perspectives revolutionizing healthcare through artificial intelligence and internet of things applications. India: IGI Global. Available from https://doi.org/10.4018/978-1-6684-5422-0.ch012, https://www.igi-global.com/book/revolutionizing-healthcare-through-artificial-intelligence/295824.

Singh, D., Divan, M., & Singh, M. (2022). Internet of Things for smart community solutions. *Sensors*, 22(2). Available from https://doi.org/10.3390/s22020640.

Solanki, M. S., & Nayak, M. M. (2020). Survey on Internet of Nano Things (IoNT). *Technology (Elmsford, N.Y.)*, 10, 2020.

Suma, V. (2021). Wearable IoT based distributed framework for ubiquitous computing. *Journal of Ubiquitous Computing and Communication Technologies*, 3(1). Available from https://doi.org/10.36548/jucct.2021.1.003.

Tang, W. H., Ho, W. H., & Chen, Y. J. (2018). Data assimilation and multisource decision-making in systems biology based on unobtrusive Internet-of-Things devices. *Biomedical Engineering Online*, 17. Available from https://doi.org/10.1186/s12938-018-0574-5, http://www.biomedical-engineering-online.com/start.asp.

Tien, J. M. (2017). Internet of Things, real-time decision making, and artificial intelligence. *Annals of Data Science*, 4 (2). Available from https://doi.org/10.1007/s40745-017-0112-5, springer.com/journal/40745.

Topel, S. D., & Al-Turjman, F. (2019). Nanosensors for the Internet of Nano-Things (IoNT): An overview internet of nano-things and wireless body area networks (WBAN). Turkey: CRC Press. Available from https://www.taylorfrancis.com/books/9780429513428, 10.1201/9780429243707-3.

Tsang, Y. P., Choy, K. L., Wu, C. H., Ho, G. T. S., Lam, C. H. Y., & Koo, P. S. (2018). An Internet of Things (IoT)-based risk monitoring system for managing cold supply chain risks. *Industrial Management & Data Systems*, 118 (7). Available from https://doi.org/10.1108/imds-09-2017-0384.

Uddin, M.H., Hossain, M.N., & Ur Rahman, A. (2021). A routing protocol for cancer cell detection using wireless nano-sensors network (WNSN). In *Advances in intelligent systems and computing* (pp. 569–578). Springer Science and Business Media, Deutschland GmbH, South Korea. Available from https://doi.org/10.1007/978-981-33-4673-4_46, http://www.springer.com/series/11156, 21945365.

Udoh, E. E., Hermel, M., Bharmal, M. I., Nayak, A., Patel, S., Butlin, M., & Bhavnani, S. P. (2023). Nanosensor technologies and the digital transformation of healthcare. *Personalized Medicine.*, 20(3). Available from https://doi.org/10.2217/pme-2022-0065, http://www.futuremedicine.com/loi/pme;jsessionid = iDlhLxr7W4pgLWINGK.

Varadan, V. K., Chen, L., & Xie, J. (2008). Nanomedicine: Design and applications of magnetic nanomaterials, nanosensors and nanosystems. Wiley. Available from https://doi.org/10.1002/9780470715611.

Varadan, V. K., Kumar, P. S., Oh, S., Kwon, H., Rai, P., Banerjee, N., & Harbaugh, R. E. (2011). e-Nanoflex sensor system: Smartphone-based roaming health monitor. *Journal of Nanotechnology in Engineering and Medicine*, 2(1). Available from https://doi.org/10.1115/1.4003479.

Vivekananthan, V., Khandelwal, G., Alluri, N. R., & Kim, S.-J. (2022). *E-skin for futuristic nanosensor technology for the healthcare system*. Informa UK Limited. Available from https://doi.org/10.1201/9781003093534-9.

Wang, L. (2019). Bio-multifunctional smart wearable sensors for medical devices. *Advanced Intelligent Systems*, 5, 2019.

Wang, W., Kumar, N., Chen, J., Gong, Z., Kong, X., Wei, W., & Gao, H. (2020). Realizing the potential of the Internet of Things for smart tourism with 5G and AI. *IEEE Network*, 34(6). Available from https://doi.org/10.1109/mnet.011.2000250.

West, D. M. (2016). How 5G technology enables the health internet of things. *Brookings Center for Technology Innovation*, 3(1), 2016.

Yang, J., Carey, P., Ren, F., Lobo, B. C., Gebhard, M., Leon, M. E., Lin, J., & Pearton, S. J. (2020). *Nanosensor networks for health-care applications nanosensors for smart cities*. United States: Elsevier. Available from https://www.sciencedirect.com/book/9780128198704, 10.1016/B978-0-12-819870-4.00023-2.

Yang, L., & Webster, T. J. (2011). Monitoring tissue healing through nanosensors nanotechnology enabled in situ sensors for monitoring health. United States: Springer New York. Available from http://www.springerlink.com/openurl.asp?genre = book&isbn = 978-1-4419-7290-3, 10.1007/978-1-4419-7291-0_2.

Zhan, K. (2021). Sports and health big data system based on 5G network and Internet of Things system. *Microprocessors and Microsystems*, 80. Available from https://doi.org/10.1016/j.micpro.2020.103363.

Zhang, Z. (2022). Artificial intelligence-enabled sensing technologies in the 5G/internet of things era: From virtual reality/augmented reality to the digital twin. *Advanced Intelligent Systems*, 7, 2022.

Zhu, H., Wu, C. K., Koo, C. H., Tsang, Y. T., Liu, Y., Chi, H. R., & Tsang, K. F. (2019). Smart healthcare in the era of Internet-of-Things. *IEEE Consumer Electronics Magazine*, 8(5). Available from https://doi.org/10.1109/MCE.2019.2923929, https://www.ieee.org/membership-catalog/productdetail/showProductDetailPage.html?product = PER262-EPC.

Smart body area networks

Ihab Nassra and Juan V. Capella

Institute of Information and Communication Technologies (ITACA), Polytechnic University of Valencia, Valencia, Spain

3.1 Introduction

In the era of digital health, integrating advanced sensors into body area networks (BANs) has emerged as a transformative approach to monitoring and managing health status. BANs, also known as wireless body area networks (WBANs), are an innovative technology that has the potential to revolutionize healthcare and improve the quality of life for millions of people worldwide. These networks, composed of wearable and implantable sensors, have transformed healthcare by providing real-time data on various physiological parameters. BANs can radically change the health care delivered by ambulances, emergency rooms, operating theaters, clinics, and homes. Furthermore, technological improvements have drastically influenced how we monitor and track our health status. Introducing BANs allows us to gather highly accurate and continuous data about our body's functioning in real time. BANs have evolved from rudimentary wearable devices to sophisticated systems capable of capturing and transmitting a plethora of physiological data. Initially limited to essential functions like heart rate monitoring and step counting, BANs now incorporate various sensors enabling tracking blood glucose levels, blood pressure, oxygen saturation, body temperature, and more. These sensors, when integrated into a BAN, provide continuous and noninvasive monitoring of vital signs, allowing for early detection of health issues and remote patient care. In recent years, integrating advanced sensors into BANs has emerged as a transformative approach in healthcare. BANs, consisting of interconnected wearable and implantable sensors, have revolutionized real-time monitoring and management of various physiological parameters. With the advent of advanced sensors, BANs have become highly efficient, accurate, and capable of providing real-time health data. One key component of BANs is advanced sensors, which play a crucial role in collecting and transmitting this data. Real-time monitoring and analysis of vital signs and other physiological parameters can aid in early detection, diagnosis, and treatment of various health conditions.

Sensor Networks for Smart Hospitals
DOI: https://doi.org/10.1016/B978-0-443-36370-2.00004-9

BAN is a network of interconnected sensors and devices worn or implanted in the human body to monitor physiological parameters, detect abnormalities, and provide real-time health information (Hasan et al., 2019). BAN can also be defined as a mechanism that enables smooth connection and data transmission across a network of implanted or wearable devices placed on or around a person's body. BAN is advantageous in domains like fitness, healthcare, and personal communication since it allows for continuous tracking of vital physiological signals, offering professionals and people unparalleled access to critical information with greater simplicity and precision. BANs have recently become prominent due to the rising prevalence of smartphones and wearable smart widgets and the widespread use of the Internet of Things (IoT). The fundamental pursuit of a BAN lies in the synchronization and prudent connection of these devices to monitor, measure, and manage an individual's physiological and biological data without impeding their movement or comfort. BANs have evolved significantly, transitioning from essential wearable devices to sophisticated systems monitoring diverse health parameters. Initially, BANs focused on simple functions like step counting and heart rate monitoring (Cavallari et al., 2014). At the heart of this technology are sensors, which play a vital role in observing several physiological parameters of the human body. BANs have gained significant attention in the healthcare industry due to their potential to revolutionize patient monitoring, disease management, and personalized healthcare. These networks enable continuous, noninvasive monitoring of vital signs and other health-related data, allowing for early detection of health issues and timely intervention. These networks utilize diverse technologies such as electrochemical, optical, piezoelectric, and microelectromechanical systems (MEMS), ensuring accuracy, reliability, and noninvasiveness. The primary purpose of BANs is to monitor health, enhance patient outcomes, promote preventive healthcare practices, and support medical diagnosis and treatment. Some advantages of using a BAN include continuous health monitoring, early detection of health issues, assistance in medical treatments, increased personal safety, and improved fitness tracking.

This chapter aims to provide a comprehensive overview of advanced sensors in BANs, exploring their capabilities, challenges, and potential impact on healthcare. This chapter also investigates the developments and clinical utility of smart wearable body sensors that have been extensively studied and reported in the literature. This chapter explores the significance of advanced sensors in BANs, their applications, the role of advanced sensors within BANs, their significance, the challenges they address, and the implications for healthcare delivery. Additionally, this chapter delves into the world of advanced sensors within BANs, shedding light on their development, key challenges, and potential applications.

3.2 Evolution of body area networks

BANs have evolved from simple wearable devices to sophisticated systems capable of monitoring a myriad of physiological signals. Initially, Dam et al. (2001) were widely regarded as the pioneers of the wireless body area sensor network sector in 2001. Even before then, in 1996, as portable electronics became more popular, Zimmerman focused on how these portable gadgets would perform in the presence of the human body. These networks were first referred to as personal area networks (PANs). Later, PAN was renamed with a more contemporary term, BAN. BAN connects several networks and devices to facilitate remote monitoring operations. One of the foremost unambiguous applications of BAN is the healthcare monitoring system.

Wireless sensor networks (WSNs) and BANs are both types of networks that use wireless communication technology to collect and transmit data. However, they differ in their applications, scale, and the nature of the nodes they use, as stated in Table 3.1 BANs emanated from WSNs. There are multiple parallels among them. Nevertheless, the features are also dissimilar due to their various application purposes. Firstly, regarding the deployment of the network, WSNs could be deployed in unreachable environments, like mountains, forests, or swamps. Multiple repetitious nodes can be positioned in the environment to avoid the issue of node failures. Thus, the number of nodes becomes higher, while in BAN, nodes are deployed on, in, or near the human body, with the total number of nodes commonly up to a few dozen (Latré et al., 2011). Secondly, regarding attributes, WSN nodes accomplish the same operations and have identical properties. Once the nodes are deployed, they may no longer require to be moved. In contrast, BAN applications use a variety of sensors based on the various signals received. Furthermore, the nodes should be small enough in size, excellent wearability, and biocompatibility. Thirdly, WSNs and BANs may be powered by batteries in terms of energy usage. WSNs could be deployed outside, as they might also be powered by solar energy or wind, whereas BANs might run on kinetic energy and body heat. Finally, the WSNs' transfer rates are almost the same, while the transfer rates of BANs differ, as the channel assignment and the data type differ between nodes in the body and on the body surface. In general, both BANs and WSNs involve the use of wireless sensors to gather and transmit data, BANs are specifically designed for use on the human body for health monitoring. In contrast, WSNs are more general-purpose networks that can be deployed in various environments for a wide range of applications.

Glucose monitors, heart rate monitors, fitness trackers, smartwatches, and implanted medical devices like insulin pumps and pacemakers are prevalent devices employed in a BAN. These gadgets may monitor different biological processes, wirelessly communicate data, and deliver real-time health and fitness information to the user. These devices can be implanted in the body as pills or implants surface mounted on the body in a fixed place or carried in various ways, such as in clothing pockets, by hand, or in bags. Devices in a BAN often interact via wireless technologies such as ZigBee, Wi-Fi, or Bluetooth, allowing for simple integration with tablets, smartphones, and other personal electronic devices or smooth sharing of information and monitoring. These widgets provide short-range, low-power communication appropriate for implanted and wearable devices. To conserve energy consumption, BAN devices often employ low-power wireless communication protocols. Nevertheless, data transfer frequency, signal strength, and the sorts of sensors utilized may have a detrimental impact on the battery life of these devices. BAN networks comprise a single central unit and several small body sensor units (BSUs) (Johny & Anpalagan, 2014). The sensors or BSUs are attached to the body or daily clothes. Various sensors are linked to a centralized processor, which transmits the data to a medical network, where healthcare specialists evaluate the user's health status. The data gathered by these sensors is transmitted wirelessly to a central hub, typically a smartphone or a

TABLE 3.1   Comparison between body area network and wireless sensor netwok.

Feature	BAN	WSN
Design	BANs are specifically designed for use on or within the human body. They consist of wearable or implantable sensors.	WSNs are larger-scale networks that can be deployed in a variety of environments, not just on the human body.
Sensors Characteristics	The sensors in BANs are typically small, lightweight, and designed to be unobtrusive. They frequently have restricted energy requirements due to the necessity for a prolonged battery life.	These nodes are self-directed and low-powered devices.
Communications	BAN devices often interact by utilizing wireless technologies such as ZigBee, Bluetooth, or Wi-Fi.	The nodes in a WSN can communicate with each other and with a Base Station (BS) using wireless communication.
Applications	BANs are predominantly used in healthcare to monitor patients' health continuously and discover any health disorders early on.	WSNs are utilized in various applications, such as surveillance, industrial process control, and environmental monitoring.
Data loss impact	More critical	Mitigated by redundant nodes
Security and privacy level	High	Lower
Biocompatibility	Very important	Not important
Power scavenge source	Thermal heat, Motion (vibration),	Solar Energy, Wind Energy
Power demand	Lower	Large
Power supply	Inaccessible and hard to replace in an implanted environment	Accessible and more readily and regularly replaced
Node lifetime	Days/months	Months/years
Replacement of nodes	Hard to replace the implanted nodes	Performed effortlessly; nodes are even disposable
Data rates	Nonhomogeneous	Homogeneous
Network topology	More variability owing to bodily movement	Most probably static or fixed
Node size	Tiny is preferable	Tiny is preferable but not necessary.
Number of nodes	Fewer and restricted in space	Several nodes are required so that a wide area is covered
Task of node	Multiple	Dedicated task
Accuracy of result	Through node accuracy and robustness	Through node redundancy
Channel	ISM (medical and industrial, scientific), body surface, medical channel	ISM
Scale	Up to centimeters to a few meters	Meters to kilometers
Monitoring	Human body physiological parameters	Environment monitoring

computer, where it is processed and analyzed. This allows for continuous health monitoring and early detection of potential health issues.

There are two types of communication in BANs based on the location of the sensors:

- *On-body communication:* This takes place among wearable devices, which are composed of sensor nodes.
- *In-body communication:* This is the connection among sensor nodes implanted into the human body.

The specific communication protocols used can vary depending on the specific requirements of the BAN, such as power consumption, data rate, and communication range.

3.3 Advanced sensor roles and types in body area networks

Sensors are the cornerstone of BANs. They are responsible for collecting the necessary data from the body. This data can include heart rate, blood pressure, body temperature, glucose levels, and more. The sensors then transmit this data wirelessly to a central device, such as a smartphone or computer, where it can be analyzed and monitored. The tiny-sized sensors in BANs can be invasive (i.e., placed into the human body) or noninvasive (i.e., attached to human skin or implemented around the human body). These gadgets do not bother the person's activity but can capture physiological data during any specific activity. For example, a patient's blood pressure, pulse rate, or temperature could be monitored during their everyday routine. A soldier's health can be monitored on the battlefield or during training sessions, and a player may be observed during a game. This enables ongoing monitoring of physiological markers (Bhatti et al., 2022). These sensors might be smaller than traditional ones.

Sensors enact primarily three tasks: sensing, processing, and communication. Sensors detect and measure physical properties or environmental changes in the sensing process, such as temperature, pressure, light, sound, motion, or chemical composition. Sensors can be designed to detect a wide range of phenomena depending on their intended application. In many cases, raw sensor data should be processed to extract meaningful information or make it more suitable for analysis or decision-making. This processing might involve filtering out the noise, calibrating measurements, converting analog signals to digital, or performing more complex computations such as pattern recognition or feature extraction. Once the sensor has collected and processed data, it often needs to transmit this information to another device or system for further analysis or action. Communication can occur through various means such as wired connections (like USB or Ethernet), wireless protocols (like Wi-Fi, Bluetooth, or Zigbee), or even through specialized networks like LoRaWAN or NB-IoT for long-range communication in IoT applications (Movassaghi et al., 2014). Table 3.2 lists invasive and noninvasive sensors (Zimmerman, 1996) that can perform the abovementioned three main tasks.

Physiological parameters may be monitored in several locations across the human body (see Fig. 3.1). Actuators are often positioned alongside these sensors to administer medications to the body. For instance, a diabetic patient's blood glucose levels are monitored. If the sensor detects a drop in glucose level, it triggers the actuator, which pumps a set amount of insulin into the body (Krames, 2002). BANs can also help disabled persons. An artificial retina, for example, converts electrical data into neural signals. It comprises a grid of tiny

TABLE 3.2   Noninvasive and invasive and sensors.

Noninvasive/wearable sensors	Invasive/implantable sensors
Blood pressure	Retina implants
Pulse oximeter	Deep brain stimulator
Electromyography (EMG)	Implantable defibrillators
Electroencephalogram (EEG)	Wireless capsule endoscope (electronic pill)
Electrocardiogram (ECG)	Pacemaker
Temperature	Electronic pill for drug delivery
Glucose sensor	Cochlear implants
Oxygen, pH value	

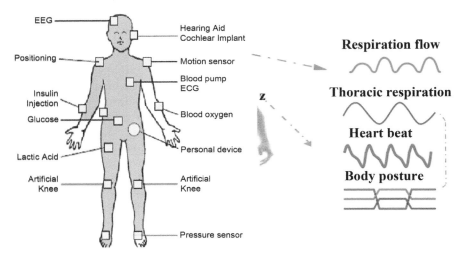

FIGURE 3.1   Human physiological parameters.

sensors that may be placed underneath the eye (Cheng et al., 2017). Sensors could be fitted to a paralyzed person's legs (or lower torso) to identify the legs' positions (Li et al., 2007).

There are many types of sensors used in BANs:

- **Biosensors:** Biosensors play a pivotal role in BANs by converting biological signals into measurable electrical signals. These sensors can detect biomolecules, enzymes, and other biological markers with high sensitivity and specificity. For instance, glucose sensors enable continuous monitoring of blood glucose levels, which is crucial for diabetes management. Biosensors are categorized into two main types:
- **Wearable Sensors:** These sensors are worn on the body and can monitor several physiological parameters. Examples include smartwatches that monitor heart rate or fitness bands that track physical activity.

- **Implantable Sensors:** These sensors are surgically implanted into the body. They can monitor internal physiological parameters [such as temperature, blood oxygen level, blood pressure, blood glucose level, and the signals related to electromyography (EMG), electroencephalogram (EEG), and electrocardiography (ECG)] that wearable sensors cannot. For instance, a sensor could be implanted into the heart to monitor heart function or into the bloodstream to monitor glucose levels.
- **Biokinetic Sensors:** These sensors monitor the angular rotation rate and the acceleration of bodily motions.
- **Ambient Sensors:** These sensors measure environmental factors like sound pressure level, humidity, light, and temperature.
- **Imaging Sensors:** Imaging sensors such as photoplethysmography (PPG) and ECG provide valuable insights into cardiovascular health by monitoring parameters like heart rate variability, arterial stiffness, and cardiac arrhythmias.
- **Motion Sensors:** Accelerometers and gyroscopes integrated into BANs enable precise motion tracking and activity recognition. These sensors facilitate monitoring physical activity levels and gait analysis, which is essential for assessing mobility and detecting abnormalities.
- **Environmental Sensors:** BANs can incorporate environmental sensors to monitor external factors such as temperature, humidity, and air quality, influencing an individual's health status and well-being.

3.3.1 Examples of implantable sensors

Implantable sensors are a crucial part of BANs, and they come in various forms to monitor different physiological parameters. The ongoing advancement of these gadgets paves the door for their widespread usage in the human body. Millions of individuals worldwide suffer from cardiovascular diseases (CVDs) and other chronic conditions such as high blood pressure, diabetes, severe joint pain, and so on. Implantable devices can connect wirelessly and can be used to assess and provide alerts to help save human lives. Baclofen pumps, medication pumps, implantable cardioverter-defibrillator (ICD), implantable cardiac devices, neurostimulators, and pacemakers are all examples of medical devices used in humans. The primary aim of all BAN systems is to enhance the users' quality of life. Yet, the technology requirements for BAN are frequently application-specific. Table 3.3 shows some of the on-body and in-body uses. Some other examples are listed as follows:

Implantable Chemical Sensors: These sensors can monitor various chemical levels in the body.

Glucose and Oxygen Sensors: These sensors are handy for people with diabetes as they can continuously monitor glucose and oxygen levels in the body (Yuce, 2013).

Neural Implants: These sensors are implanted in the nervous system and can monitor neural activity. They might be utilized for various purposes, including treating neurological illnesses, and developing brain-computer interfaces.

Cochlear Implants: Such sensors are used to restore hearing in people with severe hearing loss. They stimulate the auditory nerve directly without going via the damaged components of the ear (Ramasamy, no date).

TABLE 3.3 Characteristics of on/in-body applications.

Application type	Sensor node	Data rate	Duty cycle (per device) % per time	Power consumption	QoS (sensitive to latency)	Privacy
On-body nonmedical application	Social networking	<200 kbps	<1%	Low	No	High
	Music for headsets	1.4 Mbps	High	Relatively high	Yes	Low
	Forgotten things monitor	256 kbps	Medium	Low	No	Low
On-body medical application	Blood pressure	<10 bps	<1%	High	Yes	Medium
	SpO2	32 kbps	<1%	Low	Yes	High
	ECG	3 kbps	<10%	Low	Yes	High
In-body application	Pacemaker	Few kbps	Few kbps	Low	Yes	High
	Glucose sensor	Few kbps	<1%	Extremely high	Yes	High
	Endoscope capsule	>2 Mbps	<50%	Low	Yes	Medium

Pacemakers and Implantable Defibrillators: While not sensors in the traditional sense, these devices monitor and respond to heart rhythms, delivering electrical pulses to regulate the heartbeat.

Swallowable Devices: These include wireless capsules that can monitor various aspects of the gastrointestinal tract.

Cancer Detection: Cancer is the most significant cause of mortality globally. Sensors able to observe cancer cells can be included in BANs. For example, these sensors can detect cancers without needing a biopsy.

Diabetes Control: Diabetes is a disease that occurs when the body's capacity to use insulin is impaired. According to Preetha and Dhaya, it is the ninth most common cause of mortality due to illness (Preetha & Vel, 2016). These sensors enable continuous monitoring of blood glucose levels, which is crucial for diabetes management.

3.3.2 New generations of sensors for body sensor networks

In biological observation, a living organism is the "physical world" to be monitored. Accordingly, the sensor nodes should be nearby or implanted within the body to build a network. The demand for "invisibility" drives the development of sensor nodes for biological monitoring, which draws on all existing technological choices, ranging from microelectronics to upcoming technologies. Combining several devices within a tiny physical volume leads to "invisibility" in sensor nodes for biological surveillance. This section presents four new-generation sensors for BANs.

3.3.2.1 *Obtrusive nodes*

These nodes' weight and size make them impractical for usage. Nonetheless, they are movable and may link to other gateways or nodes. Current commercial sensors like body tracking systems and electrical heart rate that involve a marker and a wearable camera have become challenging owing to two drawbacks: first, there is excessive use of energy, which either requires a large battery or a quick charging time, and the second is an extensive sensory interface.

3.3.2.2 *Parasitic nodes*

Parasitic nodes are physical entities whose structure, weight, and size do not interfere with normal functions and are known as nodes. Body-tracking inertia and biometric clock sensors are instances of parasitic devices. These nodes should weigh tens of grams and have a few cubic centimeters of physical volume. Based on current battery technology, these nodes should consume only a few milliwatts of electrical energy. Several parasitic nodes have recently become commercially available. These gadgets reflect cutting-edge technology in wireless sensor networks (Adarsh & Kumar, 2020).

3.3.2.3 *Symbiotic nodes*

The scientific community is attempting to reinvent new technology by developing gadgets in cubic millimeters (known as smart dust) to allow various new applications of in-body biological monitoring. Nevertheless, various technical concerns should be remedied. The initial stage is to install nodes capable of providing the required energy. The body may provide the power needed by these nodes (chemical reactions in the body, temperature changes, etc.). Second, the size constraint significantly demands the integration processes and micro processing. Finally, there are issues regarding the safety requirements. Nodes must be physiologically compatible in both the long and short term. Coexistence refers to the relationship between these nodes and the target organism based on reciprocal benefits.

3.3.2.4 *Bioinspired nodes*

Bioinspired nodes are presented as the technical and architectural pinnacle of the biologically inspired node hierarchy. When these nodes reach a physical scale of a few cubic microns (or less), the interaction between the target sensor and the sensor itself ceases. Bioinspired gadgets will soon be a reality owing to nanotechnology and molecular engineering. Some research studies have shown that scale molecular devices, usually made using biomolecules, could provide some of the characteristics required in sensor nodes. These nodes are self-contained, drawing energy using chemical processes modeled from biological approaches. These devices' architectural and manufacturing procedures are analogous to natural biological processes; in addition to biological compatibility and safety, bioinspired nodes should be capable of bottom-up synthesis, reproduction, and repair.

3.4 Body area networks architecture

BAN involves several wireless sensors fitted to the human body. Such sensors constantly observe the patients' vitals for diagnosis or analysis purposes. According to Sehra and Dave, the architecture could be divided into three layers: sensors, a local server, and a cloud server. Fig. 3.2 shows a three-layer architecture of BAN.

3.4.1 First level: sensors

Sensors process the raw data from their environment and translate it into meaningful data that an observer or computer system can read. In the medical domain, sensors can process, read, and transmit vital signs, allowing remote health monitoring. Some examples of medical sensors are Chest (ABDO RES, THOR RES, AIRFLOW, and ECG), Head (EOG (R), EOG (L), EEG (sec)), Wrists (SaO2, EMG & PR).

3.4.2 Second level: local server

The local server processes the data received from the sensors. The local server could be a personal computer or a patient's smartphone. This data can be transmitted from the local server to the cloud server through the internet using a broadband connection or telecom network.

The local server performs the following jobs, as cited in Fig. 3.3:

- Data Gathering
- Data Processing
- Data Aggregation
- Data transmission

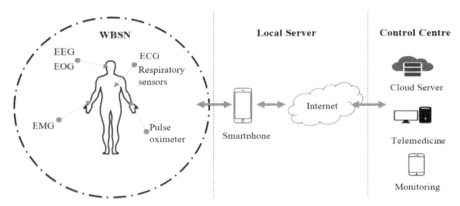

FIGURE 3.2   Three-layer architecture of body area network (Sehra & Dave, 2020).

FIGURE 3.3 Flowchart of local server functions.

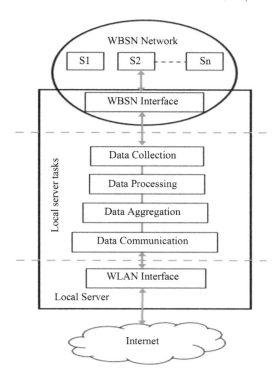

3.4.3 Third level: cloud server

The server acts as a database for all received data from several BANs where a physician examines the patients' health information. The physician can prescribe treatment/care depending on the sensors' inputs for a particular patient. After successful authorization, the doctor can access the cloud server via a web interface.

Another view of BAN architecture is described by Bangash et al. (2014), where the architecture could be divided into three-tires, as shown in Fig. 3.4:

Tier 1 (Intra BAN): In the intra-tire, the implanted biomedical or on-body sensor nodes send the data to a base station or coordinator. Zimmerman proposed this sort of communication (Zimmerman, 1996). This tier allows for both wireless and wired connection options. Intra-BAN communication is limited to the sensors and the sink. This layer has a communication range of around 2 m in and around the human body. This explains why the form of communication in this tire is short-range. Thus, Bluetooth and ZigBee are operated as communications mechanisms in this tier. The sensors monitor physiological parameters and provide the results to the sink or base station. The sink's role here is to analyze the obtained data and send it to Tier 2.

Tier 2 (Inter BAN): After the necessary data gathering and processing, base stations or coordinators send the gathered data to the sink(s) in this tire. Moreover, communication takes place between one or more access points (APs) and the sink. APs might be strategically

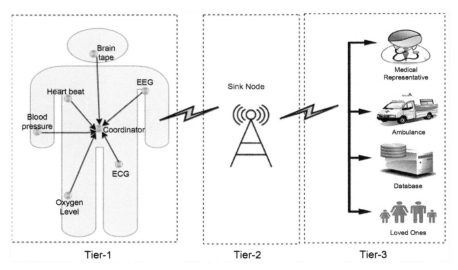

FIGURE 3.4 A three-tires architecture of wireless body sensor network (WBSN).

positioned in a dynamic environment to ensure they can successfully handle emergencies. This tier's role is to provide interconnectivity between various types of networks, such as cell phone networks (or, maybe, the Internet) and BANs. This tier allows for using wireless technologies such as Bluetooth, ZigBee, wireless local area network, cellular, and 3G/4G.

Tier 3 (Extra-BAN): In the extra tier, the sink node transmits the gathered data to a remote health center or any other destination through the Internet. This tier is intended for usage in metropolitan area networks. The medical sensor is linked to the Internet or another network to transmit data to the recipient entities, allowing healthcare staff to obtain health/medical-related data.

As illustrated in Fig. 3.4, if the environment outside the actual BAN is given consideration, the same facility can be expanded to envision an environment that can link thousands of gadgets to boost e-healthcare facilities and provide remote healthcare for hard-to-reach patients. This overarching concept is called the Internet of Medical Things (IoMT) (Tzanis, 2018). BAN can serve as the backbone for IoMT; however, when looking at the perimeter of BAN (inside Tier 2 and the core component confined to Tier 1), as this is the primary purpose of this study, anything outside BAN (i.e., anything beyond Tier 2) is considered beyond the scope of BAN's functioning.

3.5 Routing protocols in body area networks

BANs represent a significant advancement in healthcare and personal monitoring systems, where wearable and implantable devices collect physiological data and communicate with external devices for analysis and decision-making. The seamless transmission of data within BANs relies heavily on efficient routing protocols. These protocols dictate how data packets are forwarded through the network, ensuring timely and reliable information delivery. Understanding the intricacies of routing protocols in BANs is essential for optimizing network performance, conserving energy, and ensuring data integrity. Routing protocols play a crucial role in enabling efficient and reliable communication within BANs. By leveraging proximity-based, energy-efficient, QoS-aware, secure, and mobility-aware routing protocols, stakeholders can optimize network performance, conserve energy, ensure data integrity, and enhance the overall reliability of BANs. Moreover, understanding the characteristics and capabilities of different routing protocols is essential for designing and deploying BANs that meet the diverse requirements of healthcare monitoring, sports analytics, and personalized wellness applications. There are many routing protocols in BANs:

3.5.1 Proximity-based routing

Proximity-based routing protocols are well-suited for BANs due to their ability to exploit the spatial proximity of nodes. In these protocols, data packets are forwarded to nearby nodes, leveraging the physical closeness of wearable devices to establish communication links. Proximity-based routing in BANs involves routing data packets based on the physical proximity of devices rather than traditional network addresses. The purpose is to optimize communication efficiency, reduce energy consumption, and ensure reliable data delivery in dynamic environments. By minimizing the number of hops and reducing transmission delays, proximity-based routing protocols enhance the efficiency of data delivery in BANs. Examples of proximity-based routing protocols include Geographic Routing and Distance-Based Routing.

3.5.2 Energy-efficient routing

Energy efficiency is critical in BANs, where wearable and implantable devices operate on limited battery power. Energy-efficient routing protocols aim to minimize energy consumption by optimizing communication pathways and reducing unnecessary data transmissions. These protocols may employ techniques such as data aggregation, sleep scheduling, and route optimization to prolong device battery life while maintaining reliable network communication. Examples of energy-efficient routing protocols are low-energy adaptive clustering hierarchy and directed diffusion.

3.5.3 Quality of Service-aware routing

Quality of service (QoS) requirements in BANs vary depending on the application and the type of physiological data being transmitted. QoS-aware routing protocols prioritize data delivery based on predefined performance metrics such as latency, reliability, and throughput. These protocols dynamically adapt routing decisions to meet the specific QoS requirements of different types of traffic, ensuring that critical health data is delivered in a timely and reliable manner. Examples of QoS-aware routing protocols include QoS routing protocol and multi-constraint QoS routing.

3.5.4 Secure routing

Security is a paramount concern in BANs, where sensitive health data is transmitted over wireless channels. Secure routing protocols incorporate encryption, authentication, and intrusion detection mechanisms to protect data integrity and confidentiality. These protocols establish secure communication links between nodes, verify the authenticity of transmitted data, and detect and mitigate malicious activities such as eavesdropping and tampering. Examples of secure routing protocols are secure multipath routing and secure geographic routing.

3.5.5 Mobility-aware routing

In BANs, wearable devices may exhibit mobility as users move and engage in various activities. Mobility-aware routing protocols adapt to node positions and movement pattern changes to maintain connectivity and optimize routing paths. These protocols dynamically update routing tables and adjust transmission parameters based on the mobility patterns of nodes, ensuring continuous and uninterrupted communication within the network. Examples of mobility-aware routing protocols include mobility prediction-based routing and dynamic source routing.

3.6 Body area networks constraints and challenges

Communication in BANs primarily relies on a wireless connection for data transmission. The wireless medium should be capable of minimizing obstacles and amplifying the collaboration of sensor hubs with other linked gadgets. Although BANs offer significant potential for healthcare and personal use, they suffer from several constraints and challenges, as follows:

- **Limited Resources:** BANs have restricted store capacity, weak processing abilities, a short RF transmission spectrum, and a low bandwidth, which may change due to noise and other interferences (Ullah et al., 2012).
- **Heterogeneous Environment:** BAN needs to handle the issue of sensor heterogeneity sufficiently to combine various sensors regarding complexity, storage, and power efficiency. Therefore, it is necessary to boost a standard interface between the storage devices and the sensors to facilitate remote storage and transmission of sensor data from accessing the offline or online analysis and processing techniques (Bangash et al., 2014). Several types of sensor nodes are needed to monitor various health parameters of humans, which could even vary in energy consumption, processing, and storage capabilities. Hence, the heterogeneous characteristics of BANs even impose some additional challenges.
- **Data Security and Privacy:** The data yielded from BANs should be transmitted securely to guarantee the integrity and isolation of patients' data (Bhardwaj et al., 2022). Additionally, the aggregated data should be analyzed consistently and securely. Given

the sensitive nature of the data gathered by BANs, ensuring data security and privacy is paramount. Unauthorized access to this data could lead to serious privacy breaches.

- **Power Consumption:** BANs typically rely on battery power. Designing energy-efficient sensors and devices is a significant challenge, especially for implantable devices where battery replacement is not straightforward.
- **Interference:** BANs operate in the crowded wireless spectrum. Interference from other devices can affect the reliability of data transmission.
- **Wearability and Comfort:** For wearable devices, factors such as size, weight, and esthetics play a crucial role in user acceptance. The devices need to be comfortable and unobtrusive.
- **Regulatory Approval:** Obtaining regulatory approval for BANs used in medical applications can be lengthy and complex.
- **Integration with Healthcare Systems:** The data collected by BANs should be seamlessly integrated with existing healthcare systems to be useful for healthcare professionals.
- **Reliability:** Given that these networks can be used to monitor critical health parameters, they need to be highly reliable. Any malfunction could potentially have serious consequences.

Despite these challenges, the future of BANs is bright, with ongoing advancements in sensor technology, data analysis techniques, and integration with healthcare systems. As technology advances, we might anticipate more imaginative applications of these sensors, improving the quality of life for individuals worldwide.

3.6.1 Challenges in developing implantable sensors for body area networks

Developing implantable sensors for BANs presents several challenges:

Size Constraints: Implantable sensors must be small enough to fit comfortably inside the body.

Biocompatibility: The sensors' materials should be consistent with the body to avert adverse reactions.

Signal Attenuation: The human body is composed of materials that can heavily attenuate electromagnetic signals, which can degrade the quality of data transmission.

Power Efficiency: Implantable sensors typically rely on batteries for power. Designing power-efficient sensors is crucial as replacing batteries in implantable devices is not straightforward (Dinis & Mendes, 2017).

Engineering Challenges: Enhancing sensor sensitivity and selectivity while maintaining biocompatibility is a substantial challenge.

Regulatory Hurdles: Obtaining regulatory approval for such technologies might be a complicated process due to the absence of suitable protocols (Palivela, 2023).

Clinical Trials: Performing clinical trials might be challenging due to the equipment's restricted availability and high cost.

Patient-Related Obstacles: Patients may experience dread and anxiety due to a lack of knowledge about sensors. Additionally, privacy concerns should be addressed (Yogev et al., 2023).

3.6.2 Challenges related to the network layer

BANs face several challenges related to the network layer, which bears responsibility for routing data between nodes, managing network topology, and ensuring reliable communication. These challenges include:

Dynamic Topology: BANs often have dynamic topologies due to the movement of wearable or implantable devices on or within the body. Nodes may join or leave the network frequently, leading to changes in network connectivity and topology (Yaghoubi et al., 2022). The network layer must adapt to these dynamic changes efficiently, maintain connectivity between nodes, and ensure uninterrupted communication despite topology changes.

Limited Bandwidth: BANs operate in a constrained bandwidth environment, limiting the amount of data transmitted between nodes. The network layer must prioritize and manage data traffic efficiently to optimize bandwidth utilization and ensure timely delivery of critical data. Data aggregation, compression, and prioritization are essential to maximize bandwidth efficiency in BANs.

Reliability and Fault Tolerance: BAN applications often have stringent reliability and fault tolerance requirements, particularly in healthcare settings where timely and accurate data delivery is crucial. The network layer must ensure reliable communication by selecting robust routing paths, detecting and recovering from link failures, and mitigating packet loss. However, achieving reliability in BANs is challenging due to the dynamic nature of the environment, interference, and node mobility.

Security and Privacy: Security and privacy are paramount concerns in BANs due to the sensitivity of medical data and the potential for unauthorized access or tampering. The network layer must enforce secure authentication mechanisms, communication protocols, and access control policies to protect data confidentiality and integrity. Additionally, privacy-preserving techniques such as data encryption and anonymization are essential to safeguard users' privacy in BANs.

Scalability: BANs may involve many interconnected devices, particularly in healthcare environments with multiple patients and caregivers. The network layer must support scalable routing protocols and efficient resource allocation to accommodate the growing number of nodes and ensure optimal network performance. However, scalability challenges arise from the limited bandwidth, node mobility, and overhead of managing many devices in BANs.

Addressing these challenges requires innovative solutions and advancements in network layer protocols, algorithms, and techniques tailored to the unique characteristics and requirements of BANs. By overcoming these challenges, BANs can realize their full potential in revolutionizing healthcare delivery, enabling personalized monitoring, diagnosis, and treatment of medical conditions.

3.6.3 Security threats in body area networks

Ensuring the security and privacy of sensitive health data is paramount to Bans' widespread adoption and success. By addressing the various security threats discussed above through robust encryption techniques, authentication mechanisms, physical security measures, and proactive risk management strategies, stakeholders can mitigate risks and build trust in the integrity and reliability of BANs. Ultimately, a holistic approach to security is essential to harnessing the full potential of BANs while safeguarding the privacy and well-being of individuals. These interconnected wearable and implantable networks facilitate the seamless collection and transmission of physiological data. However, integrating these devices into our daily lives also brings several significant security challenges that must be addressed to ensure the privacy, integrity, and confidentiality of personal health information. There are many security threats that need to be addressed in BANs:

3.6.3.1 *Data privacy and confidentiality*

Privacy and confidentiality are paramount in BANs, where sensitive health data is constantly collected and transmitted. Unauthorized access to this data can lead to severe privacy breaches and ethical concerns. Attackers may eavesdrop on wireless transmissions or gain access to wearable devices, compromising the data's confidentiality. Encryption techniques such as advanced encryption standard and secure communication protocols like transport layer security are essential for safeguarding data privacy in BANs.

3.6.3.2 *Unauthorized access and identity spoofing*

Unauthorized access to BANs can occur when attackers impersonate legitimate users or sensor nodes to gain entry into the network. This can lead to various security threats, including data manipulation, injection of false data, or denial of service (DoS) attacks. Identity spoofing attacks can be mitigated by implementing robust authentication mechanisms such as biometric authentication, challenge-response protocols, and digital signatures. Additionally, using unique identifiers and access control mechanisms can help prevent unauthorized access to sensitive resources within the network (Siva Bharathi & Venkateswari, 2019).

3.6.3.3 *Physical security risks*

BANs are susceptible to physical security threats, particularly when sensor nodes are attached to or implanted within the human body. Malicious actors may attempt to tamper with or physically compromise these nodes, leading to data alteration or device malfunction. Ensuring the physical integrity of sensor nodes is crucial for maintaining the security and reliability of BANs. Techniques such as tamper-evident packaging, secure enclosure designs, and periodic device integrity checks can help mitigate physical security risks in BANs.

3.6.3.4 *Network denial of service attacks*

DoS attacks pose a significant threat to the availability and reliability of BANs. Attackers may flood the network with excessive traffic or exploit vulnerabilities in network protocols to disrupt communication between sensor nodes and external devices. As a result, critical health monitoring services may be disrupted, leading to potential risks to patient safety. Implementing intrusion detection and prevention systems, rate limiting mechanisms, and network segmentation techniques can help mitigate the impact of DoS attacks on BANs.

3.6.3.5 Insider threats

Insider threats, including malicious or negligent actions by authorized users or healthcare personnel, pose a significant risk to the security of BANs. Trusted individuals with access to sensitive patient data may abuse their privileges or inadvertently compromise the confidentiality and integrity of the data. Implementing strict access controls, user monitoring mechanisms, and regular security training programs can help mitigate the risks associated with insider threats in BANs (Kompara & Hölbl, 2018).

3.6.3.6 Device tampering and compromise

BANs are susceptible to device tampering and compromise, mainly when wearable devices are easily accessible. Malicious actors may attempt to tamper with or physically compromise these devices, leading to data alteration, false data injection, or device malfunction. Ensuring the physical integrity of wearable devices is crucial for maintaining the security and reliability of BANs. Techniques such as tamper-resistant packaging, secure enclosure designs, and device authentication mechanisms can help mitigate device tampering and compromise risks in BANs.

3.6.3.7 Wireless communication vulnerabilities

Wireless communication is the backbone of BANs, making them vulnerable to various wireless attacks such as eavesdropping, jamming, and man-in-the-middle attacks. Attackers may intercept wireless transmissions between wearable devices and external receivers, leading to data interception or manipulation. Employing secure communication protocols, frequency hopping techniques, and signal encryption mechanisms can help mitigate wireless communication vulnerabilities in BANs.

3.6.3.8 Eavesdropping

Eavesdropping is the act of surreptitiously listening in on a conversation (without the knowledge of the legitimate parties involved in a communication scenario). Attackers can readily intercept radio transmissions between nodes in a BAN (Agrawal, 2015).

3.6.3.9 Remote exploitation and malware

As BANs become increasingly interconnected with external networks and cloud-based services, they become susceptible to remote exploitation and malware attacks. Attackers can exploit vulnerabilities in wearable devices or associated software to gain unauthorized access, execute malicious code, or compromise the integrity of the entire network. Implementing timely software updates, device authentication mechanisms, and intrusion detection systems can help mitigate the risks associated with remote exploitation and malware in BANs (Sangaiah et al., 2019).

3.6.3.10 Impersonation attack

Impersonation assaults occur when an adversary convincingly presumes the identity of a genuine participant in a system or communication channel. If an attacker impersonates or eavesdrops on another lawful entity and acquires data, he may use it illegally.

3.6.3.11 *Replaying*

The adversary can retransmit the data signal for a certain period of time. At the receiving end, the repeated data looks to be genuine. Thus, if the adversary keeps replaying messages, the objective could be to exhaust the power source and cause the sensor to cease operating (Hajar et al., 2021).

3.6.3.12 *Forged base station attack*

In this assault, the adversary impersonates the base station. BAN's network is relatively tiny; hence, such an assault is possible. The impostor can get critical information by convincing authentic sensor nodes that this is the real base station (Khan & Pathan, 2018). Indeed, the secure transfer of data is crucial for BANs. Patient data must be protected with proper integrity, authenticity, and privacy. Additionally, only authorized entities should have access to the data. As a result, the permission component of security is equally critical. However, in this specific situation (i.e., BAN), what is crucial is the lightweight nature of the security methods, which may be implemented on implantable or wearable sensors. Notwithstanding this challenge, several secure communication models and lightweight security techniques (Hajar et al., 2021; Javadi & Razzaque, 2013) for sensor networks can be deployed to BAN scenarios simply, regardless of whether the models are server-independent or server-dependent. A BAN does not typically contain many nodes like a traditional WSN, that is, a restricted number of nodes in a network (within a reasonably local region). Attacks such as Hello flood attacks, wormhole attacks, and sinkhole attacks are unimportant to such a setting (Hajar et al., 2023).

3.7 Strategies and requirements for addressing challenges of body area networks

3.7.1 Strategies for addressing the data security issues in body area networks

Security is paramount in BANs due to the sensitivity of the health data being transmitted, the potential for unauthorized access or tampering, and the privacy concerns of individuals. BANs need to meet certain security requirements to protect the sensitive and personal data that they transmit, such as:

Confidentiality: The data should be encrypted and only accessible by authorized parties. No one else should be able to read or modify the data in transit or at rest.

Authentication: The sender and receiver of the data should be able to verify each other's identity and legitimacy. No one else should be able to impersonate or spoof them.

Integrity: The data should be protected from any alteration, deletion, or insertion by malicious parties. Any tampering with the data should be detectable and preventable.

Freshness: The data should be timely and up to date. No one else should be able to replay or reuse old data.

Availability: The data should always be accessible and reliable. No one else should be able to disrupt or deny the data transmission or reception.

Secure management: The devices and the network should be configured and maintained securely. No one else should be able to access or modify the devices' settings, keys, policies, or the network.

Access control: Access control techniques should be employed to restrict access to BAN resources based on user roles, permissions, and privileges. Role-based access control (RBAC), Attribute-based access control (ABAC), or access control lists (ACLs) may be utilized to enforce access controls and hinder unauthorized people from interacting with BAN devices and data.

Addressing the issue of data security in BANs involves several requirements and strategies:

- **Encryption:** To protect against illegal access, data transferred over the network should be encrypted. Advanced encryption algorithms can be used to ensure the data remains secure even if intercepted.
- **Authentication:** Devices within the network should be able to authenticate each other. This ensures that only authorized devices can join the network and access the data.
- **Access Control:** Implementing strict access control policies can help ensure that only authorized individuals can access the data (Jaber & Idrees, 2022). This could involve password protection, biometric authentication, or other forms of user verification.
- **Secure Software Development Practices:** Ensuring that the software running on the devices is secure is crucial. This requires adhering to safe programming practices, regular security assessments, and maintaining the software up to date with the most recent security updates.
- **Privacy-Preserving Data Aggregation:** Mechanisms can be used to aggregate sensor data to preserve privacy. This allows for valuable information to be extracted from the data without revealing sensitive personal information.
- **User Awareness and Consent:** Users should be made aware of the collected data, its use, and who has access to it. They should also be able to give or withdraw their consent for data collection (Roy et al., 2019).

Although these strategies can significantly enhance the security of BANs, no system can be 100% secure. Therefore, continuous monitoring and updating of security measures are essential. To sum up, encryption is about keeping data secret from eavesdroppers. Authentication is validating the identities of the persons engaged in a communication. Both are crucial for maintaining the integrity and security of data in BANs and other types of networks.

3.7.2 Strategies for ensuring privacy in body area networks

Ensuring privacy in a BAN is crucial due to the sensitive nature of the gathered data. Here are some key points of some privacy strategies that can be implemented in BANs:

- **Robust Security Measures:** The sensitive nature of the data gathered by BAN necessitates robust security measures to prevent breaches and ensure privacy.
- **Secure Communication:** Data communication in BAN incorporates secure methods. First, sensors should communicate via Zigbee or Bluetooth with personal device assistants (PDAs). Second, PDAs should communicate with the base station through the radio interface (Ananthi & Jose, 2021).

- **Secure Storage and Transmission:** BAN enables the safe storage and transmission of patient data to the doctor without data loss at a predetermined moment (Javadi & Razzaque, 2013).
- **AI Algorithms:** AI algorithms can solve these issues, with advancements in secure, privacy-preserving AI offering potential solutions.
- **Addressing Unique Challenges:** Most of BAN's well-known security concerns are inherited from WSNs. Nonetheless, prevalent properties of BANs, like hostile environmental conditions and extreme resource limits, provide additional specific hurdles to privacy and security assurance (Shihong, 2017).

It's important to note that while these measures can significantly enhance the privacy and security of BANs, no system can be completely immune from potential breaches. Therefore, continuous research and development are necessary to address emerging threats and vulnerabilities.

3.7.3 Strategies for improving the power efficiency of body area networks

Improving the power efficiency of implantable sensors in BANs is a critical challenge. Here are some strategies that can be employed (Yoo, 2018):

- **Energy Harvesting:** This involves powering the sensors by using the body's energy, such as heat or movement. For example, a sensor could be powered by the kinetic energy generated by body movement or the thermal energy produced by body heat.
- **Low-Power Design Techniques:** These include using low-power components, optimizing the sensor's operation to minimize power consumption, and employing power-saving modes such as sleep or standby when the sensor is not in use.
- **Efficient Data Transmission:** The way data is transmitted can significantly impact power consumption. Techniques such as data compression, efficient modulation schemes, and minimizing the transmission distance can help reduce power consumption.
- **Optimized Sensor Operation:** The sensor's operation can be optimized only to collect and transmit data when necessary. This could involve using predictive algorithms to determine when data collection is needed.
- **Advanced Battery Technologies:** Using emerging battery technologies, including micro fuel cells and solid-state batteries, can provide a longer lifespan and increased energy efficiency.
- **Wireless Power Transfer:** This involves transferring power wirelessly from an external source to the implanted sensor. This could potentially provide a continuous power supply, eliminating the need for batteries.

3.8 Body area networks applications

The rapid evolution of wireless communication, low-power integrated circuits, and physiological sensors has resulted in a new generation of BANs currently used to monitor infrastructure, agriculture, traffic, and health. Several smart physiological sensors can be combined into a wearable wireless BAN, allowing for early detection of medical disorders or computer-assisted rehabilitation. Some applications of BANs are illustrated in Fig. 3.5. There are several applications of BANs:

m-Health Monitoring

- BANs directly monitor vital signs, heart rate, skin temperature, and more, noninvasively.
- Real-time health tracking benefits patients with chronic conditions, enabling early intervention.

Sports and Fitness

- Athletes benefit from BANs by monitoring performance metrics.
- Heart rate, muscle activity, and movement patterns inform personalized training recommendations.
- BANs enhance sports performance and prevent injuries.

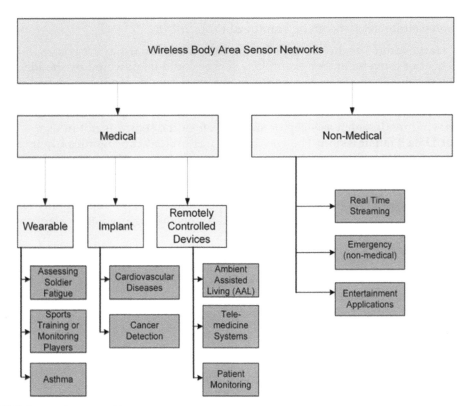

FIGURE 3.5   Applications of body area networks.

Emergency Response

- BANs play a crucial role in emergencies.
- They alert medical professionals during critical situations.
- Rapid response and accurate data transmission save lives.

3.8.1 Applications of body area networks in healthcare

Advanced sensors in BANs have widespread applications in healthcare, ranging from chronic disease management to postoperative care. For instance, continuous glucose monitoring sensors provide valuable insights for diabetic patients, facilitating timely interventions to maintain blood glucose levels within the optimal range. Similarly, wearable ECG sensors enable remote cardiac monitoring, promptly detecting abnormalities such as arrhythmias and ischemia. Furthermore, sensors integrated into smart clothing and accessories offer real-time feedback on physical activity, sleep patterns, and stress levels, promoting a holistic approach to wellness. In healthcare, BAN can be employed to monitor the patients or elderly using sensing devices that measure respiration rate, ECG, heartbeat, temperature, blood pressure, glucose level, fall detection, and walking step counting. Likewise, wearable health gadgets are also used to track patients for early warning or detection of crucial health circumstances (Marjani et al., 2017). IoT-enabled BAN applications may also be applied to keep track of health data and build statistical information about health status (Dhar et al., 2014). In populated places, sensors have many applications to tackle several real-life problems. For instance, population places may be monitored for electromagnetic fields, air pressure, vibration, light, and sound to investigate the environment's health (Rayan et al., 2021). Some real-time practices and applications of BANs in healthcare are listed below (Yang et al., 2017).

3.8.1.1 Chronic disease management

BANs equipped with advanced sensors enable continuous monitoring of vital signs and disease-specific parameters, facilitating proactive management of chronic conditions like diabetes, hypertension, and cardiovascular diseases.

3.8.1.2 Remote patient monitoring

Advanced sensors in BANs allow remote monitoring of patients, enabling healthcare practitioners to follow physiological indicators and respond quickly in case of abnormalities. This remote monitoring capability is particularly beneficial for elderly patients, individuals with chronic illnesses, and postoperative care.

3.8.1.3 Fitness and wellness tracking

BANs equipped with motion and biometric sensors are widely used for fitness tracking and wellness monitoring. These devices provide users with real-time feedback on their physical activity levels, sleep quality, and overall health, empowering them to make informed lifestyle choices.

3.8.1.4 Early disease detection

The continuous monitoring capabilities of BANs, coupled with advanced sensor technology, facilitate early detection of health problems and potential disease outbreaks. By analyzing longitudinal data trends, BANs can identify subtle changes indicative of underlying health issues, enabling timely intervention and preventive measures.

3.8.1.5 Sleep monitoring

Sleep is a paramount and vital human requirement. Healthy sleep is crucial for both mental and physical well-being. If any individual lacks good sleep, various problems and fatalities may result. The effects may include narcolepsy, a neurological illness that impairs sleep and wakefulness management, sleeping at work or while driving, and cardiovascular disease. Sleep problems impact a considerable proportion of the world's population. Polysomnography (PSG) is a diagnostic tool for monitoring sleep problems. PSG captures sleep data, which can be retained for future medical monitoring. BAN designs have been developed for detecting sleep disorders while reducing the complexity of employing a wired PSG system via sensor nodes. For example, Rajagopal and Rodriguez-Villegas (2013) developed a low-power architecture that analyzes an analog signal processing architecture on a sensor node and sleep phases using an automated sleep staging algorithm on a central node. Vicq (2007) created a prototype bio-potential sensor to monitor sleep stages remotely.

3.8.1.6 Health and well-being

BANs have the potential to give preventative treatment by detecting the emergence and progressive worsening of lifestyle illnesses. They may also track long-term progress while offering real-time training data that could be utilized to optimize the effectiveness of individual sessions.

3.8.1.7 IoT Healthcare

Integrating IoT technology in healthcare offers numerous benefits for patients, healthcare providers, and organizations. IoT has abundant applications in healthcare, such as remote monitoring of patients' health, sending an alert to a healthcare provider, tracking patients and equipment within the healthcare organization, intelligent pill dispensers that can observe patients' medication intake, intelligent beds that detect occupancy, etc. IoT-enabled remote monitoring and wearable gadgets allow patients to monitor their health status continuously, detect health issues early, and improve the management of chronic conditions, leading to better health outcomes and enhanced quality of life (Nassra & Capella, 2023). Healthcare providers can leverage IoT data analytics to gain insights into patient populations, identify trends, and deliver more personalized and effective treatments. Moreover, IoT-enabled healthcare facilities can improve operational efficiency, reduce costs, and enhance patient satisfaction by automating tasks, optimizing resource allocation, and ensuring a seamless care continuum. IoT can even assist in detecting certain health conditions in patients earlier and respond rapidly to medical crises, even if the patient is moving. IoT can enable healthcare providers to decrease the cost of services by using equipment tracking systems (Mathew et al., 2018). In general, IoT-enabled BAN applications may provide personalized care to patients while improving the quality of healthcare services.

3.8.2 Practices of body area network in sports and fitness applications

BANs have the potential to revolutionize sports and fitness, providing detailed, real-time insights into an athlete's performance and health. Thus, BANs have found significant applications in the field of sports and fitness. Outlined below are some examples of how they can be implemented:

3.8.2.1 Performance monitoring

BANs can be used to monitor an athlete's performance in real-time. They can monitor physiological data, including muscular activity, body temperature, and heart rate. This data can be used to optimize training and improve performance.

3.8.2.2 Injury prevention and rehabilitation

By monitoring an athlete's physiological data, BANs can help identify signs of potential injuries before they become serious. They can also play a crucial role in the rehabilitation process, tracking recovery and ensuring that athletes do not push themselves too hard too soon.

3.8.2.3 Sport data collection and analysis

BANs can collect high-fidelity, high-quality, low-noise, and multivariate data. This data can be analyzed utilizing machine learning and artificial intelligence (AI) techniques for time series analysis (Phatak, 2021).

3.8.2.4 Real-time feedback

BANs can provide athletes and trainers with real-time feedback about their performance. This can help them make immediate adjustments to their training regimen (McIlwraith & Yang, 2009).

3.8.3 Recent trends of body area networks in nonmedical applications

BANs can indeed be used for nonmedical applications. The potential applications of BANs are vast and continue to grow with advancements in sensor technology and wireless communication. Here are some examples:

3.8.3.1 Interactive gaming and fitness monitoring

BANs can detect motion and gestures, which can be used for interactive gaming applications. They can also monitor physical activity and vital signs during exercise, providing valuable data for fitness monitoring and performance improvement (Negra et al., 2016).

3.8.3.2 Cognitive and emotional recognition

BANs can potentially recognize cognitive states and emotional responses. This may be useful in applications such as driving assistance, where the system can detect if the driver is becoming tired or stressed (Fahmy, 2023).

3.8.3.3 *Disaster response*

In disaster events like earthquakes, terrorist attacks, or fires, BANs may aid by monitoring the vital signs of victims and rescue workers (Sen, 2023).

3.9 Existing body area networks projects and frameworks for implementing advanced sensors in real-life practices

Over the past few decades, substantial advancement has been made in incorporating advanced sensors into BANs by enabling real-time monitoring of physiological parameters and allowing for personalized, preventative care. The proliferation of wearable devices, such as smartwatches and fitness trackers, has led to the development of sophisticated sensors that can monitor several physiological biomarkers such as heart rate, blood pressure, respiratory rate, sleep patterns, and body temperature. When integrated into a BAN, these sensors provide continuous and noninvasive monitoring of vital signs, enabling remote patient care and early diagnosis of health issues.

Many studies have been undertaken on health monitoring systems. The researchers in Ahnn and Potkonjak (2013) presented the mHealth project, a cloud-based, energy-efficient mobile health monitoring system. The fundamental concept is to execute some software components in parallel in the cloud to save battery life on mobile devices. Many research initiatives have investigated prioritizing patients' health states, supporting multidirectional routing, multiinterface design, and quality of service. Their proposed system may recognize patients' emergency information and direct medical personnel to the most proper emergency care procedures. This method prioritizes crises and evaluates the most suited ambulance and treatment procedures. A priority-based, interference-sensitive monitoring system was developed by Rady et al. (2021). The system transmits patients' vital signs according to their present health status and network conditions, such as multichannel access, interference, latency, and congestion. In Alrajeh et al. (2013), researchers developed a multichannel/ multifrequency communication framework for BAN to reduce fading in health monitoring systems. The idea is to boost data rates to enable multimedia data while improving network performance.

The developments and clinical utility of smart wearable body sensors have been extensively studied and reported in the literature. Some of the frameworks for BANs are discussed below. Table 3.4 presents a brief comparison of various existing frameworks.

3.9.1 Activity as a service

Gravina et al. (2017) presented a cyber-physical framework. This approach monitors human behaviors offline or online and serves both people and communities. To assess the proposed method, the researchers utilized smart wheelchair support, physical energy calculation, and automated fall detection. They also assessed the performance by examining several metrics, such as data transmission time, memory footprint, processing load, and CPU utilization.

TABLE 3.4 Existing body area network projects and frameworks.

Framework	Target application	Intra-BAN comm.	Inter-BAN comm.	Beyond BAN comm.	Sensors
UbiMonc (Gupta et al., 2013)	Healthcare	ZigBee	Wi-Fi/ GPRS	Wi-Fi/GPRS	SpO2 Strip 2Leads ECG 3Leads ECG
Lifeguard (Montgomery, 2004)	Ambulatory physiologic monitoring for space and terrestrial applications	Wired	Internet /Bluetooth	Internet /Bluetooth	built-in accelerometer Blood temperature pulse oximeter. Respiration electrodes ECG
MIMOSA (Jantunen, 2012)	Ambient intelligence	Wibree/Bluetooth/ RFID	GPRS /UMTS	Internet	Any sensors RFID sensors
Ayushman (Kang et al., 2007)	Health monitoring	ZigBee	802.11	Internet	gait monitoring sensors. Accelerometer gyroscopic sensors oximeter EKG blood pressure.
WiMoCA (Farella et al., 2008)	Sport/gesture detection	Star topology and time table–based Medium Access Control (MAC) protocol	Bluetooth	Bluetooth/ cellular networks/ Internet/Wi-Fi	Tri-axial accelerometer
Human++ (Gyselinckx et al., 2017)	Lifestyle Assisted living. Medical Entertainment	UWB	N/A	N/A	EEG EMG ECG
PHM (Mena et al., 2018)	Healthcare	Wired	Wi-Fi	N/A	Electrocardiogram (EKG or ECG)
ASNET (Sheltami et al., 2006)	Remote health monitoring	Wired or Wi-Fi	Wi-Fi/ Ethernet	Internet/global system for mobile communications (GSM)	Blood pressure Temperature
CareNet (Jiang et al., 2011)	Remote healthcare	N/A	ZigBee	Multihop 802.11/ Internet	tri-axial accelerometer Gyroscope,
Code Blue (Shnayder et al., 2005)	Medical care	Wired	Mesh/ ZigBee	N/A	Pulse oximeter Motion

(Continued)

TABLE 3.4   (Continued)

Framework	Target application	Intra-BAN comm.	Inter-BAN comm.	Beyond BAN comm.	Sensors
SMART (Curtis et al., 2011)	Health monitoring in waiting room	Wired	802.11.b	N/A	ECG SpO2 sensor
MAHS (Kang et al., 2007)	Healthcare	Bluetooth	Wireless network	Internet	pressure Temperature Pulse Spirometer
AID-N (Sakanushi et al., 2013)	Emergency response system	Wired	ZigBee/ Mesh	Cellular networks/ Internet/Wi-Fi	ECG Blood pulse
MobiHealth (Wac et al., 2009)	Ambulatory patient monitoring	Manually	Bluetooth/ ZigBee	UMTS/GPRS	ECG
BASUMA (Falck, 2006)	Health monitoring	UWB	N/A	N/A	Spirometer SpO2 sensor reactive oxygen sensor (ROS) ECG

3.9.2 BodyCloud

Fortino et al. (2013b) constructed a large-scale BAN depending on BodyCloud structures. BodyCloud is a multitiered application-level architecture. It combines cloud computing at the SaaS (Software as a Service) level with signal processing in the node environment (SPINE). The SaaS framework is a Google-supported engine, whereas SPINE is a versatile BAN framework. Workflow, view, modality, and group are the fundamental programming concepts employed in their work.

3.9.3 CODEBLUE

Malan (2004) and Shnayder et al. incorporated wireless low-power sensors into computers and PDAs. Their presented framework, which is primarily for patients, is called Code Blue. During the test phase, the authors used the framework to examine patients and send data to their friends and family. They implemented an adaptive spanning-tree multihop routing method depending on the TinyOS Surge protocol. To reduce interference, they implemented dynamic transmission power scaling.

3.9.4 SPINE

Fortino et al. (2013a) presented an open-source programming framework called SPINE. Because of its capacity to accommodate heterogeneous components, its framework enables BAN applications and provides a platform that permits hardware and software usage when selecting.

3.9.5 TITAN

Lombriser et al. (2007) introduced the "TITAN" framework. It is used to identify context in dynamic sensor network setups. TITAN is a dynamic reconfigurable framework that uses context recognition techniques to execute reconfiguration. It is an effective system due to its features, such as quick reconfiguration, ease of programming, and high-speed processing.

3.9.6 OvulaRing

This framework was created for gynecologists and doctors to use throughout a woman's pregnancy or to determine fertility. It facilitates ovulation in women. It aids in determining when they are most ovulating and fertile, allowing them to conceive.

3.9.7 VitalPatch

VitalPatch (Tonino et al., 2019) is a wearable biosensor. This sensor detects and continually monitors eight vital indicators in real-time. The data can be accessible via a mobile platform. The vital indicators that it can monitor are listed below:

- Activity.
- Fall detection.
- Body posture.
- Skin temperature.
- Heart rate variability.
- Respiratory rate.
- Single lead ECG.
- Heart rate.

3.9.8 FreeStyle Libre

Abbott (Blum, 2018) invented the glucose monitoring device for diabetic patients. It is given to the upper arm using an applicator. This applicator is for one-time use only. When the sensor is attached, a fiber is introduced beneath the skin. According to the Abbott Diabetes Care data file, users believe this glucose monitoring technology is more user-friendly than the classic finger prick test.

3.9.9 Zio XT

IRhythm has developed a novel framework (Barrett et al., 2014). This project aims to detect the abnormal activities of the heart. This component has a continuous working time of up to 24 days. Patients can wear the Zio device when showering, sleeping, or exercising. This component can keep track of heartbeats for about 20,000 minutes.

3.10 The future scope and futuristic vision of advanced sensors in body area networks

The future of advanced sensors in BANs holds tremendous promise, with ongoing research focusing on enhancing sensor performance, reducing form factor, and improving data analytics capabilities. Nanotechnology and biocompatible materials offer opportunities for developing implantable sensors with enhanced biocompatibility and longevity. Furthermore, incorporating machine learning algorithms and AI enables predictive analytics and personalized healthcare recommendations based on individual health data. As technology continues to evolve, advanced sensors in BANs are poised to revolutionize preventive healthcare, early disease detection, and personalized medicine. For example, AI algorithms could analyze data from sensors to predict potential health issues before they become serious, allowing for early intervention.

Sensors in BANs have the potential to transform healthcare, rendering it more predictive, preventive, and personalized. As technology advances, we may see even more inventive uses for these sensors, increasing the quality of life for people worldwide. As technology advances, sensors' capabilities in BANs are expected to improve dramatically. Future sensors may be able to monitor a broader range of physiological parameters, offer more accurate readings, and even deliver real-time feedback to the user. Additionally, advancements in battery life and data transmission could make these sensors more efficient and reliable. Emerging technologies, such as blockchain, AI, and edge computing, are being integrated with IoT to enhance data analytics, improve security, and enable real-time decision-making in healthcare settings. Standardization efforts, such as developing interoperability standards and data exchange protocols, are underway to address the fragmentation and compatibility issues in IoT ecosystems. Moreover, regulatory agencies are working to establish guidelines and best practices for IoT security, data privacy, and ethical use in healthcare applications. As IoT technology continues to evolve and mature, it has the potential to transform the provision of healthcare, enhance patient outcomes, and propel innovation across the healthcare ecosystem.

Nowadays, technology plays a significant role in our lives. With the widespread usage of mobile devices and other tiny gadgets in everyday life, people now provide an ideal platform for automatically and electrically monitoring their physiological data. From a futuristic perspective, one of the significant uses of BAN that might be observed in the near future is in the healthcare sector, with virtual reality assistance. Low latency can send touch signals across a mobile network when combined with mechanicals such as special haptic gloves 5G. Using this combination of cutting-edge technology, real-time virtual surgery might be conducted with less risk. Such a system might be utilized as a training tool to teach new abilities to surgeons in faraway places, allowing them to practice and gain the necessary muscle memory. Muscle memory is frequently used interchangeably with motor learning, a type of procedural memory in which repetition consolidates a specific motor activity into memory. When an action is repeated over time, long-term muscle memory may build, allowing it to be executed without conscious effort in the future. It would be a big step forward in the medical industry if machines could move like people via remote interfaces. Sensors would be the fundamental components of any such apparatus. With advancements in IoT and CPS and an increase in the number of smart devices around us, the present platform may be better suited for the optimal use of many types of BAN applications, some of which are still unknown.

3.11 Conclusion

The field of sensor technology has witnessed remarkable advancements driven by miniaturization, improved sensitivity, power efficiency, and wireless connectivity. The proliferation of wearable devices, such as fitness trackers and smartwatches, has led to the development of sophisticated sensors that can track various physiological biomarkers such as heart rate, blood pressure, body temperature, respiratory rate, sleep patterns, and even biochemical markers. These sensors utilize diverse technologies such as electrochemical, optical, piezoelectric, and MEMs, ensuring accuracy, reliability, and noninvasiveness. With ongoing advancements in sensor technology and data analytics, the potential applications of BANs extend beyond healthcare into areas such as sports performance monitoring, workplace safety, and assisted living for older people. Despite their potential, advanced sensors in BANs face several challenges that need to be addressed. To ensure comfort and prolonged usage, miniaturization and power efficiency are crucial for wearable applications. Data security, privacy, and interoperability issues must be carefully addressed to safeguard sensitive health information and enable seamless combination with existing healthcare systems. Additionally, the regulatory landscape surrounding medical devices and data privacy regulations pose compliance challenges for sensor manufacturers and healthcare providers.

The future of advanced sensors in BANs holds tremendous promise, with ongoing research focusing on enhancing sensor performance, reducing form factor, and improving data analytics capabilities. Nanotechnology and biocompatible materials offer opportunities for developing implantable sensors with improved biocompatibility and longevity. Combining machine learning and artificial intelligence techniques enables predictive analytics and personalized healthcare recommendations based on individual health data. As technology continues to evolve, advanced sensors in BANs are poised to revolutionize preventive healthcare, early disease detection, and personalized medicine. As we navigate towards a future where technology plays an increasingly central role in healthcare, collaboration between researchers, clinicians, policymakers, and industry stakeholders will be essential to harness the transformative power of advanced sensors in BANs for the betterment of human health and well-being. Additionally, advancements in sensor miniaturization, power efficiency, and wireless communication technologies are essential to enhance the usability and adoption of BANs in diverse healthcare settings. However, addressing the associated challenges and fostering interdisciplinary collaboration will be crucial in realizing the full benefits of this transformative approach to healthcare.

References

Adarsh, A., & Kumar, B. (2020). Wireless medical sensor networks for smart e-healthcare. *Intelligent Data Security Solutions for e-Health Applications*. India: Elsevier. Available from https://www.sciencedirect.com/book/9780128195116, https://doi.org/10.1016/B978-0-12-819511-6.00015-7.

Agrawal, V. (2015). *Security and privacy issues in wireless sensor networks for healthcare* (150). Springer Science and Business Media LLC. Available from https://doi.org/10.1007/978-3-319-19656-5_32.

Ahnn, J. H., & Potkonjak, M. (2013). Toward energy-efficient and distributed mobile health monitoring using parallel offloading. In *Proceedings of the Annual International Conference of the IEEE Engineering in Medicine and Biology Society, EMBS* (pp. 7257–7261). United States. Available from https://doi.org/10.1109/EMBC.2013.6611233, 1557170X.

Alrajeh, N. A., Khan, S., Campbell, C. E.-A., & Shams, B. (2013). Multi-channel framework for body area network in health monitoring. *Applied Mathematics & Information Sciences, 7*(5). Available from https://doi.org/10.12785/amis/070511.

Ananthi, J. V., & Jose, P. S. H. (2021). A perspective review of security challenges in body area networks for healthcare applications. *International Journal of Wireless Information Networks, 28*(4). Available from https://doi.org/10.1007/s10776-021-00538-3.

Bangash, J., Abdullah, A., Anisi, M., & Khan, A. (2014). A survey of routing protocols in wireless body sensor networks. *Sensors, 14*(1). Available from https://doi.org/10.3390/s140101322.

Barrett, P. M., Komatireddy, R., Haaser, S., Topol, S., Sheard, J., Encinas, J., Fought, A. J., & Topol, E. J. (2014). Comparison of 24-hour Holter monitoring with 14-day novel adhesive patch electrocardiographic monitoring. *The American Journal of Medicine, 127*(1), 95. Available from https://doi.org/10.1016/j.amjmed.2013.10.003, e11.

Bhardwaj, T., Reyes, C., Upadhyay, H., Sharma, S. C., & Lagos, L. (2022). Cloudlet-enabled wireless body area networks (WBANs): A systematic review, architecture, and research directions for QoS improvement. *International Journal of System Assurance Engineering and Management, 13*(4). Available from https://doi.org/10.1007/s13198-021-01508-x, http://www.springer.com/engineering/production + eng/journal/13198.

Bhatti, D. S., Saleem, S., Imran, A., Iqbal, Z., Alzahrani, A., Kim, H. J., & Kim, K.-I. (2022). A survey on wireless wearable body area networks: A perspective of technology and economy. *Sensors, 22*(20), 7722. Available from https://doi.org/10.3390/s22207722.

Blum, A. (2018). Freestyle libre glucose monitoring system. *Clinical Diabetes, 36*(2). Available from https://doi.org/10.2337/cd17-0130.

Cavallari, R., Martelli, F., Rosini, R., Buratti, C., & Verdone, R. (2014). A survey on wireless body area networks: Technologies and design challenges. *IEEE Communications Surveys & Tutorials, 16*(3). Available from https://doi.org/10.1109/SURV.2014.012214.00007.

Cheng, D. L., Greenberg, P. B., & Borton, D. A. (2017). Advances in retinal prosthetic research: A systematic review of engineering and clinical characteristics of current prosthetic initiatives. *Current Eye Research, 42*(3). Available from https://doi.org/10.1080/02713683.2016.1270326.

Curtis D. Shih E. Waterman J. Guttag J. Bailey J. Stair T. Greenes R. A. Ohno-Machado L. 2011 Physiological signal monitoring in the waiting areas of an emergency room In *BODYNETS 2008 - 3rd international ICST conference on body area networks*. ICST, United States. Available from https://doi.org/10.4108/ICST.BODYNETS2008.2968, 9789639799172.

Dam, Pitchers, S., & Barnard, M. (2001). *Body area networks: Towards a wearable future.*

Dhar, S. K., Bhunia, S. S., & Mukherjee, N. (2014). Interference aware scheduling of sensors in IoT enabled healthcare monitoring system. In *Proceedings − 4th International Conference on Emerging Applications of Information Technology, EAIT 2014* (pp. 152−157). Institute of Electrical and Electronics Engineers Inc., India. Available from https://doi.org/10.1109/EAIT.2014.50, 9781479942725.

Dinis, H., & Mendes, P. M. (2017). *Recent advances on implantable wireless sensor networks.* IntechOpen. Available from https://doi.org/10.5772/intechopen.70180.

Fahmy, H. M. A. (2023). *WSNs applications.* Springer Science and Business Media LLC. Available from 10.1007/978-3-031-20709-9_3.

Falck, T. (2006). *BASUMA-the sixth sense for chronically ill patients* (p. 2006) IEEE.

Farella, E., Pieracci, A., Benini, L., Rocchi, L., & Acquaviva, A. (2008). Interfacing human and computer with wireless body area sensor networks: the WiMoCA solution. *Multimedia Tools and Applications, 38*(3). Available from https://doi.org/10.1007/s11042-007-0189-5.

Fortino, G., Giannantonio, R., Gravina, R., Kuryloski, P., & Jafari, R. (2013a). Enabling effective programming and flexible management of efficient body sensor network applications. *IEEE Transactions on Human-Machine Systems, 43*(1). Available from https://doi.org/10.1109/TSMCC.2012.2215852.

Fortino, G., Gravina, R., Guerrieri, A., & Di Fatta, G. (2013b). Engineering large-scale body area networks applications. In *Proceedings of the 8th International Conference on Body Area Networks, BodyNets 2013* (pp. 363−369). ICST, Italy. Available from https://doi.org/10.4108/icst.bodynets.2013.253721, 9781936968893.

Gravina, R., Ma, C., Pace, P., Aloi, G., Russo, W., Li, W., & Fortino, G. (2017). Cloud-based activity-aaservice cyber−physical framework for human activity monitoring in mobility. *Future Generation Computer Systems, 75*. Available from https://doi.org/10.1016/j.future.2016.09.006.

Gupta, S. K. S., Mukherjee, T., & Venkatasubramanian, K. K. (2013). *Body area networks: Safety, security, and sustainability*. Cambridge University Press. Available from https://doi.org/10.1017/CBO9781139108126.

Gyselinckx, B., Borzi, R., & Mattelaer, P. (2017). *Human+ +: Emerging technology for body area networks. Wireless technologies: Circuits, systems, and devices*. Netherlands: CRC Press. Available from http://www.tandfebooks.com/doi/book/10.1201/9780849379970, https://doi.org/10.1201/9780849379970.

Hajar, M. S., Al-Kadri, M. O., & Kalutarage, H. K. (2021). A survey on wireless body area networks: Architecture, security challenges and research opportunities. *Computers & Security, 104*102211. Available from https://doi.org/10.1016/j.cose.2021.102211.

Hajar, M. S., Kalutarage, H. K., & Al-Kadri, M. O. (2023). *Security challenges in wireless body area networks for smart healthcare*. Informa UK Limited. Available from https://doi.org/10.1201/9781003251903-15.

Hasan, K., Biswas, K., Ahmed, K., Nafi, N. S., & Islam, M. S. (2019). A comprehensive review of wireless body area network. *Journal of Network and Computer Applications, 143*. Available from https://doi.org/10.1016/j.jnca.2019.06.016.

Jaber, A. S., & Idrees, A. K. (2022). *Wireless body sensor networks: Applications, challenges, patient monitoring, decision making, and machine learning in medical applications* (105). Springer Science and Business Media LLC. Available from https://doi.org/10.1007/978-3-030-90618-4_20.

Jantunen, I. (2012). *System architecture for mobile-phone-centric ambient intelligence applications*. Doctoral dissertation, Aalto University Publication Series.

Javadi, S. S., & Razzaque, M. A. (2013). *Security and privacy in wireless body area networks for health care applications*. Springer Science and Business Media LLC. Available from https://doi.org/10.1007/978-3-642-36169-2_6.

Jiang, S., Cao, Y., Iyengar, S., Kuryloski, P., Jafari, R., Xue, Y., Bajcsy, R., & Wicker, S. (2011). CareNet: An integrated wireless sensor networking environment for remote healthcare. In *BODYNETS 2008 − 3rd International ICST conference on body area networks*. ICST. United States. Available from https://doi.org/10.4108/ICST.BODYNETS2008.2965, 9789639799172.

Johny, B., & Anpalagan, A. (2014). Body area sensor networks: Requirements, operations, and challenges. *IEEE Potentials, 33*(2). Available from https://doi.org/10.1109/MPOT.2013.2286692, http://ieeexplore.ieee.org/xpl/RecentIssue.jsp?punumber = 45&year = 2009.

Kang, E., Im, Y., & Kim, U. (2007). *Remote control multi-agent system for u-healthcare service*.

Khan, R. A., & Pathan, A.-S. K. (2018). The state-of-the-art wireless body area sensor networks: A survey. *International Journal of Distributed Sensor Networks, 14*(4). Available from https://doi.org/10.1177/1550147718768994, 155014771876899.

Kompara, M., & Hölbl, M. (2018). Survey on security in intra-body area network communication. *Ad Hoc Networks, 70*. Available from https://doi.org/10.1016/j.adhoc.2017.11.006, http://www.elsevier.com/inca/publications/store/6/7/2/3/8/0/index.htt.

Krames, E. (2002). Implantable devices for pain control: Spinal cord stimulation and intrathecal therapies. *Best Practice & Research. Clinical Anaesthesiology, 16*(4). Available from https://doi.org/10.1053/bean.2002.0263.

Latré, B., Braem, B., Moerman, I., Blondia, C., & Demeester, P. (2011). A survey on wireless body area networks. *Wireless Networks, 17*(1). Available from https://doi.org/10.1007/s11276-010-0252-4.

Li, H. B., Takizawa, K. I., Zhen, B., & Kohno, R. (2007). Body area network and its standardization at IEEE 802.15. MBAN. In *16th IST mobile and wireless communications summit*, Japan. Available from https://doi.org/10.1109/ISTMWC.2007.4299334

Lombriser, C., Roggen, D., Stäger, M., & Tröster, G. (2007). Titan: A tiny task network for dynamically reconfigurable heterogeneous sensor networks. In *Informatik aktuell* (pp. 127−138). Kluwer Academic Publishers, Switzerland. <https://www.springer.com/series/2872, https://doi.org/10.1007/978-3-540-69962-0_11>, 1431472X.

Malan, D. (2004). *Codeblue: An ad hoc sensor network infrastructure for emergency medical care*.

Marjani, M., Nasaruddin, F., Gani, A., Karim, A., Hashem, I. A. T., Siddiqa, A., & Yaqoob, I. (2017). Big IoT data analytics: Architecture, opportunities, and open research challenges. *IEEE Access, 5*. Available from https://doi.org/10.1109/ACCESS.2017.2689040, http://ieeexplore.ieee.org/xpl/RecentIssue.jsp?punumber = 6287639.

Mathew, P. S., Pillai, A. S., & Palade, V. (2018). *Applications of iot in healthcare, Lecture Notes on Data Engineering and Communications Technologies* (14). Available from springer.com/series/15362, https://doi.org/10.1007/978-3-319-70688-7_11.

McIlwraith, D., & Yang, G. Z. (2009). *Body sensor networks for sport, wellbeing and health signals and communication technology*. United Kingdom: Springer Science and Business Media Deutschland GmbH. Available from https://link.springer.com/bookseries/4748, https://doi.org/10.1007/978-3-642-01341-6_13.

Mena, L. J., Félix, V. G., Ochoa, A., Ostos, R., González, E., Aspuru, J., Velarde, P., & Maestre, G. E. (2018). Mobile personal health monitoring for automated classification of electrocardiogram signals in elderly. *Computational and Mathematical Methods in Medicine, 2018*. Available from https://doi.org/10.1155/2018/9128054.

Montgomery, K. (2004). *Lifeguard-A personal physiological monitor for extreme environments* (p. 2004) IEEE.

Movassaghi, S., Abolhasan, M., Lipman, J., Smith, D., & Jamalipour, A. (2014). Wireless body area networks: A survey. *IEEE Communications Surveys & Tutorials, 16*(3). Available from https://doi.org/10.1109/surv.2013.121313.00064.

Nassra, I., & Capella, J. V. (2023). Data compression techniques in IoT-enabled wireless body sensor networks: A systematic literature review and research trends for QoS improvement. *Internet of Things, 23*100806. Available from https://doi.org/10.1016/j.iot.2023.100806.

Negra, R., Jemili, I., & Belghith, A. (2016). Wireless body area networks: Applications and technologies. *Procedia Computer Science, 83*, 1274–1281. Available from https://doi.org/10.1016/j.procs.2016.04.266, http://www.sciencedirect.com/science/journal/18770509.

Palivela, A. (2023). The challenges in developing implantable biosensors. *Scilight, 2023*(39). Available from https://doi.org/10.1063/10.0021286.

Phatak, A. (2021). Artificial intelligence based body sensor network framework-narrative review: Proposing an end-to-end framework using wearable sensors, real-time location systems and artificial intelligence/machine learning algorithms for data collection. *Data Mining and. Sports Medicine-Open, 7*, 2021.

Preetha, A., & Vel, D. (2016). A research perspective on ubiquitous healthcare for diabetic patients. *Australian Journal of Basic and Applied Sciences, 10*(1), 2016.

Rady, A., El-Rabaie, E. L. -S. M., Shokair, M., & Abdel-Salam, N. (2021). Comprehensive survey of routing protocols for mobile wireless sensor networks. *International Journal of Communication Systems, 34*(15). Available from https://doi.org/10.1002/dac.4942.

Rajagopal, M. K., & Rodriguez-Villegas, E. (2013). Towards wearable sleep diagnostic systems for point-of-care applications. In *IEEE EMBS Special Topic Conference on Point-of-Care (POC) Healthcare Technologies: Synergy Towards Better Global Healthcare, PHT 2013* (pp. 26–29). United Kingdom. Available from https://doi.org/10.1109/PHT.2013.6461276.

Ramasamy, V. (n.d.). *Wireless sensor networks—Insights and innovations*. InTechOpen.

Rayan, R. A., Tsagkaris, C., & Iryna, R. B. (2021). The Internet of Things for healthcare: Applications, selected cases and challenges. *Studies in Computational Intelligence, 933*. Available from https://doi.org/10.1007/978-981-15-9897-5_1, http://www.springer.com/series/7092.

Roy, M., Chowdhury, C., & Aslam, N. (2019). Security and privacy issues in wireless sensor and body area networks. *Handbook of computer networks and cyber security: Principles and paradigms*. India: Springer International Publishing. Available from http://doi.org/10.1007/978-3-030-22277-2, 10.1007/978-3-030-22277-2_7.

Sakanushi, K., Hieda, T., Shiraishi, T., Ode, Y., Takeuchi, Y., Imai, M., Higashino, T., & Tanaka, H. (2013). Electronic triage system for continuously monitoring casualties at disaster scenes. *Journal of Ambient Intelligence and Humanized Computing, 4*(5). Available from https://doi.org/10.1007/s12652-012-0130-2.

Sangaiah, A. K., Shantharajah, S., & Theagarajan, P. (2019). *Privacy and security issues on wireless body area and IoT for remote healthcare monitoring intelligent pervasive computing systems for smarter healthcare*. Wiley. Available from 10.1002/9781119439004.ch10.

Sehra, K. K., & Dave, M. (2020). Privacy preserving data aggregation in wireless body sensor network. *SSRN Electronic Journal*. Available from https://doi.org/10.2139/ssrn.3734802.

Sen, S. (2023). *Wireless sensor networks* (p. 2023) IK International Pvt Ltd.

Sheltami, T., Mahmoud, A., & M. Abu-Amara, Warning and monitoring medical system using sensor networks. (2006), 2006.

Shihong, Z. (2017). A survey on secure wireless body area networks. *Journal of Security and Communication Networks, 9*, 2017.

Siva Bharathi, K. R., & Venkateswari, R. (2019). Security challenges and solutions for wireless body area networks. In *Computing, Communication and Signal Processing: Proceedings of ICCASP*, (pp. 275–283). Singapore: Springer.

Tonino, R. P. B., Larimer, K., Eissen, O., & Schipperus, M. R. (2019). Remote patient monitoring in adults receiving transfusion or infusion for hematological disorders using the vitalpatch and accelerateiq monitoring system: Quantitative feasibility study. *JMIR Human Factors*, 6(4)e15103. Available from https://doi.org/10.2196/15103.

Tzanis, G. (2018). *Healthcare data analysis in the Internet of Things era*. IGI Global. Available from https://doi.org/10.4018/978-1-5225-2255-3.ch172.

Ullah, S., Higgins, H., Braem, B., Latre, B., Blondia, C., Moerman, I., Saleem, S., Rahman, Z., & Kwak, K. S. (2012). A comprehensive survey of wireless body area networks on PHY, MAC, and network layers solutions. *Journal of Medical Systems*, 36(3). Available from https://doi.org/10.1007/s10916-010-9571-3.

Vicq. (2007). *Wireless body area network for sleep staging* (p. 2007) IEEE.

Shnayder, V., Chen, B.-R., Lorincz, K., Jones, T. R. F. F., & Welsh, M. (2005). Sensor networks for medical care. In *SenSys*, (p. 314). New York, NY, USA: Association for Computing Machinery. Available from https://doi.org/10.1145/1098918.1098979.

Wac, K., Bults, R., Van Beijnum, B., Widya, I., Jones, V.M., Konstantas, D., Vollenbroek-Hutten, M., & Hermens, H. (2009). Mobile patient monitoring: The MobiHealth system. In *Proceedings of the 31st annual international conference of the IEEE engineering in medicine and biology society: Engineering the future of biomedicine, EMBC 2009* (pp. 1238–1241). IEEE Computer Society, Switzerland. Available from https://doi.org/10.1109/IEMBS.2009.5333477, 9781424432967.

Yaghoubi, M., Ahmed, K., & Miao, Y. (2022). Wireless body area network (WBAN): A survey on architecture, technologies, energy consumption, and security challenges. *Journal of Sensor and Actuator Networks*, 11(4), 67. Available from https://doi.org/10.3390/jsan11040067.

Yang, N., Wang, Z., Gravina, R., & Fortino, G. (2017). A survey of open body sensor networks: Applications and challenges. In *14th IEEE Annual consumer communications and networking conference, CCNC 2017* (pp. 65–70). Institute of Electrical and Electronics Engineers Inc., China. Available from https://doi.org/10.1109/CCNC.2017.7983083, 9781509061969.

Yogev, D., Goldberg, T., Arami, A., Tejman-Yarden, S., Winkler, T. E., & Maoz, B. M. (2023). Current state of the art and future directions for implantable sensors in medical technology: Clinical needs and engineering challenges. *APL Bioengineering*, 7(3). Available from https://doi.org/10.1063/5.0152290.

Yoo, J. (2018). Energy-efficient body area network transceiver using body-coupled communication. *The IoT physical layer: Design and implementation*. Singapore: Springer International Publishing. Available from http://doi.org/10.1007/978-3-319-93100-5, https://doi.org/10.1007/978-3-319-93100-5_8.

Yuce, M. R. (2013). Recent wireless body sensors: Design and implementation. In *IEEE MTT-S international microwave workshop series on RF and wireless technologies for biomedical and healthcare applications, IMWS-BIO 2013 — Proceedings*. IEEE Computer Society, Australia. https://doi.org/10.1109/IMWS-BIO.2013.6756254.

Zimmerman, T. G. (1996). Personal area networks: Near-field intrabody communication. *IBM Systems Journal*, 35(3.4). Available from https://doi.org/10.1147/sj.353.0609.

4

Medical sensor network and machine learning-enabled digital twins for diagnostic and therapeutic purposes

Anna Paleczek[1] and Artur Rydosz[1,2]

[1]Biomarkers Analysis LAB, Institute of Electronics, AGH University of Science and Technology, Krakow, Poland [2]Advanced Diagnostic Equipment Sp z o.o., Krakow, Poland

4.1 Introduction

One of the challenges related to the use of artificial intelligence to diagnose diseases is the need to have a large database, that is, medical data of patients and healthy people constituting a control sample, during research often carried out in cooperation with several medical units. This often requires large financing, long-term collection of patient information and test results, as well as appropriate storage and anonymization of data, and obtaining the consent of the bioethics committee. The entire process is long and expensive and requires the participation of not only doctors but also patients. One of the possibilities to deal with this problem is the development of virtual patients, digital twins (DTs), which enable the modeling of the condition of the body, metabolic processes in diseases, and the generation of data for training artificial intelligence algorithms (Chakshu et al., 2021). Examples of the use of sensor networks and machine learning with DTs technology in health care are presented in Fig. 4.1.

There are three types of DTs: active, passive, and semiactive. In active DT, data are actively transferred to the model in online mode, and the model itself is continuously updated, while in the case of passive DTs, data are first collected and then transferred to the model in offline mode, both for training and model prediction. Semiactive DT uses a model trained on offline data, but the prediction is made on data transferred to the model in real-time (Chakshu et al., 2021).

To create a DT of a patient, it is necessary to collect data about his health condition. For this purpose, wearable devices included in wireless sensor networks and body sensor

Sensor Networks for Smart Hospitals
DOI: https://doi.org/10.1016/B978-0-443-36370-2.00005-0

networks as well as Internet of Things (IoT) technology are most often used (Cappon et al., 2023; Chen et al., 2021; Cos et al., 2021; Vats et al., 2023; Zhong et al., 2022). In the case of IoT devices used for medical purposes, the subgroup name is often used as Healthcare IoT (Pandey et al., 2021) and Medical IoT (Abirami & Karthikeyan, 2023). The sensors used to develop DTs for disease prediction and therapy monitoring are summarized in Table 4.1.

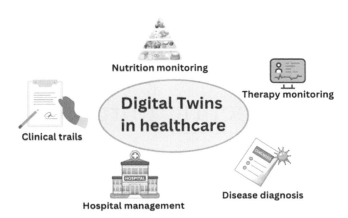

FIGURE 4.1 Examples of the use of sensor networks and machine learning with digital twins technology in health care.

TABLE 4.1   Source of data/sensor.

Type of data	Sensor	Disease	References
Voice	Smartphone microphone	Parkinson	Abirami and Karthikeyan (2023)
Blood glucose level	CGM diabetes sensor	Diabetes	Cappon et al. (2023), Shamanna et al. (2020)
Beta hydroxybutyrate level	Finger prick	Diabetes	Shamanna et al. (2020)
Body weight	Smart scale	Diabetes	Shamanna et al. (2020)
		Weight loss	Abeltino et al. (2023)
Sleep parameters, heart rate, step count	Fitbit charge 2 wristband	Diabetes	Shamanna et al. (2020)
		Pancreatectomy outcome	Cos et al. (2021)
	Xiaomi MiBand 6	Weight loss	Abeltino et al. (2023)

(Continued)

TABLE 4.1 (Continued)

Type of data	Sensor	Disease	References
Blood pressure	Blood pressure meter	Diabetes	Shamanna et al. (2020)
		Abdominal aortic aneurysm	Chakshu et al. (2021)
Laboratory blood tests	Not specified	Liver diagnosis	Rao and Mane (2019)
Arm diameter	Stretch sensor	Prevention of lymphedema	Bethencourt et al. (2021)
vital signs, heart rate (HR), respiration rate (RR), posture information and activity levels	Healthdot sensor (with accelerometer)	Recovery after surgery	van den Eijnden (2023)
activity features, including steps, walking speed, hours walking per day, activity counts (actcount), percentage active time, the number of sedentary hours per day, derived from acceleration data, as well as HR and RR derived from photoplethysmography (PPG) signals, active energy expenditure (AEE)	Elan sensor		
Breath	73 metal oxide gas sensors (JLM innovation GmbH)	Colorectal cancer	Poļaka et al. (2023)
Electronic health record (EHR), images	Hospital devices	Intensive care unit monitoring and simulation	Zhong et al. (2022)
Respiratory profile	Sensor based on ultrasounds	Respiratory behaviors	Chen et al. (2021)
Respiratory profile	Breaths per minute estimation based on changes in Wi-Fi CSI signal from ESP32	Respiratory behaviors	Khan et al. (2023)
Chronic wound images	Camera	Chronic wound management	Sarp et al. (2023)
1. Diameter of pupil, movement of head, movement of eyebrows, average closure speed of eyes, frequency of eye blinking 2. Sitting posture of body 3. Fluctuation of heart rate, temperature of skin tightness in muscles	1. Smart visual sensors 2. Kinect SD sensor 3. Smart body wearable sensors	Anxiety detection	Manocha et al. (2023)
Temperature, BPM	Wearable textile with sensors	Stress monitoring	Scheuermann et al. (2020)

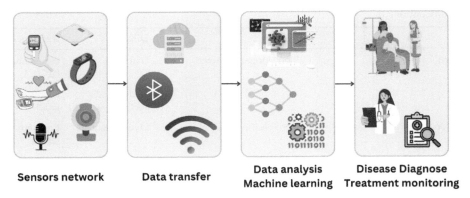

| Sensors network | Data transfer | Data analysis Machine learning | Disease Diagnose Treatment monitoring |

FIGURE 4.2   Data flow in digital twins systems for disease diagnosis and treatment monitoring.

To create a DT based on machine learning, it is necessary to implement a data collection system and communication between the device and a smartphone, server, or other data processing device. One of the possible solutions is wireless communication via Bluetooth 5.0 Low Energy (BLE), and Wi-Fi. Bethencourt et al. presented a very interesting impact of the wireless communication protocol on the worsening of the disease. The authors noticed that the use of Wi-Fi communication resulted in an increase in the temperature of the chip, which may be unfavorable for lymphedema and may worsen under the influence of heat. In the second version of the prototype, the authors used BLE, which, due to the consumption of a small amount of electricity, does not generate heat like the Wi-Fi chip (Bethencourt et al., 2021). Secure communication protocols such as HTTPS or TLS should be employed to encrypt data in transit and protect them from interception or tampering when transferring data from wearable IoT sensors to the system (Vats et al., 2023). The data flow and components of the DTs system are presented in Fig. 4.2.

In this chapter, a literature review on medical sensor networks and machine learning-enabled DTs for diagnostic and therapeutic purposes was conducted. Information regarding the preparation of data from various sensors, feature extraction techniques, as well as machine learning algorithms used in DTs systems were discussed. The explainability of machine learning models, which is important and helpful in the analysis of medical data, was also discussed.

4.2 Machine learning algorithms

One of the important stages of creating systems based on machine learning algorithms is data preprocessing. The classic stages are missing data processing, which may involve removing rows with missing information or data imputation, which means replacing missing data with other values, for example, mean, median, mode, etc. (Cos et al., 2021; Sarp et al., 2023). The next stage of preprocessing may be the use of filters, for example, Gaussian filters (Chen et al., 2021), data scale and data normalization (Paleczek & Rydosz, 2022; Połaka et al., 2023; Sarp et al., 2023).

Often, when working with data from sensors, especially those of a time series nature, it is necessary to carry out feature engineering, that is, to create new features based on the collected data. Such examples are minimum and maximum value, average value, mean of last x points, the area under the curve, and change of value (Paleczek et al., 2021; Połaka et al., 2023). In the case of time series, especially in the analysis of patient data collected 24 hours a day, it may be helpful to create features such as time of the day or a day-night variable. In addition to standard mathematical operations, it is possible to create new features using domain knowledge. van den Eijnden et al. developed algorithms to calculate the resting heart rate (RHR) and the circadian rhythm (circ) of the heart rate, heart rate recovery, etc. They also calculated the change in signal in the following days compared to the previous (van den Eijnden, 2023). Cos et al. created semantic features such as summaries of the patient's daily activity level, sleep quality, time in bed, time to fall asleep and wake up, and time to sedentary (Cos et al., 2021).

Another important issue is the division of data into training and testing sets. It is common practice to also use a validation set. Data should be divided taking into account the nature of the data set and domain knowledge. In the case of classification, it is important that data from one patient is included in only one of the sets, while in the case of time series, a common practice is to use a sliding window to generate samples (Chen et al., 2021).

There are three main types of machine learning algorithms: supervised, unsupervised, and semisupervised. The most commonly used type is supervised learning, in which we have training data that contain both features and labels (Goodfellow et al., n.d.; Kumar et al., 2022). Using this technique, depending on the data and the task, we can perform classification or regression. In classification, the task of the algorithm is to divide the data into classes, there may be two classes (binary classification) or many classes (multiclass classification). In some cases, it is possible to assign several labels to one class. Using regression algorithms, continuous data are predicted from samples (Géron, n.d.; Paleczek & Rydosz, 2022). Examples of classification are the diagnosis of diseases, the detection of cancer on imaging tests (Yang et al., 2023; Yusoff et al., 2023), the detection of falls (Inturi et al., 2023; Wang et al., 2023a), etc., while an example of a regression problem is the prediction of weight loss (Abeltino et al., 2023), blood sugar levels (Shamanna et al., 2020) and simulations of patients in the intensive care unit.

In the case of medical data, DTs are most often modeled using data from wearable sensors that collect data about the patient's health in real-time, which makes them have a time series nature.

K-nearest neighbors (KNN) is a simple algorithm that is based on finding the nearest neighbors for new data, based on most of the class or regression values among them (Abirami & Karthikeyan, 2023). Support vector machines (SVMs) are a classification tool whose objective is to determine a hyperplane that optimally separates different classes (Hussain et al., 2021). Decision trees represent a conditional structure in the form of a tree, while random forest combines multiple trees, increasing the stability and precision of classification (Rao & Mane, 2019). EXtreme gradient boosting (XGBoost) is a boosting algorithm that iteratively adds weak classifiers to the model, adapting to the errors of previous iterations, leading to a strong and flexible model (Chen & Guestrin, n.d.; Ogunleye & Wang, 2018; Paleczek et al., 2021). These various algorithms offer different approaches to solving regression and classification problems, and their appropriate choice depends on the characteristics of the data and the purpose of the analysis.

Neural networks (NNs) mimic the structure of the brain and its ability to adapt to complex patterns, which is used in both classification and regression problems. The basic element is neurones that transmit information between layers, and the learning process involves adjusting the weights of the connections between them (Géron, n.d.; Goodfellow et al., n.d.).

The long-short-term memory (LSTM) algorithm is most often used for time series prediction and classification and is a type of recurrent neural network (RNN) architecture designed to address the problem of vanishing gradients in traditional RNNs. The key advantage of LSTMs is their ability to capture long-range dependencies in sequential data by maintaining a memory cell with various gates to control the flow of information. This makes them effective in learning and remembering patterns over extended periods, which is crucial in tasks such as time-series analysis (Inturi et al., 2023; Lee & Kwak, 2022; Li et al., 2021).

Generative adversarial networks (GANs) are advanced data generation techniques in which two networks, a generator and a discriminator, compete with each other. The generator creates new data, while the discriminator tries to distinguish them from the real data. The process of training both networks leads to the generation of increasingly reliable artificial data. GANs have been used to create realistic images, texts, and even sounds (Sarp et al., 2023; Wang et al., 2023b; Zhou et al., 2023).

Machine learning algorithms used for disease detection and therapy monitoring are listed in Table 4.2.

In medical analysis model explainability is crucial for building trust, ensuring ethical and legal compliance, validating the model's performance, and improving collaboration between medical professionals and data scientists. It improves the general reliability and acceptance of machine learning models in healthcare.

In order to determine the importance of features for the final decision of the model, van den Eijnden et al. determined the Pearson correlation between the reference recovery scores and the created features per day for the training set. Such an analysis makes it possible to assess whether features originally obtained from data or engineered features have the greatest impact on the model's decision. In this case, it may also provide information to doctors on which parameters are most important to predict the recovery rate (van den Eijnden, 2023).

Feature importance and feature correlation are simple basic metrics for determining the influence of features on the model's decision. However, state-of-the-art methods are currently being used to explain AI decisions. One of them, local interpretable model-agnostic explanations (LIME) and partial dependence plot (PDP), were used in their research by Rao et al. to determine which indicator from blood tests and patient information is most important to determine the risk of liver disease (Rao & Mane, 2019). Another method, SHapley Additive exPlanations (SHAP), was used by Cos et al. to assess the impact of the collected features on the prediction of results in patients undergoing pancreatectomy. The analysis showed that the authors' results are consistent with other publications and doctors' observations. In this case, the most important role is played by neutrophil levels, calcium levels, and a history of previous surgery (Cos et al., 2021).

Identifying features with high impact on model decisions will enable physicians to better prepare the patient for treatment or surgery, paying attention to specific indicators

TABLE 4.2 Diseases that can be modeled using digital twin technology, sensors network, and machine learning algorithms.

Disease	Data	Algorithm	Purpose	References
Parkinson's disease	Voice	Optimized fuzzy-based k-nearest neighbor	diagnose	Abirami and Karthikeyan (2023)
Diabetes	Blood glucose level, blood beta hydroxybutyrate level, nutrition data, sleep parameters, heart rate, step count, blood pressure	Not specified	therapy	Shamanna et al. (2020)
Abdominal aortic aneurysm	Blood pressure in the carotid, femoral, and brachial arteries	LSTM, 1D-CNN	diagnose	Chakshu et al. (2021)
Weight loss	Weight, activity, diet	SARIMAX*, GRU, LSTM	monitoring	Abeltino et al. (2023)
Liver disease	Blood test results	Random forest classifier	diagnose, predict risk	Rao and Mane (2019)
Breast cancer	Arm diameter	Statistical methods	prevention of lymphedema	Bethencourt et al. (2021)
Recovery profile after surgery	Activity, heart rate, respiratory rate	XGBoost	Recovery monitoring	van den Eijnden (2023)
Colorectal cancer	Breath	Random forest, C4.5, artificial neural network, and Naïve Bayes	Diagnose	Poļaka et al. (2023)
Pancreatectomy	demographics, comorbidities, and clinical presentation,	random forest, gradient boosted trees (GBT), KNN, SVM with linear kernel, and logistic regression (LR) with L1 penalty	Predicting outcome	Cos et al. (2021)
Hepatitis, fibrosis and cirrhosis	Blood test results	Artificial neural networks	Diagnose	Palaniappan and Surendran (2022)
cardiovascular disease	Patient information, blood pressure, glucose levels, and activity monitoring	XGBoost	Diagnose	Vats et al. (2023)
Respiratory disorders	Lung volume, respiratory profile	Random forest classifiers	Diagnose	Chen et al. (2021)
Respiratory monitoring	Breaths per minute estimation based on changes in Wi-Fi CSI	Fine tree	Diagnose	Khan et al. (2023)

(Continued)

TABLE 4.2 (Continued)

Disease	Data	Algorithm	Purpose	References
Prioritizing pneumonia treatment	Hospital data, blood test results	1. MLP*, 2. RNN 3. RNN	1. Identify patients for intensive care 2. Assign intensive care system 3. Discontinue mechanical ventilation	Chakshu and Nithiarasu (2022)
Chronic wound treatment	Demographic data of the patient, wound characteristics, wound images	GAN	Diagnose, predict treatment progress	Sarp et al. (2023)
Stroke	EEG	SVM	Diagnose	Hussain et al. (2021)
Anxiety	Visual data, heart rate, temperature	ML–Bi-GRU	Diagnose	Manocha et al. (2023)

from blood tests, imaging tests, and information about the patient. Moreover, feature importance analysis is crucial and also helpful in disease prevention and limiting disease complications.

- Seasonal auto-regressive integrated moving average with exogenous factors (SARIMAX);
- Gated recurrent units (GRU);
- Convolutional neural network (CNN);
- Multilayer perceptron (MLP);
- Multilevel bi-gated recurrent unit (ML-Bi-GRU).

4.3 Application of digital twins

Abirami et al. proposed the architecture of the cloud-based digital twin healthcare system for Parkinson's disease diagnosis. The system consists of three layers: (1) End-user layer (patient data collection and user notification about diagnosis and suggested care service), (2) DT cloud layer (voice analysis using machine learning algorithm, Parkinson's disease detection, use of the automated case service negotiation system to negotiate with multiple care service providers to select the appropriate care service), and (3) Service layer (doctors' community). To diagnose Parkinson's disease using voice recordings, the authors trained Optimized Fuzzy Based KNN on publicly available datasets like Cerrahpasa Faculty of Medicine, Istanbul University and the University of Oxford, consisting of voice samples collected from 195 subjects. Modification of the classic k-NN classifier and the use of a fuzzy membership function to optimize the weight of all neighbors significantly reduced the prediction time and increased accuracy compared to NNs or SVM algorithms. The authors achieved 95% mean precision in both datasets (Abirami & Karthikeyan, 2023).

Constant monitoring of the disease and the patient's nutrition plays a key role in the treatment of type 2 diabetes. Complications of type 2 diabetes can be fatal, and the treatment of this disease is a complex problem, depends on many factors such as physical activity, diet, and comorbidities, and should be tailored to the patient. Therefore, the use of sensor networks, machine learning algorithms, and DTs can help in the therapy. This combination of these technologies was successfully proposed by Shamanna et al. They introduced the Twin Precision Nutrition (TPN) programm that involved 89 patients with diabetes. The sensor network contains data from CGM, fitness smart band, smart scale, and blood pressure meter. The patients entered data about their nutrition into the Web application and each sensor was connected to an application that allowed simulation of the patient's sugar metabolism after meals and prediction of blood glucose level. Such simulations enable diabetics to avoid glycaemic spikes and choose better-balanced meals. Studies showed that patients lost weight, had reduced blood sugar levels, and hemoglobin A1c (HbA1c), which are very important factors in the treatment and reduction of complications of type 2 diabetes (Shamanna et al., 2020).

One of the cardiovascular diseases that scientists are working on as a model is the abdominal aortic aneurysm (AAA). This disease occurs when an area of the aorta in the abdomen increases and can be modeled using pressure waveforms measured noninvasively on blood vessels (carotid, femoral, and brachial arteries). Such a system based on inverse analysis was proposed by Chakshu et al. It consisted of generating realistic blood pressure waveform data from (carotid, femoral and brachial arteries) and artificially generated data from the cerebellar, abdominal, and aortic roots using LSTM. The last stage of the model operation was the detection of the disease and its severity. When generating data related to the circulatory system, it is necessary to model a validated 1D hemodynamic model and realistic arterial networks based on anthropometric and hemodynamic parameters. The first DL model based on RNN generated data related to blood pressure at the end of the abdominal aortic and the second based on convolutional networks was trained to predict the diameter of AAA. The 1D-CNN model consisted of four convolutional layers, global average pooling, and fully connected layers. The generated data set included a total of 8516 patients, with 4137 healthy cases and 4392 AAA cases. Based on the data generated, the accuracy of the test set was 90.58%, however, this model has not been tested on clinical data (Chakshu et al., 2021).

Rao et al. proposed a system to predict the risk of liver disease. They used an open-source Indian Liver Patient dataset containing patient age, and results of laboratory blood tests. The Random Forest Classifier was applied to 583 samples and achieved 72% accuracy in the validation data set. The authors used the state-of-the-art Explainable AI library LIME and PDP to check the contribution of the main features to the decision of the model (Rao & Mane, 2019).

DTs can be used not only to diagnose diseases and monitor therapy, but also to simulate the nutrition and metabolic processes that occur in the body. Appropriate nutrition plays an important role in the development and prevention of diseases. Abeltino et al. created a personalized metabolic avatar for weight prediction. In their analyses, they tested models from various groups: generative models, deep learning, and statistical models. To prepare the models, data from 10 patients who monitored their diet, weight, and activity for 100 days were collected. The smart band MiBand 6 (Xiaomi Inc.®, Beijing, China) was used to monitor the activity of the patients, and the Mi Body Composition Scale (Xiaomi Inc.®, Beijing, China) to track the weight and the resting metabolic rate. Each patient used the website app (ArMOnIA, https://www.apparmonia.com) to record the meals consumed. Several models were evaluated on ten users, including the Transformer model, recursive NNs (GRUs and long short-term memory networks), and the statistical SARIMAX model. Among these, models based on GRU and LSTM demonstrated optimal and consistent predictive performance, showing the lowest root mean square errors ($0.38 \pm 0.16 - 0.39 \pm 0.18$) and acceptable interference phase computation times (12.7 ± 1.42 seconds-13.5 ± 3.60 seconds) suitable for a production environment. While the Transformer model did not significantly enhance predictive performance compared to RNNs, it did lead to a 40% increase in computational time for both forecasting and retraining. Although it had the best computational time, the SARIMAX model exhibited the poorest predictive performance among the models tested (Abeltino et al., 2023).

Cancer, a diverse group of diseases originating from abnormal cell growth, can invade nearby tissues or spread to other organs (metastasize), often resulting in death. According to the World Health Organization (WHO), cancer is the second leading global cause of death, claiming approximately 9.6 million lives in 2018. The global burden of cancer is increasing, imposing significant physical, emotional and financial challenges on individuals, families, communities, and health systems. Insufficient preparation in many low- and middle-income countries leaves numerous cancer patients without timely access to quality diagnosis and treatment. Meanwhile, health systems in certain countries contribute to increased survival rates through early detection, quality treatment, and survivorship care (Cancer & Accessed, 2023).

In patients treated for breast cancer after axillary lymph node dissection, lymphedema is often observed. To prevent it Béthencourt et al. developed a prototype using an electronic device containing the measurement circuit (sleeve with stretch sensors + conditioner) and a communication module, which can be used to measure the circumference at various points of the patient's arm and, based on statistical analyses, warn the patient about the increasing arm circumference and the possibility of developing lymphedema. The Mann—Whitney test showed that the device has a 90% chance of detecting changes in arm circumference with three measurements per day (Bethencourt et al., 2021).

Wearable devices manufactured by Philips Electronics Nederland B.V.—Healthdot sensor and Elan sensor—were used to monitor the vital parameters of patients after oncological and bariatric surgery. These sensors collected data on vital parameters such as patient activity, heart rate, and respiration rate. Based on the collected data, machine learning models were trained to predict the recovery profiles of patients. The best model turned out to be the XGBoost Regressor, which obtained a low MSE of 0.02. The system proposed by the authors is very promising; it has limitations in the form of creating reference recovery profiles, for the creation of which a uniform gold standard should have been defined to assess the patient's recovery progress (van den Eijnden, 2023).

One of the important human life parameters is respiratory parameters such as the volume of exhalation and inhalation, frequency, duration, regularity, etc. Chen et al. proposed a system using an ultrasonic wave transmitter and receiver to continuously monitor chest movements, predict respiratory behaviors of individual patients, and detect human posture and respiratory diseases such as chronic respiratory obstructive disease, asthma, apnea. The authors achieved an efficiency of posture detection of over 98% using the random forest classifier algorithm (Chen et al., 2021). Khan et al. proposed another method of monitoring patient respiration using DTs technology, using the ESP32 platform with a module based on Wi-Fi carrier state information (CSI), where small perturbations of the chest are detected as small changes in the Wi-Fi CSI data. After applying signal denoising, dimensionality reduction, and filtering, they estimated patients' breaths per minute (BPM). The authors used the estimated BPM as input to the machine learning algorithms. Of the tested, the best results were achieved by the fine tree algorithm that provides binary and multiclass classification accuracies of 96.9% and 95.8%, respectively (Khan et al., 2023).

Data that contain the composition of exhaled air, which contains more than 3000 volatile organic compounds (Paleczek & Rydosz, 2022), can be used to diagnose diseases, including cancer. The composition of breath can be examined using expensive, specialized devices, such as a gas chromatograph coupled with a mass spectrometer, and increasingly scientists are working on developing a device consisting of metal oxide gas sensors. Such devices are cheaper to produce, portable, and do not require specialized operation. This is the technology used by Połaka et al. for the prediction of colorectal cancer (CRC). They trained machine learning algorithms such as Random Forest, C4.5, Artificial NN, and Naïve Bayes on collected data from over 290 patients. The results turned out to be promising for the use of this system for the detection of CRC based on exhaled air, where the highest specificity of 84.2% was achieved using C4.5, although this algorithm did not achieve the highest precision, it had the best balance between sensitivity and specificity among the other algorithms tested by the authors (Poļaka et al., 2023).

Sarp et al. developed a DTs system for chronic wound management. Tracking the healing of chronic wounds, the system enables the prediction and adjustment of wound treatment strategies or modification of current treatment. The authors used patient demographic data, wound characteristics, and image data. The image data was collected by eKare Inc. Dataset contains wound images, ground-truth wound segmentations, and tissue classification. Researchers used this data set to train the GAN model, which was used to classify wound type, segment wound tissues, and their distribution. The model also predicted the distribution of tissues after wound treatment. The use of such a model will enable personalized wound treatment and remote monitoring by a doctor (Sarp et al., 2023).

Photos and videos can also be used to recognize the patient's emotions, which can be used to diagnose depression or stress. A system for real-time emotion detection using webcam videos was proposed by Subramanian et al. They used the MediaPipe pipeline framework, which enables the detection of characteristic points of the human body, for example, eyes, nose, arms, legs, etc. These points were used to train eight machine learning algorithms, but the best of them turned out to be Gradient Boosting, which achieved an efficiency of 99% in classifying emotions. The authors proposed that their algorithm could become part of the DTs system, which will be used to diagnose depression or stress and as a tool to monitor and plan therapy (Subramanian et al., 2022). Another system based on DTs technology for stress monitoring was proposed by Scheuermann et al. The authors used the WIWeB Smart Textile prototype (Erding) to collect 72 values from nine sensors. They tested various machine learning algorithms, of which the Random Forest Regressor achieved the smallest error in stress level prediction. The DTs technology can also be used to monitor anxiety disorders (Scheuermann et al., 2020). Manocha et al. combined the monitoring of visual, behavioral, and physical features using a sensor network consisting of smart visual sensors, a Kinect SD sensor, and wearable sensors for the smart body. Detected irregular events were classified in real time into different health severity indexes. The novel algorithm consisted of CNN for static features learning and the Multilevel Bi-Gated Recurrent Unit (ML-Bi-GRU) outperforms traditional ML and DL algorithms such as SVM, LSTM or CNN (Manocha et al., 2023).

4.4 Discussion

This chapter contains information about DT systems based on various sensors that can be used in medical sensor networks along with machine learning algorithms to diagnose diseases and monitor the course of therapy and treatment.

The most frequently used are wearable sensors such as sports bands/watches that monitor activity, continuous glucose measurement systems, scales, and cameras and microphones. The variety of data sources used requires the use of appropriate communication with the cloud. Bethencourt et al. (2021), noticed that when using Wi-Fi, the module emits additional heat, which can lead to deterioration of treatment effects, in the case of prevention of lymphedema, during which patients are advised to avoid elevated temperatures.

The collected data must be preprocessed before it is transferred to machine learning algorithms. Domain knowledge also plays an important role in this process when creating additional features, as shown by van den Eijnden (2023) and Cos et al. (2021). Depending on the defined problem and the available data, machine learning algorithms are selected. Most often, sensor data are time series, for which LSTM is a popular deep learning algorithm.

In medical applications, the use of explainability methods plays a key role. These may be classic methods for determining the correlation of features with labels or feature importance methods; they can be used mainly with classic machine learning algorithms, such as decision trees or random forests. However, modern methods such as LIME, PDP or SHAP are increasingly used, which also enable the analysis of more complex algorithms, including deep learning, for example, CNN or LSTM.

The great potential of DTs technology combined with artificial intelligence is to produce new data that can be used in preliminary research, instead of collecting data from real patients. An example is the generation of laboratory test data for ischemic stroke using a variational autoencoder. The results showed that it is impossible to distinguish real data from artificially generated data (Allen et al., 2021). This approach allows researchers to test new methods and train machine learning algorithms, explore different scenarios, validate hypotheses, and refine models on a limited number of patients, which will significantly help reduce research costs, time consumption, and the involvement of patients and medical staff.

The DTs technology combined with a network of medical sensors and machine learning algorithms opens new possibilities for disease diagnosis and therapy monitoring. Currently, most solutions are based on wearable sensors (Abeltino et al., 2023; Shamanna et al., 2020; van den Eijnden, 2023), which are a cheap and available option. It is also worth considering in the future the integration of hospital IT systems containing data from MRI, X-ray, etc. into systems containing trained machine learning and deep learning algorithms, which can help physicians in the initial diagnosis or marking risky areas and suspected disease sites in the photos.

Another solution worth developing, which is becoming more and more popular, is a gas sensor system for detecting diseases based on exhaled air (Malagù et al., 2014; Połaka et al., 2023; Wang et al., 2014). For this purpose, it is necessary to create a matrix of gas sensors and combine it with appropriate preprocessing and machine learning algorithms. Currently, breathing tests for SIBO (Foodmarble and Accessed, 2024) are known and intensive work is underway on diabetes (Neupane et al., 2016; Ochoa-Muñoz et al., 2023; Siegel et al., 2017; Wang & Wang, 2013), lung cancer (Kazeminasab et al., 2022; Oakley-Girvan & Davis, 2017; Politi et al., 2021; Ratiu et al., 2021), CRC (Malagù et al., 2014; McCarthy, 2002; Połaka et al., 2023; Sivertsen et al., 1992; Wang et al., 2014) in exhaled air. Due to the presence of biomarkers of diseases in the breath, it is possible to develop a device for noninvasive detection and monitoring of these diseases (Buszewski et al., 2007; Janssens et al., 2020; Kharitonov & Barnes, 2006; Long et al., 2020; Nowak et al., 2021). Such a device could be portable and relatively cheap, increasing the availability of tests and reducing the costs of screening, diagnostics, treatment, and then monitoring of therapy. Due to the low concentrations of biomarkers in exhaled air (Janssens et al., 2020; Khoubnasabjafari et al., 2022; Paleczek & Rydosz, 2022) and the often similarity in the chemical structure of compounds present in the breath, and therefore a similar reaction mechanism of gas sensors, it is necessary to use very sensitive and selective sensors, which is not always possible to obtain using known and available technology. However, connecting the sensor matrix with machine learning algorithms allows minimizing the cross-selectivity of these sensors and the detection of diseases with high accuracy (Ogunleye & Wang, 2018; Paleczek et al., 2021; Poļaka et al., 2023; Yang et al., 2021). Additionally, the use of explainable algorithms will allow for a detailed analysis of the results, including analysis of the significance of biomarkers for the detection of a given disease and the significance of the response of a given sensor in the matrix. The use of a device containing gas sensors in combination with already used wearables and machine learning would enable the creation of a comprehensive DT for monitoring the course of the disease, diagnosing diseases at an early stage, and testing the effect of drugs or therapies using telemedicine and cloud solutions.

4.5 Conclusions

This chapter discusses the current use of DTs in health care based on sensor networks and machine learning. The literature review showed that sensor networks may consist of various sensors, for example, CGM, microphone, camera, gas sensors, or wearable sensors such as sports bands. Appropriate data preprocessing and their analysis using domain knowledge allow you to prepare a dataset for use with machine learning algorithms. Systems based on DTs use both classic algorithms such as random trees or the algorithm of KNN neighbors, as well as their modifications such as XGBoost and more complex models such as LSTM, CNN and GAN. It is possible to apply explainability methods to models, which enable a thorough analysis of the impact of features on the model's decision and thus understanding important factors for diagnosis or monitoring of therapy, which are valuable both for data scientists and for doctors and patients. The development of medical sensor networks and machine learning-enabled DTs opens the way to fully personalized medicine and rapid diagnosis using telemedicine.

Acknowledgements

The work was partially supported by the IDUB AGH 4122 grant and the statutory activity at the Institute of Electronics AGH.

References

Abeltino, A., Bianchetti, G., Serantoni, C., Riente, A., De Spirito, M., & Maulucci, G. (2023). Putting the personalized metabolic avatar into production: A comparison between deep-learning and statistical models for weight prediction. *Nutrients*, *15*(5). Available from https://doi.org/10.3390/nu15051199, http://www.mdpi.com/journal/nutrients/.

Abirami, L., & Karthikeyan, J. (2023). Digital twin-based healthcare system (DTHS) for earlier parkinson disease identification and diagnosis using optimized fuzzy based k-nearest neighbor classifier model. *IEEE Access*, *11*. Available from https://doi.org/10.1109/access.2023.3312278.

Allen, A., Siefkas, A., Pellegrini, E., Burdick, H., Barnes, G., Calvert, J., Mao, Q., & Das, R. (2021). A digital twins machine learning model for forecasting disease progression in stroke patients. *Applied Sciences (Switzerland)*, *11*(12). Available from https://doi.org/10.3390/app11125576, https://www.mdpi.com/2076-3417/11/12/5576/pdf.

Bethencourt, L., Dabachine, W., Dejouy, V., Lalmiche, Z., Neuberger, K., Ibnouhsein, I., Chereau, S., Mathelin, C., Savy, N., Pierre, P. S., & Bousquet, N. (2021). Guiding measurement protocols of connected medical devices using digital twins: a statistical methodology applied to detecting and monitoring lymphedema. *IEEE Access, 9*. Available from https://doi.org/10.1109/ACCESS.2021.3063786, http://ieeexplore.ieee.org/xpl/RecentIssue.jsp?punumber = 6287639.

Buszewski, B., Kesy, M., Ligor, T., & Amann, A. (2007). Human exhaled air analytics: Biomarkers of diseases. *Biomedical Chromatography, 21*(6). Available from https://doi.org/10.1002/bmc.835, http://onlinelibrary.wiley.com/journal/10.1002/(ISSN)1099-0801.

Cancer and Accessed, (2023).

Cappon, G., Vettoretti, M., Sparacino, G., Del Favero, S., & Facchinetti, A. (2023). ReplayBG: A digital twin-based methodology to identify a personalized model from type 1 diabetes data and simulate glucose concentrations to assess alternative therapies. *IEEE Transactions on Biomedical Engineering, 70*(11). Available from https://doi.org/10.1109/TBME.2023.3286856, http://ieeexplore.ieee.org/xpl/RecentIssue.jsp?reload = true&punumber = 10.

Chakshu, N. K., & Nithiarasu, P. (2022). An AI based digital-twin for prioritising pneumonia patient treatment. *Proceedings of the Institution of Mechanical Engineers, Part H: Journal of Engineering in Medicine, 236*(11). Available from https://doi.org/10.1177/09544119221123431, https://journals.sagepub.com/home/PIH.

Chakshu, N. K., Sazonov, I., & Nithiarasu, P. (2021). Towards enabling a cardiovascular digital twin for human systemic circulation using inverse analysis. *Biomechanics and Modeling in Mechanobiology, 20*(2). Available from https://doi.org/10.1007/s10237-020-01393-6, http://www.springeronline.com/sgw/cda/frontpage/0,11855,1-40109-70-1167715-0,00.html.

Chen, A., Zhang, J., Zhao, L., Rhoades, R. D., Kim, D.-Y., Wu, N., Liang, J., & Chae, J. (2021). Machine-learning enabled wireless wearable sensors to study individuality of respiratory behaviors. *Biosensors and Bioelectronics, 173*112799. Available from https://doi.org/10.1016/j.bios.2020.112799.

Chen, T., & Guestrin, C. (n.d.) XGBoost: A scalable tree boosting system. In *Proceedings of the 22nd ACM SIGKDD international conference on knowledge discovery and data mining.* Available from https://doi.org/10.1145/2939672.

Cos, H., Li, D., Williams, G., Chininis, J., Dai, R., Zhang, J., Srivastava, R., Raper, L., Sanford, D., Hawkins, W., Lu, C., & Hammill, C. W. (2021). Predicting outcomes in patients undergoing pancreatectomy using wearable technology and machine learning: Prospective cohort study. *Journal of Medical Internet Research, 23*(3). Available from https://doi.org/10.2196/23595, https://www.jmir.org/2021/3/e23595/PDF.

Géron, A. (n.d.). *Hands-on machine learning with Scikit-learn and tensor flow: Concepts, tools, and techniques to build intelligent systems.*

Goodfellow, I., Bengio, Y., & Courville, A. (n.d.). *Deep learning.*

Hussain, I., Hossain, M. A., & Park, S. J. (2021) A healthcare digital twin for diagnosis of stroke. In *Proceedings of 2021 IEEE international conference on biomedical engineering, computer and information technology for health, BECITHCON 2021* (pp. 18−21). Institute of Electrical and Electronics Engineers Inc., South Korea. Available from https://doi.org/10.1109/BECITHCON54710.2021.9893641, http://ieeexplore.ieee.org/xpl/mostrecentissue.jsp?punumber = 9893559.

Inturi, A. R., Manikandan, V. M., & Garrapally, V. (2023). A novel vision-based fall detection scheme using key-points of human skeleton with long short-term memory network. *Arabian Journal for Science and Engineering, 48* (2). Available from https://doi.org/10.1007/s13369-022-06684-x, https://www.springer.com/journal/13369.

Janssens, E., van Meerbeeck, J. P., & Lamote, K. (2020). Volatile organic compounds in human matrices as lung cancer biomarkers: A systematic review. *Critical Reviews in Oncology/Hematology, 153*. Available from https://doi.org/10.1016/j.critrevonc.2020.103037, http://www.elsevier.com/locate/critrevonc.

Kazeminasab, S., Ghanbari, R., Emamalizadeh, B., Jouyban-Gharamaleki, V., Taghizadieh, A., Jouyban, A., & Khoubnasabjafari, M. (2022). Exhaled breath condensate efficacy to identify mutations in patients with lung cancer: A pilot study. *Nucleosides, Nucleotides & Nucleic Acids, 41*(4). Available from https://doi.org/10.1080/15257770.2022.2046278.

Khan, S., Alzaabi, A., Iqbal, Z., Ratnarajah, T., & Arslan, T. (2023). A novel digital twin (DT) model based on WiFi CSI, signal processing and machine learning for patient respiration monitoring and decision-support. *IEEE Access, 11*. Available from https://doi.org/10.1109/ACCESS.2023.3316508, http://ieeexplore.ieee.org/xpl/RecentIssue.jsp?punumber = 6287639.

Kharitonov, S. A., & Barnes, P. J. (2006). Exhaled biomarkers. *Chest, 130*(5). Available from https://doi.org/10.1378/chest.130.5.1541, http://www.chestjournal.org/.

Khoubnasabjafari, M., Mogaddam, M. R. A., Rahimpour, E., Soleymani, J., Saei, A. A., & Jouyban, A. (2022). Breathomics: Review of sample collection and analysis, data modeling and clinical applications. *Critical Reviews in Analytical Chemistry, 52*(7). Available from https://doi.org/10.1080/10408347.2021.1889961, http://www.tandf.co.uk/journals/titles/10408347.asp.

Kumar, A. K., Ritam, M., Han, L., Guo, S., & Chandra, R. (2022). Deep learning for predicting respiratory rate from biosignals. *Computers in Biology and Medicine, 144*. Available from https://doi.org/10.1016/j.compbiomed.2022.105338, http://www.elsevier.com/locate/compbiomed.

Lee, J.-A., & Kwak, K.-C. (2022). Personal identification using an ensemble approach of 1D-LSTM and 2D-CNN with electrocardiogram signals. *Applied Sciences, 12*(5), 2692. Available from https://doi.org/10.3390/app12052692.

Li, M., He, J., Zhou, R., Ning, L., & Liang, Y. (2021). Research on prediction model of mixed gas concentration based on CNN-LSTM network. In *ACM international conference proceeding series. association for computing machinery*. China. Available from https://doi.org/10.1145/3503047.3503110, http://portal.acm.org/.

Long, Y., Wang, C., Wang, T., Li, W., Dai, W., Xie, S., Tian, Y., Liu, M., Liu, Y., Peng, X., Liu, Y., Zhang, Y., Wang, R., Li, Q., & Duan, Y. (2020). High performance exhaled breath biomarkers for diagnosis of lung cancer and potential biomarkers for classification of lung cancer. *Journal of Breath Research, 15*(1), 016017. Available from https://doi.org/10.1088/1752-7163/abaecb.

Malagù, C., Fabbri, B., Gherardi, S., Giberti, A., Guidi, V., Landini, N., & Zonta, G. (2014). Chemoresistive gas sensors for the detection of colorectal cancer biomarkers. *Sensors (Switzerland), 14*(10). Available from https://doi.org/10.3390/s141018982, http://www.mdpi.com/1424-8220/14/10/18982/pdf.

Manocha, A., Sood, S. K., & Bhatia, M. (2023). Digital twin-assisted fuzzy logic-inspired intelligent approach for flood prediction. *IEEE Sensors Journal*. Available from https://doi.org/10.1109/JSEN.2023.3322535, http://ieeexplore.ieee.org/xpl/RecentIssue.jsp?punumber = 7361.

McCarthy, K. D. (2002). Detection of lung, breast, colorectal, and prostate cancers from exhaled breath using a single array of nanosensors. *Breast Cancer Research and Treatment*, 2002.

Neupane, S., Peverall, R., Richmond, G., Blaikie, T. P. J., Taylor, D., Hancock, G., & Evans, M. L. (2016). Exhaled breath isoprene rises during hypoglycemia in type 1 diabetes. *Diabetes Care, 39*(7), e97. Available from https://doi.org/10.2337/dc16-0461, http://care.diabetesjournals.org/content/39/7/e97.

Nowak, N., Engler, A., Thiel, S., Stöberl, A. S., Sinues, P., Zenobi, R., & Kohler, M. (2021). Validation of breath biomarkers for obstructive sleep apnea. *Sleep Medicine, 85*. Available from https://doi.org/10.1016/j.sleep.2021.06.040, http://www.elsevier.com/inca/publications/store/6/2/0/2/8/2.

Oakley-Girvan, I., & Davis, S. W. (2017). Breath based volatile organic compounds in the detection of breast, lung, and colorectal cancers: A systematic review. *Cancer Biomarkers, 21*(1). Available from https://doi.org/10.3233/CBM-170177, http://www.iospress.nl/journal/cancer-biomarkers/.

Ochoa-Muñoz, Y. H., Mejía de Gutiérrez, R., & Rodríguez-Páez, J. E. (2023). Metal oxide gas sensors to study acetone detection considering their potential in the diagnosis of diabetes: A review. *Molecules (Basel, Switzerland), 28*(3). Available from https://doi.org/10.3390/molecules28031150, http://www.mdpi.com/journal/molecules.

Ogunleye, A., & Wang, Q.G. (2018). Enhanced XGBoost-based automatic diagnosis system for chronic kidney disease. In *IEEE International Conference on Control and Automation, ICCA. 2018* (pp. 805–810). IEEE Computer Society, South Africa. Available from https://doi.org/10.1109/ICCA.2018.8444167, http://ieeexplore.ieee.org/xpl/mostRecentIssue.jsp?punumber = 6126159.

Palaniappan, R., & Surendran, S. (2022). A digital twin approach for deepened classification of patients with hepatitis, fibrosis and cirrhosis. *Journal of Physics: Conference Series, 2335*(1), 012034. Available from https://doi.org/10.1088/1742-6596/2335/1/012034.

Paleczek, A., Grochala, D., & Rydosz, A. (2021). Artificial breath classification using xgboost algorithm for diabetes detection. *Sensors, 21*(12). Available from https://doi.org/10.3390/s21124187, https://www.mdpi.com/1424-8220/21/12/4187/pdf.

Paleczek, A., & Rydosz, A. (2022). Review of the algorithms used in exhaled breath analysis for the detection of diabetes. *Journal of Breath Research, 16*(2), 026003. Available from https://doi.org/10.1088/1752-7163/ac4916.

Pandey C., Sharma S., Matta P. 2021 Body sensor network architectures in healthcare Internet-of-Things (HIoT): A survey. In *Proceedings of the 6th International Conference on Communication and Electronics Systems, ICCES 2021* (pp. 494–499). Institute of Electrical and Electronics Engineers Inc., India. Available from https://doi.org/10.1109/ICCES51350.2021.9489205, http://ieeexplore.ieee.org/xpl/mostrecentissue.jsp?punumber = 9488658.

Poļaka, I., Mežmale, L., Anarkulova, L., Kononova, E., Vilkoite, I., Veliks, V., Ļeščinska, A. M., Stonāns, I., Pčolkins, A., Tolmanis, I., Shani, G., Haick, H., Mitrovics, J., Glöckler, J., Mizaikoff, B., & Leja, M. (2023). The detection of colorectal cancer through machine learning-based breath sensor analysis. *Diagnostics*, *13*(21). Available from https://doi.org/10.3390/diagnostics13213355, http://www.mdpi.com/journal/diagnostics/.

Politi, L., Monasta, L., Rigressi, M. N., Princivalle, A., Gonfiotti, A., Camiciottoli, G., & Perbellini, L. (2021). Discriminant profiles of volatile compounds in the alveolar air of patients with squamous cell lung cancer, lung adenocarcinoma or colon cancer. *Molecules (Basel, Switzerland)*, *26*(3), 550. Available from https://doi.org/10.3390/molecules26030550.

Rao, D. J., & Mane, S. (2019). Digital twin approach to clinical DSS with explainable AI. arXiv, undefined arXiv. Available from https://doi.org/10.48550/arxiv.1910.13520, https://arxiv.org.

Ratiu, I. A., Ligor, T., Bocos-Bintintan, V., Mayhew, C. A., & Buszewski, B. (2021). Volatile organic compounds in exhaled breath as fingerprints of lung cancer, asthma and COPD. *Journal of Clinical Medicine*, *10*(1). Available from https://doi.org/10.3390/jcm10010032, https://www.mdpi.com/2077-0383/10/1/32/pdf.

Sarp, S., Kuzlu, M., Zhao, Y., & Gueler, O. (2023). Digital twin in healthcare: A study for chronic wound management. *IEEE Journal of Biomedical and Health Informatics*, *27*(11). Available from https://doi.org/10.1109/JBHI.2023.3299028, http://ieeexplore.ieee.org/xpl/RecentIssue.jsp?punumber = 6221020.

Scheuermann, C., Binderberger, T., von Frankenberg, N., & Werner, A. (2020). Digital twin: a machine learning approach to predict individual stress levels in extreme environments. In *Adjunct Proceedings of the 2020 ACM International Joint Conference on Pervasive and Ubiquitous Computing and Proceedings of the 2020 ACM International Symposium on Wearable Computers (UbiComp/ISWC '20 Adjunct)*, (pp. 657–664). New York, NY, USA: Association for Computing Machinery. Available from https://doi.org/10.1145/3410530.3414316.

Shamanna, P., Saboo, B., Damodharan, S., Mohammed, J., Mohamed, M., Poon, T., Kleinman, N., & Thajudeen, M. (2020). Reducing HbA1c in type 2 diabetes using digital twin technology-enabled precision nutrition: A retrospective analysis. *Diabetes Therapy*, *11*(11). Available from https://doi.org/10.1007/s13300-020-00931-w, http://www.springer.com/medicine/internal/journal/13300.

Sibo — Foodmarble, Accessed, (2024). 2024.

Siegel, A. P., Daneshkhah, A., Hardin, D. S., Shrestha, S., Varahramyan, K., & Agarwal, M. (2017). Analyzing breath samples of hypoglycemic events in type 1 diabetes patients: Towards developing an alternative to diabetes alert dogs. *Journal of Breath Research*, *11*(2). Available from https://doi.org/10.1088/1752-7163/aa6ac6, http://iopscience.iop.org/article/10.1088/1752-7163/aa6ac6/pdf.

Sivertsen, S. M., Bjørneklett, A., Gullestad, H. P., & Nygaard, K. (1992). Breath methane and colorectal cancer. *Scandinavian Journal of Gastroenterology*, *27*(1). Available from https://doi.org/10.3109/00365529209011161.

Subramanian, B., Kim, J., Maray, M., & Paul, A. (2022). Digital twin model: A real-time emotion recognition system for personalized healthcare. *IEEE Access*, *10*. Available from https://doi.org/10.1109/ACCESS.2022.3193941, http://ieeexplore.ieee.org/xpl/RecentIssue.jsp?punumber = 6287639.

van den Eijnden, M. A. C. (2023). Machine learning for postoperative continuous recovery scores of oncology patients in perioperative care with data from wearables. *Sensors*, *23*. Available from https://doi.org/10.3390/S23094455.

Vats, T., Singh, S. K., Kumar, S., Gupta, B. B., Gill, S. S., Arya, V., & Alhalabi, W. (2023). Explainable context-aware IoT framework using human digital twin for healthcare. *Multimedia Tools and Applications*. Available from https://doi.org/10.1007/s11042-023-16922-5, https://www.springer.com/journal/11042.

Wang, C., Ke, C., Wang, X., Chi, C., Guo, L., Luo, S., Guo, Z., Xu, G., Zhang, F., & Li, E. (2014). Noninvasive detection of colorectal cancer by analysis of exhaled breath. *Analytical and Bioanalytical Chemistry*, *406*(19). Available from https://doi.org/10.1007/s00216-014-7865-x, link.springer.de/link/service/journals/00216/index.htm.

Wang, S., Gao, J., Lu, F., You, Z., Huang, M., Fang, W., Liu, X., Li, Y., & Liu, Y. (2023a). Human motion recognition by a shoes-floor triboelectric nanogenerator and its application in fall detection. *Nano Energy*, *108108230*. Available from https://doi.org/10.1016/j.nanoen.2023.108230.

Wang, X., Guo, H., Hu, S., Chang, M. C., & Lyu, S. (2023b). *GAN-generated faces detection: a survey and new perspectives*, . *Frontiers in Artificial Intelligence and Applications* (372, pp. 2533–2542). United States: IOS Press BV. Available from https://doi.org/10.3233/FAIA230558, http://www.iospress.nl/loadtop/load.php?isbn = 19057415.

Wang, Z., & Wang, C. (2013). Is breath acetone a biomarker of diabetes? A historical review on breath acetone measurements. *Journal of Breath Research*, *7*(3), 037109. Available from https://doi.org/10.1088/1752-7155/7/3/037109.

Yang, H. Y., Wang, Y. C., Peng, H. Y., & Huang, C. H. (2021). Breath biopsy of breast cancer using sensor array signals and machine learning analysis. *Scientific Reports, 11*(1). Available from https://doi.org/10.1038/s41598-020-80570-0, http://www.nature.com/srep/index.html.

Yang, X., Wang, R., Zhao, D., Yu, F., Heidari, A. A., Xu, Z., Chen, H., Algarni, A. D., Elmannai, H., & Xu, S. (2023). Multi-level threshold segmentation framework for breast cancer images using enhanced differential evolution. *Biomedical Signal Processing and Control, 80*104373. Available from https://doi.org/10.1016/j.bspc.2022.104373.

Yusoff, M., Haryanto, T., Suhartanto, H., Mustafa, W. A., Zain, J. M., & Kusmardi, K. (2023). Accuracy analysis of deep learning methods in breast cancer classification: A structured review. *Diagnostics, 13*(4). Available from https://doi.org/10.3390/diagnostics13040683, http://www.mdpi.com/journal/diagnostics/.

Zhong, X., Babaie Sarijaloo, F., Prakash, A., Park, J., Huang, C., Barwise, A., Herasevich, V., Gajic, O., Pickering, B., & Dong, Y. (2022). A multidisciplinary approach to the development of digital twin models of critical care delivery in intensive care units. *International Journal of Production Research, 60*(13). Available from https://doi.org/10.1080/00207543.2021.2022235, http://www.tandfonline.com/toc/tprs20/current.

Zhou, T., Li, Q., Lu, H., Cheng, Q., & Zhang, X. (2023). GAN review: Models and medical image fusion applications. *Information Fusion, 91*. Available from https://doi.org/10.1016/j.inffus.2022.10.017, http://www.elsevier.com/inca/publications/store/6/2/0/8/6/2/index.htt.

5

Blockchain for security and privacy in the smart sensor network

Murat Koca

Faculty of Engineering, Department of Computer Engineering, Van Yuzuncu Yil University, Kampus, Tusba, Van, Turkey

5.1 Introduction

The combination of sensor technology and data analytics has significantly transformed the healthcare industry, leading to the emergence of intelligent healthcare networks. These networks utilize a wide range of sensors to gather patient data in real time, allowing for remote monitoring, predictive analytics, and individualized treatment plans (Aceto et al., 2018; Coelho et al., 2023; Farahani et al., 2021). The widespread use of these networks offers great potential for enhancing patient outcomes and decreasing healthcare expenses. However, it also presents significant obstacles, particularly regarding the security and confidentiality of sensitive medical data.

The healthcare industry is very susceptible to cyber threats due to the significant value of patient data and the possible consequences of breaches in terms of patient safety and confidentiality (Bisceglia et al., 2023; Ramalingam et al., 2024). Conventional centralized methods of data management, which depend on a solitary point of control, are progressively ineffective in protecting against advanced cyber threats (Popoola et al., 2023). There is an urgent requirement for inventive solutions that can enhance the security and privacy of intelligent healthcare networks while guaranteeing the smooth interchange of data among individuals involved. Blockchain fundamentally presents an innovative method for handling data, distinguished by its decentralized structure, cryptographic hashing, and consensus procedures.

Blockchain's decentralized architecture guarantees that data is not concentrated in a single location, but rather dispersed among a network of interconnected nodes. Every data block is securely connected to the one before it using cryptographic means, creating an unalterable chain. The tamper-resistant nature of blockchain makes it highly suitable for safeguarding sensitive medical data in smart healthcare networks, effectively reducing the likelihood of unwanted access, tampering, or data breaches (Majdoubi et al., 2022; Wankhede et al., 2023).

Sensor Networks for Smart Hospitals
DOI: https://doi.org/10.1016/B978-0-443-36370-2.00006-2

In addition, blockchain enables the transparent and safe exchange of data among everyone involved, via smart contracts. These self-executing contracts enforce predetermined norms and conditions, guaranteeing that data access and transactions only take place with the proper authorization. This not only improves security but also simplifies data interchange processes, promoting collaboration and interoperability throughout the healthcare ecosystem.

Furthermore, blockchain provides cutting-edge methods for safeguarding patient confidentiality, including zero-knowledge proofs and homomorphic encryption. Zero-knowledge proofs enable the verification of statements without disclosing the underlying data, whereas homomorphic encryption allows calculations to be conducted on encrypted data, maintaining anonymity during the entire process. These privacy-preserving methods enable patients to maintain authority over their medical data while yet reaping the advantages of data analysis.

In this book chapter, we will analyze the potential of blockchain technology to overcome security and privacy challenges in smart healthcare networks. By utilizing its decentralized structure, secure data storage, and privacy safeguards, blockchain technology has the potential to transform the delivery of healthcare. It can enable innovation and cooperation within the healthcare system, all while maintaining the integrity and confidentiality of patient data.

5.2 Related work

The use of blockchain technology is becoming more prominent as a viable way to enhance security and privacy within smart healthcare networks. Multiple research and projects have examined the utilization of blockchain technology in the healthcare sector, with a particular emphasis on data integrity, interoperability, patient privacy, and safe data sharing. The salient findings of these investigations are outlined below.

A crucial field of study focuses on utilizing blockchain technology to guarantee the authenticity and unchangeability of medical records and health data. Azaria et al. (2016) suggested a system that utilizes blockchain technology to manage electronic health records (EHRs) (Azaria et al., 2016). This system offers a safe and traceable way to access patient information, while also guaranteeing the accuracy and legitimacy of the data. In a similar manner, Yue et al. (2016) proposed a framework that utilizes blockchain technology to ensure the secure transfer of medical data across healthcare providers (Yue et al., 2016). This framework enables the efficient and transparent sharing of patient information while maintaining privacy.

Interoperability is a significant obstacle in healthcare, particularly in regard to the smooth transfer of data between disparate systems and organizations. Blockchain technology has been suggested as a possible remedy for addressing interoperability challenges by offering a decentralized and uniform platform for exchanging data. Dubovitskaya et al. (2017) introduced a method that uses blockchain technology to facilitate the sharing of healthcare data. This method ensures secure and efficient communication among healthcare practitioners, patients, and other involved parties.

Yaacoub et al. (2023) have recently shown, several tools and techniques that will enhance users' security operations. The tools NMAP, Maltego, and Metasploit, which are utilized by specialists to gather information about the IP of a system and identify unauthorized or foreign systems, were also assessed (Yaacoub et al., 2023).

Moreover, blockchain provides cutting-edge technologies to safeguard patient confidentiality in intelligent healthcare networks. Research has mostly concentrated on utilizing cryptographic methods, such as zero-knowledge proofs and homomorphic encryption, to guarantee the privacy of sensitive medical data. As an illustration, Soni & Singh (2021) suggested a blockchain-driven framework to securely and confidentially share genetic data. This approach enables researchers to get and examine data while safeguarding patient privacy Soni & Singh (2021).

Furthermore, numerous pilot projects and efforts have examined the pragmatic implementation of blockchain technology in the healthcare sector. An illustration of this is the MedRec project, created by academics at Massachusetts Institute of Technology (MIT), which has proven the viability of utilizing blockchain technology to oversee EHRs and facilitate the exchange of patient-centric data (Ariel, 2017).

Overall, the research emphasizes the growing fascination and capacity of blockchain technology in addressing security and privacy issues in intelligent healthcare networks. Blockchain provides a flexible and promising structure for revolutionizing healthcare delivery in the digital era, addressing concerns such as data integrity, interoperability, patient privacy, and safe data sharing. Nevertheless, further investigation and cooperation are required to surmount the obstacles in using blockchain technology and fully use its capabilities in the healthcare sector.

5.3 Smart sensor networks

A smart sensor is a sophisticated sensing device that is outfitted with integrated processing capabilities and connectivity, allowing it to independently gather, analyze, and transfer data. Smart sensors possess enhanced capabilities beyond simply providing raw data output. They are equipped with intelligence and functionality that enable them to carry out activities such as data processing, decision-making, and communication with other devices or systems.

Smart sensors possess key attributes such as:

- **Data processing**: Smart sensors have inherent processing capabilities, allowing them to scrutinize unprocessed data and extract significant insights or practical information (Plageras et al., 2018). The processing may encompass activities such as filtering, aggregation, or computing of intricate algorithms right within the sensing device.
- **Connectivity:** Smart sensors are outfitted with communication interfaces such as Wi-Fi, Bluetooth, Zigbee, or cellular networks, allowing them to send data to other devices, networks, or cloud platforms (Betta et al., 2010). This connectivity enables the instantaneous monitoring, remote manipulation, and exchange of data across dispersed systems.

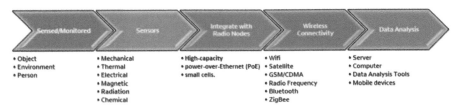

FIGURE 5.1   Working process of smart sensors.

- **Embedded Intelligence:** Smart sensors can be equipped with embedded software or firmware, allowing them to autonomously carry out tasks, adjust to varying surroundings, and react to predetermined situations or triggers. The incorporation of this advanced intelligence improves the sensor's capacity to make well-informed decisions or carry out actions based on the gathered data.
- **Energy Efficiency:** Smart sensors are specifically engineered to enhance energy utilization, thereby prolonging the lifespan of the battery or reducing power consumption to guarantee sustained functionality in areas with limited resources. Energy economy is essential for applications that necessitate extended sensor deployment or operation in remote or inaccessible areas.

Fig. 5.1 demonstrates that the operations are executed in five distinct steps. These initiate the process of gathering data that is perceived or observed from the environment, individuals, and objects. The system is connected to radio nodes with large data storage capabilities by sensors, in order to collect the needed information. Analyzed data is derived from radio nodes that are integrated and connected wirelessly. Data undergoes a process of transformation to yield specific information, which is retrieved by employing suitable methods of data analysis. The converted data is presented visually and accessible to users.

5.4 Areas of smart sensors

Smart sensors are utilized in diverse fields because of their capacity to independently gather, analyze, and communicate data. Fig. 5.2 highlights the versatility and importance of smart sensors in enabling data-driven decision-making, automation, and optimization across a variety of industries and sectors. As technology continues to advance, smart sensors are expected to play an increasingly important role in shaping the future of smart cities, connected industries, and smart infrastructure systems. Smart sensors find extensive use in various application domains, including:

- **Environmental Monitoring:** Intelligent sensors are employed to observe and assess the quality of air, water, soil, and pollution levels in urban areas, industrial sites, agricultural fields, and natural ecosystems. They aid in evaluating the ecological consequences, pinpointing the origins of pollution, and executing strategies for environmental preservation.

FIGURE 5.2   Areas of smart sensors.

- **Healthcare:** smart sensors are employed for the purpose of remotely monitoring patients, tracking health data through wearable devices, operating medical imaging equipment, and aiding in the diagnosis of medical conditions. Their responsibilities include gathering essential physiological measurements, monitoring the state of patients, ensuring compliance with drug regimens, and offering immediate health insights to tailor patient treatment.
- **Industrial Automation:** Smart sensors are essential in industrial automation for tasks including predictive maintenance, process control, quality assurance, and asset tracking. Their responsibilities include monitoring equipment performance, identifying abnormalities, optimizing production processes, and ensuring operational efficiency in the manufacturing, energy, and utility sectors.
- **Smart Buildings:** Sensors are utilized in smart buildings to manage energy consumption, detect occupancy, regulate lighting, optimize HVAC systems, and enhance security. They contribute to the reduction of energy consumption, the enhancement of occupant comfort, and the improvement of building safety and security.

- **Transportation and Logistics:** Smart sensors are utilized in transportation systems and logistics networks to track vehicles, monitor traffic, manage fleets, and track goods. They offer immediate and up-to-date insight on transportation resources, optimize the process of planning routes, enhance the flow of traffic, and improve the efficiency of the supply chain.
- **Agriculture:** Smart sensors are utilized in agriculture for precision farming, monitoring soil moisture, tracking crop health, and automating irrigation systems. They assist farmers in maximizing water utilization, overseeing crop well-being, tracking environmental circumstances, and enhancing agricultural output.
- **Smart Grids:** Smart sensors are essential components of smart grid systems, as they are responsible for monitoring and controlling the generation, transmission, distribution, and consumption of electricity. They provide real-time monitoring of energy consumption, voltage levels, grid stability, and the integration of renewable energy, hence enabling efficient and dependable electricity distribution.
- **Structural Health Monitoring:** involves the utilization of intelligent sensors to assess the condition of various infrastructure assets such as buildings, bridges, and dams. They identify and analyze structural flaws, track oscillations, evaluate load conditions, and issue advance alerts regarding probable malfunctions, thereby guaranteeing the safety and soundness of civil structures.

The variety and significance of smart sensors in facilitating data-driven decision-making, automation, and optimization across diverse industries and sectors are emphasized by these application areas. With the continuous advancement of technology, smart sensors are anticipated to have a growing and crucial impact on the development of smart cities, connected industries, and intelligent infrastructure systems.

5.5 Types of security and privacy in smart sensor systems in healthcare

The security and privacy of smart sensor systems are crucial factors that must be meticulously considered to safeguard sensitive data and guarantee the system's integrity and dependability. Security and privacy are of utmost importance for smart sensor systems in healthcare, particularly when handling sensitive patient data. The primary security and privacy safeguards employed in healthcare smart sensor technologies are as follows:

- **Data Encryption:** Employing encryption methods to safeguard confidential patient information throughout its transmission and storage (Peng & Li, 2022). This guarantees that in the event of data interception, it will remain incomprehensible without the corresponding decryption keys.
- **Access Control:** Enforcing stringent access control systems to guarantee that only authorized healthcare workers can retrieve patient data gathered by intelligent sensors. This may entail the implementation of role-based access control (RBAC) or other access control frameworks (Ni et al., 2010).
- **Authentication:** Implementing robust authentication measures, such as biometric authentication or two-factor authentication, to validate the identification of users who are accessing the smart sensor system. This measure serves to thwart illegal entry to patient data.

- **Data Integrity Verification:** Utilizing methods like as digital signatures or checksums to guarantee the integrity of patient data gathered by intelligent sensors. This aids in identifying any unauthorized alterations or efforts to tamper with the system (Koca et al., 2021).
- **Patient Consent and Transparency:** Ensuring patients are adequately informed regarding the data gathered by intelligent sensors, its intended usage, and getting their explicit agreement for its collection and processing. Data transparency fosters trust and improves privacy protection.
- **Anonymization and Pseudonymization:** Implementing methods to obfuscate or replace identifying information in patient data in order to safeguard their confidentiality. This process entails the elimination or concealment of identifiable data to avoid the recognition of specific patients.
- **Secure Communication Protocols:** To ensure the confidentiality of data exchanged between smart sensors, healthcare equipment, and data storage systems, it is recommended to employ secure communication protocols like transport layer security or virtual private networks (Chen & Horng, 2006). These protocols encrypt the data, preventing unauthorized interception or eavesdropping.
- **Physical Security Measures:** Enforcing physical security protocols to safeguard smart sensor equipment against illegal access or tampering. This includes security measures such as secured cabinets, restricted access controls, and surveillance systems implemented in healthcare facilities.
- **Regular Security Audits and Updates:** Performing routine security audits and assessments on smart sensor systems to detect and resolve any vulnerabilities or shortcomings. Regularly updating software and firmware with security patches to safeguard against known risks.
- **Regulatory Compliance:** Ensuring adherence to healthcare legislation and standards, such as the Health Insurance Portability and Accountability Act (HIPAA) (Gunn et al., 2004) in the United States or the General Data Protection Regulation (GDPR) (Hoofnagle et al., 2019) in the European Union. Adhering to these laws guarantees the protection and confidentiality of patient data obtained by intelligent sensors.

Through the implementation of these security and privacy measures, smart sensor systems in healthcare may proficiently protect patient data, uphold confidentiality, and adhere to regulatory obligations, thus fostering confidence among patients and healthcare providers.

5.6 Types of cyber attacks on smart sensor network in healthcare

Smart sensor networks are susceptible to cyber assaults that can exploit weaknesses, leading to compromised data integrity, confidentiality, and availability of services. This book chapter focuses on examining threats against smart sensors, particularly in the healthcare industry. The integration of smart sensor networks into key healthcare systems has made them increasingly susceptible to a wide range of cyber threats. Below are several prevalent cyber threats that frequently target smart sensor networks in the healthcare sector:

- **Denial of Service Attacks:** These attacks have the objective of impeding the regular operation of smart sensor networks by overwhelming them with an overwhelming amount of traffic or requests, thereby making them inaccessible to authorized users (Avcı & Koca, 2023).
- **Man-in-the-Middle Attacks:** In these attacks, involve an attacker who intercepts the communication between smart sensors and other network components (Conti et al., 2016). This interception enables the attacker to eavesdrop on sensitive data or manipulate the transmitted data.
- **Data Tampering:** Malicious actors have the potential to manipulate the data gathered by intelligent sensors, resulting in inaccurate assessments, treatment choices, or patient surveillance. Such circumstances can lead to significant repercussions for patient safety and healthcare results (Huang et al., 2021).
- **Physical Attacks:** Attackers can undermine the integrity of smart sensor equipment, install malicious software, or directly take sensitive data from the devices by having physical access to them.
- **Spoofing Attacks:** Malicious individuals may assume the identity of authentic smart sensor devices or network components in order to illicitly infiltrate healthcare systems, pilfer confidential information, or initiate additional assaults (Duo et al., 2022).
- **Ransomware Attacks:** These assaults entail the encryption of data or systems within intelligent sensor networks, followed by a demand for ransom in exchange for their decryption (Chang & Le, 2016). Ransomware has the potential to significantly disrupt hospital operations and damage the quality of patient treatment.
- **Zero-Day Exploits:** Malicious individuals can make use of undisclosed weaknesses in smart sensor devices or their software to obtain unauthorized entry, execute arbitrary commands, or engage in other harmful actions (Bilge & Dumitras, 2012).
- **Malware Infections:** Malware has the ability to infiltrate intelligent sensor networks, jeopardizing their confidentiality, integrity, and availability. Malware can be introduced through different methods, such as malicious firmware upgrades or hacked network connections (Lalonde Levesque et al., 2013).
- **Insider Threats:** Authorized personnel who have access to intelligent sensor networks may purposefully or inadvertently abuse their privileges, resulting in data breaches, system compromises, or other security problems (Georgiadou et al., 2022).
- **Social Engineering Attacks:** Adversaries can deceive healthcare staff or smart sensor network users into revealing sensitive information, such as login passwords or patient data, by employing methods like phishing or pretexting (Salahdine & Kaabouch, 2019).

In order to reduce these risks, healthcare institutions must use strong cybersecurity measures, such as encryption, access controls, network segmentation, periodic security audits, employee training, and the utilization of intrusion detection and prevention systems. In addition, it is crucial for makers of smart sensor devices to give utmost importance to security at every stage of the design, development, and deployment process.

5.7 Blockchain advantages in ensuring cyber security and privacy in smart healthcare sensor networks

Blockchain has substantial benefits in guaranteeing cybersecurity and privacy in sensor networks within smart healthcare. The decentralized and immutable ledger design of the system guarantees that sensitive patient data obtained from sensors cannot be tampered with or accessed without authorization, hence minimizing the danger of illegal access or data manipulation. Blockchain technology improves data confidentiality and strengthens resilience against cyber threats by encrypting patient data and distributing it across numerous nodes in the network. Smart contracts facilitate the enforcement of detailed access control mechanisms, permitting solely authorized healthcare personnel or companies to access and engage with patient data, thereby safeguarding privacy. Moreover, the visible and auditable characteristics of blockchain technology enable accountability and adherence to healthcare legislation like HIPAA or GDPR, promoting trust among stakeholders and guaranteeing the prioritization and safeguarding of patient privacy. In general, blockchain technology offers a strong basis for improving cybersecurity and privacy in smart health sector sensor networks. It facilitates secure sharing of data, promotes interoperability, and fosters trust within the healthcare ecosystem.

Blockchain technology provides numerous benefits in enhancing cybersecurity and safeguarding privacy in sensor networks within the smart health sector.

- **Data Integrity:** The irreversible and decentralized nature of blockchain's ledger guarantees that once data is recorded, it remains unchangeable and resistant to tampering. This feature improves the integrity of patient data gathered by intelligent health sensors, by preventing unwanted alterations and guaranteeing its correctness and dependability.
- **Secure Data Storage:** Blockchain offers a robust and unalterable approach to storing confidential patient data gathered by intelligent health sensors. The blockchain stores data in an encrypted format and distributes it among numerous nodes, thereby minimizing the chances of unwanted access or data breaches.
- **Enhanced Privacy:** Blockchain technology enables the utilization of privacy-enhancing methods, such as zero-knowledge proofs and private transactions. These methods provide the controlled release of confidential data while safeguarding the anonymity of patients and their medical records.
- **Decentralized Access Control:** Blockchain-powered access control systems let people exert enhanced authority over the individuals authorized to view their health data. Patients have the ability to allow and withdraw access privileges to their data through the use of smart contracts. This helps minimize the possibility of unlawful data access and guarantees the confidentiality of patient information.
- **Interoperability:** Blockchain enables the seamless exchange and sharing of health data among various healthcare systems and stakeholders through a unified and decentralized platform. The interoperability of healthcare systems facilitates collaboration across healthcare providers while ensuring the security and privacy of data.

- **Auditable Data Trail:** The transparent and auditable nature of blockchain enables the establishment of an unchangeable record of all data exchanges inside the smart health sensor network. The audit trail serves the function of maintaining compliance, conducting forensic investigations, and establishing accountability among network members.
- **Resilience to Cyber Attacks:** The decentralized structure and consensus procedures of blockchain provide natural resistance to cyber assaults and eliminate the risk of single points of failure. The blockchain maintains the confidentiality and availability of patient data, even if a node in the network is compromised.
- **Smart Contracts:** Smart health sensor networks can utilize blockchain-based smart contracts to automate contractual agreements and business logic. Smart contracts can implement access control measures, oversee data-sharing agreements, and enable safe transactions without the involvement of middlemen, thereby mitigating the potential for human mistakes and fraud.
- **Transparent Governance:** Blockchain technology facilitates a transparent and decentralized system of governing the smart health sensor network. Network members can collaboratively make decisions on data sharing, access control, and network policies using consensus techniques, which guarantee fairness, openness, and accountability.
- **Compliance and Regulation:** Blockchain enables adherence to healthcare standards like HIPAA and GDPR with a secure and traceable platform for storing and exchanging patient data. Adhering to regulatory regulations is crucial in order to safeguard patient privacy and prevent incurring expensive penalties due to failure to comply.

In summary, blockchain technology provides a strong and creative solution for guaranteeing cybersecurity and privacy in sensor networks within the smart health sector. It improves the reliability, confidentiality, and protection of data, while also encouraging compatibility, openness, and responsibility among healthcare participants.

5.8 Discussion

Blockchain technology provides innovative solutions to strengthen security and privacy in smart healthcare sensor networks, which are crucial in the healthcare industry where the protection of patient data is of utmost importance. Smart healthcare sensor networks can guarantee the security and confidentiality of patient data collected by sensors by utilizing blockchain's decentralized and unchangeable ledger. Every transaction logged on the blockchain is cryptographically protected and immune to modification or tampering, ensuring a reliable and open record of patient health data. The unchangeable record guarantees the integrity of personal medical information, minimizing the possibility of illegal entry, data breaches, or tampering. Consequently, it protects patient privacy and upholds the confidentiality of healthcare records.

Furthermore, the decentralized structure of blockchain eliminates the necessity for a central governing body or middleman, thus decreasing susceptibility to cyber threats and improving the durability of intelligent healthcare sensor networks. The patient data saved on the blockchain is decentralized, meaning it is spread out among several nodes in the network. This distribution of data makes it extremely difficult for unauthorized individuals to get access to or manipulate the information. This decentralized storage framework guarantees that in the event of a compromised node within the network, the integrity of the blockchain remains unaffected, hence safeguarding the security and confidentiality of patient data. In addition, blockchain technology facilitates precise access control methods via smart contracts, enabling healthcare practitioners to establish and enforce access rights according to predetermined criteria and conditions. This system guarantees that only individuals who have been granted permission, such as healthcare professionals or patients, are able to retrieve and engage with patient information. This reduces the likelihood of unlawful data retrieval or disclosure and is in accordance with regulatory standards such as HIPAA or GDPR.

In addition, blockchain technology enables secure and seamless data sharing among many participants in the smart healthcare sensor network ecosystem. Blockchain facilitates streamlined communication and cooperation among healthcare professionals, patients, researchers, and other relevant parties by offering a uniform system for data sharing. This is achieved while ensuring the protection and confidentiality of the data. Blockchain-enabled health data exchanges facilitate the secure sharing of patient data among various healthcare organizations, thereby enhancing care coordination and patient outcomes. Furthermore, blockchain technology improves trust and transparency in the healthcare sector by empowering people to exert more authority over their health data and give approval for its utilization in research or therapy endeavors. In summary, blockchain technology has the capacity to greatly transform the security and privacy of smart healthcare sensor networks. This enables enterprises to make use of the benefits of IoT technologies, while also guaranteeing the confidentiality, integrity, and accessibility of patient data.

5.9 Conclusion

Blockchain technology is increasingly being recognized as a revolutionary approach to address the significant security and privacy challenges encountered by smart healthcare sensor networks. By utilizing the decentralized and unchangeable record of blockchain, these networks can guarantee the reliability, privacy, and accessibility of patient data obtained by sensors. The decentralized architecture of blockchain mitigates risks related to centralized data storage, minimizes vulnerabilities to cyber assaults, and enhances resilience against security breaches. Furthermore, blockchain technology allows for precise control over who may access data and promotes the safe sharing of information among different parties involved in the healthcare system. This promotes transparency, trust, and the capacity for different systems to work together effectively. Healthcare organizations are increasingly using IoT technology to enhance patient care and outcomes. Blockchain is emerging as a crucial framework for safeguarding sensitive health information, preserving patient privacy, and guaranteeing compliance with regulations in smart healthcare sensor networks. The future of healthcare systems seems hopeful with the ongoing progress and acceptance of blockchain solutions. These solutions prioritize the security and privacy of patients' medical data, ensuring their well-being and anonymity.

References

Aceto, G., Persico, V., & Pescapé, A. (2018). The role of Information and Communication Technologies in healthcare: taxonomies, perspectives, and challenges. *Journal of Network and Computer Applications, 107*, 125–154. Available from https://doi.org/10.1016/J.JNCA.2018.02.008.

Ariel, C. E. (2017). *MedRec: Blockchain for medical data access, permission management and trend analysis,* 2017.

Avcı, İ., & Koca, M. (2023). Predicting DDoS attacks using machine learning algorithms in building management systems. *Electronics (Switzerland), 12*(19). Available from https://doi.org/10.3390/electronics12194142, http://www.mdpi.com/journal/electronics.

Azaria, A., Ekblaw, A., Vieira, T., & Lippman, A. (2016). MedRec: Using blockchain for medical data access and permission management. *Proceedings - 2016 2nd International Conference on Open and Big Data, OBD 2016,* 25–30. Available from https://doi.org/10.1109/OBD.2016.11.

Betta, G., Capriglione, D., Ferrigno, L., & Miele, G. (2010). Influence of Wi-Fi computer interfaces on measurement apparatuses. *IEEE Transactions on Instrumentation and Measurement, 59*(12). Available from https://doi.org/10.1109/tim.2010.2047303.

Bilge, L., & Dumitras, T. (2012). Before we knew it: An empirical study of zero-day attacks in the real world. *Proceedings of the ACM Conference on Computer and Communications Security,* 833–844. Available from https://doi.org/10.1145/2382196.2382284.

Bisceglia, M., Padilla, J., Piccolo, S., & Sääskilahti, P. (2023). On the bright side of market concentration in a mixed-oligopoly healthcare industry. *Journal of Health Economics, 90*102771. Available from https://doi.org/10.1016/j.jhealeco.2023.102771.

Chang, C. C., & Le, H. D. (2016). A provably secure, efficient, and flexible authentication scheme for ad hoc wireless sensor networks. *IEEE Transactions on Wireless Communications, 15*(1). Available from https://doi.org/10.1109/TWC.2015.2473165, http://ieeexplore.ieee.org/xpl/RecentIssue.jsp?puNumber = 7693.

Chen, C. H., & Horng, G. (2006). More robust private information retrieval scheme. *SECRYPT 2006 - International Conference on Security and Cryptography, Proceedings,* 297–302.

Coelho, K. K., Nogueira, M., Vieira, A. B., Silva, E. F., & Nacif, J. A. M. (2023). A survey on federated learning for security and privacy in healthcare applications. *Computer Communications, 207.* Available from https://doi.org/10.1016/j.comcom.2023.05.012, http://www.journals.elsevier.com/computer-communications/.

Conti, M., Dragoni, N., & Lesyk, V. (2016). A survey of man in the middle attacks. *IEEE Communications Surveys & Tutorials, 18*(3), 2027–2051. Available from https://doi.org/10.1109/COMST.2016.2548426.

Dubovitskaya, A., Xu, Z., Ryu, S., Schumacher, M., & Wang, F. (2017). Secure and trustable electronic medical records sharing using blockchain. *AMIA. Annual Symposium proceedings. AMIA Symposium,* 2017.

Duo, W., Zhou, M. C., & Abusorrah, A. (2022). A survey of cyber attacks on cyber physical systems: Recent advances and challenges. *IEEE/CAA Journal of Automatica Sinica, 9*(5), 784–800. Available from https://doi.org/10.1109/JAS.2022.105548.

Farahani, B., Firouzi, F., & Luecking, M. (2021). The convergence of IoT and distributed ledger technologies (DLT): Opportunities, challenges, and solutions. *Journal of Network and Computer Applications, 177,* 102936. Available from https://doi.org/10.1016/J.JNCA.2020.102936.

Georgiadou, A., Mouzakitis, S., & Askounis, D. (2022). Detecting insider threat via a cyber-security culture framework. *Journal of Computer Information Systems, 62*(4), 706–716. Available from https://doi.org/10.1080/08874417.2021.1903367.

Gunn, P. P., Fremont, A. M., Bottrell, M., Shugarman, L. R., Galegher, J., & Bikson, T. (2004). The health insurance portability and accountability act privacy rule a practical guide for researchers. *Medical Care, 42*(4). Available from https://doi.org/10.1097/01.mlr.0000119578.94846.f2.

Hoofnagle, C. J., van der Sloot, B., & Borgesius, F. Z. (2019). The European Union general data protection regulation: What it is and what it means. *Information & Communications Technology Law, 28*(1), 65–98. Available from https://doi.org/10.1080/13600834.2019.1573501.

Huang, D. W., Liu, W., & Bi, J. (2021). Data tampering attacks diagnosis in dynamic wireless sensor networks. *Computer Communications, 172,* 84–92. Available from https://doi.org/10.1016/J.COMCOM.2021.03.007.

Koca, M., Aydin, M. A., Sertbaş, A., & Zaİm, A. H. (2021). A new distributed anomaly detection approach for log IDS management based on deep learning. *Turkish Journal of Electrical Engineering and Computer Sciences, 25*(9). Available from https://doi.org/10.3906/elk-2102-89, https://journals.tubitak.gov.tr/elektrik/issues/elk-21-29-5/elk-29-5-15-2102-89.pdf.

Lalonde Levesque, F., Nsiempba, J., Fernandez, J. M., Chiasson, S., & Somayaji, A. (2013). A clinical study of risk factors related to malware infections. *Proceedings of the ACM Conference on Computer and Communications Security*, 97–108. Available from https://doi.org/10.1145/2508859.2516747.

Majdoubi, D. E., Bakkali, H. E., Bensaih, M., & Sadki, S. (2022). A decentralized trust establishment protocol for smart IoT systems. *Internet of Things*, 20100634. Available from https://doi.org/10.1016/j.iot.2022.100634.

Ni, Q., Bertino, E., Lobo, J., Brodi, C., Karat, C. M., Karat, J., & Trombetta, A. (2010). Privacy-aware Role-based access control. *ACM Transactions on Information and System Security*, 13(3). Available from https://doi.org/10.1145/1805974.1805980.

Peng, J., & Li, J. (2022). Agent data encryption and storage algorithm for wireless sensor networks based on blockchain technology for future smart city networks. *Journal of Testing and Evaluation*, 51(3). Available from https://doi.org/10.1520/JTE20220077, https://www.astm.org/DIGITAL_LIBRARY/JOURNALS/TESTEVAL/jote_issues.html.

Plageras, A. P., Psannis, K. E., Stergiou, C., Wang, H., & Gupta, B. B. (2018). Efficient IoT-based sensor BIG Data collection–processing and analysis in smart buildings. *Future Generation Computer Systems*, 82. Available from https://doi.org/10.1016/j.future.2017.09.082.

Popoola, O., Rodrigues, M., Marchang, J., Shenfield, A., Ikpehia, A., & Popoola, J. (2023). A critical literature review of security and privacy in smart home healthcare schemes adopting IoT & blockchain: Problems, challenges and solutions. *Blockchain: Research and Applications*100178. Available from https://doi.org/10.1016/j.bcra.2023.100178.

Ramalingam, S., Subramanian, M., Sreevallabha Reddy, A., Tarakaramu, N., Ijaz Khan, M., Abdullaev, S., & Dhahbi, S. (2024). Exploring business intelligence applications in the healthcare industry: A comprehensive analysis. *Egyptian Informatics Journal*, 25100438. Available from https://doi.org/10.1016/j.eij.2024.100438.

Salahdine, F., & Kaabouch, N. (2019). Social engineering attacks: A survey. *Future Internet*, 11(4), 89. Available from https://doi.org/10.3390/fi11040089.

Soni, M., & Singh, D. K. (2021). *Blockchain Implementation for Privacy preserving and securing the Healthcare data. 2021 10th ieee international conference on communication systems and network technologies (CSNT)* (pp. 729–734). IEEE. Available from https://doi.org/10.1109/CSNT51715.2021.9509722.E.

Wankhede, D., Gaikwad, V., Karnik, M., Mishra, V., Kekane, A., Kapase, S., & Bakkam, O. (2023). The decentralized smart contract certificate system utilizing ethereum blockchain technology. *Procedia Computer Science*, 230. Available from https://doi.org/10.1016/j.procs.2023.12.035.

Yaacoub, J. P. A., Noura, H. N., Salman, O., & Chehab, A. (2023). Ethical hacking for IoT: Security issues, challenges, solutions and recommendations. *Internet of Things and Cyber-Physical Systems*, 3. Available from https://doi.org/10.1016/j.iotcps.2023.04.002, https://www.sciencedirect.com/science/journal/26673452.

Yue, X., Wang, H., Jin, D., Li, M., & Jiang, W. (2016). Healthcare data gateways: Found healthcare intelligence on blockchain with novel privacy risk control. *Journal of Medical Systems*, 40(10). Available from https://doi.org/10.1007/s10916-016-0574-6.

Medical sensor network, blockchain and digital twin as the backbones of a connected ecosystem of smart hospitals

Xavier Fernando[1] and George Lăzăroiu[1,2,3,4]

[1]Toronto Metropolitan University, Toronto, ON, Canada [2]Curtin University, Perth, WA, Australia [3]Cardiff Metropolitan University, Cardiff, United Kingdom [4]Spiru Haret University, Bucharest, Romania

6.1 Introduction

Big healthcare data analytics, wearable sensor-based devices, digital twin and holographic simulation technologies configure smart hospital operations in virtually simulated environments. Metaverse-based healthcare monitoring and smart telemedicine diagnosis systems, 3D holographic images, and individualized patient avatars articulate immersive healthcare experiences in 3D virtual clinics. Artificial intelligence-based medical imaging and ambient health monitoring tools, blockchain-based medical data sharing, and wearable biometric sensors assist in virtual therapeutics across digital twin-based patient care units. 3D holographic visual experiences in virtual healthcare delivery across decentralized 3D virtual spaces can be attained by the use of motion sensing and digital patient twin technologies, synthetic imaging and real-time motion capture data, and wearable healthcare monitoring devices. Artificial intelligence-based medical imaging and smart wearable sensing devices, multimodal healthcare and synthetic imaging data, and cloud-based personalized healthcare and virtual consultation systems enable medical condition monitoring in smart hospital operations.

Big healthcare, physiological, and behavioral data sharing, wearable healthcare monitoring and wireless biomedical sensing devices, and deep learning-based computer vision

Sensor Networks for Smart Hospitals
DOI: https://doi.org/10.1016/B978-0-443-36370-2.00007-4

and clinical artificial intelligence algorithms shape virtual patient diagnosis and treatment in 3D virtual clinics. Virtual healthcare visits and clinical trials in virtual diagnostic environments and in a decentralized healthcare metaverse develop immersive virtual reality avatars, immersive virtual reality and motion sensing technologies, and healthcare digital twins. Multisensor medical data fusion, biomedical artificial intelligence healthcare service systems, and wearable health monitoring and multimodal sensing technologies optimize smart hospital operations in decentralized 3D virtual spaces. Cyber-physical healthcare and immersive virtual reality systems, digital twin simulation and artificial intelligence-powered diagnostic tools, and wearable haptic sensors enhance remote patient screening and personalized clinical care in virtual reality-simulated environments. Metaverse healthcare and virtual patient data, digital twin simulation and ambient computing technologies, and artificial intelligence-based diagnostic and remote sensing algorithms improve virtual healthcare visits in immersive clinical settings.

Cloud-based digital twin and holographic simulation technologies, healthcare modeling and simulation tools, and sensor-based personalized healthcare and smart telemedicine diagnosis systems can be harnessed in immersive healthcare services and virtual healthcare visits. Digital twin modeling and machine learning-based real-time data sensing tools, blockchain-empowere metaverse healthcare and tactile sensor systems, and multisensor medical data fusion can be deployed in avatar-based patient—doctor consultations and in immersive healthcare simulations in decentralized 3D virtual spaces. Cloud-based Internet of Medical Things (IoMT) and machine learning-based automated diagnostic systems, healthcare digital twins, and synthetic data and images can be leveraged in artificial intelligence-enabled healthcare delivery and in smart hospital operations across virtual healthcare environments and the medical metaverse.

6.2 Cloud computing and multimodal sensing technologies, clinical artificial intelligence and machine learning algorithms, and simulation modeling and spatial data visualization tools across blockchain- and digital twin-based medical infrastructures

Patient health status analysis and prediction, medical treatment and processes, and continuous physiological data sharing (Verma, 2022) develop on machine and deep learning techniques, the artificial Internet of Things (IoT), and cyber-physical healthcare and virtualized care systems by medical devices, sensors, and actuators. Cloud computing and multimodal sensing technologies, clinical artificial intelligence and machine learning algorithms, and big data analytics can enhance remote patient monitoring and healthcare services in terms of healthcare situation forecasting, physiological parameter changes, and automatic disease detection by patient disease risk and treatment process analysis, monitoring, and control. Simulation modeling and machine learning-based image recognition tools, networked immersive virtual reality and interactive 3D geo-visualization systems, and voice and gesture recognition technologies are instrumental in smart hospital operations. Deep learning-based image classification and spatial cognition algorithms, spatial computing and biometric sensor technologies, and predictive modeling and virtual navigation tools configure patient health status analysis and prediction.

Remote sensing and extended reality-based metaverse technologies, ambient scene detection and event forecasting tools, and visual perception and acoustic environment recognition algorithms improve smart hospital operations. Biomedical sensors and actuators assist in medical examination and patient treatment (Khan et al., 2023b) by use of IoT sensor-based health data collection and processing, real-time data visualization and cloud computing technologies, and virtual reality-based user interfaces across blockchain- and digital twin-based medical infrastructures. Remote health monitoring requires digital twin-based IoT sensors and devices with real-time sensor data mapping and control. Predictive geospatial simulation and ambient scene detection tools, dynamic routing and geospatial mapping technologies, and visual cognitive and spatial cognition algorithms can be harnessed in smart hospital operations across the blockchain-based metaverse.

Simulation modeling and spatial data visualization tools, context awareness and image processing computational algorithms, and geospatial mapping and multisensor fusion technologies can be deployed in smart hospital operations across immersive extended reality environments. Computing-based simulation and modeling techniques, clinical disease management decision-making tools, and virtual patient biometric, physiological, and behavioral data (Coorey et al., 2022) can predict disease risk by smart wearables and machine learning-based sensing and monitoring health digital twins in patient prognosis personalization. Artificial intelligence-based cyber-physical medical systems can shape clinical practice through multiple clinical and imaging devices in disease prediction and in diagnosis and treatment optimization in precision medicine. Machine learning-based image recognition and geolocation data mining tools, remote sensing data fusion techniques, and mobile location analytics can be leveraged in smart hospital operations.

Patient big data management and artificial intelligence healthcare systems can improve patient life quality and healthcare services timely and effectively (Xie et al., 2021) through blockchain-based decentralized data sharing and management reliability. Smart wearable sensing devices can optimize individualized patient condition self-management and prognosis in continuous real-time patient monitoring and in disease diagnosis and treatment by physiological parameter recording and tracking and IoT decentralized multimodal healthcare and patient physiological data transmission. Smart hospital operations require behavioral predictive analytics, deep learning-based ambient sound processing and virtual navigation tools, and haptic augmented reality and remote sensing systems.

Smart hospital operations necessitate visual imagery and digital twin simulation tools, decision and control algorithms, and immersive visualization and edge artificial intelligence computing systems. Remote healthcare data monitoring and processing (Mohammed et al., 2024) require secure and valid cyber–physical medical systems, deep and machine learning-based cloud computing and blockchain technologies, and mobile distributed fog cloud networks. Deep and reinforcement learning techniques, federated artificial intelligence systems, fog and cloud service performance, and IoMT bio-sensors integrate real-time blockchain network-based healthcare data sharing in the distributed cloud environment. Distributed sensing and environment perception technologies, ambient sound recognition and virtual navigation tools, and holographic display devices are pivotal in smart hospital operations in immersive multisensory virtual spaces.

Holographic virtual imaging and digital twin technologies, perception and cognition algorithms, and simulation modeling and deep learning-based ambient sound processing tools are instrumental in smart hospital operations. IoT-based healthcare service scalability, predictability, and convergence, patient body sensors, and fog and cloud computing technologies (Ahmad et al., 2023) enable customized healthcare through patient clinical data mining, simulation, and virtualization. Smart healthcare systems, blockchain technology, IoT sensor networking, big data analytics, and artificial intelligence deep learning algorithms can optimize patient record transmission, real-time patient health tracking and data sharing, and patient health record privacy, confidentiality, and security in disease diagnostics and cure. Wearable haptic and spatial immersive technologies, cognitive computing, IoT-based decision support systems, and movement tracking and ambient sound processing tools configure, configure smart hospital operations in immersive 3D virtual reality environments.

Behavioral modeling and spatial computing technologies, movement and behavior tracking tools, and mobile biometric data articulate smart hospital operations in the metaverse interactive environment. Medical decision support and digital personalized healthcare systems (Sadeghi & Mahmoudi, 2024) can improve patient experience by the use of IoMT data connectivity, scalability, and interoperability in integrated healthcare services and hospital care. Blockchain, digital twin, and metaverse technologies, digital distributed healthcare systems, and smart medical devices shape real-time physiological and medical data privacy and security in predictive and personalized healthcare services and disease diagnosis. Networked immersive virtual reality and visual data mining systems, geolocation data processing and spatial computing algorithms, and mobile healthcare and deep learning-based sensing technologies assist smart hospital operations. Big data computing and metaverse decentralized governance systems, spatial computing and digital twin technologies, and data visualization and cognitive navigation tools enable integrated healthcare services. Spatial computing and visual perception algorithms, cognitive mapping and simulation modeling tools, and immersive 3D and deep learning-based object detection technologies shape predictive and personalized healthcare services.

Cloud-based context-aware cyber-physical networked medical systems, real-time multimodal in-sensor computing technologies, and deep and machine learning algorithms (Shaikh et al., 2023) configure continuous patient care through data interoperability, scalability, security, and privacy. IoT wireless sensor networks, cyber-physical medical and multiagent healthcare systems, and multisource heterogeneous hospital big data processing and analysis techniques can improve patient vital sign configuration and visualization management. IoT sensor-based decentralized control and decision-making networking capabilities, real-time medical big data collection, computation, and analysis, and cloud computing-based healthcare delivery optimization are pivotal in medical data protection and privacy across healthcare virtualization architectures. Embedded sensor and actuator networking, medical data processing operations and interconnection capabilities, medical device reliability, manageability, and performance, and computational data interoperability, decentralization, and modularity articulate individualized medical treatment. Medical sensor-based vital patient data collection, mining, processing, analysis, and diagnosis, medical cloud big data dynamic reconfiguration, and cyber-physical medical system reliability, management, control, and coordination assist in healthcare resource allocation simulation and modeling. Multisource heterogeneous clinical, healthcare, and mood data mining, perception, recognition, tracking, and monitoring develop on remote and embedded smart healthcare sensor systems, cloud and wearable computing technologies, and embedded device interoperability. Cloud computing and blockchain technologies, interconnected IoT sensor and actuator networks, and remote sensor-based monitoring devices enhance data transfer availability and security in patient monitoring and control in a smart healthcare environment. Artificial intelligence deep learning algorithms, IoT cloud computing, and big data analytics can optimize medical devices by virtual networked sensors and actuators.

IoT-based disease modeling, prediction, prevention, and investigation support systems (Firouzi et al., 2021) can harness patient records and clinical data in risk prediction and tracking, disease diagnostics, prognosis, treatment, and progression, and in vital biological sign tracking and monitoring. Machine learning forecasting techniques, clinical decision support, and personalized prevention systems can be deployed in patient complication prevention, detection, diagnosis, screening, and treatment, in wearable IoT-based remote patient monitoring, and in physiological symptom and patient health status assessment. Smart interconnected healthcare devices, wearable sensor systems, digital twin and distributed ledger technologies, and machine learning algorithm-based complication prediction and risk stratification tools can be leveraged in medical data sharing and interoperability with regard to complication risk and symptom disease prediction, disease screening, diagnosis, and prognosis, and patient status monitoring. Artificial intelligence-based multisensory and blockchain technologies, machine learning predictive algorithms, and big data analytics can integrate medical data in IoT smart healthcare.

IoT-based patient data visualization, monitoring, tracking, and analysis, mobile and cloud computing networked healthcare systems, and blockchain-based patient and clinical data capturing technologies (Haleem et al., 2022) can improve healthcare delivery, diagnosis, treatment, and monitoring in precise, individualized, and customized patient care. Machine learning and computer vision algorithms, artificial intelligence- and IoT-enabled medical devices, and digital twin and virtual reality technologies can detect risk factors by real-time medical decision support and patient data management in remote healthcare services by use of electronic medical records and wearable healthcare devices. Patient health screening and tracking tools, wearable medical devices and sensors, and blockchain-based remote health and physiological data monitoring systems can be used in patient care delivery, therapy, and recovery in IoT smart healthcare by medical data gathering and analysis.

Cognitive computing and remote sensing systems, event modeling and synthetic data tools, and image recognition and cognitive artificial intelligence algorithms optimize smart hospital operations in immersive extended reality environments. 3D imaging and augmented reality visualization tools, blockchain and cloud rendering technologies, and digital twin and computer vision algorithms (Sun et al., 2022) can improve disease diagnosis and treatment through multisensor device interaction and digital patient avatars in precision medicine. Immersive medical experiences can be achieved by augmented reality and holographic simulation technologies, interconnected extended reality devices, and computer simulation and real-time motion capture tools in the medical metaverse. Immersive and interactive virtual medical environments develop on 3D imaging and intuitive visualization technologies, smart mobile healthcare devices, and IoT digital twins. Image processing computational and geospatial big data management algorithms, digital twin modeling and machine learning-based image recognition tools, and multisensor fusion and spatial immersive technologies enhance smart hospital operations. Predictive modeling and event forecasting tools, visual tracking and computer vision algorithms, and remote sensing and machine learning-based object recognition technologies improve the medical metaverse.

Ambient scene detection and image processing tools, multimodal behavioral predictive analytics, and image recognition and geospatial mapping technologies can be harnessed in smart hospital operations. Patient-specific medical interventions based on computer simulations (Wang et al., 2022a) require digital and virtual twin technologies, cloud, fog, and edge computing systems, medical imaging simulation tools, and deep learning-based realistically simulated big healthcare data. Immersive and interactive digital patient avatars are pivotal in disease identification and therapy selection, in artificial intelligence-based medical practice, and in virtual and augmented clinical trials and medical interventions. Smart medical devices, artificial intelligence-based computational medical imaging data simulation, and extended reality and blockchain technologies assist in extended reality metaverse-based healthcare interventions and clinical practice, in medical imaging-based diagnosis, and in routine treatment and therapy planning across the healthcare metaverse. Remote sensing data fusion techniques, digital twin simulation and deep learning-based ambient sound processing tools, and context awareness and acoustic environment recognition algorithms can be deployed in smart hospital operations.

Wearable sensor-based medical data, smart healthcare digital twins, and decentralized blockchain and metaverse technologies (Murala, 2023) configure diagnosis and treatment options in 3D virtual environments. Explainable artificial intelligence algorithms, blockchain-based medical record tracking and sharing, and extended reality and digital twin technologies articulate disease prevention, prediction, diagnosis, and cure in the metaverse environment. Wearable and cognitive computing technologies, metaverse-based healthcare systems, and artificial intelligence-based virtual healthcare services assist in real-time physiological indicator and clinical data monitoring, in disease progression diagnosis and forecasting, and in customized medical treatments. Wearable device-based patient physiological data, healthcare metaverse and virtual reality technologies, and decentralized medical data sharing enable predictable and explainable treatment procedures and decisions in the metaverse hospital care. Extended reality algorithms, artificial intelligence-based healthcare techniques, and IoT wearable medical devices shape accurate disease diagnosis, treatment, and prognosis in the healthcare metaverse environments. Cloud and metaverse technologies, metaverse patient avatars, and remote patient monitoring tools facilitate remote healthcare consultations and medical care. Patient medical history tracking and health data, 3D patient big data and body simulation modeling, and blockchain technology-based patient medical record tracking optimize disease diagnosis, treatment, therapy, and management in immersive virtual environments and in the healthcare metaverse.

Visual perception and spatial cognition algorithms, haptic augmented reality and cognitive computing systems, and ambient scene detection and context modeling tools can be leveraged in smart hospital operations. Blockchain-based IoMT devices and deep neural network algorithms operate in a secure interactive environment based on authentication and abnormal traffic detection mechanisms (Wang et al., 2022b) by integrating artificial intelligence and deep learning techniques, wireless sensor networks, and 5G communication tools. Smart hospital operations develop decision and control algorithms, remote sensing and machine learning-based object recognition technologies, and mobile location analytics. The blockchain-based IoMT environment integrates digital twin and distributed sensing technologies, simulation modeling and visual imagery tools, and spatial computing and image processing computational algorithms.

Smart hospital operations require geolocation data mining and cognitive mapping tools, immersive visualization and metaverse healthcare systems, and dynamic routing and digital twin technologies in immersive 3D virtual reality environments. Blockchain technologies, deep learning techniques, and IoMT-connected devices (Farouk et al., 2020) enhance sensitive medical big data security and privacy, medical big data management and analysis, vital sign tracking in remote patient monitoring, and healthcare data handling and transmission in personalized medicine. Electronic health record sharing, visual augmented reality-based medical devices, and machine learning algorithms can optimize diagnosis accuracy, treatment progress, disease condition, prediction, diagnosis, and treatment, medical big data sharing, recording, tracking, privacy, and security, and patient and clinical data transaction and analysis. Smart hospital operations necessitate geolocation data tracking and deep learning-based ambient sound processing tools, image processing computational and visual cognitive algorithms, and spatial computing and multisensor fusion technologies in the metaverse interactive environment.

Simulation modeling and synthetic data tools, haptic augmented reality and metaverse-based healthcare monitoring systems, and immersive extended reality and deep learning-based sensing technologies are pivotal in smart hospital operations across immersive interconnected 3D worlds. Cloud edge computing and blockchain technologies, computing data distributed devices, artificial IoT-based healthcare metaverse systems, and federated learning algorithms (Bashir et al., 2023) can improve personalized healthcare delivery and experiences, medical diagnosis, and patient monitoring through data management, interoperability, security, and privacy. Digital twin and spatial immersive technologies, ambient sound recognition and cognitive navigation tools, and visual perception and cognitive artificial intelligence algorithms are instrumental in smart hospital operations across immersive multisensory virtual spaces. Simulation modeling and ambient scene detection tools, image processing computational and predictive modeling algorithms, and immersive 3D and vision sensing technologies configure personalized healthcare delivery in the decentralized and interconnected metaverse.

6.3 Blockchain-based healthcare digital twin and immersive visualization systems, haptic and biometric sensor technologies, and deep learning neural network and image processing computational algorithms in smart hospital operations

Autonomous cognitive and IoT-based health monitoring systems, holographic simulation and diagnostic imaging techniques, and medical imaging devices can gather complex patient clinical data in a distributed and secure manner for medical analysis, evaluation, and prognosis (Akash & Ferdous, 2022), enabling continuous sensor-based vital sign monitoring in a multisensory environment. Haptic and biometric sensor technologies, context awareness and visual perception algorithms, and 3D generative modeling and natural language processing tools configure the blockchain-based metaverse. Haptic and biometric sensor technologies, spatial data mining and deep learning algorithms, and blockchain-based healthcare digital twin and immersive visualization systems articulate an extended reality environment. Event modeling and forecasting tools, multisensory augmented reality and spatial computing algorithms, and holographic telepresence technologies assist smart hospitals.

Digital twin- and blockchain-based context-aware smart healthcare services and virtual healthcare visits can increase patient life expectancy by deep learning sequential data processing and artificial intelligence-based diagnostic and sensing data fusion algorithms, virtual twin modeling tools, and 3D body scanning and holographic simulation technologies (Manocha et al., 2023) to provide effective medical services and identify real-time irregular physical events accurately. IoT-enabled smart healthcare monitoring devices can be pivotal in irregular event recognition by integrating user clinical history and digital twin-based medical care across 3D virtual reality environments. IoT-assisted event monitoring, clinical artificial intelligence and deep learning algorithms, and blockchain and digital twin simulation technologies can predict physical irregularities by accessing patient data archive securely through smart healthcare devices. IoT and deep learning context-aware health monitoring and event recognition systems, automated health event prediction tools, and ambient computing technologies require digital twin data-simulative, acquisition, and processing capabilities in smart healthcare with regard to avatar-based patient–doctor consultations and virtual healthcare services and clinical trials to predict irregular physical events in a decentralized healthcare metaverse.

Medical cyber-physical systems integrate digital twin and blockchain technologies, edge and cloud computing networks, and IoMT (Sahal et al., 2022) for real-time data sharing and analysis through monitoring and sensor devices, accurate risk prediction and detection, and secure decentralized decision-making. Blockchain-based digital twin networks, deep learning neural network and image processing computational algorithms, and multisensory augmented reality systems leverage distributed ledger technology wearable devices, interconnected healthcare systems, and medical sensors for semantic knowledge sharing, movement and location detection, mobile biometric data, and predictive data analytics. Generative artificial intelligence systems, metaverse and immersive engagement technologies, digital twin simulation and modeling tools, and spatial data mining algorithms optimize smart hospital operations in extended reality environments.

Human digital twin technology and networking architecture can enable remote monitoring and blockchain-based diagnostic and therapeutic services in personalized healthcare diagnosis and rehabilitation (Chen & Lin, 2023) by use of metaverse healthcare and virtualized care systems, synthetic patient data, and 3D body scanning and spatial data visualization tools in immersive healthcare simulation units. Haptic and biometric sensor technologies, spatial analytics and 3D virtual space networking tools, and simulation modeling and deep learning-based image processing algorithms enhance smart hospital operations across Web3-powered metaverse worlds. Decision intelligence and data visualization tools, digital twin and holographic virtual imaging technologies, and motion planning and spatial data mining algorithms improve blockchain-based diagnostic and therapeutic services.

Artificial intelligence and blockchain-based human digital twin modeling, motion sensing and immersive virtual simulation technologies, and machine learning-based automated diagnostic and virtual consultation systems (Okegbile et al., 2023) further personalized healthcare services and virtual patient diagnosis by use of precise medical data and physiological change analysis in sensor-based personalized healthcare. Virtual mapping and spatial data mining algorithms, 3D virtual space networking and generative modeling tools, and digital twin simulation and immersive engagement technologies can be leveraged in smart hospital operations in interactive digital worlds and in immersive extended reality environments.

Long short-term memory techniques, digital twin and blockchain technologies, and deep learning convolutional neural networks (Alqahtani et al., 2024)can improve medical treatment through real-time physiological monitoring and personal healthcare data in IoT edge computing environments. Smart hospital operations develop blockchain-based decentralized metaverse and big data computing systems, geolocation data processing and cognitive artificial intelligence algorithms, and movement and behavior tracking tools. 3D immersive environments integrate IoT-based decision support and visual perceptive systems, machine learning-based image recognition and simulation modeling tools, and environment mapping and machine learning algorithms. Smart hospital operations require immersive 3D and deep learning-based sensing technologies, digital twin simulation and geospatial analytics tools, and image processing computational and recognition algorithms.

Wireless-based sensing and signal processing technologies, machine learning and predictive analysis algorithms, and networked medical devices (Khan et al., 2023a) can improve patient care, recovery, and decision support in digital twin-based Healthcare 4.0 in terms of accurate real-time sensor data collection, virtual consultations and remote care, and patient vital sign diagnosis and monitoring. 3D virtual simulation and biometric sensor technologies, digital twin modeling and virtual navigation tools, and deep learning and 3D space mapping algorithms shape smart hospital operations in the blockchain-based metaverse. Decision intelligence and natural language processing tools, multimodal behavioral analytics, and image processing computational and context awareness algorithms optimize digital twin-based Healthcare 4.0.

Digital twin and blockchain technologies, body area sensor networks, and immersive virtual reality and smart telemedicine diagnosis systems (Yi, 2023) can secure processed and integrated patient parameters, healthcare data, and cloud-based medical records for treatment plans, enabling diagnosis and personalized care. Remote vital sign patient monitoring, efficient real-time data-driven medical resource allocation and management, and machine learning algorithms and data analysis techniques can improve treatment outcomes, health status management, simulation and prediction, and real-time abnormality detection by collected and analyzed personalized data, e.g., disease history and health risks. Digital twin and blockchain-based clinical personalized diagnostic, prognostic, and treatment optimization are instrumental in remote patient vital sign monitoring and in personalized treatment plan building across the cloud infrastructure. Blockchain network scalability and medical record systems assist digital twin-based health status tracking and management, physiological parameter modeling and simulation, and treatment plan adjustment. Cloud computing technologies and medical record systems can determine health status, treatment planning, and clinical decision-making support.

Digital twin-assisted machine learning-based smart healthcare and IoMT devices (Qu et al., 2023) can improve personalized medical services across 5G mobile networks by accurate data collection. Data mining and digital twin modeling tools, machine learning-based navigation and spatial cognition algorithms, and emotion detection and recognition technologies can be deployed in smart hospital operations. Digital twin modeling and visual perception tools, image processing computational and brain-inspired artificial intelligence algorithms, and biometric sensor and virtual modeling technologies can be leveraged in digital twin-assisted machine learning-based smart healthcare. Personalized medical services develop on spatial data visualization and behavior tracking tools, context awareness and acoustic environment recognition algorithms, and remote sensing and deep neural network technologies in blockchain-based virtual worlds.

Reliable blockchain-based cyber—physical healthcare data and services, sensor medical data fusion, and cloud-based digital twin and virtual healthcare technologies can be leveraged in medical history, risk, and patient care assessment (Ghayvat et al., 2024) for anomaly detection, diagnosis, and monitoring in smart operating rooms, in virtual diagnosis and treatment, and in avatar-based patient—doctor consultations. Smart hospital operations integrate image recognition and spatial computing technologies, visual data mining and algorithmic monitoring systems, and remote sensing and spatial cognition algorithms in the decentralized and interconnected metaverse. Smart operating rooms require movement and behavior tracking tools, vision sensing and machine perception technologies, and environment mapping and motion planning algorithms. Virtual diagnosis and treatment necessitate deep learning artificial intelligence and virtual navigation tools, remote sensing and visual perception algorithms, and voice and gesture recognition technologies.

Ambient scene detection and predictive geospatial modeling tools, immersive 3D and geospatial mapping technologies, and motion planning and visual tracking algorithms are pivotal in smart hospital operations across interactive digital worlds. Data-driven digital twin technologies, and artificial intelligence techniques, wireless biomedical sensing devices, and anthropomorphic 3D virtual avatars (Sarp et al., 2023) can optimize clinical healthcare decision support, personalized treatment, and tailored assessment by real-time data collection and processing in blockchain-empowered metaverse healthcare. Digital twin and spatial computing technologies, visual imagery and virtual navigation tools, and visual perception and deep learning-based image processing algorithms are instrumental in clinical healthcare decision support. Remote sensing and immersive metaverse technologies, ambient scene detection and remote big data management tools, and cognitive and behavioral algorithms configure blockchain-empowered metaverse healthcare in immersive extended reality environments.

5G cloud computing, digital twin and extended reality technology-enabled IoMT systems, and generative adversarial networks (Tai et al., 2022) can advance telemedical simulation by integrating accurate patient-specific data immersively in virtual healthcare services. Digital twin- and artificial intelligence-based IoMT devices, virtual healthcare and holographic simulation technologies, and healthcare modeling and simulation tools can integrate pathogenic features, remote medical data and image sharing, and physiological modeling and pathological diagnosis, predicting individual risks in customized medical services across immersive clinical settings. Sensor medical clinical data and image processing, together with clinical decision support, diagnosis, and prediction accuracy, require deep learning-based IoMT digital twin and cloud technologies, metaverse health-care data, and personalized digital avatars in mobile medical treatments. IoT-based decision support and cognitive computing systems, data visualization and spatial awareness tools, and 3D space mapping and bio-inspired computational intelligence algorithms articulate smart hospital operations. Cognitive neuro-engineering and multisensor fusion technologies, deep learning and motion planning algorithms, and 3D virtual space networking and simulation modeling tools assist virtual healthcare services across the blockchain-based metaverse.

Deep learning and ambient intelligence algorithms, wearable sensor-based devices, and digital twin and virtual healthcare technologies (Lv et al., 2024) can be deployed in medical data analysis and care services, in personalized clinical care, and in disease recognition accuracy in digital twin healthcare. Cognitive modeling and metaverse technologies, visual tracking and spatial cognition algorithms, and sensor fusion and event modeling tools enable smart hospital operations in immersive hyperconnected virtual spaces. Image processing computational and acoustic environment recognition algorithms, spatial analytics and geospatial simulation tools, and immersive visualization and interactive 3D geo-visualization systems optimize personalized clinical care. Dynamic routing and digital twin technologies, virtual simulation and motion control algorithms, and predictive geospatial simulation and event forecasting tools shape digital twin healthcare in blockchain-based virtual worlds. Visual perception and neural network-based recognition algorithms, tactile sensing and 3D modeling technologies, and behavior tracking and digital twin modeling tools enhance smart hospital operations.

Digital twin and cloud technologies, smart biomedical and wearable technology sensors, and immersive healthcare simulations (Wang et al., 2023) can detect health issues, for example, potential complications and health risks, in personalized healthcare, timely treatment options and therapeutic interventions, and precision medicine. Electronic medical records and metaverse healthcare systems can improve individualized patient outcomes, healthcare delivery, and preventative care through real-time medical data processing, sharing, and analysis. Real-time medical and patient data processing and sharing can decrease adverse reactions in patient vital sign monitoring. Digital twin-based personalized and tailored medical treatments and interventions are instrumental in adverse reaction and disease progression prediction, diagnosis accuracy, and medical error incidence decrease. Internet of Healthcare Things, digital twin and cloud computing technologies, data-driven treatment outcome option simulation tools, and digital health records can optimize digital patient treatment, therapy, and medication choice simulation and modeling by integrating medical history, health status, and physiological condition. Predictive and machine learning algorithms, real-time medical data analytics, and ambient computing and holographic simulation technologies can harness cloud- and blockchain-based digital twin patient data for real-time patient vital sign analysis with regard to detailed healthcare data collection and monitoring, treatment progress decision-making and monitoring, real-time medical data processing and transmission, interoperable healthcare data sharing, processing, and analysis, timely and accurate clinical decision support, and patient healthcare data integration and interoperability.

Artificial intelligence algorithm-based predictions and decisions (Fuller et al., 2020) can improve healthcare digital twin treatment, and patient care by remote medical data fusion, monitoring, and modeling in virtual clinical settings. Smart hospital operations develop on blockchain-based decentralized metaverse and neuromorphic computing systems, haptic sensor and immersive extended reality technologies, and simulation modeling and ambient sound processing tools. Healthcare digital twin treatment integrates biometric sensor and spatial computing technologies, geolocation data processing and deep learning-based image classification algorithms, and movement and behavior tracking tools in the metaverse interactive environment. Virtual clinical settings require remote sensing and machine vision algorithms, haptic augmented reality and visual perceptive systems, and behavior tracking and 3D virtual space networking tools in 3D immersive environments.

6.4 Blockchain-empowered metaverse healthcare systems, digital twin modeling and visual perception tools, and remote sensing and immersive metaverse technologies across 3D virtual clinics

Digital twin-enabled IoMT and clinical decision support systems, deep learning-based computer vision and healthcare artificial intelligence algorithms, and mobile fog and cloud networks (Lakhan et al., 2023) can monitor and process wearable sensor and virtual clinical data. Mobile fog and cloud computing technologies, deep and machine learning algorithms, spatial data acquisition and multiscale spatial data processing tools, and convolutional neural networks can leverage context-aware healthcare sensors for disease prediction and critical conditions in vital physiological parameter monitoring across digital twin-enabled infrastructure. Contextual awareness and predictive geospatial modeling tools, cooperative decision and control algorithms, and remote sensing and immersive metaverse technologies enable smart hospital operations. Digital twin modeling and visual perception tools, geospatial mapping and machine perception technologies, and machine learning-based predictive and remote sensing algorithms further virtual healthcare environments. Deep learning artificial and simulation modeling intelligence tools, immersive extended reality and image recognition technologies, and virtual mapping and motion planning algorithms shape vital physiological parameter monitoring.

Digital twin-based context-aware smart healthcare and metaverse-based healthcare monitoring systems, immersive healthcare and holographic simulation technologies, simulation modeling and data mining tools, and machine learning and convolutional neural network algorithms (Elayan et al., 2021) can optimize disease diagnosis and treatment, virtual healthcare delivery, and immersive healthcare experiences by abnormality detection and monitoring across virtual metaverse spaces. Cognitive and behavioral algorithms, immersive metaverse and holographic telepresence technologies, and multiscale spatial data processing and virtual navigation tools can be harnessed in smart hospital operations in extended reality environments. Geospatial mapping and immersive metaverse technologies, deep learning neural network algorithms, and spatial data acquisition and visual perception tools can be deployed in digital twin-based context-aware smart healthcare.

Digital twin and cloud computing technologies, big data analytics, and IoMT configure accurate physiological state monitoring, prediction, and diagnosis (Liu et al., 2019), reducing healthcare risks through virtual patient data modeling and simulation, sensor data, and medical resource allocation optimization. Cloud data-driven smart healthcare monitoring systems articulate healthcare digital twin and behavioral evaluation data integration and sharing through real-time physiological condition and treatment monitoring in precision medicine for accurate predictions and targeted interventions. Electronic health records, clinical information systems, and wearable sensors assist cloud healthcare services and capabilities in real-time remote evaluation, consultation, diagnosis, treatment, and monitoring. Digital twin healthcare-based cloud systems further digital twin healthcare data fusion, multigranular healthcare data mining and transmission, and physiological health data management, processing, and analysis by use of physical sensor data and wearable monitoring equipment and digital healthcare records in disease prevention. Real-time wearable device monitoring data enable collected and classified medical data transmission and analysis by wearable medical devices, digital twin healthcare technologies, and machine learning algorithms.

Artificial intelligence-based IoMT, deep and machine learning algorithms, real-time medical data processing, and cloud and edge computing systems (Khan et al., 2022) can assist in diagnosis and prognosis by real-time sensor data prediction, simulation, and analysis. Behavior simulation and modeling tools, big data and predictive analytics, and digital twin-based cyber-physical healthcare systems can detect abnormal operations by use of sensor data acquisition, analysis, processing, and integration in IoT-edge-fog-cloud computing environments. Smart hospital operations necessitate metaverse and immersive technologies, environment mapping and image processing computational algorithms, and virtual navigation and simulation modeling tools. Geolocation data processing and machine learning-based predictive algorithms, metaverse and digital twin technologies, and spatial data acquisition and visual imagery tools are pivotal in extended reality environments.

Human digital twin and 3D visualization technologies, immersive healthcare simulations, and vibrotactile actuators (De Benedictis et al., 2023) can improve preventive interventions, diagnostic capabilities, treatment delivery, and clinical processes, enabling personalized medicine. Health-related digital twin and virtual reality simulation technologies, artificial intelligence-driven diagnostic and predictive maintenance algorithms, and IoT wearable haptic sensors can enhance patient treatment and clinical procedures, reducing patient risks in preventive healthcare through physiological characteristic monitoring, wearable sensor data collection, and public health-related process planning, modeling, and replication. Deep learning and machine vision algorithms, virtual twin and holographic telepresence technologies, and multisensory augmented reality and immersive visualization systems are instrumental in smart hospital operations. IoT-based decision support and generative artificial intelligence systems, spatial data mining and image processing computational algorithms, and 3D modeling and spatial computing technologies configure preventive healthcare and personalized medicine.

Predictive digital twins, computing image processing, and virtual treatment monitoring (Aluvalu et al., 2023) configure digital patient health track records: IoT, wireless sensor data, and cloud devices are pivotal in clinical decisions, health condition evaluation, diagnosis prediction, medical history and treatment, and digital health record articulation. Cooperative decision and control algorithms, contextual awareness and simulation modeling tools, and dynamic routing and immersive extended reality technologies assist smart hospital operations. Visual perception and bio-inspired computational intelligence algorithms, spatial data acquisition and remote big data management tools, and cognitive neuro-engineering and remote sensing technologies enable health condition evaluation.

Medical digital twins developed on haptic-augmented reality navigation, IoT sensors, neural network and deep learning techniques, real-time patient monitoring capabilities, and big data analytics (Zhang & Tai, 2022) can predict clinical health status and support clinical decisions. Extended reality simulation, clinical data filtering and labeling, and virtual reality technologies enable clinical processes, treatment decision support, remote health abnormality detection and prediction, and visual rendering and haptic sensation in smart telemedicine. Smart medical devices, digital twin convolutional neural networks, physics-based rendering algorithms, and synthetic data tracking and modeling can shape data-driven feature extraction and simulation performance optimization in terms of visual and tactile sensations, risk factor and pathological type analysis, and extended reality technology-based clinical training. Autonomous cognitive and remote sensing systems, environment perception and multisensor fusion technologies, and simulation modeling and multisensory augmented reality algorithms enhance smart hospital operations across Web3-powered metaverse worlds.

Accurate disease predictions and diagnoses can be achieved by harnessing wearable sensors, enabling effective patient care (Vats et al., 2023): context-aware IoT, human digital twin technologies, and machine learning algorithms enhance medical services, patient health record examination, and healthcare system operations. Edge artificial intelligence computing and immersive visualization systems, visual cognitive and spatial data mining algorithms, and extended reality-based metaverse and haptic sensor technologies improve smart hospital operations in immersive multisensory virtual spaces. Geospatial mapping and haptic sensor technologies, spatial data mining and image processing computational algorithms, and machine learning-based image recognition and predictive geospatial modeling tools can be harnessed in smart hospital operations.

IoT sensors, holographic simulation techniques, and cloud-based personalized healthcare and smart telemedicine diagnosis systems (Shaikh et al., 2023) can optimize patient treatment in digital twin-based smart healthcare. Digital twin simulation and deep neural network technologies, deep learning-based image classification and spatial computing algorithms, and data visualization and machine learning-based image recognition tools can be harnessed in smart hospital operations. Multimodal behavioral analytics, vision sensing and 3D virtual simulation technologies, and cognitive artificial intelligence and spatial data mining algorithms improve cloud-based personalized healthcare.

Digital twin-based healthcare systems, cloud computing technologies, and machine-learning-based disease prediction, diagnosis, and treatment are instrumental in continuous physiological health monitoring and tracking for remote patients in virtual medical care facilities (Abirami & Karthikeyan, 2023) by use of mobile devices and sensors. Cloud-based digital twin healthcare and virtual decision support systems can accurately integrate IoT, machine learning, and big data for anomaly detection in remote patient health monitoring and care across smart virtual care environments by use of patient medical history and parameters. Behavioral predictive analytics, wearable haptic and spatial immersive technologies, and perception and cognition algorithms can be deployed in digital twin-based smart healthcare. Motion control and environment mapping algorithms, spatial awareness and ambient sound recognition tools, and haptic sensor and holographic telepresence technologies can be leveraged in smart hospital operations.

Digital twin-based smart and cloud-based personalized healthcare systems, 3D body scanning and mobile healthcare technologies, and healthcare body sensor networks (Xames & Topcu, 2024) can enable personalized prognosis, monitoring, and treatment in precision medicine through patient data fusion, modeling, integration, and interpretation in relation to health status. Medical wearable devices and sensors, IoMT-based clinical decision support and personalized healthcare systems, and wearable and ambient biosensors assist in disease diagnosis, medical procedures, and patient treatment. Smart hospital operations necessitate cognitive computing and artificial vision systems, deep learning-based sensing and behavioral modeling technologies, and data mining and socially-oriented location tracking tools. Remote sensing and virtual twin technologies, ambient scene detection and simulation modeling tools, and context awareness and motion planning algorithms are pivotal in precision medicine.

Health digital twin and immersive virtual simulation technologies, deep learning-based computer vision and artificial intelligence-based diagnostic algorithms, and wearable medical sensor devices (Venkatesh et al., 2024) can increase therapeutic and intervention efficacy, improve and predict patient outcomes, and reduce adverse disease effects and acute complications through patient symptom and physiological vital data analysis and handling. Artificial intelligence clinical care modeling and healthcare service systems, wireless biomedical sensing devices, and immersive healthcare and multisensory extended reality technologies can optimize personalized healthcare operations, treatment, tracking, and prediction by real-time remote individual patient care delivery monitoring and by virtual patient representation sharing and interoperability in personalized medicine. Algorithmic monitoring and metaverse decentralized governance systems, multisensor fusion and virtual modeling technologies, and computer vision and brain-inspired artificial intelligence algorithms articulate smart hospital operations in the decentralized and interconnected metaverse. Digital twin modeling and visual perception tools, machine learning-based navigation and geospatial big data management algorithms, and emotion detection and recognition technologies assist personalized healthcare operations.

Timely and accurate anomalous event detection and abnormality sign processing (Bhatia, 2023) necessitate fog computing, digital twin, blockchain technologies, IoMT, and context-aware deep learning and predictive maintenance algorithms. Movement and behavior tracking tools, image recognition and digital twin technologies, and virtual simulation and motion control algorithms enable smart hospital operations in immersive multisensory virtual spaces. Virtual navigation tools, visual cognitive and neural network-based recognition algorithms, and remote sensing and cognitive modeling technologies shape personalized medicine in immersive hyperconnected virtual spaces. Neuromorphic computing and remote sensing systems, predictive geospatial modeling and sensor fusion tools, and tactile sensing and extended reality-based metaverse technologies optimize smart hospital operations in immersive interconnected 3D worlds. Visual tracking and image processing computational algorithms, event modeling and geospatial simulation tools, and cognitive computing and interactive 3D geo-visualization systems enhance the decentralized healthcare metaverse.

Smart hospital operations develop on vision sensing and geospatial mapping technologies, multimodal behavioral predictive analytics, and spatial cognition and predictive modeling algorithms in the decentralized and interconnected metaverse. Digital twin technologies, machine and deep learning algorithms, and cyber—physical medical systems can enable timely interventions by personalized healthcare services and decision support (Khan et al., 2024) in accurate remote patient monitoring, disease diagnosis, and treatment. Artificial IoT, big data analytics, and signal processing techniques are pivotal in early proactive healthcare interventions and pathological and physiological processes by synthetic patient data augmentation accuracy and validity in Healthcare 4.0 personalized treatment plan simulation. Smart hospital operations integrate remote sensing and deep neural network technologies, geolocation data tracking and virtual navigation tools, and motion control and visual perception algorithms.

Smart healthcare and tactile sensor systems, IoMT devices and sensors, fog, edge, and cloud computing technologies, and machine learning algorithms (Kumar et al., 2023) configure clinical personalized data scalability, interoperability, integration, and transfer by assimilating severe patient condition and medical history in a decentralized healthcare metaverse. Edge computing and blockchain technologies, multimodal biomedical artificial intelligence and ambient health monitoring tools, and machine learning-based healthcare and remote sensing data fusion algorithms enable clinical patient health records and data sharing by remote patient monitoring and healthcare services, being decisive in early severe disease and health condition prediction. Cloud-based cyber-physical medical systems, cloud-based digital twin and immersive virtual simulation technologies, and ambient intelligence and predictive analytics algorithms deploy IoT-based healthcare data in remote and reliable healthcare patient data transfer by wearable health sensors in digital twin-based patient care units.

6.5 Conclusions

Smart hospital operations and virtual patient diagnosis integrate immersive healthcare and digital twin simulation technologies, holographic display devices, ambient sound processing, and artificial intelligence-based medical imaging tools in decentralized 3D virtual spaces. Remote healthcare delivery and virtual healthcare visits require 3D holographic images, wearable biometric sensors, artificial vision, and real-time healthcare monitoring systems in the medical metaverse. Virtual healthcare visits and operating rooms necessitate big healthcare data analytics, individualized patient avatars, and synthetic data and images in a decentralized healthcare metaverse. Virtual patient and synthetic imaging data, movement and behavior tracking tools, and wearable sensor-based devices are pivotal in virtual healthcare visits across virtual diagnostic environments. Motion sensing and holographic simulation technologies, multisensor medical data fusion, artificial intelligence-based medical imaging, and smart wearable sensing devices are instrumental in digital twin healthcare across 3D virtual clinics. Cyber-physical healthcare and smart telemedicine diagnosis systems, healthcare digital twins, and blockchain-based medical data sharing configure smart hospital operations in virtually simulated environments and in the medical metaverse.

Big healthcare and real-time motion capture data, motion sensing and immersive healthcare technologies, and deep learning-based computer vision and machine learning algorithms articulate personalized digital healthcare and artificial intelligence-enabled healthcare delivery in virtual diagnostic environments and in digital twin-based patient care units. Wearable healthcare monitoring and wireless biomedical sensing devices, digital patient twin and immersive virtual reality technologies, and biomedical artificial intelligence and healthcare service systems assist virtual patient diagnosis and treatment in decentralized 3D virtual spaces. Digital twin simulation and virtual navigation tools, physiological and behavioral data, and metaverse healthcare and synthetic imaging data enable medical condition monitoring and remote patient screening in virtual clinical trials across the metaverse interactive environment. 3D holographic visual and immersive healthcare experiences can be achieved by the use of diagnostic imaging techniques, wearable healthcare monitoring devices, and cloud-based personalized healthcare and virtual consultation systems in virtual metaverse spaces. Multisensor medical data fusion, virtual twin modeling and ambient health monitoring tools, and artificial intelligence-based diagnostic and spatial computing algorithms shape virtual patient diagnosis and avatar-based patient–doctor consultations in smart hospital operations in virtual diagnostic environments.

Cyber-physical healthcare and smart telemedicine diagnosis systems, healthcare modeling and simulation tools, and cloud-based digital twin and deep neural network technologies optimize virtual healthcare visits in 3D virtual clinics and in immersive clinical settings. Blockchain-empowered metaverse and sensor-based personalized healthcare systems, digital twin simulation and ambient computing technologies, and clinical artificial intelligence and deep learning-based computer vision algorithms enhance virtual therapeutics and healthcare visits in personalized clinical care across immersive networked virtual worlds. Multimodal sensing and mobile healthcare technologies, cloud-based IoT healthcare and tactile sensor systems, and artificial intelligence-powered diagnostic and virtual twin modeling tools improve immersive healthcare services and smart hospital operations in decentralized 3D virtual spaces. Geospatial analytics and context modeling tools, machine learning-based automated diagnostic and real-time healthcare monitoring systems, and deep learning-based computer vision and remote sensing algorithms can be harnessed in remote healthcare delivery in 3D virtual clinics and in the medical metaverse.

References

Abirami, L., & Karthikeyan, J. (2023). Digital twin-based healthcare system (DTHS) for earlier Parkinson disease identification and diagnosis using optimized fuzzy based k-nearest neighbor classifier model. *IEEE Access, 11*. Available from https://doi.org/10.1109/access.2023.3312278.

Ahmad, I., Abdullah, S., & Ahmed, A. (2023). IoT-fog-based healthcare 4.0 system using blockchain technology. *The Journal of Supercomputing, 79*, 3999–4020. Available from https://doi.org/10.1007/s11227-022-04788-7.

Akash, S. S., & Ferdous, M. S. (2022). A blockchain based system for healthcare digital twin. *IEEE Access, 10*. Available from https://doi.org/10.1109/ACCESS.2022.3173617, http://ieeexplore.ieee.org/xpl/RecentIssue.jsp?punumber = 6287639.

Alqahtani, A., Alsubai, S., & Bhatia, M. (2024). Digital Twin-Assisted Healthcare Framework for Adult. *IEEE Internet of Things Journal, 11*(8), 14963–14970. Available from https://doi.org/10.1109/JIOT.2023.3345331.

Aluvalu, R., Mudrakola, S., V, U. M., Kaladevi, A. C., Sandhya, M. V. S., & Bhat, C. R. (2023). The novel emergency hospital services for patients using digital twins. *Microprocessors and Microsystems, 98*. Available from https://doi.org/10.1016/j.micpro.2023.104794, https://www.journals.elsevier.com/microprocessors-and-microsystems.

Bashir, A. K., Victor, N., Bhattacharya, S., Huynh-The, T., Chengoden, R., Yenduri, G., Maddikunta, P. K. R., Pham, Q.-V., Gadekallu, T. R., & Liyanage, M. (2023). Federated learning for the healthcare metaverse:

Concepts, applications, challenges, and future directions. *IEEE Internet of Things Journal*, *10*(24). Available from https://doi.org/10.1109/jiot.2023.3304790.

Bhatia, M. (2023). IoT-inspired secure healthcare framework for adult: Blockchain perspective. *Mobile Networks and Applications*. Available from https://doi.org/10.1007/s11036-023-02263-y.

Chen, W. J., & Lin, Y. P. (2023). Event-related potential-based collaborative brain-computer interface for augmenting human performance using a low-cost, custom electroencephalogram hyperscanning infrastructure. *IEEE Transactions on Cognitive and Developmental Systems*. Available from https://doi.org/10.1109/TCDS.2023.3245048, http://ieeexplore.ieee.org/xpl/aboutJournal.jsp?punumber = 7274989.

Coorey, G., Figtree, G. A., Fletcher, D. F., Snelson, V. J., Vernon, S. T., Winlaw, D., Grieve, S. M., McEwan, A., Yang, J. Y. H., Qian, P., O'Brien, K., Orchard, J., Kim, J., Patel, S., & Redfern, J. (2022). The health digital twin to tackle cardiovascular disease—A review of an emerging interdisciplinary field. *NPJ Digital Medicine*, *5*(1). Available from https://doi.org/10.1038/s41746-022-00640-7, https://www.nature.com/npjdigitalmed/.

De Benedictis, A., Mazzocca, N., Somma, A., & Strigaro, C. (2023). Digital twins in healthcare: An architectural proposal and its application in a social distancing case study. *IEEE Journal of Biomedical and Health Informatics*, *27*(10). Available from https://doi.org/10.1109/JBHI.2022.3205506, http://ieeexplore.ieee.org/xpl/RecentIssue.jsp?punumber = 6221020.

Elayan, H., Aloqaily, M., & Guizani, M. (2021). Digital Twin for Intelligent Context-Aware IoT Healthcare Systems. *IEEE Internet of Things Journal*, *8*(23), 16749−16757. Available from https://doi.org/10.1109/JIOT.2021.3051158.

Farouk, A., Alahmadi, A., Ghose, S., & Mashatan, A. (2020). Blockchain platform for industrial healthcare: Vision and future opportunities. *Computer Communications*, *154*. Available from https://doi.org/10.1016/j.com-com.2020.02.058, http://www.journals.elsevier.com/computer-communications/.

Firouzi, F., Farahani, B., Daneshmand, M., Grise, K., Song, J., Saracco, R., Wang, L. L., Lo, K., Angelov, P., Soares, E., Loh, P.-S., Talebpour, Z., Moradi, R., Goodarzi, M., Ashraf, H., Talebpour, M., Talebpour, A., Romeo, L., Das, R., ... Luo, A. (2021). Harnessing the power of smart and connected health to tackle COVID-19: IoT, AI, robotics, and blockchain for a better world. *IEEE Internet of Things Journal*, *8*(16). Available from https://doi.org/10.1109/jiot.2021.3073904.

Fuller, A., Fan, Z., Day, C., & Barlow, C. (2020). Digital twin: Enabling technologies, challenges and open research. *IEEE Access*, *8*. Available from https://doi.org/10.1109/ACCESS.2020.2998358, http://ieeexplore.ieee.org/xpl/RecentIssue.jsp?punumber = 6287639.

Ghayvat, H., Zuhair, M., Shukla, N., & Kumar, N. (2024). Healthcare-CT: Solid PoD and blockchain-enabled cyber twin approach for healthcare 5.0 ecosystems. *IEEE Internet of Things Journal*, *11*(4). Available from https://doi.org/10.1109/JIOT.2023.3312448, http://ieeexplore.ieee.org/servlet/opac?punumber = 6488907.

Haleem, A., Javaid, M., Pratap Singh, R., & Suman, R. (2022). Medical 4.0 technologies for healthcare: Features, capabilities, and applications. *Internet of Things and Cyber-Physical Systems*, *2*. Available from https://doi.org/10.1016/j.iotcps.2022.04.001, https://www.sciencedirect.com/science/journal/26673452.

Khan, S., Alzaabi, A., Iqbal, Z., Ratnarajah, T., & Arslan, T. (2023a). A Novel Digital Twin (DT) Model Based on WiFi CSI, Signal Processing and Machine Learning for Patient Respiration Monitoring and Decision-Support. *IEEE Access*, *11*, 103554−103568. Available from https://doi.org/10.1109/ACCESS.2023.3316508.

Khan, S., Alzaabi, A., Ratnarajah, T., & Arslan, T. (2024). Novel statistical time series data augmentation and machine learning based classification of unobtrusive respiration data for respiration Digital Twin model. *Computers in Biology and Medicine*, *168*, 107825. Available from https://doi.org/10.1016/j.compbiomed.2023.107825.

Khan, S., Arslan, T., & Ratnarajah, T. (2022). Digital Twin Perspective of Fourth Industrial and Healthcare Revolution. *IEEE Access*, *10*, 25732−25754. Available from https://doi.org/10.1109/ACCESS.2022.3156062.

Khan, S., Ullah, S., Khan, H. U., & Rehman, I. U. (2023b). Digital-Twins-Based Internet of Robotic Things for Remote Health Monitoring of COVID-19 Patients. *IEEE Internet of Things Journal*, *10*(18), 16087−16098. Available from https://doi.org/10.1109/JIOT.2023.3267171.

Kumar, M., Raj, H., Chaurasia, N., & Gill, S. S. (2023). Blockchain inspired secure and reliable data exchange architecture for cyber-physical healthcare system 4.0. *Internet of Things and Cyber-Physical Systems*, *3*. Available from https://doi.org/10.1016/j.iotcps.2023.05.006, https://www.sciencedirect.com/science/journal/26673452.

Lakhan, A., Abdul Lateef, A. A., Abd Ghani, M. K., Abdulkareem, K. H., Mohammed, M. A., Nedoma, J., Martinek, R., & Garcia-Zapirain, B. (2023). Secure-fault-tolerant efficient industrial internet of healthcare things framework based on digital twin federated fog-cloud networks. *Journal of King Saud University - Computer and Information Sciences*, *35*(9). Available from https://doi.org/10.1016/j.jksuci.2023.101747, http://www.journals.elsevier.com/journal-of-king-saud-university-computer-and-information-sciences/.

Liu, Y., Zhang, L., Yang, Y., Zhou, L., Ren, L., Wang, F., Liu, R., Pang, Z., & Deen, M. J. (2019). A novel cloud-based framework for the elderly healthcare services using digital twin. *IEEE Access, 7*. Available from https://doi.org/10.1109/access.2019.2909828.

Lv, Z., Guo, J., & Lv, H. (2024). Deep learning-empowered clinical big data analytics in healthcare digital twins. *IEEE/ACM Transactions on Computational Biology and Bioinformatics, 21*(4), 660−669. Available from https://doi.org/10.1109/TCBB.2023.3252668.

Manocha, A., Afaq, Y., & Bhatia, M. (2023). Digital Twin-assisted Blockchain-inspired irregular event analysis for eldercare. *Knowledge-Based Systems, 260*, 110138. Available from https://doi.org/10.1016/j.knosys.2022.110138.

Mohammed, M. A., Lakhan, A., Zebari, D. A., Ghani, M. K. A., Marhoon, H. A., Abdulkareem, K. H., Nedoma, J., & Martinek, R. (2024). Securing healthcare data in industrial cyber-physical systems using combining deep learning and blockchain technology. *Engineering Applications of Artificial Intelligence, 129*. Available from https://doi.org/10.1016/j.engappai.2023.107612, https://www.sciencedirect.com/science/journal/09521976.

Murala, D. K., et al. (2023). MedMetaverse: Medical care of chronic disease patients and managing data using artificial intelligence, blockchain, and wearable devices state-of-the-art methodology. *IEEE Access, 11*, 138954−138985. Available from https://doi.org/10.1109/ACCESS.2023.3340791.

Okegbile, S. D., Cai, J., Niyato, D., & Yi, C. (2023). Human digital twin for personalized healthcare: Vision, architecture and future directions. *IEEE Network, 37*(2). Available from https://doi.org/10.1109/MNET.118.2200071, https://ieeexplore.ieee.org/xpl/mostRecentIssue.jsp?punumber = 65.

Qu, Z., Li, Y., Liu, B., Gupta, D., & Tiwari, P. (2023). DTQFL: A digital twin-assisted quantum federated learning algorithm for intelligent diagnosis in 5G mobile network. *IEEE Journal of Biomedical and Health Informatics*. Available from https://doi.org/10.1109/JBHI.2023.3303401, http://ieeexplore.ieee.org/xpl/RecentIssue.jsp?punumber = 6221020.

Sadeghi, M., & Mahmoudi, A. (2024). Synergy between blockchain technology and internet of medical things in healthcare: A way to sustainable society. *Information Sciences, 660*, 120049. Available from https://doi.org/10.1016/j.ins.2023.120049.

Sahal, R., Alsamhi, S. H., Brown, K. N., O'Shea, D., & Alouffi, B. (2022). Blockchain-based digital twins collaboration for smart pandemic alerting: Decentralized COVID-19 pandemic alerting use case. *Computational Intelligence and Neuroscience, 2022*. Available from https://doi.org/10.1155/2022/7786441, http://www.hindawi.com/journals/cin.

Sarp, S., Kuzlu, M., Zhao, Y., & Gueler, O. (2023). Digital twin in healthcare: A study for chronic wound management. *IEEE Journal of Biomedical and Health Informatics, 27*(11). Available from https://doi.org/10.1109/JBHI.2023.3299028, http://ieeexplore.ieee.org/xpl/RecentIssue.jsp?punumber = 6221020.

Shaikh, E., Al-Ali, A. R., Muhammad, S., Mohammad, S., & Aloul, F. (2023). Security analysis of a digital twin framework using probabilistic model checking. *IEEE Access, 11*. Available from https://doi.org/10.1109/ACCESS.2023.3257171, http://ieeexplore.ieee.org/xpl/RecentIssue.jsp?punumber = 6287639.

Sun, M., Xie, L., Liu, Y., Li, K., Jiang, B., Lu, Y., Yang, Y., Yu, H., Song, Y., Bai, C., & Yang, D. (2022). The metaverse in current digital medicine. *Clinical eHealth, 5*. Available from https://doi.org/10.1016/j.ceh.2022.07.002.

Tai, Y., Zhang, L., Li, Q., Zhu, C., Chang, V., Rodrigues, J. J. P. C., & Guizani, M. (2022). Digital-twin-enabled IoMT system for surgical simulation using rAC-GAN. *IEEE Internet of Things Journal, 9*(21). Available from https://doi.org/10.1109/JIOT.2022.3176300, http://ieeexplore.ieee.org/servlet/opac?punumber = 6488907.

Vats, T., Singh, S. K., Kumar, S., Gupta, B. B., Gill, S. S., Arya, V., & Alhalabi, W. (2023). Explainable context-aware IoT framework using human digital twin for healthcare. *Multimedia Tools and Applications*. Available from https://doi.org/10.1007/s11042-023-16922-5, https://www.springer.com/journal/11042.

Venkatesh, K. P., Brito, G., & Boulos, M. N. K. (2024). Health digital twins in life science and health care innovation. *Annual Review of Pharmacology and Toxicology, 64*(1), 159−170. Available from https://doi.org/10.1146/annurev-pharmtox-022123-022046.

Verma, R. (2022). Smart city healthcare cyber physical system: Characteristics, technologies and challenges. *Wireless Personal Communications, 122*(2). Available from https://doi.org/10.1007/s11277-021-08955-6.

Wang, G., Badal, A., Jia, X., Maltz, J. S., Mueller, K., Myers, K. J., et al. (2022a). Development of metaverse for intelligent healthcare. *Nature Machine Intelligence, 4*, 922−929. Available from https://doi.org/10.1038/s42256-022-00549-6.

Wang, J., Jin, H., Chen, J., Tan, J., & Zhong, K. (2022b). Anomaly detection in Internet of medical Things with Blockchain from the perspective of deep neural network. *Information Sciences, 617*, 133−149. Available from https://doi.org/10.1016/j.ins.2022.10.060.

Wang, E., Tayebi, P., & Song, Y. T. (2023). Cloud-based digital twins' storage in emergency healthcare. *International Journal of Networked and Distributed Computing, 11*, 75–87. Available from https://doi.org/10.1007/s44227-023-00011-y.

Xames, M. D., & Topcu, T. G. (2024). A systematic literature review of digital twin research for healthcare systems: Research trends, gaps, and realization challenges. *IEEE Access, 12*. Available from https://doi.org/10.1109/ACCESS.2023.3349379, http://ieeexplore.ieee.org/xpl/RecentIssue.jsp?punumber = 6287639.

Xie, Y., Lu, L., Gao, F., He, Sj, Zhao, Hj, Fang, Y., Yang, Jm, An, Y., Ye, Zw, & Dong, Z. (2021). Integration of artificial intelligence, blockchain, and wearable technology for chronic disease management: A new paradigm in smart healthcare. *Current Medical Science, 41*(6). Available from https://doi.org/10.1007/s11596-021-2485-0, https://rd.springer.com/journal/11596.

Yi, H. (2023). Improving cloud storage and privacy security for digital twin based medical records. *Journal of Cloud Computing, 12*(1). Available from https://doi.org/10.1186/s13677-023-00523-6.

Zhang, J., & Tai, Y. (2022). *Secure medical digital twin via human-centric interaction and cyber vulnerability resilience. Connection Science* (34, pp. 895–910). China: Taylor and Francis Ltd. Available from https://doi.org/10.1080/09540091.2021.2013443.

Digital twins and medical sensor network to analyze start-up delay in smart infusion pump

J.V. Alamelu[1] and Mythili Asaithambi[2]

[1]M S Ramaiah Institute of Technology, Bangalore, Karnataka, India [2]School of Electronics Engineering, Vellore Institute of Technology, Vellore, Tamil Nadu, India

7.1 Introduction

The digital twin (DT) is a virtual version of different verticals which is popular across many industries. The healthcare domain is leading to important breakthroughs with the DT technology. DT makes use of models driven by artificial intelligence (AI) and a significant amount of data from various Internet of Things (IoT) devices. One way to assess the performance of a physical counterpart is by using a DT. A DT in healthcare is the full-life data gathering of any patient combined with AI-powered techniques that analyze the data to respond to different clinical issues. For the related application, massive amounts of data must be collected using IoT sensors in order to build a digital model that can be tested and simulated (Haleem et al., 2023. Patients' own DT makes use of preceding insights to predict the outcome of a certain procedure, assist in selecting the most effective drug, and manage chronic illnesses. The performance of the DT in the healthcare system is based on the effective, accuracy, and reduced error to ensure patient safety. In order to achieve optimal precision and minimize errors, extensive data testing guarantees seamless real-time integration of real-time data from different sources. IoT evaluations are additionally significant in ensuring the full functionality of different sensors and devices, as well as the security and compliance of the collected data. DT is proposed to be implemented successfully to Improve Diagnostics, patient care, clinical research, strengthening of Hospital Operations, Medical Education and Diagnostics.

In clinical research, DT works with the key concept which is Patient data. AI-driven algorithms for DTs should be able to recognize abnormalities in an individual's behavior or lifestyle choices, link disparate clinical events, monitor responses and side effects to a

DOI: https://doi.org/10.1016/B978-0-443-36370-2.00008-6

specific medication, and accurate interpretation. In order to make an informed decision, healthcare professionals should assess the technology's quality and viability before utilizing algorithms and related DTs. Hospitals are compelled to use technological innovations in specific circumstances. Patients receiving chemotherapy drugs given by aerosol run the risk of experiencing severe side effects if tumor-targeting treatments miss their targets or "strike" healthy tissue (Turab & Jamil, 2023). Using a DT, they were able to replicate the movement of aerosol particles through an adult's upper airway. Furthermore, DTs could aid in medical research on brain healing. The implementation of DT is indeed required in smart hospital environments in drug infusions for various therapies and treatments. Smart infusion pumps are one among them (Polisena et al., 2018).

Smart infusion pumps are the most important drug delivery devices which are intelligent and aimed at administering drugs to patients accurately in standalone and in remote environments. These pumps are used in delivering anesthesia, hemodynamic control drugs and in mechanical ventilators. The infusion depends on different pumping mechanisms. In practice, the performance of the pump is influenced by flow rate and has an immense effect on patient safety. The factors that affect the flow rate of the pumps are start-up delay, lag time, drug absorption, syringe changeover, multiple fluids, dead volume, unintended drug bolus, volume limitation, and syringe and tubing size. Particularly, maintaining the drug flow rate can be accomplished rapidly by attaining the desired set point. The manifestation of the start-up delay is an influencing parameter for accurate flow rate. The reduction of this parameter is possible by predicting and controlling the infusion pump speed as well as a lag time of the infusion pump.

The medical device modeling, design, and verification have been carried out in open, closed-loop control environments for anesthesia pumps and multichannel chemotherapy infusion pumps (Banerjee et al., 2011). Several advancements are underway in the medical device industry in designing smart infusion pumps (Guelig et al., 2017). On average, 80 to 90% of inpatients in a hospital receive infusion therapy. Errors and malfunction have resulted in a fatality. FDA has received more than 50,000 adverse that include death. The result has triggered the medical device industry to develop safe, smart, automated infusion pump with FDA's guidelines (Hughes et al., 2015; Smith & Gray, 2020). Currently in the US, smart infusion pumps are used with wireless connectivity and cater the changes in infusion (Yu et al., 2017). Research has been handled with Becton, Dickinson Alaris pump performance relating to the drug library updates. In some situations, drug delivery is affected due to flow rate variations and miscalculations (Snijder et al., 2015). Error minimization has been achieved in smart pumps that have inbuilt drug libraries (Rajkomar & Blandford, 2012). Authors have deliberated the modeling procedures regarding the actual flow rate requirement and the need for control of infusion parameters (Sokolsky et al., 2011). The parameters that affect the flow rate such as carrier flow rate, and dead volume have been described its performance for single and multiple infusion systems has been analyzed (Maiguy-Foinard et al., 2017). The infusion medication parameters, and their calculation in terms of dosage, drip rate, flow rate, dead volume, carrier flow rate, and lag time have been elaborated in nursing calculations (Brindley, 2018). Studies on micropump design using different smart materials to obtain accurate flow rates for the administration of intravenous sedatives for dental are successful (Seo & Lee, 2016). The control of flow parameters has been handled to ensure patient safety using control algorithms even under noisy situations (Bakouri, 2014). The dosing errors and the impact of start-up delay that mitigate risk in neonatal intensive care units have been investigated for multiple infusion pump situations (Konings et al., 2017). Research on a hybrid prediction model with Artificial Neural Networks (ANN) and Support Vector Machine (SVM) to predict the remifentanil dosage for anesthetic procedures have been studied (Jove et al., 2021). SVM has been used to identify deaths due to cardiac failure and pump failure. The performance is validated through statistical metrics (Ramírez et al., 2015). Machine learning techniques K-Nearest Neighbour (KNN), Naïve Bayes, SVM, and decision trees were implemented to predict the performance of the medical device (El-Hasnony et al., 2020).

In this research work, the infusion ranges for Noradrenaline and Fentanyl have been considered for the considered parameters. Noradrenaline is typically should be infused at controlled rates and administered through a central venous catheter. The drug Fentanyl is administered as a fast infusion to relieve the patient from pain. Both drugs have a different purposes but are usually administered using smart infusion pumps. In smart infusion pumps, prediction of pump speed, and lag time is essential. The enhanced smart drug library is used to analyze the pump performance by predicting the required output parameters. Multiple regression techniques with principal components have been focused on for implementation to evaluate the prediction performance of an infusion pump. The prediction of pump speed and lag time is performed to reduce the start-up delay. Further, the predicted speed is controlled optimally by employing optimal control algorithms.

7.2 Methodology

The implementation of the DT in hospitals has to be employed based on the typical DT architecture. The architecture is usually employed as per the layer structure that is depicted in Fig. 7.1. The layer structure has the following key factors which have to be followed in a smart medical sensor network environment. The entire scheme is instantiated from the sensors, devices and modules which aids in the data acquisition, processing, representation of data, modeling using different AI and optimization algorithms. Further, the decision of the entire process has to be carried out by predicting, controlling and monitoring the acquired parameters as desired.

In the proposed work, smart infusion pump prediction and monitoring is focused and hence prediction algorithms have been considered for the infusion of the drug dosage to the patients and hence the error minimization is handled. The research workflow instigates with the preprocessing of infusion pump parameters, followed by formulation of the regression model and verification of its performance for prediction accuracy.

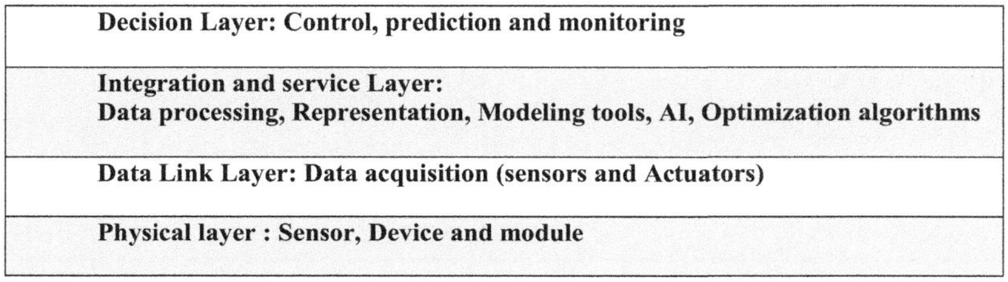

Decision Layer: Control, prediction and monitoring
Integration and service Layer: Data processing, Representation, Modeling tools, AI, Optimization algorithms
Data Link Layer: Data acquisition (sensors and Actuators)
Physical layer : Sensor, Device and module

FIGURE 7.1 Layer structure for digital twin in sensor network environment.

7.2.1 Preprocessing of infusion pump parameters

In the current work, various drug dosing and infusion flow rates for patients with a mean age of under 50 years are assessed using data from an electronic Medical Compendium. Drug dosage, infusion pump flow rate, lag time and pump speed for dead volume 0.4 mL, carrier flow rates Qc 10 mL/hour, and 50 mL/hour have been incorporated as part of the smart infusion pump dataset. The average flow rate for drugs ranging from 1 to 40 mL/hour in multiple infusion scenarios has been considered for the statistical analysis. Table 7.1 displays the descriptive statistics of the different infusion pump parameters that were derived from the electronic medical compendium. The smart drug library has been developed and it is tabulated for Noradrenaline and Fentanyl.

Utilizing the mentioned range of datasets for a smart infusion pump, a regression technique has been employed for 10 and 50 mL/hour carrier flow rates.

The current work has been performed to identify two parameters: lag time and infusion pump speed, which are calculated from manufacturer specifications for a medically graded infusion pump. Both of them are necessary in order to provide the patient with the amount they require while also shortening the infusion pump's start-up time. For two different carrier flow rates Qc of 10 and 50 mL/hour, regression models have been used. The present work is focused on lag time prediction which is an essential factor for handling start-up delays.

Regression is a typical mathematical method for predicting the dependent variable (y) from one or more independent variables (x). The primary objective of the regression method is to find the best feasible fit between the predicted and actual data. The formula for the regression analysis is in Eq. (7.1)

$$y = \beta_0 + \beta_1 x_1 + \ldots.\beta_n x_n + \epsilon \tag{7.1}$$

where y is a dependent variable, xi is the independent variable, βi is the regression coefficient, and ϵ is the error.

The training dataset is taken as D1training = (Xi,Yli), $i = 1,2,..,n$ for predicting the lag time, where Yli is the set of infusion pump lag time outputs and $Ylnewi$ is the predicted pump lag time output values derived from regression of Yli on Xi.

Initially predictions are made for both investigations using multiple linear regression models to calculate the lag time, and multicollinearity is confirmed. Further principal component regression (PCR) is applied to determine the prediction.

TABLE 7.1 Smart infusion pump parameters as used in the drug library.

S. No.	Parameter	Noradrenaline	Fentanyl
	Weight (kg)	65 ± 12	
	Drug dosage (mg/h)	1.59 ± 1.55	2.43 ± 4.72
	Infusion flow rate (mL/h)	39.9 ± 38.8	46.9 ± 94.5
	Lag time (Qc 10 mL/h)	0.056 ± 0.03	0.083 ± 0.04
	Lag time (Qc 50 mL/h)	0.02 ± 0.006	0.02 ± 0.009

7.2.2 Principal component regression

PCR is a statistical method for handling collinearity and high-dimensional data in multivariate regression analysis. When there are many associated predictor variables, it combines aspects of principal component analysis (PCA) and linear regression to enhance the performance of regression models.

When there are numerous, highly linked predictor factors, PCR can be a helpful method. The risk of overfitting is lessened, and the model's capacity for generalization is enhanced, by lowering the dimensionality. However, due to the transformation into principal components, it can be more difficult to comprehend the impact of certain predictor factors. As a result, it is crucial to interpret the results carefully.

The PCR representations are given in Eqs. (7.2)–(7.4).

The model plane y with x predictor variables and regression coefficient β is found as

$$y = \beta x + \epsilon \tag{7.2}$$

The estimated regression coefficients β are computed in ordinary least squares as

$$\beta = (x'x)^{-1}(x'y) \text{ and } R = x'x \tag{7.3}$$

where R is the correlation matrix of independent variables.

To perform PCR, we transform the independent variables into their principal components.

Mathematically, it is expressed as

$$x'x = PDP' = z'z \tag{7.4}$$

where D is a diagonal matrix of the eigenvalues of $x'x$, P is the eigenvector matrix of $x'x$ and z is a data matrix (similar in structure to X) made up of the principal components. P is orthogonal so that $P'P = I$. The new variable Z as weighted averages of the original variable X is created. To avoid multicollinearity in the data, the small eigenvalues are omitted. Later regression Y on new variables Z has been made by transforming the results back to the X scale to obtain estimates of β. These estimates will be biased, and the size of this bias is more than compensated for by the decrease in variance. The mean squared error of these estimates is less than that for least squares.

The PCRs are described as follows:

- Analyze the X matrix's primary components and record the results in Z.
- Calculate the least squares estimate A by fitting the Y (output) on Z regression.
- Set A's final element's value to zero.
- Apply $B = PA$ to transform back to the initial coefficients.

7.2.3 Prediction of speed and lag time using principal component regression

Using an essential component of the drug dosage and infusion flow rate data values, a PCA model has been created, and principal component Z has been located. Finding the least square estimated of A, with the final element of A set to 0, yields the best fit for the prediction of speed Y, which is then regressed on Z. The eigenvalues with A are then used to transform the regression coefficient back to its original value. As a result, the speed prediction has been estimated and linear regression model parameters have been produced. By comparing the measured and anticipated values, the performance of the expected speed has been examined. By calculating statistical performance indicators such as the coefficient of determination (R^2), the RMSE, the MSE, and the MAE, it has been possible to determine the average prediction error. A total of 10 and 50 mL/hour carrier flow rates have been used in the training. The prediction of lag time is performed using the same set of input data from the smart drug library dataset.

7.2.4 Statistical performance of infusion pump using regression models

The infusion pump flow rate is inversely proportional to lag time and inversely proportional to pump speed. The speed and lag time for various carrier flow rates must be estimated for each combination of drug dosage and infusion flow rate. To administer the required dosage to the patient at a controlled flow rate, the infusion pump's lag time needs to be optimized hence the start-up delay will be reduced.

The PCR regression model was used to determine the prediction for Qc of 10 and 50 mL/hour. The performance of the lag time and speed has been objectively assessed for its error and accuracy in prediction. For the set of drugs considered in the study, the prediction and residual curves for infusion pump speed and lag time have been created for two different carrier flow rates.

7.3 Prediction of lag time using principal component regression

PCR is used to estimate the lag time using 160 data points from the eMC, of which 70% are used for training and 30% for testing. Fivefold cross-validation is used to test the model's prediction accuracy and establish the statistical parameters.

In Fig. 7.2, the difference between the projected lag time and the actual values is indicated for various carrier flow rates: (A) 10 mL/hour and (B) 50 mL/hour. When predicted values are found to differ slightly from actual values, prediction accuracy is confirmed. For the majority of the samples, it is seen that the error between true and anticipated lag time is minimal.

The response curves show that the lag time for both true values and anticipated values ranges from 0 to 0.15. The displayed lag time was less for samples 1−30 than the actual value; the difference between the two is very small. More than 30 is considered to be a large data sample and thus increases the observed error between true and anticipated values. It is found that the prediction accuracy improves as the data sample rises beyond 30.

The correlation between the actual and anticipated values of lag time is displayed in Fig. 7.3A and B.

PCR is used for Qc of 10 and 50 mL/hour. The data for both forms of Qc are seen to be clustered around the diagonal line in a scatter plot, which is a more effective method of visualizing data. It's discovered that the Qc 10 and 50 mL/hour have correlation coefficients of 0.45 and 0.69, respectively. The expected lag time is statistically insignificant, and there is a weak association between the expected and actual lag times.

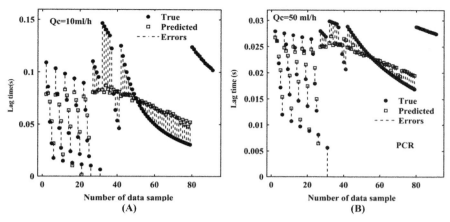

FIGURE 7.2 Variation of actual and predicted lag time for Qc (A) 10 mL/h and (B) 50 mL/h using principal component regression.

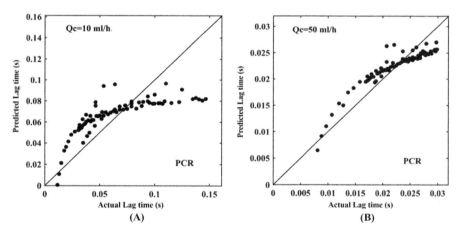

FIGURE 7.3 Correlation for actual and predicted lag time.

The residual response of the predicted lag time using PCR for both Qc variants is shown in Fig. 7.4A and B. It is shown that the residue is close to 0, which indicates the least amount of variation from the projected lag time. The residual values tend to migrate from negative values to the positive side after an anticipated lag time of 0.05, at which point they tend to move away from negative values.

However, close observation of the width of these residual values shows that the range is ± 0.05. This range is significantly low, leading to better prediction accuracy. Even though the error is lesser, the R^2 in the prediction of the lag time is not significant. The model is heteroskedastic, hence statistical significance of the independent variables is overstated and they are not significant for all the values of lag time.

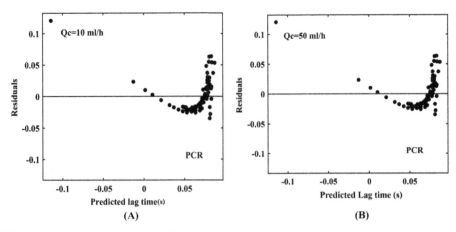

FIGURE 7.4   Residuals obtained for predicted lag time.

TABLE 7.2   Regression performance to predict lag time.

Carrier flow rate (mL/h)	Prediction accuracy (%)	Mean ± standard deviation
10	97.6	0.051 ± 0.023
50	97.2	0.0096 ± 0.003

Further, the performance of the regression model with Mean square error, mean absolute error and prediction accuracy has been tabulated in Table 7.2 along with predicted lag time for 10 and 50 mL/hour.

7.4 Conclusion

A DT is a virtual version of a real thing that can be tracked, studied, and improved. It is live and dynamic, updating with changes and incorporating knowledge from other people, machines, and the environment. This technology enhances patient care by allowing for personalized medical treatments based on genetics, physiology, family history, and other characteristics. Healthcare professionals can use robust data sources like real-time locating systems to improve the effectiveness of a DT, forecast equipment availability, and evaluate simulation-recommended changes in real-world scenarios. In this research work, start-up delay for a smart infusion pump that can be implemented in a DT environment has been analyzed. Lag time in multiple infusions is the most important factor that has to be considered along with the pump speed. The drug delivery accuracy using a smart infusion pump is facilitated with lag time. The prediction of required drug dosage in multiple infusion scenarios has been investigated using multiple regression techniques with principal components. The prediction accuracy has been identified as 97.8% and 99.7% for two different carrier flow rates 10 and 50 mL/hour. The instigation has been observed with a mean predicted lag time of 0.0051 and 0.0096 seconds for the considered carrier flow rate. The performance of the smart infusion pump when implemented with multiple regression is better and hence dead time reduction is possible in multiple infusion scenarios. The reduction in dead time is directly proportional to the start-up delay. In this paper, the performance analysis has been examined to minimize the adverse effects of providing precise drug concentration to the patients. The results obtained in this work are shown for the two different drugs considered and the same is appropriate for various drugs and the validation has been carried out. Similar results have also been obtained for the prediction performance of various drug infusions.

References

Bakouri, M. A. (2014). Sensorless physiological control of implantable rotary blood pumps for heart failure patients using modern control techniques. [Online]. <http://arxiv.org/abs/1405.2419>.

Banerjee, A., Gupta, S. K. S., Fainekos, G., & Varsamopoulos, G. (2011). Towards modeling and analysis of cyber-physical medical systems. In *Proceedings of the 4th international sympoisum of applied science biomedical communication technology - ISABEL '11* (pp. 1–5). Available from https://doi.org/10.1145/2093698.2093852.

Brindley, J. (2018). Undertaking drug calculations for intravenous medicines and infusions. *Nursing Standard: Official Newspaper of the Royal College of Nursing*, 32(20), 55–63. Available from https://doi.org/10.7748/ns.2018.e11029.

El-Hasnony, I. M., Barakat, S. I., & Mostafa, R. R. (2020). Optimized ANFIS model using hybrid metaheuristic algorithms for Parkinson's disease prediction in IoT environment. *IEEE Access*, 8, 119252–119270. Available from https://doi.org/10.1109/ACCESS.2020.3005614.

Guelig, D., et al. (2017). Design of a novel, adjustable flow rate, reusable, electricity-free, low-cost syringe infusion pump. *Journal of Medical Devices, Transactions ASME*, 11(4), 1–6. Available from https://doi.org/10.1115/1.4037935.

Haleem, A., Javaid, M., Pratap, R., & Suman, R. (2023). Biomedical technology exploring the revolution in healthcare systems through the applications of digital twin technology. *Biomedical Technology*, 4, 28–38. Available from https://doi.org/10.1016/j.bmt.2023.02.001, no. February.

Hughes, J., et al. (2015). Infusion pump-mediated mechanical hemolysis in pediatric patients. *Annals of Clinical Laboratory Science*, 45(2), 140–147.

Jove, E., et al. (2021). Hybrid intelligent model to predict the remifentanil infusion rate in patients under general anesthesia. *Logistic Journal IGPL*, 29(2), 193–206. Available from https://doi.org/10.1093/jigpal/jzaa046.

Konings, M. K., Snijder, R. A., Radermacher, J. H., & Timmerman, A. M. (2017). Analytical method for calculation of deviations from intended dosages during multi-infusion. *Biomedical Engineering Online*, 16(1), 1–28. Available from https://doi.org/10.1186/s12938-016-0309-4.

Maiguy-Foinard, A., et al. (2017). Criteria for choosing an intravenous infusion line intended for multidrug infusion in anaesthesia and intensive care units. *Anaesthia Critical Care Pain Medical*, 36(1), 53–63. Available from https://doi.org/10.1016/j.accpm.2016.02.007.

Polisena, J., Sinclair, A., Hilfi, H., Bédard, M., & Sedrakyan, A. (2018). Wireless smart infusion pumps: A descriptive analysis of the continuous quality improvement data. *Journal of Medical Biology Engineering*, 38(2), 296–303. Available from https://doi.org/10.1007/s40846-017-0302-9.

Rajkomar, A., & Blandford, A. (2012). Understanding infusion administration in the ICU through distributed cognition. *Journal of Biomedical Informatics*, 45(3), 580–590. Available from https://doi.org/10.1016/j.jbi.2012.02.003.

Ramírez, J., et al. (2015). Automatic SVM classification of sudden cardiac death and pump failure death from autonomic and repolarization ECG markers. *Journal of Electrocardiology*, 48(4), 551–557. Available from https://doi.org/10.1016/j.jelectrocard.2015.04.002.

Seo, K.-S., & Lee, K. (2016). Smart syringe pumps for drug infusion during dental intravenous sedation. *Journal of Dental Anesthia Pain Medical*, 16(3), 165. Available from https://doi.org/10.17245/jdapm.2016.16.3.165.

Smith, E. A., & Gray, G. (2020). Developing a smart infusion pump dedicated to infusion safety. *Ergonomics in design: The magazine of human factors applications*, 1–9. Available from https://doi.org/10.1177/1064804620944760, no. June.

Snijder, R. A., Konings, M. K., Lucas, P., Egberts, T. C., & Timmerman, A. D. (2015). Flow variability and its physical causes in infusion technology: A systematic review of in vitro measurement and modeling studies. *Biomedical Technology*, *60*(4), 277–300. Available from https://doi.org/10.1515/bmt-2014-0148.

Sokolsky, O., Lee, I., & Heimdahl, M. (2011, October). Challenges in the regulatory approval of medical cyber-physical systems. In *Proceedings of the 9th ACM international conference on embeded software - EMSOFT '11* (p. 227). Available from https://doi.org/10.1145/2038642.2038677.

Turab, M., & Jamil, S. (2023). *A comprehensive survey of digital twins in healthcare in the era of metaverse* (pp. 563–584).

Yu, D., Hsu, K. Y., Kim, J. H., & DeLaurentis, P. (2017). Infusion pump informatics approach to quantify impact of alerts and alarms on healthcare delivery. *Proceedings of Human Factors Ergonomics Society*, *2017*, 681–685. Available from https://doi.org/10.1177/1541931213601657.

Healthcare data management using blockchain-enabled sensor networks

Ammar Odeh

Department of Computer Science, King Hussein School of Computing Sciences, Princess Sumaya University for Technology, Amman, Jordan

8.1 Introduction

Effective data management has become a cornerstone of patient care, research, and administration in the rapidly evolving healthcare landscape. The advent of advanced technologies like sensor networks and blockchain has opened new avenues to address long-standing challenges in this domain. This overview examines the current hurdles in healthcare data management, explores the emerging role of sensor networks, and introduces blockchain technology, underscoring its potential to revolutionize how healthcare data is managed and utilized.

The healthcare data management landscape is a mix of traditional and modern systems struggling to keep up with data's ever-increasing volume and complexity. Legacy systems often lack the flexibility and scalability to manage large datasets effectively, leading to inefficiencies and potential errors.

In recent years, there has been a shift toward leveraging advanced technologies like artificial intelligence (AI) and big data analytics to enhance data management. These technologies offer robust data analysis and decision-making tools, enabling healthcare providers to derive actionable insights from their data.

Despite these advancements, the need for transformative solutions is evident. Current systems are often fragmented, and data security, privacy, and interoperability challenges remain significant. This is where integrating blockchain technology and sensor networks presents a compelling solution. By combining the real-time data collection capabilities of sensor networks with the secure, decentralized framework of blockchain, there is potential to overcome many of the existing challenges in healthcare data management.

Sensor Networks for Smart Hospitals
DOI: https://doi.org/10.1016/B978-0-443-36370-2.00009-8

8.2 Overview of healthcare data management challenges

Healthcare data management is fraught with complexities and challenges, paramount among them being the sheer volume and variety of data generated daily. With the advent of digital health records, genomic data, and imaging, the volume of data in healthcare is growing exponentially, presenting significant challenges in storage, processing, and analysis.

Compounding this issue is the paramount need for security and privacy. Healthcare data encompasses some of the most sensitive personal information, making it a prime target for breaches and cyber-attacks. Ensuring patient data's confidentiality, integrity, and availability is not just a technical necessity but also a legal imperative, with regulations such as the Health Insurance Portability and Accountability Act (HIPAA) setting stringent standards (Oakley, 2023).

Another major challenge is interoperability. Healthcare systems often operate in silos, with different providers using disparate systems that are not always compatible with each other. This lack of interoperability leads to inefficiencies, hampers care coordination, and can compromise patient safety (Stadler, 2021).

Furthermore, the regulatory and compliance landscape of healthcare data management is complex and evolving. Healthcare organizations must navigate a maze of laws and standards, often varying by region, while keeping pace with technological advancements (Fig. 8.1).

8.2.1 Integration and interoperability challenges

In healthcare data management, the hurdles of integration and interoperability stand prominent. Healthcare data often exists in isolated silos scattered across numerous systems

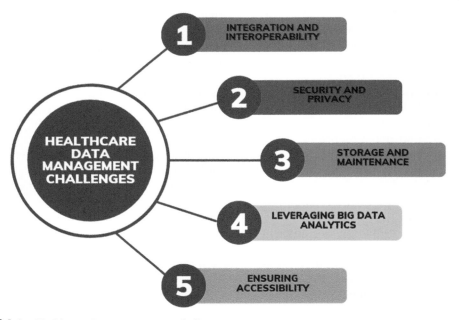

FIGURE 8.1   Healthcare data management challenges.

that lack communication synergy. Consequently, this fragmentation hinders the ability to form a comprehensive understanding of a patient's health history (Yaqoob et al., 2022).

Interoperability refers to the capacity of disparate systems to communicate and exchange information seamlessly. Integration involves the amalgamation of these varied systems to facilitate interoperability. Both aspects are crucial for healthcare organizations striving for effective data management and comprehensive patient care.

8.2.2 Challenges of security and privacy

Safeguarding security and privacy is another paramount challenge in managing healthcare data. Given the sensitive and confidential nature of health information, it is imperative to ensure robust security measures. However, the intricate nature of healthcare data often leaves it susceptible to cyber threats (Bittins et al., 2021).

Healthcare entities must implement stringent encryption protocols and restrict data access to authorized personnel only. Robust security measures and contingency plans are necessary to address potential breaches and safeguard patient data effectively.

8.2.3 Storage and maintenance issues

The task of storing and maintaining healthcare data is both complex and resource-intensive. Organizations must deploy sufficient and scalable storage solutions with healthcare data expanding unprecedentedly. It is equally important to back up data regularly and have reliable recovery systems to mitigate the impacts of outages or disasters (Palma, n.d.).

8.2.4 Leveraging big data analytics

Big data analytics involves extracting meaningful insights from large datasets, a process particularly vital in healthcare. This analysis can aid healthcare organizations in enhancing patient care, reducing costs, and making informed operational decisions. However, the complexity of healthcare data poses significant challenges to practical analysis. Organizations must equip themselves with appropriate analytical tools and expertise to unlock the potential of big data in healthcare (Rehman et al., 2022).

8.2.5 Ensuring accessibility

Data accessibility remains a significant challenge in healthcare data management. It is essential to provide authorized users with timely and easy access to necessary data, balancing this need with maintaining stringent data security. The dual requirement of securing sensitive health data while ensuring its availability can sometimes create barriers to access. To manage healthcare data effectively, organizations must navigate these challenges, providing security and Accessibility to improve patient care, reduce costs, and enhance operational decision-making (Dash et al., 2019).

8.3 Data usage in healthcare

The collected data serves multiple purposes in healthcare. Continuous and accurate data allows for a more comprehensive understanding of a patient's condition, leading to more precise diagnoses. This data informs medication dosages, therapy choices, and lifestyle recommendations in treatment planning.

In preventive care, data from sensors aids in identifying potential health risks early, allowing for timely interventions. For chronic disease management, continuous monitoring ensures that any deviation from normal parameters is quickly addressed, preventing complications (Keshta & Odeh, 2021).

A healthcare sensor is a specialized device or component engineered to detect, measure, or monitor various physiological or environmental parameters crucial to an individual's health. These sensors are tailored for healthcare environments and are pivotal in collecting valuable data for medical diagnosis, treatment, monitoring, and research. The utility of healthcare sensors spans several key areas, as elaborated as follows (Al-Fayoumi, 1990; Keshta & Odeh, 2021; Odeh et al., 2023):

Enhanced Monitoring of Vital Signs: Healthcare sensors are instrumental in continuously monitoring vital signs like heart rate, blood pressure, body temperature, respiratory rate, and oxygen saturation. These measurements are essential for a comprehensive assessment of a patient's health.

Critical Role in Disease Diagnosis and Management: Sensors are indispensable in diagnosing and managing numerous medical conditions. For instance, diabetic people use glucose sensors to monitor blood sugar levels, while electrocardiogram (ECG) sensors are essential for diagnosing and monitoring cardiac conditions.

Facilitating Remote Patient Monitoring: Healthcare sensors enable the remote monitoring of patients, which is especially beneficial for those with chronic illnesses or recovering from surgery. This capability allows healthcare professionals to keep track of patients' health, monitor their recovery, and intervene when necessary, all from a distance.

Promoting Personalized Healthcare: By collecting data specific to each individual, sensors support the customization of healthcare. This patient-specific data aids in creating tailored treatment plans, medications, and interventions, catering to the unique healthcare needs of each patient.

Aiding in Prevention and Early Detection: Sensors contribute significantly to the early detection and prevention of certain health conditions. Wearable sensors monitoring physical activity, sleep patterns, and other lifestyle factors offer insights into overall health and can signal potential health risks.

Supporting Research and Development: In the realm of medical research and development, healthcare sensors are invaluable. They facilitate the gathering of extensive datasets that researchers can analyze to discern health trends, identify patterns, and develop new treatments or interventions.

Diverse Healthcare Sensors in Use: The healthcare industry employs a wide array of sensors for various functions. Some commonly used healthcare sensors include:

Diagnostic ECGs and ECG Sensors: These devices measure the heart's electrical activity to diagnose cardiac conditions. Major manufacturers include Philips Healthcare, GE

Healthcare, Siemens Healthineers, and Medtronic. At the same time, companies like ADInstruments, Olimex, Protocentral, and DFRobot (designed for Arduino) provide more cost-effective options for ECG sensors and kits.

Blood Glucose Sensors: Essential for people with diabetes to monitor blood sugar levels. An example is the Dexcom G6 sensor.

Pulse Oximeter Sensors: These measure blood oxygen saturation, which is critical in intensive care settings. Products include the Low Noise Cabled Sensors from Masimo and the BluPRO SpO2 reusable sensors from Nihon Kohden.

Blood Pressure Sensors: These are vital for diagnosing hypertension and other cardiovascular conditions, with invasive and noninvasive sensor chips from manufacturers like Maxim Integrated and NXP Semiconductors.

Body Temperature Sensors: Used for fever diagnosis and patient temperature monitoring during treatment, with examples like the Analog Devices/Maxim Integrated MAX30205 Human Body Temperature Sensor.

Electroencephalogram (EEG) Sensors: These measure brain activity and are used for diagnosing neurological conditions. Products include advanced technologies EMG muscle sensors and EEG headbands or headsets from Muse and MindWave.

Accelerometers: Employed to track physical activity, monitor sleep, and detect falls. Renesas is a notable company developing these sensors.

Imaging Sensors: These encompass X-ray, MRI, CT, and ultrasound sensors, crucial for creating diagnostic body images. Canon Medical Systems is a notable manufacturer in this category.

As healthcare technology advances, sensors' role in patient care and medical research is poised to grow exponentially. Their integration into healthcare systems promises to enhance patient outcomes, streamline diagnostic processes, and pave the way for more personalized and efficient healthcare solutions.

Fig. 8.2 illustrates a conceptual model for healthcare data management using blockchain-enabled sensor networks. It depicts a flow of information starting with sensors monitoring patients. These sensors collect health-related data that are then recorded in electronic health records (EHRs). The data from EHRs are transferred to a blockchain network, emphasizing the decentralized nature of storing and managing this information. This blockchain network ensures the data's integrity, security, and traceability. Doctors and researchers can then access the information, indicating a streamlined flow of patient data to healthcare service providers and medical researchers for analysis and treatment purposes. This model highlights the potential for increased efficiency, security, and collaboration in managing health data through integrating sensor networks and blockchain technology.

8.4 Introduction to blockchain technology and its relevance

Blockchain technology, best known for its application in cryptocurrencies, holds immense promise in healthcare data management. At its core, blockchain is a decentralized ledger system characterized by immutability and transparency. Data entered onto a blockchain cannot be altered retroactively, ensuring data integrity—a critical factor in healthcare.

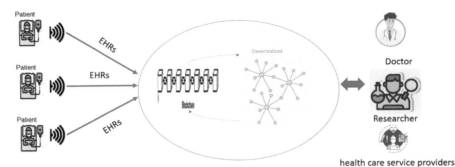

FIGURE 8.2   Conceptual model for healthcare data management using blockchain-enabled sensor networks.

The relevance of blockchain in healthcare extends to solving critical challenges in data security and traceability. It offers a secure platform for storing and sharing patient data, enhancing privacy, and reducing the risk of data breaches. Additionally, blockchain's decentralized nature addresses interoperability issues, enabling seamless exchange of information across different healthcare systems.

However, the application of blockchain in healthcare is not without its challenges. Scalability, energy consumption, and the need for a robust regulatory framework are significant barriers to its widespread adoption. Despite these hurdles, the potential benefits of blockchain in enhancing data security, patient privacy, and overall efficiency in healthcare data management are substantial.

Blockchain technology, at its core, is a digital ledger system. Unlike traditional ledgers, a central authority maintains a decentralized blockchain distributed across multiple nodes or computers. Each "block" in the blockchain contains a set of transactions or data, and every new block created is linked to the previous one, forming a chain. This linkage is secured through cryptographic principles, ensuring the data's integrity and security (Odeh & Abu Taleb, 2023).

8.4.1 Blockchain's digital ledger system

At its essence, blockchain technology functions as a digital ledger system. What sets it apart from traditional ledger systems, typically overseen by a centralized authority, is its decentralized nature. In a blockchain, the ledger is distributed across a network of nodes or computers, enhancing security and reliability. Each "block" in this chain encapsulates a set of transactions or data securely linked to the preceding block, forming a continuous chain. The security and integrity of this chain are maintained through advanced cryptographic principles, ensuring that the data within the blockchain is both secure and unalterable (McGhin et al., 2019).

8.4.2 The significance of decentralization

Decentralization stands as a cornerstone of blockchain technology. This feature is especially critical in healthcare, where data management involves many stakeholders, including hospitals, insurance companies, and patients. By decentralizing the data management system, blockchain technology eliminates the need for a single central authority. This not only bolsters security by reducing the risk of a centralized system failure but also ensures that no single entity can exert undue influence over the data. As a result, it fosters a foundation of trust and collaborative synergy among various healthcare participants, facilitating more efficient and transparent data handling (Yaqoob et al., 2022).

8.4.3 Immutability for maintaining data integrity

A key attribute of blockchain is its immutability. Once information is recorded onto a blockchain, it cannot be altered or deleted retrospectively. This characteristic is especially crucial in healthcare, where the accuracy and permanence of medical records are of utmost importance. The immutable nature of blockchain guarantees that once patient data is recorded, it remains unchanged and secure, thus protecting the data from unauthorized alterations and preserving its integrity for clinical decision-making, record-keeping, and legal compliance (Prokofieva & Miah, 2019).

8.4.4 Transparency balanced with privacy and security

Blockchain technology deftly balances transparency with privacy and security, a balancing act of critical importance in healthcare. Each transaction recorded on the blockchain is transparent and can be traced back to its origin, providing unprecedented accountability and auditability. This aspect is particularly beneficial for managing healthcare supply chains ensuring the traceability of pharmaceuticals, medical devices, and other critical healthcare supplies. Notably, while blockchain provides this transparent audit trail, it also maintains the confidentiality of sensitive patient data, ensuring that personal health information remains private and secure (Agbo et al., 2019).

8.5 How blockchain can address healthcare data management issues

8.5.1 Enhancing data security

In the healthcare sector, the protection of patient data is paramount. Blockchain technology's unique encryption and decentralized architecture provide robust defense mechanisms against hacks and data breaches. Unlike traditional centralized data storage systems, which present vulnerabilities to cyber-attacks, blockchain's distributed ledger system disperses data across a network of computers. This distribution significantly reduces the risks inherent in centralized systems and offers a more secure framework for handling sensitive healthcare data. Blockchain's cryptographic features ensure that each data transaction is securely encrypted and immutable. This means that once a piece of data is entered into the blockchain, it cannot be altered or deleted without the network's consensus, adding a layer of security. This security is particularly crucial in healthcare, where the confidentiality and integrity of patient data are not just a matter of privacy but also legal and ethical concerns (Dhillon et al., 2021).

8.5.2 Improving interoperability

Interoperability, or the ability of different healthcare systems and software to communicate and exchange data effectively, is a significant challenge in the healthcare industry. Often, patient data is fragmented across various platforms and systems, leading to inefficiencies and potential errors in patient care. Blockchain technology has the potential to serve as a unifying language between these disparate systems, enabling them to communicate seamlessly.

By creating a standardized, accessible, and secure platform, blockchain can facilitate the integration of different healthcare information systems. It allows for the collection of patient data from various sources, ensuring healthcare providers can access complete, up-to-date medical records. This unified view is essential for accurate diagnosis, treatment planning, and patient care coordination, ultimately improving patient outcomes. (Farouk et al., 2020).

8.5.3 Ensuring compliance and consent management

Compliance with regulations such as the HIPAA is crucial in healthcare data management. Blockchain technology can simplify compliance processes by providing a secure, transparent, and immutable record of all transactions. This ledger can be a definitive source for auditing purposes, ensuring that healthcare providers adhere to regulatory standards.

Moreover, blockchain introduces a novel approach to patient consent management. With blockchain, patients can control access to their medical records. They can grant or revoke consent for different healthcare providers or entities to access their data. This capability empowers patients, placing them at the center of their healthcare journey, and ensures that their data is used following their preferences and consent. This level of control and transparency aligns with the increasing emphasis on patient rights and personalized healthcare (Hasselgren et al., 2020).

8.5.4 Fraud prevention and billing

Blockchain technology can play a significant role in reducing fraud within the healthcare system. By providing an unalterable record of all transactions, blockchain makes it much more difficult for fraudulent activities to go undetected. This includes false billing, identity theft, and insurance fraud. Additionally, blockchain can streamline billing processes, reducing errors and disputes between healthcare providers and insurance companies (Li et al., 2022b).

8.5.5 Data analysis and research

Blockchain can facilitate more effective data analysis and research in healthcare. By providing a secure and comprehensive pool of patient data, researchers can access a wealth of information for medical studies while ensuring patient privacy and data integrity. This can accelerate medical research, leading to quicker development of new treatments and drugs (Upadhyay, 2020).

8.5.6 Patient engagement and empowerment

Blockchain technology can increase patient engagement and empowerment. By giving patients access to their health records and control over who can view them, blockchain fosters a more collaborative relationship between patients and healthcare providers. Patients become more involved in their healthcare decisions, leading to better health outcomes and increased patient satisfaction (Tobiano et al., 2019).

8.6 Enhanced integration of blockchain with sensor networks

The healthcare industry stands on the cusp of a technological revolution that promises to reshape how patient data is managed and utilized. At the forefront of this transformation is integrating blockchain technology with sensor networks, a convergence that heralds a new era in healthcare data management. This integration represents a synergistic alliance between cutting-edge digital ledger technology and the advanced capabilities of modern sensor networks, poised to address some of the most pressing challenges in healthcare today.

Blockchain technology, renowned for its security, transparency, and decentralization, offers a robust framework for managing the vast and sensitive data generated in healthcare settings. When combined with sensor networks, which continuously collect a wide array of patient health data, blockchain provides a solution that enhances data integrity, security, and Accessibility. This innovative integration will revolutionize healthcare by offering unprecedented data management and patient care efficiency.

Sensor networks in healthcare, encompassing a range of devices from wearable health monitors to sophisticated hospital equipment, generate a wealth of data crucial for patient diagnosis, treatment, and monitoring. Integrating these networks with blockchain technology ensures that this data is securely stored and managed and readily accessible and verifiable by authorized healthcare providers. This seamless interaction between blockchain and sensor networks enables real-time monitoring and analysis of patient data, facilitating timely medical interventions and improved patient outcomes.

Integrating blockchain with sensor networks presents a beacon of innovation and progress as the healthcare sector grapples with challenges such as data fragmentation, security vulnerabilities, and the growing demand for personalized care. It opens up new possibilities for remote patient monitoring, efficient data handling in clinical trials, and enhanced patient engagement in their healthcare journeys. However, as with any pioneering technology, this integration has challenges and considerations, including scalability, energy consumption, regulatory compliance, and user adoption.

On a global scale, blockchain integration into healthcare systems promises significant improvements. In developing countries, where healthcare infrastructure may be lacking, blockchain can provide a secure and efficient way to manage patient data, improving the quality of care. It can enhance existing healthcare systems in developed countries by improving efficiency, reducing costs, and facilitating personalized care.

Blockchain technology holds tremendous potential for transforming healthcare data management. Its ability to enhance data security, improve interoperability, and ensure compliance and consent management addresses some of the most pressing challenges in the healthcare sector. Additionally, its applications in fraud prevention, data analysis, patient engagement, and global health system improvements further underscore its potential impact.

As the healthcare industry evolves, blockchain technology could be critical in driving innovations that lead to better patient care, more efficient systems, and a more empowered patient population. However, realizing this potential will require collaboration among healthcare professionals, technologists, policymakers, and patients to navigate the technical, ethical, and regulatory challenges of this promising technology.

In this exploration, we delve into the nuances of this integration, uncovering its potential benefits, real-world applications, and the hurdles that lie ahead. As we navigate through this exciting convergence of technology, we are not just looking at incremental improvements in healthcare data management but a paradigm shift toward a more secure, efficient, and patient-centric healthcare system.

8.6.1 Expanding the potential of integration

The fusion of blockchain technology with sensor networks in the healthcare sector presents an innovative approach to managing the ever-growing volume of health data. Sensor networks, which continuously gather substantial amounts of patient information, can significantly benefit from blockchain's robust security and efficient data management capabilities. This integration ensures the integrity and security of the data and facilitates immediate access for healthcare providers, a crucial factor in timely and effective patient care (Li et al., 2022a).

8.6.2 Diverse real-world applications

The practical applications of integrating blockchain with sensor networks are extensive and varied. A prime example is remote patient monitoring, where data captured by sensors, such as vital signs or blood glucose levels, is securely uploaded to a blockchain. This enables healthcare professionals to access up-to-date patient information in real-time, enhancing the quality of remote care.

In the context of clinical trials, this integration offers a groundbreaking solution for data integrity. By recording trial data on a blockchain, researchers can create a transparent and immutable record, significantly reducing the risk of data tampering and ensuring the credibility of trial outcomes.

Another promising application is medication adherence, where sensors can track patients' medication intake and update the information on a blockchain, allowing healthcare providers to monitor compliance effectively (Hang & Kim, 2019).

8.6.3 Addressing challenges for future progress

Despite its potential, blockchain integration with sensor networks faces several challenges that must be addressed to realize its full potential. Technical challenges include scalability, as the volume of data generated by sensors can be immense, and energy consumption, particularly in blockchain operations.

Nontechnical challenges involve navigating the complex regulatory compliance landscape ensuring the integration adheres to healthcare regulations like HIPAA. Moreover, user adoption is critical; both healthcare providers and patients must be willing to embrace this new technology (Bhushan et al., 2020).

8.6.4 Looking toward a brighter future in healthcare

Looking forward, integrating blockchain with sensor networks in healthcare holds great promise. It paves the way for more personalized, efficient, and secure healthcare delivery. As technology evolves, future developments could see advancements in AI and machine learning integration, enhancing data analysis and predictive healthcare.

Continuous innovation, robust infrastructure development, and comprehensive education and training for healthcare professionals and patients are essential to leverage this integration fully. Collaborative efforts among technologists, healthcare professionals, policymakers, and patients will be crucial in overcoming these challenges.

Integrating blockchain with sensor networks represents a significant stride toward revolutionizing healthcare data management. It offers a future where healthcare is more secure, efficient, and tailored to individual patient needs, ultimately leading to improved health outcomes and a more resilient healthcare system (Farouk et al., 2020).

8.7 Technical overview of integrating blockchain with sensor networks

Integrating blockchain technology with sensor networks in healthcare forms a symbiotic relationship that leverages both technologies' strengths. Sensor networks, which include a wide array of devices from wearable health monitors to in-hospital sensors, continuously generate vast amounts of healthcare data. Integrating these networks with blockchain involves securely transmitting the data collected by sensors to a blockchain system.

This process typically begins with sensors collecting data and sending it to a local processing unit or a cloud-based system. Once the data reaches the cloud, it can be encrypted and added to a blockchain. Each data point becomes a transaction on the blockchain, creating an immutable record of the health data collected by the sensors.

Smart contracts, a key feature of blockchain, can automate responses based on the data received. For example, if a sensor detects a critical change in a patient's vital signs, a smart contract can automatically alert healthcare providers or trigger emergency protocols.

8.7.1 Ensuring security and privacy

Security in this integrated system is paramount, especially given the sensitive nature of healthcare data. Blockchain's inherent encryption and decentralization provide a robust security framework. Data encryption before it is added to the blockchain ensures that even if data is intercepted, it remains unreadable and secure. Additionally, blockchain's decentralized nature means no single point of failure, significantly reducing the risk of data breaches (Hsiao & Sung, 2021).

8.7.1.1 Enhanced security

One of the most significant benefits of integrating blockchain with sensor networks is the enhanced security of sensitive healthcare data. Blockchain's decentralized and encrypted nature provides a much more secure framework than traditional centralized databases. Each data block is linked to the previous one, making altering any information without detection extremely difficult. This feature is crucial in healthcare, where data integrity can be a matter of life and death (Hsiao & Sung, 2021; Nguyen, 2021).

8.7.1.2 Data integrity and immutability

The immutability of blockchain ensures that once sensor data is recorded, it cannot be altered retroactively. This aspect of blockchain is vital for maintaining the integrity of healthcare data. In scenarios where the accuracy of medical records is critical, such as clinical trials or chronic disease management, blockchain assures that the data has not been tampered with (Rahman et al., 2022).

8.7.1.3 Real-time data access

Blockchain enables real-time access to data collected by sensor networks. Healthcare providers can access up-to-date patient information quickly and efficiently, allowing for more timely and informed medical decisions. This real-time access is particularly beneficial in emergencies, where every second counts (Gope et al., 2019).

8.7.1.4 Blockchain-enabled sensor networks in action

One notable case study is using blockchain-enabled sensor networks in remote patient monitoring. For instance, a project might involve patients with chronic diseases wearing sensors that monitor vital signs like blood glucose or heart rate. This data is then securely recorded on a blockchain, giving doctors real-time access to patient data.

Another example is using blockchain and sensor networks to manage drug supply chains. Sensors track medication temperatures and handling conditions, recorded on a blockchain. This ensures the integrity of the drugs and compliance with safety standards (Nguyen et al., 2020).

8.8 Challenges and considerations

8.8.1 Technical challenges

Implementing blockchain in healthcare presents several technical challenges. Integrating blockchain with healthcare IT systems can be complex, requiring substantial effort and expertise. Ensuring compatibility and seamless data exchange between legacy systems and blockchain platforms is crucial.

Another technical challenge is handling large volumes of data generated in healthcare. Blockchain networks can experience reduced efficiency and increased transaction times as the volume of data grows. This issue is compounded in sensor network integrations, where real-time data collection produces continuous information (Xie et al., 2019).

Additionally, the security of blockchain systems, while robust, is attainable. The risk of 51% attacks, where a user or group gains control of most of the network's mining power, can pose a threat. However, it's more theoretical in private blockchains typically used in healthcare.

8.8.2 Ethical challenges

Ethical challenges in implementing blockchain in healthcare primarily revolve around patient data. The immutability of blockchain raises concerns about the correction of erroneous data. Once information is entered into a blockchain, rectifying mistakes can be challenging without compromising the ledger's integrity.

Privacy is another ethical concern. While blockchain can enhance data security, the transparency of the blockchain ledger could expose sensitive patient information. Balancing openness and privacy is delicate, necessitating robust encryption and strict access controls (Gross & Miller, 2019).

Informed consent for data sharing in a blockchain environment is also a crucial ethical consideration. Patients must fully know how their data is used, stored, and shared within blockchain systems, aligning with moral patient autonomy and consent standards.

8.8.3 Scalability challenges

Scalability is a significant concern when integrating blockchain with sensor networks in healthcare. Blockchain networks, particularly those using proof of work (PoW) consensus mechanisms, can suffer from slow transaction processing times and high energy consumption, which is impractical for large-scale implementations.

Sensor networks in healthcare generate vast amounts of data continuously, which can overwhelm a blockchain system not designed for high transaction throughput. This limitation can lead to data recording and access delays, hindering the real-time data analysis crucial in healthcare settings.

Several solutions are being explored to address scalability issues. These include using alternative consensus mechanisms like proof of stake (PoS) or delegated PoS, which are more energy-efficient and faster. Other approaches include off-chain transactions and sharding, where the blockchain is divided into smaller, more manageable pieces (Adavoudi Jolfaei et al., 2021).

8.8.4 Navigating regulatory landscapes

Regulatory and compliance considerations are paramount in the implementation of blockchain in healthcare. Healthcare data is subject to stringent regulations, such as the HIPAA in the United States, which sets data privacy and security standards.

Blockchain applications in healthcare must ensure compliance with these regulations, which can be challenging given blockchain's decentralized and immutable nature—for instance, HIPAA's right to erasure conflicts with blockchain's permanence, posing a compliance dilemma.

Furthermore, the global nature of blockchain networks introduces complexities in compliance with international laws and standards. Data stored on a blockchain may be subject to different regulatory requirements depending on location, necessitating careful consideration of cross-border data flows (Makinde et al., 2023).

8.9 Summary

The chapter comprehensively explores how blockchain-enabled sensor networks can address healthcare data management challenges. It begins by presenting the current landscape, a mix of outdated and modern systems that need help with the volume, security, and interoperability of healthcare data. Integrating blockchain technology with sensor networks is introduced as a solution that offers real-time data collection, enhanced security, and improved data accessibility.

Blockchain is described as an immutable and transparent decentralized digital ledger, making it suitable for sensitive healthcare data management. The technology offers solutions to problems of data security and interoperability and provides a new approach to patient consent management, addressing compliance with regulations like HIPAA.

The chapter also highlights the role of sensor networks in healthcare, which includes monitoring vital signs, managing chronic diseases, and supporting medical research. Integrating these networks with blockchain technology promises to enhance the integrity and security of healthcare data while enabling real-time monitoring and analysis, leading to better patient outcomes.

Practical applications of this integration include remote patient monitoring, clinical trials, and medication adherence. However, the chapter acknowledges that technical challenges like scalability and energy consumption, regulatory compliance, and user adoption must be addressed.

In conclusion, the chapter emphasizes the potential of blockchain and sensor networks to transform healthcare data management, making systems more secure, efficient, and patient-centered. It calls for collaboration among stakeholders to overcome technical, ethical, and regulatory challenges and realize the full benefits of these technologies.

References

Adavoudi Jolfaei, A., Aghili, S. F., & Singelee, D. (2021). A survey on blockchain-based IoMT systems: Towards scalability. *IEEE Access*, 9. Available from https://doi.org/10.1109/ACCESS.2021.3117662, http://ieeexplore.ieee.org/xpl/RecentIssue.jsp?punumber = 6287639.

Agbo, C., Mahmoud, Q., & Eklund, J. (2019). Blockchain technology in healthcare: A systematic review. *Healthcare*, 7(2), 56. Available from https://doi.org/10.3390/healthcare7020056.

Al-Fayoumi, M. A. (1990). Techniques of medical image encryption taxonomy. *Bulletin of Electrical Engineering and Informatics*, 1990.

Bhushan, B., Khamparia, A., Sagayam, K. M., Sharma, S. K., Ahad, M. A., & Debnath, N. C. (2020). Blockchain for smart cities: A review of architectures, integration trends and future research directions. *Sustainable Cities and Society*, 61. Available from https://doi.org/10.1016/j.scs.2020.102360, http://www.elsevier.com/wps/find/journaldescription.cws_home/724360/description#description.

Bittins, S., Kober, G., Margheri, A., Masi, M., Miladi, A., & Sassone, V. (2021). Healthcare data management by using blockchain technology. *Studies in Big Data, 83*. Available from https://doi.org/10.1007/978-981-15-9547-9_1, springer.com/series/11970.

Dash, S., Shakyawar, S. K., Sharma, M., & Kaushik, S. (2019). Big data in healthcare: Management, analysis and future prospects. *Journal of Big Data, 6*(1). Available from https://doi.org/10.1186/s40537-019-0217-0, https://journalofbigdata.springeropen.com.

Dhillon, V., Metcalf, D., & Hooper, M. (2021). Blockchain enabled applications: Understand the blockchain ecosystem and how to make it work for you. United States: Apress Media LLC. Available from https://doi.org/10.1007/978-1-4842-6534-5, https://link.springer.com/book/10.1007/978-1-4842-6534-5.

Farouk, A., Alahmadi, A., Ghose, S., & Mashatan, A. (2020). Blockchain platform for industrial healthcare: Vision and future opportunities. *Computer Communications, 154*. Available from https://doi.org/10.1016/j.comcom.2020.02.058, http://www.journals.elsevier.com/computer-communications/.

Gope, P., Kumar Das, A., Kumar, N., & Cheng, Y. (2019). Lightweight and physically secure anonymous mutual authentication protocol for real-time data access in industrial wireless sensor networks. *IEEE Transactions on Industrial Informatics, 15*(9). Available from https://doi.org/10.1109/tii.2019.2895030.

Gross, M. S., & Miller, R. C. (2019). Ethical implementation of the learning healthcare system with blockchain technology. *Blockchain in Healthcare Today, 2*. Available from https://doi.org/10.30953/bhty.v2.113, https://blockchainhealthcaretoday.com/e7652a1a-70b8-4ba0-ab19-6ff622f1a7de.

Hang, L., & Kim, D.-H. (2019). Design and implementation of an integrated iot blockchain platform for sensing data integrity. *Sensors, 19*(10), 2228. Available from https://doi.org/10.3390/s19102228.

Hasselgren, A., Kralevska, K., Gligoroski, D., Pedersen, S. A., & Faxvaag, A. (2020). Blockchain in healthcare and health sciences—A scoping review. *International Journal of Medical Informatics, 134*. Available from https://doi.org/10.1016/j.ijmedinf.2019.104040, http://www.elsevier.com/inca/publications/store/5/0/6/0/4/0/.

Hsiao, S. J., & Sung, W. T. (2021). Employing blockchain technology to strengthen security of wireless sensor networks. *IEEE Access, 9*. Available from https://doi.org/10.1109/ACCESS.2021.3079708, http://ieeexplore.ieee.org/xpl/RecentIssue.jsp?punumber = 6287639.

Keshta, I., & Odeh, A. (2021). Security and privacy of electronic health records: Concerns and challenges. *Egyptian Informatics Journal, 22*(2). Available from https://doi.org/10.1016/j.eij.2020.07.003, http://www.elsevier.com/wps/find/journaldescription.cws_home/723777/description#description.

Li, G., He, B., Wang, Z., Cheng, X., & Chen, J. (2022a). Blockchain-enhanced spatiotemporal data aggregation for UAV-assisted wireless sensor networks. *IEEE Transactions on Industrial Informatics, 18*(7). Available from https://doi.org/10.1109/TII.2021.3120973, http://ieeexplore.ieee.org/xpl/RecentIssue.jsp?punumber = 9424.

Li, J., et al. (2022b). A study of health insurance fraud in China and recommendations for fraud detection and prevention. *Journal of Organizational and End User Computing, 34*(4), 1−19. Available from https://doi.org/10.4018/joeuc.301271.

Makinde, A. S., Agbeyangi, A. O., & Omaji, S. (2023). Integration of blockchain into medical data security: Key features, use cases, technical challenges, and future directions. *Contemporary Applications of Data Fusion for Advanced Healthcare Informatics*. Available from https://doi.org/10.4018/978-1-6684-8913-0.ch006, https://www.igi-global.com/book/contemporary-applications-data-fusion-advanced/316653.

McGhin, T., Choo, K. K. R., Liu, C. Z., & He, D. (2019). Blockchain in healthcare applications: Research challenges and opportunities. *Journal of Network and Computer Applications, 135*. Available from https://doi.org/10.1016/j.jnca.2019.02.027, http://www.elsevier.com/inca/publications/store/6/2/2/8/9/3/index.htt.

Nguyen, G. N., Le Viet, N. H., Devaraj, A. F. S., Gobi, R., & Shankar, K. (2020). Blockchain enabled energy efficient red deer algorithm based clustering protocol for pervasive wireless sensor networks. *Sustainable Computing: Informatics and Systems, 28*. Available from https://doi.org/10.1016/j.suscom.2020.100464, http://www.elsevier.com/wps/find/journaldescription.cws_home/724189/description#description.

Nguyen, P. P., et al. (2021). *Sexually transmitted diseases*, 2021.

Oakley, A. (2023). HIPAA, HIPPA, or HIPPO: What really is the heath insurance portability and accountability act? *Biotechnology Law Report, 42*(6). Available from https://doi.org/10.1089/blr.2023.29329.aso, http://www.liebertonline.com/blr.

Odeh, A., & Abu Taleb, A. (2023). Ensemble-based deep learning models for enhancing iot intrusion detection. *Applied Sciences, 13*(21), 11985. Available from https://doi.org/10.3390/app132111985.

Odeh, A., Taleb, A. A., Alhajahjeh, T., & Navarro, F. (2023). Invisible shield: Unveiling an efficient watermarking solution for medical imaging security. *Applied Sciences, 13*(24), 13291. Available from https://doi.org/10.3390/app132413291.

Palma, F. N. S. (n.d.) Digital health beyond borders: Interoperability challenges and critical success factors in the deployment of cross-border. ePrescription in Finland and Estonia.

Prokofieva, M., & Miah, S. J. (2019). Blockchain in healthcare. *Australasian Journal of Information Systems, 23*. Available from https://doi.org/10.3127/ajis.v23i0.2203, https://journal.acs.org.au/index.php/ajis/issue/archive.

Rahman, M. S., Chamikara, M. A. P., Khalil, I., & Bouras, A. (2022). Blockchain-of-blockchains: An interoperable blockchain platform for ensuring IoT data integrity in smart city. *Journal of Industrial Information Integration, 30*100408. Available from https://doi.org/10.1016/j.jii.2022.100408.

Rehman, A., Naz, S., & Razzak, I. (2022). Leveraging big data analytics in healthcare enhancement: trends, challenges and opportunities. *Multimedia Systems, 28*(4), 1339–1371. Available from https://doi.org/10.1007/s00530-020-00736-8, http://www.springer.com/journal/530.

Stadler,A. (2021). *The health insurance portability and accountability act and its impact on privacy and confidentiality in healthcare.*

Tobiano, G., Chaboyer, W., Teasdale, T., Raleigh, R., & Manias, E. (2019). Patient engagement in admission and discharge medication communication: A systematic mixed studies review. *International Journal of Nursing Studies, 95*. Available from https://doi.org/10.1016/j.ijnurstu.2019.04.009, http://www.elsevier.com/locate/ijnurstu.

Upadhyay, N. (2020). Demystifying blockchain: A critical analysis of challenges, applications and opportunities. *International Journal of Information Management, 54*102120. Available from https://doi.org/10.1016/j.ijinfomgt.2020.102120.

Xie, J., Tang, H., Huang, T., Yu, F. R., Xie, R., Liu, J., & Liu, Y. (2019). A survey of blockchain technology applied to smart cities: Research issues and challenges. *IEEE Communications Surveys and Tutorials, 21*(3). Available from https://doi.org/10.1109/COMST.2019.2899617, http://ieeexplore.ieee.org/xpl/RecentIssue.jsp?punumber = 9739.

Yaqoob, I., Salah, K., Jayaraman, R., & Al-Hammadi, Y. (2022). Blockchain for healthcare data management: Opportunities, challenges, and future recommendations. *Neural Computing and Applications, 34*(14), 14333058. Available from https://doi.org/10.1007/s00521-020-05519-w, http://link.springer.com/journal/521.

Sensor networks and blockchain platforms for the future healthcare

Quazi Mamun

School of Computing, Mathematics and Engineering, Faculty of Business, Justice and
Behavioural Sciences Charles Sturt University, NSW, Australia

9.1 Introduction

The healthcare industry is undergoing a significant transformation propelled by technological advancements (Saeed et al., 2022). Integrating sensor networks and blockchain technology is an exciting development that offers opportunities to revolutionize healthcare delivery, patient outcomes, and data management (Arunachalam et al., 2023). This chapter explores the potential of these two technologies in shaping healthcare's future.

As the global population ages and the burden of chronic diseases increases, the demand for innovative solutions that enhance the quality of care while optimizing healthcare resources becomes more pressing. Sensor networks and blockchain technology are the most promising solutions to these challenges. Sensor networks can collect real-time data, monitor patients, and provide a holistic understanding of an individual's health. On the other hand, blockchain technology offers a decentralized and secure ledger that can record and verify transactions across a network of computers, ensuring the integrity and confidentiality of health records. (Ananth et al., 2018; Haleem et al., 2021; Kuo & Ohno-Machado, 2018).

The combination of sensor networks and blockchain technology provides a unique opportunity to overcome existing limitations in healthcare, fostering innovations in diagnostics, treatment strategies, and patient engagement (Liu et al., 2023). This chapter provides a comprehensive exploration of integrating these two technologies in the context of future healthcare. It examines the merits of sensor networks and blockchain and elaborates on how their combined utilization can address healthcare challenges.

The chapter is divided into several sections that follow a logical sequence. It begins with a background discussion that traces the historical context of sensor networks and blockchain in healthcare. The subsequent sections explore the individual contributions

Sensor Networks for Smart Hospitals
DOI: https://doi.org/10.1016/B978-0-443-36370-2.00010-4

of sensor networks and blockchain, exploring their applications and intricacies. The integration of these technologies is then examined, exploring how their collaboration can reshape healthcare delivery. The chapter also discusses the advantages and challenges of this integration, offering a nuanced perspective on its implications for security, privacy, and ethical considerations. Concrete use cases and applications are presented, illustrating the real-world impact of these technologies on healthcare.

The later sections of the chapter explore the security and privacy aspects, shedding light on the critical considerations in managing healthcare data. Finally, the chapter concludes by envisioning future trends, emerging technologies, and the evolving healthcare landscape, with sensor networks and blockchain at the forefront. The concluding remarks highlight the significance of continued research, innovation, and ethical implementation as we navigate this transformative journey into the future of healthcare.

9.2 Background

9.2.1 historical context of sensor networks in healthcare

The historical trajectory of sensor networks in healthcare is deeply intertwined with the broader evolution of information technology and the pursuit of enhanced patient care. The early roots of sensor applications in healthcare can be traced back to the mid-20th century when rudimentary sensors were employed for essential physiological monitoring (Dario et al., 2003). However, the advent of microelectronics in the latter half of the century marked a paradigm shift, enabling the development of more sophisticated and miniaturized sensors (Öberg et al., 2004).

In the 1970s and 1980s, the healthcare industry witnessed a surge in using sensors for monitoring vital signs such as heart rate, blood pressure, and temperature. Though limited in scope, these early applications laid the foundation for subsequent advancements. The late 20th century saw the emergence of wearable sensors (Gendy & Yuce, 2023; Mukhopadhyay et al., 2022), allowing individuals to monitor their health in real-time. Devices like heart rate monitors and pedometers became popular, marking a consumer-oriented approach to healthcare monitoring (He et al., 2023).

The 21st century ushered in a new era of sensor networks in healthcare, propelled by the convergence of several technological trends. The proliferation of smartphones with built-in sensors and the Internet of Things (IoT) revolutionized the landscape (Akhtar & Rehmani, 2017). Today, sensor networks encompass various devices, from wearables and implantable sensors (Wang, 2023) to ambient sensors embedded in smart homes (Beyaz, 2022). These networks enable continuous monitoring of physiological parameters and facilitate the collection of contextual data, providing a more comprehensive understanding of an individual's health (Costanzo et al., 2022).

9.2.2 Evolution of healthcare technologies and the challenges they aim to address

The evolution of healthcare technologies reflects an ongoing quest to address persistent challenges and enhance the quality of patient care. Historically, healthcare delivery was characterized by manual record-keeping, limited diagnostic tools, and a reactive rather than proactive approach to patient management. The advent of electronic health records (EHRs) in the late 20th century marked a significant milestone, streamlining data management and enhancing the accessibility of patient information (Begum et al., 2013).

As medical imaging technologies advanced, with the introduction of computed tomography and magnetic resonance imaging, diagnostic capabilities improved, enabling more accurate and noninvasive examinations. However, these advancements also introduced challenges related to the massive volumes of data generated by these technologies, necessitating robust storage, retrieval, and analysis solutions.

The late 20th century witnessed the emergence of telemedicine, driven by advancements in telecommunications. This facilitated remote consultations, improved access to healthcare in underserved areas, and laid the groundwork for the digitalization of healthcare services. Nevertheless, challenges persisted, including concerns about data security, interoperability issues among disparate systems, and the need for a comprehensive approach to patient-centered care.

9.2.3 Brief overview of sensor networks and blockchain technology

9.2.3.1 Sensor networks

Sensor networks in healthcare refer to interconnected sensors that collaboratively collect, process and transmit patient health data. These networks have evolved from early physiological monitors to encompass a spectrum of devices, from wearable fitness trackers to implantable sensors and ambient sensors embedded in intelligent environments (Raman et al., 2023).

The architecture of sensor networks typically involves the deployment of sensors on or within the body, creating a continuous data stream. These sensors capture physiological parameters such as heart rate, blood glucose levels, and activity patterns. The data generated is then transmitted to a centralized system or a cloud-based platform for further analysis.

The advent of IoT has significantly expanded the capabilities of sensor networks by enabling seamless communication between devices (Aazam et al., 2020). Wearable sensors, for instance, can communicate with smartphones or other smart devices, providing real-time feedback to users and healthcare providers. Integrating sensor networks with data analytics and artificial intelligence (AI) further enhances the interpretability of the collected data, facilitating early detection of anomalies and personalized healthcare interventions.

9.2.3.2 Blockchain technology

Initially devised as the underlying framework for cryptocurrencies, blockchain technology has evolved into a versatile and secure system with applications across various industries, including healthcare (Monrat et al., 2019). At its core, a blockchain is a decentralized and distributed ledger that records transactions across a network of computers. Each transaction, or block, is cryptographically linked to the previous one, forming a chain of blocks.

In healthcare, blockchain technology addresses critical data management, security, and interoperability challenges (Dimitrov, 2019). One of the key attributes of blockchain is its immutability; once a block is added to the chain, it cannot be altered, ensuring the integrity of the data recorded. This feature is precious in healthcare, where the accuracy and security of patient records are paramount.

Blockchain facilitates the secure and transparent sharing of health data among stakeholders. Patients, healthcare providers, and other authorized entities can access a patient's complete and unaltered medical history, promoting collaborative and patient-centric care. Smart contracts, self-executing contracts with the terms of the agreement directly written into code, further streamline processes such as billing and insurance claims (Banate, 2023).

9.2.4 Intersection of sensor networks and blockchain in healthcare

The intersection of sensor networks and blockchain technology in healthcare has gained much attention recently due to its potential for improving healthcare delivery. This convergence combines real-time data acquisition with secure, decentralized data management. The symbiotic relationship between these two technologies addresses longstanding challenges in healthcare, ranging from data silos and security concerns to the need for seamless interoperability.

Sensor networks offer real-time data acquisition and transmission, enabling healthcare professionals to monitor patients remotely and make informed decisions about their care. On the other hand, blockchain technology provides a secure, tamper-proof, and decentralized ledger for storing and managing healthcare data (Zhang et al., 2017). This combination can revolutionize healthcare by improving data security, patient empowerment, and proactive management.

In the later sections, we will explore the technical intricacies of sensor networks and blockchain technology, delving into their applications, advantages, and challenges. We will then shift our focus towards integrating these technologies, illustrating how their combined use can usher in a new era of healthcare delivery characterized by enhanced data security, patient empowerment, and proactive healthcare management. By examining use cases, security considerations, and potential future trends, this chapter aims to provide a comprehensive understanding of the transformative potential of sensor networks and blockchain in shaping the future of healthcare.

Overall, the combination of sensor networks and blockchain technology has the potential to transform the healthcare industry by improving data security, patient empowerment, and proactive healthcare management. By exploring the technical intricacies of these technologies and their integration, we can gain a deep understanding of how they can revolutionize the healthcare delivery system for the betterment of society.

9.3 Sensor networks in healthcare

Sensor networks have emerged as a transformative force in healthcare, offering a dynamic and real-time approach to monitoring and managing patients' health. This section explores sensor networks' evolution, types, and applications within the healthcare landscape.

9.3.1 Evolution of sensor networks in healthcare

The inception of sensor networks in healthcare can be traced back to the mid-20th century, with the early use of rudimentary sensors for basic physiological monitoring. The evolution gained momentum with the advent of microelectronics, enabling the development of more sophisticated and miniaturized sensors. In the late 20th century, the healthcare industry witnessed a surge in the use of sensors for monitoring vital signs such as heart rate, blood pressure (Huynh et al., 2019), and temperature.

Advancements in microsensor technologies, coupled with the proliferation of smartphones and the IoT, propelled the transformation of sensor networks in healthcare (Al-Fuqaha, 2015; Cai et al., 2019). Wearable sensors, implanted devices, and ambient sensors in smart environments became integral components of sensor networks, allowing for continuous and nonintrusive monitoring of patient's health (Gao et al., 2023).

9.3.2 Types of sensors used in healthcare

Sensor networks in healthcare encompass a diverse range of sensors designed to capture various physiological, environmental, and behavioral data. Understanding the types of sensors is essential for appreciating the breadth of data that can be collected for comprehensive health monitoring.

9.3.2.1 Physiological sensors

Physiological sensors play a pivotal role in healthcare and technology, continuously monitoring various physiological parameters. These sensors are designed to measure and record data related to bodily functions, providing valuable insights into an individual's health status. The discussion on physiological sensors encompasses their significance, applications, challenges, and advancements.

- **Significance:** Physiological sensors have become integral to modern healthcare, enabling real-time monitoring and assessment of an individual's vital signs (Cook et al., 2019). Parameters such as heart rate, blood pressure, body temperature, respiratory rate (Andreozzi et al., 2021), and electrocardiography (ECG) can be monitored using these sensors. Their significance lies in the early detection of abnormalities, facilitating timely intervention and personalized healthcare. Physiological sensors aid in clinical settings and empower individuals to manage their health proactively through wearable devices.
- **Applications:** Physiological sensors find diverse applications across various domains. In healthcare, they are used for patient monitoring, diagnostics, and disease management. Wearable devices with physiological sensors have gained popularity for fitness tracking and wellness monitoring (Park, 2023). These sensors are also employed in sports science, aviation, and the military for performance assessment and safety. Moreover, physiological sensors are crucial in research settings to gather data on human physiology and behavior studies (Zhu et al., 2017).

- **Challenges:** Despite their advancements, physiological sensors come with challenges. Sensor accuracy, reliability, and standardization remain critical concerns. Variability in individual physiology, environmental factors, and sensor calibration can affect the precision of measurements. Privacy and data security issues arise with the widespread use of wearable sensors, raising questions about protecting sensitive health information (Son et al., 2019). Furthermore, integrating diverse physiological parameters into a comprehensive monitoring system presents engineering and computational challenges.
- **Advancements:** Recent advancements in physiological sensors focus on enhancing accuracy, minimizing invasiveness, and expanding the range of measurable parameters. The miniaturization of sensors allows for an unobtrusive integration into clothing or accessories. AI and machine learning (ML) techniques analyze complex physiological data patterns, providing more nuanced insights into health conditions (Deng et al., 2023). Continuous innovation in materials and sensor technologies contributes to improved wearability and durability of these devices.

9.3.2.2 Diagnostic sensors

Diagnostic sensors significantly impact modern healthcare by facilitating the rapid and accurate identification of various medical conditions. These sensors are designed to detect specific biomarkers or physiological signals associated with diseases, enabling clinicians to make informed decisions about patient diagnosis and treatment. This short discussion will explore the significance, applications, challenges, and advancements in diagnostic sensors.

- **Significance:** Diagnostic sensors are paramount in healthcare as they enable early and precise detection of diseases. They provide a noninvasive or minimally invasive means to analyze biological samples or monitor physiological parameters, allowing for timely interventions and personalized treatment plans. The significance of diagnostic sensors lies in their potential to improve patient outcomes, reduce healthcare costs, and contribute to the overall efficiency of healthcare systems.
- **Applications:** The applications of diagnostic sensors span a wide range of medical fields. In clinical laboratories, these sensors are utilized for analyzing blood, urine, and other bodily fluids to detect specific markers associated with diseases such as diabetes, cardiovascular disorders, and infectious diseases. Point-of-care diagnostic sensors offer rapid testing outside traditional laboratory settings, facilitating immediate decisions at the bedside (Kumar et al., 2021). Molecular diagnostic sensors, including those based on DNA or RNA analysis, are crucial in identifying genetic markers associated with cancer and hereditary diseases.
- **Challenges:** Despite their significant contributions, diagnostic sensors face challenges that must be addressed. Ensuring the accuracy and reliability of diagnostic results is a persistent concern, as variations in sample quality and environmental conditions can impact sensor performance. The development of standardised protocols and validation processes is essential to establish the credibility of diagnostic sensor technologies. Additionally, issues related to the cost-effectiveness of sensor-based diagnostic methods and integrating these technologies into existing healthcare infrastructures require careful consideration.

- **Advancements:** Advancements in diagnostic sensor technologies focus on improving sensitivity, specificity, and accessibility. Nanotechnology and microfluidics have enabled the development of miniaturized sensors that require smaller sample volumes and offer rapid results. Integration with smartphone applications and telemedicine platforms has expanded the reach of diagnostic sensors, particularly in remote or resource-limited settings. Furthermore, biosensor design and material sciences advancements contribute to developing innovative sensor platforms with enhanced performance characteristics (Gharib et al., 2022; Kassal et al., 2018).

9.3.2.3 *Environmental sensors*

Ambient sensors monitor environmental factors impacting health, such as air quality, temperature, and humidity. These sensors find applications in smart homes, hospitals, and healthcare facilities to create a health-supportive environment.

- **Significance:** Environmental sensors have emerged as indispensable assets in healthcare, revolutionizing patient care and well-being. These sensors are designed to monitor and control environmental factors critical to health within medical facilities. Their significance lies in creating an atmosphere conducive to healing, minimizing infection risks, and optimizing conditions for patients and healthcare practitioners.
- **Applications:**
  - *Infection Control*: Environmental sensors are pivotal in infection prevention within healthcare settings. By monitoring air quality and detecting potential pathogens, these sensors contribute to maintaining sterile environments. In operating rooms and isolation units, they ensure that air is free from contaminants, reducing the risk of hospital-acquired infections.
  - *Temperature and Humidity Management*: Patient comfort and recovery are closely tied to environmental conditions. Sensors regulating temperature and humidity create an optimal healing environment. In patient rooms and recovery areas, these sensors contribute to maintaining a comfortable climate, supporting the healing process, and enhancing overall well-being.
  - *Ventilation Systems*: Efficient ventilation is critical in healthcare facilities. Environmental sensors monitor air circulation and quality, ensuring ventilation systems operate optimally. This is particularly crucial when airborne contaminants, such as laboratories, pharmacies, and patient rooms, must be minimized.
  - *Occupancy Monitoring*: To streamline energy usage and enhance safety, sensors monitor room occupancy. In healthcare facilities, this helps optimize lighting, heating, and cooling based on actual needs. Additionally, it aids in tracking the movement of patients and staff, contributing to better resource management.
- **Challenges:** Despite their transformative impact, deploying environmental sensors in healthcare is challenging. Ensuring compliance with healthcare regulations, addressing privacy concerns related to patient data, and achieving seamless integration with existing healthcare systems are notable hurdles. Overcoming these challenges is crucial for unlocking the full potential of environmental sensors in healthcare.
- **Advancements:** The landscape of environmental sensors in healthcare is marked by continuous advancements. The miniaturization of sensors, enhanced data analytics

capabilities, and integration with the IoT are driving progress. AI and ML applications further empower these sensors to provide predictive insights, allowing healthcare professionals to address environmental factors affecting patient well-being proactively.

9.3.2.4 Wearable sensors

Wearable sensors are integrated into devices that individuals can wear, such as smart-watches, fitness trackers, and smart clothing. These sensors continuously monitor physical activity, sleep patterns, and physiological parameters, providing valuable insights into an individual's overall well-being.

- **Significance:** Wearable sensors have ushered in a new era in healthcare, shifting the focus from reactive to proactive patient care. The importance of wearable sensors lies in their ability to continuously monitor vital health metrics, providing real-time data for patients and healthcare providers. This paradigm shift towards preventive and personalized care empowers individuals to manage their well-being actively.
- **Applications:**
  - *Health Monitoring*: Wearable sensors in devices like smartwatches and fitness trackers enable continuous health monitoring (He et al., 2023). They track vital signs such as heart rate, blood pressure, and sleep patterns, offering valuable insights into an individual's overall health. This real-time data facilitates the early detection of anomalies and empowers users to take preventive actions.
  - *Chronic Disease Management*: Patients with chronic conditions benefit immensely from wearable sensors. For conditions like diabetes, sensors can monitor glucose levels, providing timely alerts and reducing the need for frequent invasive testing. In cardiac care, wearables assist in tracking ECG patterns, enhancing the management of heart-related conditions.
  - *Physical Activity and Rehabilitation*: Wearables are pivotal in promoting physical activity and aiding rehabilitation (Abed et al., 2021). They monitor activity levels, offering personalized exercise recommendations. In rehabilitation settings, sensors track movements and adherence to prescribed exercises, enhancing the effectiveness of rehabilitation programs.
- **Challenges:** Despite their transformative potential, wearable sensors face data accuracy, user adherence, and privacy challenges. Ensuring the precision of health metrics, encouraging consistent usage, and addressing privacy concerns are critical considerations for the widespread adoption of wearable sensor technologies in healthcare.
- **Advancements:** Advancements in wearable sensor technology are rapidly evolving. Ongoing trends include smaller form factors, improved sensor accuracy, and enhanced connectivity features. AI integration enables wearables to provide more insightful and actionable data. Additionally, innovations in materials and power sources contribute to developing more comfortable, durable, and energy-efficient wearables (Hu et al., 2017).

9.3.2.5 Implantable sensors

Implantable sensors stand at the forefront of healthcare technology, introducing a transformative paradigm for monitoring and managing various medical conditions.

These miniature devices, designed for insertion within the body, furnish continuous, real-time data that holds the potential to influence patient care significantly. The following discussion delves into the significance, applications, challenges, and advancements surrounding implantable sensors, elucidating their pivotal role in modern healthcare.

- **Significance:** Implantable sensors epitomize the shift towards personalized and precision medicine. Nestled within the body, they furnish a direct and continuous monitoring solution, furnishing healthcare professionals with accurate data on physiological parameters. This real-time information facilitates timely interventions, early disease detection, and optimized treatment plans.
- **Applications:** Implantable medical devices encompass a variety of sensors designed for different healthcare applications. In chronic disease management, implantable glucose monitors play a pivotal role. These devices continuously track glucose levels, providing precise data that enables healthcare professionals to make optimal insulin adjustments for individuals with diabetes. This ensures enhanced glucose control and contributes to more effective diabetes management. In cardiovascular health, implantable heart monitors have become indispensable (Andreozzi et al., 2021). They facilitate continuous cardiac activity monitoring, enabling the early detection of arrhythmias and other heart conditions. This proactive approach significantly improves cardiovascular health outcomes by allowing timely interventions and personalized treatment plans. For individuals grappling with neurological disorders like Parkinson's, implantable neurostimulators emerge as a groundbreaking solution (Calado et al., 2020). These devices deliver targeted stimulation to specific brain areas, effectively managing symptoms and enhancing the patient's quality of life. The precision offered by implantable neurostimulators represents a significant advancement in treating neurological conditions. In orthopedics, implantable sensors are employed to detect issues at an early stage. These sensors improve treatment outcomes by providing timely information for orthopedic conditions. Early detection allows healthcare professionals to implement tailored interventions, improving patient outcomes in orthopedic care.
- **Challenges:** Implantable sensors confront various challenges that require careful consideration for seamless integration. Achieving biocompatibility is a foremost challenge, requiring meticulous design to prevent adverse reactions or tissue rejection within the patient's body. The significance of biocompatibility cannot be overstated, as any negative response could compromise the device's functionality and, consequently, the patient's well-being. Another significant hurdle involves providing a stable and durable power source for these sensors within limited space constraints (Huang et al., 2017). The longevity of the sensor is intricately tied to its power supply, impacting the duration between replacement surgeries and overall patient well-being.

Moreover, ensuring data security is critical, with the challenge of safeguarding sensitive patient data transmitted by the implant. This concern is substantial, considering the potential risks associated with unauthorized access or data breaches. Overcoming these challenges is imperative for the widespread adoption and continued advancement of implantable sensors, emphasizing the need for innovative solutions to enhance their reliability, safety, and security in healthcare applications.

9.3.3 Challenges in implementing sensor networks in healthcare

While the potential benefits of sensor networks in healthcare are substantial, several challenges must be addressed to ensure their successful implementation and widespread adoption.

9.3.3.1 Data security and privacy concerns

Implementing sensor networks in healthcare introduces several data security and privacy concerns-related challenges. One of the primary challenges is the protection of sensitive health data. Healthcare sensor networks deal with highly confidential patient information, including medical records, vital signs, and treatment plans. The critical task is safeguarding this data from unauthorized access, breaches, or cyberattacks to ensure patient privacy and confidentiality (Al-Abadi et al., 2023).

Secure data transmission is another significant challenge. The data exchanged between sensors, devices, and healthcare systems must be transmitted in a safe and encrypted manner. Unprotected data transmission could expose patient information to interception and manipulation, compromising the integrity of medical data.

Establishing robust authentication and authorization mechanisms is essential in healthcare sensor networks (Adler-Milstein & Bates, 2010). Controlling access to these networks is crucial to prevent unauthorized entry and potential privacy violations. The challenge lies in developing and maintaining effective authentication processes that ensure only authorized personnel can access patient data.

Interoperability and standardization pose challenges in integrating diverse sensor devices and systems within healthcare networks. Standardized protocols are necessary to ensure seamless data exchange. Inconsistencies in data formats and communication protocols can lead to security risks, hindering the efficient flow of information.

Endpoint security is critical, as individual sensor devices within a network can be vulnerable to cyber threats. Ensuring the security of each endpoint device, including regular updates and patches, is essential to prevent unauthorized access and potential breaches.

Balancing the need for data-driven healthcare with ethical considerations, such as obtaining informed consent from patients for data collection and sharing, is a complex challenge (Jobin et al., 2019). Respecting patient autonomy and privacy preferences while leveraging data for healthcare improvement requires careful navigation.

Data ownership, accountability, and liability issues must be clarified to build trust among patients and stakeholders (Xia et al., 2017). Determining who is responsible for data security at different stages of its lifecycle is essential for establishing a secure and accountable healthcare sensor network.

Moreover, regulatory compliance, such as adhering to healthcare data protection regulations like the Health Insurance Portability and Accountability Act (HIPAA), adds complexity to implementation. Noncompliance can lead to legal consequences and reputational damage, emphasizing the need for a comprehensive approach to regulatory adherence and data security (He et al., 2018).

Addressing these challenges requires collaboration between healthcare providers, technology developers, regulatory bodies, and policymakers to implement robust cybersecurity measures, adopt privacy-preserving technologies, and foster a data security awareness culture.

9.3.3.2 Interoperability issues

The implementation of sensor networks in healthcare encounters significant challenges related to interoperability. One major issue is the need for standardized protocols and communication formats across sensor devices and systems. Healthcare environments often deploy various sensors from various manufacturers, and these devices may use proprietary communication protocols. The absence of standardized practices hinders seamless data exchange and integration, making it difficult for different sensors to work cohesively within a network.

Interoperability challenges extend to integrating sensor data with existing healthcare information systems. EHRs and other healthcare databases may operate on different platforms or use incompatible data formats. Bridging the gap between sensor-generated data and existing healthcare systems requires robust interoperability solutions to ensure a smooth flow of information. A unified approach to data integration is needed to create a comprehensive and cohesive healthcare ecosystem.

Moreover, sensor variations in data semantics and coding standards contribute to interoperability challenges. Each sensor may use its codes and terminologies to represent health information. This diversity makes it challenging to achieve semantic interoperability, where the meaning of data is consistently understood across different systems. Standardizing data semantics is crucial for accurately interpreting and exchanging health information.

The dynamic nature of healthcare settings, with constant advancements in sensor technologies and the introduction of new devices, adds complexity to interoperability. Emerging sensors may not seamlessly integrate with legacy systems, leading to compatibility issues. Achieving backward and forward compatibility is essential to ensure that new sensor devices can work harmoniously with existing infrastructure and that older devices remain relevant as the technology evolves.

Collaboration among stakeholders, including sensor manufacturers, healthcare providers, standardization bodies, and regulatory authorities, is vital to addressing interoperability challenges. Developing and adopting industry-wide standards, such as common data models and communication protocols, can significantly improve interoperability. Additionally, establishing guidelines for seamless integration into existing healthcare systems and promoting a culture of collaboration will contribute to overcoming interoperability hurdles in sensor network implementation in healthcare.

9.3.3.3 Standardization of sensor technologies

The need for standardized protocols and technologies in sensor networks poses significant challenges in implementing these networks in healthcare. One of the key challenges is the heterogeneity of sensor devices used in healthcare settings. Different manufacturers produce sensors with varying communication protocols and data formats. Without standardized protocols, interoperability becomes a significant issue, hindering seamless communication and integration among diverse sensors.

In healthcare, where a wide range of sensors is employed for monitoring various health parameters, standardized communication protocols must be made easier for these devices to work cohesively within a network. Each sensor may utilize proprietary protocols, leading to siloed data that is challenging to integrate into a unified system. Integration is necessary for the creation of a comprehensive and interconnected healthcare environment.

The interoperability challenge extends beyond individual sensors to integrating sensor data with existing healthcare information systems, such as EHRs. These systems may operate on different platforms and employ different data formats. With standardized communication, adapting sensor-generated data to fit into existing healthcare databases becomes more complex, limiting the seamless exchange of information between sensors and established healthcare systems.

Furthermore, standardized protocols need to be revised to achieve semantic interoperability. Different sensors may use distinct coding standards and terminologies to represent health data. This diversity in semantics makes it challenging to ensure a consistent understanding of data meaning across various systems. Standardization of data semantics is crucial for accurate interpretation and effective exchange of health information among different sensors and healthcare applications.

The dynamic nature of healthcare, characterized by continuous advancements in sensor technologies, exacerbates the challenges. New sensors may enter the market with innovative features, but the need for standardized protocols can impede their integration with existing systems. Ensuring backward and forward compatibility becomes crucial to avoid the obsolescence of older devices and facilitate the seamless integration of new sensors into the healthcare infrastructure (Usmani et al., 2023).

9.3.3.4 Ethical considerations

Ethical considerations are crucial when using health data collected through sensor networks. Informed consent, data ownership, and the risk of personal health information misuse are vital issues. Informed consent means individuals must understand how their data will be collected, used, and shared before giving permission. This is especially important in sensor networks where continuous monitoring and data transmission occur (Wong et al., 2018).

Data ownership adds another layer of complexity, as the lines between personal and shared data can become blurred within sensor networks. Determining who has control and authority over the health data sensors collect raises critical ethical questions. Individuals should have a say in how their health information is used and shared, and mechanisms for transparent data ownership must be established.

The potential misuse of personal health information introduces concerns about privacy and security. Safeguarding sensitive health data from unauthorized access, breaches, or use for unintended purposes is paramount. Striking a delicate balance between harnessing the benefits of sensor networks for healthcare advancements and protecting individuals' rights and privacy is an ongoing ethical challenge (Ali et al., 2021). It requires a continuous and transparent discourse involving healthcare providers, technology developers, policymakers, and the individuals whose health data is being collected.

Ethical considerations in sensor networks extend beyond the initial consent to ongoing data management. As technologies evolve and new use cases emerge, ethical frameworks must adapt to address emerging challenges. Establishing ethical guidelines, industry standards, and regulatory frameworks becomes essential to ensure responsible and respectful practices in collecting, using, and sharing health data through sensor networks. This ongoing ethical discourse is crucial to fostering trust among individuals, promoting responsible innovation, and upholding the principles of privacy and autonomy in the increasingly interconnected landscape of healthcare technology.

9.3.3.5 Cost and resource allocation

Implementing sensor networks in healthcare requires substantial investments across multiple dimensions, encompassing infrastructure development, device procurement, and staff training. This comprehensive approach is necessary to establish a robust ecosystem to collect, transmit, and analyze health data through sensor technologies. However, the significant costs associated with these endeavors present a notable challenge, particularly for healthcare systems operating within constrained financial frameworks.

Infrastructure development involves creating the necessary network architecture, connectivity solutions, and data storage capabilities to support the seamless functioning of sensor networks. This includes deploying sensors, communication devices, and backend systems capable of handling the generated data. Procuring advanced sensor devices with the latest technologies and functionalities is another critical aspect, ensuring that the healthcare system utilizes state-of-the-art tools for accurate and real-time health monitoring.

Staff training is equally vital to ensure that healthcare professionals are proficient in utilizing sensor technologies, interpreting the generated data, and incorporating these insights into patient care. Training programs must be ongoing to keep healthcare staff updated on evolving technologies and best practices in sensor network utilization.

The challenge of cost considerations becomes particularly pronounced in healthcare systems with limited financial resources. Striking a delicate balance between the potential benefits of implementing sensor networks and the associated economic implications is imperative for the sustainable adoption of these technologies. Decision-makers must carefully evaluate the return on investment (ROI) regarding improved patient outcomes, streamlined healthcare processes, and long-term cost savings.

While sensor networks hold immense promise for revolutionizing healthcare delivery, especially in preventive care, early detection of diseases, and personalized treatment plans, the economic feasibility of these implementations must be considered. Sustainable and cost-effective strategies must be devised to ensure that the advantages of sensor networks are accessible to a broad spectrum of healthcare settings, thereby contributing to the overall enhancement of patient care and healthcare system efficiency.

9.3.3.6 Reliability and accuracy

The precision of health-related information obtained from sensors is crucial for healthcare providers to make accurate assessments, diagnoses, and treatment decisions. However, challenges related to variability in sensor accuracy, calibration issues, and potential signal interference introduce complexities that can affect the reliability of the collected data.

Variability in sensor accuracy refers to the potential differences in the performance of sensors, even within the same type or model. These variations may arise due to manufacturing discrepancies, wear and tear, or environmental factors. Calibration issues, on the other hand, pertain to the accurate alignment of sensors to established standards, ensuring that the data they produce is consistent and trustworthy. Deviations in calibration can lead to inaccuracies, compromising the reliability of the entire sensor network.

Signal interference is another factor that can impact the accuracy of sensor data. In healthcare settings, where multiple electronic devices and wireless systems coexist, the risk of signal interference is heightened. This interference may result in distorted or corrupted data, posing challenges for healthcare professionals who rely on accurate sensor information for patient monitoring and diagnosis.

Ensuring the consistency and precision of sensor-generated data is essential for healthcare providers and holds significant implications for patient trust. Patients depend on the accuracy of sensor data to receive appropriate and timely medical interventions. Any compromise in the reliability of this data can erode confidence in the effectiveness of sensor technologies and, consequently, in the overall healthcare delivery system.

9.3.4 Future directions for sensor networks in healthcare

Despite the challenges, the future of sensor networks in healthcare holds immense promise. Several trends and developments are shaping the trajectory of these networks, paving the way for more sophisticated applications and improved healthcare outcomes.

9.3.4.1 Integration with artificial intelligence

Integrating sensor networks with AI and ML algorithms represents a transformative approach to healthcare, substantially enhancing the interpretability and utility of health data. By leveraging advanced analytics, these systems can unravel intricate patterns, forecast health trends, and play a pivotal role in the early detection of diseases. This synergy empowers healthcare providers with actionable insights, contributing to more informed decision-making and improved patient outcomes.

AI and ML algorithms are adept at processing vast amounts of data generated by sensor networks, swiftly identifying meaningful correlations and patterns that might escape human observation. These technologies excel at learning from historical data, adapting to evolving circumstances, and continuously refining their predictive capabilities. Consequently, when applied to sensor data, AI and ML enable healthcare professionals to understand individual and population health dynamics better.

One significant advantage lies in the ability of these algorithms to detect subtle changes or anomalies in health data, often serving as early indicators of potential health issues. This early detection can lead to timely interventions, preventing the progression of diseases and reducing the overall burden on healthcare systems.

Moreover, integrating sensor networks with AI and ML facilitates personalized medicine by tailoring interventions based on individual health profiles. This individualized approach is particularly relevant in chronic disease management, where predicting and addressing fluctuations in health conditions can significantly enhance patient well-being.

Despite the transformative potential, challenges such as data privacy, algorithm transparency, and ethical considerations must be carefully addressed in integrating sensor networks with AI and ML. Striking a balance between harnessing the power of these technologies and safeguarding patient privacy is essential to realize the full benefits of this innovative approach to healthcare. As technology advances, the collaboration between sensor networks and AI/ML holds promises for revolutionizing healthcare delivery and improving health outcomes globally.

9.3.4.2 Edge computing for real-time processing

Edge computing entails processing data in close proximity to the data source, occurring at the network's edge rather than relying solely on centralized servers. This paradigm shift brings several advantages that are particularly beneficial in healthcare applications.

One key advantage of edge computing in healthcare sensor networks is the significant reduction in latency. By processing data closer to where it is generated, edge computing minimizes the time it takes for information to travel between the sensors and the central servers. This is crucial in healthcare scenarios where real-time data analysis is imperative, such as monitoring critical patient parameters or responding to emergencies promptly.

The decentralized nature of edge computing further facilitates real-time data analysis (Azad et al., 2024). Instead of relying on a centralized server to process data from all sensors, each sensor node can independently execute computations locally. This enhances the speed of data analysis and contributes to more efficient utilization of computing resources.

Moreover, edge computing addresses bandwidth constraints by reducing the need for continuous data transmission to centralized servers. In traditional setups, large volumes of sensor data must be constantly transmitted to a central location for processing and analysis. With edge computing, only relevant, preprocessed data or actionable insights may be transferred, optimizing bandwidth usage and minimizing the demand on network resources.

The application of edge computing in healthcare sensor networks aligns with the growing emphasis on the IoT and the desire for more distributed, responsive, and scalable healthcare systems (Sonune et al., 2017). As technology continues to evolve, leveraging edge computing in conjunction with sensor networks holds promise for enhancing healthcare applications' efficiency, responsiveness, and overall performance. However, it also raises considerations regarding data security, privacy, and the management of distributed computing resources, which need to be carefully addressed to ensure the successful implementation of this approach in healthcare settings.

9.3.4.3 Expansion of implantable sensors

Advances in miniaturization and biocompatible materials are driving the expansion of implantable sensors. These devices, placed within the body, offer a continuous and unobtrusive source of health data. Developing biodegradable sensors and energy-harvesting mechanisms further enhances the feasibility of long-term implantation.

9.3.4.4 Blockchain for secure health data exchange

Blockchain technology is increasingly being explored to address data security concerns in sensor networks. By providing a decentralized and immutable ledger, blockchain ensures the integrity and confidentiality of health data. This approach holds promise for secure health data exchange and interoperability.

9.3.4.5 Personalized medicine and treatment plans

Sensor networks contribute to the paradigm shift towards personalized medicine. The continuous monitoring of individual health parameters facilitates the tailoring of treatment plans based on real-time data, optimizing therapeutic interventions for better outcomes.

9.3.4.6 Human-centric design and user experience

Emphasizing human-centric design principles in developing wearable sensors enhances user experience and engagement. Comfortable, esthetically pleasing, and user-friendly devices encourage long-term adoption and compliance, contributing to the success of sensor networks in healthcare.

9.3.4.7 Regulatory framework development

Establishing comprehensive regulatory frameworks is essential for guiding the ethical and responsible implementation of sensor networks in healthcare. Regulatory bodies play a crucial role in defining standards, ensuring data security, and safeguarding patient rights in the context of sensor-generated health data.

9.4 Blockchain technology in healthcare

9.4.1 Introduction to blockchain technology

Conceptualized initially as the foundational framework for cryptocurrencies, blockchain technology has transcended its initial application and found a profound resonance in healthcare. This section delves into blockchain technology's principles, applications, and implications in revolutionizing healthcare systems.

9.4.2 Overview of blockchain technology

9.4.2.1 Core principles

At its core, blockchain is a decentralized and distributed ledger that records transactions across a network of computers. Each transaction, or block, is cryptographically linked to the previous one, forming a chain of blocks. This structure ensures the integrity and immutability of the data recorded on the blockchain.

9.4.2.2 Decentralization

Blockchain operates on a decentralized network, eliminating the need for a central authority or intermediary. Each participant in the network, or node, has a copy of the entire blockchain. This decentralized nature ensures transparency, reduces the risk of a single point of failure, and enhances the system's security.

9.4.2.3 Cryptographic security

Cryptography plays a pivotal role in securing transactions on the blockchain. Each transaction is secured through cryptographic algorithms, ensuring that the data is tamper-resistant. Public and private keys are employed to verify the authenticity of transactions, providing a robust layer of security.

9.4.2.4 Immutability

Once a block is added to the blockchain, it becomes immutable. This means that the data within the block cannot be altered or deleted. Immutability ensures the historical integrity of the blockchain, making it a reliable and trustworthy source of information.

9.4.2.5 Smart contracts

Smart contracts are self-executing contracts with the terms of the agreement directly written into code (Khatoon, 2020). These contracts automate and enforce the execution of contractual clauses, reducing the need for intermediaries. Smart contracts can streamline billing, insurance claims, and data-sharing agreements in healthcare (Saini et al., 2021).

9.4.3 Applications of blockchain in healthcare

Blockchain technology can address longstanding challenges in healthcare, offering solutions that enhance data security, interoperability, and transparency. Understanding the applications of blockchain in healthcare is essential for appreciating its transformative impact.

9.4.3.1 Secure health data management

Secure health data management is one of the primary applications of blockchain in healthcare. Traditional healthcare systems often grapple with issues of data breaches and unauthorized access. Blockchain's decentralized and cryptographic security features ensure the confidentiality and integrity of health records, mitigating the risks associated with centralized data repositories (Ajayi et al., 2020).

9.4.3.2 Interoperability and data sharing

Blockchain facilitates seamless interoperability and data sharing among disparate healthcare systems (Arbabi et al., 2023). Different healthcare providers, organizations, and systems can securely exchange health information through a shared and standardized ledger. This interoperability fosters a more connected and collaborative healthcare ecosystem.

9.4.3.3 Patient-controlled health records

Blockchain empowers individuals to have greater control over their health records. Patients can own and manage their health data through cryptographic keys, determining who can access their information. This shift towards patient-controlled health records aligns with patient-centric care and privacy principles.

9.4.3.4 Drug traceability and supply chain management

Blockchain ensures transparency and traceability in pharmaceutical supply chains (Dashtizadeh et al., 2022). Each pharmaceutical production, distribution, and delivery step can be recorded on the blockchain (Fernando et al., 2019). This helps prevent counterfeit drugs and enhances the efficiency of supply chain management (Musamih et al., 2021).

9.4.3.5 Clinical trials and research

Blockchain streamlines the management of clinical trial data. The entire lifecycle of a clinical trial, including patient recruitment, data collection, and results reporting, can be automated and recorded on the blockchain through smart contracts. This enhances the transparency and reliability of clinical trial data (Ramzan et al., 2023).

9.4.3.6 Identity management and authentication

Blockchain provides a robust solution for identity management and authentication in healthcare. Patients, healthcare providers, and other stakeholders can have verified and immutable identities recorded on the blockchain. This reduces the risk of identity fraud and ensures that only authorized individuals access sensitive health information.

9.4.3.7 Billing and insurance claims

The automation capabilities of smart contracts streamline billing and insurance claims processes. Through predefined rules encoded in smart contracts, the verification, processing, and settlement of billing and insurance claims can occur automatically, reducing administrative overhead and minimizing the potential for errors.

9.4.4 Unlocking healthcare potential with blockchain

Blockchain technology is bringing about a new era in healthcare, providing numerous advantages beyond traditional data management systems. By offering improved security, transparency, and more efficient processes, its implementation can transform how healthcare data is managed, leading to innovation and better patient care.

9.4.4.1 Enhanced data security

Blockchain offers enhanced data security for healthcare through its decentralized and tamper-resistant nature (Devi et al., 2023). Distributing data across a network of nodes containing a copy of the entire chain minimizes the risk of a single point of failure. The cryptographic principles used in blockchain ensure that once data is recorded, it becomes virtually immutable, preventing unauthorized alterations. Additionally, permissioned access and consensus mechanisms further fortify the system, allowing only authorized parties to validate and update information. This robust security framework not only protects sensitive healthcare data from unauthorized access but also instils trust in the integrity of the information, which is crucial for maintaining the confidentiality and accuracy of patient records.

9.4.4.2 Prevention of data breaches

Unlike traditional centralized systems, where a single breach can expose a vast amount of sensitive data, blockchain distributes information across a network of nodes.

This decentralization reduces the risk of a single point of failure, making it significantly more challenging for hackers to compromise the entire system.

The cryptographic principles employed by blockchain ensure the integrity and immutability of data. Once information is recorded in a block, it is linked to the previous block in a chain, creating a tamper-resistant structure. Any attempt to alter data in one block would require altering all subsequent blocks across the entire network, making unauthorized changes practically impossible.

Furthermore, blockchain's use of consensus mechanisms and smart contracts adds an additional layer of security (Zhou et al., 2023). Access to data is permissioned, and changes must be validated by consensus among network participants. This ensures that only authorized individuals or entities can modify the data, reducing the risk of malicious activities.

By leveraging these features, blockchain technology provides a robust defense against data breaches in healthcare, safeguarding patient information and bolstering the overall cybersecurity posture of the industry.

9.4.4.3 Patient privacy and consent

Blockchain technology introduces a sophisticated mechanism for managing patient privacy and consent in healthcare. Leveraging smart contracts, patients gain unprecedented control over their health data by defining specific access permissions and conditions for its use. This innovative approach ensures that sensitive information is shared only when explicit consent is granted by the patient, aligning seamlessly with the foundational principles of privacy and autonomy in healthcare.

With blockchain-enabled smart contracts, patients can intricately outline who can access their medical records, what type of information can be viewed, and for what purposes. These predefined conditions are encoded into the blockchain, creating a transparent and unalterable record of consent. This level of granular control empowers patients to navigate the delicate balance between sharing their health data for necessary medical purposes while maintaining a strict boundary on unauthorized access.

By incorporating blockchain's decentralized and immutable ledger, the technology establishes a trustworthy environment where patients have confidence that their privacy preferences are upheld. This enhances data security and fosters a patient-centric approach, emphasizing the importance of informed consent and putting individuals in charge of their healthcare information. In essence, blockchain offers a transformative solution that harmonizes the digital sharing of health data with the imperative need to safeguard patient privacy and autonomy.

9.4.4.4 Immutable audit trails

Creating an immutable and transparent audit trail for all transactions is one of the most significant benefits. The blockchain ledger records and timestamps every interaction with health data, whether modification or access. This feature enhances accountability and provides a comprehensive history of data activities for regulatory compliance.

The immutability of the blockchain ledger means that once the data is recorded, it cannot be altered or deleted. This feature ensures the integrity of health data, preventing any unauthorized modifications or data tampering. Moreover, the transparency of the blockchain ledger allows for easy traceability of all data activities, enabling quick identification of any unauthorized access or modification attempts.

This feature is highly beneficial for regulatory compliance, as it creates a comprehensive history of all data activities, which can be audited for compliance purposes. It also enhances accountability by recording who accessed or modified the data and when. This transparency and accountability help build trust in the healthcare system, which is essential for ensuring patient privacy and data security (Shetty et al., 2019; Vyas et al., 2020)

9.4.4.5 Cybersecurity resilience

Blockchain's resistance to tampering and unauthorized alterations contributes to its resilience against cybersecurity threats (Hasanova et al., 2019). The cryptographic consensus mechanisms used in blockchain networks make it inherently challenging for malicious actors to compromise the integrity of health data. This resilience is crucial in safeguarding healthcare systems from evolving cyber threats.

9.4.5 Challenges and considerations in implementing blockchain in healthcare

While promising, blockchain healthcare integration has challenges. Understanding these challenges is essential for devising strategies to overcome them and ensuring the successful implementation of blockchain solutions in healthcare.

9.4.5.1 Scalability

One of the primary challenges in implementing blockchain in healthcare is scalability (Chauhan, 2018). As the number of transactions and participants in the network grows, the scalability of blockchain solutions becomes a critical consideration (Gökalp et al., 2018). Ensuring that the blockchain network can handle the increasing volume of healthcare transactions is essential for widespread adoption.

9.4.5.2 Integration with existing systems

Healthcare organizations often operate with legacy systems that are not inherently compatible with blockchain technology. Integrating blockchain solutions with existing EHR systems, medical databases, and other healthcare applications poses a significant challenge (Ballal et al., 2023). Achieving seamless interoperability is crucial for effectively deploying blockchain in healthcare (Khatri et al., 2021).

9.4.5.3 Regulatory compliance

The healthcare industry is subject to stringent regulatory frameworks to ensure patient safety, privacy, and data security. Adhering to these regulations while implementing blockchain solutions requires careful consideration. Achieving compliance with existing healthcare laws and regulations is a complex process that demands collaboration between blockchain developers and regulatory bodies (Charles et al., 2019).

9.4.5.4 Standardization

The absence of standardized protocols and frameworks in the blockchain space poses challenges for interoperability (Belchior et al., 2021; Williams, 2020). Establishing industry-wide standards for healthcare blockchains is crucial to ensure that different blockchain implementations can seamlessly communicate and share data. Standardization efforts are essential for fostering a cohesive and interconnected healthcare ecosystem.

9.4.5.5 Cost and resource allocation

Implementing blockchain solutions in healthcare involves significant upfront costs, including technology infrastructure, staff training, and ongoing maintenance (Agbo & Mahmoud, 2020). For healthcare organizations with limited resources, the financial implications can hinder adoption. Striking a balance between the potential benefits and the associated costs is crucial for the sustainable deployment of blockchain in healthcare.

9.4.5.6 User education and adoption

Blockchain technology introduces a paradigm shift in managing and sharing healthcare data. Ensuring that healthcare professionals, administrators, and patients understand the principles and benefits of blockchain is essential for successful adoption. User education programs and training initiatives are crucial in fostering a positive reception and utilization of blockchain solutions.

9.4.6 Future directions for blockchain in healthcare

As blockchain technology matures, several trends and developments are shaping its future trajectory in healthcare. Exploring these future directions provides insights into the evolving landscape of blockchain in healthcare.

9.4.6.1 Federated blockchain networks

Federated Blockchain Networks hold significant promise for revolutionizing various aspects of healthcare. One primary application lies in addressing the longstanding interoperability challenge among diverse healthcare systems, by leveraging federated blockchains, a unified patient record system can be established, enabling seamless data sharing among healthcare providers. This integration enhances coordination and ensures more comprehensive care for patients by consolidating their medical information.

Another crucial aspect is the secure exchange of sensitive health data. Federated blockchains provide a decentralized and highly secured environment, utilizing immutability and cryptography to safeguard patient information during data exchanges. This ensures confidentiality, integrity, and privacy, critical elements in maintaining trust within the healthcare ecosystem.

Federated blockchain networks contribute to transparency and traceability in clinical trials and research (Hang et al., 2021). These networks offer a secure and auditable trail of research activities, ensuring data integrity in clinical trials. Collaboration among multiple research entities facilitates a more robust and reliable research environment.

Supply chain management in healthcare can also benefit significantly from federated blockchains. By tracing the entire supply chain of pharmaceuticals, these networks help prevent counterfeit drugs, authenticate medications, and ultimately enhance patient safety.

Smart contracts, a feature of blockchain technology, can be employed to automate various healthcare processes. For instance, insurance claims processing can be streamlined, reducing administrative overhead, minimizing fraudulent claims, and accelerating reimbursement procedures (Haque et al., 2021).

Federated blockchains further contribute to identity management in healthcare. Enhancing patient identity verification mitigates the risk of medical identity theft. Patients gain control over their identity information, ensuring accurate and verified data is accessible to healthcare providers.

Decentralized healthcare applications can also be developed on federated blockchain networks. These applications empower patients by giving them control over their health data, allowing selective sharing with healthcare providers and researchers.

The immutable and transparent nature of federated blockchains aids in maintaining data integrity and security in health records. Once data is recorded, it becomes tamper-resistant, providing a reliable source of information for medical professionals.

Consideration of regulatory frameworks, privacy concerns, and stakeholder collaboration is essential when implementing federated blockchain networks in healthcare. However, the potential benefits, including improved interoperability, security, and transparency, make it attractive for transforming the healthcare landscape.

9.4.6.2 Integration with emerging technologies

Blockchain's integration with emerging healthcare technologies is poised to revolutionize the industry. Teaming up with the IoT, blockchain secures and manages health data from wearables and remote monitoring, ensuring authenticity. In conjunction with AI and ML, blockchain provides a secure foundation for analyzing patient records without compromising privacy (Alzubi et al., 2021; Salim et al., 2022).

Pairing blockchain with edge computing enables decentralized patient data storage and secure local processing, while the high-speed capabilities of 5G networks, integrated with blockchain, ensure seamless data exchange and bolster the security of telemedicine transactions. Augmented reality (AR) and virtual reality simulations benefit from blockchain's secure data authentication in medical training and patient record visualization (Ivanov, 2020).

The collaboration of robotic process automation with blockchain streamlines administrative tasks and ensures transparency in the healthcare supply chain. In biotechnology, blockchain facilitates secure genomic data sharing and transparent drug development. In cybersecurity, blockchain and emerging technologies forge immutable security records and decentralized identity management, fortifying the overall cybersecurity landscape in healthcare.

9.4.6.3 Tokenization for incentive models

Tokenization in healthcare, facilitated by blockchain-based tokens, introduces innovative opportunities for establishing incentive models within the industry. The fundamental concept involves representing real-world assets or values, such as patient data or specific health-related actions, as digital tokens on a blockchain. This transformative approach opens avenues for creating dynamic and secure incentive structures that positively impact various healthcare aspects.

One notable application of tokenization is establishing reward systems for individuals contributing to health-related initiatives. Patients, for instance, can be incentivized to actively participate in wellness programs, share accurate health data, or adhere to prescribed treatment plans by distributing tokens as rewards. Securely recorded on the blockchain, these tokens are a transparent and tamper-resistant ledger of individual contributions, fostering participant trust.

Moreover, tokenization can extend to healthcare professionals and institutions. Tokens can act as tangible rewards by aligning incentives with positive outcomes, such as improved patient outcomes or adherence to evidence-based practices. This acknowledges and motivates healthcare providers and contributes to a more collaborative and patient-centric healthcare ecosystem.

Additionally, using blockchain-based tokens in healthcare can revolutionize data sharing (Taherdoost, 2023). Patients can have control over access to their health records, granting permission in exchange for tokens. This decentralized approach ensures the privacy of sensitive health information while creating a secure and traceable data exchange method between different healthcare entities.

The introduction of token-based incentives has the potential to address challenges in healthcare, such as patient engagement, data sharing, and overall system efficiency. As this innovative model evolves, it can foster a paradigm shift towards a more participatory, incentivized, and transparent healthcare ecosystem.

9.4.6.4 Cross-border health data exchange

The decentralized and secure attributes intrinsic to blockchain technology render it particularly apt to facilitate cross-border health data exchange. Within international travel, patients frequently encounter challenges in accessing and verifying their health records within foreign healthcare systems. Blockchain provides a transformative solution by establishing a unified and secure platform for patients to store their health data. Patients can control access permissions through cryptographic principles and decentralized identity management, granting healthcare providers seamless access to their records in disparate countries. This prevents the complexities of traditional data exchange methods and engenders a streamlined and secure approach.

The ramifications of blockchain-facilitated cross-border health data exchange extend beyond individual patient experiences. The secure and standardized accessibility to health records catalyzes global health collaborations, allowing researchers and healthcare professionals from diverse geographical locations to contribute to and access shared datasets. This can expedite medical research, amplify the efficacy of clinical trials, and cultivate international cooperation in addressing overarching global health challenges.

Furthermore, the ramifications of seamless health data exchange are consequential for medical tourism. Individuals seeking healthcare services abroad stand to benefit from a simplified and secure process of sharing their medical history with foreign healthcare providers. The blockchain's immutable ledger ensures the integrity of patient information, thereby contributing to a more reliable and efficient medical tourism ecosystem.

9.4.6.5 Decentralized identity solutions

Blockchain technology can potentially revolutionize how we handle identity verification processes in healthcare (Javed et al., 2021). With decentralized identity solutions built on blockchain, patients can have greater control over their identity and personal information. The self-sovereign identity recorded on the blockchain can reduce dependence on centralized identity providers, enhancing patient privacy and security.

In traditional healthcare systems, identity verification processes can take time and effort. However, these processes can be streamlined and made more efficient with blockchain technology. By leveraging blockchain-based identity solutions, healthcare providers can perform identity verification faster, more securely, and transparently.

Moreover, blockchain-based identity solutions can provide patients with access to their medical records in a secure and verifiable way. This can help improve patient outcomes by ensuring doctors can access the correct medical information when needed.

9.4.6.6 Continued regulatory framework development

As blockchain technology continues to gain ground in the healthcare industry, it is becoming increasingly important for regulatory bodies to establish comprehensive and adaptive frameworks to govern the use of this technology. These frameworks must keep pace with the rapid advancements in blockchain technology while ensuring that regulations provide clarity, protect patient rights, and foster innovation. With the right regulatory frameworks in place, blockchain has the potential to transform the healthcare industry by improving data security, streamlining processes, and enabling greater collaboration among stakeholders. However, with proper regulation, there is a risk that these benefits will be fully realized, and patient safety and privacy could be protected. Therefore, regulators must work closely with industry stakeholders to develop frameworks that balance innovation and safety.

9.5 Integration of sensor networks and blockchain

9.5.1 The synergy between sensor networks and blockchain in healthcare

The convergence of sensor networks and blockchain represents a groundbreaking paradigm in healthcare, revolutionizing how data is collected, transmitted, and stored. This section delves into the intrinsic synergy between these technologies, exploring their collaborative potential in addressing healthcare challenges and enhancing the overall efficiency of healthcare systems.

9.5.1.1 Enhancing data security

One of the fundamental challenges in healthcare is ensuring the security of sensitive patient data. Sensor networks equipped with advanced sensors and wearables generate a continuous stream of real-time health information (Ramasamy et al., 2021). Blockchain integration provides an immutable and decentralized ledger to store this data securely (Sadawi et al., 2021). Through cryptographic techniques, patient records become tamper-resistant, reducing the risk of unauthorized access and ensuring the integrity of healthcare information.

9.5.1.2 Facilitating transparent and trustworthy data exchange

Blockchain's decentralized architecture fosters transparent and trustworthy data exchange among stakeholders in the healthcare ecosystem. Smart contracts and self-executing agreements embedded in the blockchain automate and enforce predefined rules, ensuring data sharing adheres to consent and privacy preferences. This transparent and auditable framework instils trust among patients, healthcare providers, and other entities, fostering a collaborative and patient-centric approach to healthcare.

9.5.1.3 Streamlining interoperability

Interoperability has long been a challenge in healthcare, with disparate systems hindering seamless data exchange. Integrating sensor networks and blockchain facilitates interoperability by providing a standardized and secure data-sharing platform (Alam et al., 2021). Blockchain's ability to create a unified and standardized record across diverse systems enhances communication between healthcare entities, promoting a cohesive and interconnected healthcare ecosystem.

9.5.1.4 Empowering patient-centric care

The synergy between sensor networks and blockchain empowers patients to take control of their health data (Efendi et al., 2018). With wearable devices and biosensors seamlessly integrated into the sensor network, individuals can generate a comprehensive dataset of their health metrics. This data, stored on a blockchain, allows patients to grant selective access to healthcare providers, researchers, or other relevant parties, fostering patient-centric care and personalized treatment plans.

9.5.1.5 Enabling decentralized health records

Traditional health records often need to be more cohesive across various healthcare providers. Sensor networks, combined with blockchain, enable the creation of decentralized health records (Jamshed et al., 2022). Each patient owns and controls their health information securely stored on the blockchain. This decentralized approach ensures data ownership and facilitates efficient and secure sharing of health records across authorized entities, contributing to a more holistic approach to patient care.

9.5.2 How sensor data is collected, transmitted, and stored on a blockchain

This subsection delves into the intricate processes of collecting, transmitting, and storing sensor data on a blockchain. It elucidates the role of sensor networks in generating diverse health data and outlines the steps through which this data is seamlessly integrated into a blockchain framework.

9.5.2.1 Data collection through sensor networks

Sensor networks leverage a spectrum of devices, from wearables and biosensors to ambient sensors, to collect various health data. Wearable devices continuously monitor vital signs, activity levels, and other relevant metrics, while biosensors capture biological information such as glucose levels or heart rhythms. Ambient sensors within smart healthcare environments contribute additional contextual data (Lachaux et al., 2022). This collective data forms a comprehensive health profile, offering a granular view of an individual's well-being.

9.5.2.2 Real-time transmission of sensor data

The real-time nature of healthcare data is crucial for timely interventions and decision-making. Sensor data, once collected, undergoes secure and instantaneous transmission to the blockchain. This transmission is facilitated through encrypted channels, ensuring the confidentiality and integrity of the data during its journey from the sensor nodes to the blockchain nodes. Using secure communication protocols guarantees that the transmitted data remains resistant to tampering or interception.

9.5.2.3 Blockchain architecture for healthcare data

Blockchain architecture is pivotal in accommodating sensor data. A permission blockchain, where access is restricted to authorized entities, is often preferred in healthcare settings to ensure privacy and regulatory compliance. Each block in the chain contains a cryptographic hash of the previous block, creating an immutable and chronological sequence. This structure enhances security and provides an auditable trail of all sensor data transactions, reinforcing transparency and accountability.

9.5.2.4 Smart contracts orchestrating data transactions

Smart contracts, self-executing code embedded in the blockchain, play a crucial role in orchestrating data transactions. These contracts automatically enforce predefined rules and conditions governing how sensor data is accessed, shared, and utilized. For instance, a patient's consent for sharing specific health metrics with a research institution can be encapsulated in a smart contract, ensuring that data usage aligns with the patient's preferences.

9.5.2.5 Decentralized storage and retrieval

Once sensor data is transmitted and verified, it is securely stored in decentralized storage units within the blockchain. This decentralized storage ensures redundancy and resilience, mitigating the risk of data loss or corruption. Authorized entities, including healthcare providers and patients, can efficiently retrieve and access the stored data, fostering a collaborative and patient-centric approach to healthcare information management (Shibu et al., 2022).

9.5.3 Case studies demonstrating successful integration in healthcare settings

This subsection presents a series of case studies that exemplify the successful integration of sensor networks and blockchain in diverse healthcare settings. These cases showcase tangible benefits, innovative solutions, and lessons learned from real-world implementations.

9.5.3.1 Case study 1: remote patient monitoring for chronic disease management

In a regional healthcare network, sensor networks were employed to monitor patients with chronic diseases such as diabetes and hypertension. Wearable devices continuously track vital signs and securely transmit the data to a blockchain platform. Smart contracts facilitated real-time alerts for healthcare providers in case of anomalies, enabling proactive interventions. This integration improved patient outcomes, reduced hospitalizations, and enhanced patient engagement (Azbeg et al., 2023).

9.5.3.2 Case study 2: decentralized electronic health records

A consortium of healthcare providers collaborated to implement a decentralized EHRs system. Sensor data generated by patients across different healthcare facilities was stored on a blockchain, ensuring a unified and standardized health record. Patients retained control over access permissions, and healthcare providers experienced streamlined interoperability. This case demonstrated enhanced data accessibility, reduced administrative burden, and improved continuity of care (Arunachalam et al., 2023).

9.5.3.3 Case study 3: clinical trials acceleration through blockchain

In clinical research, a pharmaceutical company utilized sensor networks and blockchain to streamline clinical trials (Omar et al., 2019). Wearable devices monitored participants, and the generated data was directly recorded on a blockchain. Smart contracts facilitated automated data verification, speeding up the trial process. This integration resulted in significant cost savings, faster trial completion, and improved data integrity (Anwar et al., 2021; Kuhn et al., 2022).

9.5.3.4 Case study 4: secure and transparent drug supply chain

A multinational pharmaceutical corporation implemented a blockchain-based supply chain solution integrated with sensor networks (Alshahrani & Alshahrani, 2021). IoT-enabled sensors tracked the temperature and condition of pharmaceutical products during transportation. The sensor data, recorded on a blockchain, ensured transparency and traceability throughout the supply chain. This integration enhanced the security of pharmaceutical products, reduced the risk of counterfeiting, and ensured compliance with regulatory standards (Zhu et al., 2020).

9.5.3.5 Case study 5: wearable technology in elderly care facilities

In elderly care facilities, wearable technology and blockchain were integrated to enhance resident care. Wearables monitor residents' health parameters, including activity levels, sleep patterns, and vital signs (Nath & Thapliyal, 2021). The sensor data, encrypted and transmitted securely, was stored on a blockchain platform. Smart contracts triggered automated alerts for caregivers in case of emergencies or deviations from standard health patterns. This integration improved health monitoring, timely interventions, and increased well-being among elderly residents.

9.5.3.6 Case study 6: public health surveillance in pandemics

During a global pandemic, sensor networks and blockchain were employed for public health surveillance (Amofa et al., 2023). Wearable devices and ambient sensors collected data on symptoms, body temperature, and movement patterns (Gendy & Yuce, 2023). The encrypted data, transmitted securely to a blockchain, facilitated real-time monitoring of disease spread. Smart contracts automated contact tracing and quarantine protocols, providing authorities with actionable insights. This integration proved instrumental in controlling the pandemic, ensuring effective public health interventions (Otoum et al., 2021).

9.5.4 Future implications and challenges

As the integration of sensor networks and blockchain advances, this subsection explores the potential future implications. It anticipates challenges that may arise in the evolving landscape of healthcare technology.

9.5.4.1 Future implications

9.5.4.1.1 Accelerated research and innovation

Integrating sensor networks and blockchain is poised to accelerate research and innovation in healthcare. Real-world evidence generated from sensor data on the blockchain will expedite clinical trials, enhance drug discovery, and contribute to evidence-based medicine. The transparent and traceable nature of blockchain will foster collaborative research endeavors, opening new frontiers in medical science.

9.5.4.1.2 Emergence of decentralized healthcare ecosystems

The ongoing integration suggests the emergence of decentralized healthcare ecosystems. Patient-owned health data marketplaces, facilitated by blockchain, may become commonplace, enabling individuals to share their data for research while retaining ownership and control. This shift towards decentralization can reshape healthcare power dynamics, empowering patients and fostering equitable data exchange.

9.5.4.1.3 Improved population health management

The comprehensive data generated by sensor networks, seamlessly integrated into blockchain platforms, will contribute to improved population health management. Predictive analytics and ML algorithms applied to this rich dataset will enhance disease surveillance, early detection, and preventive interventions. This data-driven approach holds promise for addressing public health challenges and optimizing resource allocation.

9.5.4.1.4 Interconnected healthcare ecosystem

Integrating sensor networks and blockchain paves the way for a genuinely interconnected healthcare ecosystem. Wearable devices, biosensors, and ambient sensors seamlessly communicating through blockchain networks will result in holistic health monitoring. Interconnected systems will enable healthcare providers to access a unified, up-to-date health record, facilitating collaborative and integrated patient care.

9.5.4.2 *Anticipated challenges*

9.5.4.2.1 Scalability challenges

The scalability of integrated solutions remains a critical challenge. As the volume of sensor data increases and the number of participants in blockchain networks grows, scalability concerns may emerge. Innovations in consensus mechanisms, network architectures, and data storage solutions will be essential to address the scalability challenges associated with widespread adoption.

9.5.4.2.2 Regulatory evolution

The rapid evolution of healthcare technologies outpaces regulatory frameworks. As integrated solutions become more sophisticated, regulatory bodies must adapt to meet legal and ethical standards. Collaboration between technology developers and regulators is essential to navigate the regulatory landscape and establish frameworks that balance innovation with patient safety and data privacy.

9.5.4.2.3 Data ownership and consent

The issue of data ownership and consent remains a complex ethical consideration. As decentralized health data marketplaces evolve, striking a balance between data sharing for research purposes and individual consent and ownership will be crucial. Developing standardized frameworks and clear communication strategies will be essential to navigate these ethical complexities.

9.5.4.2.4 Security and privacy concerns

Despite the enhanced security offered by blockchain, security and privacy concerns persist. The potential for unauthorized access, data breaches, or vulnerabilities in sensor devices may pose threats to the integrity of health data. Continuous advancements in encryption methods, secure device protocols, and threat detection mechanisms are imperative to address evolving security challenges.

9.5.4.2.5 Technological integration and compatibility

Integrating sensor networks and blockchain requires seamless compatibility with existing healthcare infrastructures. Ensuring interoperability between diverse sensor devices, healthcare information systems, and blockchain platforms is a multifaceted challenge. Standardization efforts and collaborative initiatives are essential to harmonize technologies and achieve a cohesive healthcare ecosystem (Islam et al., 2023).

9.5.5 Ethical considerations in the integration

This subsection delves into the ethical considerations of integrating sensor networks and blockchain in healthcare. It explores the principles that guide ethical decision-making, emphasizing the importance of preserving patient autonomy, ensuring data privacy, and maintaining transparency.

9.5.5.1 Preserving patient autonomy

Integrating sensor networks and blockchain places a premium on preserving patient autonomy. Individuals should have control over their health data, deciding who can access it and for what purposes. Transparent and accessible mechanisms for granting and revoking consent and user-friendly interfaces empower patients to make informed choices about using their data in healthcare settings.

9.5.5.2 Ensuring informed consent

Informed consent is a cornerstone of ethical healthcare practices. Integrating sensor networks and blockchain necessitates transparent data collection, storage, and usage communication. Patients should be provided with clear information regarding the data types collected, the purpose of its utilization, and potential risks and benefits. Ongoing consent mechanisms embedded within blockchain smart contracts can ensure that individuals maintain control over their data throughout its lifecycle.

9.5.5.3 Privacy-preserving technologies

The deployment of privacy-preserving technologies is imperative in maintaining the confidentiality of health data. Techniques such as zero-knowledge proofs and homomorphic encryption, integrated into blockchain platforms, enable secure and private transactions. Embracing privacy-enhancing technologies safeguards individuals from unauthorized access and upholds the principle of medical confidentiality.

9.5.5.4 Transparent governance structures

Transparent governance structures are vital in ensuring ethical decision-making and accountability. Clear guidelines on data access, usage, and sharing should be established, and mechanisms for auditing and oversight should be in place (Hripcsak et al., 2014). Ethical governance structures build trust among stakeholders, assuring patients and healthcare providers that the integration is conducted with integrity and adherence to ethical principles.

9.5.5.5 Equity in data access

The integration should prioritize equitable access to healthcare data. Ensuring that diverse populations, including underrepresented groups, benefit from advancements requires proactive measures. Addressing biases in data collection, algorithms, and access ensures that healthcare solutions are inclusive, improving outcomes for all demographic groups.

9.5.5.6 Addressing bias and fairness

The potential for bias in healthcare algorithms demands ethical scrutiny. As sensor data feeds into decision-making processes, there is a risk of perpetuating existing biases. Rigorous evaluation, algorithmic decision-making transparency, and continuous bias monitoring are crucial ethical considerations. Addressing bias ensures that healthcare interventions are fair and do not perpetuate existing disparities.

9.5.5.7 Cultural sensitivity

Integrating sensor networks and blockchain must respect cultural diversity and sensitivity. Ethical considerations should encompass cultural nuances because healthcare beliefs and practices vary across cultures (Altay et al., 2021). Efforts to incorporate cultural competence into the design and implementation of integrated solutions foster inclusivity and respect for diverse perspectives.

9.5.6 Reflection on the transformative potential

This subsection reflects on the transformative potential of integrating sensor networks and blockchain in healthcare. It explores the broader implications for patient outcomes, healthcare delivery, and the evolution of the healthcare ecosystem.

9.5.6.1 Patient-centric outcomes

The integration holds profound implications for patient-centric outcomes. Empowering patients with control over their health data, facilitating personalized medicine, and enabling proactive interventions through real-time monitoring contribute to improved health outcomes. The shift towards patient-centricity aligns with the broader movement towards value-based care, emphasizing positive outcomes and patient satisfaction.

9.5.6.2 Enhanced efficiency in healthcare delivery

Integrated solutions offer the potential to enhance efficiency in healthcare delivery. Streamlining data exchange, interoperability, and automated processes through smart contracts reduces administrative burdens. Timely access to accurate and comprehensive health records facilitates faster decision-making, reducing the lag time in diagnoses and interventions. Enhanced efficiency contributes to a more responsive and agile healthcare system.

9.5.6.3 Empowering healthcare providers

Healthcare providers stand to gain significant empowerment through integration. Access to real-time, comprehensive patient data supports evidence-based decision-making. Automated alerts triggered by smart contracts enable proactive interventions, preventing complications and hospitalizations. The empowerment of healthcare providers translates to improved patient care, increased job satisfaction, and a more resilient healthcare workforce.

9.5.6.4 Data-driven research and innovation

The integration fuels a data-driven approach to research and innovation in healthcare. The wealth of sensor data, securely stored on a blockchain, becomes a valuable resource for researchers. Accelerated clinical trials, advanced predictive analytics, and collaborative research endeavors are facilitated, driving innovation and contributing to developing cutting-edge medical solutions.

9.5.6.5 Reshaping the healthcare ecosystem

The transformative potential extends to reshaping the entire healthcare ecosystem. Decentralized health data ownership, interconnected systems, and equitable data exchange foster a paradigm shift in how healthcare is perceived and delivered. The integration paves the way for a more collaborative, transparent, and patient-centric healthcare ecosystem, transcending traditional boundaries and silos.

9.6 Advantages and challenges of sensor networks and blockchain in healthcare

9.6.1 Benefits of employing sensor networks in healthcare

Sensor networks have ushered in a new era of healthcare by offering many benefits that positively impact patient care, treatment outcomes, and the overall efficiency of healthcare systems.

9.6.1.1 Real-time patient monitoring

One of the primary advantages of sensor networks is the ability to enable real-time patient monitoring. Wearable sensors, implanted devices, and ambient sensors provide continuous data streams, allowing healthcare providers to monitor vital signs, activity levels, and other relevant parameters without needing physical presence (Wagholikar & Wagholikar, 2023). This real-time monitoring is crucial for patients with chronic conditions, facilitating early intervention and personalized care.

9.6.1.2 Early detection of health issues

Sensor networks contribute to the early detection of health issues by continuously collecting and analyzing data. Changes in physiological parameters or activity patterns that may indicate the onset of a health issue can be identified promptly. This early detection enhances the effectiveness of preventive measures, reducing the likelihood of complications and hospitalizations (Luo et al., 2022).

9.6.1.3 Enhanced chronic disease management

Individuals with chronic diseases, such as diabetes, cardiovascular disorders, and respiratory conditions, benefit from sensor networks in managing their conditions effectively. Continuous monitoring of relevant health metrics and data analytics enables personalized treatment plans and timely medication adjustments. This proactive approach to chronic disease management improves patient outcomes and quality of life.

9.6.1.4 Improved patient engagement

Sensor networks empower patients to engage in their healthcare journey actively. Through wearable sensors and mobile applications, individuals can track their physical activity, monitor vital signs, and receive real-time feedback. This increased awareness and involvement foster a sense of ownership over one's health, promoting healthier lifestyle choices and adherence to treatment plans.

9.6.1.5 Efficient remote patient monitoring

Remote patient monitoring, facilitated by sensor networks, enables healthcare providers to monitor patients outside traditional healthcare settings. This is especially valuable for individuals in rural or underserved areas, allowing them to access healthcare services without frequent travel. The efficiency of remote patient monitoring contributes to cost savings and improved accessibility to care.

9.6.1.6 Data-driven personalized medicine

Sensor networks generate vast amounts of individualized health data, paving the way for data-driven personalized medicine. By analyzing a patient's unique physiological and behavioral patterns, healthcare providers can tailor treatment plans to specific needs. This personalized approach enhances treatment efficacy, reduces adverse effects, and optimizes healthcare outcomes.

9.6.1.7 Streamlined clinical trials

In research and development, sensor networks streamline clinical trials by automating data collection and ensuring the accuracy of trial outcomes. Wearable sensors and smart devices provide researchers with real-time insights into participants' health metrics, improving the efficiency of data collection and analysis. This accelerates the pace of clinical research and innovation.

9.6.1.8 Enhanced public health surveillance

Sensor networks contribute to public health surveillance by monitoring environmental factors, detecting disease outbreaks, and identifying trends in population health. Ambient sensors can track air quality, temperature, and other parameters, providing valuable data for early warning systems and proactive public health interventions.

9.6.2 Challenges of sensor networks in healthcare

While the benefits of sensor networks in healthcare are substantial, several challenges must be addressed to ensure their widespread adoption and seamless integration into healthcare systems.

9.6.2.1 Data security and privacy concerns

The continuous generation and transmission of health data raise significant concerns regarding data security and privacy. Protecting sensitive health information from unauthorized access, data breaches, and cyberattacks is paramount to maintaining patient trust and regulatory compliance (Rehman et al., 2023). Addressing these concerns requires robust encryption methods, secure data storage, and adherence to privacy regulations.

9.6.2.2 Interoperability issues

Interoperability remains a significant challenge in the implementation of sensor networks. Healthcare systems often use diverse devices and platforms that may not seamlessly communicate with each other. Achieving interoperability requires developing and adopting standardized protocols, ensuring that different sensor devices can exchange data seamlessly and contribute to a cohesive healthcare ecosystem.

9.6.2.3 Standardization of sensor technologies

The lack of standardized protocols and technologies in the sensor network space hinders interoperability and complicates the integration of diverse sensor devices. Establishing industry-wide standards is crucial for promoting compatibility and facilitating the widespread adoption of sensor networks. Standardization efforts should address communication protocols, data formats, and device interfaces.

9.6.2.4 Ethical considerations

As we increasingly rely on technology to monitor and collect health data through sensor networks, we must consider the ethical implications of such practices. One of the main concerns is informed consent, which means that individuals must be fully aware of how their data will be collected, used and shared. Moreover, data ownership is crucial to ensure that individuals can control their data and decide who can access it. Finally, there is the risk of potential misuse of personal health information, leading to discrimination or other negative consequences. Therefore, it is essential to have ongoing ethical discourse and to balance the benefits of sensor networks and individuals' rights and privacy. This will help ensure that health data is collected, used and shared responsibly and ethically.

9.6.2.5 Cost and resource allocation

Implementing sensor networks in healthcare involves creating a system of interconnected devices that can collect and transmit data about patients. This can include everything from wearable devices that track vital signs to sensors that monitor environmental conditions. However, creating such a system requires significant investments in infrastructure, device procurement, and staff training. The financial implications can challenge and hinder adoption for smaller healthcare organizations with limited resources.

Therefore, healthcare organizations must balance the potential benefits of implementing sensor networks and the associated financial costs. This will help ensure the sustainable deployment of sensor networks in healthcare. By carefully weighing the benefits against the costs, healthcare organizations can determine the best way to implement sensor networks in a practical and financially feasible way.

9.6.2.6 Reliability and accuracy

Sensor data is essential in healthcare decision-making. This data can include patient vital signs, medication administration, and other clinical metrics that healthcare providers rely heavily on to make informed decisions. However, the accuracy and reliability of this data are critical. Any variations in sensor accuracy, calibration issues, or potential signal interference can negatively impact the reliability of the collected data. As a result, healthcare providers must ensure the consistency and precision of sensor-generated information to maintain the trust of patients and other healthcare providers. By doing so, healthcare providers can make more informed decisions and help provide better care to their patients.

9.6.2.7 *Integration with existing healthcare systems*

Integrating sensor networks with existing healthcare systems is an essential step towards enhancing the quality and efficiency of healthcare services. However, this process can be challenging due to the diverse array of legacy technologies and protocols used in the healthcare industry. As a result, compatibility issues may arise when connecting sensor devices with HER systems or medical databases.

To achieve seamless integration, it is essential to ensure that the sensor devices are compatible with the existing healthcare systems and can communicate effectively. This can be accomplished using standardized protocols and interfaces widely accepted in the healthcare industry.

Achieving seamless integration is vital for maximizing the utility of sensor-generated data within the broader healthcare infrastructure. By integrating sensor networks with existing healthcare systems, healthcare providers can gain access to real-time data that can be used to improve patient outcomes and reduce costs. This can help healthcare providers make more informed decisions and enhance the overall quality of care they provide to their patients.

9.6.2.8 *Regulatory compliance*

The healthcare industry is one of the most regulated industries in the world, and this is because it deals with people's health, safety, and personal data. Healthcare providers must adhere to strict regulatory frameworks that ensure patient safety, privacy, and data security. This is particularly important when implementing sensor networks to monitor patients' health and well-being.

Achieving compliance with existing healthcare laws and regulations is a complex process that demands collaboration between sensor technology developers and regulatory bodies. Developers must ensure that their technology meets the requirements set out by regulatory bodies. In contrast, regulatory bodies must ensure that the technology is safe, secure, and meets the needs of patients. Failure to comply with these regulations can result in severe consequences for healthcare providers, including fines, legal action, and damage to their reputation.

Therefore, it is crucial to carefully consider the regulatory requirements when implementing sensor networks in healthcare. This includes understanding the laws and regulations that apply to your specific use case, working closely with regulatory bodies to ensure compliance, and implementing robust security measures to protect patient data and maintain privacy. By doing so, healthcare providers can leverage the benefits of sensor technology while ensuring that patient safety, privacy, and data security are not compromised.

9.6.3 Ongoing research and developments in sensor networks

The field of sensor networks in healthcare is dynamic, with ongoing research and developments aimed at addressing the challenges above and unlocking further potential.

9.6.3.1 *Advances in sensor technology*

Ongoing research focuses on advancing sensor technology to improve accuracy, reliability, and functionality. Miniaturization, increased sensor sensitivity, and the developing of novel sensor materials contribute to the evolution of sensors used in healthcare applications. These advancements enhance the quality of data collected and expand the range of measurable parameters.

9.6.3.2 Machine learning for data analysis

Integrating ML algorithms with sensor networks is a promising avenue for enhancing data analysis. ML models can identify patterns, predict health trends, and provide valuable insights from the vast datasets generated by sensor networks. This approach contributes to more accurate diagnostics and personalized treatment strategies.

9.6.3.3 Edge computing for real-time processing

Research is ongoing to integrate edge computing with sensor networks to enable real-time data processing closer to the data source. This approach minimizes latency, reduces the need for continuous data transmission to centralized servers, and addresses bandwidth constraints. Implementing edge computing enhances the efficiency of sensor networks in healthcare applications.

9.6.3.4 Blockchain for data security

Exploring the integration of blockchain technology with sensor networks is a research area focused on enhancing data security and privacy. Blockchain's decentralized and immutable ledger can address unauthorized data access and tampering concerns. Research is ongoing to evaluate the feasibility of employing blockchain with sensor networks for secure health data management.

9.6.3.5 Ethical frameworks for data use

Research in developing ethical frameworks for data collected through sensor networks is crucial. This includes addressing issues of informed consent, data ownership, and the responsible use of health information. Establishing clear ethical guidelines ensures that the deployment of sensor networks aligns with principles of privacy, autonomy, and patient rights.

9.6.3.6 Standardization initiatives

Ongoing efforts in standardization aim to create standard protocols and frameworks for sensor networks. To enhance interoperability, standardization initiatives address communication protocols, data formats, and device interfaces. Collaborative endeavors involving industry stakeholders, research institutions, and regulatory bodies contribute to developing cohesive standards.

9.6.4 Benefits of employing blockchain in healthcare

Blockchain technology introduces transformative benefits to the healthcare sector, addressing longstanding challenges and revolutionizing how health data is managed and shared.

9.6.4.1 Enhanced data security

The decentralized and cryptographic nature of blockchain significantly enhances data security in healthcare. Blockchain employs advanced cryptographic techniques to secure health data, ensuring that it is stored and transmitted in a tamper-resistant manner. This heightened security reduces the risk of data breaches and unauthorized access.

9.6.4.2 Immutability and transparency

Once data is recorded on the blockchain, it becomes immutable, meaning it cannot be altered or deleted. This immutability ensures the integrity of health records, providing a transparent and unchangeable history of data activities. Immutability is particularly crucial for maintaining the accuracy and trustworthiness of health information.

9.6.4.3 Interoperability and data sharing

Blockchain facilitates interoperability by providing a standardized and shared ledger. Different healthcare entities, including hospitals, clinics, and insurance providers, can securely exchange health information on a common platform. This interoperability fosters a more connected and collaborative healthcare ecosystem, reducing data silos and improving overall efficiency (Sharma et al., 2023).

9.6.4.4 Patient-controlled health records

Blockchain empowers patients with greater control over their health records. Patients can own and manage their health data through cryptographic keys, determining who can access specific information. This shift towards patient-controlled health records aligns with patient autonomy and privacy principles, enabling individuals to manage their healthcare information actively.

9.6.4.5 Streamlined clinical trials and research

Blockchain streamlines clinical trial data management by providing a secure and transparent platform for recording and verifying trial-related information. Smart contracts automate various aspects of clinical trials, including patient recruitment, consent management, and data sharing. This automation enhances clinical research efficiency and accelerates the development of new treatments.

9.6.4.6 Supply chain traceability

Blockchain ensures transparency and traceability in pharmaceutical supply chains (Hepp et al., 2018). Each pharmaceutical production, distribution, and delivery step can be recorded on the blockchain, reducing the risk of counterfeit drugs and enhancing overall supply chain management. This application is critical for ensuring the authenticity and safety of medications.

9.6.4.7 Improved billing and insurance processes

Using smart contracts in blockchain facilitates the automation of billing and insurance processes. Smart contracts execute predefined rules for verifying, processing, and settling billing and insurance claims. This automation reduces administrative overhead, minimizes the potential for errors, and streamlines financial transactions within the healthcare ecosystem (Banate, 2023).

9.6.5 Challenges of implementing blockchain in healthcare

Despite its transformative potential, implementing blockchain in healthcare poses challenges that must be carefully navigated for successful adoption and integration.

9.6.5.1 Scalability

Scalability is a significant challenge in blockchain implementations, especially as the volume of healthcare transactions grows. Blockchain networks must handle increasing data loads and transaction volumes without compromising performance. Ongoing research and technological advancements are directed towards developing scalable solutions suitable for the demands of healthcare systems.

9.6.5.2 Integration with existing systems

Healthcare organizations often operate with legacy systems that are not inherently compatible with blockchain technology. Integrating blockchain solutions with existing EHR systems, medical databases, and other healthcare applications poses a significant challenge. Achieving seamless integration is crucial for the effective deployment of blockchain in healthcare.

9.6.5.3 Regulatory compliance

Adhering to existing healthcare regulations while implementing blockchain solutions requires careful consideration. The decentralized and transparent nature of blockchain introduces novel considerations regarding compliance with data protection laws, patient privacy regulations, and other healthcare-specific regulations. Collaboration between blockchain developers and regulatory bodies is essential to ensure compliance.

9.6.5.4 Standardization

The absence of standardized protocols and frameworks in the blockchain space hinders interoperability and complicates the integration of diverse blockchain solutions. Establishing industry-wide standards for healthcare blockchains is crucial to ensure that different implementations can seamlessly communicate and share data. Standardization efforts are pivotal in fostering a cohesive and interconnected healthcare ecosystem.

9.6.5.5 Cost and resource allocation

The initial costs associated with implementing blockchain solutions in healthcare, including infrastructure, training, and development, can be substantial. Healthcare organizations must carefully assess the ROI and allocate resources effectively to ensure the sustainability of blockchain deployments. Striking a balance between the potential benefits and financial considerations is crucial for widespread adoption.

9.6.5.6 User education and adoption

Blockchain technology introduces a paradigm shift in managing and sharing healthcare data. Ensuring that healthcare professionals, administrators, and patients understand the principles and benefits of blockchain is essential for successful adoption. Robust user education programs, training initiatives, and change management strategies are crucial in fostering a positive reception and effective utilization of blockchain solutions.

9.6.5.7 Governance and consensus mechanisms

Establishing governance structures and consensus mechanisms within healthcare blockchain networks is a challenge that requires careful consideration. Determining how decisions are made, resolving disputes, and ensuring equitable participation in the network are essential aspects of blockchain governance. Striking the right balance between decentralization and governance is critical for healthcare blockchains to function effectively.

9.6.5.8 Energy consumption

The energy consumption associated with blockchain consensus mechanisms, such as proof-of-work, raises environmental concerns. Research and development efforts are directed towards exploring alternative consensus mechanisms that are more energy-efficient. Sustainable blockchain solutions that minimize environmental impact are crucial for aligning with broader societal and environmental goals.

9.6.6 Ongoing research and developments in blockchain

Continuous research and development initiatives focus on addressing the challenges associated with implementing blockchain in healthcare and expanding its potential applications.

9.6.6.1 Scalability solutions

Research is ongoing to develop scalable solutions for blockchain networks, particularly in healthcare (Ismail et al., 2019; Salim et al., 2022). Proposals include layer-two scaling solutions, sharding, and other approaches to increase transaction throughput without compromising decentralization. Advancements in scalability solutions aim to make blockchain technology more adaptable to the demands of healthcare systems.

9.6.6.2 Interoperability standards

Efforts are underway to establish interoperability standards for healthcare blockchains. Standardizing communication protocols, data formats, and interfaces ensures that different blockchain implementations can seamlessly exchange information. Collaborative initiatives involving industry stakeholders, standardization bodies, and healthcare organizations contribute to developing interoperability standards.

9.6.6.3 Regulatory

The evolving nature of blockchain technology requires a corresponding evolution in regulatory frameworks. Ongoing research explores regulatory considerations specific to healthcare blockchains, addressing data protection, patient privacy, and compliance with existing healthcare laws (Durneva et al., 2020; Tandon et al., 2020). Adaptive regulatory frameworks provide clarity and guidance for the responsible implementation of blockchain in healthcare.

9.6.6.4 Privacy-preserving techniques

Research focuses on integrating privacy-preserving techniques into blockchain implementations to enhance the confidentiality of health data. Zero-knowledge proofs, homomorphic encryption, and other cryptographic methods are explored to ensure that sensitive information remains confidential while benefiting from blockchain's transparency and security features.

9.6.6.5 Smart contract innovation

Smart contracts are computer programs that automatically execute the terms of a contract when certain predefined conditions are met. They are a fundamental building block for blockchain applications. In the healthcare industry, smart contracts have the potential to address various challenges, such as complex healthcare workflows, adherence to regulatory requirements, and automating intricate processes.

Ongoing research is exploring innovative uses of smart contracts in healthcare. For instance, (Antunes et al., 2018) propose using smart contracts to automate clinical trial processes, ensuring regulatory compliance and reducing the time and cost associated with traditional clinical trials. The authors also suggest using smart contracts to manage patients' consent to participate in a clinical trial, ensuring transparency and privacy.

Moreover, advancements in smart contract capabilities contribute to the broader utility of blockchain in healthcare scenarios. For example, smart contracts can automate the payment process, ensuring timely and accurate payment to healthcare providers.

9.6.6.6 Decentralized identity solutions

Research and development efforts are focused on decentralized identity solutions within blockchain networks. Creating secure and verifiable digital identities on the blockchain reduces reliance on centralized identity providers. This innovation aligns with principles of self-sovereign identity, enhancing security and privacy in healthcare interactions (Asamoah et al., 2020).

9.6.6.7 Integration with emerging technologies

Integrating blockchain with other emerging technologies, such as AI, the IoT, and edge computing, is a frontier of ongoing research. Exploring synergies between blockchain and these technologies enhances the capabilities of healthcare systems, enabling real-time data processing, predictive analytics, and seamless connectivity.

9.6.6.8 Social and ethical implications

Blockchain technology can transform healthcare by improving data security, interoperability, and accessibility. However, its implementation also raises significant social and ethical concerns that must be carefully considered.

One critical ethical consideration is patient privacy. Blockchain's immutable and decentralized ledger system can enhance data security and protect against unauthorized access.

Still, it can also make correcting errors or removing sensitive information from the system more complex. Therefore, it is essential to ensure that patient data is only accessible to authorized parties and that patients have control over their personal health information.

Another ethical consideration is the potential impact on vulnerable populations. Blockchain can improve healthcare access and reduce costs, but it could also exacerbate existing inequalities if certain groups are excluded from the system. Therefore, it is vital to ensure that blockchain is deployed in a way that promotes equity and social justice.

A recent study published in the Journal of Medical Internet Research highlights the importance of examining blockchain's social and ethical implications in healthcare. The study concludes that a comprehensive ethical framework is needed to ensure that the deployment of blockchain aligns with ethical principles, respects patient rights, and fosters positive social outcomes (Zhang et al., 2018).

While blockchain has the potential to revolutionize the healthcare industry, it is essential to carefully consider its implementation's social and ethical implications to ensure that it aligns with ethical principles and promotes positive social outcomes.

9.7 Use cases and applications in healthcare: a comprehensive exploration

9.7.1 Introduction to use cases in healthcare

Integrating sensor networks and blockchain technology in healthcare opens the door to many use cases, revolutionizing patient care, treatment strategies, and healthcare management. This section delves into a detailed exploration of specific use cases, highlighting the transformative impact on remote patient monitoring, personalized medicine, and preventive healthcare. Through real-world examples of successful implementations, we uncover the tangible benefits and implications for patient outcomes.

9.7.2 Remote patient monitoring: enhancing healthcare beyond the clinic

9.7.2.1 Real-time vital sign monitoring

Sensor networks facilitate real-time monitoring of patients' vital signs, providing healthcare providers with immediate insights into physiological parameters such as heart rate, blood pressure, and oxygen saturation. Wearable sensors and connected devices enable continuous data collection, allowing healthcare professionals to detect anomalies promptly and intervene in emergencies.

9.7.2.2 Chronic disease management

Remote patient monitoring proves instrumental in managing chronic diseases effectively. Patients with diabetes, hypertension, and heart disease can use wearable sensors to track their health metrics. The collected data, transmitted securely through sensor networks, empowers healthcare providers to adjust treatment plans quickly, preventing complications and improving long-term health outcomes.

9.7.2.3 Postoperative and rehabilitation monitoring

Sensor networks aid in postoperative monitoring and rehabilitation following surgeries or medical interventions. Wearable devices track patients' movements, activity levels, and recovery progress. This data assists healthcare professionals in tailoring rehabilitation programs, ensuring optimal recovery, and minimizing the risk of postoperative complications.

9.7.2.4 Elderly care and fall detection

Sensor networks play a pivotal role in elderly care by continuously monitoring seniors' activities. Wearable and ambient sensors detect changes in movement patterns, alerting caregivers or healthcare providers to potential fall risks (Agrawal et al., 2023; Jain & Semwal, 2022). This proactive approach enhances the safety and well-being of the elderly population, allowing for timely interventions and support (Luo et al., 2022).

9.7.3 Personalized medicine: tailoring treatments to individual needs

9.7.3.1 Genetic and biomarker monitoring

Sensor networks contribute to the era of personalized medicine by enabling the monitoring of genetic markers and biomarkers. Implantable sensors and genetic monitoring devices offer real-time insights into a patient's genetic profile and specific biomolecular indicators (Firouzi et al., 2023). This information guides personalized treatment plans, optimizing drug efficacy and minimizing adverse effects.

9.7.3.2 Medication adherence monitoring

Ensuring patient adherence to medication regimens is a critical aspect of personalized medicine. Sensor-enabled medication packaging and wearable devices track medication intake in real-time. This data helps healthcare providers monitor adherence and allows timely interventions if patients deviate from prescribed treatment plans.

9.7.3.3 Adaptive treatment plans

Sensor networks empower healthcare providers to dynamically adjust treatment plans based on individual responses and ongoing health data. Continuous monitoring of patient's physiological parameters and health behaviors allows for adaptive interventions. For instance, in oncology, real-time data can inform modifications to chemotherapy dosages, minimize side effects, and improve treatment outcomes.

9.7.3.4 Allergen and environmental sensing

Personalized medicine extends beyond biological factors to include environmental considerations. Sensor networks equipped with allergen and environmental sensors assist individuals with allergies or sensitivities. Patients can make informed decisions to avoid triggers by providing real-time information about environmental conditions, enhancing their overall quality of life.

9.7.4 Preventive healthcare: anticipating and mitigating health risks

9.7.4.1 Early disease detection

Sensor networks contribute to preventive healthcare by enabling early detection of potential health risks. Continuous monitoring of physiological parameters and health metrics allows for identifying subtle changes that may indicate the onset of diseases. Early detection facilitates timely interventions, improving the chances of successful treatment and recovery.

9.7.4.2 Lifestyle and wellness tracking

Wearable sensors and smart devices with lifestyle tracking features empower individuals to monitor their wellness proactively. Sensor networks provide a comprehensive overview of individuals' lifestyles, from physical activity and sleep patterns to dietary habits. This information guides personalized recommendations for healthier living, preventing the development of lifestyle-related diseases.

9.7.4.3 Immunization and disease surveillance

Sensor networks contribute to public health initiatives by enhancing immunization tracking and disease surveillance. Smart vaccine vials equipped with sensors monitor temperature and storage conditions, ensuring the efficacy of vaccines. Additionally, ambient sensors contribute to disease surveillance by detecting patterns indicative of potential outbreaks, enabling timely public health responses.

9.7.4.4 Environmental health monitoring

Sensor networks extend their impact to environmental health monitoring, aiding in identifying factors that may pose health risks. Air quality sensors, for example, contribute to the detection of pollutants and allergens. This information benefits individual health and informs public health strategies to address environmental contributors to diseases.

9.7.5 Examples of successful implementations and impact on patient outcomes

9.7.5.1 Case study: continuous glucose monitoring in diabetes management

Continuous glucose monitoring (CGM) systems exemplify the success of sensor networks in diabetes management. CGM devices continuously measure glucose levels, providing real-time data to individuals with diabetes and their healthcare providers. This technology has improved glycemic control, reduced hypoglycemic events, and enhanced quality of life for individuals managing diabetes.

9.7.5.2 Case study: remote monitoring in heart failure management

Remote patient monitoring has demonstrated significant success in managing heart failure patients. Wearable sensors and connected devices monitor vital signs, fluid retention, and activity levels. Through early detection of deteriorating health indicators, healthcare providers can intervene promptly, reducing hospital readmissions and improving overall outcomes for heart failure patients.

9.7.5.3 Case study: blockchain-enabled electronic health records

Integrating blockchain in EHRs has streamlined data management and enhanced security. Blockchain's immutable ledger ensures the integrity of patient records, reducing the risk of data tampering and unauthorized access. This innovation has positively impacted data sharing among healthcare providers, fostering collaboration and improving the continuity of care.

9.7.5.4 Case study: wearable sensors in parkinson's disease management

Wearable sensors tailored for Parkinson's patients continuously monitor motor symptoms and movement patterns. This real-time data assists neurologists in adjusting medication dosages and optimizing treatment plans. By facilitating personalized care, wearable sensors improve symptom management and enhance the quality of life for individuals with Parkinson's disease.

9.7.6 Charting the future of sensor networks and blockchain in healthcare

The use cases and applications of sensor networks and blockchain technology in healthcare represent a paradigm shift towards patient-centric, personalized, and preventive care. Remote patient monitoring, personalized medicine, and preventive healthcare initiatives showcase the tangible benefits of these technologies in improving patient outcomes, enhancing treatment efficacy, and fostering a proactive approach to healthcare.

Real-world examples and successful implementations underscore the transformative impact of sensor networks and blockchain on various facets of healthcare delivery. As technology evolves and research advances, the potential for further innovation in healthcare use cases becomes increasingly promising.

The journey towards a future where healthcare is not just reactive but anticipatory, not just standardized but personalized, is unfolding through integrating sensor networks and blockchain. As technology continues to evolve, and as research advances, the potential for further innovation in healthcare use cases becomes increasingly promising.

9.7.6.1 Future directions in remote patient monitoring

The future of remote patient monitoring holds immense potential for expanding the scope of monitored parameters. Integrating advanced sensor technologies, such as biosensors and imaging devices, will provide a more comprehensive understanding of patients' health status. Additionally, incorporating AI algorithms for predictive analytics will enable the early identification of health trends and potential complications.

9.7.6.2 Advancements in personalized medicine

The trajectory of personalized medicine is set to advance with breakthroughs in genomics, proteomics, and metabolomics. Emerging technologies, such as liquid biopsy sensors and point-of-care genetic testing devices, will empower individuals with real-time insights into their genetic predispositions and allow healthcare providers to tailor treatments with unprecedented precision. The convergence of data from wearables, genetic monitoring, and lifestyle factors will further refine personalized medicine approaches.

9.7.6.3 Pioneering preventive healthcare initiatives

The future of preventive healthcare will witness the integration of emerging technologies, including IoT devices, environmental sensors, and advanced analytics. Smart cities and connected ecosystems will contribute to a holistic approach to health, where data from various sources collaborates to identify and mitigate potential health risks. Innovative interventions, driven by sensor networks, will focus on addressing social determinants of health and promoting overall well-being.

9.7.6.4 Exploring new frontiers in blockchain applications

Integrating blockchain in healthcare will extend beyond EHRs to explore novel applications. Decentralized clinical trials powered by blockchain technology will streamline trial processes, enhance data integrity, and facilitate global collaboration. Smart contracts in healthcare will automate administrative tasks, reducing inefficiencies and ensuring transparent and accountable workflows. Moreover, blockchain-enabled supply chain solutions will continue to play a pivotal role in providing the authenticity and traceability of pharmaceuticals.

9.7.6.5 Patient empowerment and informed decision-making

A key theme in the future of healthcare will be the increasing empowerment of patients through sensor networks and blockchain applications. Patients will have greater control over their health data, making informed decisions about their care plans and treatment options. The democratization of health information will foster a collaborative relationship between patients and healthcare providers, contributing to a more patient-centric healthcare landscape.

9.7.6.6 Ethical considerations and privacy safeguards

As sensor networks and blockchain technologies become more ingrained in healthcare, ethical considerations and privacy safeguards will take center stage. Ongoing research will explore robust ethical frameworks for using health data, ensuring that individuals' rights and autonomy are respected. Privacy-preserving technologies, including advanced encryption and decentralized identity solutions, will be integral in maintaining the confidentiality of sensitive health information.

9.7.6.7 Interconnected healthcare ecosystems

The future of healthcare will witness the emergence of interconnected ecosystems where sensor networks and blockchain seamlessly integrate with other healthcare technologies. Interoperability standards will play a pivotal role in ensuring the fluid exchange of information between different devices, platforms, and healthcare stakeholders. This interconnectedness will contribute to more holistic and collaborative approaches to patient care.

9.7.6.8 Global impact and access to healthcare

Sensor networks and blockchain can potentially address global healthcare challenges, particularly in underserved regions. Decentralized healthcare systems, enabled by blockchain, can facilitate the secure and transparent sharing of health information across borders.

Additionally, sensor-based technologies can support telemedicine initiatives (Ganesh et al., 2020), providing remote communities access to essential healthcare services.

9.8 Security and privacy in healthcare: safeguarding patient data in the digital era

9.8.1 Introduction: the imperative of data security and patient privacy

Maintaining robust data security and safeguarding patient privacy in healthcare have become paramount in the digital transformation. As healthcare systems increasingly rely on sensor networks and blockchain technology to streamline processes and enhance patient care, addressing security and privacy concerns becomes critical to successful implementation.

This section delves into the multifaceted landscape of security and privacy in healthcare, exploring the imperative of protecting patient data, elucidating how blockchain enhances security in healthcare data transactions, and navigating the intricate realm of regulatory compliance and ethical considerations.

9.8.2 The imperative of data security in healthcare

9.8.2.1 Patient confidentiality and trust

Patient confidentiality is the bedrock of trust in healthcare. The digitalization of health records, while offering unprecedented benefits in accessibility and Efficiency, introduces new challenges to maintaining patient confidentiality. Ensuring that sensitive health information remains secure from unauthorized access is a legal and ethical obligation and fundamental to fostering patient trust in healthcare systems.

9.8.2.2 Cybersecurity threats

The healthcare sector is an attractive target for cyberattacks due to its wealth of valuable data. Healthcare data is a treasure trove for malicious actors, from personal identification information to sensitive medical records. Cybersecurity threats, including ransomware attacks, data breaches, and identity theft, pose significant risks to patient safety and the integrity of healthcare systems.

9.8.2.3 Vulnerabilities in traditional healthcare systems

Traditional healthcare systems, reliant on centralized databases and legacy infrastructure, are susceptible to vulnerabilities. The concentration of data in a central repository makes these systems attractive targets for cybercriminals. Addressing the security shortcomings of traditional systems is a prerequisite for transitioning towards more secure and resilient healthcare infrastructures.

9.8.3 Blockchain: reinventing security in healthcare data transactions

9.8.3.1 Decentralization and distributed ledger technology

As a decentralized and distributed ledger technology, blockchain offers a paradigm shift in how healthcare data is stored and accessed. By eliminating a single point of control, blockchain reduces the risk of unauthorized access and data manipulation. Each participant in the network maintains a copy of the ledger, creating a transparent and tamper-resistant system.

9.8.3.2 Immutable and transparent record-keeping

The immutability of blockchain ensures that once data is recorded, it cannot be altered or deleted. This feature enhances the integrity of healthcare data transactions, providing a verifiable and transparent record of every interaction. Immutable record-keeping not only safeguards against data tampering but also instils confidence in the accuracy and authenticity of health information.

9.8.3.3 Encryption and cryptographic security

Blockchain employs advanced cryptographic techniques to secure data transactions. Each transaction is encrypted and linked to the previous one, creating a chain of blocks resistant to tampering. Cryptographic security enhances the confidentiality of patient data, mitigating the risk of unauthorized access and ensuring that only authorized parties can decrypt and access sensitive health information.

9.8.3.4 Smart contracts for access control

Smart contracts and self-executing agreements encoded on the blockchain enable programmable access control to healthcare data. Access permissions can be predefined and executed automatically based on predetermined conditions. This feature ensures that only authorized individuals or entities can access specific patient information, enhancing data privacy and reducing the risk of data breaches.

9.8.3.5 Consensus mechanisms for trust

Blockchain's consensus mechanisms, such as proof-of-work or proof-of-stake, contribute to the establishment of trust in healthcare data transactions. The decentralized nature of consensus mechanisms ensures that no single entity can manipulate the data or transactions. This trust-building aspect is fundamental in healthcare, where the accuracy and reliability of patient data are paramount.

9.8.4 Regulatory compliance and ethical considerations

9.8.4.1 Healthcare data protection regulations

Adherence to healthcare data protection regulations is a cornerstone of ensuring security and privacy. Regulations, such as the HIPAA in the United States, set stringent requirements for protecting patient health information. Its decentralized and secure architecture aids healthcare organizations in meeting and exceeding regulatory standards (He et al., 2018).

9.8.4.2 General data protection regulation compliance

The General Data Protection Regulation (GDPR), applicable in the European Union, imposes stringent requirements on the processing and protecting personal data. Healthcare organizations leveraging blockchain must navigate the GDPR landscape to ensure compliance. Blockchain's transparency and user consent principles align with GDPR principles, facilitating a harmonious integration.

9.8.4.3 Interplay of ethics and technology

Ethical considerations play a pivotal role in the intersection of technology and healthcare. The responsible use of sensor networks and blockchain demands an ethical framework prioritizing patient autonomy, consent, and the responsible stewardship of health data. Striking a balance between technological innovation and ethical principles is imperative for fostering a healthcare ecosystem prioritizing patient well-being.

9.8.4.4 Informed consent in blockchain transactions

Blockchain transactions involving healthcare data necessitate a reimagining of the informed consent process. Patients must be adequately informed about the nature of blockchain technology, its implications for data security and privacy, and how their health information will be utilized. Transparent communication and empowering patients to make informed choices contribute to ethical and consensual data transactions.

9.8.4.5 Addressing bias and fairness

The deployment of sensor networks and blockchain in healthcare must be vigilant against perpetuating biases and inequalities. Whether for data analysis or smart contracts, algorithms used in healthcare systems must undergo rigorous scrutiny to ensure fairness and avoid exacerbating existing disparities. Ethical considerations extend beyond technical aspects to encompass the societal impact of technological implementations.

9.8.5 Challenges and considerations in security and privacy

9.8.5.1 Scalability challenges

While blockchain holds immense promise for enhancing security, scalability remains a challenge. As healthcare data transactions increase, blockchain networks must scale to accommodate the demand. Research and development efforts focus on scalability solutions, such as layer-two protocols and sharding, to ensure the viability of blockchain in large-scale healthcare systems.

9.8.5.2 Interoperability imperatives

Achieving interoperability between blockchain networks and existing healthcare systems is crucial for seamless data exchange. The diversity of healthcare stakeholders, each with its systems and protocols, necessitates standardized interfaces and communication protocols. Interoperability initiatives aim to bridge the gap between disparate systems, fostering a cohesive and interconnected healthcare ecosystem.

9.8.5.3 Education and adoption challenges

Educating healthcare professionals, administrators, and patients about the intricacies of blockchain technology poses a significant challenge. Adopting new technologies requires a cultural shift, and stakeholders must be well-informed about blockchain's benefits, risks, and ethical considerations in healthcare. Robust education and training programs are essential for fostering a technology-literate healthcare workforce.

9.8.5.4 Evolving regulatory landscape

The regulatory landscape surrounding healthcare data is dynamic, with constant updates and revisions. Healthcare organizations leveraging blockchain must remain vigilant to regulation changes and adapt their practices accordingly. Monitoring regulatory developments and proactive engagement with regulatory authorities ensure ongoing compliance and ethical data practices.

9.8.5.5 Security audits and vulnerability management

Continuous security audits and vulnerability management are imperative in ensuring the ongoing resilience of blockchain-enabled healthcare systems. Regular audits assess the robustness of security measures, identify potential vulnerabilities, and recommend mitigating actions. Proactive vulnerability management involves promptly addressing identified weaknesses to thwart security threats preemptively.

9.8.5.6 Ethical decision-making in data governance

Ethical decision-making becomes central as healthcare organizations navigate the complexities of data governance in a blockchain-driven landscape. Establishing ethical guidelines for data sharing, consent management, and algorithmic fairness requires thoughtful consideration. Ethical frameworks should be dynamic, adapting to technological advancements and evolving societal expectations.

9.8.6 Future trajectories in security and privacy

9.8.6.1 Quantum-resistant blockchain

The advent of quantum computing threatens existing cryptographic systems, including those used in blockchain. Future trajectories in security involve the development of quantum-resistant blockchain technologies. Research and innovation in quantum-resistant cryptography aim to fortify blockchain against emerging quantum threats, ensuring the continued security of healthcare data.

9.8.6.2 Privacy-preserving technologies

Advancements in privacy-preserving technologies are pivotal for addressing concerns related to data exposure in blockchain. Zero-knowledge proofs, homomorphic encryption, and other cryptographic techniques enable secure data transactions without revealing the underlying information. Integrating privacy-preserving technologies in healthcare blockchain systems enhances patient privacy while maintaining the benefits of decentralized ledgers.

9.8.6.3 Federated learning for enhanced privacy

Federated learning, a decentralized ML approach, holds promise in healthcare for preserving patient privacy while enabling collaborative data analysis. Instead of centralizing data for analysis, federated learning allows models to be trained across distributed datasets. This approach minimizes the need for raw data sharing, addressing privacy concerns associated with centralized data repositories.

9.9 Future trends and directions: pioneering the next frontier in healthcare transformation

9.9.1 Introduction

9.9.1.1 Anticipating the evolution of sensor networks and blockchain in healthcare

The healthcare landscape is on the cusp of a transformative era driven by integrating sensor networks and blockchain technology. As we delve into the future, this section explores emerging trends, envisions predictions for future developments, and contemplates the potential impact on healthcare delivery, research, and patient outcomes.

9.9.2 Emerging trends in sensor networks for healthcare

9.9.2.1 Advancements in wearable sensor technologies

The trajectory of wearable sensor technologies is poised for significant advancements (Prada & Forero, 2022). Miniaturization, improved battery life, and enhanced sensor capabilities will empower patients with a broader array of health-monitoring devices. Wearables will extend beyond fitness tracking to encompass continuous monitoring of vital signs, enabling proactive healthcare interventions and personalized treatment plans.

9.9.2.2 Integration of biosensors and biochemical sensors

The future holds the integration of advanced biosensors and biochemical sensors into healthcare sensor networks. These sensors, capable of detecting specific biomarkers and physiological indicators, will provide real-time insights into a patient's health status. Applications range from early detection of diseases to personalized medication management, revolutionizing diagnostic capabilities.

9.9.2.3 Expansion of ambient and environmental sensors

Ambient and environmental sensors will be integral in capturing contextual data for comprehensive health monitoring. These sensors will assess factors such as air quality, temperature, and exposure to environmental pollutants. Integrating these data points with individual health profiles will enable a holistic understanding of the impact of surroundings on patient well-being.

9.9.2.4 Smart implants and intra-body sensors

The advent of smart implants and intra-body sensors is set to redefine healthcare monitoring at the microscale. Implanted devices with sensor capabilities will provide real-time data from within the body. This innovation holds promise for precisely monitoring chronic conditions, targeting drug delivery, and detecting physiological anomalies early.

9.9.3 Evolving landscape of blockchain technology in healthcare

9.9.3.1 Interoperability solutions for seamless data exchange

One of the critical future trends in blockchain for healthcare is the development of interoperability solutions. As healthcare ecosystems diversify, interoperable blockchain networks will facilitate seamless data exchange between disparate systems. Standardized protocols and interfaces will be instrumental in creating a cohesive and interconnected healthcare infrastructure.

9.9.3.2 Quantum-secure blockchain architectures

With the looming advent of quantum computing, the development of quantum-secure blockchain architectures becomes imperative. Future blockchain implementations will incorporate cryptographic techniques resilient to quantum threats, ensuring the long-term security of healthcare data. This proactive approach anticipates the evolving landscape of cybersecurity.

9.9.3.3 Integration of decentralized identity solutions

Decentralized identity solutions will be integral to blockchain implementations in healthcare. Patients, providers, and other stakeholders will have secure, self-sovereign identities on the blockchain, streamlining access management and enhancing data security. This shift towards a decentralized identity aligns with privacy principles and patient empowerment.

9.9.3.4 Smart contracts for automated healthcare processes

The evolution of smart contracts in healthcare will extend beyond basic access control to automated healthcare processes. Smart contracts will streamline administrative tasks, automate claims processing, and facilitate transparent and efficient billing. These self-executing agreements will enhance operational efficiency, reduce errors, and ensure adherence to predefined rules.

9.9.4 Predictions for future developments and innovations

9.9.4.1 Integration of artificial intelligence with sensor networks

A significant prediction for the future is the seamless integration of AI with sensor networks. AI algorithms will analyze vast datasets generated by sensors, providing actionable insights for healthcare professionals. ML models will contribute to early disease detection, personalized treatment recommendations, and predictive healthcare analytics.

9.9.4.2 Convergence of blockchain with Internet of Things

The convergence of blockchain with the IoT will redefine data integrity and security in connected healthcare devices. Blockchain's decentralized architecture will enhance the trustworthiness of IoT-generated data, mitigating the risk of tampering or malicious interference. This synergy will be pivotal in ensuring data reliability from interconnected devices.

9.9.4.3 Emergence of patient-owned health data marketplaces

A paradigm shift in healthcare data ownership is anticipated with the emergence of patient-owned health data marketplaces. Blockchain will enable patients to control access to their health data, deciding when and how it is shared. These decentralized marketplaces will foster a transparent and equitable health information exchange, empowering individuals and incentivizing data sharing for research.

9.9.4.4 Integration of augmented reality in healthcare visualization

Integrating AR with sensor networks promises to transform healthcare visualization. AR applications will overlay real-time health data onto a patient's physical environment, providing clinicians with immersive insights during diagnostics and surgeries. This innovation could enhance precision in medical procedures and training (Ferreira-Brito et al., 2023).

9.9.5 Potential impact on healthcare delivery, research, and patient outcomes

9.9.5.1 Revolutionizing personalized medicine

The combined impact of advanced sensor networks and blockchain on healthcare is poised to revolutionize personalized medicine. Continuous monitoring of individual health parameters and secure and interoperable health records on the blockchain will enable tailored treatment plans. The shift towards personalized medicine promises more effective interventions and improved patient outcomes.

9.9.5.2 Accelerating drug discovery and clinical research

Integrating blockchain in clinical research and sensor-generated real-world evidence will accelerate drug discovery and development. Decentralized clinical trials, facilitated by blockchain, will enhance participant recruitment, data integrity, and transparency. This transformative approach will streamline research processes, bringing new therapies to market more efficiently.

9.9.5.3 Enhancing population health management

Sensor networks and blockchain will be pivotal in advancing population health management strategies. Real-time data from wearables, environmental sensors, and health records on the blockchain will facilitate proactive interventions to address public health challenges. The potential to identify and respond to emerging health trends at a population level holds promise for preventive healthcare initiatives.

9.9.5.4 Shaping the future of telemedicine and remote patient monitoring

Integrating sensor networks and blockchain will significantly enhance Telemedicine and remote patient monitoring. Secure and decentralized health records will enable seamless sharing of patient information across telehealth platforms. The continuous stream of real-time data from wearables will empower healthcare providers to monitor and manage patients remotely, enhancing accessibility and quality of care.

9.9.6 Ethical considerations and societal implications

9.9.6.1 Ethical governance of artificial intelligence and machine learning algorithms

The ethical governance of AI and ML algorithms, utilized with sensor networks, becomes paramount. Ensuring fairness, transparency, and accountability in algorithmic decision-making will be essential to prevent biases and disparities in healthcare outcomes. Ethical guidelines must evolve with technological advancements to uphold patient trust and societal values.

9.9.6.2 Inclusive access and addressing digital divides

Deploying advanced sensor networks and blockchain solutions in healthcare necessitates a concerted effort to address digital divides. Inclusive access to these technologies is essential to prevent exacerbating existing healthcare disparities. Initiatives focusing on digital literacy, accessibility, and equitable distribution of technological resources will be crucial in ensuring that the benefits of healthcare innovation reach diverse populations.

9.9.6.3 Privacy-preserving practices in health data sharing

As healthcare transitions towards patient-owned data marketplaces and decentralized health information exchange, privacy-preserving practices must be at the forefront. Striking a balance between data sharing for research and protecting individual privacy requires robust cryptographic solutions, transparent consent mechanisms, and ongoing dialogs on ethical data stewardship.

9.9.6.4 Ethical use of augmented reality in healthcare

Integrating AR in healthcare visualization introduces ethical considerations related to patient consent and the responsible use of immersive technologies. Establishing guidelines for ethical AR applications in medical settings is essential to ensure patient autonomy, minimize potential psychological impacts, and foster a collaborative and ethical environment in healthcare practices.

9.9.7 Overcoming challenges on the path to future innovations

9.9.7.1 Addressing regulatory frameworks for emerging technologies

The dynamic nature of emerging technologies necessitates continuous evolution in regulatory frameworks. Policymakers and regulatory bodies must proactively engage with technological advancements, ensuring that regulations are adaptive, proportionate, and conducive to innovation. Collaborative efforts between industry stakeholders and regulators are crucial in shaping frameworks that balance innovation with patient safety and ethical considerations.

9.9.7.2 Research and development in scalability solutions

Scalability remains a persistent challenge in blockchain implementations. Future research and development efforts should focus on scalability solutions and exploring innovations such as layer-two protocols, sharding, and consensus algorithm enhancements.

These endeavors are essential to ensure blockchain can support the growing volume of healthcare transactions without compromising Efficiency and speed.

9.9.7.3 Education and training for healthcare professionals

The successful integration of sensor networks and blockchain in healthcare relies on the preparedness of healthcare professionals. Robust education and training programs should be implemented to familiarize professionals with the intricacies of these technologies. Ensuring clinicians, administrators, and support staff are well-versed in the ethical and practical aspects of sensor networks and blockchain will be integral to the successful adoption and implementation.

9.9.7.4 Public awareness and patient engagement

Public awareness and patient engagement are pivotal in shaping the future of healthcare technologies. Educating patients about sensor networks' benefits, risks, and ethical considerations and blockchain fosters informed decision-making. Building trust through transparent communication and involving patients in the design and governance of healthcare technologies contribute to a patient-centric and inclusive future.

9.9.8 Collaboration and partnerships in driving innovation

9.9.8.1 Interdisciplinary collaboration

The convergence of sensor networks and blockchain in healthcare necessitates interdisciplinary collaboration. Researchers, engineers, healthcare professionals, policymakers, and ethicists must collaboratively navigate the complex intersection of technology, healthcare, and ethics. Interdisciplinary forums and collaborative initiatives will foster a holistic approach to innovation, ensuring that diverse perspectives contribute to the development of future healthcare solutions.

9.9.8.2 Industry collaboration for standards and protocols

Industry collaboration is indispensable in establishing standards and protocols for seamlessly integrating sensor networks and blockchain. Collaborative efforts between technology providers, healthcare institutions, and regulatory bodies will contribute to developing interoperable and universally accepted frameworks. Standardization initiatives will enhance compatibility, facilitate data exchange, and accelerate the adoption of transformative technologies.

9.9.8.3 Engaging with ethical and societal organizations

Engaging with ethical and societal organizations is crucial in navigating the ethical implications of emerging healthcare technologies. Collaborating with bioethics committees, patient advocacy groups, and societal organizations ensures that ethical considerations remain at the forefront of technological development. This engagement fosters a shared responsibility in shaping a future where innovation aligns with societal values and ethical principles.

9.10 Conclusion: shaping the future of healthcare through sensor networks and blockchain

The fusion of sensor networks and blockchain in healthcare promises to revolutionize how we understand, deliver, and experience healthcare. However, adopting these technologies necessitates active engagement with patients and the public. Educating individuals about the benefits, risks, and ethical considerations fosters a sense of empowerment and shared responsibility. Involving patients in decision-making processes, particularly concerning data sharing and consent, contributes to a patient-centric approach and builds trust in the healthcare ecosystem.

Regulatory bodies play a pivotal role in shaping the trajectory of healthcare technologies. Collaboration between industry stakeholders and regulatory bodies is essential to create agile frameworks that foster innovation while upholding the highest safety and ethical practice standards. As sensor networks and blockchain evolve, regulatory frameworks must adapt to ensure patient safety, data privacy, and ethical use.

Ethical oversight and governance mechanisms must be ingrained in deploying sensor networks and blockchain in healthcare. Bioethics committees, institutional review boards, and ethical guidelines should be dynamic and responsive to technological advancements. Continuous dialog on ethical considerations ensures that adopting these technologies aligns with societal values and prioritizes the well-being of individuals and communities.

Healthcare industry stakeholders should continue investing in emerging technologies, supporting research and development initiatives, pilot projects, and innovation hubs. This investment is instrumental in unlocking the full potential of sensor networks and blockchain, driving advancements that benefit patients and the healthcare ecosystem.

The interdisciplinary nature of healthcare technologies calls for sustained collaboration between various domains. Researchers, clinicians, technologists, ethicists, and policymakers should engage in ongoing dialogs to address emerging challenges, share insights, and collectively shape the future of healthcare. Interdisciplinary collaboration ensures a holistic approach considering the diverse perspectives necessary for successful innovation and adoption.

As the healthcare industry navigates this transformative journey, it is essential to remain mindful of the ethical considerations and societal implications. The responsible deployment of these technologies demands a vigilant approach, ensuring that the benefits are equitably distributed, privacy is safeguarded, and patients have agency over their health information. Encouragement is extended to researchers, healthcare professionals, policymakers, and industry leaders to embrace the evolution of sensor networks and blockchain in healthcare.

In conclusion, let us embark on this journey with a shared vision—where sensor networks and blockchain converge to create a healthcare landscape that transcends boundaries, empowers individuals, and lays the foundation for a healthier, more connected tomorrow. The possibilities are boundless, and the responsibility is collective. Together, let us pave the way for a future where innovation and compassion intersect, shaping a healthcare ecosystem that prioritizes the well-being of humanity.

References

Aazam, M., Zeadally, S., & Harras, K. A. (2020). Health fog for smart healthcare. *IEEE Consumer Electronics Magazine*, 9(2), 96−102. Available from https://doi.org/10.1109/MCE.2019.2953749.

Abed, H., Bellemare-Rousseau, S., Bélanger-Huot, B., Ahadi, M., Drouin, É., Roudjane, M., Dugas, M.-A., Miled, A., & Messaddeq, Y. (2021). A wire-free and fiber-based smart t-shirt for real-time breathing rate monitoring. *IEEE Sensors Journal*, 22(5), 4463−4471.

Adler-Milstein, J., & Bates, D. W. (2010). Paperless healthcare: Progress and challenges of an IT-enabled healthcare system. *Business Horizons*, 53(2). Available from https://doi.org/10.1016/j.bushor.2009.10.004.

Agbo, C. C., & Mahmoud, Q. H. (2020). Blockchain in healthcare: Opportunities, challenges, and possible solutions. *International Journal of Healthcare Information Systems and Informatics (IJHISI)*, 15(3). Available from https://doi.org/10.4018/IJHISI.20200701052020.

Agrawal, D. K., Usaha, W., Pojprapai, S., & Wattanapan, P. (2023). Fall risk prediction using wireless sensor insoles with machine learning. *IEEE Access*, 11. Available from https://doi.org/10.1109/ACCESS.2023.3252886, http://ieeexplore.ieee.org/xpl/RecentIssue.jsp?punumber = 6287639.

Ajayi, O., Abouali, M., & Saadawi, T. (2020). Secured inter-healthcare patient health records exchange architecture. In *2020 IEEE international conference on blockchain (blockchain)* (pp. 456−461). Rhodes, Greece. https://doi.org/10.1109/Blockchain50366.2020.00066.

Akhtar, F., & Rehmani, M. H. (2017). Energy harvesting for self-sustainable wireless body area networks. *IT Professional*, 19(2). Available from https://doi.org/10.1109/MITP.2017.34.

Al-Abadi, A. A. J., Mohamed, M. B., & Fakhfakh, A. (2023). Impact of availability attacks on enabling IoT-based healthcare applications. In *2023 International Wireless Communications and Mobile Computing (IWCMC)* (pp. 1666−1671). Marrakesh, Morocco. https://doi.org/10.1109/IWCMC58020.2023.10183010.

Al-Fuqaha, A., et al. (2015). Internet of things: A survey on enabling technologies, protocols, and applications. *IEEE Communications Surveys & Tutorials*, 17(4), 2347−2376. Available from https://doi.org/10.1109/COMST.2015.2444095.

Alam, S. R., Jain, S., & Doriya, R. (2021). Security threats and solutions to IoT using Blockchain: A review. In *2021 5th international conference on intelligent computing and control systems (ICICCS)* (pp. 268−273). Madurai, India. https://doi.org/10.1109/ICICCS51141.2021.9432325.

Ali, A., Rahim, H. A., Pasha, M. F., Dowsley, R., Masud, M., Ali, J., & Baz, M. (2021). Security, privacy, and reliability in digital healthcare systems using blockchain. MDPI AG, Malaysia. *Electronics (Switzerland)*, 10(16). Available from https://doi.org/10.3390/electronics10162034, https://www.mdpi.com/2079-9292/10/16/2034/pdf.

Alshahrani, W., & Alshahrani, R. (2021). Assessment of Blockchain technology application in the improvement of the pharmaceutical industry. In *2021 International Conference of Women in Data Science at Taif University* (pp. 1−6). https://doi.org/10.1109/WIDSTAIF52235.2021.9430210

Altay, A., Learney, R., Güder, F., & Dincer, C. (2021). Sensors in blockchain. *Trends in Biotechnology*. Available from https://api.semanticscholar.org/CorpusID:235169173.

Alzubi, O. A., Alzubi, J. A., Shankar, K., & Gupta, D. (2021). Blockchain and artificial intelligence enabled privacy-preserving medical data transmission in Internet of Things. John Wiley and Sons Inc, Jordan. *Transactions on Emerging Telecommunications Technologies*, 32(12). Available from https://doi.org/10.1002/ett.4360, http://onlinelibrary.wiley.com/journal/10.1002/(ISSN)2161-3915.

Amofa, S., Lin, X., Xia, Q., Xia, H., & Gao, J. (2023). Blockchain-based health data sharing for continuous disease surveillance in smart environments. In *Proceedings of the international conference on parallel and distributed systems - ICPADS* (pp. 185−192). IEEE Computer Society, China. Available from https://doi.org/10.1109/ICPADS56603.2022.00032, 9781665473156.

Ananth, C., Karthikeyan, M., & Mohananthini, N. (2018). A secured healthcare system using private blockchain technology. *Journal of Engineering Technology.*, 6, 42−54.

Andreozzi, E., Centracchio, J., Punzo, V., Esposito, D., Polley, C., Gargiulo, G. D., & Bifulco, P. (2021). Respiration monitoring via forcecardiography sensors. *Sensors*, 21(12). Available from https://doi.org/10.3390/s21123996, https://www.mdpi.com/1424-8220/21/12/3996/pdf.

Antunes, R. S., Seewald, L. A., Rodrigues, V. F., Da Costa, C. A., Gonzaga, L., Righi, R. R., Maier, A., Eskofier, B., Ollenschläger, M., Naderi, F., Fahrig, R., Bauer, S., Klein, S., & Campanatti, G. (2018). A survey of sensors in healthcare workflow monitoring. *ACM Computing Surveys*, 51(2). Available from https://doi.org/10.1145/3177852, http://dl.acm.org/citation.cfm?id = J204.

Anwar, A., Goyal, S. B., & Ghosh, A. (2021). Tracking clinical trials and enhancement of security & control with blockchain for medical record. In *2021 IEEE 6th international conference on computing, communication and automation (ICCCA)* (pp. 632–636). Arad, Romania. Available from https://doi.org/10.1109/ICCCA52192.2021.9666276.

Arbabi, M. S., Lal, C., Veeraragavan, N. R., Marijan, D., Nygard, J. F., & Vitenberg, R. (2023). A Survey on blockchain for healthcare: Challenges, benefits, and future directions. *IEEE Communications Surveys and Tutorials*, 25(1). Available from https://doi.org/10.1109/COMST.2022.3224644, http://ieeexplore.ieee.org/xpl/RecentIssue.jsp?punumber = 9739.

Arunachalam, S., Shanthi, H. J., Sivagurunathan, G., Das, S., Anand, D., & Raj, M. T. (2023). Cloud-based decentralized smart healthcare for patient monitoring on deep learning. In *Proceedings of the 2nd international conference on applied artificial intelligence and computing, ICAAIC 2023* (pp. 459–466). Institute of Electrical and Electronics Engineers Inc., India. 9781665456302. Available from https://doi.org/10.1109/ICAAIC56838.2023.10141120, http://ieeexplore.ieee.org/xpl/mostRecentIssue.jsp?punumber = 10140172.

Asamoah, K. O., Xia, H., Amofa, S., Amankona, O. I., Luo, K., Xia, Q., Gao, J., Du, X., & Guizani, M. (2020). Zero-Chain: A blockchain-based identity for digital city operating system. *IEEE Internet of Things Journal*, 7(10). Available from https://doi.org/10.1109/JIOT.2020.2986367, http://ieeexplore.ieee.org/servlet/opac?punumber = 6488907.

Azad, T., Newton, M. A. H., Trevathan, J., & Sattar, A. (2024). Hierarchical decentralized edge interoperability. *IEEE Internet of Things Journal*, 11(8). Available from https://doi.org/10.1109/JIOT.2023.3340298, http://ieeexplore.ieee.org/servlet/opac?punumber = 6488907.

Azbeg, K., Ouchetto, O., & Jai Andaloussi, S. (2023). Access control and privacy-preserving blockchain-based system for diseases management. *IEEE Transactions on Computational Social Systems*, 10(4), 1515–1527. Available from https://doi.org/10.1109/TCSS.2022.3186945.

Ballal, S., Chandre, Y., Pise, R., Sonare, B., & Patil, S. (2023). Blockchain-based decentralized platform for electronic health records management. In *IEEE International Conference on Blockchain and Distributed Systems Security, ICBDS 2023*. Institute of Electrical and Electronics Engineers Inc., India. Available from https://doi.org/10.1109/ICBDS58040.2023.10346392, http://ieeexplore.ieee.org/xpl/mostRecentIssue.jsp?punumber = 10346238. 9798350333763.

Banate, H. (2023). Decentralised application for health insurance management using blockchain. In *14th International Conference on Computing Communication and Networking Technologies (ICCCNT)*. Available from https://doi.org/10.1109/ICCCNT56998.2023.103080502023.

Begum, M., Mamun, Q., & Kaosar, M. (2013). A privacy-preserving framework for personally controlled electronic health record (PCEHR) system. In *Proceeding 2nd Australian eHealth Informatics and Security Conference, held on the 2nd-4th December, 2013 at Edith Cowan University, Perth, Western Australia*. Available from https://doi.org/10.4225/75/579706bc40a9a.

Belchior, R., Vasconcelos, A., Guerreiro, S., & Correia, M. (2021). A survey on blockchain interoperability: Past, present, and future trends. *ACM Computing Surveys*, 54(8). Available from https://doi.org/10.1145/347114, Article 168.

Beyaz, M.I. (2022). An implantable sensor for arterial pressure monitoring with minimal loading: Design and finite element validation. In *Proceedings of IEEE Sensors*. Institute of Electrical and Electronics Engineers Inc., Turkey. Available from https://doi.org/10.1109/SENSORS52175.2022.9967260, http://www.ieee.org/sensors, 21689229.

Cai, G., Fang, Y., Wen, J., Han, G., & Yang, X. (2019). QoS-aware buffer-aided relaying implant WBAN for healthcare IoT: Opportunities and challenges. *IEEE Network*, 33(4). Available from https://doi.org/10.1109/mnet.2019.1800405.

Calado, A., MacCiantelli, G., Errico, V., Gruppioni, E., & Saggio, G. (2020). Evaluation of dedicated bluetooth low energy wireless data transfer for an implantable EMG sensor. In *ACM International Conference Proceeding Series* (pp. 52–57). Association for Computing Machinery, Italy. Available from https://doi.org/10.1145/3441233.3441239, http://portal.acm.org/, 9781450388283.

Charles, W., Marler, N., Long, L., & Manion, S. (2019). Blockchain compliance by design: Regulatory considerations for blockchain in clinical research. *Frontiers in Blockchain*, 2. Available from https://doi.org/10.3389/fbloc.2019.00018.

Chauhan, A. (2018). Blockchain and scalability. In *2018 IEEE international conference software quality reliability secure and. companion* (pp. 122–128). Available from https://doi.org/10.1109/QRS-C.2018.00034

Cook, D. J., Schmitter-Edgecombe, M., Jönsson, L., & Morant, A. V. (2019). Technology-enabled assessment of functional health. *IEEE Reviews in Biomedical Engineering*, 12, 319–332. Available from https://doi.org/10.1109/RBME.2018.2851500.

Costanzo, I., Sen, D., Rhein, L., & Guler, U. (2022). Respiratory monitoring: Current state of the art and future roads. *IEEE Reviews in Biomedical Engineering, 15*. Available from https://doi.org/10.1109/rbme.2020.3036330.

Dario, P., Hannaford, B., & Menciassi, A. (2003). Smart surgical tools and augmenting devices. *IEEE Transactions on Robotics and Automation, 19*(5), 782—792. Available from https://doi.org/10.1109/TRA.2003.817071.

Dashtizadeh, M., Meskaran, F., & Tan, D. (2022). A secure blockchain-based pharmaceutical supply chain management system: Traceability and detection of counterfeit Covid-19 vaccines. In *2022 IEEE 2nd Mysore sub section international conference (MysuruCon)* (pp. 1—5). Mysuru, India. https://doi.org/10.1109/MysuruCon55714.2022.9972646

Deng, Z., Guo, L., Chen, X., & Wu, W. (2023). Smart wearable systems for health monitoring. *Sensors, 23*, 2479. Available from https://doi.org/10.3390/s23052479.

Devi, T., Kamatchi, S.B., & Deepa, N. (2023). Enhancing the security of healthcare data using blockchain technology. In *2023 International Conference on Computer Communication and Informatics (ICCCI)* (pp. 1—7), Coimbatore, India. Available from https://doi.org/10.1109/ICCCI56745.2023.10128545.

Dimitrov, D. V. (2019). Blockchain applications for healthcare data management. *Healthcare Information Research., 25*(1), 51—56. Available from https://doi.org/10.4258/hir.2019.25.1.51.

Durneva, P., Cousins, K. C., & Chen, M. (2020). The current state of research, challenges, and future research directions of blockchain technology in patient care: Systematic review. *Journal of Medical Internet Research, 22*. Available from https://api.semanticscholar.org/CorpusID:221140373.

Efendi, S., Siregar, B., & Pranoto, H. (2018). Concept designs of patient information security using e-health sensor shield platform on blockchain infrastructure. *In Proceedings of MICoMS 2017 (Emerald Reach Proceedings Series)* (Vol. 1, pp. 641—646). Emerald Publishing Limited, Leeds. Available from https://doi.org/10.1108/978-1-78756-793-1-00100.

Fernando, E., Meyliana, & Surjandy. (2019). The success factor of implementation blockchain technology in the pharmaceutical industry: A literature review. In *2019 6th international conference information technology computer. electronic engineering. ICITACEE 2019* (pp. 1—5). Available from https://doi.org/10.1109/ICITACEE.2019.8904335.

Ferreira-Brito, F., Ferreira, J., Vieira, M., Guerreiro, J., & Guerreiro, T. (2023). Digital therapeutics with virtual reality and sensors. In *UbiComp/ISWC 2023 Adjunct - Adjunct Proceedings of the 2023 ACM International Joint Conference on Pervasive and Ubiquitous Computing and the 2023 ACM International Symposium on Wearable Computing* (pp. 611—614). Association for Computing Machinery, Inc, Portugal. Available from https://doi.org/10.1145/3594739.3611327, http://dl.acm.org/citation.cfm?id = 3594739, 9798400702006.

Firouzi, F., Jiang, S., Chakrabarty, K., Farahani, B., Daneshmand, M., Song, J., & Mankodiya, K. (2023). Fusion of IoT, AI, edge—fog—cloud, and blockchain: Challenges, solutions, and a case study in healthcare and medicine. *ieee internet of things journal, 10*(5). Available from https://doi.org/10.1109/jiot.2022.3191881.

Ganesh, D., Seshadri, G., Sokkanarayanan, S., Bose, P., Rajan, S., & Sathiyanarayanan, M. (2020). AutoImpilo: Smart automated health machine using IoT to improve telemedicine and telehealth. In *Proceedings of the international conference on smart technologies in computing, electrical and electronics, ICSTCEE 2020* (pp. 134—138). Institute of Electrical and Electronics Engineers Inc. Undefined. Available from https://doi.org/10.1109/ICSTCEE49637.2020.9277223, http://ieeexplore.ieee.org/xpl/mostRecentIssue.jsp?punumber = 9276205, 9781728172132.

Gao, F., Liu, C., Zhang, L., Liu, T., Wang, Z., Song, Z., Cai, H., Fang, Z., Chen, J., Wang, J., Han, M., Wang, J., Lin, K., Wang, R., Li, M., Mei, Q., Ma, X., Liang, S., Gou, G., & Xue, N. (2023). Wearable and flexible electrochemical sensors for sweat analysis: A review. *Microsystems & Nanoengineering, 9*(1). Available from https://doi.org/10.1038/s41378-022-00443-6.

Gendy, M. E. G., & Yuce, M. R. (2023). Emerging technologies used in health management and efficiency improvement during different contact tracing phases against COVID-19 pandemic. *In IEEE Reviews in Biomedical Engineering, 16*, 38—52. Available from https://doi.org/10.1109/RBME.2022.3219433.

Gharib, G., Bütün, İ., Muganlı, Z., Kozalak, G., Namlı, İ., Sarraf, S. S., Ahmadi, V. E., Toyran, E., van Wijnen, A. J., & Koşar, A. (2022). Biomedical applications of microfluidic devices: A review. *Biosensors, 12*(11). Available from https://doi.org/10.3390/bios12111023, http://www.mdpi.com/journal/biosensors/.

Gökalp, E., Gökalp, M. O., Çoban, S., & Eren, P. E. (2018). Analysing opportunities and challenges of integrated blockchain technologies in healthcare. *Lecture Notes in Business Information Processing, 333*, 174—183. Available from https://doi.org/10.1007/978-3-030-00060-8_13, http://www.springer.com/series/7911.

Haleem, A., Javaid, M., Singh, R. P., Suman, R., & Rab, S. (2021). Blockchain technology applications in healthcare: An overview. *International Journal of Intelligent Networks, 2*. Available from https://doi.org/10.1016/j.ijin.2021.09.005, https://www.sciencedirect.com/journal/international-journal-of-intelligent-networks.

Hang, L., Kim, B. H., Kim, K. H., Kim, D. H., & Parameshachari, B. D. (2021). A Permissioned Blockchain-Based Clinical Trial Service Platform to Improve Trial Data Transparency. *BioMed Research International*, *2021*. Available from https://doi.org/10.1155/2021/5554487.

Haque, A.B., Muniat, A., Ullah, P.R., & Mushsharat., S. (2021). An automated approach towards smart healthcare with blockchain and smart contracts. In *Proceedings - IEEE 2021 International Conference on Computing, Communication, and Intelligent Systems, ICCCIS 2021* (pp. 250–255). Institute of Electrical and Electronics Engineers Inc., Bangladesh. Available from https://doi.org/10.1109/ICCCIS51004.2021.9397158, http://ieeexplore.ieee.org/xpl/mostRecentIssue.jsp?punumber = 9396788, 9781728185293.

Hasanova, H., Baek, U. J., Shin, M. G., Cho, K., & Kim, M. S. (2019). A survey on blockchain cybersecurity vulnerabilities and possible countermeasures. *International Journal of Network Management*, *29*(2). Available from https://doi.org/10.1002/nem.2060, http://onlinelibrary.wiley.com/journal/10.1002/(ISSN)1099-1190.

Hepp, T., Sharinghousen, M., Ehret, P., Schoenhals, A., & Gipp, B. (2018). On-chain vs. off-chain storage for supply- and blockchain integration. *IT - Information Technology*, *60*(5-6). Available from https://doi.org/10.1515/itit-2018-0019.

He, X., Alqahtani, S., & Gamble, R. (2018). Toward privacy-assured health insurance claims. In *2018 IEEE international conference on Internet of Things (iThings) and IEEE green computing and communications (GreenCom) and IEEE cyber, physical and social computing (CPSCom) and IEEE smart data (SmartData)* (pp. 1634–1641). Available from https://doi.org/10.1109/Cybermatics_2018.2018.00273.

He, T., Chen, J., He, B.-G., Wang, W., Zhu, Z.-L., & Lv, Z. (2023). Toward wearable sensors: Advances, trends, and challenges. *ACM Computing Surveys*, *55*(14s). Available from https://doi.org/10.1145/3596599, Article 333.

Hripcsak, G., Bloomrosen, M., FlatelyBrennan, P., Chute, C. G., Cimino, J., Detmer, D. E., Edmunds, M., Embi, P. J., Goldstein, M. M., Hammond, W. E., Keenan, G. M., Labkoff, S., Murphy, S., Safran, C., Speedie, S., Strasberg, H., Temple, F., & Wilcox, A. B. (2014). Health data use, stewardship, and governance: ongoing gaps and challenges: A report from AMIA's 2012 health policy meeting. *Journal of the American Medical Informatics Association*, *21*(2). Available from https://doi.org/10.1136/amiajnl-2013-002117.

Huang, J., Xing, C.-C., & Wang, C. (2017). Simultaneous wireless information and power transfer: Technologies, applications, and research challenges. *IEEE Communications Magazine*, *55*(11), 26–32. Available from https://doi.org/10.1109/MCOM.2017.1600806.

Huynh, T. H., Jafari, R., & Chung, W.-Y. (2019). Noninvasive cuffless blood pressure estimation using pulse transit time and impedance plethysmography. *IEEE Transactions on Biomedical Engineering*, *66*(4), 967–976. Available from https://doi.org/10.1109/TBME.2018.2865751.

Hu, F., Liu, X., Shao, M., Sui, D., & Wang, L. (2017). Wireless energy and information transfer in WBAN: An overview. *IEEE Network*, *31*(3). Available from https://doi.org/10.1109/mnet.2017.1600246.

Islam, M. A., Islam, M. A., Jacky, M. A. H., Al-Amin, M., Miah, M. S. U., Khan, M. M. I., & Hossain, M. I. (2023). Distributed ledger technology based integrated healthcare solution for Bangladesh. *IEEE Access*, *11*. Available from https://doi.org/10.1109/ACCESS.2023.3279724, http://ieeexplore.ieee.org/xpl/RecentIssue.jsp?punumber = 6287639.

Ismail, L., Materwala, H., & Zeadally, S. (2019). Lightweight blockchain for healthcare. *IEEE Access*, *7*, 149935–149951. Available from https://api.semanticscholar.org/CorpusID:204864140.

Ivanov, V. M. (2020). *Advances in augmented reality (AR) for medical simulation and training* (p. 3).

Jain, R., & Semwal, V. B. (2022). A novel feature extraction method for preimpact fall detection system using deep learning and wearable sensors. *IEEE Sensors Journal*, *22*(23), 22943–22951. Available from https://doi.org/10.1109/JSEN.2022.3213814.

Jamshed, M. A., Ali, K., Abbasi, Q. H., Imran, M. A., & Ur-Rehman, M. (2022). Challenges, *applications, and future of wireless sensors in internet of things: A review*. *IEEE Sensors Journal*, *22*(6). Available from https://doi.org/10.1109/JSEN.2022.3148128, http://ieeexplore.ieee.org/xpl/RecentIssue.jsp?punumber = 7361.

Javed, I. T., Alharbi, F., Bellaj, B., Margaria, T., Crespi, N., & Qureshi, K. N. (2021). Health-id: A blockchain-based decentralized identity management for remote healthcare. *Healthcare (Switzerland)*, *9*(6). Available from https://doi.org/10.3390/healthcare9060712, https://www.mdpi.com/2227-9032/9/6/712/pdf.

Jobin, A., Ienca, M., & Vayena, E. (2019). The global landscape of AI ethics guidelines. *Nature Machine Intelligence*, *1*(9), 389–399. Available from https://doi.org/10.1038/s42256-019-0088-2.

Kassal, P., Steinberg, M. D., & Steinberg, I. M. (2018). Wireless chemical sensors and biosensors: A review. *Sensors and Actuators, B: Chemical*, *266*, 228–245.

Khatoon, A. (2020). A blockchain-based smart contract system for healthcare management. *Electronics, 9*(1), 94. Available from https://doi.org/10.3390/electronics9010094.

Khatri, S., Alzahrani, F. A., Ansari, M. T. J., Agrawal, A., Kumar, R., & Khan, R. A. (2021). A systematic analysis on blockchain integration with healthcare domain: Scope and challenges. *IEEE Access, 9.* Available from https://doi.org/10.1109/ACCESS.2021.3087608, http://ieeexplore.ieee.org/xpl/RecentIssue.jsp?punumber = 6287639.

Kuhn, D. R., Roberts, J. D., Ferraiolo, D., & DeFranco, J. (2022). A distributed ledger technology design using hyperledger fabric and a clinical trial use case. In *2022 IEEE 29th annual software technology conference (STC)* (pp. 168–173). Gaithersburg, MD, USA. Available from https://doi.org/10.1109/STC55697.2022.00031.

Kumar, D., Ding, X., Du, W., & Cerpa, A. (2021). Building sensor fault detection and diagnostic system. In *BuildSys 2021 - Proceedings of the 2021 ACM International Conference on Systems for Energy-Efficient Built Environments* (pp. 357–360). Association for Computing Machinery, Inc, United States. Available from https://doi.org/10.1145/3486611.3491122, Available from http://dl.acm.org/citation.cfm?id = 3486611, 9781450391146.

Kuo, T. T., & Ohno-Machado, L. (2018). Modelchain: Decentralized privacy-preserving healthcare predictive modeling framework on private blockchain networks. arXiv, United States arXiv. Available from https://doi.org/10.48550/arxiv.1802.01746, https://arxiv.org/.

Lachaux, K., Maitre, J., Bouchard, K., Lussier, M., Bottari, C., Couture, M., Bier, N., Giroux, S., & Gaboury, S. (2022). Managing the fall risk in smart homes using monocular cameras, ambient sensors and an interactive social robot. In *IEEE international conference on blockchain, smart healthcare and emerging technologies, SmartBlock4Health 2022.* Institute of Electrical and Electronics Engineers Inc., Canada. Available from https://doi.org/10.1109/SmartBlock4Health56071.2022.10034526, http://ieeexplore.ieee.org/xpl/mostRecentIssue.jsp?punumber = 10035029, 9781665460149.

Liu, S., Xue, B., Yan, W., Rwei, A. Y., & Wu, C. (2023). Recent advances and design strategies towards wearable near-infrared spectroscopy. *IEEE Open Journal of Nanotechnology, 4,* 25–35. Available from https://doi.org/10.1109/OJNANO.2022.3226603.

Luo, J., Bai, R., He, S., & Shin, K. G. (2022). Pervasive pose estimation for fall detection. *ACM Transactions on Computing for Healthcare, 3*(3). Available from https://doi.org/10.1145/3478027, https://health.acm.org/index.cfm.

Monrat, A. A., Schelén, O., & Andersson, K. (2019). A survey of blockchain from the perspectives of applications, challenges, and opportunities. *IEEE Access, 7,* 117134–117151. Available from https://doi.org/10.1109/ACCESS.2019.2936094.

Mukhopadhyay, S. C., Suryadevara, N. K., & Nag, A. (2022). Wearable sensors for healthcare: Fabrication to application. *Sensors, 22,* 5137. Available from https://doi.org/10.3390/s22145137.

Musamih, A., Salah, K., Jayaraman, R., Arshad, J., Debe, M., Al-Hammadi, Y., & Ellahham, S. (2021). A blockchain-based approach for drug traceability in healthcare supply chain. *IEEE Access, 9.* Available from https://doi.org/10.1109/access.2021.3049920.

Nath, R. K., & Thapliyal, H. (2021). Wearable health monitoring system for older adults in a smart home environment. In *Proceedings of IEEE computer society annual symposium on VLSI, ISVLSI* (pp. 390–395). IEEE Computer Society, United States. Available from https://doi.org/10.1109/ISVLSI51109.2021.00077, http://ieeexplore.ieee.org/xpl/conhome.jsp?punumber = 1000807, 21593477.

Öberg, P. Å., Togawa, T., & Spelman, F. A. (Eds.), (2004). *Sensors in medicine and health care: Sensors applications* (1st ed.). Wiley-VCH. Available from https://doi.org/10.1002/3527601414.

Omar, I. A., Jayaraman, R., Salah, K., & Simsekler, M. C. E. (2019). Exploiting ethereum smart contracts for clinical trial management. In *Proceedings of IEEE/ACS international conference on computer systems and applications, AICCSA.* IEEE Computer Society, United Arab Emirates. Available from https://doi.org/10.1109/AICCSA47632.2019.9035341, http://ieeexplore.ieee.org/xpl/conferences.jsp, 21615330.

Otoum, S., Al Ridhawi, I., & Mouftah, H. T. (2021). Preventing and controlling epidemics through blockchain-assisted AI-enabled networks. *IEEE Network, 35*(3), 34–41. Available from https://doi.org/10.1109/MNET.011.2000628, May/June 2021.

Park, J. (2023). A stretchable and biocompatible epidermal sensor for continuous monitoring of skin temperature and humidity. *Advanced Functional Materials, 51,* 2023.

Prada, E. J. A., & Forero, L. M. S. (2022). A belt-like assistive device for visually impaired people: Toward a more collaborative approach. *Cogent Engineering, 9*(1)2048440.

Raman, R., Meenakshi, R., Rukmani Devi, D., Kaul, M., Jayaprakash, S., & Murugan, S. (2023). IoT applications in sports and fitness: Enhancing performance monitoring and training. In *2nd International Conference on*

Smart Technologies for Smart Nation, SmartTechCon 2023 (pp. 137–141). Institute of Electrical and Electronics Engineers Inc., India. Available from https://doi.org/10.1109/SmartTechCon57526.2023.10391301, http://ieeexplore.ieee.org/xpl/mostRecentIssue.jsp?punumber = 10391093, 9798350305418.

Ramasamy, L. K., Khan K P, F., Imoize, A. L., Ogbebor, J. O., Kadry, S., & Rho, S. (2021). Blockchain-based wireless sensor networks for malicious node detection: A survey. *EEE Access, 9.* Available from https://doi.org/10.1109/ACCESS.2021.3111923, http://ieeexplore.ieee.org/xpl/RecentIssue.jsp?punumber = 6287639.

Ramzan, S., Aqdus, A., Ravi, V., Koundal, D., Amin, R., & Al Ghamdi, M. A. (2023). Healthcare applications using blockchain technology: Motivations and challenges. *IEEE Transactions on Engineering Management, 70*(8). Available from https://doi.org/10.1109/TEM.2022.3189734, https://ieeexplore.ieee.org/servlet/opac?punumber = 17.

Rehman, M., Javed, I. T., Qureshi, K. N., Margaria, T., & Jeon, G. (2023). A cyber secure medical management system by using blockchain. *IEEE Transactions on Computational Social Systems, 10*(4). Available from https://doi.org/10.1109/TCSS.2022.3215455, http://ieeexplore.ieee.org/servlet/opac?punumber = 6570650.

Sadawi, A. A., Hassan, M. S., & Ndiaye, M. (2021). A survey on the integration of blockchain with IoT to enhance performance and eliminate challenges. *IEEE Access, 9,* 54478–54497. Available from https://doi.org/10.1109/ACCESS.2021.3070555.

Saeed, N., Loukil, M. H., Sarieddeen, H., Al-Naffouri, T. Y., & Alouini, M. S. (2022). Body-centric terahertz networks: Prospects and challenges. *IEEE Transactions on Molecular, Biological, and Multi-Scale Communications, 8*(3). Available from https://doi.org/10.1109/TMBMC.2021.3135198, https://www.ieee.org/membership-catalog/productdetail/showProductDetailPage.html?product = PER475-ELE.

Saini, A., Zhu, Q., Singh, N., Xiang, Y., Gao, L., & Zhang, Y. (2021). A smart-contract-based access control framework for cloud smart healthcare system. *IEEE Internet of Things Journal, 8*(7). Available from https://doi.org/10.1109/jiot.2020.3032997.

Salim, M. M., Park, L., & Park, J. H. (2022). A Machine Learning based Scalable Blockchain architecture for a secure Healthcare system. In *2022, the 13th international conference on information and communication technology convergence (ICTC)* (pp. 2231–2234). Jeju Island, Republic of Korea. Available from https://doi.org/10.1109/ICTC55196.2022.9952962.

Sharma, I., Kaushik, K., & Chhabra, G. (2023). Augmenting transparency and reliability for national health insurance scheme with distributed ledger. In *2023 4th international conference on electronics and sustainable communication systems (ICESC)* (pp. 1399–1405). Available from https://doi.org/10.1109/ICESC57686.2023.10193127.

Shetty, S., Liang, X., Bowden, D., Zhao, J., & Zhang, L. (2019). Blockchain-based decentralized accountability and self-sovereignty in healthcare systems. In H. Treiblmaier, & R. Beck (Eds.), *business transformation through blockchain* (pp. 81–98). Palgrave Macmillan. Available from https://doi.org/10.1007/978-3-319-99058-3_5.

Shibu, A., Anirudh, A., Anilkumar, A.T., Radhakrishnan, A., & Izudheen, S. (2022). Secure storage and retrieval of electronic health records. In *Proceedings of International Conference on Computing, Communication, Security and Intelligent Systems (IC3SIS 2022)*. Institute of Electrical and Electronics Engineers Inc., India. Available from https://doi.org/10.1109/IC3SIS54991.2022.9885484, http://ieeexplore.ieee.org/xpl/mostRecentIssue.jsp?punumber = 9885260, 9781665468831.

Sonune, S., Kalbande, D., Yeole, A., & Oak, S. (2017). Issues in IoT healthcare platforms: A critical study and review. In *Proceedings of 2017 International Conference on Intelligent Computing and Control, I2C2 2017* (pp. 1–5). Institute of Electrical and Electronics Engineers Inc., India. Available from https://doi.org/10.1109/I2C2.2017.8321898, 9781538603741.

Son, H. X., Nguyen, M. H., Vo, H. K., et al. (2019). Toward a privacy protection based on access control model in hybrid cloud for healthcare systems. In *International joint conference: 12th international conference on computational intelligence in security for information systems (CISIS 2019) and 10th international conference on european transnational education (ICEUTE 2019)* (pp. 77–86). Springer.

Taherdoost, H. (2023). The role of blockchain in medical data sharing. *Cryptography, 7*(3), 36. Available from https://doi.org/10.3390/cryptography7030036.

Tandon, A., Dhir, A., Islam, N., & Mäntymäki, M. (2020). Blockchain in healthcare: A systematic literature review, synthesizing framework and future research agenda. *Computers in Industry, 122.* Available from https://doi.org/10.1016/j.compind.2020.103290, https://www.journals.elsevier.com/computers-in-industry.

Usmani, U. A., Happonen, A., & Watada, J. (2023). Secure integration of IoT-enabled sensors and technologies: Engineering applications for humanitarian impact. In *2023, the 5th international congress on human-computer interaction, optimization and robotic applications (HORA)* (pp. 1–10). Istanbul, Turkiye. Available from https://doi.org/10.1109/HORA58378.2023.10156740.

Vyas, J. D., Han, M., Li, L., Pouriyeh, S., & He, J. S. (2020). Integrating blockchain technology into healthcare. In *ACMSE 2020 - Proceedings of the 2020 ACM Southeast Conference* (pp. 197–203). Association for Computing Machinery, Inc, United States. Available from https://doi.org/10.1145/3374135.3385280, http://dl.acm.org/citation.cfm?id = 3374135, 9781450371056.

Wagholikar, S., & Wagholikar, O. (2023). Application of wearables in healthcare management: Recent trends and futuristic approach. In *OPJU international technology conference on emerging technologies for sustainable development, OTCON 2022*. Institute of Electrical and Electronics Engineers Inc., India. Available from https://doi.org/10.1109/OTCON56053.2023.10113968, http://ieeexplore.ieee.org/xpl/mostRecentIssue.jsp?punumber = 10113898, 9781665492942.

Wang, Y. (2023). This study presents a hybrid wearable system using bioimpedance, ECG, and accelerometer data for stress and sleep monitoring to improve mental health management. *Sensors, 24*, 2023.

Williams, I. (2020). Cross-chain blockchain networks, compatibility standards, and interoperability standards. IGI Global. Available from https://doi.org/10.4018/978-1-7998-3632-2.ch010.

Wong, M. C., Yee, K. C., & Nohr, C. (2018). Socio-technical consideration for blockchain technology in healthcare: The technological innovation needs clinical transformation to achieve the outcome of improving quality and safety of patient care. *Studies in Health Technology and Informatics, 247*, 636–640.

Xia, Q., Sifah, E. B., Asamoah, K. O., Gao, J., Du, X., & Guizani, M. (2017). MeDShare: Trust-less medical data sharing among cloud service providers via blockchain. *IEEE Access, 5*. Available from https://doi.org/10.1109/ACCESS.2017.2730843, http://ieeexplore.ieee.org/xpl/RecentIssue.jsp?punumber = 6287639.

Zhang, X., Schmidt, D. C., & White, J. (2018). Blockchain in healthcare: The rise of the ecosystem. *Journal of Medical Internet Research, 20*(5)e10129.

Zhang, P., White, J., Schmidt, D.C., & Lenz, G. (2017). Applying software patterns to address interoperability in blockchain-based healthcare apps. arXiv, United States arXiv https://arxiv.org, https://doi.org/10.48550/arxiv.1706.03700.

Zhou, S., Li, K., Xiao, L., Cai, J., Liang, W., & Castiglione, A. (2023). A systematic review of consensus mechanisms in blockchain. *Mathematics, 11*(10), 2248. Available from https://doi.org/10.3390/math11102248.

Zhu, P., Hu, J., Zhang, Y., & Li, X. (2020). A blockchain based solution for medication anti-counterfeiting and traceability. *IEEE Access, 8*. Available from https://doi.org/10.1109/access.2020.3029196.

Zhu, X., Wang, Y., Wang, C., Yang, H., Wang, X., & Yang, M. (2017). Developing a driving fatigue detection system using physiological sensors. In *Proceedings of the 29th Australian conference on computer-human interaction* (pp. 566–570). Association for Computing Machinery. https://doi.org/10.1145/3152771.3156188.

Digital twin and sensor networks for healthcare monitoring frameworks

Amirhossein Danesh[1], Shaker El-Sappagh[1,2] and Tamer Abuhmed[1]

[1]College of Computing and Informatics, Sungkyunkwan University, Suwon, South Korea
[2]Faculty of Computer Science and Engineering, Galala University, Suez, Egypt

10.1 Introduction

In the modern landscape, digital twin (DT) technology, known for creating virtual replicas of physical entities, has found widespread applications across diverse domains. Its utility in manufacturing optimizes design and maintenance processes (Digital twins improve real-life manufacturing, n.d.), while in healthcare, it plays a pivotal role in personalized medicine and enhancing patient care (Venkatesh et al., 2022). This technology is instrumental in the automotive and aerospace industries for vehicle testing and maintenance (Examining the Data on Digital Twin in the Automotive Industry, 2023), while in urban planning, it contributes to efficient city modeling and traffic optimization. DTs are equally valuable in the energy sector for managing power systems and in construction for assisting in building lifecycle management (Ammar et al., 2022). Moreover, their use extends to retail for optimizing logistics, and to environmental monitoring in promoting sustainable practices.

In the healthcare domain, DTs generate virtual representations of patients, medical equipment, and entire healthcare systems. These digital models are essential for ongoing, real-time monitoring, and offer predictive analysis capabilities that significantly improve treatment methodologies (Shengli, 2021). This enhancement stems from the integration of diverse data sources, including current physiological data and extensive historical health records (Saracco, 2023). Integrating sophisticated technologies into DTs, such as the Internet of Things (IoT), blockchain, and artificial intelligence (AI), significantly enhances their capabilities. For instance, AI was applied for several applications for medical diagnosis (Abuhmed et al., 2021; Ali et al., 2023; El-Sappagh et al., 2020, 2023), progression detection (Abuhmed et al., 2021; El-Sappagh et al., 2021, 2023; Rahim et al., 2023a, 2023b; Saleh et al., 2023), and security applications (Abdukhamidov et al., 2023; Abuhamad, 2018; Abuhamad et al., 2020, 2009), to name a few (Yüksel et al., 2023). These technologies facilitate the collection and examination of intricate data sets, providing healthcare professionals with deeper insights into patient conditions and healthcare processes. As a result, DTs in healthcare refine decision-making, leading to more effective patient care management and improved overall healthcare outcomes (Ferdousi, 2022). Current applications of DT technology in healthcare include real-time patient monitoring, predictive diagnostics, treatment optimization, and the facilitation of personalized medicine, all contributing to a significant evolution in healthcare delivery and patient outcomes. This aligns with the broader trajectory of innovation in the sector, fostering a shift toward more personalized and resilient healthcare systems (Vallée, 2023).

This paper presents a comprehensive analysis of the development and present status of DT technology within the healthcare industry. Through a thorough review of contemporary research articles, it explores the existing implementations of DTs in healthcare, as well as their potential future development. An integral component of this review is a comprehensive survey that aims to delineate the current landscape, and forecast future trends of DT in healthcare. This survey is critical to understanding how DT technology can continue to evolve and bring transformative changes to healthcare practices and patient care, thereby underscoring its potential impact and utility in the future of healthcare technology. The key contributions of this article may be summarized as follows:

- *Advancements in sensor networks for DTs*: Recent wireless sensor network (WSN) protocols in DTs are reviewed, focusing on energy efficiency, reliable data forwarding, and network longevity, integrating new sensor technologies for real-time health monitoring.
- *Case studies on DTs in chronic disease management*: DT applications in managing type 2 diabetes (T2D) are analyzed, highlighting the effective use of IoT and machine learning (ML) of the twin precision treatment program.
- *Human digital twin (HDT) frameworks*: HDT frameworks for diabetes management of the elderly are explored, including their architecture, and personalized treatment strategies.
- *Evaluation of DT applications and challenges*: DT applications in healthcare are assessed, identifying challenges in sensor technology, data integration, and security, and underline the need for interdisciplinary solutions.
- *Strategic framework for healthcare DT implementation*: A strategy for integrating DTs with AI in healthcare is proposed, aiming to enhance patient care and healthcare practices.

In summary, our survey provides a comprehensive view of the role of DTs in enhancing healthcare, emphasizing personalized care and predictive health management, and laying the groundwork for prospective studies and practical applications. The subsequent sections of this paper are structured as follows: Section 10.2 offers a succinct review of the DT, surveying key literature and validations. Section 10.3 then outlines crucial DT technologies and models in healthcare. Sections 10.4 and 10.5 next define and outline the concept and characteristics, respectively, of DTs, while Section 10.6 explores DT infrastructure, focusing on AI and ML roles in healthcare DT. Meanwhile, Section 10.7 explores DT frameworks, while Section 10.8 covers energy-efficient DTs and sensor tech in health monitoring. Section 10.9 next discusses the benefits of the DT in disease management and hospital system optimization, while Section 10.10 details the role of DTs in managing illnesses like diabetes and tumors, presenting two diabetes and human brain case studies. Finally, Sections 10.11 and 10.12 overview the tools and challenges, respectively, of the DT in healthcare, while Section 10.13 concludes the paper.

10.2 Related work

The last seven years have seen a significant upsurge of interest in the DT concept, spanning both the academic and industrial domains. This surge coincides with a notable increase in the volume of publications with the development of innovative processes, the emergence of new concepts, and the identification of a wide range of potential benefits associated with DTs, as illustrated in Fig. 10.1. In the existing literature, several review articles have investigated different facets of DTs in healthcare, focusing explicitly on the application of DTs in healthcare and their relevance to medical case studies (Danesh et al., 2024). Nevertheless, the recent and specific intersection of DTs and healthcare still needs to be examined, to acquire thorough and detailed insight into the potential of this emerging field within healthcare. Shengli (2021) highlights the applications, models, and implementation of human digital twins (HDTs), focusing on the challenges in accurately modeling and simulating human health behavior. These challenges include integrating diverse health data, technological limitations in simulation, and the need for the secure and ethical handling of personal data, which are all essential for effective HDTs. Ferdousi (2022) provides an overview of the well-being digital twin (WDT), highlighting challenges such as societal acceptance, healthcare worker adoption, data integration, and system scalability, and emphasizing the potential of DTs for personalized treatment and enhancing patient care. Sahal et al. (2022a) introduce the enhancement of healthcare through personal digital twins (PDTs), integrating them with blockchain and AI for personalized care; the paper addresses challenges like data privacy, security, scalability, and ethical

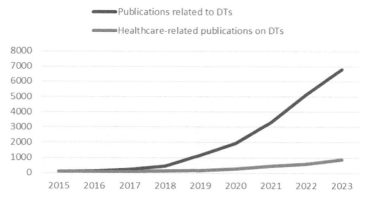

FIGURE 10.1 Comparative annual publication trends for digital twins (DTs) and healthcare-specific DTs from 2015 to 2023.

considerations, focusing on PDT applications in various healthcare scenarios, including COVID-19 management and personalized medicine. Furthermore, Chen (2023) describes its potential in personalized treatment and health monitoring; the challenges identified include societal acceptance, data integration, and system scalability. Additionally, De Benedictis et al. (2023) review DTs in healthcare, covering applications in patient care and public health, and highlight the lack of standardization in healthcare DTs. It discusses the role of AI in DT data processing, and identifies key challenges like standardization, security, privacy, and ethical considerations, emphasizing the need for future improvements in connectivity and process optimization. Furthermore, Huang et al. (2022) discuss DTs in healthcare as personalized, data-driven models, emphasizing ethical risks, like privacy, algorithmic bias, and data misuse. It suggests a process-oriented ethical framework to manage these risks, and highlights limitations, such as the limited literature, and potential oversight of genetic data risks. El-Sappagh et al., (2021, 2023) and Rahim et al. (2023a) examine healthcare DTs, emphasizing digital replication of health phenomena and challenges in data handling, security, and privacy, addressing issues like inadequate data frameworks, security breaches, and the need for sophisticated data collection and secure storage. Lastly, Björnsson et al. (2020) describe DTs in healthcare as computational models for individualized patient treatment and drug selection, utilizing ML and AI for their construction and analysis; the paper's limitations involve addressing technical, medical, ethical, and theoretical challenges in the clinical implementation of DTs, requiring extensive research comparable to the Human Genome Project. Table 10.1 provides a comprehensive overview of prior research contributions and limitations in healthcare DTs, and compares these studies with the current survey, particularly in terms of DT applications, and their connections to AI and blockchain.

10.3 Methodology and research questions

We delve into the advantages inherent in the integration of DT within the healthcare sector, while simultaneously delineating their distinctive attributes. Our systematic approach is founded on a rigorous methodology with well-defined parameters. The inclusion criteria are peer-reviewed studies that are published in English between January 2013 and December 2023 that focus on the practical application of DTs in healthcare environments and provide empirical outcomes. We exclude nonpeer-reviewed articles, publications outside the specified timeframe, and studies not directly related to the healthcare application of DTs. This selection process was designed to minimize biases, and was informed by a comprehensive search across databases, such as PubMed, Scopus, and IEEE Xplore, using a variety of search terms related to "Digital Twins" and "healthcare technology." The deliberate search and review strategy yielded 75 relevant articles, compiling a robust dataset for our analysis. Table 10.2 presents the research questions guiding our inquiry, which are informed by a seminal reference framework designed for intelligent, personalized healthcare enabled by DTs. This framework integrates data from diverse medical sensors and wearables, providing insights into metrics, such as body temperature, cardiac rate, arterial pressure, glucose levels, and indicators related to physical fitness. Our analysis spans a range of healthcare domains, highlighting the potential of the DT in

TABLE 10.1 Healthcare digital twin technology comparison between the previous work and our present survey. IOT/CPS, IOT/Cyber-Physical Systems (CPS).

Ref.	Main rfeature	DT	AI	Block chain	IOT/CPS	Application	Limitations
Shengli (2021)	Presents the HDT as a digital replica of individuals for health management, integrating complex personal data.	✓	✓	✓	✓	Use of HDT for full lifecycle management in healthcare.	Key challenges are complex data integration, and ethical and privacy concerns.
Ferdousi (2022)	Analyzes WDT and its role in improving individual well-being.	✓	✓	—	✓	Enhancing individual well-being.	Data limitations, AI trust concerns, and the need for healthcare expertise.
Sahal, Alsamhi, Brown (2022)	Describes how personal DTs improve healthcare by enabling precise decision-making and treatment optimization.	✓	✓	—	✓	Personalized care is improved through the combination of blockchain and AI.	Do not identify perfect requirements for better optimization.
Chen (2023)	Examines the networking architecture and essential technologies of HDT within PH applications.	✓	✓	—	—	Personalized treatment and health monitoring	Standardization of HDT networking technologies across different healthcare systems.
De Benedictis et al. (2023)	Utilizing Utilizes DT technology to enforce social distancing for virus containment in the workplace.	✓	✓	—	✓	Patient treatment, physician training, and public health management.	Needs more accurate scalability and adaptability to various workplaces and lack of specific environmental factors.
Huang et al. (2022)	Identifies ethical concerns associated with DTs in personalized healthcare services.	✓	✓	—	—	Enabling highly personalized medical care and treatment.	Framework may hinder ethical risk evaluation for DT information in healthcare systems.
Ogunseiju et al. (2021)	Shows how the DT framework enhances ergonomic management via bi-directional mapping.	✓	✓	—	—	Influential DT in the Healthcare industry.	Limitations include scalability, sensor constraints, and feedback effectiveness.
Akash and Ferdous (2022)	Utilizes mathematical data model for patient data collection (Blockchain based).	✓	—	✓	—	Distributed epidemic notification.	Challenges include data collection, security risks, and storage/analysis complexities.
Björnsson et al. (2020)	Finds that DT personalizes medicine and clarifies SDTC strategy.	✓	—	✓	—	Individualized medicine.	Limitations include technical, medical, and ethical in DTs' implementation.
	This work	✓	✓	✓	✓	Utilization of DTs & sensors in healthcare monitoring.	Security risks, and complexities in analysis.

TABLE 10.2   Inquiries and correlating approaches in research.

Number	Question	Section
Q1	What is the role of the DT in healthcare, its characteristics, and infrastructure?	4,5
Q2	How secure is the information used in constructing a DT?	5
Q3	How does ML contribute to DTs in the healthcare domain?	6
Q4	What are the existing DT frameworks?	7
Q5	What are the current applications of DTs in healthcare for specific diseases, hospitals, medical processes?	8
Q6	How can DT help in diabetes and human brain sickness?	9
Q7	What are the simulation packages for implementing DTs in healthcare?	10
Q8	What are the existing challenges in implementing DTs in the healthcare sector?	11

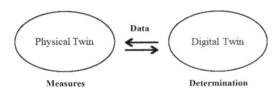

FIGURE 10.2   The seamless coexistence of the digital and physical twins.

automating decision-making processes, and in managing conditions like diabetes, tumors, and brain health data complexities. Additionally, applying a strategic reference model to these conditions offers multiple benefits to patients, healthcare professionals, and researchers. We articulate the research objectives and key questions addressed by this study, which cover the conceptualization of DTs, their foundational framework, and the array of potential applications and usage scenarios. The adoption of this meticulous research methodology enables systematic exploration of the technical aspects of the deployment of DTs in healthcare, contributing significantly to the advancement of this transformative technology within the industry.

10.4 Background

10.4.1 The origin of the digital twin

The DT has gained considerable prominence in recent years, emerging as a focal point in research. A plethora of scholarly works underscores its pivotal role in modern industries (Vohra, 2022). DTs are often utilized for monitoring, analyzing, and optimizing the performance of physical assets, systems, or processes, see Fig. 10.2. They can be employed for proactive servicing, and to optimize performance, enhance design, and conduct virtual testing and experimentation. DTs have found utility in manufacturing, agriculture, and product design (Sahal et al., 2022a). In the realm of biomedical sciences, DTs contribute to cardiovascular diagnostics (Lu et al., 2022), and regulate insulin infusion (Rivera et al., 2020), exemplifying their versatile applications. DTs applications are envisaged to support personalized medication (Chen, 2023), and forecast immune system responses in humans (Liu, 2019). For example, precision and accuracy in healthcare can be enhanced by proactively analyzing data to anticipate potential health issues and take appropriate actions. This proactive optimization approach is labeled as a Wellness DT, which focuses on improving the well-being of individuals.

10.4.2 Digital twin definitions and concept

As the amount of research on DTs grows, numerous definitions have emerged. However, common core components can be found in every DT development. Many researchers have defined DTs in their own unique ways, as shown in Table 10.3, while others have cited different definitions proposed by their peers. The definition of a DT that receives the most citations is as follows: "A comprehensive simulation integrates Multiphysics, multiscale, and probabilistic aspects for an as-built vehicle or system. Utilizing the most advanced physical models, sensor updates, and more, it faithfully mirrors the lifespan of its corresponding airborne twin" (Glaessgen & Stargel, 2012).

The fundamental components of a DT, including modeling, IoT, and simulation, are already widely acknowledged and well-established. The essence of DTs can be encapsulated as follows: a tangible entity has its virtual counterpart, with a link that facilitates the movement of data from the physical world to the digital domain. This linkage facilitates the exchange of data and knowledge from the digital domain to the physical world, as illustrated in Fig. 10.3.

The study commenced by delineating essential principles through an exhaustive examination of literature sourced from the Google Scholar and Scopus databases. A targeted search was undertaken for articles including the term "Digital Twin" or "Digital Twins" in their titles. The selected papers comprised a diversity of sources, including scholarly journals, conference publications, investigative studies, and authoritative encyclopedic references. These documents were thoroughly examined to address several essential questions: the characterization of a DT, the technologies employed, the digital patient, and current applications in various industries, especially healthcare, as well as the challenges and opportunities associated with this emerging technology.

10.4.3 The importance of the digital twin in healthcare

DTs offer significant benefits in healthcare due to their unique capabilities. Fig. 10.4 shows the advantages of DTs within the healthcare domain:

Increased accuracy: DTs allow for the generation of a digital replication of a patient's anatomy or physiological systems, enabling more accurate and detailed analysis. This enhanced accuracy can facilitate precise diagnosis, treatment planning, and the monitoring of diseases (Melesse et al., 2021).

TABLE 10.3 Conceptualizing digital twins: varied definitions and interpretations.

Ref.	Definition
Glaessgen and Stargel (2012)	"A digital twin acts as a digital representation of a physical system or entity, employed for comprehending, forecasting, and enhancing its operational efficiency."
Singh et al. (2021)	"A digital twin represents a real-time digital replica of a physical object or system, facilitating data analysis and simulations for the purpose of monitoring and optimizing performance."
Park et al. (2019)	"A digital twin is defined as a comprehensive virtual model of a real-world system, incorporating all its physical details and functional elements."
Alam and El Saddik (2017)	"A digital twin represents an exact cybernetic duplicate of a physical system, accurately mirroring all its functionalities."
Milazzo et al. (2018)	"The digital twin encompasses collected data, structured information, and various models detailing the physical progression of equipment. It replicates the authentic equipment evolution, preemptively identifying potential failures."
Barszcz and Zabaryłło (2019)	"The "Digital Twin" methodology involves a streamlined numerical model."
Bruynseels et al. (2018)	"A Digital Twin intricately links a physical system, such as a specific machine, with its computer model to closely mirror the architecture, dynamics, and real-time state of the system."
Wuttke et al. (2020)	"Digital twins involve developing virtual simulations of processes, products, or services to predict system behavior and identify potential issues before implementation."
Schluse and Rossmann (2016)	"A "digital twin" is a virtual portrayal of a real-world entity, whether a person, software system, or physical object such as a machine, component, or environmental element."
Reitz et al. (2019)	"In general, the term "Digital Twin" encompasses two main aspects: the management layer of a Cyber-Physical System (CPS), and its corresponding simulation models."
Steinmetz et al. (2018)	"A comprehensive simulation of a vehicle or system integrates advanced physical models, sensor updates, and fleet history to mirror the operational life of its flying twin."
Ardanza et al. (2019)	"They act as digital depictions of real systems, capturing not just their 3D physical features, but also their behavioral traits."
Liau et al. (2018)	"A Digital Twin constitutes a digital representation of an actual production system, used for optimization, monitoring, diagnosis, and prediction by integrating AI, machine learning, and software analytics with substantial physical system data."
Tao et al. (2019)	"The digital twin of a product encompasses physical components, virtual models, and linked data, thus merging the tangible and digital worlds. The physical entities represent the concrete products utilized by users."
Liu et al. (2019)	"The "Digital Twin" is a cutting-edge technology providing realistic models of current processes and interactions. It uses integrated simulations, optimal physical models, and sensor feedback to accurately reflect its real-life equivalent."
Bohlin et al. (2018)	"A "Digital Twin" entails employing a digital replica of a physical system for instantaneous optimization. This concept includes a comprehensive portrayal of a component, product, or system, encompassing all critical data across present and future lifecycle stages."

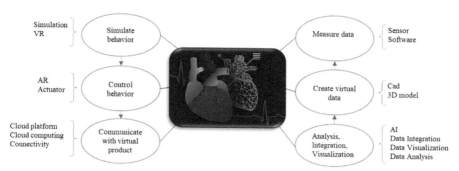

FIGURE 10.3 The idea of digital twin encompasses the linkage between the tangible reality and the virtual domain, enabling the seamless exchange of information between them.

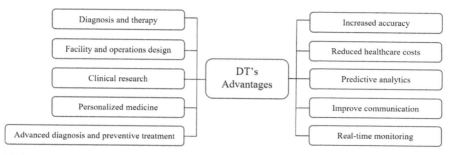

FIGURE 10.4 Advantages of digital twin within the healthcare domain.

Reduced healthcare costs (*labor, etc.*): DTs can potentially reduce healthcare costs by optimizing resource utilization, streamlining processes, and minimizing the need for physical interactions. This has the potential to result in cost reductions concerning personnel expenditures and research initiatives (Corral-Acero et al., 2020).

Predictive analytics: DTs facilitate the examination of current patient data coupled with historical information, enabling predictive analytics to recognize potential health risks, forecast disease progression, and customize treatments to suit individual requirements. This proactive approach can lead to better patient outcomes and early intervention (Sahal et al., 2022b).

Improved communication: DTs enhance communication within the healthcare community by providing a collaborative virtual platform. This enables seamless collaboration, information sharing, and interdisciplinary decision-making, leading to improved patient DTs facilitating the continuous monitoring of patient health, making the information available instantaneously, and allowing medical professionals to continuously monitor vital statistics, medication compliance, and various health metrics. This real-time monitoring improves patient outcomes, reduces hospital readmissions, and lowers overall healthcare costs (Barbiero et al., 2021), concurrently enabling the tracking of chronic conditions and overall well-being. Through the assimilation of data from wearable devices, electronic health records, and

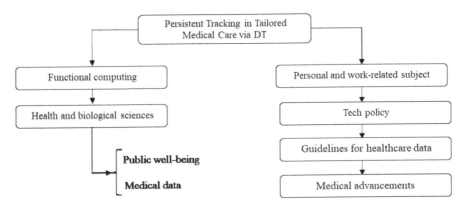

FIGURE 10.5   Personalized monitoring in healthcare using digital twin technology.

environmental sensors, a DT can provide continuous monitoring and analysis of an individual's health condition. This allows for the early identification of abnormalities, proactive interventions, and personalized recommendations for lifestyle modifications (Ahmed et al., 2022). Fig. 10.5 illustrates a flow chart of seamless monitoring in individualized healthcare via DTs.

Drug development: DTs can have a substantial impact on drug development by simulating the impact of new drugs on virtual patient models. This allows researchers to refine dosages, predict efficacy, and identify potential side effects, before initiating clinical trials (Melesse et al., 2021). Additionally, they play a role in the creation and manufacture of novel vaccines.

Advanced diagnosis and preventive treatment: DTs can aid in advanced diagnosis by integrating patient-specific data and generating real-time insights. This enables healthcare professionals to detect diseases at an early stage, and develop personalized preventive treatment plans (Hassani et al., 2022).

Personalized medicine: DTs can facilitate personalized medicine by considering individual patient characteristics, genetic profiles, and environmental factors. This allows healthcare providers to customize treatment approaches, and enhance outcomes for individual patients (Abuhmed et al., 2021).

Clinical research: DTs can support clinical research by providing virtual representations of patients, enabling simulations, and experiments. This allows researchers to test hypotheses, evaluate treatment strategies, and generate evidence for more effective healthcare interventions (Attaran & Celik, 2023). They also facilitate the study of infected patients' data for future research and the identification of promising paths for further research among real individuals.

Facility and operations design: DTs can be used to design healthcare facilities and optimize operational processes. They enable simulation-based planning, resource allocation, and workflow optimization, resulting in improved efficiency and cost-effectiveness. Blockchain provides a decentralized and immutable ledger that ensures the integrity and traceability of data generated by DTs. This is particularly important in healthcare, where sensitive patient information is involved (Huang et al., 2022).

Diagnosis and therapy: DTs assist in diagnosis and therapy by integrating patient data, medical imaging, and predictive models. They support healthcare professionals in decision-making, treatment planning, and the monitoring of real-time patient progress (Ogunseiju et al., 2021).

10.5 Digital twin characteristics

DT applications have several characteristics. These attributes are summarized as follows.

Connectivity: The instantaneous transfer of data within the tangible object or product and its DT is facilitated by establishing an electronic connection. This connection is instituted through sensors placed on the physical object, collecting, and transmitting data via diverse integration technologies. As a result, businesses, products, and customers can achieve enhanced connectivity. DTs, comprising a combination of IoT, AI, and ML, undergo software analysis along with spatial network graphs, enabling the creation of dynamic digital simulations that mirror the behavior and development of their real-world counterparts (Glaessgen & Stargel, 2012; Steinmetz et al., 2018). The process involves data integration from diverse sources to accurately represent the current state and operational conditions of the DT. This self-learning educational model leverages sensor data from various aspects of its operating environment for its analysis. Moreover, the digital model of the DT integrates historical data from prior machine operations to enhance its comprehensive representation.

Homogenization: DTs represent a digital innovation that both results from, and facilitates data uniformity. Through this uniformity and the separation of data from its physical embodiment, the concept of DTs is conceived. With DTs, an increasing amount of data pertaining to physical objects can be stored and processed in digital format, leading to enhanced efficiency and cost-effectiveness in transportation and analysis. As a result, the creation of DTs offers the potential for reduced costs and more efficient evaluation, prediction, and issue resolution, compared to traditional methods that rely on mathematical models, and that wait for physical failures to occur (Abuhamad et al., 2020; Steinmetz et al., 2018).

Privacy and security: Ensuring the security of data utilized for constructing a DT is of the utmost significance. Strong protocols are commonly enforced to guarantee the confidentiality, accuracy, and accessibility of data throughout the process. The significant communication chain of big data underscores the necessity of creating statistical data related to location (Yang et al., 2021). Effective privacy measures are highly demanded to safeguard the disclosure of patient-associated location information. Privacy guarantees the continual protection of confidential patient information in every scenario without any proactive involvement from the individual; their privacy remains unbreeched. In contrast to conventional frameworks, the transformation and security of data are achieved directly through human intervention (Abouelmehdi et al., 2017). Being proactive involves anticipating vulnerabilities and potential risks to an individual's crucial healthcare data, aiming to prevent privacy breaches from occurring, rather than responding to them after they have occurred (Jimenez et al., 2020).

Reprogrammability: An integral aspect of DT technology lies in its reprogrammability, enabling the modification of physical products. By employing sensors, AI-based tools, and predictive analytics, DTs can autonomously adapt to ensure optimal functionality of the physical item. This reprogrammable attribute has led to the emergence of new features (Dhanaraj et al., 2023). For example, in the case of an engine, DTs can monitor its operation, and if needed, replace the engine, resulting in an upgraded version of the device.

Digital trail: The existence of a digital trail can lead to the occurrence of another digital trail. This trail can prove valuable in investigating and determining the cause of malfunction or unexpected failure in the digital version of a specific device' digital version (Dhanaraj et al., 2023).

Feedback process: The key feature of DTs is the feedback process of quality experience. This loop involves the transmission of interactions with analyzed data to the user, the generation and analysis of new sensory data, and the continuous looping back of information for further user engagement. Fig. 10.6 illustrates the characteristics of the DT.

10.6 Technological infrastructure of digital twin in the medical domain

The technological infrastructure of DTs, as illustrated in Fig. 10.7, encompasses various components that enable the functionality and capabilities of these virtual representations. It is noteworthy that AI and ML play vital roles in healthcare DT technology. AI processes intricate medical data to construct detailed virtual patient replicas, while ML refines predictions through data learning, synergizing to enhance virtual simulations. This collaboration advances precision medicine, offering actionable insights that have the potential to transform patient care (Fuller et al., 2020). The IoT is integral to the technological structure of DTs, with its devices proving crucial for collecting real-time environmental data, and ensuring accurate digital replication of physical entities. The role of the IoT extends to various sectors, including smart manufacturing, healthcare, and urban planning, optimizing operational efficiency, patient care, and resource management (Armeni et al., 2022). Big data analytics is essential in handling and interpreting the extensive datasets generated by DTs, supporting informed decision-making, and enhancing operational efficacy. In the context of cyber-physical systems (CPS), the fusion of computation, networking, and physical operations, bolstered by real-time data from sensors and actuators, is foundational to

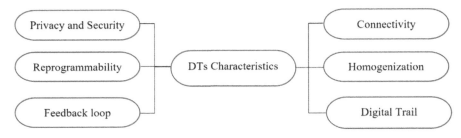

FIGURE 10.6   Digital twin's characteristics.

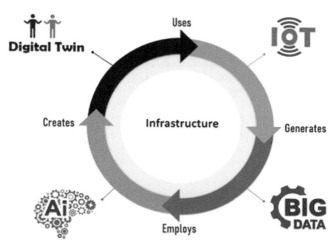

FIGURE 10.7 The technological infrastructure of digital twins and their relationship.

DT functionality. CPS is particularly significant in manufacturing for process automation, and in smart cities for efficient resource management (Armeni et al., 2022). Image Processing in DTs is crucial for analyzing and modifying visual data from the physical twin, especially in healthcare for disease diagnosis, and in industry for quality control (Sun et al., 2023). Lastly, 3D Reconstruction in DTs transforms physical objects and environments into three-dimensional digital models, supporting accurate replication for detailed simulations in architecture and manufacturing (Barricelli et al., 2019). The comprehensive integration of these technological components enhances the functionality of DTs, while also holding immense potential for revolutionizing diverse industries and improving overall outcomes in modern healthcare practices. Table 10.4 provides examples of previous technology infrastructures, illustrating the breadth of applications and advancements in the field:

10.7 Digital twin frameworks in healthcare

A framework for DTs offers a systematic method for establishing and deploying DT technology, guaranteeing precision, dependability, and the efficient enhancement of system or process performance. When utilized in conjunction with IoT devices, AI, and data analytics, the DT framework creates a virtual patient duplicate, promoting collaboration among healthcare professionals and patient engagement (Rivera et al., 2020). The suggested DT framework combines interconnected devices, database administration, and AI in a three-step process to generate a virtual patient duplicate. This facilitates enhanced healthcare engagement and patient collaboration. IoT sensors capture and transmit real-time vital signs, while the DT replica ensures advanced data management. Processed data is utilized for analytics and ML algorithms. This platform enables ongoing health monitoring, timely anomaly identification, precise prescription, controlled experimentation, outcome tracking, lifestyle enhancement, and improved patient communication, resulting in

TABLE 10.4 Digital twin technology infrastructures with example.

Ref.	Technological infrastructure of DT	Explanation	Example
Armeni et al. (2022)	Internet of Things (IoT)	Sensor devices and data infrastructure accumulate real-time patient information, encompassing vital signs to improve DT accuracy.	Monitoring patient blood pressure, heart rate, and oxygen levels using wearable devices.
Kamel Boulos and Zhang (2021)	Artificial Intelligence (AI)	AI techniques including ML and DL, analyze data, recognize patterns, and enhance treatment optimization in DTs.	Predicting medication response from historical data and detecting early vital sign deterioration patterns.
Armeni et al. (2022)	Big Data Analytics	Diverse patient data (health records, genomics, and behavior) are processed for meaningful DT insights.	Personalizing cancer treatment via genomic analysis, mining health records for population studies.
Sun et al. (2023)	Image Processing	Medical images (MRI, CT) are analyzed for relevant info in DT models.	Extracting anatomical features for surgery planning, analyzing brain scans for neurological disorders.
Sun et al. (2023)	3D Reconstruction	3D models are created from medical images by software tools and algorithms from medical images for precise anatomical representation.	Constructing a 3D heart model for cardiovascular planning; producing a virtual dental model for orthodontics.
Barricelli et al. (2019)	Cyber-Physical Systems (CPS)	A group of tangible items engage with a virtual counterpart over a network, resulting in the creation of the DT.	Remote monitoring of a patient's vitals, transmission for real-time twin analysis, and the adjustment of medication based on the twin's suggestions.

diverse benefits for the healthcare system. Fig. 10.8 shows a typical example of a medical healthcare architecture for patient monitoring using the Internet of Medical Things (IoMT). Fig. 10.9 illustrates the DT framework in healthcare:

Computing and prediction phase: In healthcare, the processing and prediction phase includes gathering patient information via IoT wearable sensors, transmitting real-time body indicators like pulse rate, blood pressure, and oxygen level, and then storing it in a cloud-based database. ML methods are utilized to examine and enhance the data, construct classifiers, and create predictive models to identify anomalies (Table 10.5). The outcomes are saved in a secure cloud database, and are accessible to patients and other components for feedback, correction, and model enhancement (Elayan et al., 2021).

Monitoring and adjustment stage: During the monitoring and restoration stage, healthcare professionals employ predictive analytics results to deliver personalized treatments and guidance informed by their expertise. This complements clinical diagnosis and improves patient care. Through the ongoing incorporation live data into forecasting

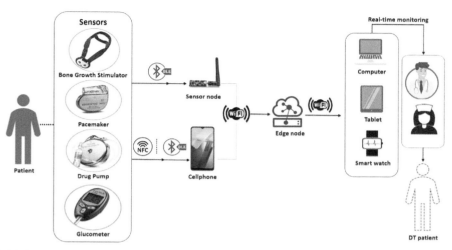

FIGURE 10.8 Example of digital twin framework in healthcare. IoMT architecture (Data is conveyed from patients' IoT sensor devices (on the left) to edge nodes through mounted devices (in the center), and then routed to the HDT architecture. Finally, the information is disseminated to medical staff using suing such a smartwatch application.)

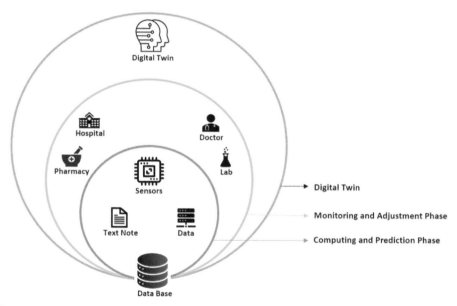

FIGURE 10.9 The DT framework in healthcare.

models, deviations in body metrics can be identified, health risks can be vigilantly tracked, and appropriate treatments can be recommended (Popa et al., 2021). Healthcare providers can rectify, validate, and offer informative feedback to optimize the model while having access to the result information. For example, from wearable

TABLE 10.5 Types of data, classifiers, and analyses commonly used in digital twin technology for healthcare.

Ref.	Application	Type of data	Common vlassifier	Analysis	Reason
Ooka et al. (2021)	Predictive Modeling	Patient vitals, lab results	Random Forest	Predicting patient deterioration	Vital signs and lab results offer vital patient health info. Random Forest, chosen for its complex data handling and accurate predictions, aids in anticipating deterioration for timely intervention.
Saeedi et al. (2023)	Image Analysis	Medical images (MRI, CT scans)	Convolutional Neural Network	Detecting tumors in radiological images	Medical images contain rich visual information. CNNs excel in analyzing images by learning intricate patterns, crucial for effective tumor detection.
Huang et al. (2018)	Personalized Medicine	Genomic data, medical history	Support Vector Machine	Predicting drug responses based on genetics	Genomic data informs treatment response. SVM classifies using genetic variations, aiding personalized medicine.
Lin et al. (2023)	Real-time Monitoring	Wearable sensor data (ECG, EEG)	LSTM	Detecting abnormal heart rate patterns	Wearable sensors provide ongoing data. LSTMs excel in time-series analysis, capturing heart rate patterns for irregularity detection.
Lee et al. (2023)	Clinical Text Analysis	Electronic health records, notes	Natural Language Processing	Extracting disease outcomes from clinical text	Clinical notes hold unstructured data. NLP parses text, extracting patient outcomes for analysis and prediction.
Clermont et al. (2007)	Physiological Modeling	Organ behavior simulations	Differential Equations	Simulating drug interactions on organ systems	Physiological models simulate real-world behavior. Differential equations model complex processes, like drug interactions, for virtual testing.
Schober and Vetter (2021)	Predictive Analytics	Patient historical data	Logistic Regression	Estimating readmission risk	Historical data unveils patterns. Logistic Regression suits binary outcomes like readmission risk, identifying high-risk patients.

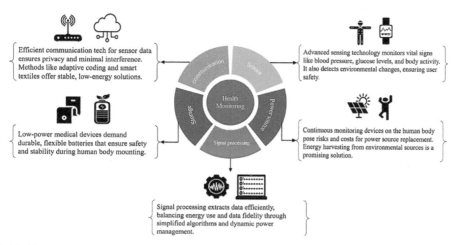

FIGURE 10.10 A system for monitoring all-day is comprised of the following components. sensors, signal processing, communication, storage, and power source.

devices, if any issues are identified, alerts are generated to healthcare professionals, who can access the DT's information, and review the patient's condition (Dhanaraj et al., 2023).

The essential elements needed to construct the comprehensive monitoring system are categorized into five main groups: sensors, signal processing, communication, energy storage, and power suppliers, as illustrated in Fig. 10.10.

Complementing the effectiveness of these monitoring systems is the advent of DT technology, which excels in real-time patient monitoring, accurate diagnosis, and precision treatment. This harnesses real-time health data collected from wearable devices and mobile phones to promptly identify anomalies, facilitating tailored and effective treatment. This personalized approach is achieved through the application of sophisticated computer algorithms and principles from the field of bioinformatics. Ultimately, this technology is instrumental in increasing patient survival rates and elevating the overall quality of life (Milenković et al., 2006). An exemplary embodiment of such technology is the AMON project, detailed in Sun et al. (2022). The AMON project is dedicated to the development of an advanced wearable telemonitoring and alert system. This innovative system is designed to continuously collect and evaluate medical data, offering effective medical emergency detection and management. Furthermore, it seamlessly connects patients to medical centers, ensuring a holistic and streamlined approach to patient care.

Comparison phase: During the comparison phase, patients with comparable conditions collaborate to improve their DTs and the overarching framework. By comparing the current patient's outcomes with those of similar cases, the predictive models acquire more dependable insights from real-life situations, thereby enhancing accuracy. This enables healthcare practitioners to make informed decisions by leveraging current data, as well as historical records and future predictions from other patients (Elayan et al., 2021). They can simulate, adjust, or prevent comparable experiences based on this comprehensive knowledge. For example, a patient's cardiac digital replica can be used to compare real-time information from heart sensors with the virtual representation. This process helps identify irregularities and deviations from anticipated operation, enabling the timely identification of potential cardiac problems, and guiding personalized treatment decisions (Dhanaraj et al., 2023).

10.8 Integrating sensors into healthcare digital twin

Sensors and the IoT in healthcare are foundational in this technological evolution, where sensors detect various physical inputs, and are crucial in patient monitoring and disease diagnosis (Islam et al., 2023). They form the basis for IoT in healthcare, a network that facilitates enhanced healthcare services through data collection and analysis, including remote monitoring and efficient resource management (Pradhan et al., 2021). The interplay between IoT and DT in healthcare is particularly transformative, with DTs being virtual representations of patients or processes updated in real-time (Abdulmalek et al., 2022). This synergy leads to predictive analysis, personalized treatment, improved patient outcomes, and operational efficiency (Ahila et al., 2023). Addressing the challenges in this domain, creating protocols for DTs in environments with limited resources is vital, focusing on optimizing energy efficiency, ensuring reliable data forwarding, and prolonging network lifespan (Redeker et al., 2021). In this regard, WSNs play a critical role, utilizing cost-effective, integrated wireless nodes for real-time monitoring across various settings. These networks process and transmit data to control centers, forming the basis of DTs following specific protocols.

Recent technological advancements have significantly improved sensor technology, energy-efficient circuits, and connectivity, leading to the development of compact, intelligent physiological sensors. These sensors, integral for monitoring vital signs, are seamlessly integrated into wireless networks for continuous health monitoring and real-time medical record updates (Milenković et al., 2006). They operate in two main scenarios: within hospitals using WSNs, and in wearable devices that communicate with mobile apps through technologies like Bluetooth and ZigBee, facilitating real-time monitoring, and enabling doctors to swiftly evaluate patient health risks (Jimenez et al., 2020). Furthermore, physiological sensors are increasingly becoming part of Wearable wireless body/personal area networks (WWBANs); these consist of lightweight, low-cost sensors (Jovanov et al., 2005). WWBANs allow for discreet, continuous health monitoring, providing immediate feedback on health status and timely updates to medical records (Velez & Miyandoab, 2019). This technology is invaluable for computer-assisted rehabilitation and early disease detection (Negra et al., 2016). As sensor technology advances, the precision and variety of the data collected improve, leading to the creation of more accurate and comprehensive DTs, essential in the evolving landscape of healthcare technology (Rishani, 2018). In addition to the broad range of sensors integrated into IoT and WWBAN systems, certain sensors, as depicted in Fig. 10.11, have gained prominence for their specific applications in healthcare.

Fitbit Charge 2 device: It is a popular fitness tracker that comes equipped with a variety of sensors that are designed to monitor and trace different facets of the subject's

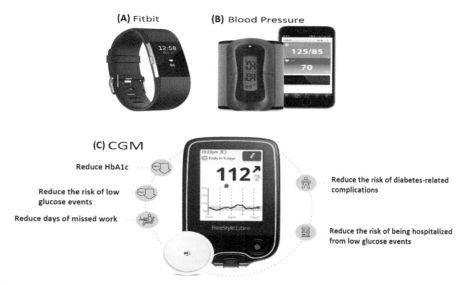

(A) Fitbit

(B) Blood Pressure

(C) CGM

Reduce HbA1c

Reduce the risk of low glucose events

Reduce days of missed work

Reduce the risk of diabetes-related complications

Reduce the risk of being hospitalized from low glucose events

FIGURE 10.11 Various wearable sensors in the healthcare field.

well-being and physical activity, like recording types of heart rate measuring movement, monitoring sleep patterns, or managing stress.

Heart Rate Sensor: One of the key features of Fitbit Charge 2 is its heart rate sensor, which continuously monitors the subject's heart rate throughout the day, and during exercise. This sensor utilizes photoplethysmography (PPG) technology, which measures blood flow through the skin to calculate heart rate.

TD-3140 Arm Blood Pressure sensor: This sensor is crafted for noninvasive measurement of systolic and diastolic blood pressure, as well as pulse rate. It utilizes an inflatable cuff on the upper arm and features Bluetooth communication, a backlit display, detection of irregular heartbeats (IHB), 200MB memory capacity, and compatibility with the MbH BP app for cardiovascular assessment (Taidoc, 2020).

Abbott Libre Pro CGM sensor: The continuous glucose monitoring (CGM) sensor is a medical device that provides real-time data on the levels of glucose in individuals diagnosed with diabetes. It consists of a sensor with a needle inserted into the subcutaneous tissue of the abdomen, quantifying an electrical signal that corresponds to the concentration of glucose in the interstitial fluid. A transmitter relays the signal to a portable device, which displays it on a monitor (Facchinetti, 2016).

Table 10.6 lists commonly used sensor types in healthcare DT applications, along with their corresponding roles. These sensors have a crucial function in overseeing different dimensions of patient health, enabling accurate and dynamic representations within the DT framework.

Although DTs in healthcare present various advantages, certain challenges and issues related to sensors must be addressed through collaboration among healthcare professionals, engineers, and technology experts, as presented in Table 10.7.

TABLE 10.6 Different type of sensors and their application in digital twin.

Challenges/Problems	Description	Reference
Continuous glucose monitoring (CGM)	Diabetes management, glucose level monitoring	Alam and El Saddik (2017)
Electrocardiogram (ECG)	Cardiac health monitoring, detecting abnormal heart rhythms	Al-Zyoud et al. (2022)
Electroencephalogram (EEG)	Neurological disorders, brain-computer interfaces	Islam et al. (2022)
Blood pressure sensors	Hypertension management, personalized monitoring	Barbiero et al. (2021)
Pulse oximeters	Respiratory health monitoring, chronic respiratory conditions	Khan (2023)
Temperature sensors	Fever monitoring, environmental health analysis	Barnabas and Raj (2020)
Accelerometers and IMUs	Physical therapy, gait analysis, rehabilitation	Alcaraz et al. (2019)
Respiratory rate sensors	Respiratory health, sleep disorders	Troncoso et al. (2021)
Oxygen saturation sensors	Monitoring blood oxygen levels	Al-Zyoud et al. (2022)
Heart rate monitors	Cardiac health monitoring, exercise tracking	Rivera et al. (2020)
Oxygen flow sensors	Oxygen therapy management	Buhagiar et al. (2022)
Blood oxygen sensors	Monitoring oxygen levels in critical care	Luna et al. (2022)
Body position sensors	Monitoring body posture and movements	Ogunseiju et al. (2021)
Glucometers	Blood glucose measurement	Gupta et al. (2021)
Magnetic resonance imaging (MRI)	Neuroimaging, creating detailed brain DT	Voigt et al. (2021)
Computed tomography (CT) scanners	3D models for surgical planning and intervention	Sun et al. (2023)
Electrooculogram (EOG) sensors	Eye movement monitoring, sleep tracking	Hu et al. (2022)
Electromyogram (EMG) sensors	Muscle activity monitoring, prosthetic control	Dai et al. (2022)

10.9 Digital twins applications in the healthcare domain

The healthcare industry is rapidly adopting DT technology, as depicted in Fig. 10.12. This innovative approach serves as a virtual counterpart to the physical devices, machinery, and systems utilized in healthcare. It facilitates assessment and monitoring without the need for close physical proximity (Javaid et al., 2023). Through the infusion of real-time data into a virtual model, the assimilation of dynamic information across various healthcare settings, it enables informed decision-making and process improvement, and comprehensive management throughout the healthcare sector's lifecycle. System dynamics can be understood by employing various tools, such as devices, mechanisms, or living organisms, to identify issues, implement modifications, and mitigate risks in healthcare settings.

TABLE 10.7 Challenges of sensors.

Challenges/problems	Description	Ref.
Accuracy and Reliability	Ensuring sensors provide accurate and reliable data for an accurate representation of the patient's condition.	Rishani (2018)
Data Integration and Compatibility	Integrating data from different sensors with varying data formats and protocols into a cohesive DT system.	Clay et al. (2021)
Sensor Placement and Patient Comfort	Determining the optimal placement of sensors for accurate data capture while considering patient comfort.	Appelboom et al. (2014)
Data Security and Privacy	Protecting sensitive patient information generated by sensors through proper data security and privacy measures.	Masood et al. (2018)
Maintenance and Calibration	Regular maintenance, calibration, and quality control of sensors to ensure accurate measurements and performance.	Martins et al. (2020)
Signal interference	Managing signal interference that can affect sensor accuracy and reliability in healthcare environments.	Liu et al. (2021)
Power management	Efficiently managing power consumption of sensors to ensure uninterrupted data collection and prolong sensor lifespan.	Sodhro et al. (2020)
Sensor Validation and Calibration	Validating and calibrating sensors to maintain accuracy and consistency of measurements over time.	Kim et al. (2019)
Sensor data synchronization	Ensuring timely and accurate synchronization of sensor data in complex DT systems.	Satyanarayana et al. (2022)
Cost and scalability	Addressing the cost considerations and scalability challenges associated with sensor deployment in healthcare.	Ye et al. (2001)

This approach facilitates the development of optimal solutions and the effective communication of accurate data.

10.9.1 Literature of digital twin in the medical domain

Healthcare organizations can harness DTs to assess product and equipment performance, enhance customer satisfaction, and inform well-rounded decisions for operations and strategy in multiple domains. These domains include areas like automotive, aerospace, cargo shipping, smart cities, and healthcare within the industrial IoT, especially in a smart context (Fuller et al., 2020). Table 10.8 presents a comprehensive summary of DTs in the medical field, detailing their various application techniques

Morrison et al. (2018) focus on the significant role of computational modeling in medical device regulation, emphasizing its application in simulating device performance, and human-body interactions, and incorporating DTs into design and software applications. The discussion includes the use of deep learning and (Q)SAR models in chemical toxicology, which are essential for regulatory submissions. The versatility of this approach extends from simulating device functions and anatomy to employing "virtual patients" to predict outcomes and facilitate virtual trials in imaging systems. By leveraging big data

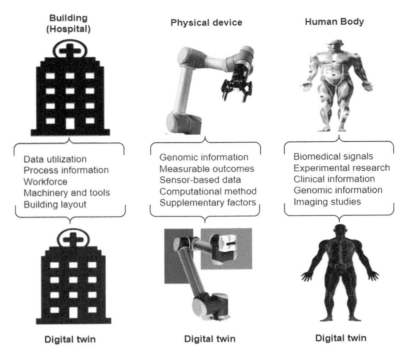

FIGURE 10.12   In the healthcare domain, virtual replicas can be employed to digitally gather, oversee, and assess data concerning the human body, medical apparatus, and healthcare establishments.

and deep learning, these methods provide insights throughout the product lifecycle, and are crucial in the regulatory approval process, ensuring device safety and efficacy. The FDA's integration of these advanced methods into its regulatory framework marks a shift towards a more technologically focused approach to medical device innovation and decision-making regulation.

Schwartz et al. (2020) introduce the DT model, which pivots from Big Data to a more personalized healthcare approach through N-of-1 research. This model utilizes time-sequenced data to provide individualized insights, enhancing precision medicine and augmenting traditional research methods. It encompasses digital technologies in healthcare to improve lifestyle, health, wellness, and chronic disease management. Utilizing mobile health tech, biosensors, wearables, and connected devices, the DT approach monitors various biometric and psychological parameters, showing promising results in personalized health management. These applications, effective in real-world healthcare settings, leverage diverse health datasets to provide actionable insights, signifying a significant shift towards tailored healthcare and wellness monitoring.

Corral-Acero et al. (2020) delineate the emergence of precision cardiology, an area within the broader spectrum of precision medicine, through the innovative employment of DT technology in healthcare. This avant-garde methodology is pivotal in customizing therapeutic interventions for individual patients, particularly in the realm of cardiovascular health.

TABLE 10.8 Overview and comparison of the applications of digital twin s in the medical field.

Ref.	Dataset used	Applications in healthcare	AI model	Technique used	Limitation
Shamanna et al. (2020)	64 individuals diagnosed with Type 2 Diabetes.	Type 2 Diabetes.	TPN ML algorithms with glucose monitoring.	ML algorithm analyzing CGM and food intake data for dietary guidelines	limited sample size, absence of a control group, and a brief study duration.
Morrison et al. (2018)	Medical device and human body interaction data.	Device simulation, virtual trials.	DL, (Q)SAR.	Computational modeling, data analysis.	Data accuracy, model validation.
Schwartz et al. (2020)	Time-sequenced, biometric, and psychological data.	Personalized health and chronic disease management.	—	DT approach with wearables and big data.	Data privacy, integration, and accuracy.
Corral-Acero et al. (2020)	Patient-specific cardiovascular data.	Precision cardiology and disease management.	Advanced AI and statistical algorithms.	Mechanistic and AI-driven models for DTs.	Data integration and clinical application accuracy.
Sahal, et al. (2022b)	wearable sensors, medical devices.	COVID-19 pandemic management using a medical cyber-physical system.	ML and DL for risk assessment.	Blockchain-based DTs framework with AI and IoT.	Model validation.
Shamanna et al. (2020)	CGM readings, food intake.	Type 2 diabetes management.	ML for glycemic response.	DT, CGM, IoT, and ML integration.	Model accuracy, patient adherence.
Barbiero et al. (2021)	Multi-tissue expression data.	Predictive healthcare, complex disease management.	GNNs, GANs.	Computational modeling with AI.	Theoretical focus, real-world application testing.

The cornerstone of this approach is the meticulous integration of voluminous patient-specific data, which facilitates the precise prediction and amelioration of cardiovascular diseases (CVDs). This integration is achieved through a harmonious combination of mechanistic models—rooted to gain a comprehensive grasp of physiological processes and the fundamental tenets of physics and chemistry—and sophisticated statistical models, which are the progeny of advanced AI algorithms and extensive data analysis. In this scholarly work, the emphasis on the role of computational models and simulations in cardiovascular medicine is salient. This analysis culminates in the creation of exhaustive and dynamic DTs, representing a significant technological leap in the medical field. The findings gleaned from this innovative approach exhibit immense potential, indicating substantial advancements in diagnosis, treatment, and prognostication within cardiovascular medicine. The paper propounds the application of this DT technology within actual clinical settings, marking a transformative stride in the clinical decision-making and operational workflows of cardiology.

Sahal et al. (2022b) present a blockchain-based DTs framework that is designed for pandemic alert systems, with a focus on addressing COVID-19 challenges. This framework enables decentralized, intelligent decision-making, which is crucial for implementing measures like quarantine and lockdown, and is underpinned by secure, transparent data exchange through blockchain technology. Structured into four key layers—physical, DTs, data analytics, and decision-making—it integrates human and nonhuman entities, virtual replicas of physical elements, and an analytical layer for processing and decision support. The framework operates within the healthcare domain, harnessing the combined power of DTs, blockchain, IoT, and AI, to create robust medical cyber-physical systems. It leverages AI, particularly ML and deep learning, to analyze extensive data from diverse sources, addressing the critical need for precise risk assessments in decentralized systems. Practical in its application, the framework is designed for real-world healthcare scenarios, particularly pandemic management. It employs a systematic approach, including data collection from historical ledger databases, dividing data into training and testing sets, and utilizing ML techniques for predictive modeling. The effectiveness of these models is measured using standard ML metrics. The comprehensive approach of the framework implies the use of extensive datasets, including inputs from wearable sensors and medical devices, which are crucial for constructing detailed DTs.

Shamanna et al. (2020) introduce the twin precision nutrition (TPN) Program, a pioneering approach in the healthcare sector for managing T2D. Utilizing DT Technology, this program integrates CGM, IoT technology, dietary data, and an ML algorithm. It offers personalized nutritional guidance to patients, helping them avoid foods that elevate blood glucose, and suggesting healthier alternatives. This unique program, applied in a real-world setting, showed substantial improvements in diabetic health metrics over a 90-day period. Patients demonstrated a marked decrease in HbA1c levels, substantial reduction in insulin resistance, and weight loss, while many were able to discontinue diabetes medication. The AI model employed, processing CGM and dietary intake data, predicted postprandial glycemic responses, tailoring dietary advice to individual needs. Key challenges include ensuring the AI model's accuracy, and patient adherence to the program. The dataset for the model comprised daily CGM readings and food intake records, providing comprehensive health and nutrition data for the analysis. This study illustrates the potential of integrating technology with healthcare to enhance disease management and patient outcomes in T2D.

Barbiero et al. (2021) introduce a novel DT model, integrating advanced AI techniques like graph neural networks (GNNs) and generative adversarial networks (GANs), to provide a comprehensive, multidimensional perspective of patients' health conditions. This model represents a significant shift in healthcare, moving toward a more preventive and interdisciplinary approach. It encapsulates the complexity of the human body at various levels—from organs to cells—through intricate mathematical modeling. The efficacy of this model was demonstrated in simulated clinical cases, emphasizing its capability to forecast critical health metrics and generate detailed multitissue expression data, which is particularly beneficial in understanding and managing complex diseases, like SARS-CoV-2 infection. This innovative approach addresses the challenge of melding multiscale computational modeling with AI, aiming for a system that is both accurate and interpretable. While the study primarily explores theoretical and simulated scenarios, it lays the groundwork for potential real-world applications, marking a progressive step toward personalized, predictive healthcare.

DTs offer a secure space for assessing alterations that impact the efficiency of devices, machinery, and systems (Ahmed et al., 2022). Employing machines, processes, or living organisms facilitates the real-time comprehension of system dynamics, enabling prompt identification of issues, and the implementation of necessary adjustments or procedures.

10.9.2 Case studies of digital twin medical applications

DTs for specific diseases involve developing virtual duplicates or models that replicate the behavior and characteristics of a patient's condition, leveraging data from various sources, including medical imaging, patient records, and real-time monitoring. These replicas enable personalized simulations and targeted interventions (Sahal et al., 2022a). For example, the DT concept optimizes the understanding and management of CVD, a primary contributor to global mortality, predominantly associated with ischemic heart disease. In response to the constraints of existing risk assessment approaches, personalized medicine, which utilizes omics data and computational techniques for tailored treatments, is being adopted. In the context of CVD, DT research is a burgeoning interdisciplinary domain centered on numerical simulation models, including some earlier models that were designed for real-time cyber-physical systems (Coorey et al., 2022). Fig. 10.13 illustrates the utilization of DT technology in the management of specific diseases. It shows how virtual models of disease states are created for conditions such as diabetes, cancer, neurological disorders, CVDs, and infectious diseases. These models can predict responses to changes in lifestyle, treatments, and the progression of diseases, aiding in personalized healthcare planning.

Fig. 10.14 presents the role of DT technology in enhancing hospital and medical processes. It covers aspects such as patient engagement, safety, monitoring, and surgery planning. Additionally, it touches on the utility of DTs in managing hospital facilities, monitoring medical equipment, and optimizing operational workflows to improve efficiency and reduce costs.

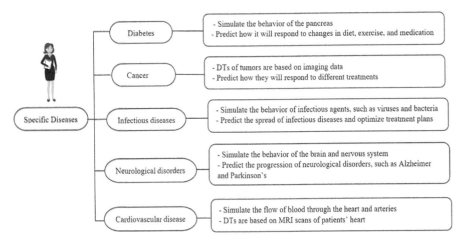

FIGURE 10.13   Fundamental elements of digital twins for specific diseases.

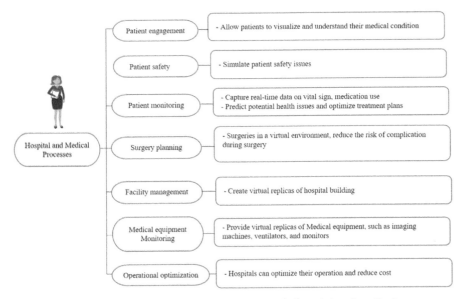

FIGURE 10.14   Fundamental elements of digital twins for specific hospital and medical processes.

10.10 Digital twin applications in diabetes and the human brain

Diabetes is a persistent and potentially life-threatening ailment that is marked by the body's incapacity to generate or efficiently utilize insulin, resulting in elevated blood glucose levels (BGLs). One of the most prevalent diseases globally, it poses significant health risks, and requires continuous medical attention and lifestyle management to prevent complications (World Health Organization WHO, 2023).

DT technology has emerged as a revolutionary tool in the management and treatment of diabetes. In diabetes care, DTs can simulate an individual's glucose metabolism, and predict the impact of diet, exercise, and medication on blood sugar levels. This has profound implications for personalized treatment plans, and helps in fine-tuning insulin dosages and dietary recommendations to achieve optimal glycemic control (Artificial Intelligence Offers Significant Rate of Remission for Type 2 Diabetes Compared to Standard Care, 2023). DT technology in diabetes management addresses key issues by predicting blood sugar fluctuations, and preventing hyperglycemic and hypoglycemic events. It supports personalized medicine, considering individual physiological traits for more effective treatment (Smith et al., 2019). Additionally, integration with wearable devices allows continuous glucose tracking and personalized insights. In research, DTs aid in understanding diabetes progression and complications, simulating disease evolution to develop new therapeutic and preventive strategies (Shamanna, Joshi, et al., 2021).

Fig. 10.15 shows different metrics to assess the efficacy of the DT technology in diabetes management.

10.10.1 HbA1c reduction

HbA1c (glycated hemoglobin): Glycated hemoglobin is a crucial marker of long-term blood glucose control. A significant reduction in HbA1c indicates improved diabetes management and better glycemic outcomes (Shamanna et al., 2020), changes in HbA1c will happen over a period of at least 6 weeks, and CGM sensors or fingerstick glucose meters are commonly used to measure BGL. The long short-term memory model (LSTM) ML model is usually applied to the reduction of HbA1c. Table 10.9 shows the A1C value and subject condition.

Insulin resistance reduction: Measuring the reduction in insulin resistance is essential to evaluating the effectiveness of DT technology in improving insulin sensitivity, which is a key factor in diabetes management (Shamanna et al., 2020). Becoming more active and Weight loss are probably the best ways to combat insulin resistance.

Weight loss: Assessing the extent of weight loss achieved through DT-enabled precision nutrition therapy can indicate the impact of the intervention on overall health and metabolic control (Morrison et al., 2018).

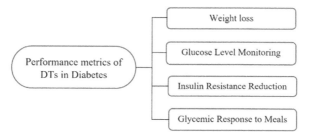

FIGURE 10.15 Performance metrics of DTs in Diabetes.

TABLE 10.9 A1C value and subject condition.

A1C value	ADA diagnosis
5.6% or less	Normal
5.6%−6.3%	Prediabetes
6.4% more	Diabetes

Glucose level monitoring: Monitoring changes in glucose levels is fundamental in diabetes management. A reduction in BGL signifies improved glycemic control, and a positive response to the intervention (Shamanna et al., 2020).

Glycemic response to meals: In type 1 diabetes, analyzing the glycemic response to meals using metabolic DTs can inform personalized insulin dosing strategies for meals with varying compositions of fat and protein (Smith et al., 2019).

It is worth noting that these metrics are specific to the studies mentioned in the provided references, and may vary depending on the DT technology and diabetes management approach being used. When evaluating the performance of DT technology in diabetes, these metrics help determine its efficacy in improving glycemic control, patient outcomes, and the potential for personalized and precision approaches to diabetes management.

10.10.2 Diabetes case studies

10.10.2.1 Diabetes case study 1: digital twin precision treatment program

The study, "A retrospective analysis of glycemic variability, body mass index (BMI), and blood pressure among individuals with diabetes participating in the DT Precision Treatment Program" (Shamanna, Dharmalingam, et al., 2021), addresses the significant challenges of T2D, a condition marked by increased health risks, medication use, and healthcare costs. Fluctuations in blood sugar levels are key factors in diabetes-related complications. To tackle these issues, the study focuses on the use of virtual DTs, specifically through the twin precision treatment (TPT) program. This program employs full-body DT technology, IoT, ML algorithms, and personalized nutrition, aiming to assess and treat individual metabolic impairments in T2D patients. The study leverages Whole Body DT technology, creating dynamic digital models of the metabolic processes of patients. This approach is supported by AI techniques, such as rule-based systems, traditional ML, and DL, complemented by IoT for data collection via body sensors and mobile apps. These integrated technologies offer a personalized, comprehensive strategy for managing T2D, focusing on individual patient needs and conditions.

The implementation of AI algorithms was a pivotal aspect of this study. The researchers employed a range of algorithms, including gradient-boosted decision trees (GBDT), deep learning neural networks, and LSTMs, to analyze the collected data. These algorithms yielded impressive results: glucose variability was maintained below 18%, and the mean glycemic variability was recorded at 17.34%. Additionally, there was a notable decrease in the BMI from (29.23−27.43) kg/m^2, and a significant reduction in both systolic and diastolic blood pressure. The datasets used in this study were diverse, encompassing information gathered from blood tests, and nutritional information entered using a specialized mobile app. This comprehensive monitoring allowed for in-depth understanding of each patient's health state, facilitating personalized treatment strategies. Study participants used a Fitbit Charge 2, Bluetooth-enabled blood pressure meter, and Bluetooth Smart Scale for daily health monitoring, along with daily blood BHB level measurements and CGM using an Abbott Libre Pro sensor. All data were transmitted to the TPT Program's platform, and were accessible through the Twin app.

The practical utilization of DT technology demonstrated in this study underscores its potential for transforming healthcare practices. The technology was successfully applied in managing T2D, resulting in reduced glycemic variability, BMI, and blood pressure. Moreover, the reliance on antihypertensive medications significantly decreased among patients. Nevertheless, the study's retrospective design, limited sample size, and absence of a control group were recognized as constraints. These factors highlight the necessity for additional research, specifically in the context of randomized case-control studies, to validate and expand upon these findings. The results of the study underscore the significant transformative capacity of DT technology in healthcare, paving the way for more personalized and effective treatment methods. Fig. 10.16 shows the architecture of the patient under the TPT program.

10.10.2.2 Diabetes case study 2: elderly type 2 diabetes management

In this case, we explore the management of elderly type 2 diabetes (E-T2D) through the utilization of the HDT framework. By leveraging diverse patient-specific information, a

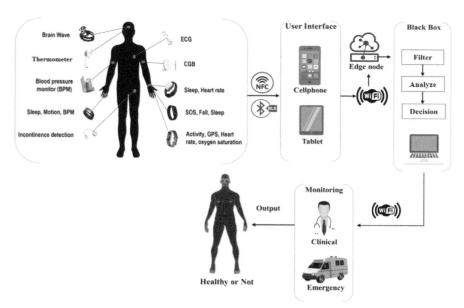

FIGURE 10.16   DT architecture for diabetes patients under the TPT program.

series of models are constructed for management and prediction, customizing diabetes treatment for patients with E-T2D (Thamotharan et al., 2023).

DTs in healthcare, particularly Human HDTs, are becoming a fundamental aspect of tailoring treatments for individuals (Ardanza et al., 2019). The increasing commonality of IoT devices capable of linking with user equipment to instantly amass, retain, analyze, and deliver notifications, even though mobile apps or built-in sensors, is now a standard trend. Merging patient simulations with live data allows for profound comprehension of patient states, effective condition control, anticipation of future events, tracking of current patient status, and the facilitation of informed choices. Furthermore, integrating virtual scenarios, interactive models, and specialized knowledge-based databases could enhance the capacity to intelligently supervise and alert users (Barricelli et al., 2019). The HDT is comprised of three elements: the patient DT (PT), a virtual DT (VT), and their interactions. The distinctive strength of the HDT lies in its capacity to manage historical and real-time data. This technology can harness data to enhance tailored treatment strategies, suggest lifestyle adjustments, refine patient management, and curtail expenses for E-T2D patients. Moreover, the HDT forecasts upcoming patient situations, and prevents instances of elevated and reduced blood sugar levels, providing proactive prescriptions (Thamotharan et al., 2023).

10.10.2.2.1 The diabetes human digital twin framework

The foundational elements of the Human DT framework include the PT, VT, and interfaces. The PT represents the real patient, and its virtual representation is based on past data, sensor measurements, contextual details, and a range of data inputs. The VT serves as the digital counterpart of the PT, facilitating E-T2D management. Interfaces connect PT to VT, transmitting data like sensor measurements, or insights, such as food effects on T2D. A robust interface is essential for the synchronized development of both PT and VT. These components, working in harmony, provide tailored healthcare services for elderly individuals with T2D diabetes (E-T2D). Fig. 10.17 illustrates the HDT framework that is comprised of four modules: data aggregation, future prediction based on historical data, diagnostic utilization for anticipating patient variations, and personalized insulin infusion management to regulate BGLs. Each module serves specific tasks within the system (Thamotharan et al., 2023).

10.10.2.2.2 The implementation of human digital twin

Data module in IoMT: The Human DT's IoMT architecture is organized into three layers: transfer, perception, and application. In the perception layer, small-scale sensors employ NFC to measure BGLs, and send the data to a mobile app for transmission. Physical activity and vital signs (heart rate) are detected using an accelerometer, gyros, MAX30100-based monitor, (DS18B20) temperature, and (CCS2210) activity sensor. RF (NRF24L01 and RFM69HCW modules) and/or Wi-Fi communication are used to collect sensed information by the sensor node. BGLs are tracked by the Freestyle Libre Pro sensor. Utilizing NFC and BLE interfaces, the mobile app gathers data, transmitting it to the edge node through Wi-Fi. A compact database within the edge node stores and retrieves data at 15-minute intervals. The edge node interacts with additional devices and the cloud through Wi-Fi connections. Stakeholders utilize web interfaces to observe

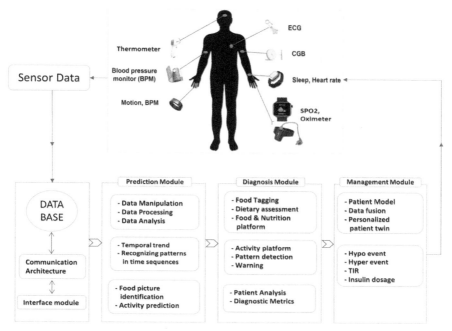

FIGURE 10.17 First, a data module collects current information; Secondly, a forecasting module predicts forthcoming values by analyzing past and present data. Thirdly, a diagnostic component utilizes real-time measurements and predictions to identify potential interventions and forecast variances among patients. Finally, a management module tailors insulin administration to maintain optimal blood glucose levels.

current or past data patterns. Fig. 10.8 provides a schema of the envisioned IoMT structure:

Prediction module: The forecasting module encompasses the subsequent components: (i) prediction of time-series, (ii) algorithm for identifying food images, and (iii) examination of structured temporal data. These elements leverage patient context, clinical temporal data, and supplementary information to predict the future trends in BGLs (Sahal et al., 2022b). The LSTM model is employed to predict BGLS, addressing problems related to gradient vanishing and exploding commonly encountered with recurrent neural networks (Khanna, 2022). LSTM has the capability to manage extended delays, handle noise, and cope with data loss, offering increased flexibility for fine-tuning network parameters.

The customization module facilitates accurate insulin infusion, effectively regulating BGLs within specified ranges according to individual patient characteristics. It employs a semiparametric regression model to address fluctuations in BGLs that are attributed to geriatric factors. The adaptive model is derived from data samples, enabling tailored insulin infusion tailored to individual conditions. Its goal is to address E-T2D management and construct a personalized HDT (Khanna, 2022).

Conclusion: The HDT allows for personalized and accurate insulin infusion tailored to individual patient factors. It aggregates various data types, including contextual, clinical, and patient-specific data, to provide deeper insights. The results indicate that customizing diabetes care through HDT enhances duration within the desired glucose range, diminishes the occurrences of hyper and hypo events, and efficiently controls diabetes by minimizing insulin infusion.

10.10.3 Human brain case studies

10.10.3.1 *Human brain case study 1: tumor detection*

DTs are valuable for maintaining medical devices, including magnetic resonance imaging (MRI) scanners. Actual MRI images of the individual were employed to generate and observe a simulation of the patient's brain. This replica is supplemented with extensive details obtained from the individual's medical records and real-time sensor data, including mobile EEG technologies. EEG recordings and IoT environment data contribute to enhancing the judgment capabilities of the DT.

The algorithm for detecting brain tumors employs contrast analysis of brightness in MRI scans, where tumors commonly display a unique, and often more pronounced, level of brightness. To achieve this, a clustering technique was employed, specifically the K-means method, which minimizes the square of the distance between data points and the center of the cluster (Moftah et al., 2010). This process involves colorized clustering, directly utilizing the 3D MRI image (Fig. 10.18), where the third dimension signifies the RGB combination of each pixel. Clusters are established using K-means, signifying distinct combinations of RGB components. The ideal number of clusters is predetermined using the knee rule. Contemplating the within-cluster sum of Squares or sum of squared errors (SSE) metric for each scan involves the computation of the sum of Euclidean distances between elements within clusters and their respective cluster centers (Sarris et al., 2023).

The dataset consists of 248 MRI images sourced from 11 Radiopaedia cases (Huang et al., 2022) and the MRI Scans for Brain Tumor Identification dataset (Ogunseiju et al., 2021). Among these images, 59.91% belonged to patients with brain tumors, while 40.09% were from healthy patients.

A high-value class was chosen from the clustered image. A dynamic circular mask with a customizable radius was generated for pixel isolation. If the covered region surpasses a

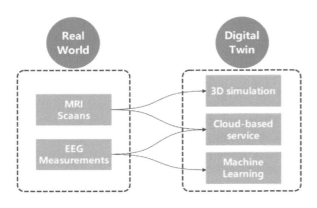

FIGURE 10.18 Processing magnetic resonance imaging scans leads to the creation of 3D models of the brain, and aids in tumor detection.

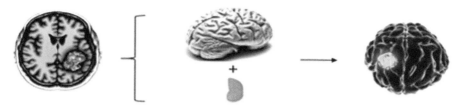

FIGURE 10.19 An magnetic resonance imaging scan detects the tumor (highlighted in yellow), which is followed by the meticulous construction of a comprehensive three-dimensional representation of the brain and the tumor based on the scan results.

certain threshold, it is recognized as a tumor. The radius adapts to each subject; and if detection fails, it decreases for another attempt. The successful tumor localization is evident from the initial steps in Fig. 10.19. Subsequently, the 3D model is formed by combining visualizations of both the tumor and brain segments.

Conclusion: The algorithm for tumor detection was employed on 248 scans with a varying radius of 30–100 cm. Higher radius values correlated with increased accuracy. The algorithm aimed to distinguish MRI scans of individuals without health issues, as well as those with tumors, yielding accuracy ranging from 0.85% to 0.96% (mean 0.92%); however, the limited number of healthy patient samples in the dataset potentially compromised the realism and reliability of the algorithm's performance. This outcome underscores the critical need for a more robust and comprehensive dataset that includes a balanced proportion of healthy and tumor-affected scans, ensuring a more realistic assessment and improvement of the algorithm's efficacy. Such refinements are essential to enhancing the reliability and accuracy of tumor detection, thereby advancing the application of DT technology in medical diagnostics and treatment planning.

10.10.3.2 Human brain case study 2: digital twin for stroke patients

This case study demonstrates how a DT can benefit stroke patients in healthcare by utilizing EEG data and ML methods. By employing EEG data and advanced ML techniques, we achieved our objectives. We enlisted 48 stroke patients and 75 individuals in good health for the study. Portable EEG devices (headsets) were employed to collect EEG data from these participants. Thorough data analysis was conducted to identify key features that could effectively discriminate between the two groups (Hussain et al., 2021).

Fig. 10.20 illustrates the transmission of raw EEG data from the EEG headset, collected during resting and working phases, and walking to the nearby MiniPC app using Bluetooth low energy (BLE). The API running on the Jetson Nano utilizes a communication protocol to send EEG data, formatted in JSON, to an Elasticsearch database hosted in the cloud. The Apache Spark server handles data preprocessing and feature extraction. Subsequently, a machine-learning algorithm acquires knowledge, and forecasts the neurological condition of the patient. A digital counterpart amalgamates biological information, findings from experiments, computational simulations, and results from clinical trials. The interpreted data can be displayed in specialized platforms for designated medical professionals, aiding in the diagnosis, clinical actions, and decision-making process.

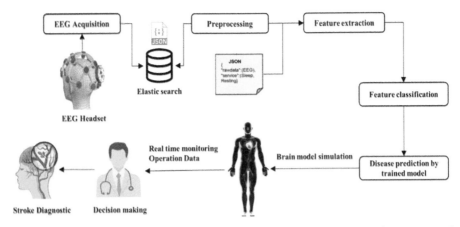

FIGURE 10.20 The EEG headset transmits data to a nearby PC via Bluetooth. The information is subsequently transmitted to a cloud-based database using a messaging protocol in JSON format. Preprocessing, feature extraction, and machine learning on an Apache Spark server predict neurological status. Creating a digital twin integrates biological data, models, and trial outcomes for post-stroke care prognosis. The analyzed data is visualized in portals for doctors' diagnostics and decisions.

To distinguish neurological traits between acute patients and individuals in good health, we employed support vector machine (SVM), logistic regression, and random forest models. Our analytical approach encompassed hypothesis tests and descriptive statistics, notably the t-test for independent samples. Statistical analysis was executed using IBM SPSS 24 software, with ML studies conducted using IBM SPSS Modeler 18 software (Hussain et al., 2021).

The stroke group had a mean revised brain symmetry index (rsBSI) of 0.263 with a standard deviation of 0.088, while the control group had a mean rsBSI of 0.143 with a standard deviation of 0.053. A higher Brain Symmetry Score after revision suggests cortical damage in one hemisphere due to a stroke. The classification results for the EEG feature dataset show SVM achieved 76% accuracy, while the Random tree model showed the highest sensitivity of 74% in predicting stroke patients. The SVM algorithm achieved the highest precision of 77% (Hussain et al., 2021).

In summary, the investigation illustrated the utility of specific brain activity measurements in effectively distinguishing between individuals recovering from strokes, and those in good health, across various mental states. Employing an ML model (SVM), the data was classified with 76% accuracy. This DT framework holds the potential to aid clinical decisions in stroke prevention and poststroke treatment.

10.11 Packages and tools for implementing digital twins in healthcare

The available simulation packages and tools provide various features to develop DTs in healthcare, including modeling complex hospital systems and simulating specific medical conditions for patients (Lim et al., 2020). Table 10.10 lists notable platforms:

Organizations have a range of comprehensive tools at their disposal for DT applications, such as ANSYS, Predix, Siemens' MindSphere, and PTC's Thingworx, each with its

TABLE 10.10 Different platform of digital twin and their specifications.

Package/ platform	Real-time data processing	Model	Programming language	Services	Ref.
Azure DT	High	–	C#, Java, JavaScript, Python	Simulation, diagnosis and prognosis services	Microsoft (2023)
Predix DT	High	–	Java, Node.js, Python, etc.	Simulation & optimization services	Electric (2023)
Siemens DT	High	–	Java, C++, etc.	Simulation service	Siemens (2023)
PTC's Thingworx	High	Rule modeling	JavaScript, Web technologies	Diagnosis and prognosis services	ThingWorx Inc (2023)
IBM Watson IoT	High	–	Java, Node.js, Python, etc.	Simulation & optimization services	Cognitive IoT for Heathcare (2023)
GE DT Solutions	High	–	Java, Python, etc.	Simulation & optimization services	Ge Digital (2023)
ANSYS	Moderate	Physical & behavioral modeling	Python, scripting languages	Simulation, diagnosis and prognosis services	Procario (2023)
MATLAB®	Moderate	Rule, physical modeling	MATLAB, C, C++, etc.	Simulation, diagnosis and prognosis services	Mathworks (2023)
3D Experience	Moderate	Physical & geometry modeling	Python, C++, Java, etc.	Simulation services	Systèmes (2023)

unique strengths. For example, Azure and IBM Watson are notable in IoT and AI, while Siemens and ANSYS excel in engineering and manufacturing, Predix specializes in heavy industry analytics, Thingworx integrates IoT and augmented reality (AR), MATLAB® is known for its algorithmic complexity, and 3D Experience focuses on 3D design. The selection of a specific DT platform depends on the unique needs of the industry, ranging from optimizing facility management and equipment maintenance to enhancing healthcare practices through personalized patient treatment and monitoring. As the DT domain continues to evolve, these platforms are poised to play a significant role in advancing various sectors, including healthcare, by improving patient outcomes.

DT includes virtual representations, and requires building models like anatomical, functional, behavioral, and finite element analysis (Hu et al., 2021). These tasks rely on enabling technologies, such as sensors, advanced data processing, and AI. Tools like MRI scans, CT scans, 3D modeling software, and medical simulation platforms support modeling and simulation (Systèmes, 2023). Standardization of data and models in common formats, protocols, and standards is crucial for these diverse technologies and tools to collaborate effectively in advancing medical knowledge and patient care.

10.12 Challenges of digital twin in healthcare

The incorporation of DT technology into the healthcare sector offers transformative potential, yet it is essential to critically evaluate the challenges and limitations that accompany its implementation. This section delves into the complex landscape of DTs in healthcare, elucidating the key hurdles that necessitate comprehensive consideration.

AI, data integration and accuracy: Digital replicas encounter numerous comparable problems and hurdles encountered in contemporary AI and substantial data analysis (Guidance, 2021). These encompass challenges related to data presence and quality, data fusion and compatibility, data exchange involving intellectual property concerns, cross-platform and system data confidentiality and security, and concerns over AI predisposition, along with deficiencies in explication and reproducibility. The smooth integration of a range of patient data originating from different origins represents a pivotal undertaking. Ensuring the accuracy and reliability of this integrated data is crucial to preserving the integrity and effectiveness of the resultant DT.

Data privacy and security: Securing patient information becomes of paramount importance, particularly in the context of merging sensitive health data to generate DTs. These data fuel patient-oriented models, while upholding data integrity and privacy. Constructing a PDT-centered intelligent personalized healthcare system necessitates rigorous adherence to data privacy regulations, enabling healthcare to advance its services, while remaining compliant (Dillenseger et al., 2021).

Model complexity and validation: Creating precise physiological models within DTs presents a complex task, due to the intricacies of real-world biological systems. The intricacy of human physiology adds complexity to creating a PDT (Kayvanpour et al., 2015). This is heightened by the interplay among bodily components, raising complexity. Additionally, data-centric approaches for PDTs must incorporate past patient data for analysis (Rasheed et al., 2020). Consequently, constructing a robust human healthcare DT model to establish a tangible personalized healthcare framework proves demanding.

Ethical and regulatory adherence: The integration of DT technology introduces ethical considerations, particularly concerning patient autonomy, data ownership, and privacy. Adherence to evolving healthcare regulations and ethical frameworks poses intricate challenges that require thoughtful navigation. Ethical concerns arise with human health DTs, given their involvement with sensitive individual data (Bruynseels et al., 2018). The primary ethical challenge pertains to forecasting disease risks, and effectively communicating these predictions with patients.

Interoperability and standardization: Facilitating smooth communication and interaction among different devices and systems within the healthcare environment necessitates the adoption of standardized data formats and communication protocols. This affects confidentiality, data transfer, transparency, rights, and alignment between virtual and real worlds. Global standards would hasten the adoption and realization trends of the DT (Alazab et al., 2022).

Budgetary considerations: Although the potential advantages of DTs are significant, the financial commitment needed for their creation, integration, and upkeep might burden healthcare budgets. Assessing the cost-effectiveness and enduring value is crucial for informed decision-making (Retiwalla, n.d.).

Tackling these intricate challenges is crucial to unlocking the complete capabilities of DTs in advancing healthcare. By thoughtfully deliberating, fostering innovation, and encouraging collaboration, the healthcare industry can leverage the revolutionary potentials that DT technology brings forth.

Limitations of the applied ML/DL algorithms: In the context of healthcare DTs, the application of ML and DL methodologies is confronted with several pivotal challenges. These include biases inherent in training data, leading to potential inaccuracies in model outputs Furthermore, the complex nature of DL models, particularly deep neural networks, poses significant issues regarding interpretability, rendering the decision-making process opaque (Jin et al., 2022). Additionally, the generalizability of these models is a concern, as when applied to novel data sets, performance can vary significantly (Mak et al., 2018). Finally, the dependency on extensive and diverse datasets for effective model training is often hampered by data privacy and availability concerns in the healthcare domain (Beam & Kohane, 2018). These limitations underscore the critical need for robust, ethical, and transparent methodologies in the implementation of ML and DL within healthcare DTs.

10.13 Conclusion

In this paper, we explored the integration of DT technology into the healthcare domain, highlighting its considerable impact on patient care, diagnosis, and treatment strategies. By combining real-time patient data, computational models, and advanced analytics, DTs offer a versatile platform for simulating and analyzing complex physiological processes. This platform enables personalized insights for healthcare providers, leading to timely decisions, tailored recommendations, early disease detection, and optimized treatments. The study also discussed the challenges and progress in WSN DT protocols with advanced sensors for comprehensive health monitoring, enabling accurate digital replicas. We proposed a reference framework that envisions the integration of DTs and AI for intelligent personalized healthcare services. We also discussed specific applications of DT in healthcare, including personalized diabetes care, individualized management of T2D of the elderly, precise tumor detection, and proactive stroke prevention. However, it is crucial to acknowledge challenges, such as data security, model accuracy, and ethical considerations. Collaboration among medical professionals, engineers, data scientists, and regulatory bodies is essential to harness the full potential of DT technology, ultimately improving patient outcomes, and reshaping healthcare paradigms.

Acknowledgment

This work was supported by the National Research Foundation of Korea(NRF) grant funded by the Korea government(MSIT)(No. 2021R1A2C1011198), (Institute for Information & communications Technology Planning & Evaluation) (IITP) grant funded by the Korea government (MSIT) under the ICT Creative Consilience Program (IITP-2021−2020-0−01821), and AI Platform to Fully Adapt and Reflect Privacy-Policy Changes (RS-2022-II220688).

References

Abdukhamidov, E., Abuhamad, M., Woo, S. S., Chan-Tin, E., & Abuhmed, T. (2023). Hardening interpretable deep learning systems: Investigating adversarial threats and defenses. *IEEE Transactions on Dependable and Secure Computing*. Available from https://doi.org/10.1109/TDSC.2023.3341090, http://ieeexplore.ieee.org/xpl/RecentIssue.jsp?punumber = 8858.

Abdulmalek, S., Nasir, A., Jabbar, W. A., Almuhaya, M. A. M., Bairagi, A. K., Khan, M. A.-M., & Kee, S.-H. (2022). IoT-based healthcare-monitoring system towards improving quality of life: A review. *Healthcare*, 10(10), 1993. Available from https://doi.org/10.3390/healthcare10101993.

Abouelmehdi, K., Beni-Hssane, A., Khaloufi, H., & Saadi, M. (2017). Big data security and privacy in healthcare: A review. *Procedia Computer Science*, 113, 73–80. Available from https://doi.org/10.1016/j.procs.2017.08.292, http://www.sciencedirect.com/science/journal/18770509.

Abuhamad, M. et al. (2018) Large-scale and language-oblivious code authorship identification. In *Proceedings of the ACM conference on computer and communications security*. South Korea: Association for Computing Machinery. Available from https://doi.org/10.1145/3243734.3243738.

Abuhamad, M., Abuhmed, T., Mohaisen, D., & Nyang, D. (2020). AUToSen: Deep-learning-based implicit continuous authentication using smartphone sensors. *IEEE Internet of Things Journal*, 7(6). Available from https://doi.org/10.1109/JIOT.2020.2975779, http://ieeexplore.ieee.org/servlet/opac?punumber = 6488907.

AbuHmed, T., Nyamaa, N., & Nyang, D. H. (2009). Software-based remote code attestation in wireless sensor network. *GLOBECOM - IEEE Global Telecommunications Conference*. Available from https://doi.org/10.1109/GLOCOM.2009.5425280.

Abuhmed, T., El-Sappagh, S., & Alonso, J. M. (2021). Robust hybrid deep learning models for Alzheimer's progression detection. *Knowledge-Based Systems*, 213106688. Available from https://doi.org/10.1016/j.knosys.2020.106688.

Ahila, A., Dahan, F., Alroobaea, R., Alghamdi, W. Y., Mohammed, M. K., Hajjej, F., Alsekait, D. M., & Raahemifar, K. (2023). A smart IoMT based architecture for E-healthcare patient monitoring system using artificial intelligence algorithms. *Frontiers in Physiology*, 14. Available from https://doi.org/10.3389/fphys.2023.1125952, http://www.frontiersin.org/Physiology/archive/.

Ahmed, I., Ahmad, M., & Jeon, G. (2022). Integrating digital twins and deep learning for medical image analysis in the era of COVID-19. *Virtual Reality and Intelligent Hardware*, 4(4). Available from https://doi.org/10.1016/j.vrih.2022.03.002, http://www.keaipublishing.com/en/journals/virtual-reality-and-intelligent-hardware/.

Akash, S. S., & Ferdous, M. S. (2022). A blockchain based system for healthcare digital twin. *IEEE Access*, 10. Available from https://doi.org/10.1109/ACCESS.2022.3173617, http://ieeexplore.ieee.org/xpl/RecentIssue.jsp?punumber = 6287639.

Alam, K. M., & El Saddik, A. (2017). C2PS: A digital twin architecture reference model for the cloud-based cyber-physical systems. *IEEE Access*, 5. Available from https://doi.org/10.1109/ACCESS.2017.2657006, http://ieeexplore.ieee.org/xpl/RecentIssue.jsp?punumber = 6287639.

Alazab, M., Khan, L. U., Koppu, S., Ramu, S. P., Iyapparaja, M., Boobalan, P., Baker, T., Maddikunta, P. K. R., Gadekallu, T. R., & Aljuhani, A. (2022). Digital twins for healthcare 4.0—Recent advances, architecture, and open challenges. *IEEE Consumer Electronics Magazine*, 12(6), 29–37.

Alcaraz, J. C., Moghaddamnia, S., Fuhrwerk, M., & Peissig, J. (2019). Efficiency of the memory polynomial model in realizing digital twins for gait assessment. *European Signal Processing Conference*, 2019. Available from https://doi.org/10.23919/EUSIPCO.2019.8903143, http://eusipco2019.org/.

Ali, S., Abuhmed, T., El-Sappagh, S., Muhammad, K., Alonso-Moral, J. M., Confalonieri, R., Guidotti, R., Del Ser, J., Díaz-Rodríguez, N., & Herrera, F. (2023). Explainable artificial intelligence (XAI): What we know and what is left to attain trustworthy artificial intelligence. *Information Fusion*, 99101805. Available from https://doi.org/10.1016/j.inffus.2023.101805.

Al-Zyoud, I., Laamarti, F., Ma, X., Tobón, D., & El Saddik, A. (2022). Towards a machine learning-based digital twin for non-invasive human bio-signal fusion. *Sensors*, 22(24), 9747. Available from https://doi.org/10.3390/s22249747.

Ammar, A., Nassereddine, H., AbdulBaky, N., AbouKansour, A., Tannoury, J., Urban, H., & Schranz, C. (2022). Digital twins in the construction industry: A perspective of practitioners and building authority. *Frontiers in Built Environment*, 8. Available from https://doi.org/10.3389/fbuil.2022.834671, journal.frontiersin.org/journal/built-environment.

Appelboom, G., Camacho, E., Abraham, M. E., Bruce, S. S., Dumont, E. L. P., Zacharia, B. E., D'Amico, R., Slomian, J., Reginster, J. Y., Bruyère, O., & Connolly, E. S. (2014). Smart wearable body sensors for patient self-assessment and monitoring. *Archives of Public Health, 72*(1). Available from https://doi.org/10.1186/2049-3258-72-28, http://www.archpublichealth.com/.

Ardanza, A., Moreno, A., Segura, Á., de la Cruz, M., & Aguinaga, D. (2019). Sustainable and flexible industrial human machine interfaces to support adaptable applications in the Industry 4.0 paradigm. *International Journal of Production Research, 57*(12). Available from https://doi.org/10.1080/00207543.2019.1572932, http://www.tandfonline.com/toc/tprs20/current.

Armeni, P., Polat, I., De Rossi, L. M., Diaferia, L., Meregalli, S., & Gatti, A. (2022). Digital twins in healthcare: Is it the beginning of a new era of evidence-based medicine? A critical review. *Journal of Personalized Medicine, 12*(8). Available from https://doi.org/10.3390/jpm12081255, http://www.mdpi.com/journal/jpm.

Artificial Intelligence Offers Significant Rate of Remission for Type 2 Diabetes Compared to Standard Care (2023) Whole body digital twin is, reverse diabetes and metabolic diseases. American Diabetes Association.

Attaran, M., & Celik, B. G. (2023). Digital twin: Benefits, use cases, challenges, and opportunities. *Decision Analytics Journal, 6.* Available from https://doi.org/10.1016/j.dajour.2023.100165, https://www.journals.elsevier.com/decision-analytics-journal.

Barbiero, P., Viñas Torné, R., & Lió, P. (2021). Graph representation forecasting of patient's medical conditions: Toward a digital twin. *Frontiers in Genetics, 12.* Available from https://doi.org/10.3389/fgene.2021.652907, https://www.frontiersin.org/journals/genetics#.

Barnabas, J., & Raj, P. (2020). The human body: A digital twin of the cyber physical systems. *Advances in Computers, 117.* Available from https://doi.org/10.1016/bs.adcom.2019.09.004, http://www.elsevier.com/wps/find/bookdescription.cws_home/705045/description#description.

Barricelli, B. R., Casiraghi, E., & Fogli, D. (2019). A survey on digital twin: Definitions, characteristics, applications, and design implications. *IEEE Access, 7.* Available from https://doi.org/10.1109/access.2019.2953499.

Barszcz, T., & Zabaryłło, M. (2019). Concept of automated malfunction detection of large turbomachinery using machine learning on transient data. *Diagnostyka, 20*(1). Available from https://doi.org/10.29354/diag/100399, http://www.diagnostyka.net.pl/pdf-100399-32504?filename = Concept%20of%20automated.pdf.

Beam, A. L., & Kohane, I. S. (2018). Big data and machine learning in health care. *JAMA - Journal of the American Medical Association, 319*(13). Available from https://doi.org/10.1001/jama.2017.18391, https://jamanetwork.com/journals/jama/articlepdf/2675024/jama_beam_2018_vp_170174.pdf.

Danesh, A., Juraev, F., El-Sappagh, S., & Abuhmed, T. (2024). Integrating digital twin technology with dynamic ensemble learning for sepsis prediction in intensive care units. *Journal of Intelligence and Information Systems, 30*(2), 25−59.

De Benedictis, A., Mazzocca, N., Somma, A., & Strigaro, C. (2023). Digital twins in healthcare: An architectural proposal and its application in a social distancing case study. *IEEE Journal of Biomedical and Health Informatics, 27*(10). Available from https://doi.org/10.1109/JBHI.2022.3205506, http://ieeexplore.ieee.org/xpl/RecentIssue.jsp?punumber = 6221020.

Björnsson, B., Borrebaeck, C., Elander, N., Gasslander, T., Gawel, D. R., Gustafsson, M., Jörnsten, R., Lee, E. J., Li, X., Lilja, S., Martínez-Enguita, D., Matussek, A., Sandström, P., Schäfer, S., Stenmarker, M., Sun, X. F., Sysoev, O., Zhang, H., & Benson, M. (2020). Digital twins to personalize medicine. *Genome Medicine, 12*(1). Available from https://doi.org/10.1186/s13073-019-0701-3, https://genomemedicine.biomedcentral.com.

Bohlin, R., Hagmar, J., Bengtsson, K., Lindkvist, L., Carlson, J. S., & Söderberg, R. (2018). Data flow and communication framework supporting digital twin for geometry assurance. *ASME International Mechanical Engineering Congress and Exposition, Proceedings (IMECE), 2.* Available from https://doi.org/10.1115/IMECE2017-71405, http://www.asmedl.org/journals/doc/ASMEDL-home/proc/.

Bruynseels, K., de Sio, F. S., & van den Hoven, J. (2018). Digital twins in health care: Ethical implications of an emerging engineering paradigm. *Frontiers in Genetics, 9.* Available from https://doi.org/10.3389/fgene.2018.00031, https://www.frontiersin.org/articles/10.3389/fgene.2018.00031/full.

Buhagiar, A. J., Freitas, L., Scott, W. E., & Larsen, P. G. (2022). Digital Twins for organ preservation devices. *Lecture Notes in Computer Science (including subseries lecture notes in artificial intelligence and lecture notes in bioinformatics), 13704,* 22−36. Available from https://doi.org/10.1007/978-3-031-19762-8_3, https://www.springer.com/series/558.

Chen, J. (2023). *Networking technologies for enabling human digital twin in personalized healthcare applications: A comprehensive survey,* 2023.

Clay, I., Angelopoulos, C., Bailey, A. L., Blocker, A., Carini, S., Carvajal, R., Drummond, D., McManus, K. F., Oakley-Girvan, I., Patel, K. B., Szepietowski, P., & Goldsack, J. C. (2021). Sensor data integration: A new cross-industry collaboration to articulate value, define needs, and advance a framework for best practices. *Journal of Medical Internet Research*, 23(11), e34493. Available from https://doi.org/10.2196/34493.

Clermont, G., Vodovotz, Y., & Rubin, J. (2007). Equation-based models of dynamic biological systems. *Endothelial Biomedicine*. United States: Cambridge University Press. Available from http://doi.org/10.1017/CBO9780511546198, 10.1017/CBO9780511546198.192.

Cognitive IoT for Heathcare. (2023), 2023.

Coorey, G., Figtree, G. A., Fletcher, D. F., Snelson, V. J., Vernon, S. T., Winlaw, D., Grieve, S. M., McEwan, A., Yang, J. Y. H., Qian, P., O'Brien, K., Orchard, J., Kim, J., Patel, S., & Redfern, J. (2022). The health digital twin to tackle cardiovascular disease—A review of an emerging interdisciplinary field. *NPJ Digital Medicine*, 5(1). Available from https://doi.org/10.1038/s41746-022-00640-7, https://www.nature.com/npjdigitalmed/.

Corral-Acero, J., Margara, F., Marciniak, M., Rodero, C., Loncaric, F., Feng, Y., Gilbert, A., Fernandes, J. F., Bukhari, H. A., Wajdan, A., Martinez, M. V., Santos, M. S., Shamohammdi, M., Luo, H., Westphal, P., Leeson, P., DiAchille, P., Gurev, V., Mayr, M., ... Lamata, P. (2020). The 'Digital Twin' to enable the vision of precision cardiology. *European Heart Journal*, 41(48). Available from https://doi.org/10.1093/eurheartj/ehaa159.

Dai, Y., Wang, J., & Gao, S. (2022). Advanced electronics and artificial intelligence: Must-have technologies toward human body digital twins. *Advanced Intelligent Systems*, 4(7). Available from https://doi.org/10.1002/aisy.202100263.

Digital twins improve real-life manufacturing (n.d.). MIT Technology Review Insights.

Dhanaraj, R. K., Murugesan, S., Balusamy, B., & Balas, V. E. (2023). *Digital Twin Technologies for Healthcare* (4). IET.

Dillenseger, A., Weidemann, M. L., Trentzsch, K., Inojosa, H., Haase, R., Schriefer, D., Voigt, I., Scholz, M., Akgün, K., & Ziemssen, T. (2021). Digital biomarkers in multiple sclerosis. *Brain Sciences*, 11(11), 1519. Available from https://doi.org/10.3390/brainsci11111519.

Elayan, H., Aloqaily, M., & Guizani, M. (2021). Digital twin for intelligent context-aware IoT healthcare systems. *IEEE Internet of Things Journal*, 8(23). Available from https://doi.org/10.1109/JIOT.2021.3051158, http://ieeexplore.ieee.org/servlet/opac?punumber = 6488907.

G. Electric, (2023), 2023.

El-Sappagh, S., Abuhmed, T., Riazul Islam, S. M., & Kwak, K. S. (2020). Multimodal multitask deep learning model for Alzheimer's disease progression detection based on time series data. *Neurocomputing*, 412. Available from https://doi.org/10.1016/j.neucom.2020.05.087, http://www.elsevier.com/locate/neucom.

El-Sappagh, S., Alonso-Moral, J. M., Abuhmed, T., Ali, F., & Bugarín-Diz, A. (2023). Trustworthy artificial intelligence in Alzheimer's disease: State of the art, opportunities, and challenges. *Artificial Intelligence Review*, 56(10). Available from https://doi.org/10.1007/s10462-023-10415-5, https://www.springer.com/journal/10462.

El-Sappagh, S., Saleh, H., Sahal, R., Abuhmed, T., Islam, S. M. R., Ali, F., & Amer, E. (2021). Alzheimer's disease progression detection model based on an early fusion of cost-effective multimodal data. *Future Generation Computer Systems*, 115. Available from https://doi.org/10.1016/j.future.2020.10.005, https://www.journals.elsevier.com/future-generation-computer-systems.

Examining the Data on Digital Twin in the Automotive Industry. Altair Engineering Inc, (2023).

Facchinetti, A. (2016). Continuous glucose monitoring sensors: Past, present and future algorithmic challenges. *Sensors*, 16(12), 2093. Available from https://doi.org/10.3390/s16122093.

Ferdousi, R. (2022). Digital twins for well-being: An overview. *Digital Twin*, 1, 2022.

Fuller, A., Fan, Z., Day, C., & Barlow, C. (2020). Digital twin: Enabling technologies, challenges and open research. *IEEE Access*, 8. Available from https://doi.org/10.1109/ACCESS.2020.2998358, http://ieeexplore.ieee.org/xpl/RecentIssue.jsp?punumber = 6287639.

Ge Digital, Digital twin solutions. (2023).

Glaessgen, E.H., & Stargel, D.S. (2012). The digital twin paradigm for future NASA and U.S. air force vehicles. In *53rd AIAA/ASME/ASCE/AHS/ASC structures, structural dynamics and materials conference 2012*. United States.

Gupta, D., Kayode, O., Bhatt, S., Gupta, M., & Tosun, A. S. (2021). Hierarchical federated learning based anomaly detection using digital twins for smart healthcare. *Proceedings - 2021 IEEE 7th International Conference on Collaboration and Internet Computing, CIC 2021*, 16–25. Available from https://doi.org/10.1109/CIC52973.2021.00013, http://ieeexplore.ieee.org/xpl/mostRecentIssue.jsp?punumber = 9706610.

Hassani, H., Huang, X., & MacFeely, S. (2022). Impactful digital twin in the healthcare revolution. *Big Data and Cognitive Computing*, 6(3). Available from https://doi.org/10.3390/bdcc6030083, http://www.mdpi.com/journal/BDCC.

Hu, W., Zhang, T., Deng, X., Liu, Z., & Tan, J. (2021). Digital twin: A state-of-the-art review of its enabling technologies, applications and challenges. *Journal of Intelligent Manufacturing and Special Equipment, 2*(1). Available from https://doi.org/10.1108/jimse-12-2020-010.

Hu, Z., Lou, S., Xing, Y., Wang, X., Cao, D., & Lv, C. (2022). Review and perspectives on driver digital twin and its enabling technologies for intelligent vehicles. *IEEE Transactions on Intelligent Vehicles, 7*(3). Available from https://doi.org/10.1109/TIV.2022.3195635, http://ieeexplore.ieee.org/xpl/tocresult.jsp?isnumber = 7433488&punumber = 7274857.

Huang, P.-H., Kim, K.-H., & Schermer, M. (2022). Ethical issues of digital twins for personalized health care service: Preliminary mapping study. *Journal of Medical Internet Research, 24*(1), e33081. Available from https://doi.org/10.2196/33081.

Huang, S., Nianguang, C. A. I., Pacheco, P. P., Narandes, S., Wang, Y., & Wayne, X. U. (2018). Applications of support vector machine (SVM) learning in cancer genomics. *Cancer Genomics and Proteomics, 15*(1). Available from https://doi.org/10.21873/cgp.20063, http://cgp.iiarjournals.org/content/15/1/41.full.pdf + html.

Hussain, I., Hossain, M.A., & Park, S.J. (2021). A healthcare digital twin for diagnosis of stroke. In *Proceedings of 2021 IEEE international conference on biomedical engineering, computer and information technology for health, BECITHCON 2021* (pp. 18–21). doi: 10.1109/BECITHCON54710.2021.9893641, http://ieeexplore.ieee.org/xpl/mostRecentIssue.jsp?punumber = 9893559

Inc (2023). | Industrial IoT Software.

Islam, M. R., Kabir, M. M., Mridha, M. F., Alfarhood, S., Safran, M., & Che, D. (2023). Deep learning-based IoT system for remote monitoring and early detection of health issues in real-time. *Sensors, 23*(11). Available from https://doi.org/10.3390/s23115204, http://www.mdpi.com/journal/sensors.

Islam, M. S., Hussain, I., Rahman, M. M., Park, S. J., & Hossain, M. A. (2022). Explainable artificial intelligence model for stroke prediction using EEG signal. *Sensors, 22*(24). Available from https://doi.org/10.3390/s22249859, http://www.mdpi.com/journal/sensors.

Javaid, M., Haleem, A., & Suman, R. (2023). Digital twin applications toward Industry 4.0: A review. *Cognitive Robotics, 3*. Available from https://doi.org/10.1016/j.cogr.2023.04.003, https://www.sciencedirect.com/science/journal/26672413.

Jimenez, J. I., Jahankhani, H., & Kendzierskyj, S. (2020). Health care in the cyberspace: medical cyber-physical system and digital twin challenges. *Internet of Things*. Available from https://doi.org/10.1007/978-3-030-18732-3_6, http://www.springer.com/series/11636.

Jin, D., Sergeeva, E., Weng, W. H., Chauhan, G., & Szolovits, P. (2022). Explainable deep learning in healthcare: A methodological survey from an attribution view. *WIREs Mechanisms of Disease, 14*(3). Available from https://doi.org/10.1002/wsbm.1548, https://onlinelibrary.wiley.com/journal/26929368.

Jovanov, E., Milenkovic, A., Otto, C., & Groen, P. C. D. (2005). A wireless body area network of intelligent motion sensors for computer assisted physical rehabilitation. *Journal of Neuroengineering and Rehabilitation, 2*. Available from https://doi.org/10.1186/1743-0003-2-6, http://www.jneuroengrehab.com/content/2/1/6, United States.

Kamel Boulos, M. N., & Zhang, P. (2021). Digital twins: From personalised medicine to precision public health. *Journal of Personalized Medicine, 11*(8). Available from https://doi.org/10.3390/jpm11080745, https://www.mdpi.com/2075-4426/11/8/745/pdf.

Kayvanpour, E., Mansi, T., Sedaghat-Hamedani, F., Amr, A., Neumann, D., Georgescu, B., Seegerer, P., Kamen, A., Haas, J., Frese, K. S., Irawati, M., Wirsz, E., King, V., Buss, S., Mereles, D., Zitron, E., Keller, A., Katus, H. A., Comaniciu, D., ... Berger, T. (2015). Towards personalized cardiology: Multi-scale modeling of the failing heart. *PLoS One, 10*(7), e0134869. Available from https://doi.org/10.1371/journal.pone.0134869.

Khan, S. (2023). Digital twins-based internet of robotic things for remote health monitoring of COVID-19 patients. *IEEE Internet Things Journal, 2023*.

Khanna, N. N. (2022). Cardiovascular/stroke risk stratification in diabetic foot infection patients using deep learning-based artificial intelligence: An investigative study. *Journal of Clinical Medicine., 2022.*

Kim, J., Campbell, A. S., de Ávila, B. E. F., & Wang, J. (2019). Wearable biosensors for healthcare monitoring. *Nature Biotechnology, 37*(4). Available from https://doi.org/10.1038/s41587-019-0045-y, http://www.nature.com/nbt/index.html.

Lee, R. Y., Kross, E. K., Torrence, J., Li, K. S., Sibley, J., Cohen, T., Lober, W. B., Engelberg, R. A., & Curtis, J. R. (2023). Assessment of natural language processing of electronic health records to measure goals-of-care discussions as a clinical trial outcome. *JAMA Network Open, 6*(3), E231204. Available from https://doi.org/10.1001/jamanetworkopen.2023.1204, https://jamanetwork.com/journals/jamanetworkopen.

Liau, Y., Lee, H., & Ryu, K. (2018). Digital twin concept for smart injection molding. *IOP Conference Series: Materials Science and Engineering, 324*(1), 012077. Available from https://doi.org/10.1088/1757-899x/324/1/012077.

Lim, K. Y. H., Zheng, P., & Chen, C. H. (2020). A state-of-the-art survey of digital twin: Techniques, engineering product lifecycle management and business innovation perspectives. *Journal of Intelligent Manufacturing, 31* (6). Available from https://doi.org/10.1007/s10845-019-01512-w, http://www.kluweronline.com/issn/0956-5515/.

Lin, H., Zhang, S., Li, Q., Li, Y., Li, J., & Yang, Y. (2023). A new method for heart rate prediction based on LSTM-BiLSTM-Att. *Measurement, 207*112384. Available from https://doi.org/10.1016/j.measurement.2022.112384.

Liu, J., Zhou, H., Liu, X., Tian, G., Wu, M., Cao, L., & Wang, W. (2019). Dynamic evaluation method of machining process planning based on digital twin. *IEEE Access, 7*. Available from https://doi.org/10.1109/ACCESS.2019.2893309, http://ieeexplore.ieee.org/xpl/RecentIssue.jsp?punumber = 6287639.

Liu, Q., Mkongwa, K. G., & Zhang, C. (2021). Performance issues in wireless body area networks for the healthcare application: A survey and future prospects. *SN Applied Sciences, 3*(2). Available from https://doi.org/10.1007/s42452-020-04058-2, springer.com/snas.

Liu, Y., et al. (2019). A novel cloud-based framework for the elderly healthcare services using digital twin. *IEEE Access, 7*, 49088–49101. Available from https://doi.org/10.1109/ACCESS.2019.2909828.

Lu, W., Zheng, Q., Xu, N., & Feng, J. (2022). The human digital twin brain in the resting state and in action. *arXiv, China arXiv*. Available from https://doi.org/10.48550/arXiv.2211.15963, https://arxiv.org.

Luna, J., Ungab, G. A. M. D., Abrougui, K., Dahir, H., Khattab, A., & Kumar, R. (2022). Digital twin for cardiology. *Digital Twin for Healthcare: Design, Challenges, and Solutions*. Available from https://doi.org/10.1016/B978-0-32-399163-6.00018-4, https://www.sciencedirect.com/book/9780323991636.

Mak, G. C. K., Kwan, M. Y. W., Mok, C. K. P., Lo, J. Y. C., Peiris, M., & Leung, C. W. (2018). Influenza A(H5N1) virus infection in a child with encephalitis complicated by obstructive hydrocephalus. *Clinical Infectious Diseases, 66*(1). Available from https://doi.org/10.1093/cid/cix707, http://cid.oxfordjournals.org/content/by/year.

Martins, A. B., Farinha, J. T., & Cardoso, A. M. (2020). Calibration and certification of industrial sensors – A global review. *WSEAS Transactions on Systems and Control, 15*. Available from https://doi.org/10.37394/23203.2020.15.41, http://wseas.org/wseas/cms.action?id = 4073.

Masood, I., Wang, Y., Daud, A., Aljohani, N. R., & Dawood, H. (2018). Towards smart healthcare: Patient data privacy and security in sensor-cloud infrastructure. *Wireless Communications and Mobile Computing, 2018*. Available from https://doi.org/10.1155/2018/2143897, https://www.hindawi.com/journals/wcmc/.

Mathworks (2023). Digital Twin.

Melesse, T. Y., Di Pasquale, V., & Riemma, S. (2021). Digital twin models in industrial operations: State-of-the-art and future research directions. *IET Collaborative Intelligent Manufacturing, 3*(1). Available from https://doi.org/10.1049/cim2.12010, https://ietresearch.onlinelibrary.wiley.com/journal/25168398.

Microsoft (2023). Azure digital twins.

Milazzo, M. F., Ancione, G., Scionti, G., & Bragatto, P. A. (2018). *Assessment and management of ageing of critical equipment at seveso sites*. Informa UK Limited. Available from 10.1201/9781351174664-205.

Milenković, A., Otto, C., & Jovanov, E. (2006). Wireless sensor networks for personal health monitoring: Issues and an implementation. *Computer Communications, 29*(13-14). Available from https://doi.org/10.1016/j.comcom.2006.02.011.

Moftah, H. M., Ella Hassanien, A., & Shoman, M. (2010). 3D brain tumor segmentation scheme using K-mean clustering and connected component labeling algorithms. *Proceedings of the 2010 10th international conference on intelligent systems design and applications, ISDA'10*, 320–324. Available from https://doi.org/10.1109/ISDA.2010.5687244.

Morrison, T. M., Pathmanathan, P., Adwan, M., & Margerrison, E. (2018). Advancing regulatory science with computational modeling for medical devices at the FDA's office of science and engineering laboratories. *Frontiers in Medicine, 5*. Available from https://doi.org/10.3389/fmed.2018.00241, https://www.frontiersin.org/articles/10.3389/fmed.2018.00241/full.

Negra, R., Jemili, I., & Belghith, A. (2016). Wireless body area networks: Applications and technologies. *Procedia Computer Science, 83*, 1274–1281. Available from https://doi.org/10.1016/j.procs.2016.04.266, http://www.sciencedirect.com/science/journal/18770509.

Ogunseiju, O. R., Olayiwola, J., Akanmu, A. A., & Nnaji, C. (2021). Digital twin-driven framework for improving self-management of ergonomic risks. *Smart and Sustainable Built Environment, 10*(3). Available from https://doi.org/10.1108/SASBE-03-2021-0035, http://www.emeraldinsight.com/products/journals/journals.htm?id = sasbe.

Ooka, T., Johno, H., Nakamoto, K., Yoda, Y., Yokomichi, H., & Yamagata, Z. (2021). Random forest approach for determining risk prediction and predictive factors of type 2 diabetes: Large-scale health check-up data in Japan. *BMJ Nutrition, Prevention and Health, 4*(1). Available from https://doi.org/10.1136/bmjnph-2020-000200, https://nutrition.bmj.com/.

Park, K. T., Nam, Y. W., Lee, H. S., Im, S. J., Noh, S. D., Son, J. Y., & Kim, H. (2019). Design and implementation of a digital twin application for a connected micro smart factory. *International Journal of Computer Integrated Manufacturing, 32*(6). Available from https://doi.org/10.1080/0951192X.2019.1599439, http://www.tandfonline.com/loi/tcim20.

Popa, E. O., van Hilten, M., Oosterkamp, E., & Bogaardt, M. J. (2021). The use of digital twins in healthcare: Socio-ethical benefits and socio-ethical risks. *Life Sciences, Society and Policy, 17*(1). Available from https://doi.org/10.1186/s40504-021-00113-x, https://lsspjournal.biomedcentral.com/.

Pradhan, B., Bhattacharyya, S., Pal, K., & Sadiq Fareed, M. M. (2021). IoT-based applications in healthcare devices. *Journal of Healthcare Engineering, 2021*. Available from https://doi.org/10.1155/2021/6632599.

Procario, J. (2023). Pillars for change: ANSYS CTO talks digital twins, vertical health care, and more at IEEE.

Rahim, N., Abuhmed, T., Mirjalili, S., El-Sappagh, S., & Muhammad, K. (2023a). Time-series visual explainability for Alzheimer's disease progression detection for smart healthcare. *Alexandria Engineering Journal, 82*. Available from https://doi.org/10.1016/j.aej.2023.09.050, http://www.elsevier.com/wps/find/journaldescription.cws_home/724292/description#description.

Rahim, N., El-Sappagh, S., et al. (2023b). Prediction of Alzheimer's progression based on multimodal deep-learning-based fusion and visual explainability of time-series data. *Information Fusion, 92*, 363—388. Available from https://doi.org/10.1016/j.inffus.2022.11.028.

Rasheed, A., San, O., & Kvamsdal, T. (2020). Digital twin: Values, challenges and enablers from a modeling perspective. *IEEE Access, 8*. Available from https://doi.org/10.1109/ACCESS.2020.2970143, http://ieeexplore.ieee.org/xpl/RecentIssue.jsp?punumber = 6287639.

Redeker, M., Weskamp, J. N., Rossl, B., & Pethig, F. (2021). Towards a digital twin platform for industrie 4.0. *Proceedings - 2021 4th IEEE international conference on industrial cyber-physical systems, ICPS 2021*, 39—46. Available from https://doi.org/10.1109/ICPS49255.2021.9468204, http://ieeexplore.ieee.org/xpl/mostRecentIssue.jsp?punumber = 9467798.

Reitz, J., Schluse, M., & Roßmann, J. (2019). *Industry 4.0 beyond the factory: An application to forestry.* Springer Science and Business Media LLC. Available from 10.1007/978-3-662-59317-2_11.

Retiwalla, R. (n.d.). *Digital twins in healthcare: Revolutionizing patient care.*

Rishani, N. (2018). *Wearable, epidermal, and implantable sensors for medical applications.*

Rivera, L.F., Villegas, N.M., Jiménez, M., Tamura, G., Angara, P., & Müller, H.A. (2020). Towards continuous monitoring in personalized healthcare through digital twins. In *CASCON 2019 Proceedings - Conference of the centre for advanced studies on collaborative research - Proceedings of the 29th annual international conference on computer science and software engineering* (pp. 329—335).

Saeedi, S., Rezayi, S., Keshavarz, H., & R. Niakan Kalhori, S. (2023). MRI-based brain tumor detection using convolutional deep learning methods and chosen machine learning techniques. *BMC Medical Informatics and Decision Making, 23*(1). Available from https://doi.org/10.1186/s12911-023-02114-6, https://bmcmedinformdecismak.biomedcentral.com/.

Sahal, R., Alsamhi, S. H., & Brown, K. N. (2022a). Personal digital twin: A close look into the present and a step towards the future of personalised healthcare industry. *Sensors, 22*(15). Available from https://doi.org/10.3390/s22155918, http://www.mdpi.com/journal/sensors.

Sahal, R., Alsamhi, S. H., Brown, K. N., O'Shea, D., & Alouffi, B. (2022b). Blockchain-based digital twins collaboration for smart pandemic alerting: Decentralized COVID-19 pandemic alerting use case. *Computational Intelligence and Neuroscience, 2022*. Available from https://doi.org/10.1155/2022/7786441, http://www.hindawi.com/journals/cin.

Saleh, H., El-Rashidy, N., Abuhmed, T., & El-Sappagh. S. (2023). LSTM deep learning model for Alzheimer's disease prediction based on cost-effective time series cognitive scores. In *5th Novel Intelligent and Leading Emerging*

Sciences Conference, NILES 2023 — Proceedings (pp. 1–6). doi: 10.1109/NILES59815.2023.10296640, http://ieeex-plore.ieee.org/xpl/mostRecentIssue.jsp?punumber = 10296538

Saracco, R. (2023). *Digital twins for healthcare*, 2023.

Sarris, A. L., Sidiropoulos, E., Paraskevopoulos, E., & Bamidis, P. (2023). *Towards a digital twin in human brain: Brain tumor detection using k-means* (302). IOS Press. Available from 10.3233/shti230345.

Satyanarayana, T. V. V., Mohana Roopa, Y., Maheswari, M., Patil, M. B., Tamrakar, A. K., & Prabhu Shankar, B. (2022). A secured IoT-based model for human health through sensor data. *Measurement: Sensors*, 24100516. Available from https://doi.org/10.1016/j.measen.2022.100516.

Schluse, M., & Rossmann, J. (2016). From simulation to experimentable digital twins: Simulation-based development and operation of complex technical systems. In *ISSE 2016 - 2016 international symposium on systems engineering - Proceedings Papers*. doi: 10.1109/SysEng.2016.7753162.

Schober, P., & Vetter, T. R. (2021). Logistic regression in medical research. *Anesthesia and Analgesia*, 132(2). Available from https://doi.org/10.1213/ANE.0000000000005247, http://journals.lww.com/anesthesia-analgesia/toc/publishahead.

Schwartz, S. M., Wildenhaus, K., Bucher, A., & Byrd, B. (2020). Digital twins and the emerging science of self: Implications for digital health experience design and "small" data. *Frontiers in Computer Science*, 2. Available from https://doi.org/10.3389/fcomp.2020.00031, http://www.frontiersin.org/journals/computer-science.

Shamanna, P., Dharmalingam, M., Sahay, R., Mohammed, J., Mohamed, M., Poon, T., Kleinman, N., & Thajudeen, M. (2021). Retrospective study of glycemic variability, BMI, and blood pressure in diabetes patients in the digital twin precision treatment program. *Scientific Reports*, 11(1). Available from https://doi.org/10.1038/s41598-021-94339-6.

Shamanna, P., Joshi, S., Shah, L., Dharmalingam, M., Saboo, B., Mohammed, J., Mohamed, M., Poon, T., Kleinman, N., Thajudeen, M., & Keshavamurthy, A. (2021). Type 2 diabetes reversal with digital twin technology-enabled precision nutrition and staging of reversal: A retrospective cohort study. *Clinical Diabetes and Endocrinology*, 7(1). Available from https://doi.org/10.1186/s40842-021-00134-7.

Shamanna, P., Saboo, B., Damodharan, S., Mohammed, J., Mohamed, M., Poon, T., Kleinman, N., & Thajudeen, M. (2020). Reducing HbA1c in type 2 diabetes using digital twin technology-enabled precision nutrition: A retrospective analysis. *Diabetes Therapy*, 11(11). Available from https://doi.org/10.1007/s13300-020-00931-w.

Shengli, W. (2021). Is human digital twin possible? *Computer Methods and Programs in Biomedicine Update*, 1100014. Available from https://doi.org/10.1016/j.cmpbup.2021.100014.

Siemens, A. (2023). *A passion for digital twins*, 2023.

Singh, M., Fuenmayor, E., Hinchy, E. P., Qiao, Y., Murray, N., & Devine, D. (2021). Digital twin: Origin to future. *Applied System Innovation*, 4(2). Available from https://doi.org/10.3390/asi4020036, https://www.mdpi.com/2571-5577/4/2/36/pdf.

Smith, T. A., Seron, M. M., Goodwin, G. C., Medioli, A. M., King, B. R., Smart, C. E., Harris, M., Oneal, D. N., Rafferty, J., & Howley, P. (2019). 1058-P: The use of metabolic digital twins to personalize mealtime insulin dosing in type 1 diabetes clinical management. *Diabetes*, 68(Supplement_1). Available from https://doi.org/10.2337/db19-1058-p.

Sodhro, A. H., Zongwei, L., Pirbhulal, S., Sangaiah, A. K., Lohano, S., & Sodhro, G. H. (2020). Power-management strategies for medical information transmission in wireless body sensor networks. *IEEE Consumer Electronics Magazine*, 9(2). Available from https://doi.org/10.1109/MCE.2019.2954053, https://www.ieee.org/membership-catalog/productdetail/showProductDetailPage.html?product = PER262-EPC.

Steinmetz, C., Rettberg, A., Ribeiro, F. G. C., Schroeder, G., & Pereira, C. E. (2018). Internet of things ontology for digital twin in cyber physical systems. *Brazilian Symposium on Computing System Engineering, SBESC*, 2018, 154–159. Available from https://doi.org/10.1109/SBESC.2018.00030, http://ieeexplore.ieee.org/xpl/mostRecentIssue.jsp?punumber = 6472847.

Sun, T., He, X., Song, X., Shu, L., & Li, Z. (2022). The digital twin in medicine: A key to the future of healthcare? *Frontiers in Medicine*, 9. Available from https://doi.org/10.3389/fmed.2022.907066, journal.frontiersin.org/journal/medicine.

Sun, T., He, X., & Li, Z. (2023). Digital twin in healthcare: Recent updates and challenges. *Digital Health*, 9. Available from https://doi.org/10.1177/20552076221149651, 205520762211496.

Systèmes, D. (2023). *Virtual Twin Experiences in Life Sciences & Healthcare*, 2023.

Systèmes, D. (2023). Put digital-driven proactive quality to work for you. In *1tce4zx*_ga*MTg1NTM0MzkxNy4xNzAx MTUyNTk0*_ga_DYJDKXYEZ4*MTcwMTE1MjU5My4xLjEuMTcwMTE1MjYyNS4yOC4wLjA.

Taidoc. (2020). *Arm blood pressure monitor*, 2020.

Tao, F., Sui, F., Liu, A., Qi, Q., Zhang, M., Song, B., Guo, Z., Lu, S. C. Y., & Nee, A. Y. C. (2019). Digital twin-driven product design framework. *International Journal of Production Research*, *57*(12). Available from https://doi.org/10.1080/00207543.2018.1443229, http://www.tandfonline.com/toc/tprs20/current.

Thamotharan, P., Srinivasan, S., Kesavadev, J., Krishnan, G., Mohan, V., Seshadhri, S., Bekiroglu, K., & Toffanin, C. (2023). Human digital twin for personalized elderly type 2 diabetes management. *Journal of Clinical Medicine*, *12*(6), 2094. Available from https://doi.org/10.3390/jcm12062094.

Troncoso, Á., Ortega, J. A., Seepold, R., & Madrid, N. M. (2021). Non-invasive devices for respiratory sound monitoring. *Procedia Computer Science*, *192*, 3040−3048. Available from https://doi.org/10.1016/j.procs.2021.09.076, http://www.sciencedirect.com/science/journal/18770509.

Vallée, A. (2023). Digital twin for healthcare systems. *Frontiers in Digital Health*, *5*. Available from https://doi.org/10.3389/fdgth.2023.1253050, https://www.frontiersin.org/journals/digital-health#.

Velez, F. J., & Miyandoab, F. D. (2019). Wearable technologies and wireless body sensor networks for healthcare. *Wearable Technologies and Wireless Body Sensor Networks for Healthcare*. Available from https://doi.org/10.1049/PBHE011E, https://shop.theiet.org/wearable-tech-wireless-hb.

Venkatesh, K. P., Raza, M. M., & Kvedar, J. C. (2022). Health digital twins as tools for precision medicine: Considerations for computation, implementation, and regulation. *NPJ Digital Medicine*, *5*(1). Available from https://doi.org/10.1038/s41746-022-00694-7, https://www.nature.com/npjdigitalmed/.

Vohra, M. (2022). *Overview of digital twin digital twin technology: Fundamentals and applications*. Wiley. Available from 10.1002/9781119842316.ch1.

Voigt, I., Inojosa, H., Dillenseger, A., Haase, R., Akgün, K., & Ziemssen, T. (2021). Digital twins for multiple sclerosis. *Frontiers in Immunology*, *12*. Available from https://doi.org/10.3389/fimmu.2021.669811, https://www.frontiersin.org/journals/immunology#.

WHO Guidance (2021). Ethics and governance of artificial intelligence for health.

World Health Organization (WHO), (2023). Diabetes Fact Sheet, 2023, [Online].

Wuttke, H. D., Henke, K., & Hutschenreuter, R. (2020). Digital twins in remote labs. *Lecture Notes in Networks and Systems*, *80*. Available from https://doi.org/10.1007/978-3-030-23162-0_26, springer.com/series/15179.

Yang, D., Karimi, H. R., Kaynak, O., & Yin, S. (2021). Developments of digital twin technologies in industrial, smart city and healthcare sectors: A survey. *Complex Engineering Systems*, *1*(1). Available from https://doi.org/10.20517/ces.2021.06, https://www.oaepublish.com/articles/ces.2021.06.

Ye, F., Chen, A., Lu, S., & Zhang, L. (2001). A scalable solution to minimum cost forwarding in large sensor networks. In *Proceedings - International conference on computer communications and networks, ICCCN 2001-*. doi: 10.1109/ICCCN.2001.956276.

Yüksel, N., Börklü, H. R., Sezer, H. K., & Canyurt, O. E. (2023). Review of artificial intelligence applications in engineering design perspective. *Engineering Applications of Artificial Intelligence*, *118*. Available from https://doi.org/10.1016/j.engappai.2022.105697, https://www.journals.elsevier.com/engineering-applications-of-artificial-intelligence.

Wireless body area network for e-health application

Kamal Das[1] and Soumen Moulik[2]

[1]SRM University-AP, Mangalagiri, Andhra Pradesh, India [2]NIT Meghalaya, Bijni Complex, Shillong, Meghalaya, India

11.1 Introduction

The confluence of healthcare and technological innovation has given rise to wireless body area networks (WBANs), marking a revolutionary paradigm shift in medical care and health monitoring delivery. WBANs represent a transformative integration of wearable sensors, efficient communication technologies, and cutting-edge advancements like the Internet of Things (IoT), machine learning (ML). These networks are designed to monitor physiological parameters in real-time, allowing for personalized and proactive healthcare solutions (Qadri et al., 2020). The widespread adoption of WBANs is primarily propelled by the strategic placement of sensors on or inside the human body. These sensors are diverse, each dedicated to monitoring specific aspects of an individual's health. Electrocardiogram (ECG) and electroencephalogram (EEG) sensors track cardiac and brain activities. In contrast, blood pressure sensors, temperature sensors, and glucose monitors continuously capture vital signs, facilitating the early detection of anomalies and ensuring timely interventions. Additional sensors, such as motion sensors, respiratory rate sensors, and environmental sensors contribute to a holistic health profile, paving the way for comprehensive health monitoring. The communication backbone of WBANs is equally pivotal, ensuring seamless data transmission from sensors to monitoring systems or healthcare providers. Technologies like Bluetooth, Zigbee, IEEE 802.15.6 and IPV6 Over Low-Power Wireless Personal Area Networks (6LoWPAN) are tailored to specific use cases ranging from short- range, low-power communication to long-range connectivity (Cavallari et al., 2014; Chen et al., 2011; Ullah et al., 2012). The integration of WBANs with emerging technologies amplifies their impact on healthcare. As integral components of the IoT ecosystem, WBANs facilitate health data exchange, enabling remote monitoring, predictive analytics, and patient engagement. ML and AI analyze the copious amounts of data

Sensor Networks for Smart Hospitals
DOI: https://doi.org/10.1016/B978-0-443-36370-2.00012-8

generated by WBANs, unlocking the potential for early disease detection, personalized treatment plans, and informed decision-making. This chapter explores the various aspects of WBANs, including the sensors used, the communication technologies involved, and their integration with emerging technologies such as IoT, ML and blockchain.

11.2 Wireless body area network architecture

The architecture of WBAN communication is classified into three Tiers, as shown in Fig. 11.1 (Latré et al., 2011; Movassaghi et al., 2014; Negra et al., 2016). Tier-1 communication depicts the communication of raw sensed data between the body sensor devices and the hub associated with a single WBAN. This is also known as intra-WBAN communication. Tier-2 communication, also called inter-WBAN communication, represents the communication of data within multiple WBANs or between the hub of WBANs and the nearest access point. Tier-3 communication denotes the communication of data between the access points and the external medical servers through the Internet. This is also known as beyond-WBAN communication. A brief description of these communication tiers is given below.

11.2.1 Intra-wireless body area network communication

The intra-WBAN or Tier-1 communication range is approximately 2 meter around a human body. Intra-WBAN comprises heterogeneous wearable sensor devices and a central coordinator or Hub. Different body sensors, such as a respiratory sensor, a blood pressure

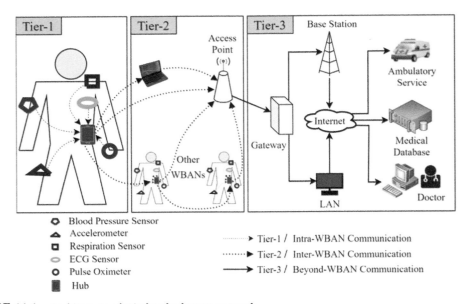

FIGURE 11.1   Architecture of wireless body area network.

sensor, an ECG sensor, a pulse oximeter, and an accelerometer collect raw data by sensing the corresponding physiological parameters and transmit the raw data to the Hub through a wireless communication medium, as represented by dashed lines in Hub processes and aggregates these collected data locally and transmits them, sometimes partially, to remote medical servers over the internet for 24×7 health monitoring (Baker et al., 2017). The communication in this tier primarily happens between the sensor devices and the Hub using star topology. Multi-hop communication is also possible in peer-to-peer topologies where individual sensor devices serve as source nodes, and the Hub acts as a sink. In this communication tier, quality of service (QoS) provisioning is challenging as it comprises sensor devices with limited resources. According to the application requirement, other network topologies such as ring, mesh, tree, and hybrid are also used in WBAN (Bertrand, 2015; Jafer et al., 2020; Moungla et al., 2014; Vera et al., 2019; Youssef et al., 2015).

11.2.2 Inter-wireless body area network communication

In Inter-WBAN, communication takes place between the hubs of different WBANs or between the hubs of different WBANs and access points. Access point deployment is a practical component of the infrastructure. However, it is also potential to conceive of an ad hoc infrastructure in which the deployment of access points is dynamic, like in the case of medical emergency care response or disaster site circumstances (Gao et al., 2007). The infrastructure-based design is utilized by the majority of WBAN applications, providing a few benefits such as more bandwidth, centralized management with security control, and flexibility. It is also appropriate for use in homes, offices, and hospitals (Curtis et al., 2011).

11.2.3 Beyond wireless body area network communication

Beyond-WBAN communication involves the Internet, external medical servers, and authorized medical personnel such as doctors and nurses to establish an end-to-end e-Health system with remote access to patients' medical records. The database is another essential component of this tier as it maintains end-user profiles and medical history. Authorized doctors can access these records anytime, making emergency care more effective. Moreover, data analytics provides a pathway for ubiquitous healthcare by facilitating automated messages to the end-users in case any abnormal health data is detected in real-time. Beyond-WBAN communication also covers ambulatory healthcare services, which is vital in emergencies.

11.3 Wearable sensor devices and microcontrollers

WBANs rely on various hardware, such as a diverse range of sensors and microcontrollers. Each sensor device is designed to monitor specific physiological parameters and gather essential data for healthcare and remote monitoring applications. These sensors play a pivotal role in providing real-time information about a patient's health status, enabling timely intervention, early disease detection, and continuous health assessment. Similarly, the microcontrollers are hardware devices that facilitate different operations on the sensed data.

11.3.1 Wearable sensors

In this section, we will explore the various types of sensors and other hardware commonly used in WBANs and their applications (Fig. 11.2).

11.3.1.1 Electrocardiogram sensors

ECG sensors are fundamental in WBANs, monitoring the electrical activity of the heart (Varon et al., 2015). ECG sensors typically consist of leads or electrodes placed on the chest, wrists, and ankles, which record the electrical signals generated by the heart's contractions. This data is essential for assessing heart health and diagnosing arrhythmias or cardiac anomalies. WBANs equipped with ECG sensors can provide real-time monitoring of heart rate, rhythm, and ST-segment changes, facilitating early detection of cardiac events and enabling timely intervention.

11.3.1.2 Electroencephalogram sensors

EEG sensors measure electrical activity in the brain, offering insights into neurological health. They consist of electrodes placed on the scalp to capture brain wave patterns. WBANs employing EEG sensors are used in applications such as monitoring epilepsy patients to detect seizures or assessing sleep quality. They can provide valuable data for diagnosing neurological disorders and guiding treatment (Casson et al., 2018).

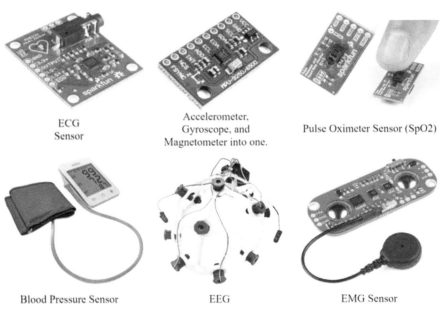

ECG
Sensor

Accelerometer,
Gyroscope, and
Magnetometer into one.

Pulse Oximeter Sensor (SpO2)

Blood Pressure Sensor

EEG

EMG Sensor

FIGURE 11.2   Wearable sensors.

11.3.1.3 Blood pressure sensors

These sensors are designed to monitor blood pressure, a vital sign that provides critical information about a person's cardiovascular health. Blood pressure sensors can be integrated into wearable devices or cuffs, allowing continuous monitoring of systolic and diastolic pressures (Bijender & Kumar, 2021). In patients with hypertension or cardiovascular diseases, WBANs equipped with blood pressure sensors help in tracking blood pressure variations throughout the day, aiding in medication management and risk assessment.

11.3.1.4 Temperature sensors

Body temperature is a crucial parameter for assessing general health and diagnosing conditions such as fever or hypothermia. WBANs incorporate temperature sensors to monitor changes in body temperature. These sensors can be placed on the skin's surface or within wearable devices, pro- viding continuous monitoring of temperature and enabling early identification of anomalies (Kuzubasoglu et al., 2021).

11.3.1.5 Glucose monitors

For individuals with diabetes, continuous glucose moni- toring is a game-changer in disease management. Glucose sensors can be implanted or worn externally, constantly measuring glucose levels in the interstitial fluid. These sensors offer real-time data that aids in insulin dosing, dietary decisions, and glycemic control. WBANs equipped with glucose monitors provide a new level of freedom for diabetes patients, reducing the need for invasive blood glucose tests (Kim et al., 2018; Zafar et al., 2022).

11.3.1.6 Respiratory rate sensors

Respiratory rate sensors are essential for assessing lung function and detecting disorders such as sleep apnea. These sensors can be integrated into wearable devices, detecting chest or abdominal movements associated with breathing (Kundu et al., 2013). By monitoring respiratory rates, WBANs help healthcare professionals assess lung health and intervene in cases of abnormal breathing patterns.

11.3.1.7 Motion and activity sensors

Accelerometers and gyroscopes are used to measure motion and activity levels (Atallah et al., 2010). These sensors are particularly valuable in tracking physical activity, posture, and mobility. WBANs equipped with motion sensors find applications in rehabilitation and elderly care. They can provide insights into the progress of rehabilitation exercises or detect falls among the elderly, sending alerts for immediate assistance. These sensors, collectively or individually, enable WBANs to provide a holistic view of a patient's health and well-being. They facilitate remote monitoring, early disease detection, and personalized healthcare. The integration of these sensors into WBANs not only improves patient care but also has the potential to reduce healthcare costs by preventing complications, hospitalizations, and unnecessary medical visits. As sensor technology continues to advance, the capabilities of WBANs will expand, contributing to more precise and efficient healthcare delivery.

Arduino　　　　　　ESP8266　　　　　　Raspberry Pi

FIGURE 11.3　Microcontrollers.

11.3.2 Microcontrollers

The Arduino microcontroller is a versatile open-source platform for developing WBANs (Mahmood et al., 2017). Arduino's compact size, low power consumption, and extensive community support make it ideal for creating wearable health devices. In WBANs, Arduino facilitates seamless communication between various sensors, such as heart rate monitors and temperature sensors, allowing real-time data collection and transmission to a central hub. The micro-controller's compatibility with wireless communication modules, such as Bluetooth and Wi-Fi, ensures efficient and reliable data exchange. This integration empowers healthcare professionals to remotely monitor patients, track health trends, and provide timely interventions. The Arduino microcontroller's user-friendly nature and adaptability continue to drive innovations in the burgeoning field of wireless health monitoring. Microcontrollers like the ESP8266 and Raspberry Pi are also suitable for developing WBANs due to their compact dimensions and energy-efficient designs (Kalpana & Annadurai, 2021; Keshamoni, 2019; Ramya & Jagadeesan, 2019) (Fig. 11.3).

11.4 Communication standards

Communication technology is a critical component of WBANs as it facilitates the seamless transfer of data from sensors to monitoring systems or healthcare providers. The choice of communication technology in a WBAN is essential to ensure real-time data transmission, and energy efficiency. Many communication standards have been developed to pave the way for e-Health applications, such as Bluetooth Low Energy (BLE), IEEE 802.15.4, IEEE 802.15.6, and 6LoWPANs. This section will explore the various communication technologies employed in WBANs and their specific use cases and advantages (Table 11.1).

11.4.1 Bluetooth low energy

Bluetooth is a low-power short-range wireless communication technology with a master-slave architecture, introduced by the IEEE 802.15.1 standard (IEEE, 2002). It has been developed to substitute serial cables with wireless connections. Nowadays, it is also used to connect controllers, actuators, sensors and essential wireless infrastructures. One of the main advantages of Bluetooth is its availability. In a piconet, a master device may communicate with up to seven slaves. Compared to classical Bluetooth, BLE provides low

TABLE 11.1 Comparison between different communication standards.

Parameters	BLE	IEEE 802.15.4	IEEE 802.15.6	6LoWPAN
Range	Up to 10 m	1–100 m	Up to 10 m	1–100 m
Maximum nodes	8	65536	256	IPv6 addressing
Topology	Star	Star, P2P, Tree, Mesh	One-hop star, two-hop star	Mesh
Spread spectrum	FHSS	DSSS	-	DSSS
Frequency band	2.4 GHz ISM; 2400, 868, 915 MHz	NB: 402, 420, 863, 902, 950 MHz, 2.3 GHz, and 2.4 GHz; UWB: 3494.4–4492.8 MHz, 6489.6–9984.0 MHz; HBC: 21 MHz	2400, 868, 915 MHz	
Transmission time	Up Mbps to 1	20–250 Kbps	Up to 10 Mbps	20–250 Kbps
Protocol stack	PHY to Application Layer	Data Link and Physical Layer	MAC and PHY	Network Adaptation Layer
Radio layer	Bluetooth Radio	IEEE 802.15.4	IEEE 802.15.6	IEEE 802.15.4
Modulation	GFSK	O-QPSK, BPSK	DBPSK, DQPSK, D8PSK, GMSK	O-QPSK
MAC access	TDMA	TDMA, CSMA/CA	TDMA, CSMA/CA, Polling, Slotted ALOHA	TDMA, CSMA/CA

cost and low energy consumption, while providing a similar communication range. BLE mainly focuses on healthcare and medical applications. The ultra-low-power requirement of BLE makes it suitable for small devices with limited battery life, such as wearable technologies. Fig. 11.4 illustrates the protocol stack of BLE comprises the controller and the host. All the applications are used on the top of the GATT and GAP layers. BLE uses L2CAP to fragment large packets from the upper layers into the maximum packet size of BLE packets on the sender side, and recombine small packets from the link layer on the receiver side. HCI allows communication between the host and the controller.

11.4.1.1 Open challenges in Bluetooth low energy-based communication

The open challenges of BLE-based communication are as follows:

Devising a method of safe long-term key exchange or pairing in BLE to avoid key leakage. This is highly vulnerable to the possibility of forcing connecting devices to regenerate their keys.

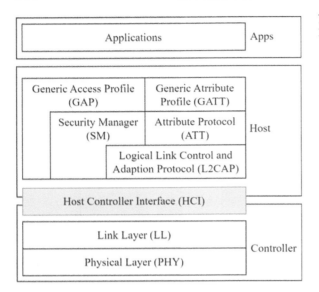

FIGURE 11.4 Bluetooth low energy (BLE) Protocol Stack.

Avoiding dependency on other networks such as wireless local area network (WLAN) or Long-Term Evolution while translating the Bluetooth packets to IP packets, by bringing seamless IPv6 connectivity in the core specification of BLE.

Optimal chipsets and hardware specifications are required in BLE-based communications to enable energy harvesting and storage.

11.4.2 IEEE 802.15.4 standard for low-rate wireless personal area networks

The IEEE 802.15.4 standard (Committee, 2011) allows both star and peer-to-peer topologies. The devices that communicate between each other using this standard can be divided into two groups—full-function devices (FFDs) and reduced-function devices (RFDs). An FFD can serve as a PAN coordinator, whereas an RFD is intended for comparatively simple tasks, such as sensing and transmitting the sensed data to the coordinator. PAN coordinators mostly operate in beacon-enabled mode in which they send periodical beacon frames to synchronize communication with the attached devices. The slotted carrier sense multiple access algorithm is used in this mode. The duration of time between two consecutive beacon transmissions is known as superframe. This interval is also known as Beacon Interval (BI). The structure of a superframe is illustrated in Fig. 11.5. Along with BI, the structure of superframe is also defined by another variable—superframe duration (SD), which refers to the active portion of superframe. Along with the active portion, a superframe may consist of an inactive portion, in which the devices can enter into sleep mode. The length of the active and inactive portions solely depends on the values of BI and SD, which in turn decided by two PAN Information Base (PIB) attributes——Beacon order (BO) and superframe order (SO), respectively, as illustrated in Fig. 11.5. Furthermore, the active portion is divided into two parts—one part is contention access period (CAP) and the other

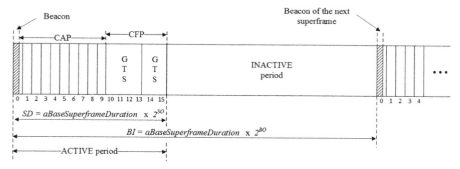

FIGURE 11.5 Superframe structure of IEEE 802.15.4 MAC.

part is contention-free period (CFP). The CFP consists of guaranteed time slots (GTSs). The coordinator allocates these GTSs to the sensor nodes according to their GTS requests to the coordinator. On the contrary, CAP allows contention among the sensor devices using a slotted CSMA-CA algorithm to provide access to the channel. The primary essence of this algorithm is to sense the channel before transmitting, which is also known as Clear Channel Assessment (CCA). The algorithm flows through different paths based on the channel condition and the values of three variables—contention window, number of back-off (NB) stages and backoff exponent (BE). Three MAC parameters—macMinBE, mac-MaxBE, and macMaxCSMABackoffs play important roles in this algorithm.

11.4.2.1 Open challenges in IEEE 802.15.4-based communication

The open challenges of IEEE 802.15.4-based works are as follows:

- Context-aware tuning of MAC PIB attributes.
- In place of random backoff selection, judicious choice of BE values in order to optimize various network performance metrics such as delay, power consumption, and throughput.
- Introducing prioritization schemes for data traffic and sensor devices based on their urgency to access the channel and other relevant criteria can be a potential future scope.
- Devising efficient GTS allocation and scheduling mechanisms. Presently, a maximum of seven GTS slots may be allocated in a superframe period, which causes a significant problem of scalability for dense networks.
- Optimization of the duty cycle period is another important open concern. Dynamic duty cycle-based approaches are required to manage nodes' access to the channel during both the inactive and active periods of the superframe to conserve energy without compromising other important performance.

11.4.3 IEEE 802.15.6

In 2012, the IEEE task group proposed a new standard called IEEE 802.15.6 for WBANs (Association, 2012). This standard serves in various medical and nonmedical applications, enabling connectivity of ultra-low-power wireless sensor devices inside and outside the human body. The standard is specifically designed for use with a broad range of data rates, low power consumption, short-range, and a large number of nodes (256) per body area network. The IEEE 802.15.6 standard can achieve up to 10 Mbps data rates while being extremely low power. The standard's main characteristics are multiple data rates, device and traffic prioritization, multiple access methods, and radio interfaces.

In IEEE 802.15.6, the hub shall operate in one of the following three access modes——(i) Beacon mode with beacon periods, (ii) nonbeacon mode with beacon periods, and (iii) nonbeacon mode without beacon periods. Beacon mode with beacon periods is the most useful access mode where the hub divides the time axis into equal-length beacon periods (superframes). Except for the inactive superframe, the hub broadcasts beacon frames in each beacon period. Beacon frames consist of all the information about the network and superframe structure. The hub broadcasts a beacon frame at the start of every superframe period. The superframe structure of the IEEE 802.15.6 MAC consists of two exclusive access periods (EAP1 and EAP2), two random access periods (RAP1 and RAP2), two managed access periods (MAP1 and MAP2) and an optional CAP period. Fig. 11.6 illustrates the superframe structure of the IEEE 802.15.6 standard in beacon mode with beacon periods. EAPs, RAPs, and CAP are the CAPs where nodes contend for resource allocation using either CSMA/CA or slotted ALOHA random access mechanism. The EAP1 and EAP2 periods are used for the transmission of emergency data. User priority (UP) value is determined in the range of 0 to 7 based on traffic classification. The frames with high importance are given a high UP value. The highest UP frame is Emergency data or medical implant event report (UP7). The RAP1, RAP2, and CAP periods are used to transmit all kinds of traffic. The MAP periods are used for downlink, uplink, bilink, and delay bilink allocation intervals. In MAP periods, type I/II polling mechanism is used for channel allocation. Except for RAP1, the length of all other access periods can have zero in a beacon period, as stated in the standard.

11.4.3.1 Open challenges in IEEE 802.15.6-based communication

The limitations and open challenges of IEEE 802.15.6-based works are as follows:

- Efficient algorithms are required to reduce energy consumption and energy harvesting of sensor nodes.
- Adaptability with the mobility of the human body and posture is an important open area to explore. Unexpected changes in human body movements and positions can degrade the performance of a WBAN.
- Context-aware methods for window size selection are required to serve application-specific requirements. The standard-specified binary exponential backoff algorithm suffers from overlapping backoff assignment, which causes collisions in WBAN.
- Designing dynamic superframe structure by adjusting the length of various access phases which will be adaptable to the nature of applications.

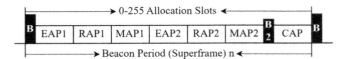

FIGURE 11.6 Superframe structure of the IEEE 802.15.6 standard in beacon mode with beacon periods.

- Sensor prioritization is required and can be done based on various parameters such as packet generation rate and buffer status for fair slot allocation to sensor devices.
- Efficient coexistence mechanisms are required to prevent intra-WBAN interference as well as inter-WBAN interference with neighboring WBANs.

11.4.4 IPV6 over low-power wireless personal area networks

In several aspects, IPv6 suits well to sensing and monitoring applications: its almost infinite address space allows increasingly ubiquitous computing for the future. Furthermore, combination with Internet architecture facilitates flexibility, principled optimization, and creativity in each layer of the stack. To support this perception, in 2005, IETF established the 6LoWPAN working group to standardize the use of IPv6 over IEEE 802.15.4 (Shelby & Bormann, 2011). In the 6LoWPAN network protocol stack, the physical layer and MAC layers are specified by the IEEE 802.15.4 standard. The network layer is defined by the IETF 6LoWPAN standard with the Internetwork layer using the IETF IPv6 protocol and the transport layer using either user datagram protocol or transmission control protocol. Protocol stack and end-to-end architecture for sensor-augmented healthcare systems using 6LoWPAN are illustrated in Fig. 11.7. 6LoWPAN also defined how IPv6 datagrams can be transmitted over IEEE 802.15.4 communication links and perform essential IPv6 neighbor discovery functionality (e.g., duplicate address detection, address resolution) in a network with overlapping broadcast domains.

11.4.4.1 Open challenges in 6LoWPAN-based communication

The open challenges in 6LoWPAN-based works are as follows:

- Neighbor discovery is another critical problem in 6LoWPAN. Here, the main challange is to propose a method that requires the least amount of packet transmission for a node to maintain contact with neighnoring nodes and routers. 6LoWPAN uses duplicate address request and the duplicate address confirmation between 6LoWPAN Routers and the 6LoWPAN border router for duplicate address detection. Therefore, introducing a method for duplicate address detection over multiple hops is another key issue in 6LoWPAN.

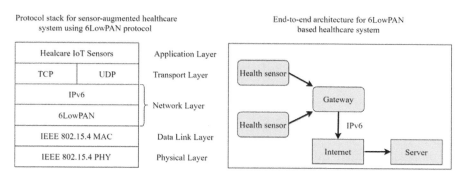

FIGURE 11.7   Protocol stack and end-to-end architecture for healthcare systems using 6LoWPAN.

- Header compression in 6LoWPAN is another pressing issue. Compression and decompression of the headers must be performed based on the context exchanged before communication; otherwise receiving node will not understand the packet.

11.5 Integration with emerging technologies

WBANs represent a crucial intersection between healthcare and technology. These networks, equipped with a myriad of sensors and robust communication technologies, have proven to be highly adaptable to the integration of emerging technologies. In this section, we will delve into how WBANs are harmoniously incorporating emerging technologies such as the IoT, ML, and Blockchain to enhance healthcare services, improve patient outcomes, and revolutionize healthcare as we know it.

11.5.1 Internet of Things

The IoT is a paradigm that describes the interconnection of everyday objects to the internet, enabling them to collect and exchange data. WBANs are an integral part of the IoT ecosystem, as they provide a continuous stream of real-time health data, making them valuable data sources for the broader IoT. The integration of WBANs and IoT opens up numerous possibilities for improved healthcare:

11.5.1.1 *Seamless data exchange*

WBAN sensors can seamlessly exchange data with IoT platforms, electronic health records, and healthcare provider systems. This connectivity enables healthcare professionals to access comprehensive and up-to-date patient data for more informed decision-making.

11.5.1.2 *Remote monitoring and management*

WBANs allow for remote monitoring of patients in real-time. This is particularly valuable for chronic disease management, postoperative care, and elderly patient care. Healthcare providers can receive alerts and notifications based on real-time sensor data, enabling timely interventions. Advancements in technology have evolved, enabling the development of solutions for remote patient monitoring and wirelessly connected healthcare surveillance (Nwibor et al., 2023; Pathak et al., 2021; Siam et al., 2023; Wan et al., 2018).

11.5.1.3 *Health data aggregation*

IoT-enabled WBANs can aggregate data from multiple patients and sensors, creating a large pool of health-related information (Othman et al., 2022; Rezaeibagha et al., 2021; Ullah et al., 2021; Zhang & Dong, 2022). This data can be analyzed to identify trends and anomalies, aiding in disease prediction, public health monitoring, and research.

11.5.1.4 Enhanced wearable devices

IoT integration encourages the development of smarter wearable devices. These wearables can interact with other IoT devices, such as smart home systems, to create an interconnected ecosystem. For instance, a WBAN-enabled smartwatch can integrate with a home's climate control system to help manage temperature for patients with temperature-sensitive conditions (Fu et al., 2021; Haghi et al., 2017; Metcalf et al., 2016; Verma et al., 2022).

Patient Engagement: WBANs within the IoT ecosystem can provide data to patients and caregivers, enabling better self-management of health conditions. Patients can actively engage with their health data, leading to improved adherence to treatment plans and a more significant role in their healthcare (Gaur, 2022; Ikawati et al., 2023; Mitchell, 2021).

11.5.2 Machine learning and artificial intelligence

ML and artificial intelligence (AI) are pivotal in the analysis and interpretation of the vast amount of data generated by WBANs. These technologies enable more proactive and personalized healthcare services (Abdellatif et al., 2023; Ullah et al., 2019). The integration of ML and AI with WBANs offers numerous benefits:

11.5.2.1 Early disease detection

ML algorithms can continuously analyze sensor data from WBANs to identify early warning signs of various medical conditions, including irregular heart rhythms, sleep disorders, or fluctuations in blood glucose levels. Early detection can lead to timely intervention and improved patient outcomes (Abdel-Basset et al., 2020; Basheer et al., 2021; Casella et al., 2023; El-Hasnony et al., 2020; Hosseinzadeh et al., 2021; Sciarrone et al., 2021).

11.5.2.2 Personalized treatment recommendations

ML models can analyze patient data from WBANs to provide personalized treatment recommendations (Sanjay et al., 2021). For instance, a WBAN can track a diabetic patient's glucose levels and suggest insulin dose adjustments based on the data, thus optimizing glycemic control (Ihnaini et al., 2021).

11.5.2.3 Predictive analytics

ML can analyze long-term trends in patient data to create predictive models. These models can forecast health issues, enabling healthcare providers to take preventive measures (K. & K., 2020). For example, ML models can predict the likelihood of falls in elderly patients and suggest interventions to reduce the risk.

11.5.2.4 Real-time decision support

AI-powered systems can provide real-time decision support for healthcare professionals. When integrated with WBANs, AI can analyze data in real-time and offer suggestions or alerts to medical staff, helping them make quicker and more accurate decisions (Comito et al., 2020; Fahmy et al., 2022; Moreira et al., 2019).

11.5.2.5 Data processing

WBANs generate a significant amount of data. ML and AI can process and categorize this data, reducing the burden on healthcare providers and facilitating more efficient data management (Baker et al., 2017).

11.5.3 Blockchain technology

Blockchain technology is gaining traction in healthcare due to its potential to enhance data security, transparency, and patient privacy (Dakhel & Hassan, 2020; Hasan et al., 2022; Ren et al., 2019). Integrating blockchain with WBANs offers several advantages:

Data Security: Blockchain provides a secure and immutable ledger for patient data. Data from WBANs, including sensor readings, medical history, and treatment records, can be securely stored on the blockchain. This ensures the integrity of health records and reduces the risk of unauthorized access or tampering.

Data Ownership and Control: Patients can have greater control over their health data. They can grant access to their data to specific healthcare providers or researchers while maintaining ownership and the ability to revoke access at anytime.

Interoperability: Blockchain can facilitate interoperability between different healthcare systems and WBANs. It creates a standardized format for health data, making it easier to share and integrate information across various healthcare settings.

Consent Management: Blockchain allows for the creation of smart contracts that govern data access and sharing. Patients can define who can access their data and under what circumstances. This enhances patient privacy and consent management.

Research and Clinical Trials: Blockchain can stream- line the process of data sharing for medical research and clinical trials. Researchers can access anonymized data securely, and clinical trial data can be stored transparently for regulatory purposes.

The integration of blockchain technology with WBANs addresses the growing concerns about data privacy, security, and interoperability in healthcare. It empowers patients to take control of their health data while providing healthcare providers with a secure and standardized platform for data exchange.

11.6 Applications of wireless body area networks

WBANs exhibit a broad spectrum of applications, ranging from military and healthcare to sports and entertainment. These applications can be categorized into medical and nonmedical domains, with the overarching objective of enhancing users' quality of life. It is essential to recognize that the technological requirements for WBANs are application-specific and tailored to meet the unique demands of diverse use cases (Movassaghi et al., 2014; Negra et al., 2016).

11.6.1 Medical applications

WBANs hold immense potential to reshape the landscape of healthcare by introducing real-time patient monitoring and early diagnosis of life-threatening diseases. As demographic trends predict the global population aged over 60 will increase to 2.1 billion by 2050, the demand for medical care is expected to rise significantly (Zhou, 2019). The use of WBANs is seen as a pivotal solution to address these challenges. Continuous monitoring of physiological attributes, such as blood pressure, heart rate, and body temperature, lies at the core of WBAN applications in the medical field. The ability to detect abnormal conditions promptly allows for swift action, as data collected by sensors can be transmitted to gateways or coordinators, such as cell phones. These coordinators then relay the information through cellular networks or the Internet to remote locations, such as emergency centers or doctors' offices.

11.6.1.1 Disability assistance

WBANs prove beneficial in monitoring soldiers, policemen, and firefighters in challenging environments. This includes the use of cameras, biometric sensors, GPS, and wireless networking for improved communication and centralized monitoring, potentially reducing the risk of injuries and enhancing care (Domingo, 2012). Some research has been conducted to monitor and assist people with disabilities in improving their living conditions and fostering greater autonomy and independence. The authors in Lopes (2020) introduce a taxonomy for IoT architectures and outline requirements for assisting individuals with disabilities. The proposed IoT architecture aligns with existing specifications, considering healthcare stakeholders' perspectives and generic requirements. The article addresses challenges in designing IoT architectures for people with disabilities. The authors in Molleapaza-Huanaco et al. (2020) introduce an innovative solution leveraging electrooculography (EOG) technology to enable real-time monitoring and control of smart home environments tailored for individuals with motor disabilities. The platform integrates a graphical user interface that responds to specific eye movements, allowing users to manage various aspects of their home environment, such as doors, windows, lighting, temperature, and TV functions. Singh et al. (2015) present a home- assisted and cost-effective living system catering to individuals with disabilities and homebound elderly. Authors Stojmenski et al. (2016) proposed a smart home platform aiding individuals with physical disabilities, utilizing 3D cameras to interpret facial expressions for environment control, catering to those with motor disabilities.

11.6.1.2 Human performance management

Athletes can optimize their training schedules with WBANs, which offer monitoring parameters, motion capture, and rehabilitation support. Real-time feedback facilitates performance improvement and reduces the risk of injuries resulting from incorrect training. Authors in Fu and Liu (2013) proposed a system to monitor athletes' physiological parameters during sports activities utilizing body area networks. The system aims to enhance performance and prevent injuries by providing real-time data analysis. It explores the feasibility and effectiveness of BANs in sports monitoring, emphasizing their potential to optimize athletic performance and health management. Authors in Meena et al. (2014) study the use of WBANs for tracking and analyzing physical activities. It investigates the design and implementation of WBAN-based systems for real-time monitoring, emphasizing their potential in healthcare, sports, and fitness applications. Mustafa et al. (2023) proposed a symmetric TDMA mechanism to enhance the performance of body sensor networks in sports applications to optimize energy consumption and reduce interference by synchronizing sensor communication schedules. This approach offers potential improvements in data transmission reliability and efficiency for monitoring athletes' physiological parameters during sports activities.

11.6.1.3 Sleep staging

Monitoring sleep patterns is a critical aspect of healthcare. WBANs contribute to reducing or preventing conditions such as Myocardial Infarction by continuously monitoring episodic events and other abnormal conditions. The article by Kim et al. (2021) addresses the challenges of supporting an ageing population by proposing an unobtrusive IoT-based system for monitoring sleep quality in older people. It employs accelerometers and motion sensors to assess sleep-wake conditions, aiding in the early detection of sleep disorders. The authors in Rahim and Karmakar (2013) proposed a novel approach for sleep apnea monitoring in WBANs using sensor cooperation and network coding. By employing cooperative communication among sensors and network coding techniques, the system enhances reliability and efficiency in detecting sleep apnea events, offering promising advancements in healthcare technology. The research by Yacchirema et al. (2018) proposes a system integrating real- time monitoring and treatment support for elderly obtrusive sleep apnea (OSA) patients. Employing fog computing and cloud-based big data analysis, it predicts air quality and enhances system efficiency, achieving high effectiveness in OSA treatment guidance.

11.6.1.4 Cancer detection

WBAN-based sensors with the capability to monitor cancer cells in the human body could revolutionize cancer diagnosis. Continuous monitoring without the need for biopsies enables timely analysis and treatment (Mahmood et al., 2021). The article by Rajput et al. (2022) suggests a cost-effective wearable microstrip patch antenna for breast cancer detection. By employing microwave imaging methods, the antenna targets identifying irregular tissue characteristics in the breast. The authors in Sarestoniemi et al. (2022) introduce a study on a monitoring vest with flexible ultrawideband (UWB) antennas for breast cancer detection. Using on-body antennas, it identifies differences in UWB radio channel characteristics indicative of cancerous tissue. Simulation results illustrate signal propagation variances caused by tumors, suggesting the potential for a portable telemedicine application for self-monitoring and early breast cancer detection. The article by Menon & Rodrigue (2023) proposes an efficient early breast cancer detection method using UWB radar. It introduces a novel algorithm to process radar signals, enhancing tumor detection accuracy. This noninvasive approach shows promise for improving early diagnosis of breast cancer, potentially leading to better patient outcomes.

11.6.1.5 Patient monitoring

WBANs play a crucial role in monitoring vital signals and providing real-time feedback on the recovery process. They can transmit measurements such as heart rate, body temperature, respiration rate, blood pressure, and body implant parameters. Additionally, WBANs facilitate drug administration in hospitals, aid rehabilitation, and provide interfaces for diagnostics. The authors in Montón et al. (2008) present a WBAN employing the Zigbee/IEEE 802.15.4 standard to facilitate seamless patient data monitoring. The system connects diverse body sensors to a portable hub, enabling connectivity to external networks like IEEE 802.11 and GPRS. It predicts physiological states concerning wakefulness, fatigue, and stress, enhancing health services with low power consumption, cost-effectiveness, and versatile sensor connectivity. Jafer et al. (2020) designed a system for monitoring physiological signals remotely using a WBAN. The system enables real-time monitoring of vital signs such as heart rate, temperature, and blood pressure, facilitating healthcare applications outside clinical settings. Gupta et al. (2021) proposed a system that leverages wireless technology to monitor patients' health remotely. It integrates sensors in wearable devices to collect vital signs and transmits data to a central hub for analysis.

11.6.1.6 Telemedicine systems

WBANs facilitate extended periods of unobtrusive ambulatory health monitoring. Integrating WBANs ensures continuous, real-time transmission of vital signals, enabling healthcare professionals to remotely monitor patients. This technology enhances telemedicine by providing a reliable and efficient platform for prolonged health surveillance, contributing to improved patient care (Chakraborty et al., 2013). Authors in Latha and Vetrivelan (2020) explore telemedicine methods for emergencies via WBANs. It introduces Bayes' theorem for predicting emergencies and sending alerts based on observed evidence. Network characteristics like data rate and latency are analyzed for medical decision-making.

11.6.1.7 Other works

In addition to the abovementioned applications, numerous research studies focusing on medical applications have been undertaken. Choudhury et al. (2021) proposed a physique-based approach for human activity recognition utilizing ensemble learning techniques and smartphone sensors. By incorporating accelerometer and gyroscope data, the system achieves improved accuracy in identifying human activities, enhancing the potential for health monitoring and fitness tracking applications. The authors in Choudhury et al. (2020) introduced a cloud-based real-time human activity recognition system utilizing a wearable device with sensors and a WiFi module to collect and transmit movement data to the cloud. ML algorithms are employed for activity classification. Bisoi et al. (Bisoi et al., 2023) proposed a method for human activity recognition based on conditional temporal attention learning models. It employs temporal attention mechanisms to capture sequential sensor data dependencies, enhancing activity recognition task accuracy. The authors in Roy et al. (2022) and Saxena et al. (2021) proposed a human fall prediction mechanism using wearable sensor devices and ML algorithms. Moulik and Majumdar (2019) designed a system named FallSense to detect human falls accurately using a combination of sensors, including accelerometers, infrared transmitter-receiver pairs, and ultrasonic sensors in an IoT environment. By employing a fuzzy inference system, FallSense merges data from multiple sensors to determine the likelihood of a fall.

11.6.2 Nonmedical application

Nonmedical applications of WBANs are equally diverse, spanning various domains that contribute to enhancing the overall quality of life.

11.6.2.1 Sports and fitness

WBANs revolutionize sports and fitness monitoring by providing real-time feedback on athletes' vital signs, movement patterns, and biomechanics (Raković & Lutovac, 2015). WBANs optimize training routines, prevent injuries by detecting deviations, and track postexercise recovery status. This technology enables data-driven coaching for performance enhancement and personalized training programs. By offering insights into athletes' physiological responses, WBANs elevate training precision and effectiveness, maximizing athletic performance and minimizing the risk of overtraining or fatigue. Authors in Serrani and Aliverti (2022) explore the feasibility of utilizing an embedded platform for acquiring biopotentials during sports activities. It investigates the platform's potential for real- time monitoring of physiological signals, aiming to enhance sports performance and safety through continuous biometric data collection. Crandall et al. (2022) designed a WBAN system to monitor skiers' flexibility and motion during skiing activities. The system enables real-time data collection to analyze and enhance skiing performance.

11.6.3 Augmented reality and virtual reality

WBANs enable dynamic adjustments to gameplay based on players' real-time emotional and physical states, enhancing engagement and immersion. It facilitates biofeedback training for stress management and emotional regulation through interactive AR/VR simulations. Additionally, WBAN-enabled multiplayer experiences foster social interaction and competition by incorporating players' physiological feedback, elevating the overall gaming experience to new levels of realism and interactivity. Beyond gaming, WBANs integrated with AR technology find applications in various sectors, such as industry, education, and retail. In industry, AR overlays real-time data onto workers' field of vision while monitoring their health and safety using WBANs, while in education, AR-enhanced learning experiences are tailored to students' physiological responses. Similarly, AR shopping experiences in retail are personalized based on shoppers' preferences and biometric data collected through WBANs, creating a more immersive and interactive shopping environment. Chen et al. (2021) proposed a smartphone platform equipped with sensors to track users' movements accurately, allowing for intuitive control in VR experiences. This approach maximizes interactivity and improves user engagement in mixed-reality games. The article by Zhang et al. (2020) explores utilizing virtual reality (VR) to visualize college asset management within the IoT framework. It investigates how VR technology enhances the understanding and management of campus assets, offering immersive solutions for efficient IoT-driven asset monitoring and control in educational institutions. Ward and Gittens (2022) proposed an augmented reality system to help users find suitable study spaces, utilizing IoT devices like repurposed cell phones and Arduino technology for sensing environmental elements.

11.6.3.1 Worker safety in hazardous environments

WBANs have the potential to enhance worker safety in hazardous settings by consistently observing both vital signs and surrounding environmental factors. These networks rapidly notify workers of dangers such as extreme temperatures or harmful gases, facilitating quick reactions and evacuation procedures. In critical situations, WBANs send distress signals and location information to facilitate rescue operations. Moreover, they contribute to adherence to safety standards by recording data and facilitating predictive analysis for risk evaluation, thus ensuring the protection of workers and improving workplace safety measures overall. De Fazio et al. (2022) introduced a smart shirt with integrated sensors and energy harvesters that monitor vital signs and environmental conditions in hazardous workplaces. Data are wirelessly transmitted to the cloud for processing and storage, with a mobile app enabling connectivity in WiFi-limited areas. Hinze et al. (2022) introduced a novel wearable IoT solution, the Hakituri project, designed to enhance workplace safety in New Zealand's forestry industry. It integrates wearables, networking, and data analytics, offering real-time alerts and dynamic network setups tailored for rugged outdoor environments, significantly improving worker health and safety. Authors in Ranjan et al. (2022) introduced a wearable ear muff equipped with sensors to detect hazardous noise levels, a mask to filter toxic gases, and smoke sensors to prevent fire accidents. Antolín et al. (2017) present a wearable wireless sensor network for monitoring harmful gases in industrial settings. It introduces a customized sensor node using LR-WPAN protocol to measure CO_2 levels. Integrated with a web app, it enables remote monitoring and early hazard detection, enhancing worker safety.

11.6.3.2 Emotion detection

WBANs use wearable bio-sensors like ECG, electromyograph, EEG, and electrodermal activity to track physiological signals such as heart rate and skin conductivity in order to detect emotions. Integrated into accessories such as watches and earrings, WBANs provide real-time insights into emotional states. This technology finds applications in mental health monitoring and enhancing human—computer interaction. Zamkah et al. (2020) proposed a system that employs cortisol and antistress hormones as key stress biomarkers for forthcoming wearable sensors to enable easier real-time tracking of emotional stress. The article by Costa et al. (2019) introduces the Emotional Smart Wristband, integrated with iGenda, to detect emotional states and adjust home environments accordingly, which benefits communities like retirement homes. iGenda acts as an interface and information center, aiming to create specific emotions. Yang et al. (2017) proposed a real-time emotion detection system using EEG measurements that employs a headband with printed signal acquisition electrodes and OpenViBE software. Shu et al. (2020) proposed an emotional recognition method using heart rate data from smart bracelets.

11.6.3.3 Defense

WBAN finds crucial applications in defense sectors because it enhances soldier monitoring, communication, and overall situational awareness. WBAN enables real-time health monitoring of soldiers, tracking vital signs and detecting injuries promptly. It also facilitates communication between soldiers and command centers, providing critical updates on battlefield conditions and troop movements (Varghese & Nene, 2018). Additionally, WBAN can integrate with other defense systems, such as drones or surveillance devices, amplifying their effectiveness in surveillance and reconnaissance missions. Kang et al. (2020) proposed a framework for secure automated messaging and data fusion to address challenges in reducing data size while maintaining accuracy in ad hoc networks like LPWAN and WBAN. Authors in Conroy et al. (2022) proposed a wearable-based early infection warning system to mitigate COVID-19s impact on workforce productivity. Utilizing ML, it predicts infections before symptoms manifest. The article Langleite et al. (2021) explores how IoT can be incorporated into military activities, showcasing practical hurdles using a sample wearable device. It contributes valuable insights into the feasibility and implications of IoT technology in enhancing military effectiveness, emphasizing the need to address operational concerns in its implementation. Authors in Raja and Bagwari (2018) highlight the significance of the military assistance and surveillance system (MASS) in enhancing national security. MASS integrates advanced features like a land information system, multisensor data fusion, and IoT-based communication to aid soldiers in critical missions.

11.7 Challenges and future directions

WBANs revolutionize healthcare, sports monitoring, and human—computer interaction with small sensors and actuators on or inside the body, enabling real-time monitoring. However, realizing the full potential of WBANs requires overcoming several significant challenges and navigating a direction towards future innovation and advancement.

11.7.1 Challenges in wireless body area network

11.7.1.1 Physical layer challenges

WBANs encounter physical layer challenges primarily due to the unique communication characteristics within the human body. Issues like signal attenuation, multipath fading, and interference from biological tissues pose obstacles to reliable and efficient data transmission. Overcoming these challenges necessitates innovative antenna design, modulation techniques tailored for body-centric communication, and signal processing algorithms optimized for the body's electromagnetic properties. Few efforts have been made to mitigate physical layer challenges. Article by El-Mohandes et al. (2018) presents an UWB digital baseband transceiver for WBANs, minimizing power and area through algorithmic and architectural modifications, enhancing BCH coding, and achieving low power and area usage in CMOS technology. Authors in Tseng et al. (2016) introduced an efficient cross- layer reliable retransmission scheme in IEEE 802.15.6 to address signal interference and improve transmission reli- ability. The article by El-Mohandes et al. (2018) introduced a low-power, efficient architecture for a narrowband WBAN transceiver at 2.4 GHz, focusing on high data reliability and scalability. It achieves adjustable data rates with low power consumption and demonstrates a 1% packet error rate at 9.6 dB SNR.

11.7.1.2 MAC layer challenges

At the MAC layer, WBANs face resource allocation, contention resolution, and energy efficiency challenges. The dynamic nature of WBANs, with nodes frequently moving and changing positions, complicates medium access control. Moreover, the stringent energy constraints of WBAN devices demand efficient protocols for scheduling transmissions and minimizing idle listening. Developing MAC protocols that strike a balance between energy efficiency, latency, and throughput remains a significant challenge in WBAN research. MAC layer challenges can be mitigated using dynamic superframe structures and efficient contention-based channel access protocols. Authors in Das et al. (2022) and Das & Moulik (2023) proposed dynamic superframe and slot allocation schemes to balance energy efficiency and throughput in heterogeneous scenarios. Articles by Das and Moulik (2021), Fourati et al. (2018), and Saboor et al. (2020) introduced CSMA-based channel allocation algorithms to improve network performance by reducing idle listening time and collisions.

11.7.1.3 Quality of service challenges

Ensuring QoS in WBANs is crucial for reliable and timely data delivery, especially in healthcare applications where real-time monitoring is critical. However, WBANs operate in dynamic and unpredictable environments, leading to fluctuating channel conditions, packet losses, and varying data priorities. Balancing conflicting requirements such as latency, reliability, and energy efficiency poses a significant challenge. Designing QoS-aware proto- cols capable of adapting to changing network conditions and prioritizing critical data streams is essential to meeting the stringent QoS requirements of WBAN applications. Deepak et al. (Deepak & Babu, 2018) proposed an efficient channel access scheme for WBANs to enhance the reliability of transmitting emergency physiological data. An analytical model is presented to compute the average delay and reliability of emergency data frames, demonstrating significant improvements over the IEEE 802.15.6 standard scheme. Das et al. (2023) proposed an optimal method for selecting relay nodes as a substitute for the two-hop star topology extension of IEEE 802.15.6 to improve packet delivery ratio, network lifespan, and throughput. Samanta and Misra (2018) introduced a dynamic connectivity establishment and scheduling scheme utilizing price-based selection and coalition game theory to improve QoS by minimizing delays and maximizing throughput.

11.7.1.4 Energy efficiency

WBAN nodes are typically powered by energy-constrained batteries, making energy efficiency a critical concern. The energy demands of continuous sensing, processing, and wireless communication can quickly deplete these batteries, leading to a shortened operational lifespan. Developing energy-efficient protocols, low-power hardware, and energy-harvesting techniques is crucial to addressing this challenge. The article by Shukla et al. (2021) explores a spectral and energy-efficient WBAN for smart healthcare. It employs cognitive radio (CR) technology to optimize spectrum use, prioritizes sensor nodes based on applications, and implements energy harvesting protocols for cooperation. Hu et al. (2022) introduced a cross-layer MAC protocol for RF-powered energy harvesting WBANs. It features dynamic superframe scheduling, TS strategy for energy harvesting, and transmission power adjustment to improve energy efficiency and network performance in long-term health monitoring applications. The article by Kim & Kim (2023) proposed an adaptive scheduling and power control scheme for multiobjective optimization in personalized WBANs, addressing the limitations of existing approaches by integrating priority-based scheduling and deep reinforcement learning power control to improve QoS, reliability, and energy efficiency.

11.7.1.5 Reliability and security

Ensuring reliable and secure communication within WBANs is essential, especially when dealing with sensitive health data. Interference from other wireless devices, signal attenuation due to body tissues, and potential cyber-attacks pose significant challenges. Designing robust encryption schemes, authentication protocols, and interference mitigation techniques is essential to safeguarding data integrity and user privacy. The authors in Zia et al. (2023) discussed the significance of securing healthcare data in WBANs and introduced a novel authentication protocol for WBANs to improve scalability, security, and efficiency compared to existing protocols. Yin et al. (2023) proposed lightweight and secure numeric comparison protocol (LSNCP) for Bluetooth in WBANs. LSNCP reduces the computational load compared to NCP by introducing new logic expressions. Security is verified through GNY logic and a modified Bellare-Rogaway model. Theoretical analysis and experiments demonstrate LSNCP's improved performance for healthcare, metaverse, and blockchain applications. Zhang and Dong (2022) proposed a privacy-preserving aggregation scheme that ensures secure data collection, supports the anonymity of multiple receivers, and prevents leakage. It's lightweight and cost-efficient, addressing the limitations of existing schemes.

11.7.2 Future directions

As we look towards the future of WBANs, technological advancements and research efforts are poised to address current challenges and unlock new potential. Future developments in WBANs will focus on enhancing sensor capabilities, optimizing communication technologies, and advancing integration with emerging technologies. These efforts will pave the way for WBANs to play an even more significant role in healthcare delivery, disease management, and wellness monitoring. The potential pathways for future development are detailed below:

- Continued advancements in miniaturization technology will enable the development of smaller, lightweight WBAN devices seamlessly integrated into everyday clothing and accessories.
- WBANs will leverage contextual information to adaptively respond to changing environmental conditions and user requirements, optimizing resource utilization and enhancing system performance.
- Integrating multiple sensing modalities within WBANs will provide a more comprehensive view of user health, enabling early detection of abnormalities and proactive intervention strategies.

- Research into wireless power transfer and energy harvesting techniques will prolong device lifespan and enable perpetual operation of WBAN nodes without the need for frequent battery replacements.
- Leveraging AI and ML algorithms will empower WBANs with advanced data analytics capabilities for predictive modeling, anomaly detection, and personalized healthcare decision support.

11.8 Conclusion

WBANs have emerged as a transformative technology with wide-ranging applications in healthcare, sports, and beyond. This chapter has provided a comprehensive overview of WBANs, covering various aspects, including architecture, hardware and sensors, different communication standards, integration with emerging technologies, applications, challenges, and future directions. WBANs offer a promising avenue for continuously monitoring physiological parameters, enabling personalized healthcare, and enhancing quality of life. Despite their potential, WBANs face challenges in energy efficiency, security, and interoperability. However, ongoing research and technological advancements address these challenges and pave the way for future innovations in WBANs. Integrating WBANs with emerging technologies like IoT, AI, and ML holds immense promise for further enhancing their capabilities and expanding their applications. As WBANs continue to evolve, they are poised to play a pivotal role in shaping the future of healthcare and human-centric technologies.

References

Abdel-Basset, M., Ding, W., & Abdel-Fatah, L. (2020). The fusion of Internet of Intelligent Things (IoIT) in remote diagnosis of obstructive sleep apnea: A survey and a new model. *Information Fusion* (61). Egypt: Elsevier B.V. Available from https://doi.org/10.1016/j.inffus.2020.03.010, http://www.elsevier.com/inca/publications/store/6/2/0/8/6/2/index.htt.

Abdellatif, A. A., Mhaisen, N., Mohamed, A., Erbad, A., & Guizani, M. (2023). Reinforcement learning for intelligent healthcare systems: A review of challenges, applications, and open research issues. *IEEE Internet of Things Journal*.

Antolín, D., Medrano, N., Calvo, B., & Pérez, F. (2017). A wearable wireless sensor network for indoor smart environment monitoring in safety applications. *Sensors, 17*(2), 365. Available from https://doi.org/10.3390/s17020365.

Association, I. S. (2012). IEEE standard for local and metropolitan area networks-part 15.6: Wireless body area networks. *IEEE std., 802*(6), 2012.

Atallah, L., Lo, B., King, R., & Yang, G. Z. (2010). Sensor placement for activity detection using wearable accelerometers. *International conference on body sensor networks, BSN 2010* (pp. 24–29). United Kingdom. Available from https://doi.org/10.1109/BSN.2010.23.

Baker, S. B., Xiang, W., & Atkinson, I. (2017). *Internet of Things for smart healthcare: Technologies, challenges, and opportunities, . IEEE Access* (5). Australia: Institute of Electrical and Electronics Engineers Inc. Available from http://ieeexplore.ieee.org/xpl/RecentIssue.jsp?punumber = 6287639, 10.1109/ACCESS.2017.2775180.

Basheer, S., Alluhaidan, A. S., & Bivi, M. A. (2021). Real-time monitoring system for early prediction of heart disease using Internet of Things. *Soft Computing, 25*(18). Available from https://doi.org/10.1007/s00500-021-05865-4, http://springerlink.metapress.com/app/home/journal.asp?wasp = h83ak0wtmr5uxkah9j5m&referrer = parent& backto = browsepublicationsresults,466,533.

Bertrand, A. (2015). Distributed signal processing for wireless EEG sensor networks. *IEEE Transactions on Neural Systems and Rehabilitation Engineering, 23*(6). Available from https://doi.org/10.1109/TNSRE.2015.2418351.

Bijender., & Kumar, A. (2021). Flexible and wearable capacitive pressure sensor for blood pressure monitoring. *Sensing and Bio-Sensing Research, 33*, 100434. Available from https://doi.org/10.1016/j.sbsr.2021.100434.

Bisoi, M., Balabantaray, B. K., & Moulik, S. (2023). Human activity recognition using CTAL model. In *Lecture Notes in Networks and Systems* (pp. 347–356). Springer Science and Business Media, Deutschland GmbH, India. Available from https://doi.org/10.1007/978-981-19-7867-8_28, https://www.springer.com/series/15179 23673389.

Casson, A. J., Abdulaal, M., Dulabh, M., Kohli, S., Krachunov, S., & Trimble, E. (2018). Electroencephalogram, seamless healthcare monitoring: Advancements in wearable, attachable, and invisible devices.

Casella, E., Cantor, M. C., Setser, M. M. W., Silvestri, S., & Costa, J. H. (2023). *A machine learning and optimization framework for the early diagnosis of bovine respiratory disease.* IEEE Access.

Cavallari, R., Martelli, F., Rosini, R., Buratti, C., & Verdone, R. (2014). A survey on wireless body area networks: Technologies and design challenges. *IEEE Communications Surveys and Tutorials, 16*(3). Available from https://doi.org/10.1109/SURV.2014.012214.00007, http://ieeexplore.ieee.org/xpl/RecentIssue.jsp?punumber = 9739.

Chakraborty, C., Gupta, B., & Ghosh, S. K. (2013). A review on telemedicine-based WBAN framework for patient monitoring. *Telemedicine and e-Health, 19*(8). Available from https://doi.org/10.1089/tmj.2012.0215, http://www.liebertpub.com/publication.aspx?pub_id = 54.

Chen, K. Y., Lee, J. D., & Zhang, T. J. (2021). The body sensor suit with mixed reality interactive games. In *IEEE International conference on consumer electronics-Taiwan, ICCE-TW 2021.* Institute of Electrical and Electronics Engineers Inc., Taiwan. Available from https://doi.org/10.1109/ICCE-TW52618.2021.9603144, http://ieeexplore.ieee.org/xpl/mostRecentIssue.jsp?punumber = 9601161 9781665433280.

Chen, M., Gonzalez, S., Vasilakos, A., Cao, H., & Leung, V. C. M. (2011). Body area networks: A survey. *Mobile Networks and Applications, 16*(2). Available from https://doi.org/10.1007/s11036-010-0260-8.

Choudhury, N. A., Moulik, S., & Choudhury, S. (2020). Cloud-based real- time and remote human activity recognition system using wearable sensors. In *2020 IEEE International Conference on Consumer Electronics-Taiwan (ICCE-Taiwan).* IEEE.

Choudhury, N. A., Moulik, S., & Roy, D. S. (2021). Physique-based human activity recognition using ensemble learning and smartphone sensors. *IEEE Sensors Journal, 21*(15). Available from https://doi.org/10.1109/JSEN.2021.3077563, http://ieeexplore.ieee.org/xpl/RecentIssue.jsp?punumber = 7361.

Comito, C., Falcone, D., & Forestiero, A. (2020). Current trends and practices in smart health monitoring and clinical decision support. In *Proceedings - 2020 IEEE International Conference on Bioinformatics and Biomedicine, BIBM 2020* (pp. 2577–2584). Institute of Electrical and Electronics Engineers Inc., Italy. Available from https://doi.org/10.1109/BIBM49941.2020.9313449, http://ieeexplore.ieee.org/xpl/mostRecentIssue.jsp?punumber = 9312958 9781728162157.

Committee, L. S. (2011). Part 15.4: Wireless medium access control (MAC) and physical layer (PHY) specifications for low-rate wireless personal area networks (LR-WPANs). *IEEE Computer Society.*

Conroy, B., Silva, I., Mehraei, G., Damiano, R., Gross, B., Salvati, E., Feng, T., Schneider, J., Olson, N., Rizzo, A. G., Curtin, C. M., Frassica, J., & McFarlane, D. C. (2022). Real-time infection prediction with wearable physiological monitoring and AI to aid military workforce readiness during COVID-19. *Nature Research, United States Scientific Reports, 12*(1). Available from https://doi.org/10.1038/s41598-022-07764-6, http://www.nature.com/srep/index.html.

Costa, A., Rincon, J. A., Carrascosa, C., Julian, V., & Novais, P. (2019). Emotions detection on an ambient intelligent system using wearable devices. *Future Generation Computer Systems, 92*. Available from https://doi.org/10.1016/j.future.2018.03.038.

Crandall, A. S., Mamolo, S., & Morgan, M. (2022). SkiMon: A wireless body area network for monitoring ski flex and motion during skiing sports. *Sensors, 22*(18). Available from https://doi.org/10.3390/s22186882, http://www.mdpi.com/journal/sensors.

Curtis, D., Shih, E., Waterman, J., Guttag, J., Bailey, J., Stair, T., Greenes, R. A., & Ohno-Machado, L. (2011). Physiological signal monitoring in the waiting areas of an emergency room. In *2008 - 3rd International ICST Conference on Body Area Networks.* ICST, United States. Available from https://doi.org/10.4108/ICST.BODYNETS2008.2968 9789639799172.

Dakhel, M., & Hassan, S. (2020). A secure wireless body area network for e-health application using blockchain. In *Communications in Computer and Information Science* (pp. 395–408). Springer, Iraq. Available from https://doi.org/10.1007/978-3-030-38752-5_31, http://www.springer.com/series/7899.

Das, K., & Moulik, S. (2021). PBCR: Parameter-based backoff counter regulation in IEEE 802.15.6 CSMA/CA. In *2021 International Conference on COMmunication Systems and NETworkS, COMSNETS 2021* (pp. 565–571). Institute of Electrical and Electronics Engineers Inc., India. Available from https://doi.org/10.1109/COMSNETS51098.2021.9352747, http://ieeexplore.ieee.org/xpl/mostRecentIssue.jsp?punumber = 9352735 9781728191270.

Das, K., Moulik, S., & Chang, C. Y. (2022). Priority-based dedicated slot allocation with dynamic superframe structure in IEEE 802.15.6-based wireless body area networks. *IEEE Internet of Things Journal*, 9(6). Available from https://doi.org/10.1109/JIOT.2021.3104800, http://ieeexplore.ieee.org/servlet/opac?punumber = 6488907.

Das, K., Ray, R., & Moulik, S. (2023). Optimal relaying nodes selection for IEEE 802.15.6-based two-hop star topology WBAN. *Internet of Things*, 22, 100740. Available from https://doi.org/10.1016/j.iot.2023.100740.

De Fazio, R., Al-Hinnawi, A.-R., De Vittorio, M., & Visconti, P. (2022). An energy-autonomous smart shirt employing wearable sensors for users' safety and protection in hazardous workplaces. *Applied Sciences*, 12(6), 2926. Available from https://doi.org/10.3390/app12062926.

Deepak, K. S., & Babu, A. V. (2018). Improving reliability of emergency data frame transmission in IEEE 802.15.6 wireless body area networks. *IEEE Systems Journal*, 12(3). Available from https://doi.org/10.1109/JSYST.2017.2717189, https://ieeexplore.ieee.org/xpl/mostRecentIssue.jsp?punumber = 4267003.

Domingo, M. C. (2012). An overview of the Internet of Things for people with disabilities. *Journal of Network and Computer Applications*, 35(2). Available from https://doi.org/10.1016/j.jnca.2011.10.015.

El-Hasnony, I. M., Barakat, S. I., & Mostafa, R. R. (2020). Optimized ANFIS model using hybrid metaheuristic algorithms for parkinson's disease prediction in IoT environment. *IEEE Access* (8). Egypt: Institute of Electrical and Electronics Engineers Inc. Available from https://doi.org/10.1109/ACCESS.2020.3005614, http://ieeexplore.ieee.org/xpl/RecentIssue.jsp?punumber = 6287639.

El-Mohandes, A. M., Shalaby, A., & Sayed, M. S. (2018). Efficient low-power digital baseband transceiver for IEEE 802.15.6 narrowband physical layer. *IEEE Transactions on Very Large Scale Integration (VLSI) Systems*, 26(11). Available from https://doi.org/10.1109/TVLSI.2018.2862348.

Fahmy, K. A., Yahya, A., & Zorkany, M. (2022). A decision support healthcare system based on IoT and neural network technique. *Journal of Engineering, Design and Technology*, 20(3). Available from https://doi.org/10.1108/JEDT-08-2020-0317, http://www.emeraldinsight.com/info/journals/jedt/jedt.jsp.

Fourati, H., Idoudi, H., & Saidane, L. A. (2018). Intelligent slots allocation for dynamic differentiation in IEEE 802.15.6 CSMA/CA. *Ad Hoc Networks* (72). Tunisia: Elsevier B.V. Available from http://www.elsevier.com/inca/publications/store/6/7/2/3/8/0/index.htt, 10.1016/j.adhoc.2018.01.007.

Fu, D., Chen, L., Cheng, Z., & Tsai, S.-B. (2021). Integration of wearable smart devices and internet of things technology into public physical education. *Mobile Information Systems* (2021)). Available from https://doi.org/10.1155/2021/6740987.

Das, K., & Moulik, S. (2023). Boss: Bargaining-based optimal slot sharing in ieee 802.15. 6-based wireless body area networks. *IEEE Internet of Things Journal*, 10(4) 2945–2953.

Fu, Y., & Liu, J. (2013). Monitoring system for sports activities using body area networks. In *Proceedings of the 8th International Conference on Body Area Networks, BodyNets 2013* (pp. 408–413). ICST, China. Available from https://doi.org/10.4108/ist.bodynets.2013.253675 9781936968893.

Gao, T., Massey, T., Selavo, L., Crawford, D., Chen, B. R., Lorincz, K., Shnayder, V., Hauenstein, L., Dabiri, F., Jeng, J., Chanmugam, A., White, D., Sarrafzadeh, M., & Welsh, M. (2007). The advanced health and disaster aid network: A light-weight wireless medical system for tiage. *IEEE Transactions on Biomedical Circuits and Systems*, 1(3). Available from https://doi.org/10.1109/TBCAS.2007.910901.

Gaur, L. (2022). *Internet of Things in healthcare*. Springer Science and Business Media LLC. Available from 10.1007/978-981-16-9476-9_6.

Gupta, M., Tanwar, S., Rana, A., & Walia, H. (2021). Smart healthcare mon- itoring system using wireless body area network. In *9th International Conference on Reliability, Infocom Technologies and Optimization (Trends and Future Directions)(ICRITO)*. IEEE.

Haghi, M., Thurow, K., & Stoll, R. (2017). Wearable devices in medical internet of things: Scientific research and commercially available devices. *Korean Society of Medical Informatics, Germany Healthcare Informatics Research*, 23(1). Available from https://doi.org/10.4258/hir.2017.23.1.4, http://pdf.medrang.co.kr/Hir/2017/023/Hir023-01-02.pdf.

Hasan, K., Chowdhury, M. J. M., Biswas, K., Ahmed, K., Islam, M. S., & Usman, M. (2022). *A blockchain-based secure data-sharing framework for software defined wireless body area networks*, . *Computer Networks* (211). Australia: Elsevier B.V. Available from http://www.journals.elsevier.com/computer-networks/, 10.1016/j.comnet.2022.109004.

Hinze, A., Bowen, J., & König, J. L. (2022). Wearable technology for hazardous remote environments: Smart shirt and Rugged IoT network for forestry worker health. *Smart Health*, 23, 100225. Available from https://doi.org/10.1016/j.smhl.2021.100225.

Hosseinzadeh, M., Koohpayehzadeh, J., Bali, A. O., Asghari, P., Souri, A., Mazaherinezhad, A., Bohlouli, M., & Rawassizadeh, R. (2021). A diagnostic prediction model for chronic kidney disease in internet of things platform. *Multimedia Tools and Applications*, 80(11). Available from https://doi.org/10.1007/s11042-020-09049-4, https://link.springer.com/journal/11042.

Hu, J., Xu, G., Hu, L., Li, S., & Xing, Y. (2022). An adaptive energy efficient MAC protocol for RF energy harvesting WBANs. *IEEE Transactions on Communications*, 71(1), 2022.

IEEE (2002). Standard for part 15.1: Wireless medium access control (MAC) and physical layer (PHY) specifications for wireless personal area networks (WPAN).

Ihnaini, B., Khan, M. A., Khan, T. A., Abbas, S., Daoud, M. S., Ahmad, M., & Khan, M. A. (2021). A smart healthcare recommendation system for multidisciplinary diabetes patients with data fusion based on deep ensemble learning. *Computational Intelligence and Neuroscience* (2021). China: Hindawi Limited. Available from http://www.hindawi.com/journals/cin, 10.1155/2021/4243700.

Ikawati, V., Saepudin, D., Susanto, B., Munandar, A., Nurba, H. P., & Prihatmanto, A. S. (2023). Individual health profiling using multimodal sensors on smart health care. In *Proceeding of 2023 17th International Conference on Telecommunication Systems, Services, and Applications, TSSA 2023*. Institute of Electrical and Electronics Engineers Inc., Indonesia. Available from https://doi.org/10.1109/TSSA59948.2023.10366913, http://ieeexplore.ieee.org/xpl/mostRecentIssue.jsp?punumber = 10366508 9798350309164.

Jafer, E., Hussain, S., & Fernando, X. (2020). A wireless body area network for remote observation of physiological signals. *IEEE Consumer Electronics Magazine*, 9(2). Available from https://doi.org/10.1109/MCE.2019.2953736, https://www.ieee.org/membership-catalog/productdetail/showProductDetailPage.html?product = PER262-EPC.

K., G. P., & K., K. P. (2020). Application of IoT in predictive health analysis—A review of literature. *International Journal of Management, Technology, and Social Sciences*. Available from https://doi.org/10.47992/ijmts.2581.6012.0089.

Kalpana, S., & Annadurai, C. (2021). A novel energy efficient architecture for wireless body area networks. *Personal and Ubiquitous Computing, Personal and Ubiquitous Computing*, 2021.

Kang, J. J., Yang, W., Dermody, G., Ghasemian, M., Adibi, S., & Haskell-Dowland, P. (2020). No soldiers left behind: an IoT-based low-power military mobile health system design. *IEEE Access* (8). Australia: Institute of Electrical and Electronics Engineers Inc. Available from http://ieeexplore.ieee.org/xpl/RecentIssue.jsp?punumber = 6287639, 10.1109/ACCESS.2020.3035812.

Keshamoni, K. (2019). Design and architecture of wireless body area network using android application. *International Journal of Informatics and Communication Technology (IJ-ICT*, 8(2), 71. Available from https://doi.org/10.11591/ijict.v8i2.pp71-76.

Kim, J., Campbell, A. S., & Wang, J. (2018). Wearable non-invasive epidermal glucose sensors: A review. *Talanta* (177). United States: Elsevier B.V. Available from https://doi.org/10.1016/j.talanta.2017.08.077, https://www.journals.elsevier.com/talanta.

Kim, J. Y., Chu, C. H., & Kang, M. S. (2021). IoT-based unobtrusive sensing for sleep quality monitoring and assessment. *IEEE Sensors Journal*, 21(3). Available from https://doi.org/10.1109/JSEN.2020.3022915, http://ieeexplore.ieee.org/xpl/RecentIssue.jsp?punumber = 7361.

Kundu, S. K., Kumagai, S., & Sasaki, M. (2013). A wearable capacitive sensor for monitoring human respiratory rate. *Japanese Journal of Applied Physics*, 52(4S), 04CL05. Available from https://doi.org/10.7567/jjap.52.04cl05.

Kuzubasoglu, B. A., Sayar, E., Cochrane, C., Koncar, V., & Bahadir, S. K. (2021). Wearable temperature sensor for human body temperature detection. *Journal of Materials Science: Materials in Electronics*, 32(4). Available from https://doi.org/10.1007/s10854-020-05217-2, https://rd.springer.com/journal/10854.

Kim,, B.-S. Shah, B., & Kim, K.-I. (2023). Adaptive scheduling and power control for multi-objective optimization in IEEE 802.15. 6 based personalized wireless body area networks. *IEEE Transactions on Mobile Computing*, 22(11), 6251–6268.

Langleite, R., Griwodz, C., & Johnsen, F. T. (2021). Military applications of internet of things: Operational concerns explored in context of a prototype wearable. Available from https://www.ffi.no/en/publications-archive/military-applications-of-internet-of-things-operational-concerns-explored-in-context-of-a-prototype-wearable.

Latha, R., & Vetrivelan, P. (2020). Wireless body area network (WBAN)-based telemedicine for emergency care. *Sensors (Switzerland), 20*(7). Available from https://doi.org/10.3390/s20072153, https://www.mdpi.com/1424-8220/20/7/2153/pdf.

Latré, B., Braem, B., Moerman, I., Blondia, C., & Demeester, P. (2011). A survey on wireless body area networks. *Wireless Networks, 17*(1). Available from https://doi.org/10.1007/s11276-010-0252-4.

Lopes, V. (2020). Internet of Things feasibility for disabled people. *Transactions on Emerging Telecommunications Technologies, 31*(12), 2020.

Mahmood, A. S., Jafer, E., Hussain, S., & Fernando, X. (2017). Wireless body area network development for remote patient health observing. In *IHTC 2017 - IEEE Canada International Humanitarian Technology Conference 2017* (pp. 26–31). Institute of Electrical and Electronics Engineers Inc., Iraq. Available from https://doi.org/10.1109/IHTC.2017.8058193 9781509062645.

Mahmood, S. N., Ishak, A. J., Saeidi, T., Soh, A. C., Jalal, A., Imran, M. A., & Abbasi, Q. H. (2021). Full ground ultra-wideband wearable textile antenna for breast cancer and wireless body area network applications. *Micromachines, 12*(3). Available from https://doi.org/10.3390/mi12030322, http://www.mdpi.com/journal/micromachines.

Meena, R., Ravishankar, S., & Gayathri, J. (2014). Monitoring physical activities using wban. *International Journal of Computer Science and Information Technologies, 5*(4), 2014.

Metcalf, D., Milliard, S. T. J., Gomez, M., & Schwartz, M. (2016). Wearables and the internet of things for health: Wearable, interconnected devices promise more efficient and comprehensive health care. *IEEE Pulse, 7*(5). Available from https://doi.org/10.1109/MPUL.2016.2592260, http://pulse.embs.org/pastissues.html.

Mitchell, K. (2021). Internet of things-enabled smart devices, health- care body sensor networks, and online patient engagement in COVID-19 prevention, screening, and treatment. *American Journal of Medical Research, 8*(1), 2021.

Menon, M. D., Rodrigue, J. (2023). Efficient ultra wideband radar based non invasive early breast cancer detection. *IEEE Access, 11*, 84214–84227.

Molleapaza-Huanaco, J., Charca-Morocco, H., Juarez-Chavez, B., Equino-Quispe, R., Talavera-Suarez, J., & Mayhua-Lopez. E. (2020). IoT platform based on EOG to monitor and control a smart home environment for patients with motor disabilities. In *Proceedings - 2020 13th International Congress on Image and Signal Processing, BioMedical Engineering and Informatics, CISP-BMEI 2020* (pp. 784–789). Institute of Electrical and Electronics Engineers Inc., Peru. Available from https://doi.org/10.1109/CISP-BMEI51763.2020.9263534, http://ieeexplore.ieee.org/xpl/mostRecentIssue.jsp?punumber = 9263486 9780738105451.

Montón, E., Hernandez, J. F., Blasco, J. M., Hervé, T., Micallef, J., Grech, I., Brincat, A., & Traver, V. (2008). Body area network for wireless patient monitoring. *IET Communications, 2*(2). Available from https://doi.org/10.1049/iet-com:20070046.

Moreira, M. W. L., Rodrigues, J. J. P. C., Korotaev, V., Al-Muhtadi, J., & Kumar, N. (2019). A comprehensive review on smart decision support systems for health care. *IEEE Systems Journal, 13*(3). Available from https://doi.org/10.1109/jsyst.2018.2890121.

Moulik, S., & Majumdar, S. (2019). FallSense: An automatic fall detection and alarm generation system in IoT-enabled environment. *IEEE Sensors Journal, 19*(19). Available from https://doi.org/10.1109/jsen.2018.2880739.

Moungla, H., Jarray, A., Karmouch, A., & Mehaoua, A. (2014) Cost-effective reliability-and energy-based intra-WBAN interference mitigation. In *Proceedings - IEEE Global Communications Conference, GLOBECOM* (pp. 2399–2404). France. Available from https://doi.org/10.1109/GLOCOM.2014.7037167, https://ieeexplore.ieee.org/xpl/conhome/1000308/all-proceedings.

Movassaghi, S., Abolhasan, M., Lipman, J., Smith, D., & Jamalipour, A. (2014). Wireless body area networks: A survey. *IEEE Communications Surveys and Tutorials, 16*(3). Available from https://doi.org/10.1109/SURV.2013.121313.00064, http://ieeexplore.ieee.org/xpl/RecentIssue.jsp?punumber = 9739.

Mustafa, M. M., Khalifa, A. A., & Cengiz, K. (2023). A symmetric TDMA mechanism to optimize the performance of the body sensor network for sports application. In *HORA 2023 - 2023 5th International Congress on Human-Computer Interaction, Optimization and Robotic Applications, Proceedings*. Institute of Electrical and Electronics Engineers Inc., India. Available from https://doi.org/10.1109/HORA58378.2023.10156665, http://ieeexplore.ieee.org/xpl/mostRecentIssue.jsp?punumber = 10156655 9798350337525.

Negra, R., Jemili, I., & Belghith, A. (2016). Wireless body area networks: Applications and technologies. In *Procedia Computer Science* (pp. 1274–1281). Elsevier, Tunisia. Available from https://doi.org/10.1016/j.procs.2016.04.266, http://www.sciencedirect.com/science/journal/18770509 1877050983.

Nwibor, C., Haxha, S., Ali, M. M., Sakel, M., Haxha, A. R., Saunders, K., & Nabakooza, S. (2023). Remote health monitoring system for the estimation of blood pressure, heart rate, and blood oxygen saturation level. *IEEE Sensors Journal*, 23(5). Available from https://doi.org/10.1109/JSEN.2023.3235977, http://ieeexplore.ieee.org/xpl/RecentIssue.jsp?punumber = 7361.

Othman, S. B., Almalki, F. A., Chakraborty, C., & Sakli, H. (2022). Privacy-preserving aware data aggregation for IoT-based healthcare with green computing technologies. *Computers and Electrical Engineering*, 101, 2022.

Pathak, N., Misra, S., Mukherjee, A., & Kumar, N. (2021). HeDI: Healthcare device interoperability for IoT-based e-health platforms. *IEEE Internet of Things Journal*, 8(23). Available from https://doi.org/10.1109/JIOT.2021.3052066, http://ieeexplore.ieee.org/servlet/opac?punumber = 6488907.

Qadri, Y. A., Nauman, A., Zikria, Y. B., Vasilakos, A. V., & Kim, S. W. (2020). The future of healthcare internet of things: A survey of emerging technologies. *IEEE Communications Surveys & Tutorials*, 22(2). Available from https://doi.org/10.1109/comst.2020.2973314.

Rahim, A., & Karmakar, N. C. (2013). Sensor cooperation in wireless body area network using network coding for sleep apnoea monitoring system. In *Proceedings of the 2013 IEEE 8th International Conference on Intelligent Sensors, Sensor Networks and Information Processing: Sensing the Future, ISSNIP 2013* (pp. 432–436). Australia. Available from https://doi.org/10.1109/ISSNIP.2013.6529829.

Raja, P., & Bagwari, S. (2018). IoT based military assistance and surveillance. In *Proceedings - 2nd International Conference on Intelligent Circuits and Systems, ICICS 2018* (pp. 345–348). Institute of Electrical and Electronics Engineers Inc., India. Available from https://doi.org/10.1109/ICICS.2018.00076, http://ieeexplore.ieee.org/xpl/mostRecentIssue.jsp?punumber = 8476190 9781538664834.

Rajput, A., Powar, S., Punekar, P., Rahate, G., Sontakke, P., & Ayane, S. (2022). Design of low cost wearable microstrip patch antenna for breast cancer detection. In *6th International Conference on Computing, Communication, Control and Automation, ICCUBEA 2022*. Institute of Electrical and Electronics Engineers Inc., India. Available from https://doi.org/10.1109/ICCUBEA54992.2022.10010742, http://ieeexplore.ieee.org/xpl/mostRecentIssue.jsp?punumber = 10010701 9781665484510.

Raković, P., & Lutovac, B. (2015). A cloud computing architecture with wireless body area network for professional athletes health monitoring in sports organizations-Case study of Montenegro. In *Proceedings - 2015 4th Mediterranean Conference on Embedded Computing, MECO 2015 - Including ECyPS 2015, BioEMIS 2015, BioICT 2015, MECO-Student Challenge 2015* (pp. 387–390). Institute of Electrical and Electronics Engineers Inc., Montenegro. Available from https://doi.org/10.1109/MECO.2015.7181950 9781479989997.

Ramya, B., & Jagadeesan, S. (2019). Human health monitoring system over internet in wireless body area networks. *Journal of Public Health Research and Development*, 10(2). Available from https://doi.org/10.5958/0976-5506.2019.00433.9, http://www.indianjournals.com/ijor.aspx?target = ijor:ijphrd&volume = 10&issue = 2&article = 184&type = pdf.

Ranjan, S., Kumar, N. S., Chandrasekaran, G., Sowmiya, K., Varalakshmi, K., Priyadarshi, N., Bhaskar, M., & Kumar, N. (2022). Atmospheric mon itoring and fire prevention electronic system for mining workers. In *IEEE 9th Uttar Pradesh Section International Conference on Electrical*.

Ren, Y., Leng, Y., Zhu, F., Wang, J., & Kim, H.-J. (2019). Data storage mechanism based on blockchain with privacy protection in wireless body area network. *Sensors*, 19(10), 2395. Available from https://doi.org/10.3390/s19102395.

Rezaeibagha, F., Mu, Y., Huang, K., & Chen, L. (2021). Secure and efficient data aggregation for IoT monitoring systems. *IEEE Internet of Things Journal*, 8(10). Available from https://doi.org/10.1109/JIOT.2020.3042204, http://ieeexplore.ieee.org/servlet/opac?punumber = 6488907.

Roy, A., Mukherjee, R., Moulik, S., & Chakrabarti, A. (2022). human fall prediction using ensemble learning technique. In *Proceedings - 2022 IEEE International Conference on Consumer Electronics - Taiwan, ICCE-Taiwan 2022* (pp. 545–546). Institute of Electrical and Electronics Engineers Inc., India. Available from https://doi.org/10.1109/ICCE-Taiwan55306.2022.9868977, http://ieeexplore.ieee.org/xpl/mostRecentIssue.jsp?punumber = 9868970 978166547050.6.

Saboor, A., Ahmad, R., Ahmed, W., Kiani, A. K., Alam, M. M., Kuusik, A., & Le Moullec, Y. (2020). Dynamic slot allocation using non overlapping backoff algorithm in IEEE 802.15.6 WBAN. *IEEE Sensors Journal*, 20(18). Available from https://doi.org/10.1109/JSEN.2020.2993795, http://ieeexplore.ieee.org/xpl/RecentIssue.jsp?punumber = 7361.

Samanta, A., & Misra, S. (2018). Dynamic connectivity establishment and cooperative scheduling for QoS-aware wireless body area networks. *IEEE Transactions on Mobile Computing*, 17(12). Available from https://doi.org/10.1109/TMC.2018.2813370, http://ieeexplore.ieee.org/xpl/RecentIssue.jsp?puNumber = 7755.

Sanjay, J. P., Deepak, T. N., & Manimozhi, M. (2021). Prediction of health problems and recommendation system using machine learning and IoT. In *3rd IEEE International Virtual Conference on Innovations in Power and Advanced Computing Technologies, i-PACT 2021*. Institute of Electrical and Electronics Engineers Inc., India. Available from https://doi.org/10.1109/i-PACT52855.2021.9696622, http://ieeexplore.ieee.org/xpl/mostRecentIssue.jsp?punumber = 9696358 9781665426916.

Sarestoniemi, M., Reponen, J., Sonkki, M., Myllymaki, S., Pomalaza-Raez, C., Tervonen, O., & Myllyla, T. (2022). Breast cancer detection feasibility with UWB flexible antennas on wearable monitoring vest. In *IEEE International Conference on Pervasive Computing and Communications Workshops and other Affiliated Events, PerCom Workshops 2022* (pp. 751−756). Institute of Electrical and Electronics Engineers Inc., Finland. Available from https://doi.org/10.1109/PerComWorkshops53856.2022.9767512, http://ieeexplore.ieee.org/xpl/mostRecentIssue.jsp?punumber = 9766442 9781665416474.

Saxena, U., Moulik, S., Nayak, S. R., Hanne, T., & Sinha Roy, D. (2021). Ensemble-based machine learning for predicting sudden human fall using health data. *Mathematical Problems in Engineering* (2021). India: Hindawi Limited. Available from http://www.hindawi.com/journals/mpe/contents.html, 10.1155/2021/8608630.

Sciarrone, A., Bisio, I., Garibotto, C., Lavagetto, F., Staude, G. H., & Knopp, A. (2021). Leveraging IoT wearable technology towards early diagnosis of neurological diseases. *Journal on Selected Areas in Communications, 39*(2). Available from https://doi.org/10.1109/JSAC.2020.3021573, http://ieeexplore.ieee.org/xpl/tocresult.jsp?isnumber = 5678773.

Serrani, A., & Aliverti, A. (2022). Feasibility study of an embedded platform for biopotentials acquisition during sports activities. In *IEEE International Workshop on Sport, Technology and Research, STAR 2022 - Proceedings* (pp.13−18). Institute of Electrical and Electronics Engineers Inc., Italy. Available from https://doi.org/10.1109/STAR53492.2022.9859660, http://ieeexplore.ieee.org/xpl/mostRecentIssue.jsp?punumber = 9859560 9781665486019.

Shelby, Z., & Bormann, C. (2011). *The wireless embedded Internet* (6). John Wiley & Sons, 2011.

Shu, L., Yu, Y., Chen, W., Hua, H., Li, Q., Jin, J., & Xu, X. (2020). Wearable emotion recognition using heart rate data from a smart bracelet. *Sensors, 20*(3), 718. Available from https://doi.org/10.3390/s20030718.

Shukla, A. K., Upadhyay, P. K., Srivastava, A., & Moualeu, J. M. (2021). Enabling co-existence of cognitive sensor nodes with energy harvesting in body area networks. *Sensors Journal, 21*(9). Available from https://doi.org/10.1109/JSEN.2021.3062368, http://ieeexplore.ieee.org/xpl/RecentIssue.jsp?punumber = 7361.

Singh, V. K., Baghoriya, S., & Bohara, V. A. (2015). HELPER: A home assisted and cost effective living system for people with disabilities and homebound elderly. In *IEEE International Symposium on Personal, Indoor and Mobile Radio Communications, PIMRC* (pp. 2115−2119). Institute of Electrical and Electronics Engineers Inc., India. Available from https://doi.org/10.1109/PIMRC.2015.7343647 9781467367820.

Stojmenski, A., Joksimoski, B., Chorbev, I., & Trajkovikj, V. (2016). Smart home environment aimed for people with physical disabilities. In *Proceedings - 2016 IEEE 12th International Conference on Intelligent Computer Communication and Processing, ICCP 2016* (pp.13−18). Institute of Electrical and Electronics Engineers Inc., North Macedonia. Available from https://doi.org/10.1109/ICCP.2016.7737115 9781509038992.

Siam, A. I., El-Affendi, M. A., Elazm, A. A., El-Banby, G. M., El-Bahnasawy, N. A., Abd El-Samie, F. E., & Abd El-Latif, A. H. (2023). Portable and Real-Time IoT-Based Healthcare Monitoring System for Daily Medical Applications. *IEEE Transactions on Computational Social Systems, 10*(4), 1629−1641. Available from https://doi.org/10.1109/TCSS.2022.3207562.

Tseng, H. W., Wu, R. Y., & Wu, Y. Z. (2016). An efficient cross-layer reliable retransmission scheme for the human body shadowing in IEEE 802.15.6-based wireless body area networks. *IEEE Sensors Journal, 16*(9). Available from https://doi.org/10.1109/JSEN.2016.2523461, http://ieeexplore.ieee.org/xpl/RecentIssue.jsp?punumber = 7361.

Ullah, A., Azeem, M., Ashraf, H., Alaboudi, A. A., Humayun, M., & Jhanjhi, N. Z. (2021). Secure healthcare data aggregation and transmission in IoT - A survey. *IEEE Access* (9). Pakistan: Institute of Electrical and Electronics Engineers Inc. Available from https://doi.org/10.1109/ACCESS.2021.3052850, http://ieeexplore.ieee.org/xpl/RecentIssue.jsp?punumber = 6287639.

Ullah, F., Islam, I. U., Abdullah, A. H., & Khan, A. (2019). Future of big data and deep learning for wireless body area networks. *Springer briefs in computer science*. Pakistan: Springer. Available from https://doi.org/10.1007/978-981-13-3459-7_5, http://www.springer.com/series/10028.

Ullah, S., Higgins, H., Braem, B., Latre, B., Blondia, C., Moerman, I., Saleem, S., Rahman, Z., & Kwak, K. S. (2012). A comprehensive survey of wireless body area networks on PHY, MAC, and network layers solutions. *Journal of Medical Systems, 36*(3). Available from https://doi.org/10.1007/s10916-010-9571-3.

Varghes,e V., & Nene, M. J. (2018). Role of body area network in battlefield of things. In *2018 3rd International Conference for Convergence in Technology, I2CT 2018*. Institute of Electrical and Electronics Engineers Inc., India. Available from https://doi.org/10.1109/I2CT.2018.8529445, http://ieeexplore.ieee.org/xpl/mostRecentIssue. jsp?punumber = 8509796 9781538642733.

Varon, C., Caicedo, A., Testelmans, D., Buyse, B., & Van Huffel, S. (2015). A novel algorithm for the automatic detection of sleep apnea from single-lead ECG. *IEEE Transactions on Biomedical Engineering, 62*(9). Available from https://doi. org/10.1109/TBME.2015.2422378, http://ieeexplore.ieee.org/xpl/RecentIssue.jsp?reload = true&punumber = 10.

Vera, D., Costa, N., Roda-Sanchez, L., Olivares, T., Fernández-Caballero, A., & Pereira, A. (2019). Body area networks in healthcare: A brief state of the art. *Applied Sciences, 9*(16), 3248. Available from https://doi.org/ 10.3390/app9163248.

Verma, D., Singh, K. R., Yadav, A. K., Nayak, V., Singh, J., Solanki, P. R., & Singh, R. P. (2022). *Internet of things (IoT) in nano-integrated wearable biosensor devices for healthcare applications, . Biosensors and Bioelectronics: X* (11). India: Elsevier Ltd. Available from https://doi.org/10.1016/j.biosx.2022.100153, https://www.journals.elsevier.com/biosensors-and-bioelectronics-x.

Wan, J., Al-Awlaqi, M., Li, M., Grady, M., Gu, X., Wang, J., & Cao, N. (2018). Wearable IoT enabled real-time health monitoring system. *EURASIP Journal on Wireless Communications and Networking, 2018*(1), 2018.

Ward, S., & Gittens, M. (2022). Locating optimal study areas using augmented reality and low cost IoT devices. In *IEEE Games, Entertainment, Media Conference, GEM 2022*. Institute of Electrical and Electronics Engineers Inc., Barbados. Available from https://doi.org/10.1109/GEM56474.2022.10017619, http://ieeexplore.ieee.org/xpl/mostRecentIssue.jsp?punumber = 10017435 9781665461382.

Yacchirema, D. C., Sarabia-Jacome, D., Palau, C. E., & Esteve, M. (2018). A smart system for sleep monitoring by integrating IoT with big data analytics. *IEEE Access* (6). Ecuador: Institute of Electrical and Electronics Engineers Inc. Available from https://doi.org/10.1109/ACCESS.2018.2849822, http://ieeexplore.ieee.org/xpl/RecentIssue.jsp?punumber = 6287639.

Yang, W., Tudor, Y., & John. (2017). A real-time wearable emotion detection headband based on EEG measurement, author = Wei. *Physical, 263*, 2017.

Yin, H., Huang, X., Xing, B., Huang, J., Sun, X., Li, J., Chai, S., Zhang, D., Bakar, R. A., & Wang, W. (2023). LSNCP: Lightweight and secure numeric comparison protocol for wireless body area networks. *IEEE Internet of Things Journal, 10*(5), 13247–13263.

Youssef, S. B. H., Rekhis, S., & Boudriga, N. (2015). Design and analysis of a WBAN-based system for firefighters. In *IWCMC 2015 - 11th International Wireless Communications and Mobile Computing Conference* (pp. 526–531). Institute of Electrical and Electronics Engineers Inc., Tunisia. Available from https://doi.org/10.1109/IWCMC.2015.7289139 9781479953448.

Zafar, H., Channa, A., Jeoti, V., & Stojanović, G. M. (2022). Comprehensive review on wearable sweat-glucose sensors for continuous glucose monitoring. *Sensors, 22*(2). Available from https://doi.org/10.3390/s22020638, https://www.mdpi.com/1424-8220/22/2/638/pdf.

Zamkah, A., Hui, T., Andrews, S., Dey, N., Shi, F., & Sherratt, R. S. (2020). Identification of suitable biomarkers for stress and emotion detection for future personal affective wearable sensors. *Biosensors, 10*(4). Available from https://doi.org/10.3390/bios10040040, https://www.mdpi.com/2079-6374/10/4/40.

Zhang, J., & Dong, C. (2022). Secure and lightweight data aggregation scheme for anonymous multi-receivers in WBAN. *IEEE Transactions on Network Science and Engineering, 10*(1), 2022.

Zhang, X., Zheng, B., & Pan, L. (2020). Using virtual reality technology to visualize management of college assets in the internet of things environment. *IEEE Access* (8). China: Institute of Electrical and Electronics Engineers Inc. Available from https://doi.org/10.1109/ACCESS.2020.3019836, http://ieeexplore.ieee.org/xpl/RecentIssue.jsp?punumber = 6287639.

Zhou, M. (2019). *Aging population a global challenge*, 2019.

Zia, M., Obaidat, M. S., Mahmood, K., Shamshad, S., Saleem, M. A., & Chaudhry, S. A. (2023). A provably secure lightweight key agreement protocol for wireless body area networks in healthcare system. *IEEE Transactions on Industrial Informatics, 19*(2). Available from https://doi.org/10.1109/TII.2022.3202968, http://ieeexplore.ieee.org/xpl/RecentIssue.jsp?punumber = 9424.

Anonymity preserving security protocol for wireless body area networks: towards the secure remote patient healthcare monitoring

Vincent Omollo Nyangaresi[1,2]

[1]Department of Computer Science & Software Engineering, Jaramogi Oginga Odinga University of Science and Technology, Bondo, Kenya [2]Department of Applied Electronics, Saveetha School of Engineering, SIMATS Deemed University, Chennai, Tamil Nadu, India

12.1 Introduction

The deployment of the Internet of Things (IoT) in scenarios such as intelligent transportation, smart homes, smart healthcare system, smart cities and smart grids has increased convenience in people's lives and energy savings (Bordel et al., 2021; Nyangaresi, 2021a; Vivekanandan et al., 2021). In particular, IoT applications in the healthcare system can potentially reduce the costs associated with most treatments (Sowjanya & Dasgupta, 2020). Wireless body area networks (WBANs) have been developed for this purpose, where the patient's health conditions can be continuously monitored from remote locations. This is facilitated by availing real-time patient data to the healthcare providers over public channels or through the cloud. In its basic form, a WBAN comprises miniature and lightweight physiological sensors and actuators, which may be implanted in or patched on the patients' bodies or integrated into patients' clothing (Fotouhi et al., 2020; Jones & Katzis, 2018).

The collected real-time data is thereafter transmitted to e-health cloud servers accessible to medical professionals, who can then treat patients at any time and from any place (Alzahrani et al., 2021). In so doing, WBANs enable emergency medical assistance and remote diagnosis or treatment using implantable or wearable sensors (Movassaghi et al., 2014; Shen et al., 2018). For instance, patient blood oxygen saturation can be monitored

Sensor Networks for Smart Hospitals
DOI: https://doi.org/10.1016/B978-0-443-36370-2.00013-X

using wearable pulse oximeter sensors, glycemic index can be analyzed in real-time using implantable blood glucose sensors to trigger insulin pumps, while electrocardiograms (ECGs) sensors can perceive patient ECG variations among heart disease patients (Seyedi et al., 2013). Upon collection of these physiological data from the patients, it can be transmitted to remote healthcare control centers for analysis, decision-making and appropriate action (Alzahrani et al., 2021; Shen et al., 2016).

Apart from patient treatment, WBANs are deployed to monitor people with various medical conditions such as Alzheimer's disease or initial assessment of diseases prior to medical diagnosis by experts. Remote monitoring of patients with highly infectious diseases such as COVID-19 is also possible, so as to reduce contact levels. In addition, the promotion of elderly living standards, emergency health responses such as heart attack, and computer-assisted rehabilitation are other potential application domains of WBANs. Clearly, WBANs aid medical professionals and patients to have efficient, cheaper and reliable healthcare.

In spite of the potential benefits of WBANs, many security and privacy challenges lurk in these networks. According to (He et al., 2016), data confidentiality, nonrepudiation, integrity, authenticity and availability are key security goals in this environment. Since these networks transmit and process sensitive and private patient data, any form of compromise of WBANs can have life-threatening consequences (Kaur et al., 2018; Wang et al., 2020). As pointed out in Sowjanya and Dasgupta (2020), data security assurance is one of the requirements for the adoption of WBANs. Similarly, security and privacy issues in WBANs have been highlighted in Shen et al. (2018) and Halford et al. (2015) to be of significance during the deployment of these networks. The open nature of the deployed wireless communication channel between the physiological sensors and the remote medical servers exposes the exchanged data to numerous security and privacy attacks (Nyangaresi & Mohammad, 2021). Consequently, the secure transmission of patient data between the sensors and healthcare providers, as well as secure storage over the cloud is paramount (Sowjanya & Dasgupta, 2020).

To address these privacy and security challenges, authentication protocols are required to ensure that only legitimate medical professionals access the sensor-collected data (Alzahrani et al., 2021; Fotouhi et al., 2020). In WBANs, the sensors have limited computing power and are battery-powered (Wang et al., 2020), which presents some challenges in the design of these authentication protocols. As such, the deployed authentication schemes must be lightweight in terms of the cryptographic operations involved, messages exchanged and the memory required (Mohd et al., 2018; Nyangaresi & Ogundoyin, 2021). The contributions of this paper include the following:

- A biometric-based authentication algorithm is developed for secure data access in WBANs.
- Pseudonyms and random nonces are deployed to offer anonymity and untraceability of the communicating entities over public wireless channels.
- Extensive lemmas formulations and proofs are executed to show the robustness of the proposed algorithm in both Dolev—Yao and Canetti-Krawczyk models.
- Formal security analysis is carried out using Burrows—Abadi—Needham (BAN) logic to show the establishment of a session key after successful mutual authentication.
- Performance evaluation is executed to show that this algorithm exhibits the least execution time and bandwidth requirements.

The rest of this chapter is organized as follows: Section 12.2 discusses the related work while Section 12.3 describes the system model. On the other hand, Section 12.4 details the proposed algorithm, while Section 12.5 gives an elaboration of the security analysis of the proposed algorithm. Towards the end, Section 12.6 highlights the performance evaluation of the proposed algorithm. Finally, Section 12.7 concludes the paper and gives future directions.

12.2 Related work

The security and privacy issues in WBANs have attracted great attention from the research community and hence a myriad of authentication protocols have been presented. For instance, certificateless authentication schemes have been developed in He et al. (2015) and Xiong and Qin (2015). Although certificateless schemes solve key escrow problems, they have high computation and resource requirements. Similarly, the protocols in He et al. (2016) and Gope and Hwang (2016a), Kumari et al. (2016), Srinivas et al. (2017), Wazid et al. (2018), and Wei et al. (2018) have high computation costs and may not offer untraceability and perfect forward key secrecy. On the other hand, the anonymous authentication protocol presented in Gope and Hwang (2016b) is susceptible to denial of service (DoS) attacks and lacks both session key agreement and forward key secrecy (Li et al., 2018a). The secure framework presented in Hu et al. (2016) involves computationally expensive bilinear pairing operations that are not practical for WBAN sensors (Nyangaresi et al., 2020; Yao et al., 2015).

Two lightweight authentication protocols are introduced in Aman et al. (2017) and Zhao et al. (2016) based on PUFs. Although these schemes are efficient, the physical Unclonable Function (PUF)-based assumptions are not ideal for many WBANs (Alzahrani et al., 2021). On the other hand, the lightweight schemes in Amin et al. (2018) and Kumari and Om (2016) are susceptible to offline guessing and traceability attacks (Fotouhi et al., 2020).

A three-factor authentication protocol based on elliptic curve cryptography (ECC) is presented in Li et al. (2018b). Although this scheme provides crucial security features, it has high computation overheads. Using public key cryptography (PKC), two security schemes have been developed in Sangari and Manickam (2014) and (Li et al., 2014). Unfortunately, PKC-based protocols introduce complexities in the management of certificates (Nyangaresi, 2021b). On the other hand, the patient healthcare monitoring scheme in Xu et al. (2019) is susceptible to impersonation, replay and key compromise attacks. In addition, it cannot uphold both privacy and anonymity. Although the scheme in Ibrahim et al. (2016) offers mutual authentication, it is vulnerable to de-synchronization attacks. Similarly, the protocol in Farash et al. (2017) provides mutual authentication but is susceptible to traceability attacks (Wu et al., 2016). The ECC scheme in Yao et al. (2015) offers session key encryption but these keys are not elements of the elliptic curve group. Consequently, this protocol is susceptible to collusion attacks.

The two-factor authentication protocol in Jiang et al. (2016) can provide some levels of untraceability. However, this technique cannot withstand session-specific temporary information leak attacks and may permit unauthorized logins (Li et al., 2018b). Similarly, the two-factor authentication scheme in Wu et al. (2018) is robust against session key, privileged insider, traceability and offline guessing attacks. However, it cannot assure forward key secrecy. To address problems with digital signature protocols, identity-based security schemes have been developed in Shen et al. (2017) and Li et al. (2015). Unfortunately, the invasion of the key generation center may compromise the security of these protocols. In addition, identity-based schemes may lead to leakage of the real identities of the communicating entities (Nyangaresi & Petrovic, 2021). Although the ciphertext-policy attribute-based encryption schemes in Li et al. (2019), Liu et al. (2019), and Zhang et al. (2019) provide revocability and traceability protection, they have extensive computation overheads due to bilinear pairing operations (Nyangaresi, 2021c). For the same reasons, the ECC and identity-based schemes in Irshad et al. (2017a, 2017b) are computationally expensive for WBAN sensors. The anonymous authentication technique in Liu et al. (2014) has low computational requirements, but cannot withstand public key replacement attacks (Xiong, 2014).

To address high computational complexity for bilinear pairing operations, the scheme in He et al. (2018) outsources these pairing operations to the cloud. However, this may potentially compromise the privacy of the patient's health-related data (Lin et al., 2017). On the other hand, the signature-based technique introduced in Zhang et al. (2013) cannot withstand adversarial tracing attacks, and its pairing operations are not efficient for the WBAN sensors (Nyangaresi et al., 2021).

It is evident that the conventional authentication protocols have security, performance or privacy issues and hence are not suitable for deployment in WBANs. In addition, the need for access to the patients' encrypted data by multiple medical workers implies that they share a common secret key. Although symmetric encryption-based techniques are ideal for this situation, the leakage of this shared secret key compromises the security of the entire healthcare system (Sowjanya & Dasgupta, 2020). On their part, conventional public key encryption schemes such as Rivest−Shamir−Adleman require an extra overhead for public key management or digital certificates (Nyangaresi & Morsy, 2021). Although identity-based encryption techniques can address digital certificate issues in public key encryption schemes, they fail to offer support for one-to-many communications.

12.3 System model

The proposed algorithm comprises the system administrator (SA), gateway node (GWN), body sensor units (BSUs), medical server units (MDUs), and the inference terminals (INTs). Here, the SA is in charge of both the MDUs and INTs. For simplicity, the INTs are incorporated into MDUs and are responsible for automated decision-making based on the received patient data from the BSUs. Fig. 12.1 shows the system architecture of the proposed algorithm.

As shown in Fig. 12.1 the BSUs collect data from the patient after which they send it through wireless channels to the GWN. The collected data items pertaining to physiological changes that may be associated with a myriad of diseases such as heart attack, diabetes, COVID-19 among others. Since the sensors are limited in terms of computation and transmission power, the GWN amalgamates data from various sensors before forwarding

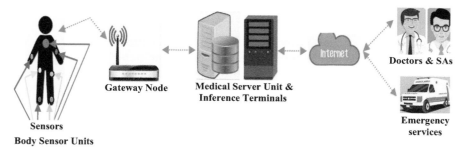

FIGURE 12.1   System architecture.

TABLE 12.1   Symbols and descriptions.

Symbol	Description
$\acute{Y}_{SK}$	GWN's secret key
ID_{SA}	SA's unique identifier
δ	SA's secret token
β_{SA}	SA's biometrics
S_P	SA's pseudonym
ID_{BSU}	BSU's unique identifier
S_P	BSU's pseudonym
$\dot{G}_{SK}$	BSU's long term secret key
$\acute{K}_i$	Random nonce
H_S	Helper string
SK_D	Secret key data
$h(.)$	One-way hashing operation
Φ	Session key shared between SA & BSU
$\parallel$	Concatenation operation
$\oplus$	XOR operation

it to the hospital information systems such as MSUs and INTs. These servers may be cloud-based and hence medical professionals may deploy the wireless public channels to access patient data that may facilitate some emergency interventions. Table 12.1 gives the symbols used in this paper and their descriptions.

As shown in Table 12.1, the proposed algorithm utilized a number of cryptographic primitives such as secret keys, one-way hashing, exclusive-or operations, and random number generators among others.

12.4 The proposed algorithm

In this algorithm, the fuzzy extractor is utilized to perform both key generation and secret key reproduction. To achieve this, the SA's biometric data β_{SA} is employed as input while the helper string is taken as H_S. The output of the generation function $G_P(.)$ is a random string SK_D that serves as the secret key data. On the other hand, during the reproduction process, H_S and β_{SA} serve as inputs to output the initial SK_D. In terms of execution, three major phases are implemented, which include entity registration, mutual authentication and key agreement as discussed below.

12.4.1 Registration phase

At the onset of SA and BSUs registration, the GWN generates a secret key $\bar{Y}_{SK}$. Thereafter, the SA and the BSUs are registered at the GWN. This is a five-step procedure as described below.

Step 1: The SA chooses unique identifier ID_{SA} and secret token δ. Next, the SA imprints biometrics β_{SA} to the MSU's INT before choosing nonce $\acute{K}_1$. This is followed by the computation of $(SK_D, H_S) = G_P(\beta_{SA})$, $S_P = h(ID_{SA} \| \acute{K}_1)$ and $A_1 = h(\acute{K}_1 \| ID_{SA} \| \delta)$ as shown in Fig. 12.2. Finally, the

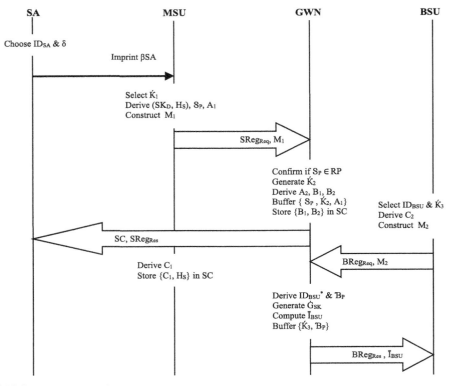

FIGURE 12.2 Registration phase.

INT constructs message $M_1 = \{S_P, A_1\}$ that is sent to the GWN together with registration request $SReg_{Req}$ through some secure channels.

Step 2: After receiving M_1, the GWN confirms whether S_P is already registered in its repository RP. Provided that $S_P \notin RP$, the GWN generates nonce $Ḱ_2$ that is utilized to derive $A_2 = h(S_P \| \bar{Y}_{SK} \| Ḱ_2)$, $B_1 = A_2 \oplus A_1$ and $B_2 = h(A_2 \| A_1)$. Next, the GWN buffers S_P together with $Ḱ_2$ and A_1. Thereafter, GWN stores security parameter pair $\{B_1, B_2\}$ into a smart card (SC) that is then issued to the SA in registration response message $SReg_{Res}$.

Step 3: Upon receipt of the SC, the SA through the MSU derives $C_1 = h(SK_D \| \delta)$ before storing security parameter pair $\{C_1, H_S\}$ into the SC.

Step 4: To start off BSU registration, the BSU selects its unique identity ID_{BSU} and nonce $Ḱ_3$. Next, it derives $C_2 = h(Ḱ_3) \oplus ID_{BSU}$. It then composes message $M_2 = \{C_2, Ḱ_3\}$ before sending it together with registration request $BReg_{Req}$ to the GWN via secure channels.

Step 5: On receiving M_2, the GWN derives $ID_{BSU}{}^* = C_2 \oplus h(Ḱ_3)$ and $B_P = h(ID_{BSU} \| Ḱ_3)$. This is followed by the random generation of BSU's secret key $Ġ_{SK}$. Next, the GWN computes $\bar{I}_{BSU} = h(B_P \| \bar{Y}_{SK} \| Ġ_{SK})$ and buffers security parameter pair $\{Ḱ_3, B_P\}$ in its memory. Finally, the GWN sends $\bar{I}_{BSU}$ together with registration response $BReg_{Res}$ to the BSU over some secure channels.

12.4.2 Authentication and key agreement

In order to access the patient data collected by the BSUs, the SA located in a remote health facility has to log in and authenticate to the GWN. This involves the following five steps.

Step 1: The SA inputs ID_{SA} and δ to the MSU followed by the imprint of β_{SA}. Next, the MSU computes $SK_D = R_P(\beta_{SA}, H_S)$, $Ḱ_1 = C_1 \oplus h(SK_D \| \delta)$, $S_P = h(ID_{SA} \| Ḱ_1)$ and $A_1 = h(Ḱ_1 \| ID_{SA} \| \delta)$. This is followed by the extraction of $A_2 = B_1 \oplus A_1$ and the derivation of $B_2{}^* = h(A_2 \| A_1)$. It then checks whether $B_2{}^* \stackrel{?}{=} B_2$ and if the two parameters are not the same, the login session is terminated. However, if they are equivalent, the MSU generates nonce $Ḱ_4$ that is utilized in the derivation of $H_1 = h(A_2 \| ID_{BSU}) \oplus Ḱ_4$ and $H_2 = h(A_2 \| ID_{BSU} \| Ḱ_4)$. Finally, it constructs $M_3 = \{S_P, H_1, H_2\}$ and sends it together with the login request Log_{Req} to the GWN over insecure channels.

Step 2: Upon receipt of M_3, the GWN retrieves $Ḱ_2$ from its RP that it deploys to compute $A_2{}^* = (S_P \| \bar{Y}_{SK} \| Ḱ_2)$, $Ḱ_4 = h(A_2{}^* \| ID_{BSU}) \oplus H_1$ and $H_2{}^* = h(A_2 \| ID_{BSU} \| Ḱ_4)$. This is followed by the confirmation of whether $H_2{}^* \stackrel{?}{=} H_2$ such that the login attempt is terminated if the two parameters are not equal. However, if the two are identical, the GWN generates nonce $Ḱ_5$ before computing $\bar{I}_{BSU} = h(h(ID_{BSU} \| Ḱ_3) \| \bar{Y}_{SK} \| Ġ_{SK})$, $H_3 = h(ID_{BSU} \| B_P \| \bar{I}_{BSU}) \oplus Ḱ_5$ and $H_4 = h(\bar{I}_{BSU} \| B_P \| Ḱ_5)$. The GWN then composes message $M_4 = \{H_3, H_4\}$ that is then sent to the BSU together with Log_{Req} over insecure channels as shown in Fig. 12.3.

Step 3: After receiving M_4 from the GWN, the BSU computes $Ḱ_5 = h(B_P \| \bar{I}_{BSU}) \oplus H_3$, $H_4{}^* = h(B_P \| \bar{I}_{BSU} \| Ḱ_5)$. Next, it confirms whether $H_4{}^* \stackrel{?}{=} H_4$ such that if they are not the same, authentication session is terminated, otherwise the BSU generates nonce $Ḱ_6$ and derives session key $\Phi = h(B_P \| \bar{I}_{BSU} \| Ḱ_6)$ and $H_5 = h(\Phi \| \bar{I}_{BSU} \| Ḱ_6)$. It then composes $M_5 = \{H_5\}$ before sending it to the GWN together with login response Log_{Res}.

Step 4: On receiving M_5, the GWN re-computes $\Phi^* = h(B_P \| \bar{I}_{BSU} \| Ḱ_6)$ and $H_5{}^* = h(\Phi^* \| \bar{I}_{BSU} \| Ḱ_6)$. Afterwards, it checks whether $H_5{}^* \stackrel{?}{=} H_5$ such that the authentication session is

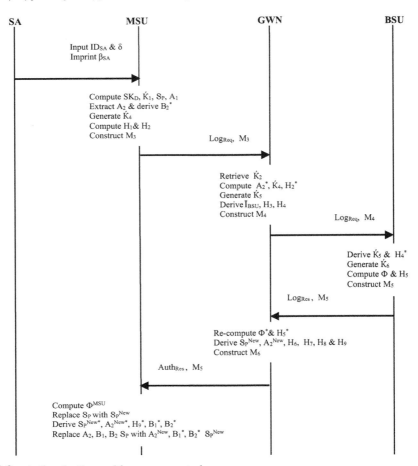

FIGURE 12.3 Authentication and key agreement phase.

terminated if the two are not identical. However, if the two are equal, the GWN derives $S_P^{New} = h(\acute{K}_5 \| S_P)$, $A_2^{New} = h(S_P^{New} \| \bar{Y}_{SK} \| \acute{K}_5)$, $H_6 = (\acute{K}_4 \| A_2^*) \oplus S_P^{New}$, $H_7 = (\acute{K}_4 \| A_2^*) \oplus A_2^{New}$, $H_8 = (\acute{K}_4 \| A_2^*) \oplus \Phi^*$ and $H_9 = (\Phi^* \| \acute{K}_4 \| A_2^{New} \| S_P^{New})$. Next, the GWN constructs $M_6 = \{H_6, H_7, H_8, H_9\}$ and sends it together with authentication response $Auth_{Res}$ to the MSU over insecure channels.

Step 5: After obtaining M_6, the MSU computes $\Phi^{MSU} = H_8 \oplus (\acute{K}_4 \| A_2)$ and checks whether $\Phi^{MSU} \stackrel{?}{=} \Phi^*$. Upon successful session key agreement, the GWN substitutes S_P with S_P^{New}. This is followed by the derivation of $S_P^{New}{}^* = H_6 \oplus (\acute{K}_4 \| A_2)$, $A_2^{New*} = H_7 \oplus (\acute{K}_4 \| A_2)$ and $H_9^* = (\Phi^{MSU} \| \acute{K}_4 \| A_2^{New} \| S_P^{New})$. Next, the MSU confirms whether $H_9^* \stackrel{?}{=} H_9$ such that the session is terminated if they are not similar. However, if the two values are equal, the MSU derives $B_1^* = A_2^{New} \oplus A_1$ and $B_2^* = h(A_2^{New} \| A_1)$. Afterwards, it substitutes A_2, B_1, B_2 and S_P with A_2^{New}, B_1^*, B_2^* and S_P^{New} respectively. Consequently, the SA through the MSU, GWN and the BSU have successfully authenticated each other and share a common session key for traffic protection.

12.5 Security analysis

In this section, both formal and informal security analyses are executed to demonstrate the security features offered by the proposed algorithm.

12.5.1 Formal security analysis

In this sub-section, the BAN logic is deployed to demonstrate the existence of strong mutual authentication among the communicating entities. To achieve this, the notations in Nyangaresi and Rodrigues (2022) and logic rules in Nyangaresi and Moundounga (2021) are utilized. Thereafter, the following eight security goals are formulated:

Goal-1 $\text{GWN} | \equiv \text{MSU} | \equiv (\acute{K}_4)$
Goal-2 $\text{GWN} | \equiv (\acute{K}4)$
Goal-3 $\text{BSU} | \equiv \text{GWN} | \equiv (\acute{K}_5)$
Goal-4 $\text{BSU} | \equiv (\acute{K}5)$
Goal-5 $\text{GWN} | \equiv \text{BSU} | \equiv \text{BSU} \overset{\Phi}{\leftrightarrow} \text{GWN}$
Goal-6 $\text{GWN} | \equiv \text{BSU} \overset{\Phi}{\leftrightarrow} \text{GWN}$
Goal-7 $\text{MSU} | \equiv \text{GWN} | \equiv MSU \overset{\Phi}{\leftrightarrow} \text{GWN}$
Goal-8 $\text{MSU} | \text{MSU} \overset{\Phi}{\leftrightarrow} \text{GWN}$

To achieve the BAN logic proofs, the initial state assumptions (ISAs) below are formulated.

$\text{ISA}_1: \text{GWN} | \left(\text{MSU} \overset{A_2}{\leftrightarrow} \text{GWN} \right)$

$\text{ISA}_2: \text{GWN} | \equiv \#(\acute{K}_4)$

$\text{ISA}_3: \text{BSU} | \left(\text{GWN} \overset{\text{ID}_{\text{BSU}}}{\leftrightarrow} \text{BSU} \right)$

$\text{ISA}_4: \text{BSU} | \equiv \#(\acute{K}_5)$

$\text{ISA}_5: \text{GWN} | \equiv \left(\text{BSU} \overset{\overline{Y}_{\text{SK}}}{\leftrightarrow} \text{GWN} \right)$

$\text{ISA}_6: \text{GWN} | \equiv \#(\text{ID}_{\text{BSU}})$

$\text{ISA}_7: \text{MSU} | \equiv \left(\text{MSU} \overset{\acute{K}_4}{\leftrightarrow} \text{GWN} \right)$

$\text{ISA}_8: \text{MSU} | \equiv \#(S_P^{\text{New}})$

$\text{ISA}_9: \text{GWN} | \equiv \text{MSU} \Rightarrow \left(\text{GWN} \overset{A_2}{\leftrightarrow} \text{MSU} \right)$

$\text{ISA}_{10}: \text{BSU} | \equiv \text{GWN} \Rightarrow \left(\text{BSW} \overset{\text{ID}_{\text{BSU}}}{\leftrightarrow} \text{GWN} \right)$

$\text{ISA}_{11}: \text{GWN} | \equiv \text{BSU} \Rightarrow \left(\text{BSU} \overset{\Phi}{\leftrightarrow} \text{GWN} \right)$

$\text{ISA}_{12}: \text{MSU} | \equiv \text{GWN} \Rightarrow \left(\text{MSU} \overset{\Phi}{\leftrightarrow} \text{GWN} \right)$

During the mutual authentication and key agreement procedures, messages $M_3 = \{S_P, H_1, H_2\}$, $M_4 = \{H_3, H_4\}$, $M_5 = \{ H_5\}$ and $M_6 = \{H_6, H_7, H_8, H_9\}$ are exchanged. These messages are idealized as follows:

M_3: MSU → GWN: $(S_P, ID_{BSU}, Ќ_4)_{A_2}$

M_4: GWN → BSU: $(ID_{BSU}, B_P, Ќ_5)_{\bar{I}_{BSU}}$

M_5: BSU → GWN: $(B_P, Ќ_5, \bar{I}_{BSU})_{\hat{Y}_{SK}}$

M_6: GWN → MSU: $(S_P^{New}, A_2^{New}, \Phi)_{Ќ_4}$

The main BAN logic proofs (BLPs) are executed using the Message Meaning Rule (MMR), Jurisdiction Rule (JR), Nonce Verification Rule (NVR), Believe Rule (BR), Freshness Rule (FR), idealized messages and ISAs.

Based on M_3, BLP_1 is obtained:

BLP_1: GWN◁ $(ID_{BSU}, S_P, Ќ_4)_{A_2}$

On the other hand, the application of MMR in ISA_1 yields BLP_2.

BLP_2: GWN| ≡ MSU| ∼ $(ID_{BSU}, S_P, Ќ_4)$

The application of FR in ISA_2 yields BLP_3.

BLP_3: GWN| ≡ #$(ID_{BSU}, S_P, Ќ_4)$

However, the utilization of NVR in both BLP_2 and BLP_3 results in BLP_4.

BLP_4: GWN| ≡ MSU| ≡$(ID_{BSU}, S_P, Ќ_4)$

Using BR in BLP_4 yields BLP_5.

BLP_5: GWN| ≡ MSU| ≡$(Ќ_4)$, and hence Goal -1 is attained.

On the other hand, based on M_4, BLP_6 is derived.

BLP_6: BSU◁ $(ID_{BSU}, B_P, Ќ_5)_{\bar{I}_{BSU}}$

The application of MMR in ISA_3 yields BLP_7.

BLP_7: BSU| ≡ GWN| ∼ $(ID_{BSU}, B_P, Ќ_5)$

However, using FR in ISA_4 yields BLP_8.

BLP_8: BSU| ≡ #$(ID_{BSU}, B_P, Ќ_5)$

Applying NVR in both BLP_7 and BLP_8 results in BLP_9.

BLP_9: BSU| ≡ GWN| ≡$(ID_{BSU}, B_P, Ќ_5)$

Using BR in BLP_9 yields BLP_{10}.

BLP_{10}: BSU| ≡ GWN| ≡$(Ќ_5)$, achieving Goal-3.

On the other hand, based on M_5, BLP_{11} is obtained.

BLP_{11}: GWN◁ $(B_P, Ќ_5, \bar{I}_{BSU})_{\hat{Y}_{SK}}$

The application of MMR in both BLP_{11} and ISA_5 results in BLP_{12}.

BLP_{12}: GWN| ≡ BSU| ∼ $(B_P, Ќ_5, \bar{I}_{BSU})$

Using FR in ISA_6 yields BLP_{13}.

BLP_{13}: GWN| ≡ #$(B_P, Ќ_5, \bar{I}_{BSU})$

However, the application of NVR in both BLP_{12} and BLP_{13} results in BLP_{14}.

BLP_{14}: GWN| ≡ BSU| ≡$(B_P, Ќ_5, \bar{I}_{BSU})$

Based on BLP_{14} and $\Phi = h(B_P \| \bar{I}_{BSU} \| Ќ_6)$, BLP_{15} is obtained.

BLP_{15}: GWN| ≡ BSU| ≡ BSU $\overset{\Phi}{\leftrightarrow}$ GWN, thus Goal - 5 is achieved.

According to M_6, BLP_{16} is obtained.

BLP_{16}: MSU◁ $(S_P^{New}, A_2^{New}, \Phi)_{\hat{Y}_{SK}}$

Applying MMR in both ISA_7 and BLP_{16} yields BLP_{17}.

BLP_{17}: MSU| ≡ GWN| ∼ $(S_P^{New}, A_2^{New}, \Phi)_{\hat{Y}_{SK}}$

On the other hand, using FR in both ISA_8 and BLP_{17} results in BLP_{18}.

BLP_{18}: MSU| ≡ # $(S_P^{New}, A_2^{New}, \Phi)$

Using NVR in both BLP_{17} and BLP_{18} yields BLP_{19}.

BLP_{19}: $MSU| \equiv GWN| \equiv (S_P^{New}, A_2^{New}, \Phi)$

Applying BR in BLP_{19} results BLP_{20}.

BLP_{20}: $MSU| \equiv GWN| \equiv (\Phi)$

Based on BLP_{20}, BLP_{21} is obtained.

BLP_{21}: $MSU| \equiv GWN| \equiv MSU \overset{\Phi}{\leftrightarrow} GWN$, therefore Goal -7 is attained

The application of JR in both BLP_5 and ISA_9 results in BLP_{22}.

BLP_{22}: $GWN| \equiv (Ќ_4)$, hence achieving Goal-2.

On the other hand, using JR in both BLP_{10} and ISA_{10} yields BLP_{23}.

BLP_{23}: $BSU| \equiv (Ќ_5)$, therefore Goal-4 is attained.

Using JR in both BLP_{15} and ISA_{11} results BLP_{24}.

BLP_{25}: $GWN| \equiv BSU \overset{\Phi}{\leftrightarrow} GWN$, attaining Goal-6.

Finally, JR is applied in both BLP_{21} and ISA_{12} to obtain BLP_{25}.

BLP_{25}: $MSU| \equiv MSU \overset{\Phi}{\leftrightarrow} GWN$, thus Goal-8 is attained.

The attainment of all eight goals demonstrates the existence of a session key among the communicating entities after successful mutual authentication procedures.

12.5.2 Informal security analysis

In this section, it is shown that the developed algorithm is robust under both Dolev-Yao and Canetti-Krawczyk models. The assumptions of these two models are articulated in Nyangaresi (2021d). To accomplish this, the following eleven theorems are formulated and proofed.

Theorem 1: *The proposed algorithm offers strong mutual authentication and key agreement.*

Proof. During the mutual authentication procedures, messages $M_3 = \{S_P, H_1, H_2\}$, $M_4 = \{H_3, H_4\}$, $M_5 = \{H_5\}$ and $M_6 = \{H_6, H_7, H_8, H_9\}$ are exchanged among the BSU, MSU and the GWN. To authenticate the SA, the MSU performs $B_2^* \overset{?}{=} B_2$ check, while the MSU is authenticated by the GWN by checking whether $H_2^* \overset{?}{=} H_2$ and $H_5^* \overset{?}{=} H_5$. On the other hand, the BSU authenticates the GWN by confirming whether $H_4^* \overset{?}{=} H_4$. Similarly, the MSU authenticates the GWN by checking if $H_9^* \overset{?}{=} H_9$. In addition, the BSU derives session key $\Phi = h(B_P \| Ī_{BSU} \| Ќ_6)$ while the GWN re-computes session key $\Phi^* = h(B_P \| Ī_{BSU} \| Ќ_6)$. On its part, the MSU re-computes session key $\Phi^{MSU} = H_8 \oplus (Ќ_4 \| A_2)$. After successful mutual authentication, the session key is set as $\Phi^{MSU} = \Phi^* = \Phi$ and hence the exchanged traffic is sufficiently protected.

Theorem 2: *Offline guessing attacks are curbed in the proposed algorithm.*

Proof. The goal of this attack is for an adversary to decipher the SA's unique identity ID_{SA} and secret token δ in polynomial time. Suppose that an attacker succeeds in extracting parameters $\{B_1, B_2, C_1$ and $H_S\}$ stored in the SC through power analysis. Thereafter, an attempt is made to decipher ID_{SA} and δ. However, B_1 and B_2 are masked with A_2 in A_1. In addition, A_2 is masked with both $Ȳ_{SK}$ and $Ќ_2$ and as such, ID_{SA} and δ cannot be extracted from B_1 and B_2. Suppose now that an attacker attempts to simultaneously guess

ID_{SA} and δ. However, the masking of these parameters with SA's biometric β_{SA} renders this guessing computationally infeasible.

Theorem 3: *DoS attacks are effectively thwarted in the proposed algorithm.*

Proof. The aim of the attacker here is to block the SA from accessing the data in the BSUs. To accomplish this, an attacker captures messages $H_6 = (\acute{K}_4 \| A_2^*) \oplus S_P^{New}$, $H_7 = (\acute{K}_4 \| A_2^*) \oplus A_2^{New}$, $H_8 = (\acute{K}_4 \| A_2^*) \oplus \Phi^*$ and $H_9 = (\Phi^* \| \acute{K}_4 \| A_2^{New} \| S_P^{New})$. Thereafter, an adversary generates bogus nonce $\acute{K}_{Bogus}$ which it utilizes to construct fake message $H_9^{Bogus} = H_9 \oplus \acute{K}_{Bogus}$. An adversary then attempts to re-send message set $\{H_6, H_7, H_8, H_9^{Bogus}\}$. However, upon receiving $M_6 = \{H_6, H_7, H_8, H_9\}$, the MSU confirms whether $H_9^* \overset{?}{=} H_9$ such that the session is terminated if they are not similar. Consequently, attacker initiated messages are easily detected and eliminated from the communication session.

Theorem 4: *The proposed algorithm preserves user and device anonymity.*

Proof. Suppose that an attacker is interested in capturing the SA's real identity ID_{SA} to be utilized in tracing the SA. However, in the proposed algorithm, ID_{SA} and BSU's unique identifier ID_{BSU} are enciphered together with nonces $\acute{K}_1$ in $A_1 = h(\acute{K}_1 \| ID_{SA} \| \delta)$ and $\acute{K}_3$ in $\bar{I}_{BSU} = h(h(ID_{BSU} \| \acute{K}_3) \| \tilde{Y}_{SK} \| \dot{G}_{SK})$. In addition, $S_P = h(ID_{SA} \| \acute{K}_1)$ is substituted with $S_P^{New} = h(\acute{K}_5 \| S_P)$, at the GWN since this parameter is transmitted over insecure channels. As such, it is impossible for an adversary to determine SA's and BSU's true identities.

Theorem 5: *Man-in-the-middle and packet replay attacks are curbed in the proposed algorithm.*

Proof. The assumption made in these attacks is that an adversary is capable of intercepting exchanged messages $M_3 = \{S_P, H_1, H_2\}$, $M_4 = \{H_3, H_4\}$, $M_5 = \{H_5\}$ and $M_6 = \{H_6, H_7, H_8, H_9\}$ over the open wireless networks. Thereafter, an attempt is made to construct login message $B_2^* = h(A_2 \| A_1)$, where $A_1 = h(\acute{K}_1 \| ID_{SA} \| \delta)$ and $A_2 = h(S_P \| \tilde{Y}_{SK} \| \acute{K}_2)$. By *Theorem 4*, an attacker cannot decipher ID_{SA} and hence valid login message cannot be constructed at the MSU. In addition, any attempt to masquerade as a legitimate SA to forward previously exchanged messages will fail since parameters $A_2 = h(S_P \| \tilde{Y}_{SK} \| \acute{K}_2)$, $B_1 = A_2 \oplus A_1$, $B_2 = h(A_2 \| A_1)$ and $S_P = h(ID_{SA} \| \acute{K}_1)$ needed to accomplish this are substituted with their refreshed counterparts $A_2^{New} = h(S_P^{New} \| \tilde{Y}_{SK} \| \acute{K}_5)$, $B_1^* = A_2^{New} \oplus A_1$, $B_2^* = h(A_2^{New} \| A_1)$ and $S_P^{New} = h(\acute{K}_5 \| S_P)$ respectively. The incorporation of nonces $\acute{K}_1$ and $\acute{K}_5$ in these messages render them session specific and hence replayed messages will be easily detected.

Theorem 6: *The proposed algorithm is resilient against forgery attacks.*

Proof. The goal of this attack is for the adversary to derive valid messages $H_1 = h(A_2 \| ID_{BSU}) \oplus \acute{K}_4$, $H_2 = h(A_2 \| ID_{BSU} \| \acute{K}_4)$, $H_3 = h(ID_{BSU} \| B_P \| \bar{I}_{BSU}) \oplus \acute{K}_5$, $H_4 = h(\bar{I}_{BSU} \| B_P \| \acute{K}_5)$, $H_5 = h(\Phi \| \bar{I}_{BSU} \| \acute{K}_6)$, $H_6 = (\acute{K}_4 \| A_2^*) \oplus S_P^{New}$, $H_7 = (\acute{K}_4 \| A_2^*) \oplus A_2^{New}$, $H_8 = (\acute{K}_4 \| A_2^*) \oplus \Phi^*$ and $H_9 = (\Phi^* \| \acute{K}_4 \| A_2^{New} \| S_P^{New})$. However, it can be seen that these messages incorporate nonces $\acute{K}_4$, $\acute{K}_5$ and $\acute{K}_6$ and secret tokens $A_2 = h(S_P \| \tilde{Y}_{SK} \| \acute{K}_2)$ and $\bar{I}_{BSU} = h(B_P \| \tilde{Y}_{SK} \| \dot{G}_{SK})$. In addition, one-way hashing operation is executed in all these messages, which renders them collision-resistant. Here, it is infeasible to derive valid H_1 and H_2 without A_2 on the SA side. Since A_2 incorporates GWN's secret keys $\bar{Y}_{SK}$ and $\acute{K}_2$ which are unavailable to the adversary, this attack flops. On the other hand, at the GWN, messages H_3, H_4, H_6, H_7, H_8 and H_9 require A_2, $\acute{K}_4$, $\acute{K}_5$, B_P and $\bar{I}_{BSU}$ which are unavailable to the adversary. Similarly, on the patient's BSU side, H_5 is masked with $\bar{I}_{BSU}$ and $\acute{K}_6$. Consequently, it is not possible to forge the exchanged messages in the proposed algorithm.

Theorem 7: *Privileged insider attacks are thwarted in the proposed algorithm.*

Proof. Suppose that we have some SA who is malicious at the MSU side who has access to the registration parameters S_P, A_1 belonging to a particular legitimate SA. Using power analysis technique, this privileged insider successfully retrieves security parameters $\{B_1, B_2, C_1$ and $H_S\}$. Thereafter, an attempt is made to decipher the legitimate user's unique identifier ID_{SA} and secret token δ. However, the derivation of ID_{SA} and δ requires biometric secret key $SK_D = R_P(\beta_{SA}, H_S)$ which cannot be computed due to the unavailability of SA's biometric data β_{SA}.

Theorem 8: *The proposed algorithm is robust against session disclosure attack.*

Proof. Suppose that an attacker has captured messages $H_8 = (\acute{K}_4 \| A_2{}^*) \oplus \Phi^*$ and $H_9 = (\Phi^* \| \acute{K}_4 \| A_2{}^{New} \| S_P{}^{New})$ and is interested in computing session key $\Phi^* = h(B_P \| \bar{I}_{BSU} \| \acute{K}_6)$ from these messages. However, this requires knowledge of $\bar{I}_{BSU}$ and $\acute{K}_6$. Since $\bar{I}_{BSU} = h(h(ID_{BSU} \| \acute{K}_3) \| \bar{Y}_{SK} \| \dot{G}_{SK})$ is encapsulated using GWN's master key $\bar{Y}_{SK}$, BSU's long term secret key $\dot{G}_{SK}$ and nonce $\acute{K}_3$, the derivation of Φ^* will fail. Similarly, without nonces $\acute{K}_4$ and $\acute{K}_6$, the derivation of Φ^* is infeasible.

Theorem 9: *Impersonation attacks are effectively prevented in the proposed algorithm.*

Proof. The aim of this attack is to compute exchanged messages through masquarading as a legitmate network entity. During the authentication and key agreement phase, messages $M_3 = \{S_P, H_1, H_2\}$, $M_4 = \{H_3, H_4\}$, $M_5 = \{H_5\}$ and $M_6 = \{H_6, H_7, H_8, H_9\}$ are exchanged. Here, $H_1 = h(A_2 \| ID_{BSU}) \oplus \acute{K}_4$, $H_2 = h(A_2 \| ID_{BSU} \| \acute{K}_4)$, $H_3 = h(ID_{BSU} \| B_P \| \bar{I}_{BSU}) \oplus \acute{K}_5$, $H_4 = h(\bar{I}_{BSU} \| B_P \| \acute{K}_5)$, $H_5 = h(\Phi \| \bar{I}_{BSU} \| \acute{K}_6)$, $H_6 = (\acute{K}_4 \| A_2{}^*) \oplus S_P{}^{New}$, $H_7 = (\acute{K}_4 \| A_2{}^*) \oplus A_2{}^{New}$, $H_8 = (\acute{K}_4 \| A_2{}^*) \oplus \Phi^*$ and $H_9 = (\Phi^* \| \acute{K}_4 \| A_2{}^{New} \| S_P{}^{New})$. Clearly, all transmitted messages are encapsulated in nonces $\acute{K}_4$, $\acute{K}_5$ and $\acute{K}_6$ which are randomly selected by each of the network entity. Considering message H_3, it is evident that ID_{BSU}, B_P, $\bar{I}_{BSU}$ and $\acute{K}_5$ are needed for its accurate derivation. However, $\bar{I}_{BSU} = h(h(ID_{BSU} \| \acute{K}_3) \| \bar{Y}_{SK} \| \dot{G}_{SK})$ and $B_P = h(ID_{BSU} \| \acute{K}_3)$ are masked with nonces $\acute{K}_3$ and secret keys $\bar{Y}_{SK}$ and $\dot{G}_{SK}$. As such, it is impossible to derive this message for possible GWN impersonation.

Theorem 10: *The proposed algorithm is robust against traceability attacks.*

Proof. In the proposed algorithm, the SA's unique identifier ID_{SA} is encapsulated in $S_P = h(ID_{SA} \| \acute{K}_1)$ and $A_1 = h(\acute{K}_1 \| ID_{SA} \| \delta)$. Considering S_P, it is refreshed as $S_P{}^{New} = h(\acute{K}_5 \| S_P)$ at the GWN and updated accordingly to thwart any offline guessing and tracing attacks. In addition, all exchanged messages $M_3 = \{S_P, H_1, H_2\}$, $M_4 = \{H_3, H_4\}$, $M_5 = \{H_5\}$ and $M_6 = \{H_6, H_7, H_8, H_9\}$ incorporate nonces and other intermediary parameters which are refreshed after every successful session. For instance, at the MSU, parameters A_2, B_1, B_2 and S_P are substituted with A_2^{New}, B_1^*, B_2^* and S_P^{New} respectively. Consequently, it is cumbersome to deploy these messages to trace down any particular network entity.

Thereom 11: *De-synchronization attacks are curbed in the proposed algorithm.*

Proof. Suppose that an attacker is interested in preventing the SA from receiving messages $\{H_6 = (\acute{K}_4 \| A_2^*) \oplus S_P^{New}$, $H_7 = (\acute{K}_4 \| A_2^*) \oplus A_2^{New}$, $H_8 = (\acute{K}_4 \| A_2^*) \oplus \Phi^*$ and $H_9 = (\Phi^* \| \acute{K}_4 \| A_2^{New} \| S_P^{New})\}$ from the GWN. If this happens, then the SA will be totally de-synchronized with the GWN. However, any attacker initiated de-synchronization will flop since the SA verifies whether $H_9^* \overset{?}{=} H_9$ such that the session is terminated if they are dissimilar. In addition, upon this session termination, S_P is not updated with S_P^{New} and hence de-synchronization attacks are kept at bay.

12.6 Performance evaluation

In the analysis of authentication and key agreement protocols, execution time and bandwidth requirements are the most utilized parameters. Therefore, in this section, the proposed algorithm is evaluated in terms of these two metrics as discussed below.

12.6.1 Execution time

During the authentication phase in WBANs, some of the cryptographic operations executed include chaotic map function (T_C), one-way hashing (T_H), fuzzy extraction (T_{FE}), symmetric encryption and decryption (T_S). Based on the values in Challa et al. (2017) and Srinivas et al. (2018), Table 12.2 gives the execution times of these cryptographic operations.

In the proposed algorithm's login, authentication and key agreement phases, one-way hashing and fuzzy extraction operations are executed. On the MSU side, $1T_{FE}$ and $6T_H$ are executed, while only $4T_H$ operations are carried out on the BSU. On the other hand, $9T_H$ operations are executed on the GWN. As such, $1T_{FE}$ and $19T_H$ cryptographic operations are required in the proposed algorithm as shown in Table 12.3.

TABLE 12.2 Cryptographic execution time.

Cryptographic operation	Time (ms)
T_C	17.1
T_H	0.32
T_{FE}	17.1
T_S	5.6

TABLE 12.3 Execution time comparisons.

Scheme	User	GWN	BSU	Total (ms)
Srinivas et al. (2017)	$2T_S + 8T_H$	$T_S + 4T_H$	$2T_S + 4T_H$	$5T_S + 16T_H = 33.12$
Kumari et al. (2016)	$2T_C + 2T_S + 4T_H$	$2T_S + 6T_H$	$2T_C + 3T_H$	$4T_C + 4T_S + 13T_H = 94.96$
Wazid et al. (2018)	$T_{FE} + 14T_H$	$9T_H$	$9T_H$	$T_{FE} + 33T_H = 27.66$
Proposed	$T_{FE} + 6T_H$	$9T_H$	$4T_H$	$1T_{FE} + 19T_H = 23.18$

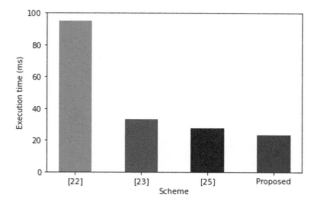

FIGURE 12.4 Execution time comparisons.

TABLE 12.4 Parameter lengths.

Cryptographic operation	Length (bits)
One-way hashing	160
Chaotic map	1024
Identities	160
Nonces	128
Timestamps	32

As shown in Fig. 12.4, the protocol in Kumari et al. (2016) have the highest execution time followed by the schemes in Srinivas et al. (2017) and Wazid et al. (2018) respectively.

However, the proposed algorithm has the lowest execution time and hence is suitable for the resource-constrained WBANs sensors.

12.6.2 Bandwidth requirements

For communication overhead computations, the values in Challa et al. (2017) and Srinivas et al. (2018) are deployed in which all one-way hashing and identities are 160 bits long, while chaotic map, random numbers and timestamps are 1024 bits, 128 bits and 32 bits respectively as shown in Table 12.4.

TABLE 12.5   Bandwidth requirement comparisons.

Scheme	Bandwidth (bits)
Srinivas et al. (2017)	5344
Kumari et al. (2016)	5248
Wazid et al. (2018)	1696
Proposed	1600

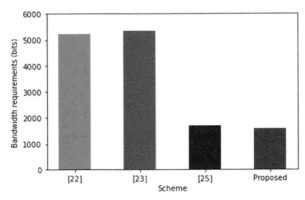

FIGURE 12.5   Bandwidth requirement comparisons.

During the login, authentication and key agreement phases of the proposed algorithm, messages $M_3 = \{S_P, H_1, H_2\}$, $M_4 = \{H_3, H_4\}$, $M_5 = \{H_5\}$ and $M_6 = \{H_6, H_7, H_8, H_9\}$ are exchanged among the BSU, MSU and the GWN. The bandwidth requirements are derived as follows:

M_3:$\{S_P = H_1 = H_2 = 160\} = 480$ bits
M_4:$\{H_3 = H_4 = 160\} = 320$ bits
$M_5 = \{H_5 = 160\} = 160$ bits
M_6: $\{H_6 = H_7 = H_8 = H_9 = 160\} = 640$ bits

As such, the total bandwidth requirement in the proposed algorithm is 1600 bits. Table 12.5 presents the bandwidth requirements of the proposed algorithm as well as those of other schemes.

Based on Fig. 12.5, the scheme in Srinivas et al. (2017) has the highest bandwidth requirements followed by the schemes in Kumari et al. (2016) and Wazid et al. (2018) respectively. On the other hand, the proposed algorithm has the least bandwidth requirements.

As such, our algorithm is the most applicable in WBAN where the sensors are power-limited and hence need to send only a few bits during the authentication and key agreement phase.

12.7 Conclusion

Numerous authentication schemes have been developed to provide secure remote patient healthcare monitoring. These protocols are basically based on conventional techniques such as public key infrastructure, device identity, bilinear pairings, ECC, and digital signatures or certificates among other approaches. However, it has been shown that the majority of these schemes incur extensive computation and communication overheads. In addition, some of these protocols are still susceptible to numerous security and privacy attacks. On the other hand, the developed algorithm is shown to be robust against the majority of these attacks. Compared with other related approaches, the developed algorithm incurs the lowest execution time and bandwidths. It is therefore truly lightweight and hence applicable in WBANs where the physiological sensors are resource-constrained.

References

Alzahrani, B. A., Irshad, A., Albeshri, A., & Alsubhi, K. (2021). A provably secure and lightweight patient-healthcare authentication protocol in wireless body area networks. *Wireless Personal Communications, 117*(1), 47−69.

Aman, M. N., Chua, K. C., & Sikdar, B. (2017). *A light-weight mutual authentication protocol for IoT systems.* in 2017 IEEE global communications conference (pp. 1−6). IEEE.

Amin, R., Islam, S. H., Kumar, N., & Choo, K. K. R. (2018). An untraceable and anonymous password authentication protocol for heterogeneous wireless sensor networks. *Journal of Network and Computer Applications, 104*, 133−144.

Bordel, B., Alcarria, R., Robles, T., & Iglesias, M. S. (2021). Data authentication and anonymization in IoT scenarios and future 5G networks using chaotic digital watermarking. *IEEE Access, 9*, 22378−22398.

Challa, S., Wazid, M., Das, A. K., Kumar, N., Reddy, A. G., Yoon, E. J., & Yoo, K. Y. (2017). Secure signature-based authenticated key establishment scheme for future iot applications. *IEEE Access, 5*, 3028−3043.

Farash, M. S., Chaudhry, S. A., Heydari, M., Sadough, S., Mohammad, S., Kumari, S., & Khan, M. K. (2017). A lightweight anonymous authentication scheme for consumer roaming in ubiquitous networks with provable security. *International Journal of Communication Systems, 30*(4), e3019.

Fotouhi, M., Bayat, M., Das, A. K., Far, H. A. N., Pournaghi, S. M., & Doostari, M. A. (2020). A lightweight and secure two-factor authentication scheme for wireless body area networks in health-care IoT. *Computer Networks, 177*, 107333.

Gope, P., & Hwang, T. (2016a). A realistic lightweight anonymous authentication protocol for securing real time application data access in wireless sensor networks. *IEEE Trans Industrial Electronics, 63*(11), 7124−7132.

Gope, P., & Hwang, T. (2016b). An efficient mutual authentication and key agreement scheme preserving strong anonymity of the mobile user in global mobility networks. *Journal of Network and Computer Applications, 62*, 1−8.

Halford, T. R., Courtade, T. A., Chugg, K. M., & Li, X. (2015). Energy-efficient group key agreement for wireless networks. *IEEE Transactions on Wireless Communications, 14*(10), 5552−5564.

He, D., Zeadally, S., Kumar, N., & Lee, J. H. (2016). Anonymous authentication for wireless body area networks with provable security. *IEEE Systems Journal, 11*(4), 2590−2601.

He, D., Zeadally, S., & Wu, L. (2015). Certificateless public auditing scheme for cloud-assisted wireless body area networks. *Journal of IEEE Systems Journal, 2015*, 1−10.

He, Q., Zhang, N., Wei, Y., & Zhang, Y. (2018). Lightweight attribute based encryption scheme for mobile cloud assisted cyber-physical systems. *Computer Network, 140*, 163−173.

Hu, C., Li, H., Huo, Y., Xiang, T., & Liao, X. (2016). Secure and efficient data communication protocol for wireless body area networks. *IEEE Trans Multi-Scale Computer System, 2*(2), 94−107.

Ibrahim, M. H., Kumari, S., Das, A. K., Wazid, M., & Odelu, M. V. (2016). Secure anonymous mutual authentication for star two-tier wireless body area networks. *Computer Methods and Programs in Biomedicine, 135*, 37−50.

Irshad, A., Chaudhry, S. A., Xie, Q., Li, X., Farash, M. S., Kumari, S., & Wu, F. (2017a). An enhanced and provably secure chaotic map-based authenticated key agreement in multi-server architecture. *Arabian Journal for Science and Engineering, 43*, 811−828.

Irshad, A., Sher, M., Nawaz, O., Chaudhry, S. A., Khan, I., & Kumari, S. (2017b). A secure and provable multi-server authenticated key agreement for TMIS based on Amin et al. scheme. *Multimedia Tools and Applications, 76*(15), 16463−16489.

Jiang, Q., Ma, J., Wei, F., Tian, Y., Shen, J., & Yang, Y. (2016). An untraceable temporal-credential based two-factor authentication scheme using ECC for wireless sensor networks. *Journal of Network and Computer Applications, 76*, 37−48.

Jones, R. W., & Katzis, K. (2018). 5G and wireless body area networks. *IEEE Wireless communications and networking conference workshops (WCNCW)* (2018, pp. 373−378). IEEE.

Kaur, H., Kumar, N., & Batra, S. (2018). An efficient multi-party scheme for privacy preserving collaborative filtering for healthcare recommender system. *Future Generation Computer Systems, 86*, 297−307.

Kumari, S., Li, X., Wu, F., Das, A. K., Arshad, H., & Khan, M. K. (2016). A user friendly mutual authentication and key agreement scheme for wireless sensor networks using chaotic maps. *Future Generation Computer Systems, 63*, 56−75.

Kumari, S., & Om, H. (2016). Authentication protocol for wireless sensor networks applications like safety monitoring in coal mines. *Computer Networks, 104*, 137−154.

Li, J., Chen, X., Li, M., Li, J., Lee, P., & Lou, W. (2014). Secure deduplication with efficient and reliable convergent key management. *IEEE Transactions on Parallel and Distributed Systems, 25*(6), 1615−1625.

Li, J., Wang, S., Li, Y., Wang, H., Wang, H., Wang, H., & You, Z. (2019). An efficient attribute- based encryption scheme with policy update and file update in cloud computing. *IEEE Transactions on Industrial Informatics, 15* (12), 6500−6509.

Li, X., Niu, J., Kumari, S., Wu, F., & Choo, K. K. R. (2018a). A robust biometrics based three-factor authentication scheme for global mobility networks in smart city. *Future Generation Computer Systems, 83*, 607−618.

Li, X., Niu, J., Kumari, S., Wu, F., Sangaiah, A. K., & Choo, K. K. R. (2018b). A three-factor anonymous authentication scheme for wireless sensor networks in internet of things environments. *Journal of Network and Computer Applications, 103*, 194−204.

Li, X., Niu, J., Liao, J., & Liang, W. (2015). Cryptanalysis of a dynamic identity-based remote user authentication scheme with verifiable password update. *International Journal of Communication Systems, 28*(2), 374382.

Lin, G., Hong, H., & Sun, Z. (2017). A collaborative key management protocol in cipher- text policy attribute-based encryption for cloud data sharing. *IEEE Access, 5*, 9464−9475.

Liu, J., Zhang, Z., Chen, X., & Kwak, K. S. (2014). Certificateless remote anonymous authentication schemes for wireless body area networks. *IEEE Transactions on Parallel & Distributed Systems, 25*(2), 332−342.

Liu, Z., Xu, J., Liu, Y., & Wang, B. (2019). Updatable ciphertext-policy attribute-based encryption scheme with traceability and revocability. *IEEE Access, 7*, 66832−66844.

Mohd, B. J., Hayajneh, T., Ahmad Yousef, K. M., Khalaf, Z. A., & Bhuiyan, M. Z. A. (2018). Hardware design and modeling of lightweight block ciphers for secure communications. *Future Generation. Computer System, 83*, 510−521.

Movassaghi, S., Abolhasan, M., Lipman, J., Smith, D., & Jamalipour, A. (2014). Wireless body area networks: A survey. *IEEE Communication. Survey. Tutorial, 16*(3), 1658−1686.

Nyangaresi, V. O. (2021a). Lightweight Key Agreement and Authentication Protocol for Smart Homes . *IEEE Africon* (2021, pp. 1−6). IEEE.

Nyangaresi, V.O. (2021b). Provably secure protocol for 5G HetNets. In *2021 IEEE International conference on microwaves, antennas, communications and electronic systems (COMCAS)* (pp. 17−22). IEEE.

Nyangaresi, V. O. (2021c). Hardware assisted protocol for attacks prevention in ad hoc networks. *International conference for emerging technologies in computing* (pp. 3−20). Cham: Springer.

Nyangaresi, V. O. (2021d). ECC based authentication scheme for smart homes. *International symposium ELMAR* (2021, pp. 5−10). IEEE.

Nyangaresi, V. O., & Mohammad, Z. (2021). Privacy preservation protocol for smart grid networks. *International telecommunications conference (ITC-Egypt)* (2021, pp. 1−4). IEEE.

Nyangaresi, V. O., & Morsy, M. A. (2021). Towards privacy preservation in internet of drones. *2021 IEEE 6th international forum on research and technology for society and industry (RTSI)*, (pp. 306−311). IEEE.

Nyangaresi, V. O., & Moundounga, A. R. A. (2021). Secure data exchange scheme for smart grids. In *2021 IEEE 6th International forum on research and technology for society and industry (RTSI)* (pp. 312–316). IEEE.

Nyangaresi, V. O., & Ogundoyin, S. O. (2021). Certificate based authentication scheme for smart homes. *3rd Global power, energy and communication conference (GPECOM)* (2021, pp. 202–207). IEEE.

Nyangaresi, V. O., & Petrovic, N. (2021). Efficient PUF based authentication protocol for internet of drones. *International telecommunications conference (ITC-Egypt)*, (2021, pp. 1–4). IEEE.

Nyangaresi, V. O., & Rodrigues, A. J. (2022). Efficient handover protocol for 5G and beyond networks. *Computers & Security, 113*, 1–12, 102546.

Nyangaresi, V. O., Rodrigues, A. J., & Abeka, S. O. (2020). Efficient group authentication protocol for secure 5G enabled vehicular communications. *16th International computer engineering conference (ICENCO)* (2020, pp. 25–30). IEEE.

Nyangaresi, V. O., Rodrigues, A. J., & Taha, N. K. (2021). Mutual authentication protocol for secure VANET data exchanges. *International conference on future access enablers of ubiquitous and intelligent infrastructures* (pp. 58–76). Cham: Springer.

Sangari, A.S., & Manickam, J.M. L. (2014). public key cryptosystem based security in wireless body area network. In *Proceedings of the 2014 IEEE international conference on circuit, power and computing technologies* (pp. 1609–1612). IEEE.

Seyedi, M., Kibret, B., Lai, D. T., & Faulkner, M. (2013). A survey on intrabody communications for body area network applications. *IEEE Transactions on bio-medical Engineering, 60*(8), 2067–2079.

Shen, J., Chang, S., Shen, J., Liu, Q., & Sun, X. (2018). A lightweight multi-layer authentication protocol for wireless body area networks. *Future Generation Computer Systems, 78*, 956–963.

Shen, J., Liu, D., Lai, C., Ren, Y., & Xingming, S. (2017). A secure identity-based dynamic group data sharing scheme for cloud computing. *Journal of Internet Technology*, 1–9.

Shen, J., Tan, H., Moh, S., Chung, I., & Wang, J. (2016). An efficient RFID authentication protocol providing strong privacy and security. *Journal of Internet Technology, 17*(3), 443–455.

Sowjanya, K., & Dasgupta, M. (2020). A ciphertext-policy attribute based encryption scheme for wireless body area networks based on ECC. *Journal of Information Security and Applications, 54*, 102559.

Srinivas, J., Das, A. K., Wazid, M., & Kumar, N. (2018). Anonymous lightweight chaotic map-based authenticated key agreement protocol for industrial internet of things. *IEEE Transactions on Dependable and Secure Computing, 17*(6), 1133–1146.

Srinivas, J., Mishra, D., & Mukhopadhyay, S. (2017). A mutual authentication framework for wireless medical sensor networks. *Journal of Medical Systems, 41*(5), 80.

Vivekanandan, M. K., Sastry, V. N., & Srinivasulu Reddy, U. (2021). BIDAPSCA5G: Blockchain based Internet of Things (IoT) device to device authentication protocol for smart city applications using 5G technology. *Peer-to-Peer Networking and Applications, 14*(1), 403–419.

Wang, J., Han, K., Fan, S., Zhang, Y., Tan, H., Jeon, G., & Lin, J. (2020). A logistic mapping-based encryption scheme for wireless body area networks. *Future Generation Computer Systems, 110*, 57–67.

Wazid, M., Das, A. K., & Vasilakos, A. V. (2018). Authenticated key management protocol for cloud-assisted body area sensor networks. *Journal of Network and Computer Applications, 123*, 112–126.

Wei, F., Vijayakumar, P., Shen, J., Zhang, R., & Li, L. (2018). A provably secure password-based anonymous authentication scheme for wireless body area networks,. *Computers & Electrical Engineering, 65*, 322–331.

Wu, F., Li, X., Sangaiah, A. K., Xu, L., Kumari, S., Wu, L., & Jian, S. (2018). A lightweight and robust two factor authentication scheme for personalized healthcare systems using wireless medical sensor networks. *Future Generation Computer Systems, 82*, 727–737.

Wu, F., Xu, L., Kumari, S., Li, X., Das, A. K., Khan, M. K., & Baliyan, R. (2016). A novel and provably secure authentication and key agreement scheme with user anonymity for global mobility networks. *Security and Communication Networks, 9*(16), 3527–3542.

Xiong, H. (2014). Cost-effective scalable and anonymous certificateless remote authentication protocol. *IEEE Transactions on Information Forensics & Security, 9*(12), 2327–2339.

Xiong, H., & Qin, Z. (2015). Revocable and scalable certificateless remote authentication protocol with anonymity for wireless body area. *Networks, IEEE Transactions on Information Forensics & Security, 10*(7), 1.

Xu, Z., Xu, C., Chen, H., & Yang, F. (2019). A lightweight anonymous mutual authentication and key agreement scheme for WBAN. *Concurrency and Computation: Practice and Experience, 31*(14), e5295.

Yao, X., Chen, Z., & Tian, Y. (2015). A lightweight attribute-based encryption scheme for the internet of things. *Future Generation Computer System, 49*(C), 104–112.

Zhang, L., Hu, G., Mu, Y., & Rezaeibagha, F. (2019). Hidden ciphertext policy attribute-based encryption with fast decryption for personal health record system. *IEEE Access, 7,* 33202–33213.

Zhang, L., Liu, J., & Sun, R. (2013). An Efficient and lightweight certificateless authentication protocol for wireless body area networks. *IEEE Computer society international conference on intelligent networking and collaborative systems* (pp. 637–639). IEEE.

Zhao, M., Yao, X., Liu, H., & Ning, H. (2016). Physical unclonable function based authentication protocol for unit IoT and ubiquitous IoT. *International conference on identification, information and knowledge in the internet of things (IIKI)* (2016, pp. 179–184). IEEE.

Wireless sensor networks for smart healthcare

Venkata Krishna Reddy M[1], Premkumar Chithaluru[1,2],
Manoj Kumar[3,4] and Pallati Narsimhulu[5]

[1]Department of Computer Science and Engineering, Chaitanya Bharathi Institute of Technology
(Autonomous), Hyderabad, Telangana, India [2]Department of Information Technology, Mahatma
Gandhi Institute of Technology, Hyderabad, Telangana, India [3]School of Computer Science,
FEIS, University of Wollongong in Dubai, Dubai, United Arab Emirates [4]MEU Research Unit,
Middle East University, Amman, Jordan [5]Department of Computer Engineering and
Technology, Chaitanya Bharathi Institute of Technology, Hyderabad, Telangana, India

13.1 Introduction

A person's day-to-day actions can be tracked through the usage of an autonomous system defined as a WSN. Defense, science, industry, business, and other sectors can all benefit from these networks' serviceperson's. The sensor nodes developed by WSN have many applications in the realms of medicine, athletics, the arts, and also, the military, the space program, consumer electronics, and the fire department, all while using very little power. WSNs allow us to keep tabs on people's whereabouts, actions, and crucial physiological signals from afar over the internet. This results in monetary savings. There is a growing need for these gadgets, and meeting that demand requires addressing problems with availability, fault tolerance, reliability, QoS, and safety. Because of issues with constant evolution and finite resources like storage, energy, and bandwidth. Unfortunately, WSNs have not been able to meet all of the aforementioned conditions.

New WSN-based medical technologies promise significant improvements in care and significant reductions in costs, and the healthcare industry is jumping on board. There has been a rapid increase in the number of implanted and wearable medical devices that use wireless technology to regulate human activities and measure a wide variety of physiological data. Biosensor and actuator-equipped implantable devices can control heart rates,

Sensor Networks for Smart Hospitals
DOI: https://doi.org/10.1016/B978-0-443-36370-2.00014-1

monitor hypertension, and other conditions, stimulate nerves functionally, detect glaucoma, and track pressure in the cranium and bladder, among other applications (Sindhu et al., 2016). WSN devices are used for physiological monitoring, assisting the motion of artificial limbs, and serving as little "base stations" for data collection and dissemination. In the not-too-distant future (Yuce & Khan, 2011), doctors will be able to monitor medicine use via tiny transponders implanted in pills.

To detect chronic ailments such as coronary heart disease, asthma, diabetes, and a host of others, and to notify patients in case of emergency, it is made up of intelligent sensor nodes that do not interfere with normal living. This allows for multiple miniature body sensor units (BSUs) to communicate wirelessly with a central body central unit (BCU) worn on the body. Around 1995, researchers first began to think of using wireless personal area network (WPAN) technologies to enable communication on, close to, and all around the body of a human being, marking the beginning of the current generation of WSN technology. Around 2001, this specific use of WPAN was given the moniker body area network (BAN) to indicate that it exclusively facilitates communications on, within, and immediately surrounding the human body. WPAN wireless technologies can be used as gateways in a WSN (Mahn, 2013) system, allowing for greater transmission ranges.

Because of its multidisciplinary nature, the field of BANs has the potential to usher in a new era of low-cost, constantly-available online medical record updates. Wearable WSNs that incorporate a variety of intelligent physiological sensors (Clark, 2009) have the potential to aid in early disease identification and computer-assisted rehabilitation. Embedding noninvasive biosensors all over the human body and unobtrusive is crucial to the success of this field. Sensors implanted in human bodies will record a range of physiological data to track the patient's health wherever they may be. Data will be sent wirelessly to a remote computer for processing.

13.1.1 Types of wireless sensor networks

Three distinct kinds of WSNs exist, distinguished by the entity that makes decisions based on information gathered by a network of sensors.

13.1.1.1 Dependent wireless sensor network

Dependent wireless body area sensor networks (Yao, 2014) are networks in which a third party, such as a doctor, nurse, or medical center, makes decisions based on data obtained from a network of sensors. Someone else receives the data and uses it to make a diagnosis. The next course of action, if any, or medication prescribed for the patient will be determined by the third party based on the information gathered. Such a system has wireless or cellular connections to other systems. The benefit of a dependent WSN is that it enables simultaneous analysis of all vital signs and diagnoses. However, this long-distance communication can run into trouble if the third party we are trying to reach is too preoccupied to respond. When this occurs, the patient's condition may deteriorate.

13.1.1.2 Independent wireless sensor network

Although they share the same goal as dependent WSNs, independent WSNs (Varshney, 2006) use a slightly different approach to reaching that goal. Actuators, which are also included in an independent WSN alongside sensor nodes, allow for immediate, independent action on the human body in response to sensor data or through direct human contact. When seconds count in a crisis, an independent WSN's ability to make instantaneous decisions and activate hardware actuators is invaluable. The body control unit (BCU) can function locally without any external network connections. As a result, there will be fewer transmissions and less drain on the battery. However, if BCU has not been trained to recognize a certain condition, complications may arise.

13.1.1.3 Sensible wireless sensor network

This network incorporates features from both of the aforementioned networks. Actuator nodes make autonomous judgments if the issue is straightforward, but they involve a third party if it is more complicated. If the doctor does not respond within a predetermined length of time due to being too busy, SWSN will make the call.

13.1.2 Features of wireless sensor network sensor nodes

WSN nodes have a variety of characteristics that make them ideal for a wide range of cutting-edge uses. Very few of them are as low in energy.

13.1.2.1 Economies of scale

Because the nodes make efficient use of electricity and are dispersed over a relatively small area, they have a longer lifespan, and a lower amount of connections are needed for the development of the network as well as their replacement if they become damaged. As a consequence of all of this, the costs associated with establishing a network will be reduced.

13.1.2.2 Ease of wearing

Nodes are utilized that are not only lightweight but also tiny in size, making it possible to conveniently transport them from one place to another by carrying them on your person or in a bag.

13.1.2.3 Conservation of energy

The design of the nodes ensures that they use a negligible amount of power. The employment of power management strategies allows for more effective management of the network's power resources, which in turn extends the amount of time that nodes in the network can function normally.

13.1.2.4 Variety of sensors

WSNs make use of a wide variety of sensors, some of which measure temperature, others heart rate, and so on. The data storage, processing power, and power requirements of these sensor nodes all vary widely.

13.1.3 Benefits of wireless sensor network

When compared to conventional methods of patient monitoring, it has been proven that WSNs are superior.

- Wires attached to a person and leading to a screen meant that the person being monitored had to remain in the hospital until their monitoring was complete. The patient was unable to get out of bed. However, as a result of advancements in medical technology, with the introduction of wireless body sensor networks, patients are no longer restricted to staying in one area; they can receive care anywhere, from the comfort of their own home or office to a remote location far from any hospital.
- The innovative approach of using sensors has resulted in user-friendly ways for tracking motion, body temperature, and other data from the human body, especially when compared to prior systems. Data can be retrieved whenever needed and stored for later use on a computer, PDA, or other mobile device.
- In the past, health monitoring systems required a tangled web of connections to function. To monitor the human body, wireless body sensor networks rely on tiny gadgets that can exchange data wirelessly.
- The ability to keep monitors on your health is a major perk of using a WSN. Fitness trackers and other types of wearable technology may keep tabs on a person's vitals such as their pulse, blood pressure, and even how well they sleep. Sending this data to a centralized location allows for in-depth analysis and the construction of a personalized health profile. Those people suffering from chronic illnesses like diabetes or cardiovascular disease will gain significantly from this.
- Increased security is yet another benefit of a WSN. In the event of an emergency, wearable electronics like smartwatches can be set to send out alerts. In the event of an emergency, such as a fall or an abnormal heart rate, a smartwatch can notify the appropriate people. Those with limited mobility or who live alone may benefit greatly from this.
- The use of a WSN has also been linked to enhanced athletic and physical performance. Fitness trackers and other forms of wearable technology can track your activity and offer useful insights into how you're doing. You can use this data to see where you're excelling and where you need to work on improving.

13.2 Hardware

Communication in a WSN is carried out via a wide variety of small devices.

13.2.1 Sensor node's architecture

Detecting signals, digitizing and managing those signals for multiple-access communication, and then wirelessly transferring them via a transceiver are the three primary functions of a sensor node. The signals picked up from the human body are weak and accompanied by background noise. Signal amplification is performed initially, and then

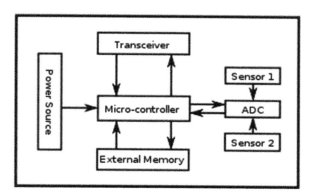

FIGURE 13.1   Design of sensor node.

the amplified signal is filtered to get rid of the unwanted noise. After being digitized by the A/D converter, the analog signals are then stored in the microcontroller. Fig. 13.1 demonstrates the architecture of the sensor node.

Finally, the microcontroller packages this information into packets and transmits them via transceiver to the web. The battery's power is distributed efficiently thanks to the microcontroller. To do this, power management techniques are used to turn off the devices while they are in a sleep state.

13.2.2 Types of sensor nodes

13.2.2.1 Gas sensor

It measures the concentration of oxygen in the blood and the rate at which carbon dioxide is being exhaled during exercise or rest.

13.2.2.2 Pulse sensor

The oxygen saturation level is detected by this sensor. The individual clips a sensor onto their finger, toe, earlobe, etc., and the sensor emits a light signal that penetrates the skin. Hemoglobin concentration in arterial blood is measured by comparing the amount of oxygenated hemoglobin to the total amount of hemoglobin in the blood. The ratio of the amount of light absorbed by oxygenated hemoglobin to the total amount of hemoglobin in the artery is the unit of measurement.

13.2.2.3 Blood sugar

A blood glucose level is determined by drawing a drop of blood on a strip of glucose-sensitive molecules from a person's finger. A Glucometer, which provides a numerical reading, is used to analyze the collected sample. However, optical sensing and infrared technology have made glucose monitoring possible. High hemoglobin on arterial hemoglobin concentration.

13.2.2.4 Temperature sensors

These sensors can detect both the relative humidity of an individual's immediate environment and his core temperature. An alert signal is sent out if the readings show a deviation from normalcy that is greater than a predetermined threshold.

13.2.2.5 Electroencephalogram sensor

The brain's electrical activity can be measured with this sensor. Humans' scalps are electrodes in a variety of locations to achieve this. Electrodes pick up data on the brain's electrical activity and transmit it to an amplifier, which then draws patterns. There must be some form of functional connection between brain areas if their electrical activities are synchronized.

13.2.2.6 Electrocardiogram sensor

An electrocardiogram (ECG) is a graph that displays the heart's electrical activity and is used to diagnose cardiac problems and monitor the efficacy of treatment. Humans have electrodes attached to their chests, arms, and other bodily parts. Electrode potential difference generates the ECG signal.

13.2.2.7 Blood pressure

This sensor measures blood pressure using an oscillometric method, providing accurate readings for both the systolic and diastolic readings.

13.3 Software and architecture of wireless sensor network

13.3.1 Software

Multiple types of software are needed for a WSN to operate well. Most nodes employ event-driven software, where a specific action is taken in response to the occurrence of an event, to maximize the efficiency of power consumption. WSN software also includes operating systems, which handle things similar to the scheduling of tasks, administration of memory, and optimization of power consumption. Along with RIOT, LiteOS, ERIKA Enterprise, and Contiki, TinyOS is a popular operating system option. Windows Silverlight, iOS, and Android are examples of base station operating systems that power smartphones.

13.3.2 Architecture

Sensor nodes in a WSN are typically quite small and diverse. Several sensor nodes, seen in Fig. 13.2, are positioned over a human body to perform numerous activities. A blood pressure monitor is one example; an electrocardiogram, electroencephalogram, etc. are all measured by various devices. These hubs are often referred to as "BSUs". These BSUs are responsible for intra-WSN/tier-1 communication and for communicating with one another. These sensor nodes relay their information to a central hub called the BCU. Inter WSN/tier-2 communication explains how information moves from one location to

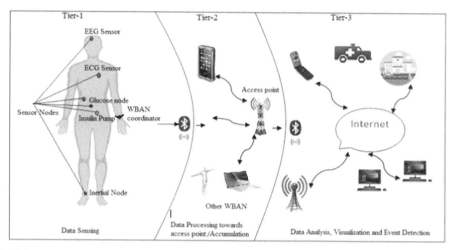

FIGURE 13.2 Depicts the overall design of a wireless sensor network.

another system. Existing wireless technologies like Bluetooth, ZigBee, etc. are utilized to transmit the data from these devices to an access point. At this point, the information reaches the gateway, which mediates communications between several networks. Networks in the healthcare industry may consist of hospitals, telephone lines, or a centralized facility.

Once information is uploaded to the web, it can be accessed anywhere in the globe. Information gathered in these facilities may be filed away in database servers for later use in patient diagnosis, research, or record-keeping. To prevent abuse, some security measures can be implemented to limit access to a select group of verified users. Our iPods or mobile phones can also be used to collect and hold this data, which can then be transmitted to a computer at a later time. Doctors can make a diagnosis and give the patient his medication without ever leaving their chairs.

13.3.3 Topology

The topology of a sensor network describes the structure of its nodes. One hub, subdivided into extended star topologies systems with one or two hops, has been approved by the IEEE 802 TG6. The simplest topology, consisting of a single hub, is depicted in Fig. 13.3. In a topology with only a single hop, frames can be sent between individual nodes and the central hub. Frames in a two-hop stretched star topology relay through a node instead of directly between the hub and the nodes. A WBSN uses a wireless communication channel for coordination between its hubs and nodes based on the arrival time of packets.

In addition to these, the Mesh and hybrid topologies are two that work well with WBSNs. In a mesh topology, all of the nodes are physically connected, but in a hybrid topology, several topologies are combined.

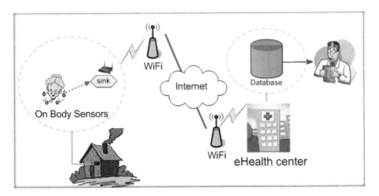

FIGURE 13.3   Topology of wireless sensor networks.

13.3.4 Wireless body area network technologies

Wireless BAN may necessitate many innovations at various stages. Here is a detailed look at the most prominent WSN technology proposals. (Negraa & Jemilia, 2016; Salehi, 2016)

13.3.4.1 IEEE 802.15.6

The first WSN standard, IEEE 802.15.6 provides a wide variety of communications in and around the human body for both medical and nonmedical applications. Multiple frequency bands are used for data transmission in the IEEE 802.15.6 standard (Yuce & Khan, n.d.) such as 400, 800, 900 MHz, 2.3, and 2.4 GHz NarroWSNd (NB) band, the 3.111.2 GHz Ultra-Wideband (UWB)4 band, and the 1050 MHz human body communication (Dangi et al., 2014) band. A huge number of nodes (256 per BAN), minimal energy use over a short range, and the ability to prioritize nodes based on application demands are just a few of the reasons why this technology is so promising, this standard represents a significant advancement in the field of wearable WSNs. CSMA/CA (Yuce & Khan, n.d.) or a slotted Aloha access process manages the channel access. The three distinct security algorithms it defines provide for a wide range of possible implementations. The IEEE 802.15.6 allows for extremely less energy communication with data speeds up to 10 Mbps. While it is capable of accounting for some types of body motion (such as a person walking in a straight line), it is not a good fit for the kinds of scenarios required by the burgeoning field of WSN applications, including activities like swimming, running, jogging, and sitting. The throughput needs of most WSN applications may be met by this standard, which reaches a maximum of 680 Kbps. However, it can't handle the demands of new applications that rely on high-quality video and audio transfers.

13.3.4.2 IEEE 802.11

Specifications are laid out in the IEEE 802.11 standard for WLANs. Wi-Fi is a wireless networking technology that, when used with an access point (AP) or in ad hoc mode, enables users to access the Internet with broadband speeds by IEEE 802.11 standards. Streaming large amounts of data is a breeze with its high-speed wireless networking, videoconferencing, and audio/conversational capability. The widespread availability of Wi-Fi capable mobile devices is a huge benefit, but the devices' high power requirements are a major drawback.

13.3.4.3 802.15.4 and Zigbee

When it comes to low-power wireless network technologies, ZigBee is among the most widely adopted options. Because of its 128-bit security feature, ZigBee is well-suited for low-data-rate radio-frequency applications with long battery lives that require safe networking. Many years can pass between battery changes for ZigBee-enabled devices thanks to their ability to enter sleep mode. There are two distinct components to ZigBee technology. First, the ZigBee alliance establishes the concept of "application layers," which includes the network, security, and application software levels. Additionally, IEEE 802.15.4 specifies the physical and media access control layers. This standard specifies the use of unclotted/slotted "CSMA/CA (Carrier Sense Multiple Access with Collision Avoidance)" mechanisms for wireless channel access and the allocation and management of guaranteed time slots (GTSs). The ZigBee standard allows for wireless communication in the 915 MHz, 868 MHz, and 2.4 GHz ranges. Since many wireless systems operate at once, the frequency band, 2.4 GHz is very congested, making Zigbee less than ideal for WSN applications. Zigbee's low data rate (250 Kbps) is another drawback that prevents it from being suitable for use in highly-trafficked, real-time WSN systems. In reality, the low data rate makes it impractical to use in healthcare settings with several patients, but it's perfect for individual use.

13.3.4.4 Bluetooth

It's a standard for wireless communications over short distances to keep data safe. Piconets allow for simultaneous communication between up to eight devices, using a single piece of hardware as the controller and the remaining devices serving as clients throughout the network. Among Bluetooth's, most appealing features is the ease with which various Bluetooth-enabled devices can pair with one another and exchange data in nearly any location on Earth. Also important is the fact that no direct line of sight between devices is required for communication to take place.

As a result, many different kinds of smartphones use it to communicate with one another to enable various data and speech applications. To minimize interference, Devices that use Bluetooth technology do so in the ISM (Industrial, Scientific, and Medical) band at 2.4 GHz and hop between 79 channel spacing of 1 MHz and a nominal repetition rate of 1600 Hz. Bluetooth's range is 1–100 m, and its top speed is 3 Mbps.

13.4 Issues and challenges and applications

13.4.1 Issues

13.4.1.1 Band selection

Different applications running on a WSN have varying bandwidth needs. Healthcare applications necessitate a low data transfer rate. ZigBee is the ideal wireless technology for this kind of use. UWB's reduced latency is ideal for use in time-sensitive applications. This means that picking the right bands is essential.

13.4.1.2 Interoperability

In a WSN, devices use a variety of frequencies and must use protocols such as ZigBee, Bluetooth, and others to connect. Because of this, interoperability may become an issue. These networks must be compatible with those of varying specifications.

13.4.1.3 Interference

WSNs must be close to other equipment and networks. Therefore, the data signals may be subject to distortion. Tissues within the body, heat radiation, etc., can also play a role. There should be no hiccups or dropped connections between these networks.

13.4.1.4 Fault tolerance

WSN relies on constant connectivity and error-free communication notwithstanding challenges presented by elements like disconnections and the surrounding environment.

13.4.1.5 Scheduling

Every one of a WSN's packets is unique. While the delivery of some packets is time-sensitive, the delivery of others is just as important. Decisions and plans must be made based on the data packets currently being transmitted over the network. Based on this plan, we prioritize which data packets will be transmitted first.

13.4.1.6 Control packets overhead

The control packets slow down the network because they don't carry any data. These packets are a major source of wasted energy.

13.4.2 Challenges

13.4.2.1 Deployment restriction

The WSN should be something that can be worn and is not too bulky or annoying. It shouldn't disrupt or add extra work to the user's normal routine. In an ideal world, the user wouldn't even notice the technology was monitoring their activity; in other words, the system would be "transparent."

13.4.2.2 Performance consistency

The WSN's effectiveness should be reliable. When the WSN is turned off and back on, the sensor readings should still be reliable and in calibration. Strong and reliable wireless connections are required for a wide range of user scenarios.

13.4.2.3 Safeguarding systems and individual devices

It would take significant effort to ensure secure and accurate transmission. Ensure patient security data is only taken from their specialized system and not combined with other patients' data. Data created by WSN should be safe and limited in access.

13.4.2.4 *Continuous tracking*

Some users, such as those at risk of cardiac arrest, may prefer that their WSNs operate continuously, while others, such as those at risk of falls, may only require WSNs to function while they are walking or moving. The amount of energy used and the lifespan of the BAN before the energy source is depleted are both affected by the level of monitoring.

13.4.2.5 *QOS and reliability*

The data transmitted by WBSN must be reliable and error-free. BAN's medical applications place a premium on ensuring the secure delivery of sensitive information at all times. Due to the potentially catastrophic effects of inaccurate or corrupted data, reliability and quality of service are essential for such mission-critical applications.

13.4.2.6 *Privacy and security*

Depending on the use case, WSN may store data that is vital to the operation of the system, and any changes to that data could have catastrophic consequences, even death. Because of this, there must be reliable methods for determining whether or not the requesting party is authorized to access the requested data. Also, make sure no tampering occurs between the sender and the receiver by keeping data intact.

13.4.3 Applications

The healthcare industry is a likely early adopter of WSNs due to their potential utility in areas like constant monitoring (Ullah et al., 2012) and logging of vital parameters of patients with chronic conditions including diabetes, asthma, and heart attacks. In the case of a diabetic patient, a WSN network may trigger the administration of insulin through a pump if their blood sugar level falls below a predetermined threshold, while in the case of a heart attack patient, the network could send an alarm to the hospital if the patient's vital signs changed.

This technology could also be used in the military or for homeland security purposes. The extension of this technology into new domains may further facilitate communication by allowing for the unobtrusive transfer of data between humans and machines.

13.4.3.1 *Military*

WSN has numerous defensive applications. Some of them include evaluating soldiers' hydration levels, monitoring their whereabouts, and measuring their core body temperature. When a soldier is injured, the data can be used to determine what kind of medical attention they need; when their strength, precision, and focus need to be increased; and when friendly fire incidents can be reduced by informing them of their precise location and identity at regular intervals.

13.4.3.2 *Emotion detection*

WSN can also be used to keep tabs on people's feelings. The human body produces a substance called serotonin in the brain and the intestine. When serotonin levels drop, people feel melancholy, and when they rise, they feel either happy or anxious. This molecule allows us to deduce an individual's emotional state.

13.4.3.3 Personal health monitoring

WSN allows for the continuous monitoring of vital signs in patients with conditions like heart disease, asthma, and diabetes. Home ECG and EMG monitoring allows patients to collect their own data for review by their physicians.

13.4.3.4 Medical

The use of BANs in remote patient monitoring has the potential to be extremely beneficial. Neither the patient nor the doctor needs to be physically present at the clinic. Patients' vital signs, including blood glucose, heart rate, blood pressure, etc., can be monitored and treated even when they are at home. Eventually, doctors will be able to keep tabs on patients no matter where they are and provide them with any medication they need. Patients will no longer need to be physically attached to bulky monitoring equipment.

13.5 Wireless sensor network in healthcare

13.5.1 Applications and use cases

13.5.1.1 Telemetry heart arrhythmia patients

Coronary heart illness is a common cause of cardiac arrhythmia (Yao, 2014). Coronary heart disease affects around one million Americans. The success of medication treatment for arrhythmia can be tracked by taking regular ECG readings from the patient. A cardiologist can monitor the patient's vital signs remotely via General Packet Radio Service (GPRS) transmission from the patient's home or other location, saving both time and money. The goal is to identify unusual patterns rapidly so that corrective action can be taken. In this scenario, we'll analyze how both patients and cardiologists can save time and money.

13.5.1.2 Emergency medical services via telemedicine

The trauma patient WSN will provide vital signs to the hospital trauma team from the scene. Paramedics wear trauma team WSNs with audio and wireless connection to the hospital. The goal of this scenario is to assess if mobile communications can enhance care quality and reduce response time to accidents. Telemetry technology can save time, improve therapy, and increase patient recovery possibilities. Measure parameters such as breathing frequency, oxygen saturation, heart rate, blood pressure, pupil size, responses, and fluid intake. The scenario will utilize GPRS and Universal Mobile Telecommunications System (UMTS) networks.

13.5.1.3 Environmental patient rehabilitation

Patients in this case are chronic respiratory patients who can improve their functional level through rehabilitation. The purpose of this research is to determine whether or not wireless health monitoring WSN can be used to implement remotely supervised outdoor training programs based on the regulation of walking speed. The physiotherapist can monitor the patient's exercise progress online and offer suggestions and corrections as needed. It is anticipated that there can be major benefits, both financially and socially, from allowing patients to undergo physical exercise in their local settings. Pulse oximetry, electrocardiogram, and mobility will be assessed, and the patient and remote physiotherapist will be able to communicate with one another via audio.

13.5.1.4 High-risk pregnant women integrated homecare

High-risk pregnancies might lead to prolonged hospital stays due to pregnancy-related problems. Admission is important for intensive patient and unborn child monitoring. Continuous monitoring at home can delay hospitalization, minimize costs, and provide greater security for the mother and unborn child. The WSN is used to monitor patients at home and send biosignals (maternal and fetal) to the hospital. An additional purpose of the scenario is to assess if the proposed remedy delays hospitalization and lowers costs. The scenario uses GPRS and Universal Mobile Telecommunications System(UMTS).

13.5.1.5 Monitoring vital signs in respiratory failure patients

The individuals in this scenario have respiratory insufficiency from chronic pulmonary illnesses. These individuals require ongoing medical attention to prevent deterioration of their condition. In addition to regular check-ups, patients require home oxygen therapy, requiring continuous supervision. Wireless health monitoring WSNs are used to detect diseases early and improve home care for identified patients by identifying intervention needs. The projected benefits include fewer check-ups and hospitalizations, and saving time and money. Measured parameters include pulse rate, oxygen saturation, and accelerometer signals.

13.5.1.6 Assistive living environments

The aging population, rising healthcare costs, and priority for independence drive the development of innovative assisted-living technology for safe and autonomous aging (Movassaghi et al., 2013). This field uses home automation to enhance quality of life and promote independence. Assisted living facilities are a viable option for disabled and elderly individuals who require support but do not require 24/7 monitoring or emergency assistance.

13.5.1.7 Home-based healthcare support

Patients with several chronic diseases, including the elderly, can receive remote help and home-based care through the use of GPRS. Patients will wear wireless health monitoring nurse-WSNs to track their recovery status at home or in other locations, while nurses will utilize wireless health monitoring nurse-WSNs to take vitals during in-home nursing shifts. The wireless health remote monitoring strategy aims, among other things, to improve patient's access to healthcare specialists without overburdening existing infrastructure. Blood pressure, heart rate, temperature, glucose, and spirometry are among the parameters that will be measured.

Human health depends on measuring and monitoring physiological processes, parameters, and traits. Telemedicine, optoelectronics, and micro and nanosensors are being optimized.

Data acquired from the body can avoid injuries and aid in timely and accurate medicine administration, such as using customized drug release devices. Innovative wearable health monitoring technologies incorporated into telemedicine networks can detect aberrant situations early and prevent significant repercussions. Continuous ambulatory monitoring can aid patients during diagnostic procedures, chronic disease management, and monitored recuperation from acute events or surgeries.

Consumers and patients alike can use WHMS to keep tabs on vital signs like blood pressure and heart rate thanks to a variety of wearable gadgets. These gadgets provide more reliable health reports for patients than regular screenshots. This enables more accurate treatment for the patient's condition. WHMS can aid in disease prevention by identifying trends rapidly as a starting point.

13.5.2 Biometric sensors

Biometric security is the result of the marriage between human physical characteristics and digital technology in the form of biometric sensors. To compare a biometric sample in real-time with those already on file, these semiconductor devices come integrated with a database of templates and algorithms. The benefit of these gadgets has already been seen in many domains, and new ones are constantly being developed. They have been labeled as cutting-edge biometric technology, so you know they'll do a good job of identifying you.

13.5.2.1 *Metrics of biometric sensor*

A biometric sensor uses a variety of different algorithms to produce highly accurate user authentication. The main elements of these devices include analog-to-digital converters, which are responsible for translating analog biometric data into digital codes. Physical characteristics are used by these devices to create templates, such as fingerprints, face metrics, vein structures in hands, and others. These biometric security systems allow for quick identification and verification, among other benefits. This technology comes in semiconductor, optical, and ultrasonic sensors, now in the market.

13.6 Real-time health monitoring and usage

Through a case study, we show how sensors can be used for real-time glucose monitoring in WSN.

13.6.1 Use case

A diabetic old woman checks her blood sugar regularly with a sensor that reports its readings to the hospital's server. Metformin and Glimepiride were prescribed and dietary changes were recommended during her most recent doctor's appointment. The doctor is watching the old woman closely to make sure she maintains her diet until her next scheduled monthly check-up. The doctor, meanwhile, is curious about the efficacy of the drug at this time. The old woman needs to come in earlier than her scheduled check-up if her blood sugar level remains high for even a week. She also runs the danger of hypoglycemia (low blood sugar), which could cause her to black out. Therefore, the doctor is concerned that she has ready access to emergency medical care should she have severe hypoglycemia. Finally, the doctor should be able to access this data in an emergency with the help of a wearable body access network, which consists largely of glucose monitoring sensors.

In light of the foregoing, it seems clear that a glucose-measuring device that doubles as a hypoglycemia warning is required. For this sensor system to be useful in the identification of hypoglycemia, it must function continuously and not rely on the initiative of the user to collect samples. The use of a continuous glucose sensor in conjunction with a tunable insulin delivery system has the potential to significantly improve blood glucose control, which is of enormous use in the treatment of hyperglycemia. The use of a continuous glucose sensor is recommended.

One possibility is an acute subcutaneously implanted glucose sensor that utilizes the concept of enzyme electrodes to detect hydrogen peroxide. A small, needle-like sensor is inserted beneath the skin once every three to seven days, and the data is processed by an electronic control unit (ECU). This sensor has been made to be as small as a needle for injecting insulin, is soft, and can be implanted subcutaneously with a 21-gauge needle. The group (Tavera et al., 2021) has created a wearable, battery-powered ECU that regulates the sensor potential, stores the current, and processes it. By temporarily connecting the ECU to a portable personal computer, we can perform an in vivo calibration operation by entering the data of two distinct blood glucose concentrations and the accompanying currents. Complex algorithms based on methods from mathematical morphology are used to process signals.

To translate sensor readings into a rough estimate of glucose content, a two-point in vivo calibration process has been designed. This technique involves taking two readings of blood sugar, one before and one after a dose of glucose (or after eating). It is possible to estimate the subcutaneous glucose concentration, G, using the following formula: $G = (I - I_o)/S$, (Kaur & Kang, 2019) where I is the current measured in the absence of glucose and S is the sensitivity of the assay in vivo, both determined by linear extrapolation from measured values of the current. Subcutaneous implantation of a glucose sensor in rats, dogs, and human volunteers has verified the efficacy of this method. The software used for sensor calibration is based on the detection of a plateau in sensor output, which initiates a request for blood glucose measurement (Rahangdale, 1973). An alarm will now sound if the ECU's estimated glucose concentration falls below a user-defined hypoglycemia threshold.

13.7 Conclusion and future trends

WSN has practical uses in fields such as medicine, the arts, and physical fitness. In the next years, it may prove to be a game-changing technology, with implications far beyond the domains discussed in the article and several new opportunities for developers to capitalize on as a result.

Although efforts are being made to address problems including latency, interference, and dynamic topology, additional efforts are needed to make this technology user-friendly and convenient. The sports and entertainment industries are evolving, creating new chances for those interested in pursuing careers in this field. While the current limitations of WSN in terms of data transfer and available resources to boost the battery life of individual nodes are significant, these issues will be mitigated in the not-too-distant future.

Research into establishing reliable, secure, and efficient communication between sensors that are installed on the human body to monitor the health status of patients and the activities of people in their daily lives has received considerable attention in recent years. This article provides a comprehensive summary of the various aspects that have been under study in recent years in wireless body sensor networks. The goal of this article was to provide a foundation for scholars interested in working in this area by introducing a selection of the limited literature on the topic of bio-medical sensors in WSNs for health monitoring. It is not required to apply all of the examined methods in a single setting, as they can be adopted and used by the existing aims and rules. It may be stated that increased network implementation costs and the shorter service life of the network can be predicted if WSNs are created without considering issues such as dependability, security, and energy consumption.

However, the ability to tailor a service to the individual is seen as crucial to the success of new ventures. Working with any of the health case scenarios is thus possible through the development of an appropriate model, the use of highly accurate and appropriate sensors, and the upkeep of a high level of security and accuracy. This will enable medical centers to get sickness data and take the necessary corrective action.

References

Clark, D. (2009). Take two digital pills and call me in the morning. *Wall Street Journal*, 2009.

Dangi, K., Grewal, S., & Panda. (2014). *Challenges in wireless body area network—A survey*. ICROIT, IEEE.

Kaur, P., & Kang, S. S. (2019). Hybrid routing protocol for wireless body area networks. *International Journal of Innovative Technology and Exploring Engineering*, 8(10). Available from https://doi.org/10.35940/ijitee. J9273.0881019, https://www.ijitee.org/wp-content/uploads/papers/v8i10/J92730881019.pdf.

Mahn, T. G. (2013). Wireless medical technologies: Navigating government regulation in the new medical age. *Fishs Regulatory & Government Affairs Group*, 2013.

Movassaghi, S., Abolhasan, M., & Lipman, J. (2013). A review of routing protocols in wireless body area networks. *Journal of Networks*, 8(3). Available from https://doi.org/10.4304/jnw.8.3.559-575, http://ojs.academypublisher.com/index.php/jnw/article/view/jnw0803559575/6729.

Negraa, R., & Jemilia, I. (2016). *Abdelfettah Belghitha,b, Wireless body area networks: Applications and technologies. The second international workshop on recent advances on machine-to machine communications* (p. 2016) Elsevier.

Rahangdale, H. (1973). A review on WMSN (wireless medical sensor networks) for health monitoring systems. *ECS Transactions*, 1973.

Salehi, A., et al. (2016). *IEEE 802.15.6 standards in wireless body area networks from a health care point of view. In* 22nd Asia pacific conference. IEEE.

Sindhu, S., Vashisth, S., & Chakarvarti, S. K. (2016). A review on wireless body area network (WBAN) for health monitoring system: Implementation protocols. *Communications on Applied Electronics*, 4(7). Available from https://doi.org/10.5120/cae2016652130.

Tavera, C. A., Ortiz, J. H., Khalaf, O. I., Saavedra, D. F., & Aldhyani, T. H. H. (2021). Wearable wireless body area networks for medical applications. *Computational and Mathematical Methods in Medicine*, 2021. Available from https://doi.org/10.1155/2021/5574376, http://www.hindawi.com/journals/cmmm/.

Ullah, S., Higgins, H., Braem, B., Latre, B., Blondia, C., Moerman, I., Saleem, S., Rahman, Z., & Kwak, K. S. (2012). A comprehensive survey of wireless body area networks. *Journal of Medical Systems*, 36(3). Available from https://doi.org/10.1007/s10916-010-9571-3.

Varshney, U. (2006). Patient monitoring using infrastructure-oriented wireless LANs. *International Journal of Electronic Healthcare*, 2(2). Available from https://doi.org/10.1504/IJEH.2006.008829, http://www.inderscience.com/ijeh.

Yao, H. J. (2014). Wireless Body Area Network and its Health Applications. In *Microwave Conference Proceedings*, Asia Pacific, IEEE.

Yuce, M. R., & Khan, J. Y. (2011). *Wireless body area networks: Technology, implementation and applications.* Australia: Pan Stanford Publishing Pte. Ltd.. Available from http://www.panstanford.com/books/9789814241571.html, 10.4032/9789814241571.

Yuce, M.R., & Khan, J.Y. (n.d.) Wireless body area networks: Technology, implementation and applications.

Wireless body area networks for healthcare in smart hospital

Daniel Godfrey and Ki-Il Kim

Department of Computer Science and Engineering, Chungnam National University, Daejeon, Republic of Korea

14.1 Introduction

Wireless body area network (WBAN) is implemented as one ad hoc network which consists of wearable and implantable sensors strategically placed on or inside the human body. These sensors collaboratively collect and transmit vital physiological data wirelessly, forming a dynamic network that plays a pivotal role in healthcare, sports, and wellness applications (Bhatti et al., 2022; Yaghoubi et al., 2022). According to a study conducted by the World Health Organization, it is suggested that the rate of deaths caused by chronic diseases, such as diabetes, asthma, and heart-related illnesses is expected to increase by as much as 15% by the year 2030. Following that, the need for more medical systems and personnel is expected to increase significantly. Hence the a need for improved systems to monitor and detect the severity of health conditions. The recent advancement in the field of the Internet of Things (IoT) technology has made way for wide applications that involve monitoring of physical activities of medical specialists remotely and in some cases autonomously (Singh et al., 2020; Wu et al., 2019). The use of WBAN has seen a significant increase in recent years caused by the simultaneous increase of different types of wireless sensors that support varied types of IoT applications. Physiological medical information collected by wearable or implanted medical devices is designed to forward real-time medical data to a remote server or a sink node where medical personnel can use them to monitor a patient's health status and offer medical support. A good example of bio-signals collected can be blood pressure, heart rate, temperature, blood sugar level and electrocardiogram.

As compared to typical ad hoc and wireless sensor networks, WBANs have several characteristics that allow them to guarantee flexible and reliable medical monitoring in real-time such as:

Sensor Networks for Smart Hospitals
DOI: https://doi.org/10.1016/B978-0-443-36370-2.00015-3

- **Miniaturization and wear-ability:** One of the defining features of WBANs is their emphasis on miniaturization and wear-ability. These networks utilize tiny, lightweight sensors that can be comfortably worn or even implanted on the body. This miniaturization allows for unobtrusive integration, enabling continuous monitoring without disrupting the daily activities of the user (Majumder et al., 2019).
- **Real-time monitoring and medical applications:** WBANs enable continuous monitoring of crucial physiological parameters, that play a pivotal role in early disease detection and facilitate personalized patient care (Chen et al., 2010; Momoda & Hara, 2015). WBANs excel in providing real-time monitoring of vital medical information, making them well-suited for applications where immediate feedback is crucial. Whether in emergency response scenarios or sports performance analysis, WBANs enable ubiquitous monitoring, contributing to enhanced situational awareness and timely interventions.
- **Communication and networking:** Seamless communication among sensor nodes is achieved through the implementation of wireless communication technologies, specifically designed for short-range technologies such as Bluetooth, Zigbee, or ultra-wideband (UWB) (Preethichandra et al., 2023). Moreover, advanced routing protocols are required to build networks, recover link failures, maintain acceptable data transfer latency, and support a vast range of data rates to meet the necessary requirements to support multihops.
- **Energy-efficiency:** Given the inherent constraints of wearable devices, energy efficiency is of paramount concern in WBAN design. To address this challenge, low-power sensor nodes and energy-efficient communications protocols are implemented, extending the operational lifetime of devices and minimizing the need for frequent battery replacements (Guo & Syed, 2022).
- **Security and privacy:** As WBANs handle sensitive health data, robust security measures are of utmost importance. Encryption, authentication, and privacy-preserving techniques are integrated into WBAN protocols to safeguard against unauthorized access and protect patient confidentiality, ensuring the secure transmission of vital health information (Noor et al., 2021).

The latest advancements of WBAN play a key role in enhancing the quality of patients' lives through improvements in real-time monitoring, short response to medical emergencies, and reduction of both medical costs and the long operational hours of medical staff. Despite these benefits, applications in WBAN still face numerous challenges, such as security and privacy concerns, which have become major issues due to the sensitivity of the personal medical data collected. Unauthorized network attacks from intruders could lead to critical medical states for patients or even prove fatal. Beyond security challenges, WBANs encounter several other obstacles and concerns that can affect their normal operations. Interoperability issues among different WBAN devices and standards pose a significant challenge, impacting the well-coordinated functioning of sensor nodes. Moreover, power consumption remains a critical concern, necessitating innovative solutions to ensure prolonged device operation without frequent battery replacements. The complexity of managing the large-scale data generated by WBANs introduces challenges in data storage, processing, and interpretation, highlighting the need for robust frameworks for effective data management (Abiodun et al., 2019).

14.1.1 Standardization and overview of wireless body area networks communications

The IEEE 802.15.6 standard (IEEE standard for local and metropolitan area networks - Part 15.6: Wireless body area networks, 2012) supporting WBAN communication specifies the physical and the Medium Access Control (MAC) layers for short-range, low power and highly reliable wireless communication. To satisfy the application requirements of WBAN, this standard defines three physical layers which are; the narrowband (NB) to support seven frequency bands at different data rates, the UWB for simple and durable implementation at low power consumption and the human body communication (HBC) to support data transmission using the electric field communication technology.

The IEEE 802.15.6 standard describes WBAN as an integrated information technology infrastructure consisting of normal sensor nodes and a centralized sink node. WBAN adopts two types of communication topologies which can either be a single hop or a multihop communication type. In single-hop communication, data is transmitted directly from one sensor node to another without intermediate nodes. Each sensor node communicates directly with the sink node or another specific node within the network. Meanwhile, in multihop communication, data is relayed through multiple intermediate sensor nodes before reaching the sink node. Instead of communicating directly with the destination, a sensor node forwards data to its neighboring nodes until it reaches the desired destination.

Fig. 14.1 describes a scenario depicting applications of WBAN showing all its major components and its simplified communication architecture. There are generally three types of communication within the WBAN architecture:

- **Tier-1:** Intra-WBAN communication: refers to communication that occurs at the lowest level within the WBAN. It involves direct communication between sensor nodes located within the same WBAN on or around the body of an individual. Tier-1 Intra-BAN communication facilitates the exchange of data among nearby sensor nodes, enabling local information processing and coordination.

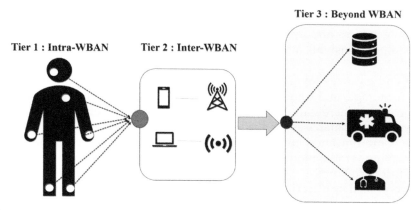

FIGURE 14.1   Simplified wireless body area network scenario.

- **Tier-2:** InterWBAN communication: refers to communication that occurs at a higher level within the WBAN architecture. It involves interactions between different WBANs or subnetworks within a larger WBAN system. This communication level may include the exchange of aggregated data, coordination between WBAN clusters, or the transmission of information between WBAN nodes and a central monitoring or control unit.
- **Tier-3:** Beyond WBAN communication: this layer encompasses all communication channels outside the WBAN network itself. This may include communication between WBAN nodes and external devices or systems, such as smartphones, personal computers, medical servers, or other networks (e.g., the Internet). Extra-communication enables data exchange between the WBAN and external entities for purposes such as data analysis, remote monitoring, or integration with broader healthcare systems.

In the diagram above, we see that wireless nodes distributed across the human body are connected to the end server or a wireless sink node in either a single or multihop manner. The entire architecture can be divided into five layers which are as follows:

- **Physiological sensors layer:** This layer comprises the physiological sensors deployed on or around the human body to collect various types of biological data. These sensors monitor vital signs such as heart rate, blood pressure, body temperature, oxygen saturation, and other physiological parameters relevant to healthcare monitoring. The physiological sensors layer forms the foundation of the WBAN network by capturing real-time health data from the individual.
- **Communication layer:** The layer facilitates the transmission of data collected by the physiological sensors to other nodes within the WBAN network. It includes wireless communication protocols and technologies that enable seamless data exchange between sensor nodes, coordinator nodes, and the sink node. Common communication technologies used in WBANs include Bluetooth, Zigbee, UWB, and others optimized for low-power, short-range communication.
- **Data processing layer:** This layer is responsible for aggregating, processing, and analyzing the data collected by the physiological sensors. This layer may include coordinator nodes or processing units within the WBAN network that perform tasks such as data fusion, anomaly detection, signal processing, and feature extraction. Data processing algorithms and techniques are applied to the collected physiological data to extract meaningful insights and derive actionable information for healthcare applications.
- **Sink node and gateway layer:** This particular layer serves as centralized points for data aggregation, storage, and transmission in the WBAN network. The sink node acts as a central repository where data from multiple sensor nodes is collected and forwarded to external systems or databases for further analysis. Gateway nodes may also be included to facilitate communication between the WBAN network and external networks or devices, enabling remote monitoring, data sharing, and integration with broader healthcare infrastructures.
- **External access and applications layer:** It enables interaction between the WBAN network and external entities, such as healthcare professionals, caregivers, or other healthcare systems. This layer encompasses interfaces, applications, and services that

allow authorized users to access WBAN data, monitor patient health status, provide interventions, and integrate WBAN data with electronic health records or telemedicine platforms External access may be facilitated through web portals, mobile apps, or dedicated healthcare software interfaces.

The structure of this chapter is divided into different parts, each describing a different part of WBAN technology. Section 14.1 gives a detailed introduction to WBANs, highlighting their fundamental principles and significance in healthcare applications. This section describes a scenario illustrating the application of WBANs in real-life scenarios. Following this, Section 14.2 provides an in-depth examination of advancements in WBAN protocols, encompassing the protocol stack of WBANs in the physical (PHY), MAC, and routing layers. Section 14.3 identifies emerging research trends and challenges for network layers in WBANs. It also discusses potential areas for future exploration and development. This section ends by highlighting the importance of addressing these research directions to further advance the field of WBANs and maximize their potential impact. Finally, this chapter concludes by presenting the key findings and insights presented in the chapter. It reflects on the evolution of WBAN technology and its transformative impact on healthcare and beyond while emphasizing the importance of ongoing research and collaboration to continue pushing the boundaries of WBAN innovation.

14.2 Advancement in wireless body area networks

As explained before, WBANs have undergone significant advancements across various aspects, contributing to their efficacy in healthcare, sports, and wellness monitoring. This section explores these advancements, focusing on the protocol stack, routing protocols, and innovative applications of WBAN technology. Defined in the 802.15.6 standard is the data link layer namely the MAC layer that supports the three PHY layers, the NB, UWB and the HBC layers as shown in Fig. 14.2.

The PHY layer which is the lowest layer of the architecture, deals with the physical attributes and measures bit error rate, probability of error and data rate. It is responsible for the transmission and reception of data, clear channel assessment and activation and

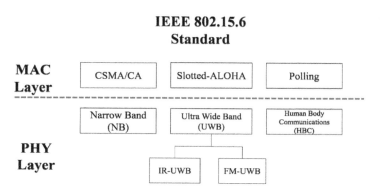

IEEE 802.15.6 Standard

FIGURE 14.2 IEEE 802.15.6 medium access control and physical layers.

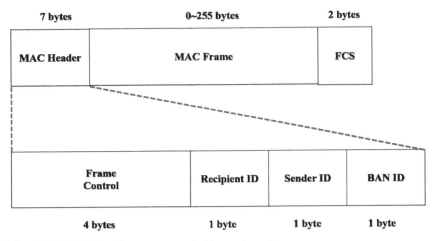

FIGURE 14.3   IEEE 802.15.6 medium access control frame format.

deactivation of the radio transceiver. Nodes in WBANs are organized into one or two hop star networks whereby a single coordinator controls the entire WBAN consisting of a number of nodes ranging from zero to mMaxBANSize nodes. The IEEE 802.15.6 standard also defines the MAC frame format, communication modes and access mechanisms of WBANs. Shown in Fig. 14.3, there is the 56-bit-sized message header frame format for MAC. This format has a variable length frame body of a maximum length of 255 octets and an 18-bit frame check sequence. The MAC header consists of an additional 32-bit frame control that carries frame type information such as beacon, acknowledgment, or other control frames, 8-bit recipient identification (ID) and 8-bit sender ID that carries address information of the recipient and the sender of the data frame, and finally, the 8-bit WBAN ID field that describes information on the WBANs in which the transmission is active.

14.2.1 Considerations in each layer

The protocol stack of WBANs is made up of the PHY and the MAC layers, which perform important roles in ensuring efficient communication and resource management within the network. Recent advancements in these layers have led to improved performance, reliability, and energy efficiency of WBANs.

- **PHY Layer:** Advancements in PHY include developments in modulation techniques, antenna designs, and transmission power control, enabling higher data rates, enhanced signal reliability, and reduced power consumption. These improvements are essential for supporting diverse sensor nodes and applications in WBANs.
- **MAC Layer:** The MAC layer governs access to the shared wireless medium and is responsible for coordinating communication between multiple sensor nodes in the network. Recent advancements in MAC protocols have focused on minimizing

contention and collision, optimizing channel access mechanisms, and supporting quality of service (QoS) requirements for different types of WBAN applications.

- **Network Layer:** The routing protocols designed for WBAN environments are critical for establishing efficient communication paths between sensor nodes and facilitating data exchange within the network. Advancements in routing protocols aim to address the unique characteristics and challenges of WBANs, such as limited energy resources, dynamic topology, and mobility. Such routing schemes can be divided into several groups based on the objective or the parameter of interest during optimization process. There are several routing protocol categorizations.
- **Energy-Efficient Routing:** New routing protocols prioritize energy efficiency by minimizing the energy consumption of sensor nodes during data transmission and routing operations. These protocols employ techniques such as duty cycling, data aggregation, and route optimization to prolong the operational lifetime of WBAN devices.
- **Reliable and Adaptive Routing:** Advanced routing protocols incorporate mechanisms for reliable data delivery and adaptability to changing network conditions. These protocols utilize dynamic routing metrics, route redundancy, and error recovery mechanisms to ensure robust communication and fault tolerance in WBANs.

14.2.2 Innovative applications of wireless body area networks technology

WBAN technology has seen innovative applications across various domains, including healthcare, sports, and wellness monitoring. These applications leverage the unique capabilities of WBANs to provide real-time data collection, analysis, and feedback, enabling personalized and proactive interventions.

- **Healthcare Monitoring:** WBANs are used for continuous monitoring of physiological parameters, early detection of health anomalies, and remote patient management. Applications include cardiac monitoring, fall detection, medication adherence tracking, and telemedicine services.
- **Sports Performance Analysis:** In sports and fitness, WBANs are employed to monitor athletes' biometric data, track movement patterns, and analyze performance metrics in real-time. These applications aid in optimizing training routines, preventing injuries, and enhancing athletic performance.
- **Wellness Monitoring:** WBANs support wellness monitoring initiatives by tracking individuals' activity levels, sleep patterns, and stress levels. Wearable WBAN devices provide users with insights into their lifestyle habits, promoting behavior modification and preventive healthcare practices.

14.3 Routing challenges in wireless body area networks

The common network topology for WBANs is a one-hop star network configuration due to their ease of management as well as implementation. However, there are some issues to be addressed for one-hop networks in the aspects of power consumption and

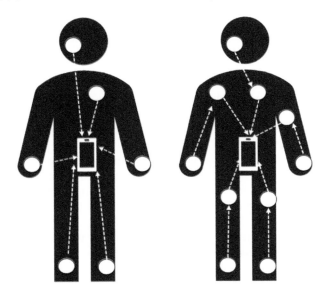

FIGURE 14.4 The type of wireless body area networks.

(A) Single-hop networks   (B) Multi-hop networks

network interference. To solve these problems, it is more feasible to introduce multihop networks where intermediate nodes relay data as shown in Fig. 14.4. As shown in Fig. 14.3, multihop networks are more scalable for the case of a large number of sensors through multiple paths (Kim et al., 2015). Furthermore, multihop networks are expected to extend network lifetime and reliability through less energy consumption and interference.

In multihop networks, a routing protocol is employed to decide the next hop. Unlike typical wireless networks, some important features such as limited bandwidth, battery and computing power in an implanted sensor node for WBANs demand different requirements in designing routing protocols. Also, network environments characterized by human motions. This indicates that previous general and typical ad hoc routing protocols cannot guarantee performance without any modification and changes. There are so many good comprehensive surveys and review papers for routing in WBANs. Most of them provide the categorization of current routing protocols and present comparisons of them in the aspects of benefits and disadvantages. Due to the strong dependency on the application, the selection of a routing protocol relies on the requirement of the application as well as supporting metrics in protocols. Among these approaches, in this chapter, we describe two key features for routing protocols in WBAN, that is, mobility and temperature awareness. In addition, we introduce feasible simulation tools for performance evaluation in WBAN.

14.3.1 Mobility models in wireless body area networks

The mobility model is the key constraint for protocol design for mobile ad hoc networks since it changes topology at a time. mobility of nodes causes frequent changes in the network topology, and this leads to link breakage and increases reinitiating of the route discovery process. But, in the opposite feature, mobility can improve throughput and provide multiple paths.

There are many mobility models (Camp et al., 2002) for typical ad hoc networks such as the random waypoint model. But, these models are designed for specific mobile patterns for humans. Thus, the new mobility model should be designed for human postural changes. As for this research, (Kim et al., 2017) presented a comprehensive survey paper for the mobility model. In this work, the mobility model is categorized as individual and group.

In addition to this general model, some specific mobility model for WBAN was suggested by Misra et al. (2015). In this work, they present a mobility model called random room mobility, which is used to capture the dynamics of WBAN user mobility within the building. This model is used to evaluate the performance of extra-WBAN communication to demonstrate its suitability for medical applications. In this model, a user is assumed to move within the building from one room to another by selecting random speed. This is very similar to the random waypoint model with pause time. However, the direction for the next movement is strictly limited to the one of rooms in the building. Fig. 14.5 shows the example of a patient movement in a hospital. According to the actions in each room, different staying times, that is, pause times are given. Another mobility model called the body Gauss—Markov mobility model (Liu et al., 2018) was presented for movement patterns that can reveal real human body movements by combining it model and the human mobility model. In this model, two patterns, a steady walking pace or a slow running speed, are assumed. Especially, for human walking, discrete four steps are modeled.

Based on the strong relationship between the mobility model and routing protocol, Singh et al. (2022) presented the experimental results for the impact of the mobility model on performance in routing protocol to achieve the appropriate value for diverse parameters in the routing protocols.

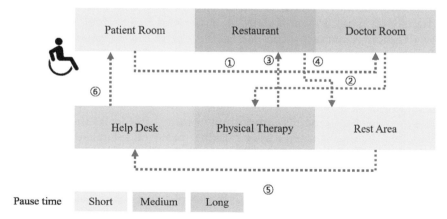

FIGURE 14.5   Example of user movement in a hospital.

14.3.2 Mobility-aware routing protocol in wireless body area networks

Mobility-aware routing protocols are designed to deal with topology changes due to movements in body posture. The basic procedure for mobility-aware protocol is to set the communication cost factor which determines the next hop for relay. Most of the approach is to predict the location of sensor nodes with mobility models. Research work till 2017 is well surveyed by Kim et al. (2017) so we address some important protocols and recent work.

In this research area, a novel Mobility Handling Routing Protocol (Karmakar et al., 2017) for WBAN was proposed as a representative approach. This approach makes use of human mobility through posture detection and ensures seamless connectivity for cardiac patients to deal with hand movement properly. Mobility-supporting adaptive threshold-based thermal-aware energy-efficient multi-hop protocol (Javaid et al., 2013) and its variants such as mobility threshold-based stability increased throughput to the sink using MultihoP routing protocol (M-TSIMPLE) (Navya & Deepalakshmi, 2017) were presented. These protocols build the tree structure by requesting a join procedure quickly whenever a node moves.

As an alternative scheme, multipath routing protocol (Akbar et al., 2022) can handle mobility issues in an appropriate way. In the proposed scheme, a sensor node establishes two paths, that is, primary and secondary. To achieve this, all nodes are supposed to have both radio frequency (RF) and body-coupled communication transceivers. The former is to transmit the normal data whereas the latter is for emergency data or in case of breakage of the primary path. The sensor node switches to another path according to failure and recovery.

Recently, machine learning technology has improved the mobility-supporting protocol for WBAN. These approaches make use of enhanced recognition of moving human body posture with machine learning technology. At first, a Posture Aware Dynamic Data Delivery (PA-DDD) protocol was presented by Goyal et al. (2021). It employs an improved initial Centroid K-means clustering technique for the classification of various human body postures to recognize human body posture. Another approach is to predict the forward node for homogeneous and heterogeneous configuration of the nodes through the Adam moment estimation (Adam) optimizer. Based on the results of output in the Adam network, the transmitting node sends data to either the forwarding node or sink node directly. The decision is made by comparing the energy of the predicted forward node with a predetermined value.

14.3.3 Thermal aware routing protocol in wireless body area networks

In addition to previous mobility-supporting routing protocols, the most outstanding feature of WBANs is the thermal-aware routing protocol (Shahzad, 2022). For a biomedical purpose and contains, each implanted sensor node in WBANS should prevent temperature rise which may cause damage to body tissues. To do this, routing protocol should be designed to make use of various available routes while avoiding temperature rise. Before discussing details for routing protocol for thermal aware features, it is demanded to review the amount of radiation power absorbed by the human tissue per unit of weight to measure harmfulness. Most of the research work for this is based on specific absorption rate (SAR) (Dewhirst et al., 2003) which is computed with the electrical conductivity of the tissue, E is the electric field induced by the radiation, and p is the tissue density. SAR indicates the rate at which radiation energy is absorbed by tissue per unit weight and computes the thermal change in human tissue (Yaghoubi et al., 2022).

$$SAR = \frac{\sigma |E|^2}{\rho} \, w/kg$$

The strong relationship between thermal exposure given in the equation (Yaghoubi et al., 2022) and damage indicates that heat delivery can lead to homogeneous normal tissues behaving in a heterogeneous way. Thus, it is very important to design a communication protocol to prevent the effect of temperature rise. Generally, the temperature rise of a sensor node is caused by the both activities of the radio transmitter/receiver of nodes during data exchange and their internal circuitry during data processing. This generated heat is likely to be harmful to the human body which is monitored through WBAN. There are some good research reviews and survey papers for thermal-aware routing protocol. In this chapter, we will describe the representative research work and recent work. Fig. 14.6 shows the categorization of existing protocol with metrics.

As shown in Fig. 14.6, thermal-aware routing protocols make use of either single or multiple metrics. Fundamentally, temperature of nodes is main metric to decide the relay node. But, total temperature of the route and RSSI level can be used as metric.

Thermal-aware routing algorithm (TARA) (Tang et al., 2005) is known as the first research work in this research area. The main procedure is to avoid the hotspot node whose temperature is higher than predetermined threshold value. To achieve this, a sensor node continuously measures the temperature itself as well as estimates the temperature of neighboring node. When a node receives a packet to the hotspot, it buffers it until the temperature of the hotspot node becomes below than threshold. If the hotspot node becomes

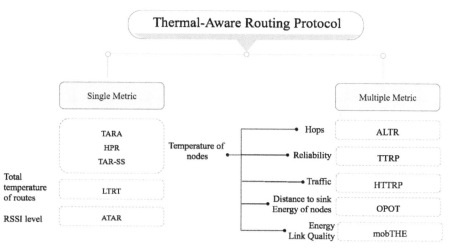

FIGURE 14.6 Categorization of thermal-aware routing protocol with a number of metrics.

normal, the packet is relayed. Otherwise, it is dropped. After TARA was proposed, variants and other protocols have been proposed to address temperature issues. One issue is to prevent the hotspot node instead of avoiding it. For this purpose, hotspot-preventing routing (HPR) (Bag & Bassiouni, 2008) was suggested to prevent the formation of hotspots through a threshold to control the temperature of nodes. In HPR, a path between source and destination is established by the shortest path algorithm. In the found path, if there is a hotspot node along the path, the packet is delivered to one of neighbors with the lowest temperature. To prevent hotspot nodes, HPR maintains the threshold that consists of hotspot nodes. A hotspot node is inserted into the threshold if it has a temperature higher than the mean of the temperatures of the transmitter and its neighbors. The main deficit of this type of protocol is a longer hop than the normal one to avoid the hotspot nodes. This problem contributes to developing a new routing protocol. Fig. 14.7 shows the different established paths in TARA and hotspot-preventing routing (HPR). Even though both schemes avoid the hotspot node successfully, a different path is selected according to the principle of hop and path-based selection.

The least total route temperature (LTRT) (Takahashi, 2008) was proposed to reduce the number of hops and temperature of nodes along the path instead of one of the next hops. The key feature of LTRT is to route packets along the path with the lowest temperature. This procedure is done by building the weighted graph with cost as a node's temperature. The Dijkstra's algorithm to find the lowest cost is accomplished. The shortest path is updated according to the variation of temperature repeatedly. However, LTRT can cause a short network lifetime since load balance is not considered at all. When it comes to hop count for temperature rise, it helps to reduce the number of hops between source and destination. As fewer nodes are along the path, heat generation in a whole network is achieved. A thermal aware routing protocol (ATAR) was suggested by Ghrfran et al. in Jamil (2019). focused on this balanced network by adjusting transmission power properly. More details, the transmission power is adjusted with the received signal strength indicator (RSSI) read from its neighbor.

Despite its advantage of thermal-aware routing protocol, single metric cannot deal with changes in networks environments such as human posture change. So, multiple metrics are employed for thermal-aware routing protocol (TARP). Basically, temperature of node

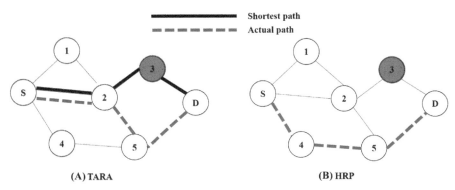

FIGURE 14.7   Comparison of path establishment in thermal-aware routing algorithm and HRP.

is one of metrics, however, different metrics were proposed to improve the performance. The example includes hop, reliability and traffic pattern. Moreover, metrics more than two also was considered as shown in Bouldjadj (2022).

The primary goal of thermal-aware routing algorithm based on traffic control (TRATC) (Maymand et al., 2017) was to reduce the temperature rise of nodes while controlling the network traffic in the proper level. To achieve this, TRATC employs two threshold values to manage traffic volume and temperature of nodes. The first threshold is for the temperature of a node. If the temperature of a node is less than this value, the next hop is selected according to the number of remaining hops and residual energy. Otherwise, a node controls the incoming traffic from the neighboring nodes. Secondly, if the temperature of a node increases beyond the second threshold in a case of failed traffic control, a node requests the neighbors to deliver packets along the shortest path. For this purpose, number of hops, temperature, and the energy of nodes are exchanged and used to choose the next hop. Optimum path optimum temperature routing protocol (OPOT) (Banuselvasaraswathy & Rathinasabapathy, 2020) operates like TRATC in that a next hop is chosen as a relay node from one of neighbors. OPOT is likely to choose the relay node with the minimum distance to the sink, low temperature and high residual energy. In addition to these three metrics, OPOT supports three traffic classes as well as priorities. By combination of class and priority, if the temperature of node is greater than predetermined value, it forwards the high priority paths. Otherwise, it concerns routing for all traffics.

Heat generation problem in intrabody nanonetworks (IBN) that focus on the nanosensors in the Terahertz (THz) band was addressed in Javaheri (2021). In this work, the authors have proposed a temperature-aware routing protocol (TA-IBN) by excluding data collection through the hotspots area. In addition, data freshness to report more accurate information is concerned. This approach contributes to reducing antenna radiation exposure time. To demonstrate better performance than the existing scheme, the nano-SIM tool is used for evaluation.

14.3.4 Recent thermal-aware routing protocol in wireless body area networks

Recently, TARPs tend to improve the performance by employing several processing technologies such as fuzzy logic and optimization technology. Fuzzy logic has been widely used for many research areas in wireless sensor networks. In Alakhras et al. (2020), it is proved that localization can be improved through fuzzy logic to solve challenging issues for position in wireless sensor networks. Also, another outstanding research area to use fuzzy logic is clustering. Fuzzy logic can be the solution for clustering by accomplishing one of the following purposes, that is, cluster header selection, fuzzy logic combined algorithm, fuzzy logic for energy harvesting and fuzzy logic using reliability for clustering (Verma et al., 2023). Fuzzy logic for security-awareness and fuzzy logic routing for other types of wireless sensor networks are suggested as future research challenges. In addition to the two research areas above, routing is the most popular research area to utilize fuzzy logic as studied by Maryem et al. (2020). Due to many constraints such as energy consumption and network lifetime, fuzzy logic is the most useful scheme to implement routing protocol in wireless sensor networks.

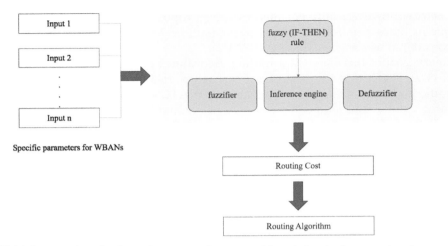

FIGURE 14.8 Procedure for thermal-aware routing protocol for wireless body area networks.

Like typical wireless sensor networks, a fuzzy logic-based routing protocol for WBANs has been recently proposed. Fuzzy logic can be combined with TARP which is based on decision with measured metrics that is imprecise and nonnumerical information. Fig. 14.8 shows how to use fuzzy logic for TARP. Several parameters specified for WBANs are input for fuzzy interference system while quantitative cost is output. Based on this output value, routing algorithm decides the next hop.

As an example of a recent fuzzy logic thermal-aware routing protocol, a new scheme called temperature-aware routing protocol based on fuzzy logic (TARPFL) was proposed by Suh et al. (2023). The authors have chosen temperature, buffer occupancy and Received Signal Strength (RSS) for this routing protocol with current and expected values. Unlike most existing schemes that take current value in this category, expected values in the next period are considered. Retransmission of lost packet can lead to temperature rise on a node, RSS value belongs to expected value. By combining these three values in a three level, twenty-seven fuzzy rules are listed. According to this rule, if the link is ranked as "ACCEPTABLE," it is chosen as next hop. In addition, if the multiple links are considered, one of links in the possible set is randomly selected.

A swarm intelligence multiobjective fuzzy protocol was proposed to introduce a swarm intelligence multiobjective fuzzy logic in Aryai et al. (2023a). It consists of two components, that is, a fuzzy inference system (FIS) and automatic rule tuning using a whale optimization algorithm (WOA). In the FIS, input includes residual energy, distance, reliability, bandwidth, temperature, path loss and estimation energy consumption while the output does the next hop node. Also, Mamdani's rules of the FIS are automatically tuned with the mentioned WOA.

While the previous two protocols target efficient routing in one WBAN, the authors have proposed a new fuzzy logic-based and thermal-aware clustering and routing scheme for multiWBANs in Javaid (2023). In this work, fuzzy logic controller is employed for clustering with temperature of cluster head, number of similar neighbors, number of neighbors, remaining energy and path loss. After cluster header is chosen for one WBANs, interWBANs communication is accomplished between each header.

In addition to fuzzy logic, several intelligent algorithms have been continually applied into thermal-aware routing protocol for WBANs. We will explain some research work in the category. First, priority-based energy-efficient, delay and temperature aware routing algorithm (PEDTARA) was proposed by Ahmed et al. (n.d.). It is fundamentally based on Multiobjective genetic chaotic spider monkey optimization (MGCSMO) and the incorporation of both chaotic and genetic operators for prioritized routing process. It aims for two types of data packets such as normal and emergency transmission. According to the type of data, three different routing algorithms are chosen. For example, optimal shortest path routing for normal data is chosen while energy-efficient emergency routing for high-priority critical data is employed. In this process, traffic priority routing includes temperature factors for node selection. Also, evaluation results reveal that PEDTARA outperforms rather than traditional approach in the aspects of several metrics such as temperature and network lifetime.

14.3.5 Further research challenges in the network layer in wireless body area networks

We have described the multihop networks and specific routing protocols for WBANs. Until now, routing protocols have attracted many researchers' interests by adapting traditional protocols in a way of considering specific features of WBANs. However, there are some issues to be addressed and mentioned.

- **Multiobjective Routing Protocols:** As compared with single objective routing protocol, multiobjective routing protocol aim to provide the most suitable route by taking into requirements account. Reliability, energy efficiency, network lifetime, and other QoS are well-known requirement. To consider and attempt optimization for multiobjective, machine learning can be good approach. Some research work introducing Q-learning algorithm in Aryai et al. (2023b) and Bedi et al. (2022) has continuously proposed. But, network architecture and appropriate machine learning algorithms should be developed.
- **Secure Routing Protocol:** Sensed value in WBANs is related to personal information so it is essential to preserve privacy for that. Some research work such as (Roshini & Kiran, 2023) has been proposed to address this issue. However, due to computing and energy limitations, current schemes need to be revised to achieve low-cost goals by considering lightweight communication approach.
- **Network Architecture:** Most of the research work for routing protocol has been developed under flat architecture. However, it is known that the hierarchical approach has benefits in the aspects of energy consumption. However, it also has the disadvantage of complexity to construct and maintain the cluster architecture. This is very crucial for the sensor node for energy and temperature. In addition to this traditional approach, Software Defined Networks (SDN) for WBANs (Hasan et al., 2020; Masood et al., 2024) has attracted many researchers recently. It can provide traffic engineering functions for WBANs and enable to implement intelligent routing.

- **Performance Evaluation:** Most of the research work was evaluated through simulation (Liu et al., 2021; Sharma et al., 2022). Even though some modules for WBANs in network simulators such as NS-3 and OMNET++ have been released, they are not enough for accurate evaluation due to important missing components such as mobility models for gesture. Thus, it is the best option to develop a new WBANs simulator which provides a specific model for features of WBANs in MAC and PHY layers. Furthermore, it is more desirable to implement the real model and evaluate it.

14.4 Conclusions

In this chapter, we provided a comprehensive survey for WBAN to implement healthcare applications in smart hospitals. Due to outstanding features for network environments, communication protocols should be designed and developed by considering them. Among them, we focused on a routing protocol for WBANs. Specially, two routing protocols, mobility and thermal-aware routing protocol have been introduced and explained. Finally, some remaining research challenges have been suggested for further research trends. Even though four issues have been addressed, there are still open issues to be studied in this research area.

Acknowledgment

This work was supported by Institute for Information & communications Technology Planning & Evaluation (IITP) grant funded by the Korea government (MSIT)(No.RS-2022-II221200, Convergence security core talent training business(Chungnam National University)) and the Basic Science Research Program through the National Research Foundation of Korea (NRF) funded by the Ministry of Education under Grant RS2023-00237300

References

Abiodun, A. S., Anisi, M. H., & Khan, M. K. (2019). Cloud-based wireless body area networks: Managing data for better health care. *IEEE Consumer Electronics Magazine, 8*(3). Available from https://doi.org/10.1109/mce.2019.2892244.

Ahmed, O., Hu, M., & Ren, F. (no date) PEDTARA: Priority-based energy efficient, delay and temperature aware routing algorithm using multi-objective genetic chaotic spider monkey optimization for critical data transmission in WBANs.

Akbar, S., Mehdi, M. M., Jamal, M. H., Raza, I., Hussain, S. A., Breñosa, J., Espinosa, J. C. M., Barrera, A. E. P., & Ashraf, I. (2022). Multipath routing in wireless body area sensor network for healthcare monitoring. *Healthcare, 10*(11), 2297. Available from https://doi.org/10.3390/healthcare10112297.

Alakhras, M., Oussalah, M., & Hussein, M. (2020). A survey of fuzzy logic in wireless localization. *Eurasip Journal on Wireless Communications and Networking, 2020*(1). Available from https://doi.org/10.1186/s13638-020-01703-7, http://www.springerlink.com/content/1687-1499/.

Aryai, P., Khademzadeh, A., Jafarali Jassbi, S., & Hosseinzadeh, M. (2023a). SIMOF: Swarm intelligence multi-objective fuzzy thermal-aware routing protocol for WBANs. *Journal of Supercomputing, 79*(10). Available from https://doi.org/10.1007/s11227-023-05102-9, https://www.springer.com/journal/11227.

Aryai, P., Khademzadeh, A., Jafarali Jassbi, S., Hosseinzadeh, M., Hashemzadeh, O., & Shokouhifar, M. (2023b). Real-time health monitoring in WBANs using hybrid metaheuristic-driven machine learning routing protocol (MDML-RP). *AEU - International Journal of Electronics and Communications, 168*. Available from https://doi.org/10.1016/j.aeue.2023.154723, http://www.elsevier.com/aeue.

Bag, A., & Bassiouni, M. A. (2008). Hotspot preventing routing algorithm for delay-sensitive applications of in vivo biomedical sensor networks. *Information Fusion*, 9(3). Available from https://doi.org/10.1016/j.inffus.2007.02.001.

Banuselvasaraswathy, B., & Rathinasabapathy, V. (2020). Self-heat controlling energy efficient OPOT routing protocol for WBAN. *Wireless Networks*, 26(5). Available from https://doi.org/10.1007/s11276-020-02303-5.

Bedi, P., Das, S., Goyal, S. B., Shukla, P. K., Mirjalili, S., & Kumar, M. (2022). A novel routing protocol based on grey wolf optimization and Q learning for wireless body area network. *Expert Systems with Applications*, 210. Available from https://doi.org/10.1016/j.eswa.2022.118477, https://www.journals.elsevier.com/expert-systems-with-applications.

Bhatti, D. S., Saleem, S., Imran, A., Iqbal, Z., Alzahrani, A., Kim, H. J., & Kim, K.-I. (2022). A survey on wireless wearable body area networks: A perspective of technology and economy. *Sensors*, 22(20), 7722. Available from https://doi.org/10.3390/s22207722.

Bouldjadj, S. (2022). Thermal aware routing protocols for wireless body area networks: Review and open research issues. *Karbala International Journal of Modern Science*, 8(3). Available from https://doi.org/10.33640/2405-609X.3244, https://kijoms.uokerbala.edu.iq/cgi/viewcontent.cgi?article = 3244&context = home.

Camp, T., Boleng, J., & Davies, V. (2002). A survey of mobility models for ad hoc network research. *Wireless Communications and Mobile Computing*, 2(5). Available from https://doi.org/10.1002/wcm.72.

Chen, H., Wu, W., & Lee, J. (2010). A WBAN-based real-time electroencephalogram monitoring system: Design and implementation. *Journal of Medical Systems*, 34(3). Available from https://doi.org/10.1007/s10916-008-9242-9.

Dewhirst, M.W., Viglianti, B.L., Lora-Michiels, M., Hoopes, P.J., & Hanson, M. (2003). Thermal dose requirement for tissue effect: Experimental and clinical findings. In *Proceedings of SPIE - The international society for optical engineering*, United States (pp. 37–57). 10.1117/12.476637.

Goyal, R., Patel, R. B., Bhaduria, H. S., & Prasad, D. (2021). An efficient data delivery scheme in WBAN to deal with shadow effect due to postural mobility. *Wireless Personal Communications*, 117(1). Available from https://doi.org/10.1007/s11277-019-06997-5, http://www.springerlink.com/content/0929-6212.

Guo, K., & Syed, S. A. S. (2022). Energy efficiency based lifetime improvement for wireless body area network. *IET Communications*, 16(7). Available from https://doi.org/10.1049/cmu2.12381, https://ietresearch.onlinelibrary.wiley.com/journal/17518636.

Hasan, K., Ahmed, K., Biswas, K., Saiful Islam, M., & Ameri Sianaki, O. (2020). Software-defined application-specific traffic management for wireless body area networks. *Future Generation Computer Systems*, 107. Available from https://doi.org/10.1016/j.future.2020.01.052, https://www.journals.elsevier.com/future-generation-computer-systems.

IEEE Standard for local and metropolitan area networks (2012). Part 15.6: Wireless body area networks, IEEE std, 802.

Jamil, F. (2019). *Adaptive thermal aware routing protocol for wireless body area network*.

Javaheri, D. (2021). Temperature-aware routing protocol for intrabody nanonetworks. *Journal of Network and Computer Applications*, 2021.

Javaid, N., Abbas, Z., Fareed, M. S., Khan, Z. A., & Alrajeh, N. (2013). M-ATTEMPT: A new energy-efficient routing protocol for wireless body area sensor networks. *Procedia Computer Science*, 19. Available from https://doi.org/10.1016/j.procs.2013.06.033.

Javaid, S. (2023). A new energy-efficient and temperature-aware routing protocol based on fuzzy logic for multi-WBANs. *Ad Hoc Networks, Ad Hoc Networks*, 2023.

Karmakar, K., Biswas, S., & Neogy, S. (2017). MHRP: A novel mobility handling routing protocol in wireless body area network. In *Proceedings of the 2017 international conference on wireless communications, signal processing and networking, WiSPNET 2017* (pp. 1939–1945). Institute of Electrical and Electronics Engineers Inc., India. 10.1109/WiSPNET.2017.8300099.

Kim, B.-S., Kim, K., & Kim, K.-I. (2017). A Survey on Mobility Support in Wireless Body Area Networks. *Sensors*, 17(4), 797. Available from https://doi.org/10.3390/s17040797.

Kim, T.Y., Youm, S., Jung, J.J., & Kim, E.J. (2015). Multi-hop WBAN construction for healthcare IoT systems. In *Proceedings - 2015 International Conference on Platform Technology and Service, PlatCon 2015*. Institute of Electrical and Electronics Engineers Inc. South Korea 10.1109/PlatCon.2015.20. 9781479918881 27 28.

Liu, Q., Mkongwa, K. G., & Zhang, C. (2021). Performance issues in wireless body area networks for the healthcare application: a survey and future prospects. *SN Applied Sciences*, 3(2). Available from https://doi.org/10.1007/s42452-020-04058-2, springer.com/snas.

Liu, Y., Liu, D., & Yue, G. (2018). BGMM: A body gauss-markov based mobility model for body area networks. *Tsinghua Science and Technology, 23*(3). Available from https://doi.org/10.26599/TST.2018.9010005, http://ieeexplore.ieee.org/xpl/RecentIssue.jsp?punumber = 5971803.

Majumder, S., Mondal, T., & Deen, M. J. (2019). A simple, low-cost and efficient gait analyzer for wearable healthcare applications. *IEEE Sensors Journal, 19*(6). Available from https://doi.org/10.1109/JSEN.2018.2885207, http://ieeexplore.ieee.org/xpl/RecentIssue.jsp?punumber = 7361.

Maryem, M., Abdelghani, E.O., & Belkassem, T. (2020). Routing in wireless sensor networks using fuzzy logic: A survey. In *2020 International Conference on Intelligent Systems and Computer Vision, ISCV 2020*. Institute of Electrical and Electronics Engineers Inc., Morocco http://ieeexplore.ieee.org/xpl/mostRecentIssue.jsp?punumber = 9199645. 10.1109/ISCV49265.2020.9204318. 9781728180410.

Masood, F., Khan, W. U., Alshehri, M. S., Alsumayt, A., & Ahmad, J. (2024). Energy efficiency considerations in software-defined wireless body area networks. *Engineering Reports, 6*(3). Available from https://doi.org/10.1002/eng2.12841, https://onlinelibrary.wiley.com/journal/25778196.

Maymand, L., Ayatollahitafti, V., & Gandomi, A. (2017). Traffic control thermal-aware routing in body area networks. *Journal of Soft Computing Decision Support Systems*, 2017.

Misra, S., Mahapatro, J., Mahadevappa, M., & Islam, N. (2015). Random room mobility model and extra-wireless body area network communication in hospital buildings. *IET Networks, 4*(1). Available from https://doi.org/10.1049/iet-net.2014.0009, http://digital-library.theiet.org/content/journals/iet-net.

Momoda, M., & Hara, S. (2015). A cooperator-assisted wireless body area network for real-time vital data collection. *Eurasip Journal on Wireless Communications and Networking, 2015*(1). Available from https://doi.org/10.1186/s13638-015-0459-2, http://www.springerlink.com/content/1687-1499/.

Navya, V., & Deepalakshmi, P. (2017). Mobility supported threshold based stability increased throughput to sink using multihop routing protocol for link efficiency in wireless body area networks (M-TSIMPLE). In *Proceedings of the 2017 IEEE International Conference on Intelligent Techniques in Control, Optimization and Signal Processing, INCOS 2017* (pp. 1–7). Institute of Electrical and Electronics Engineers Inc. India 10.1109/ITCOSP.2017.8303107.

Noor, F., Kordy, T. A., Alkhodre, A. B., Benrhouma, O., Nadeem, A., & Alzahrani, A. (2021). Securing wireless body area network with efficient secure channel free and anonymous certificateless signcryption. *Wireless Communications and Mobile Computing*, 2021. Available from https://doi.org/10.1155/2021/5986469, https://www.hindawi.com/journals/wcmc/.

Preethichandra, D. M. G., Piyathilaka, L., Izhar, U., Samarasinghe, R., & De Silva, L. C. (2023). Wireless body area networks and their applications—A review. *IEEE Access, 11*. Available from https://doi.org/10.1109/ACCESS.2023.3239008, http://ieeexplore.ieee.org/xpl/RecentIssue.jsp?punumber = 6287639.

Roshini, A., & Kiran, K. V. D. (2023). Hierarchical energy efficient secure routing protocol for optimal route selection in wireless body area networks. *International Journal of Intelligent Networks, 4*. Available from https://doi.org/10.1016/j.ijin.2022.11.006.

Shahzad, Y. (2022). IoT based thermal aware routing protocols in wireless body area networks: Survey: IoT based thermal aware routing in WBAN. *IET Communications*, 2022.

Sharma, S., Tripathi, M.M., & Mishra, V.M. (2022). Comparative analysis of routing protocols in wireless body area network (WBAN). In *Proceedings of 2nd international conference on innovative practices in technology and management, ICIPTM 2022*. Institute of Electrical and Electronics Engineers Inc., India. http://ieeexplore.ieee.org/xpl/mostRecentIssue.jsp?punumber = 9752773. 10.1109/ICIPTM54933.2022.9754202. 9781665466431 703 706.

Singh, R., Sinha, S., Anand, S., & Sen, M. (2020). Wireless body area network: An application of IoT and its issuses—A survey. *Advances in Intelligent Systems and Computing, 1120*, 285–293. Available from https://doi.org/10.1007/978-981-15-2449-3_24, http://www.springer.com/series/11156.

Singh, S., Prasad, D., Rani, S., Singh, A., Alharithi, F. S., & Almotiri, J. (2022). Wireless body area routing protocols impact analysis on entity mobility models with static sink node. *Applied Sciences (Switzerland), 12*(11). Available from https://doi.org/10.3390/app12115655, https://www.mdpi.com/2076-3417/12/11/5655/pdf?version = 1654164365.

Suh, B., Kim, H. J., Lim, B., Shah, B., & Kim, K. I. (2023). Design of fuzzy logic based-temperature-aware routing protocol. *Open Public Health Journal, 16*(1). Available from https://doi.org/10.2174/18749445-v16-230818-2022-159, https://openpublichealthjournal.com/contents/volumes/V16/e187494452307200/e187494452307200.pdf.

Takahashi, D. (2008). Temperature aware routing for telemedicine applications in embedded biomedical sensor networks. *EURASIP Journal of Wireless Communications Networks*, 2008.

Tang, Q., Tummala, N., Gupta, S. K. S., & Schwiebert, L. (2005). TARA: Thermal-aware routing algorithm for implanted sensor networks. *Lecture Notes in Computer Science, 3560*, 206−217. Available from https://doi.org/10.1007/11502593_17, http://www.springeronline.com/sgw/cda/frontpage/0,11855,4-40356-69-1180994-0,00.html.

Verma, S., Bhatia, S., Zeadally, S., & Kaur, S. (2023). Fuzzy-based techniques for clustering in wireless sensor networks (WSNs): Recent advances, challenges, and future directions. *International Journal of Communication Systems, 36*(16). Available from https://doi.org/10.1002/dac.5583, http://onlinelibrary.wiley.com/journal/10.1002/(ISSN)1099-1131.

Wu, F., Wu, T., & Yuce, M. R. (2019). An Internet-of-Things (IoT) network system for connected safety and health monitoring applications. *Sensors, 19*(1), 21. Available from https://doi.org/10.3390/s19010021.

Yaghoubi, M., Ahmed, K., & Miao, Y. (2022). Wireless body area network (WBAN): A survey on architecture, technologies, energy consumption, and security challenges. *Journal of Sensor and Actuator Networks, 11*(4). Available from https://doi.org/10.3390/jsan11040067, http://www.mdpi.com/journal/jsan.

Internet of medical things for accurate and sustainable medical decision making in heart disease management

Philippe Ea, Osman Salem and Ahmed Mehaoua

Center Borelli UMR 9010, Université Paris Cité, Paris, France

15.1 Introduction

The evolution of healthcare technology has witnessed transformative shifts, with the integration of the Internet of Things (IoT) into medical applications marking a significant milestone. The synergy of healthcare and IoT has given rise to the Internet of Medical Things (IoMT). This paradigm leverages interconnected devices and sensors to enhance patient care, monitor health parameters, and streamline medical processes (Razdan & Sharma, 2022; Srivastava et al., 2022).

As technological advancements accelerated, medical devices became smarter and more interconnected, paving the way for IoMT to revolutionize the healthcare landscape. IoMT encompasses a diverse array of devices, ranging from wearable fitness trackers and vital sign monitors to implantable sensors and smart medical imaging systems (Pradhan et al., 2021).

At its core, IoMT is founded on the seamless integration of medical devices and data-driven technologies, facilitating real-time monitoring, data collection, and analysis. This interconnected ecosystem has proven instrumental in preventive healthcare, remote patient monitoring, and the development of intelligent diagnostic tools (Baskar et al., 2020). However, the evolving nature of healthcare challenges necessitates continuous advancements in IoMT to ensure the delivery of efficient and accurate healthcare services (Zeadally et al., 2020).

Sensor Networks for Smart Hospitals
DOI: https://doi.org/10.1016/B978-0-443-36370-2.00016-5

In this context, our research delves into the application of machine learning (ML) and deep learning (DL) techniques within the IoMT framework for the detection of heart disease. Cardiovascular diseases, including heart disease, remain a leading cause of mortality worldwide, underscoring the critical need for effective diagnostic tools (Ciumărnean et al., 2022; Vogel et al., 2021). In recent years, the integration of ML and DL techniques into healthcare has presented an encouraging avenue for improving diagnostic accuracy. This study focuses on leveraging these advancements to develop a robust model for heart disease detection, with a keen focus on addressing the challenges of data privacy, noise introduction, and the intricacies of model updates.

Medical sensors, often integrated into wearable devices, play an important role in modern healthcare. These sensors, ranging from electrocardiograms (ECGs) to blood pressure monitors, provide a continuous stream of physiological data. Leveraging this wealth of information, our study seeks to develop models capable of real-time heart disease detection. For instance, an ECG sensor can capture the electrical activity of the heart, offering valuable insights into cardiac health. Blood pressure monitors, pulse oximeters, and other medical sensors contribute additional dimensions to the dataset, enriching the diagnostic potential of our models.

One persistent challenge in dynamic medical data analysis is the phenomenon of catastrophic forgetting. This occurs when a model trained on one set of data significantly degrades its performance when presented with new or updated information (Ebrahimi et al., 2021). Our approach aims to mitigate this challenge by incorporating model updates. These updates, driven by techniques like elastic weight consolidation (EWC) for DL models and warm start for traditional ML models, facilitate continuous learning without compromising prior knowledge. By doing so, our models adapt to evolving data distributions while retaining their proficiency in diagnosing heart disease.

In envisioning a practical deployment of our approach, we introduce the concept of a personal area network (PAN). This network integrates various medical sensors into a unified, user-centric system. Unlike traditional monitoring approaches that require constant human oversight, our PAN operates autonomously, continuously collecting and processing health-related data. Importantly, the PAN prioritizes data security by avoiding external data transfers, ensuring that sensitive health information remains localized to the individual.

Moreover, this commitment to data privacy empowers the inclusion of highly personalized features in the PAN. We anticipate the integration of such features sourced from a user's PAN. These features may include physiological signals, lifestyle information, and contextual data. For instance, a sensor capturing sleep patterns or stress levels could provide additional layers of information, contributing to a holistic understanding of an individual's health.

Furthermore, the PAN is designed to proactively raise alerts in cases where the collected data suggests potential signs of heart disease. This ensures that users are promptly notified of any concerning health indicators. Users receiving such alerts can then seek timely medical attention, enhancing the proactive nature of our healthcare solution.

This research makes several noteworthy contributions to the field of dynamic medical data analysis and personalized healthcare:

- We present robust ML and DL models for heart disease detection, addressing challenges related to noise introduction, and the issue of catastrophic forgetting. Our models, particularly random forest (RF), extra trees (ET), and gradient boosting (GB), consistently demonstrate superior performance.

- To tackle the challenge of catastrophic forgetting, we introduce a strategy for continuous learning through model updates.
- We also propose the concept of a PAN. It operates autonomously, ensuring continuous data collection and processing while prioritizing data security by avoiding external data transfers. This concept lays the foundation for user-centric and privacy-focused healthcare solutions.
- Our approach facilitates the inclusion of personalized features. These features encompass physiological signals, lifestyle information, and contextual data, providing a holistic view of an individual's health. The PAN's proactive alert system enhances user safety by notifying individuals of potential signs of heart disease, prompting timely medical attention.

In summary, this study endeavors to advance cardiovascular disease diagnosis through the integration of medical sensors, ML and DL models, and a user-centric PAN. By addressing challenges such as catastrophic forgetting, ensuring data security, and incorporating personalized features, we aim to contribute to the evolution of dynamic medical data analysis and redefine the landscape of personalized healthcare.

15.2 Related work

In recent years, the application of ML and DL techniques in healthcare has garnered significant attention due to their potential to transform medical diagnosis and treatment. This section provides an overview of the existing literature.

The integration of ML in healthcare has witnessed remarkable strides, contributing to the development of intelligent diagnostic tools and personalized treatment strategies. Numerous studies have explored the efficacy of ML algorithms in analyzing medical data. DL, with its ability to automatically extract intricate features from complex datasets, has demonstrated great performance in tasks such as medical image analysis, disease prediction, and treatment recommendation.

Khanam et al. compared several ML models to detect diabetes on a dataset of 768 patients (Khanam & Foo, 2021). Among the seven models compared, logistic regression (LR) and support vector machine (SVM) obtained commendable results, with accuracies of around 78%. Notably, a customized neural network algorithm achieved an impressive accuracy of 88.57%, showcasing the potential of DL.

Another work by Saru et al. focused on diabetes as well (Saru & Subashree, 2019). They applied a bootstrapping resampling technique to enhance the accuracy of the decision tree (DT). They got an accuracy of 94.4% and a miss rate of 5.6%. Ahmed et al. worked on the same dataset and introduced a fused ML approach combining SVM and artificial neural network (ANN), leveraging the strength of both algorithms (Ahmed et al., 2022). The proposed method reached an improved accuracy of 94.87% and a miss rate of 5.13% only.

The potential of DL is further demonstrated by Butt et al., who implemented multilayer perceptron (MLP) and long-short-term memory (LSTM) (Butt et al., 2021). They obtained accuracies of 86.08% and 97.26%, respectively, surpassing traditional methods like RF, which achieved 77.4%.

In the context of heart disease, Li et al. proposed a heart disease identification technique using a fast conditional mutual information feature selection algorithm (Li et al., 2020). They used a dataset containing features such as age, chest pain, blood pressure, thallium, etc. Their proposed approach achieved an accuracy of 92.37% and outperformed other existing methodologies.

Kavitha et al. used a hybrid ML algorithm (Kavitha et al., 2021). They combined RF and DT to perform predictions on a heart disease dataset and managed to surpass both RF and DT when used individually with an accuracy of 88.7%.

Advanced techniques are also explored in the healthcare domain. Chen et al. proposed the utilization of federated learning (FL) along with cyclic knowledge distillation (Chen et al., 2023). This methodology allows them to include further personalized features as data privacy is guaranteed. On seven benchmark datasets, their framework showcased improved accuracies, with scores approximately 10% higher overall.

Another work analyzed the potential of graph neural networks (GNN) (Kwak et al., 2020). Kwak et al. compared their GNN models with other algorithms to study adverse drug reactions. In their graph, nodes represent medical codes, while the edges represent the relationship between them. The implementation resulted in an enhanced Area Under the Receiver Operating Characteristic (AUROC) curve performance of 0.795.

In the context of dynamic data, where models need to adapt to changes over time, incremental learning (IL) strategies become imperative. IL addresses the challenges associated with catastrophic forgetting and enables models to adapt to new information without compromising past knowledge. Such techniques have been widely used, even outside the medical field.

For instance, Chen et al. investigated the Bayesian generative regularization (BGR) to overcome catastrophic forgetting (Chen, 2021). By combining generative and discriminative loss, they demonstrate the efficacy of their approach in comparison to multiple state-of-the-art approaches. On one of the tested datasets, BGR outperformed other methods by more than 15%.

In a similar vein, Shi et al. tackled the problem in incremental few-shot learning (Shi et al., 2021). Their approach involves searching for flat local minima of the base training objective function, which is then used to fine-tune the model's parameters. Through multiple training and testing sessions, their methodology consistently outperformed others, achieving slightly higher accuracies in most sessions.

The synthesis of these diverse elements forms the foundation for our research. Our study builds upon these concepts, aiming to contribute novel insights into the domain of heart disease detection within the dynamic and interconnected landscape of IoMT.

15.3 Proposed approach

A healthcare dataset from Ramakrishnan is used to conduct our study (Ramakrishnan, 2019). It is associated with several significant global public health concerns such as hypertension, stroke, and heart disease. In this study, our target feature will be heart disease.

This dataset contains various other features, including clinical measures such as average glucose level or body mass index (BMI). Features related to lifestyle such as smoking status or work type are also present, providing interesting information.

First, before using our models, we performed thorough data preprocessing by removing instances with undefined values. Moreover, we resampled the classes to balance them. These steps help us to ensure the readiness of our data for our models by reducing the potential presence of bias in their predictions.

After these preparations, we can train and test our models. We partitioned our dataset into two sets using a 60/40 split ratio. The first one is used for initial training and testing of the models, while we will introduce noise into the second one to simulate new data and update our models. A fivefold cross-validation is applied to ensure the robustness of each model and to mitigate the risk of overfitting, meaning the risk that our model will learn too much specific insight from the training data.

We carefully selected ML and DL models, each chosen for their ability to perform IL on new unseen data without having to start learning from scratch each time. The classifiers adopted are LR, RF, ET, GB, MLP, ANN, convolutional neural network (CNN), and LSTM. This diverse set of algorithms takes advantage of unique strengths and characteristics to contribute to a complete analysis and an in-depth comparison.

15.3.1 Gamma distribution

Additionally, we explored data augmentation techniques using the 40% subset, as we recognize the paramount need for a diverse dataset to fortify our models' robustness and capabilities of generalization when confronted with unseen data. Our primary emphasis was on a crucial numerical feature—the average glucose level. This value holds pivotal importance as it is usually monitored in most health problem research, owing to its well-established correlations with cardiovascular health. To introduce controlled noise into the data, we opted for the gamma distribution with $k = 2$ and $\theta = 2$. This selection was steered by its propensity to model nonnegative, right-skewed data as we can see in Fig. 15.1.

The gamma distribution for a random variable x, with a specific shape k and scale θ parameters, offers a flexible probability density function detailed in the following equation:

$$f(x;k,\theta) = \frac{1}{\theta^k \cdot \Gamma(k)} \cdot x^{k-1} \cdot e^{-\frac{x}{\theta}}$$

$\Gamma(k)$ represents the gamma function evaluated at the value k. For all positive integers k, it is defined as follows: $\Gamma(k) = (k-1)!$

Given that the distribution of $\Gamma(2,2)$ is mostly centered around small values, it provided us with the opportunity to add minor variations while also allowing for the potential introduction of outliers. For each row in the remaining 40% of the preprocessed dataset, we generated a random number from the $\Gamma(2,2)$ distribution. Subsequently, we calculated the mean and standard deviation of the average glucose level for each class. Finally, we updated the original value of each sample by adding the product of the standard deviation and the generated number to the mean average glucose level for the corresponding class. The whole process is summarized in the following equation where μ and σ represent the

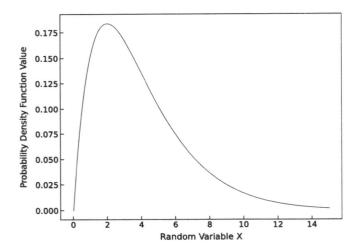

FIGURE 15.1   Probability density function of the gamma (2, 2) distribution the graph illustrates the probability density of a random variable following the gamma distribution with shape parameter 2 and scale parameter 2.

mean and standard deviation of the average glucose level for the corresponding class respectively, while Rand is the random number generated from the $\Gamma(2, 2)$ distribution:

$$\text{New Average Glucose Level} = \mu + (\sigma \times \text{Rand})$$

This meticulous process not only introduced realistic variations in the average glucose level values but also included potential outliers. These new and unseen data will be used to update our models through IL. This step ensures the adaptability of our models to changing data distributions and the evolution of the medical landscape. We will also be able to strengthen our models against outliers. We employed distinct IL strategies for DL models and traditional ML models.

15.3.2 Elastic weight consolidation

For our DL models, which include CNN and LSTM, we implemented the EWC technique. EWC is a regularization method that is designed to enable models to retain previously acquired knowledge while learning new tasks, preventing the issue of catastrophic forgetting. In our implementation, we start by obtaining the model weights before the new training task. Then we compute the gradients of the previous loss about these weights. These gradients represent the sensitivity of the model's parameters to the previous task. In the final step, we compute the importance scores based on the squared gradients. These scores indicate the most influential model parameters for preserving past knowledge. The EWC loss term is defined as follows:

$$\text{EWC}_\theta = \sum_i \frac{1}{2} \cdot \text{Squared Gradient}(\theta_i)(\theta_i - \theta_{\text{old}_i})^2$$

Here, EWC_θ represents the EWC loss, θ_i is the current model weights, θ_{old_i} is the previous model weights and SquaredGradient(θ_i) quantifies the sensitivity of θ_i to changes. By adding the EWC loss to the primary loss during training, our DL models effectively balance the acquisition of new knowledge with the retention of previous task information, resulting in adaptive and robust models.

15.3.3 Warm start

For our traditional ML models, we employed a warm start approach to update them. Warm start initialization involves initializing these models with previously learned weights and hyperparameters from the original training. This strategy offers benefits for traditional models when updating them with new data because it allows them to begin training from a point close to their previous state. In a warm start, the model's initial parameter values are set based on the knowledge acquired from previous training. For instance, the weights in LR or the decision boundaries in tree-based models like RF are initialized to values that are likely to be close to the optimal ones for the new task. The warm start strategy is particularly effective when the tasks share similar feature spaces or underlying patterns. The impact of these advantages is observed in the accelerated convergence and improved performance of the models, making it a valuable technique in our approach.

This combination of EWC for DL models and warm start for traditional ML models ensures that our models can efficiently adapt to changes in the data distribution and learn from new data, enabling them to provide reliable medical decision support.

15.3.4 Feature reduction

Moreover, to further improve our models, we intend to conduct a similar process of updating our models. However, in this second experiment, we incorporate a feature selection process into the mix, offering an additional layer of refinement to our IoMT system. We employ the recursive feature elimination with cross-validation (RFECV) technique. It plays a key role in optimizing each model's feature set, making them more efficient in processing medical data and improving their generalization capabilities. RFECV operates as a strategic tool for determining the most relevant features within our dataset. It recursively fits a model and evaluates it using cross-validation. During this process, the importance of each feature is ranked, and the least informative ones are removed at each iteration. The goal is to find the optimal subset of characteristics that results in the highest accuracy for the model used. The advantages of RFECV are multiple. First, it helps prevent overfitting by only retaining the most informative features, reducing noise, and improving the generalization to unseen data. Second, by focusing on a reduced feature set, our models can perform more efficiently, making them well-suited for real-time decision-making tasks. This dimensionality reduction can lead to more lightweight sensors or data capture devices, for example, making them more user-friendly and efficient for healthcare practitioners. Furthermore, with less data to analyze, our models can provide quicker and more responsive decisions, securing timely responses in case of emergencies.

In summary, our models, comprising DL and traditional ML, are initially trained and tested on a healthcare dataset. However, to introduce variability and simulate real-world variations, we explore data augmentation into a key feature: the average glucose level, which is essential in heart disease management. By carefully using the gamma distribution, we introduce controlled noise and create unseen data containing outliers. Subsequently, we employ EWC and warm start techniques to update the models with these new data efficiently. Furthermore, we attempt to improve the model efficiency through RFECV, simplifying model designs and potentially allowing lightweight data capture. This holistic approach aims to empower healthcare professionals and everyday users with versatile and effective IoMT technologies for decision support.

15.4 Experimental results

15.4.1 Exploratory data analysis

We begin our study with an exploration of the dataset, which serves as the basis for our investigations. It contains a collection of features, each potentially delivering insights into heart disease management. These features include:

- **Sex:** The gender for each individual.
- **Age:** Age is a widely recognized factor in heart disease risk.
- **Hypertension:** The presence or absence of hypertension, synonymous with high blood pressure.
- **Ever married:** Whether the person ever got married.
- **Work type:** The occupation of individuals may influence their daily activity level and standard of living.
- **Residence type:** Urban and rural environments can offer different lifestyle patterns and access to healthcare.
- **Average glucose level:** Elevated glucose levels are usually associated with diabetes.
- **BMI:** BMI is a measure of body fat based on height and weight.
- **Smoking status:** Whether or not the person has ever smoked.
- **Stroke history:** Stroke history can provide insight into a person's overall cardiovascular health.
- **Heart disease:** Our target variable, indicates whether an individual has heart disease. Understanding the factors contributing to this label is the primary goal of our research.

With these features, we can explore their contributions to heart disease prediction and also facilitate the development of understandable models. We carefully balanced our classes to have approximately 5000 samples in each of them and guarantee the robustness of our models.

Continuing our analysis, we examine the distributions of key features among individuals with and without heart disease. The kernel density estimation (KDE) plots, in Figs. 15.2 and 15.3, illustrate these distributions for BMI and average glucose levels respectively. KDE provides a smoothed representation of the underlying data distribution. The density on the y-axis is a measure of how densely the data points are distributed across different values of the feature. It indicates the likelihood of encountering a data point with

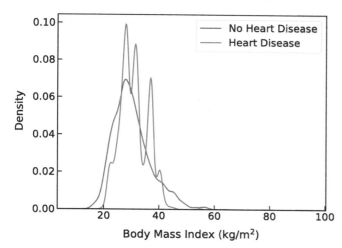

FIGURE 15.2 Body mass index (BMI) distribution per class the distribution of BMI across different classes, providing insights into its variability and potential correlations with heart disease risk.

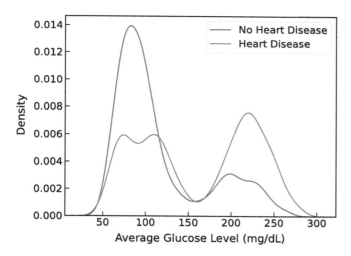

FIGURE 15.3 Average glucose level distribution per class the distribution of average glucose level across different classes, providing insights into its variability and potential correlations with heart disease risk.

a specific feature value. Peaks on the KDE plot represent highly concentrated data, while lower areas suggest sparser regions.

Essential knowledge can be gained regarding the variations in these characteristics among people with and without heart disease. As illustrated in Fig. 15.2, we observe that BMI tends to center around 30 kg/m² for individuals in good health. Intriguingly, for individuals with heart disease, the KDE plot for BMI shifts slightly higher, centering around a value above 30. Moreover, it displays a narrower distribution, suggesting that individuals with heart disease tend to have less variability in BMI compared to those without heart disease. This subtle shift and reduced variability in BMI may constitute interesting diagnostic information and avenues for our models.

In Fig. 15.3, we observe that a striking contrast emerges in the distribution of average glucose levels. Significantly, we can discern a pronounced bimodal distribution for both individuals with and without heart disease. The initial peak, spanning between 60 and 110 mg/dL, typically corresponds to normal glucose levels according to the World Health Organization's guidelines (World Health Organization, 2023). Conversely, the second peak, centered around 180 and 250 mg/dL, frequently indicates individuals with diabetes. This stark difference in glucose level distributions between the two classes emphasizes the potential connection between heart disease and diabetes. Indeed, the prominence of the second peak, representing higher average glucose levels, among individuals with heart disease implies a possible association between elevated glucose levels and heart disease. Consequently, this underscores the importance of vigilant glucose level monitoring, particularly for individuals with heart disease, as elevated glucose levels may serve as an indicator of heightened risk.

Furthermore, our analysis of feature importance for the RF model, provided in Fig. 15.4, reveals the powerful role that average glucose levels play in its decision-making process. This visualization helps us gauge the importance of each feature within our dataset. Although we only present the feature importance for the RF model, it is important to stress that most models displayed similar rankings, albeit with minor variations in feature significance values. We observe that both average glucose levels and BMI emerge as highly influential factors for the RF model, with corresponding importance scores of approximately 36% and 27%. This emphasis on average glucose levels motivated our decision to introduce gamma-distributed noise into this feature, recognizing its central role in predicting heart disease risk. In contrast, the remaining features have importance scores below 10%. For instance, the gender of the individual, work type, and residence type demonstrate limited to negligible significance in influencing the RF model's decisions.

Our main goal is to evaluate the effectiveness of our proposed approach, which combines data augmentation, model updates, and feature selection. As explained in the preceding section, we first split our dataset into a 60/40 ratio. The first subset served as the

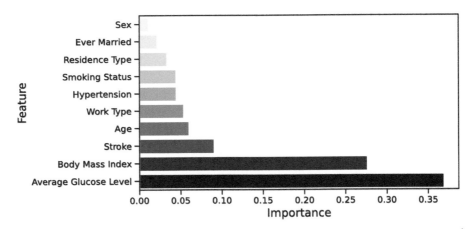

FIGURE 15.4 Feature importance for random forest (RF) model analysis of feature importance for the RF model.

basis for training and testing the performance of our models. Then, we introduced noise in the average glucose level within the remaining 40% of the original dataset, following a $\Gamma(2,2)$ distribution. This second subset underwent a two-step evaluation: an initial test using the pretrained models, followed by model updates using EWC for DL models and warm start for ML models. During our experimentation, we used a fivefold cross-validation to consolidate our results. Beyond these steps, we investigated the influence of feature selection by conducting identical experiments with RFECV to assess its impact on the performance of our models.

15.4.2 Evaluation metrics

Now we can move forward to the presentation of our results. Several evaluation metrics are used to perform a complete assessment of the efficiency of each model:

- **Accuracy:** Represents the fraction of true predictions. It serves as a fundamental measure of overall model performance. This metric can be misleading when dealing with imbalanced datasets, however, this is not the case here.

$$\text{Accuracy} = \frac{\text{True Positives} + \text{True Negatives}}{\text{Total Predictions}}$$

- **Precision:** Measures the accuracy of positive predictions by calculating the fraction of positive predictions that are indeed correct. It quantifies how exact a model is when it labels an individual as a heart disease victim.

$$\text{Precision} = \frac{\text{True Positives}}{\text{True Positives} + \text{False Positives}}$$

- **Recall:** Evaluates the ability of a model to capture all positive instances by computing the ratio of all actual positive examples that the model correctly predicts. In essence, it assesses how effectively a model avoids missing instances of heart disease.

$$\text{Recall} = \frac{\text{True Positives}}{\text{True Positives} + \text{False Negatives}}$$

- **F1-score:** Combines both precision and recall to provide a balanced measure. It is particularly robust when dealing with imbalanced datasets where one class significantly outweighs the other. In our study, the f1-score provides an overall assessment of a model's accuracy in detecting heart disease while minimizing errors. A classifier can only achieve a high f1-score if both its precision and recall are high.

$$\text{F1} - \text{score} = 2 \cdot \frac{\text{Precision} \cdot \text{Recall}}{\text{Precision} + \text{Recall}}$$

- **Area Under the Receiver Operating Characteristic (ROC) Curve (AUC):** The ROC curve plots the false positive rate against the true positive rate across multiple threshold values. The AUC represents the area under this curve and operates as an effective measure of overall model performance. A higher AUC indicates superior model performance in distinguishing between the presence and absence of heart disease.

- **Training time and single prediction time:** Measure the total time needed to train and predict a single instance, respectively. It is imperative to achieve fast processing times, as we aim for quick solutions for IoMT devices. Therefore, a balance between accuracy and speed is crucial.

15.4.3 Results without feature reduction

Throughout this section, diverse figures and tables are displayed to provide detailed insights into our research. Figs. 15.5–15.7 depict the ROC curves obtained from our models using the original features. A detailed numerical analysis of the performance of each model can be found in Table 15.1.

Our investigation begins with the examination of ROC curves, which offer a visual overview of the efficiency of each model. In Fig. 15.5, illustrating results from the baseline test using original data, RF and ET models emerge as standout classifiers, boasting

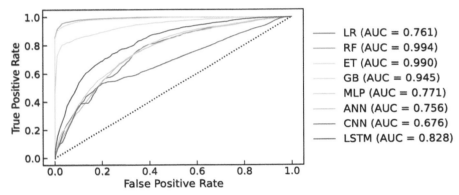

FIGURE 15.5   Basic classification illustration of the receiver operating characteristic curves obtained initially.

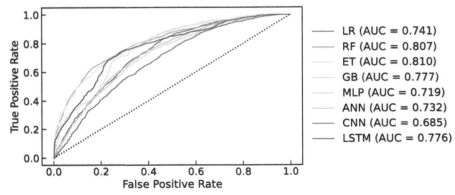

FIGURE 15.6   Test on augmented data before incremental learning (IL) illustration of the receiver operating characteristic curves obtained on augmented data before IL.

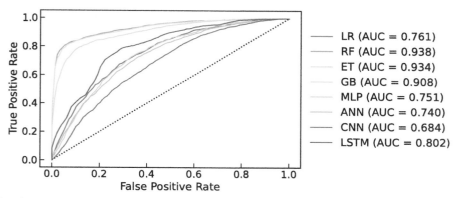

FIGURE 15.7 Test on augmented data after incremental learning (IL) illustration of the receiver operating characteristic curves obtained on augmented data after IL.

impressive AUC values of 0.994 and 0.99, respectively. GB follows closely with a great AUC of 0.945. However, DL models show relatively underwhelming performance, with AUC scores mainly below 0.8.

Then we test these trained models with the new data where $\Gamma(2, 2)$ noise is included in the average glucose level. We can immediately see in Fig. 15.6 that the ROC curves are mostly gathered around the same area. The models that were performing well were significantly lower. For instance, RF, ET, and GB lost more than 0.15 in their AUC scores which are only around 0.8 now. All the other models are displaying more or less worse ROC curves too.

However, updating the models through the warm start for ML classifiers and EWC for DL ones improved the results as depicted in Fig. 15.7. Our three best models so far: RF, ET, and GB, came back to extremely satisfying results with scores higher than 0.9. DL models have not shown any spectacular improvement after the update, even if their AUC values still increased a little. Once again, they do not seem to be as reliable as the three ones cited previously.

Table 15.1 confirms these observations. Indeed, we can observe the exceptional performance of RF and ET during the initial testing, performed without any feature reduction. Their metrics are remarkable, all exceeding 0.95. After the update, while their performance slightly lowered by approximately 0.1 in each metric, they still stood as the most reliable classifiers. An intriguing aspect of our findings is the trade-off between precision and recall, which allows us to take note of some important insights. Some models, such as CNN postupdate, achieve a recall score of 0.99 on the augmented data, demonstrating their proficiency in identifying actual positive instances. However, we can note that precision and accuracy scores are only at 0.5. Therefore, half of the cases predicted as positive are, in fact, false positives. This means that these models tend to classify most cases as positive. Such behavior could be problematic in real-life situations. For example, misclassifying a healthy patient as having heart disease is a scenario best avoided. Thus, achieving well-balanced metrics is imperative in this critical domain. Finally, we also witness the significance of updating the models. The overall performance of all the classifiers declined when confronted with the augmented data, but increased after updating with warm start or EWC.

TABLE 15.1   Comparison of results obtained without feature reduction.

Model	Accuracy	Precision	Recall	F1-score	AUC
LR	0.69	0.69	0.71	0.70	0.761
	0.57	0.53	0.98	0.69	0.741
	0.69	0.68	0.72	0.70	0.761
RF	0.96	0.98	0.94	0.96	0.994
	0.75	0.79	0.68	0.73	0.807
	0.87	0.88	0.84	0.86	0.938
ET	0.95	0.97	0.93	0.95	0.990
	0.74	0.77	0.68	0.72	0.810
	0.86	0.85	0.86	0.86	0.934
GB	0.88	0.90	0.85	0.87	0.945
	0.71	0.66	0.81	0.73	0.777
	0.83	0.83	0.83	0.83	0.908
MLP	0.71	0.68	0.77	0.72	0.771
	0.55	0.52	0.99	0.68	0.719
	0.69	0.68	0.70	0.69	0.751
ANN	0.69	0.71	0.66	0.67	0.756
	0.50	0.50	0.99	0.66	0.732
	0.65	0.61	0.84	0.70	0.740
CNN	0.65	0.63	0.71	0.66	0.676
	0.50	0.50	0.99	0.66	0.685
	0.50	0.50	0.99	0.66	0.684
LSTM	0.75	0.76	0.74	0.75	0.828
	0.66	0.61	0.87	0.72	0.776
	0.73	0.72	0.74	0.73	0.802

Note: For each model, the first row displays the initial results, the second row showcases the test results of the trained models on augmented data, and the third row illustrates the test results on the augmented data after retraining.

15.4.4 Results with feature reduction

After reviewing the results on the original dataset, we will examine the outcomes of our experiments after employing RFECV for dimensionality reduction. Figs. 15.8–15.10 present ROC curves generated using the reduced feature set, offering insights into the performance of each model in this context. Additionally, the breakdown of numerical performance metrics can be found in Table 15.2.

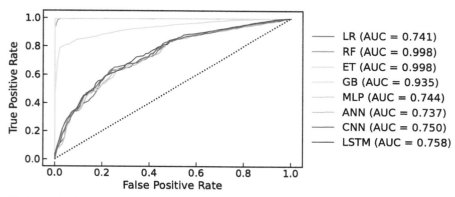

FIGURE 15.8   Basic classification with recursive feature elimination with cross-validation (RFECV) illustration of the receiver operating characteristic curves obtained initially with RFECV.

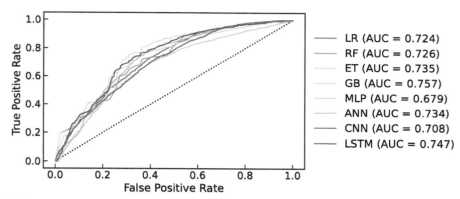

FIGURE 15.9   **Test on augmented data with recursive feature elimination with cross-validation (RFECV) before incremental learning** (IL). Illustration of the receiver operating characteristic curves obtained on augmented data with RFECV before IL.

In our study, we performed RFECV with the RF model as the underlying model for feature selection. This technique resulted in the creation of a reduced dataset containing only three crucial features besides our target feature: average glucose level, BMI, and the presence of a stroke. This is not surprising as these features were the most relevant, as showcased in Fig. 15.4. The use of RFECV with the RF model not only simplified the dataset but also retained the most influential features, thereby simplifying the modeling process and improving interpretability.

In Figs. 15.8–15.10, the ROC curves demonstrate a certain degree of consistency with the initial results obtained without RFECV, albeit with some minor fluctuations. Fig. 15.8 highlights two models that stand out: RF and ET. Both of them showcase exceptional discriminatory ability with an AUC score of 0.998. GB follows closely with an AUC of 0.935, while the remaining models tend to cluster in a similar performance range. When evaluating performance on the augmented data, in Fig. 15.9, a notable performance decline is

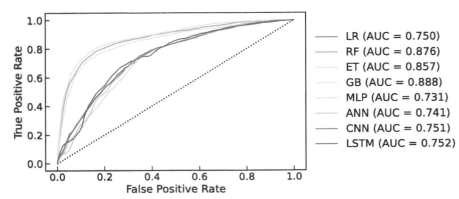

FIGURE 15.10   Test on augmented data with recursive feature elimination with cross-validation (RFECV) after incremental learning (IL). Illustration of the receiver operating characteristic curves obtained on augmented data with RFECV after IL.

apparent once again. In this context, GB and LSTM outperform the other models with an AUC score exceeding 0.745. Subsequently, upon updating the classifiers, RF, ET, and GB display performance improvement, as shown in Fig. 15.10. However, this enhancement is insufficient to restore their original efficiency on the initially reduced data, as emphasized in Table 15.2. Considering the RFECV-based feature selection approach, ET and RF initially emerged as the top-performing models on the original data, consistently achieving all metrics at 0.98 or 0.99. However, postupdate, GB surpasses them, achieving an AUC of 0.888 and performance metrics around 0.8. Thus, while RFECV aids in improving efficiency on the base data, it results in lower performance on the data augmented with noise in comparison to the baseline approach without feature reduction.

In addition to all these evaluations, we must consider the computational efficiency of these models. This will be particularly useful for real-time applications. Figs. 15.11 and 15.12 provide insights into the time efficiency of each model used for both training and predictions. For the training times, it is evident that MLP and LSTM have longer training times, superior to 1.5 seconds, in their initial training on the full dataset. In contrast, other models like LR, ANN, and CNN tend to be more time-efficient during training. However, we saw previously that their performance is not that good which makes this computational efficiency quite irrelevant. Our three best models, RF, ET, and GB display an average training time of around 1 second.

Remarkably, when applying RFECV, there is a significant reduction in training times. The reduced dataset results in more efficient training without sacrificing model performance in the case of RF and ET on original data as we saw in Table 15.2. This is particularly advantageous when time constraints are a concern. When we look at the training times after applying RFECV, we observe that the gap between different models narrows significantly and the overall training times are under 0.5 seconds except for MLP and LSTM. This demonstrates the usefulness of feature selection in reducing computational complexity, making it an attractive option for real-time or resource-constrained applications. These observations also apply to training times during updates when implementing

TABLE 15.2 Comparison of results obtained with recursive feature elimination with cross-validation.

Model	Accuracy	Precision	Recall	F1-score	AUC
LR	0.67	0.67	0.67	0.67	0.741
	0.56	0.53	0.98	0.69	0.724
	0.69	0.66	0.76	0.71	0.750
RF	0.98	0.98	0.99	0.98	0.998
	0.62	0.68	0.40	0.51	0.726
	0.81	0.80	0.80	0.80	0.876
ET	0.99	0.98	0.99	0.99	0.998
	0.68	0.69	0.64	0.66	0.735
	0.79	0.78	0.79	0.78	0.857
GB	0.87	0.90	0.85	0.87	0.935
	0.68	0.62	0.89	0.73	0.757
	0.82	0.81	0.82	0.81	0.888
MLP	0.66	0.72	0.58	0.62	0.744
	0.62	0.58	0.82	0.68	0.679
	0.68	0.66	0.69	0.67	0.731
ANN	0.67	0.64	0.78	0.70	0.737
	0.60	0.55	0.96	0.70	0.734
	0.64	0.59	0.90	0.71	0.741
CNN	0.67	0.72	0.55	0.60	0.750
	0.53	0.51	0.99	0.67	0.708
	0.68	0.64	0.79	0.70	0.751
LSTM	0.68	0.70	0.64	0.66	0.758
	0.56	0.52	0.97	0.68	0.747
	0.70	0.67	0.77	0.72	0.752

Note: For each model, the first row displays the initial results, the second row showcases the test results of the trained models on augmented data, and the third row illustrates the test results on the augmented data after retraining.

our proposed approach. The update times display similar variations as the basic training. Notably, using RFECV yields faster update times, which is consistent with our analysis.

When examining the time required for single predictions, as depicted in Fig. 15.12, we see a similar pattern. The models show variations in prediction time, with some being more efficient than others. Notably, DL models such as ANN, CNN, and LSTM necessitate more time for predictions, exceeding 0.1 milliseconds. Conversely, LR, GB, and MLP can

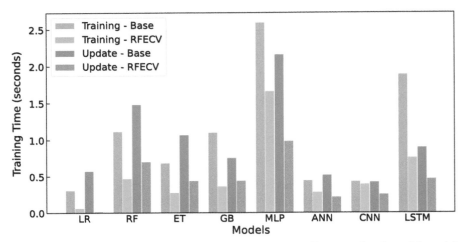

FIGURE 15.11   **Training and updating time for our models.** Time efficiency of each model used for training and updates.

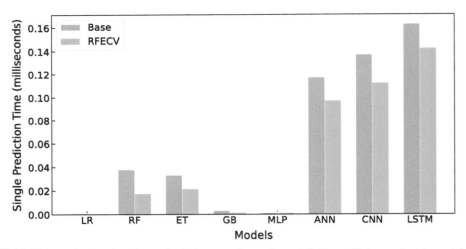

FIGURE 15.12   **Prediction time for a single instance for each model.** Time efficiency of each model used for predictions.

produce nearly instantaneous results. RF and ET slightly require more time for predictions. Once again, the application of RFECV results in decreased processing times for all models, further cementing the benefits of dimensionality reduction. The reduced set of features is responsible for a minor decrease in the computational time required for each prediction in models such as RF, ET, ANN, CNN, and LSTM. This can be of utmost importance in situations where quick decisions are necessary, as is often the case in medical diagnosis.

Our findings underscore the importance of considering not only the predictive accuracy of models but also their efficiency in terms of training and test times. RFECV presents itself as a valuable strategy, as it leads to more time-efficient training and testing. Although the performance using RFECV deteriorated further postupdate compared to the baseline approach, the efficiency of RF and ET preupdate is superior. However, the update still enabled our models to enhance their performance as fresh augmented data was incorporated.

15.5 Conclusion

Throughout our study, we explored various techniques to identify a model capable of assisting healthcare professionals in diagnosing heart disease. We aimed to establish a classifier that could maintain superior performance, sustainability, and resistance to potential data alterations, such as those resulting from the introduction of noise following a $\Gamma(2, 2)$ distribution in the average glucose levels. We also compared the speed of the models tested to determine the fastest ones.

During our experiments, three models emerged: RF, ET, and GB. Except for when RFECV was used with augmented data, the first two models consistently obtained extremely high results and were the top performers overall during the study. However, in that specific scenario, GB achieved better results with an AUC score of 0.888 and metrics around 0.8. Before the update, both RF and ET obtained AUC scores higher than 0.990 whether RFECV was used or not. Without RFECV, they still showcased an impressive performance after the update, with AUC scores exceeding 0.93.

One noticeable trend in our results is the relatively inferior performance of DL models when compared to traditional ML models. The size of our dataset might be a key factor contributing to this discrepancy. Typically, DL models perform better on larger datasets, and our outcomes emphasize the significance of having abundant data to unlock their complete potential. Nevertheless, privacy regulations make it a challenging task to gather a substantial amount of high-quality medical data.

The frequency of model updates raises important considerations as well, especially in dynamic domains like healthcare. Overly frequent updates may lead to overfitting or instability, while infrequent updates could result in models missing critical changes in data distribution. Balancing the update schedule to ensure optimal model performance remains a vital area of investigation. It is worth noting that several frequent updates, if not well-controlled, might lead to a gradual degradation in prediction accuracy and the phenomenon of catastrophic forgetting. Conversely, complete retraining from scratch may have drawbacks too. Significant shifts in data distribution or the emergence of new information could necessitate this process. The balance between update frequency and retraining is an important aspect that still has to be studied.

Eventually, we aimed to develop an approach suitable for deployment on an IoT device dedicated to individual users. This device would enable local data processing, eliminating the need to transfer sensitive information to external entities. Therefore, in a personalized health monitoring scenario, we envision the potential incorporation of additional and highly individualized features sourced from a user's PAN. These features may encompass private data such as physiological signals, lifestyle details, and contextual knowledge. This research serves as a foundational step toward realizing the vision of localized, user-centric healthcare technology. As we move ahead, exploring the potential value of these personalized features and their integration into the current models is a promising direction for revolutionizing the field of dynamic medical data analysis.

References

Ahmed, U., Issa, G. F., Khan, M. A., Aftab, S., Khan, M. F., Said, R. A. T., Ghazal, T. M., & Ahmad, M. (2022). Prediction of diabetes empowered with fused machine learning. *IEEE Access, 10*. Available from https://doi.org/10.1109/access.2022.3142097.

Baskar, S., Mohamed Shakeel, P., Kumar, R., Burhanuddin, M. A., & Sampath, R. (2020). A dynamic and interoperable communication framework for controlling the operations of wearable sensors in smart healthcare applications. *Computer Communications, 149*. Available from https://doi.org/10.1016/j.comcom.2019.10.004.

Butt, U. M., Letchmunan, S., Ali, M., Hassan, F. H., Baqir, A., & Sherazi, H. H. R. (2021). Machine learning based diabetes classification and prediction for healthcare applications. Hindawi limited, Malaysia. *Journal of Healthcare Engineering, 2021*. Available from https://doi.org/10.1155/2021/9930985, http://www.hindawi.com/journals/jhe/contents/.

Chen, P.H. et al. (2021). *Proceedings of machine learning research*.

Chen, Y., Lu, W., Qin, X., Wang, J., & Xie, X. (2023). MetaFed: Federated learning among federations with cyclic knowledge distillation for personalized healthcare. *IEEE Transactions on Neural Networks and Learning Systems*. Available from https://doi.org/10.1109/TNNLS.2023.3297103, http://ieeexplore.ieee.org/xpl/RecentIssue.jsp?punumber = 5962385.

Ciumărnean, L., Milaciu, M. V., Negrean, V., Orăşan, O. H., Vesa, S. C., Sălăgean, O., Iluţ, S., & Vlaicu, S. I. (2022). Cardiovascular risk factors and physical activity for the prevention of cardiovascular diseases in the elderly. *International Journal of Environmental Research and Public Health, 19*(1), 207. Available from https://doi.org/10.3390/ijerph19010207.

Ebrahimi, S., Petryk, S., Gokul, A., Gan, W., Gonzalez, J. E., Rohrbach, M., & Darrell, T. (2021). Remembering for the right reasons: Explanations reduce catastrophic forgetting. *Applied AI Letters, 2*(4). Available from https://doi.org/10.1002/ail2.44.

Kavitha, M., Gnaneswar, G., Dinesh, R., Sai, Y.R., & Suraj, R.S. (2021). Heart disease prediction using hybrid machine learning model. In *Proceedings of the 6th international conference on inventive computation technologies, ICICT 2021* (pp. 1329−1333). <http://ieeexplore.ieee.org/xpl/mostRecentIssue.jsp?punumber = 9358464>, https://doi.org/10.1109/ICICT50816.2021.9358597.

Khanam, J. J., & Foo, S. Y. (2021). A comparison of machine learning algorithms for diabetes prediction. *ICT Express, 7*(4). Available from https://doi.org/10.1016/j.icte.2021.02.004, https://www.journals.elsevier.com/ict-express/.

Kwak, H., Lee, M., Yoon, S., Chang, J., Park, S., & Jung, K. (2020). Drug-disease graph: predicting adverse drug reaction signals via graph neural network with clinical data. *Lecture notes in computer science (including subseries lecture notes in artificial intelligence and lecture notes in bioinformatics)* (pp. 633−644). https://www.springer.com/series/558, https://doi.org/10.1007/978-3-030-47436-2_48.

Li, J. P., Haq, A. U., Din, S. U., Khan, J., Khan, A., & Saboor, A. (2020). Heart disease identification method using machine learning classification in E-healthcare. *IEEE Access, 8*. Available from https://doi.org/10.1109/ACCESS.2020.3001149, http://ieeexplore.ieee.org/xpl/RecentIssue.jsp?punumber = 6287639.

Pradhan, B., Bhattacharyya, S., & Pal, K. (2021). IoT-based applications in healthcare devices. *Journal of Healthcare Engineering, 2021*. Available from https://doi.org/10.1155/2021/6632599, http://www.hindawi.com/journals/jhe/contents/.

Ramakrishnan, A. (2019). *Healthcare dataset stroke data*.

Razdan, S., & Sharma, S. (2022). Internet of Medical Things (IoMT): Overview, emerging technologies, and case studies. *IETE Technical Review (Institution of Electronics and Telecommunication Engineers, India), 39*(4). Available from https://doi.org/10.1080/02564602.2021.1927863, http://www.tandfonline.com/loi/titr20#.V1U9n01f3cs.

Saru, S., & Subashree, S. (2019). Analysis and prediction of diabetes using machine learning. *International Journal of Emerging Technology and Innovative Engineering, 5*(4), 2019.

Shi, G., Chen, J., Zhang, W., Zhan, L. M., & Wu, X. M. (2021). Neural information processing systems foundation Hong Kong overcoming catastrophic forgetting in incremental few-shot learning by finding flat minima. *Advances in Neural Information Processing Systems, 9*, 6747–6761. Available from https://papers.nips.cc/.

Srivastava, J., Routray, S., Ahmad, S., Waris, M. M., & Asghar, M. Z. (2022). Internet of Medical Things (IoMT)-based smart healthcare system: Trends and progress. *Computational Intelligence and Neuroscience, 2022*. Available from https://doi.org/10.1155/2022/7218113.

Vogel, B., Acevedo, M., Appelman, Y., Bairey Merz, C. N., Chieffo, A., Figtree, G. A., Guerrero, M., Kunadian, V., Lam, C. S. P., Maas, A. H. E. M., Mihailidou, A. S., Olszanecka, A., Poole, J. E., Saldarriaga, C., Saw, J., Zühlke, L., & Mehran, R. (2021). The Lancet women and cardiovascular disease commission: Reducing the global burden by 2030. *The Lancet, 397*(10292). Available from https://doi.org/10.1016/s0140-6736(21)00684-x.

World Health Organization (2023). L. R. Mean fasting blood glucose. <https://www.who.int/data/gho/indicator-metadata-registry/imr-details/2380> (accessed 15.09.23).

Zeadally, S., Siddiqui, F., Baig, Z., & Ibrahim, A. (2020). Smart healthcare: Challenges and potential solutions using internet of things (IoT) and big data analytics. *PSU Research Review, 4*(2). Available from https://doi.org/10.1108/PRR-08-2019-0027, http://www.emeraldgrouppublishing.com/journal/prr.

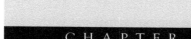

CHAPTER

16

Blockchain and smart contracts for wearable health sensing

Jose Cedeño (Ricardo),
Carlos Sánchez-Torres (Eduardo) and Jesus Favela
Department of Computer Science, Center for Scientific Research and Higher Education of
Ensenada, Baja California, Mexico

16.1 Introduction: the role of smart sensors in e-health and m-health

The proliferation of mobile and wearable devices has led to their unprecedented integration into our daily lives (Ray et al., 2019). Mobile and wearable sensing is becoming a popular approach to infer patterns of activity and behavior to help us understand how they affect health and well-being. E-health refers to the use of digital technologies and telecommunications (computers, internet, mobile devices) for online healthcare services. E-health is often applied alongside traditional nondigital (offline) healthcare services. Health systems are taking advantage of these advances to offer their services remotely and with minimal disruption to the patient's daily activities. This is how e-health (Eysenbach, 2001) emerged with the aim of improving access, efficiency, and the quality of personalized healthcare through the fusion of wearable sensing devices and digital systems on the Internet. Mobile devices include an array of sensors able to collect location, audio, image, text, physiological signals, among other data, from which additional information can be inferred using activity recognition techniques (Kwapisz et al., 2011).

One of the main applications of ubiquitous computing is in health and well-being, taking advantage of the capacity of the sensors in these devices to expand access to services and reduce costs. These applications reange from remote health monitoring, intelligent emergency management systems, and access to health data (Bardram, 2008). This field has been referred to as "Pervasive Health" and has attracted the attention of healthcare providers, leading to the emergence of mobile health (m-Health) (Kotz et al., 2016). The digitization of health services has led to an increase in the volume and type of health

Sensor Networks for Smart Hospitals
DOI: https://doi.org/10.1016/B978-0-443-36370-2.00017-7

data collected and the analyses that can be carried out with it (Porsdam Mann et al., 2021). This volume of information is expected to increase as patients are more willing to participate in decision-making about their health and more devices and sensors are deployed.

Unfortunately, the devices that collect this massive amount of data implement light security measures as they have limited resources (Zhang et al., 2016). These sensors tend to be part of a client-server architecture where all the collected data is centralized in a database and sent or consulted using REST APIs. For this reason, digitized health services suffer from many of the issues associated with large, centralized server systems: data sharing and consent management, access control, authentication, and user trust (Kotz et al., 2016). A failure in the security of these systems could lead to cyberattacks that compromise the user's personal information, making them victims of identity theft or an incident that puts their health at risk due to the loss of information critical for a correct medical diagnosis. The risks go beyond technical factors; the actions of dishonest parties directly cause the leakage, misuse, or commercialization of patient data for profit.

Although the most naive solution might be to prohibit the use of patient or user data in general, we must understand the critical importance of such data in improving health services. The correct approach is to generate "fair data," which is compliant with being locatable, accessible, interoperable, and reusable (FAIR) (Dunning et al., 2017) and the adequate use of such data, complying with the principles of collective benefit, authority control, responsibility and ethics (CARE) (Leonelli et al., 2021). In this chapter, we propose the use of blockchain technology for its ability to function as a decentralized, distributed, and democratic transaction log and information storage. Its node-based structure allows the platform's functions, such as data registration and storage, to be shared among its participants so that the workload is distributed without the need for a main server. Each node has a copy of the network state, so if one fails, the information is available on the rest. This participatory structure allows decisions to be made not by an institution or legal person but by consensus to the satisfaction of the majority.

To convey the benefits of using blockchain on health data from smart sensors, we describe a reference architecture (Angelov et al., 2012) for the fair collection and use of mobile and wearable sensing data, named traceable health data (TRHEAD). The blockchain-based architecture supports building systems capable of collecting sensing data while respecting user privacy, providing control and authorship over it by recording each operation in the blocks of the chain and guaranteeing consciously collected data for the training of machine learning (ML) models.

The chapter is organized as follows: In Section 16.2 we introduce blockchain technology, its associated terms and its uses in the healthcare domain. We then present the requirements for a platform that guarantees the fair collection and use of data from mobile and wearable sensors. Section 16.3 illustrates the problem by presenting use scenarios and the roles involved in them, including their rights and responsibilities. We introduce the TRHEAD reference architecture in Section 16.4. Section 16.5 describes the implementation of a mobile sensing system based on TRHEAD and a sensing campaign conducted with this system that led to the conscious training of an ML model. Finally, Section 16.6 presents our conclusions and directions for future work.

16.2 Blockchain for healthcare

A blockchain is a set of nodes that cooperate to maintain a participatory and democratic network (Aste et al., 2017). Unlike a centralized server, decisions in the network are carried out through consensus mechanisms in which its nodes participate directly. This decentralized nature protects the network from adversarial attacks since consensus must be reached by the majority. Thus, the more nodes there are the greater the security offered.

In healthcare, the use of blockchain allows maintaining a general and immutable record of medical procedures clinical procedures and diagnostic test results, reducing the number of medical practices and monitoring required when the patient is transferred to another institution. This saves time and resources for both practitioners and patients; the latter will be able to see where their information goes with complete transparency. Pharmaceutical companies can eliminate the problems of drug manipulation and counterfeiting by tracking each of their assets (Haleem et al., 2021). As a relatively new technology, blockchain has had limited dissemination outside the field of ICT. It is often mistakenly labeled as just the basis for the rise of cryptocurrencies. However, its features meet many of the needs for privacy, availability, authenticity, security, and traceability of the information management process required by healthcare institutions.

The network itself is not capable of handling the internal processes of healthcare institutions, for that, some applications, known as smart contracts, are built on top of this network. Like any contract, a smart contract establishes the terms of an agreement. But unlike a traditional one, the terms are executed as code on a blockchain. Smart contracts allow developers to create applications that benefit from the security, reliability, and accessibility of the blockchain, while offering sophisticated peer-to-peer features, from lending and insurance to logistics and gaming.

16.2.1 Smart contracts

A smart contract is code that runs on the blockchain to facilitate, execute, and enforce the terms of an agreement between untrusted parties. It can be considered a system that releases digital assets to all or some of the parties involved once predefined rules have been met. Compared to traditional contracts, smart contracts do not rely on a trusted third party to function, which results in low transaction costs. Different blockchain platforms can be used to deploy smart contracts, with Ethereum being one of the most widely used. This is largely due to the availability of the Solidity language that allows the creation of custom contracts and is Turing complete. Smart contracts can be applied in asset management, e-commerce, and music rights management (Alharby & Moorsel, 2017).

These contracts allow different functionalities to be programmed and various services to be built. They act as intelligent software agents to automatically manage certain transactions when preassigned conditions are met on a blockchain network, making them suitable for automatable internal processes, as they eliminate the need for third-party interference (Omar et al., 2020).

In 2018, Hölbl et al. (2018) described the construction of networks with some restrictions for participants (consortium and private networks) to give the network better control over access and record creation.

Smart contracts add many functionalities to a blockchain but have yet to experience widespread use in healthcare. Current trends in blockchain research in healthcare indicate that it is mainly used for data sharing, health records, and access control, but rarely for other scenarios, such as supply chain management or prescription drug management. Therefore, the potential of blockchain remains unexploited. Most research presents a novel framework, architecture, or model that uses blockchain technology in healthcare systems. Furthermore, technical details about the blockchain elements used, such as the platform, consensus algorithm, type (public, private, consortium), or the use of smart contracts, are often not provided.

16.2.2 Decentralized applications

Decentralized applications (DApps) operate on blockchains, thus offering no central control, or transparency by making the code publicly available, security, and ownership. End users interact directly with DApps, making transparent the complexity behind them that supports such services. They act as a mediating element between the end-user and the blockchain-based infrastructure.

16.2.3 Non-fungible tokens

A nonfungible token (NFT) is a cryptographic asset on a blockchain that contains unique identification information and codes that separate them from each other (Taherdoost, 2023). Unlike fungible assets like Bitcoin, where each unit is identical, each NFT has its own distinct identity and value. This is achieved through the inclusion of special codes and information directly embedded within the token.

The use of NFTs in the healthcare sector is being explored in applications such as tokenizing medical records, tracking supplies, and securing access to medical devices. This is made possible due to their ability to ensure transparent ownership, track provenance, and facilitate secure data sharing.

16.2.4 Requirements for mobile and wearable data sensing

Considering the risks associated with the gathering and use of personal data from mobile and wearable sensors, the following principles should guide the management of such data:

Data traceability allows data consumers to know the path the data has taken before reaching a dataset, database, or repository, allowing them to verify that it has not been altered or its integrity has been compromised. Tracing the specific device used to collect data is important when training models with data from devices from different sensors, perhaps with different accuracies or temporal frequencies. Furthermore, ML models should be able to trace back to the data used for their training, which could help understand decisions made by the model (eXplainable AI) or motivate retraining if issues are reported about the reliability of the data and its labeling.

Data provenance lets us know that the data was collected legally, labeled correctly, and not generated synthetically (Shumailov et al., 2023). However, these principles often involve research processes that compromise the identity of the patient who generated the data or allow the determination of information about the patient that cannot be revealed. For example, collecting data from a smart band can provide geolocation information that, when subjected to manual or computer scrutiny, can reveal the residence and places frequented by the user of the sensor (Kalnis et al., 2007).

Another principle should be respect for the patient's privacy, which should not be confused with the protection of their data, since despite making it public for consumption, any connection with the identity of the person who generated it could be removed. Another option is the creation of a layer of anonymity between the patient and their data, an electronic identity isolated from the information of the natural person towards which to focus the traceability and provenance of the data.

Consent is essential in this context and includes the patient's right to control and know how their data is being used, as well as the lifetime of the data. When data is collected for a clinical study, the decision to deny or revoke consent for its use must be respected, and this should not be a condition for the provision of a service if it is not strictly necessary, according to relevant regulations such as the general data protection regulation (GDPR https://gdpr.eu/).

Data availability responds to the need to always have the data available and implies that the service that provides it does not stop due to technical factors or is reduced because it cannot respond to demand. It is linked to the absence of bias, which means having sufficient quantity and variability in the data to include representations of all the classes to which a product is directed. This allows products such as ML algorithms to be trained without bias and to respond correctly instead of tilting their responses towards a dominant class in the training dataset.

To comply with these principles, the platform must be supported by a technology that is:

- **Transparent:** Where the traceability and provenance of the data can be assured.
- **Participative:** Where a user can defend the right to respect their privacy and to consent.
- **Decentralized:** So that the information is available from multiple providers and the platform reaches more users, while increasing the variety of data that is collected.

16.3 Roles and use scenarios for the FAIR use of mobile/wearable data in healthcare

Fairness in data usage should not only be present in the treatment of data but also considered as an economic-social process and regulated as such. To inform the design of the TRHEAD architecture, we describe the three main roles involved in the process and design scenarios that illustrate its use and benefits.

16.3.1 Roles for data gathering and usage

We identified the following main roles in the process of generating data from mobile/ wearable sensors, its curation, and proper use. These individuals and organizations will sign contracts with other roles as part of the workflow for the fair use of data.

Data generators or data holders: They are responsible for sensing their own data using a DApp or storing large volumes of other people's data. These are usually individuals or patients with wearable sensors or organizations that compile large databases that collect data from a group of users.

Data generators have the right to be rewarded for the data they contribute in the form of currency, service, or recognition; for their privacy to be respected and to control access to their data. On the other hand, they must accept the nonrefutability of the operations they perform on their data, including consent provided on its use, at least until they revoke it.

Data curators: They clean, filter, and/or label data, just to mention some of the tasks they must perform to generate volumes of data with the required quality to obtain valuable information from them.

Curators have the right to be rewarded for their work in curating and/or labeling data in the form of currency, services, and recognition; and to have their work recognized as an asset independent of the data on which it is based and to backtrack data to trustworthy sources to verify its provenance. In contrast, they have the duty to accept the nonrefutability of the operations they perform on users' data and the one they produce, respect the privacy of the users, and respect the usage of legal mechanisms such as consent letters according to the approval of an ethics committee.

Data consumer: These individuals and organizations consume data and generate information from it in scientific articles, new social or economic services, and ML models.

The consumers of data have the right to know the data provenance of the assets they acquire and consume, to receive the data under the terms agreed during the transaction, and to obtain rights to models generated with this data under the terms of the agreement. They are responsible for ensuring that the data they received was consciously collected as authorized by the generators and for using the data under the terms agreed to in the consent letter or similar.

16.3.2 Use scenarios

Departing from the roles described above, we present specific use scenarios to illustrate how the integration of blockchain technologies promotes healthcare data collection, control, and consumption activities. Each scenario focuses on one of these roles.

16.3.2.1 Scenario 1. Data generator uses a blockchain-supported tool to gather and publish data transparently

Alice accepts to participate in a study about sleep apnea by signing a letter of consent in a DApp on her smartphone, which states that she will receive US$1 in BTC per night of data and that her identity will not be known to data curators and consumers. Before she goes to sleep, she activates the app to capture the sounds she generates while sleeping.

The data will be uploaded to the platform created for the study. After several days of this routine, Alice is informed that a data curator has consumed her data by creating a "dataset" with the corresponding credit to her account being made. She checks her transaction log and, in the "Consumption Purpose Statement" section, finds the address of a University website in whose repository the dataset is located. Alice is satisfied to know that her data will help researchers at the University conduct a study to improve the quality of life of sleep apnea patients.

16.3.2.2 Scenario 2. Data curator labels and publishes a dataset

The DigitalHealth Center manages the medical records of its patients that have been collected, organized, and labeled by its medical staff. The data contained in these records belong to the institution since its patients have signed a letter of consent for their use under certain conditions. These medical records are stored in their platform together with the patients' letters of consent to ensure the fidelity of their provenance (data provenance). The center allows these data to be made available free of charge for research purposes but not the letters of consent. In order to have access to the signed consents, the consumer must agree to provide free participation to the institution of any result obtained under the following terms: If the result is a service, permanent license for the use of such service and subsequent versions; if it is a set of processed data, access for its consumption; if it is an article of scientific value, recognition to DigitalHealth as the source of the data.

Carlos is a data curator with experience in audio voice analysis and is asked to process the data files of interviews with older adults conducted in a geriatric clinic. His work includes preprocessing the audio files, generating transcripts of the utterances, and adding relevant metadata, which do not compromise privacy, such as gender, age, and diagnosis. He uploads the results of his work to the platform, making them available for consumption under the condition that credit to its blockchain wallet for the amount of US$100 in BTC, and the DigitalHealth Center is exempt from payment in accordance with the terms stipulating access to patient consent letters.

A research group working on biomarkers for dementia purchases the dataset curated by Carlos as they are interested in creating and eventually commercializing a machine-learning model to infer dementia from voice recordings. They agree to access the letters of consent from the DigitalHealth Center in exchange for a permanent license for its use.

16.3.2.3 Scenario 3. Data consumer creates a sensing campaign to create a dataset to consciously train a machine learning model

Elsa investigates the effect of a moisturizer on young fair-skinned women for the pharmaceutical company Vitalia. For this purpose, she initiates a sensing campaign to collect images of the faces of fair-skinned women between 15 and 30 years of age. Users of Vitalia products that match the inclusion criteria and have expressed their interest in participating in sensing studies are notified of the sensing campaign initiated by Elsa. The young women who decide to participate must upload photos of their faces each day before applying the cream and afterward using the DApp the company created using a blockchain-based platform. The images are uploaded in sections created for the study by each user, which include letters of consent allowing full use of the multimedia content stored in them. From the analysis of the data collected, Elsa obtained evidence that the cream reduces the appearance of skin blemishes. The results of the research are published in an article with sample images of some of the women participating in the study to visualize the effect of the cream. The legal department of the pharmaceutical company informs Elsa that one of the participants whose photo was published alleges that this was done without her consent and has caused her psychological damage, for which she plans to sue the company. The researcher proceeds to generate a digital version of the letter of consent signed by the complainant through the platform and sends it to the legal department for disposition. The matter is settled without escalation.

16.4 A blockchain-based architecture for FAIR data collection and use in pervasive healthcare

The scenarios described above illustrate the services required from a platform aimed at providing blockchain support for the fair gathering and usage of health data from mobile and wearable sensors:

- A user interface to allow users to collect, upload, and use health-related data from smart sensors.
- The ability to connect with various mobile and wearable sensors to collect data.
- A reliable registry of all the operations taking place on the platform to assure data traceability.
- Connection storage services for the secure preservation and controlled sharing of the data obtained from the sensors, additional data from their curated versions and letters of consent.
- An ML platform that can consciously train models from data legally obtained for such use. Models generated through this platform allow for the traceability of the provenance of the data used for its training, including the consent provided by data creators and curators.

These functionalities must be implemented, respecting the privacy of the users and the consent they provide for the use of their data. Rather than implementing a specific system that satisfy these requirements, we propose a reference architecture to serve as a basis to implement a variety of applications for the conscious use of health data from smart sensors such as the ones described in the scenarios above.

16.4.1 The traceable health data reference architecture

TRHEAD is a reference architecture for the fair collection and use of sensing data to train ML models consciously. TRHEAD is blockchain-based to gather users' data while protecting their privacy, provide control and ownership of those while registering every transaction using smart contracts (traceability) and train ML models with these consciously/ethically gathered data. The architecture includes a client application that is responsible for safeguarding the user identity and linking it to its e-wallet address. The trained models will be distributed as stand-alone instances of a computational notebook and can be traced to the digital consent letters that allow the consumption of the data used to train them.

The architecture (see Fig. 16.1) is composed of a DApp as a graphical interface for user interaction that executes the libraries that allow communication with the blockchain. The blockchain itself functions as a decentralized, immutable public registry of the operations carried out on the platform and the NFTs (smart contracts) that represent the rights over the data. Another component is a cloud storage system, which is used to store both the health data and the metadata associated with the NFTs that are recorded on the chain. To consume the data stored in the cloud for the conscious training of ML models, the use of a computing notebook is proposed, although the range of possibilities is much wider.

We next describe in more detail the components of the proposed reference architecture.

Dapp: A DApp is the interface of the user (Data Generator, Curator or Consumer) to his wallet in order to sign with it all transactions and manage its assets, either internal network credit or NFTs. Data generators and data holders can upload the healthcare data in their possession to the platform and automatically generate NFTs that represent ownership over these assets, allowing them to control their access and maintain traceability of its consumption.

Data curators can purchase these NFTs with internal platform credit and with them a digital letter of consent for their consumption specifying the term and extent of their privileges over them. This is for the purpose of reprocessing, segmenting, and tagging the data to create a new set of value-added data that can be of greater use to consumers.

Consumers, for their part, can consume the raw data from the platform, preferring data already processed and/or labeled by specialists, or directly requiring an ML model already trained using the data found on the platform. Each of these options includes corresponding digital letters of consent and payment in network credit.

Data storage and sharing: To support storage and data-sharing services, we propose the use of the IPFS protocol, a decentralized file-sharing network that provides THREAD and its users with decentralized storage. Even though it is part of the Web3 movement, it isn't a blockchain, despite sharing similar features.

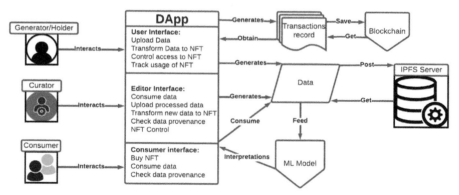

FIGURE 16.1   The traceable health data reference architecture.

THREAD's intention is to give each user their own encrypted database for medical records within IPFS. When a data generator wishes to share information and a data consumer is in search of a fair dataset, they can negotiate a mutual agreement, typically embodied in a smart contract. Yet, transparency is the cornerstone of this process. While actual patients and data scientists may not dwell on the Web3 technological complexities, they undoubtedly prioritize the security and portability of their data.

Blockchain: A key component of the TRHEAD architecture is a blockchain backbone. Unlike a centralized server, decisions on a "blockchain" are made through consensus mechanisms in which its nodes directly participate. This decentralized nature protects the network from adversarial attacks, since consensus must be reached by a majority and, therefore, the more nodes there are, the greater the security provided.

In the TRHEAD architecture, the blockchain is the regulating entity of all operations, stores data usage records, and controls the privileges that are held over them. Whenever an operation is performed on the data, the e-wallet address of the initiator of the operation and of all those who intervened or were involved in it is recorded, which allows for automatic, public, and immutable traceability of the operation.

Smart contracts are responsible for carrying out these operations when the conditions for their execution are met, and their main advantage is that they automate the agreement between peers, without the need for the intervention of a third party. This allows the chain to become a kind of ledger that everyone can consult, but only those who pass a test established by the network of nodes can edit it to ensure that no invalid records are introduced. This test is known as a consensus mechanism and is generally focused on preventing a group of malicious individuals from manipulating the network to their benefit, either by centralizing operations on their nodes or by carrying out adversarial attacks.

Machine learning platform: ML represents a paradigm shift in the discovery of the causality of health conditions and the overall improvement of healthcare systems. Data science applied to healthcare allows medical records to become raw material for training models that help healthcare professionals refine diagnoses and patients be more proactive towards the monitoring and control of their disease. In the proposed architecture, these models are end consumers for ethically collected data and will be distributed as basic versions focused on specific functions such as medical diagnosis or monitoring progress in medical interventions.

The ML platform in TRHEAD would be capable of distributing the training between several nodes of a "blockchain" through the use of a library such as Distributed Tensor Flow. The consensus mechanism of the chain would be used to choose and reward the nodes that participate in the tasks according to their reliability and the magnitude of their contribution to the final result. The data stored in the distributed storage system would be retrieved by a smart contract running on the blockchain and its storage addresses made available to the distributed model training service for the creation of models that would be stored back and registered in the chain as new assets.

16.4.2 A platform for fair health mobile data collection and usage

Following the TRHEAD reference architecture, we implemented a platform upon which applications for gathering and using health mobile data can be implemented.

A DApp as a web application was implemented using ReactJS to connect to the user's wallet through a browser extension. A different interface might be required for each role to support the operations they need to perform, such as gathering data from mobile and wearable sensors, signing a letter of consent or paying for the use of digital assets.

For data storage and sharing we use OrbitDB, a distributed peer-to-peer database that uses IPFS as its backend. It offers five data models for storing data: log, feed, key-value, docs, and counter. Data gathered using smart sensors is stored in the document database provided by OrbitDB from which it can be shared with Data Consumers. On the other hand, we ensure traceability by providing watermarks through Steganography on binary files, such as images and videos.

As blockchain backbone, we use the Vara Network, a stand-alone layer-1 decentralized network built and running on top of Gear Protocol. Gear Protocol (https://docs.substrate. io/) is a Substrate-based smart-contract platform that enables anyone to develop and run a dApp in Vara Network as well as other networks powered by the Gear Protocol's runtime and technology. The Vara network provides a distributed, immutable, and public record of the operations performed on the data handled in the platform. When a new dataset is uploaded from the DApp, it will be stored in the Gear Technologies IPFS, and an NFT will be created with its information and access control in that storage.

These transactions are signed in the chain with the e-wallet address of the user who uploaded the data, ensuring traceability. Finally, the CID that identifies the data uploaded in the IPFS is retrieved by the interface and sent to the computing notebook that is used to train ML models with this consciously collected data. We reiterate that the utilities of this data, once ready for consumption, can go far beyond due to the wide range of possibilities offered by a custom computational notebook.

TRHEAD uses EvaNotebook (https://notebook.sanchezcarlosjr.com) to generate consciously-trained ML models. EvaNotebook is a computational notebook designed to operate within a browser environment with tools to manage decentralized datasets and build transparent applications for data scientists and end-users. Its design lends itself to ETL operations but with an emphasis on Web3 and blockchain. It achieves this with the assistance of a decentralized database and incorporates various application protocols, including WebRTC, WebSockets, libP2P, IPFS, and OrbitDB. ETL stands for Extract, Transform, and Load. These are operations that data scientists apply to various sources to construct a data warehouse for further analysis. ML models trained with EvaNotebook can be certified as consciously trained if they are developed with data from the blockchain that can be traced, and it is used respecting the terms of the letters of consent signed by the data generators and holders. Thus, EvaNotebook supports the responsible and ethical development of AI.

16.5 Using the traceable health data architecture for the conscious training of a machine learning model

We describe the implementation and use of a sensing platform based on the TRHEAD reference architecture and the platform derived from it. The system should allow gathering data from sensors in a mobile device and uploading the data using a REST API for its consumption. The data will be used to create an ML model. All operations will be registered using a smart contract on the blockchain.

The purpose of the system was to gather photos of users imitating the facial expressions of a social robot (Rocha & Muchaluat-Saade, 2023). The model trained with this data will be used by the robot during social interaction.

A DApp was implemented as a web application. The app has access to the camera in the device to take pictures and upload them to an IPFS server and send the smart contract the metadata of the image and its CID. The app can also be used to validate images from other users (acting as a data curator) and sign a letter of consent (see Fig. 16.2).

The user gets credit for each photo uploaded and for each photo validated by other users. However, if the user incorrectly validates a photo, or the photo he uploads is not properly validated by others he will be penalized with credits being removed from his wallet.

The Moonbeam network was used to display the smart contract with the images and metadata that resulted from the sensing campaign.

Nine individuals participated in the sensing campaign that lasted one week, and produced a total of 255 validated images of five facial expressions (sad, surprised, happy, angry, and neutral).

A script in EvaNotebook was used to download the dataset from the IFPS server and train a model to recognize the expressions using an instance of the you only look once (YOLO) architecture, which uses a convolutional neural network for object detection. The model was trained using 5-k-fold cross-validation. The resulting model has a F1 score of 90%.

More importantly, the model itself is registered with a smart contract as an asset. The model can be traced back to the data. Thus, if for instance errors are found in the labeling

FIGURE 16.2 User interface of the decentralized applications (DApp) user interface of the DApp.

of some of the data, the model can be flagged for re-training. Similarly, if any issues are found with the consent on the use of some of the data this can be traced to all models created with such dataset.

16.6 Conclusions

Healthcare data is sensitive, if used inadequately, it can create risks to the privacy and security of individuals and could lead to inappropriate treatment or questionable medical evidence. As smart sensors, incorporated in mobile and wearable devices are increasingly being used to gather data for healthcare and wellbeing, they are becoming part of medical records, being used for personalized medicine and to create models that infer how our activities and behaviors influence our health. In contrast with medical records, which are mostly created, updated and stored in clinics and hospitals, the data from mobile and wearable sensors is mostly recorded by the individuals themselves and kept in their accounts in diverse repositories.

In addition, ML is increasingly being used to create models from user data for diagnosis, health monitoring and risk assessment. There are risks of data misuse, however, which has fueled a current for the ethical and responsible use of AI in healthcare (Babic et al., 2021) aimed at supporting transparency and trust in models. It is widely recognized that the quality of the data used to train these supervised ML models greatly influences their reliability (Volovici et al., 2022).

It is therefore understood as a necessity to collect this data in a secure manner, where the user's identity is not compromised, and in a controlled manner, giving each participant recognition for his or her contribution. These tasks, when assigned to an institution composed of human personnel, are exposed to known adversities such as human error during classification, data leaks and the tendency to bias.

In the face of this problem, blockchain technology offers an automated and democratic way to govern the interaction of users with their data on the network. As discussed earlier in this text, smart contracts can automate tasks related to the recording of transactions on data and act as digital representations of the data and the privileges associated with controlling their access.

However, there are limitations associated with the use of this technology to manage medical records. The consensus mechanisms used by the blockchain are not perfect and it is possible for a malicious group of people to cover a high enough percentage of the network to influence on-chain decisions to their benefit. The very democratic nature of the network makes it vulnerable to divisions among its participants that result in the fragmentation of the network into what is known as "forks," sometimes irreconcilably.

We must consider that for the optimal functioning of these IT solutions associated with a blockchain, the volume of participants associated with it must reach considerable numbers. This means that the greater the number of connected nodes, the greater the robustness and credibility of the network, since transactions are validated by more participants. Similarly, in the field of medical data consumption for the improvement of diagnoses, the greater the number of participants, the greater the variety of data captured and the lesser the bias in them. We can infer then that network participants and network users need not necessarily be two independent groups. We advocate for a future in which patients are empowered with control over their medical data and participate in the preservation and fair use of it by becoming nodes in the network that manages it.

Clearly there is still a long way to go towards this goal, to achieve mass participation of nontechnical users in the blockchain requires an appealing and self-explanatory interface, due to its technical complexity. Moreover, the privacy of medical data is a recurring and critical issue when handling personal patient information. Today we already have approaches to solve this problem such as Federated Learning, thanks to which patient data never leave the capturing device, for example the patient's cell phone, but only the metrics needed for training ML models are shared. However, this approach does not cover other scenarios such as remote diagnosis where the doctor must have direct access to the medical records, also the metrics that are shared in Federated Learning can be used to retrieve the original data. For these cases, as discussed above, the use of traditional or homomorphic encryption is recommended.

References

Alharby, M., & Moorsel, A. V. (2017). Blockchain-based smart contracts: A systematic mapping study. *Fourth International Conference on Computer Science and Information Technology*, 125−140. Available from https://doi.org/10.5121/csit.2017.71011.

Angelov, S., Grefen, P., & Greefhorst, D. (2012). A framework for analysis and design of software reference architectures. *Information and Software Technology*, 54(4). Available from https://doi.org/10.1016/j.infsof.2011.11.009.

Aste, T., Tasca, P., & Di Matteo, T. (2017). Blockchain technologies: The foreseeable impact on society and industry. *Computer*, 50(9). Available from https://doi.org/10.1109/MC.2017.3571064.

Babic, B., Gerke, S., Evgeniou, T., & Cohen, I. G. (2021). Beware explanations from AI in health care. *Science (New York, N.Y.)*, 373(6552). Available from https://doi.org/10.1126/science.abg1834.

Bardram, J. E. (2008). Pervasive healthcare as a scientific discipline. *Methods of Information in Medicine*, 47(3). Available from https://doi.org/10.3414/ME9107.

Dunning, A., De Smaele, M., & Böhmer, J. (2017). Are the FAIR data principles fair? *International Journal of Digital Curation*, 12(2). Available from https://doi.org/10.2218/ijdc.v12i2.567.

Eysenbach, G. (2001). What is e-health? *Journal of Medical Internet Research*, 3(2), e20. Available from https://doi.org/10.2196/jmir.3.2.e20.

Haleem, A., Javaid, M., Singh, R. P., Suman, R., & Rab, S. (2021). *Blockchain technology applications in healthcare: An overview*. International Journal of Intelligent Networks (2). India: KeAi Communications Co. Available from https://doi.org/10.1016/j.ijin.2021.09.005, https://www.sciencedirect.com/journal/international-journal-of-intelligent-networks.

Hölbl, M., Kompara, M., Kamišalić, A., & Zlatolas, L. N. (2018). A systematic review of the use of blockchain in healthcare. *Symmetry*, 10(10). Available from https://doi.org/10.3390/sym10100470, https://www.mdpi.com/2073-8994/10/10/470/pdf.

Kalnis, P., Ghinita, G., Mouratidis, K., & Papadias, D. (2007). Preventing location-based identity inference in anonymous spatial queries. *IEEE Transactions on Knowledge and Data Engineering*, 19(12). Available from https://doi.org/10.1109/TKDE.2007.190662.

Kotz, D., Gunter, C. A., Kumar, S., & Weiner, J. P. (2016). Privacy and security in mobile health: A research agenda. *Computer*, 49(6). Available from https://doi.org/10.1109/MC.2016.185.

Kwapisz, J. R., Weiss, G. M., & Moore, S. A. (2011). Activity recognition using cell phone accelerometers. *ACM SIGKDD Explorations Newsletter*, 12(2). Available from https://doi.org/10.1145/1964897.1964918.

Leonelli, S., Lovell, R., Wheeler, B. W., Fleming, L., & Williams, H. (2021). From FAIR data to fair data use: Methodological data fairness in health-related social media research. *Big Data and Society*, 8(1). Available from https://doi.org/10.1177/20539517211010310, journals.sagepub.com/home/bds.

Omar, I. A., Jayaraman, R., Salah, K., Simsekler, M. C. E., Yaqoob, I., & Ellahham, S. (2020). Ensuring protocol compliance and data transparency in clinical trials using Blockchain smart contracts. *BMC Medical Research Methodology, 20*(1). Available from https://doi.org/10.1186/s12874-020-01109-5, http://www.biomedcentral.com/bmcmedresmethodol/.

Porsdam Mann, S., Savulescu, J., Ravaud, P., & Benchoufi, M. (2021). Blockchain, consent and prosent for medical research. *Journal of Medical Ethics, 47*(4). Available from https://doi.org/10.1136/medethics-2019-105963.

Ray, P. P., Dash, D., & De, D. (2019). A systematic review and implementation of IoT-based pervasive sensor-enabled tracking system for dementia patients. *Journal of Medical Systems, 43*(9). Available from https://doi.org/10.1007/s10916-019-1417-z, https://link.springer.com/journal/10916.

Rocha, M., & Muchaluat-Saade, D. (2023). Friendly Robot for Education and Healthcare: FRED. In *2023 ACM International Conference on Interactive Media EXperiences Workshops (IMXw23)* (pp. 19–22). ACM. Available from https://doi.org/10.1145/3604321.3604342.

Shumailov, I., Shumaylov, Z., Zhao, Y., Gal, Y., Papernot, N., & Anderson, R. (2023). The curse of recursion: Training on generated data makes models forget. *arXiv*. Available from https://doi.org/10.48550/arXiv.2305.17493, https://arxiv.org.

Taherdoost, H. (2023). Non-fungible tokens (NFT): A systematic review. *Information, 14*(1), 26. Available from https://doi.org/10.3390/info14010026.

Volovici, V., Syn, N. L., Ercole, A., Zhao, J. J., & Liu, N. (2022). Steps to avoid overuse and misuse of machine learning in clinical research. *Nature Medicine, 28*(10). Available from https://doi.org/10.1038/s41591-022-01961-6, https://www.nature.com/nm/.

Zhang, J., Xue, N., & Huang, X. (2016). A secure system for pervasive social network-based healthcare. *IEEE Access, 4*. Available from https://doi.org/10.1109/access.2016.2645904.

CHAPTER

17

Blockchain technology for health insurance

Anupam Tiwari

Institution of Electronics and Telecommunication Engineers, New Delhi, India

17.1 Introduction

In the landscape of health insurance (HEI), the association of blockchain technology (BCT) (Zheng et al., 2017) marks a critical shift toward a more secure, transparent, and efficient paradigm. This chapter delves into the complex convergences of BCT and HEI, analyzing the transformative potential this disruptive technology brings around an industry laden with multiple challenges. From cryptographic foundations ascertaining data integrity to the decentralized framework revolutionizing claims processing, we navigate the technical intricacies that corroborate blockchain applications. Elaborating beyond theoretic frameworks, we delve into real-world use cases, sorting out how BCTs immutability and transparency can extenuate fraud dangers. As we dissect the multifarious implications, this chapter aims to provide a comprehensive apprehension of how BCT stands poised to redefine the very framework of HEI, introducing novel levels of security, trust, and operational efficiency.

17.2 Blockchain technology

BCT is a decentralized and secure system that fundamentally specifies data storage and transaction verification (Thuraisingham, 2020). At its core, a blockchain is a chain of blocks, with each block indexing a list of transactions. These blocks are cryptographically linked through a process known as hashing. Each block contains a unique identifier called a hash, which is rendered by applying one hash function to the block's data, letting in the hash of the previous block. This interlinked structure creates a chain of blocks, where the hash of each block serves as a digital fingerprint and is essential for asserting the integrity of the entire chain. The linkage through hashes ensures that any alteration in one block

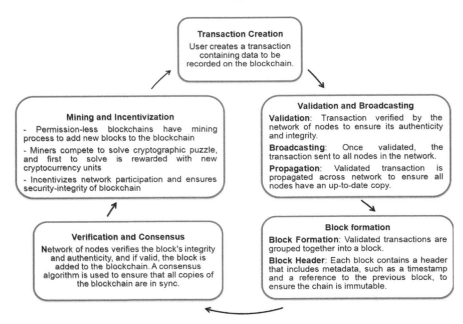

FIGURE 17.1   Blockchain process sequence.

would call for changing subsequent blocks, making the blockchain immune to tampering. The decentralized and consensus-driven nature of blockchain coalesced with this cryptographic chaining, sets up a transparent and secure ledger for recording transactions across a network. Fig. 17.1 depicts a typical chain of events in a BCT schema.

17.2.1 Blockchain: an amalgamation of technologies

Blockchain is an amalgamation of multiple technologies and concepts few of which are enumerated below with brief explanation:

17.2.1.1 Byzantine fault tolerance

Byzantine fault tolerance is a vital property that ascertains the network's ability to arrive at consensus and keep the integrity of the distributed ledger even if some nodes are faulty or malicious (Alboaie et al., 2021). This resiliency is essential for blockchain-based applications, as it forbids manipulation or modification of the ledger, preserving the trustless and secure nature of the technology.

17.2.1.2 Consensus mechanisms

Pivotal in blockchain networks, consensus mechanisms (Deng et al., 2022) assure agreement among participating nodes on the validity of transactions. In decentralized systems, attaining consensus forbids double-spending and ensures the integrity of the ledger. Bitcoin's Proof-of-Work, Ethereum's transition to Proof-of-Stake, and other consensus algorithms like Delegated Proof-of-Stake represent diverse approaches to achieving agreement within distributed networks.

17.2.1.3 Cryptography

Suffices as the foundation for securing transactions and assuring data integrity. Utilizing advanced mathematical algorithms, it encrypts sensitive data, such as transaction details and user identities, to defend against unauthorized access. Public and private key pairs impart pseudonymous identities to user nodes, facilitate secure data transmission and user authentication, fortifying the confidentiality and authenticity of blockchain transactions.

17.2.1.4 Decentralization

Decentralization decimates reliance on any central agency, administering control across a network of nodes (Geekiyanage Don & Motalebi, 2021). This assures transparency, resilience, and censorship resistance, mitigating single points of failure and raising trust in the integrity of the distributed ledger data. The decentralized nature of blockchain authorises individuals within the network, bringing up a paradigm shift away from conventional centralised systems.

17.2.1.5 Digital signatures

Digital signatures (Sadkhan & Sadkhan, 2022) allow a secure method for verifying the authenticity of transactions. Applying asymmetric cryptography, each participant possesses a unique private key to digitally sign transactions, while a representing known public key allows others to verify the signature. This checks data integrity and nonrepudiation, raising the trustworthiness of transactions within the decentralized network.

17.2.1.6 Distributed ledger technology

Refers to the fundamental infrastructure of blockchain, enabling a decentralized, secure, and transparent record of transactions. Unlike conventional centralized ledgers, DLT holds a distributed copy of the ledger across multiple node participants on the network, fostering trust and decimating the need for intermediaries.

17.2.1.7 Forks (hard forks/soft forks)

Forks (Misic et al., 2019) are substantial alterations to the rules governing a blockchain network which can be generally classified into hard forks and soft forks. Hard forks are backward-incompatible alterations that necessitate all nodes to upgrade their application/software to hold consensus. Soft forks, on the other hand, are backward-compatible alterations that let in older versions of the software to proceed operating without interrupting the network. Hard forks are used to apply major changes while soft forks are used for minor changes or bug fixes.

17.2.1.8 Hash functions

Cryptographic algorithms that play a critical role in securing blockchain transactions. Hash functions convert data of any size into a fixed-length output, known as a hash value, which is peculiar to that data. This unique and lasting property makes them crucial for maintaining data integrity and preventing tampering in blockchain networks. Common hash functions used in blockchain include SHA-256, SHA-3, MD5, BLAKE2, RIPEMD MurmurHash, etc.

17.2.1.9 Merkle trees

Also known as hash trees, are cryptographic data structures that render effective data verification and are usually used in BCT to verify the integrity of large datasets without the need of downloading the entire data set from nodes. In merkle trees, each node comprises a hash value, which is unique peculiar fingerprint to dataset it represents. By combining the hash values of child nodes, parent nodes are created, forming a hierarchical data structure. The root hash value corresponds to the entire dataset, and any changes to the data will result in a different root hash value, facilitating easy detection of tampering or corruption.

17.2.1.10 Patricia trees

Used for storing and retrieving key-value pairs expeditiously, particularly when keys share common prefixes.

17.2.1.11 Merkle patricia trie

Combines the strengths of both. It stores data like a Patricia tree and adds a Merkle tree on top for data integrity checks. Such MPT hybrids are used in Ethereum blockchain.

Nodes: Nodes can be thought of as networked computers running blockchain software. They have the following functions to perform:

- **Store the entire ledger:** Each node has a copy, ruling out single points of failure.
- **Validate transactions:** Assure transactions follow the predefined rules.
- **Relay information:** They connect and sync with other nodes, disseminating updates and keeping everyone with same data.
- **Mine new blocks:** Some nodes aka miners compete to add new transaction batches (blocks) to the chain as part of respective consensus mechanism

Without nodes, the blockchain wouldn't exist. They're the backbone, ensuring transparency, security, and the magic of decentralization.

17.2.1.12 Peer-to-peer network

P2P network are cardinal to decentralized systems, allowing for direct communication and data sharing amidst participant nodes without intermediaries or any need of third parties. Each node in the network keeps a copy of the entire blockchain, bringing up redundancy and assuring data consistency. P2P in blockchain is majorly responsible for:

- **No gatekeepers:** No single entity controls the network, forbidding censorship and manipulation.
- **Direct communication:** Nodes talk to each other, sharing data and updates without depending upon a central agency or authority.
- **Increased resilience:** No single point of failure, if one node goes down, others keep the network humming.

- **Enhanced security:** Tampering is near impossible, as every node verifies and stores the entire ledger.

17.2.1.13 Public and private keys

These establish a cardinal cryptographic pairing mechanism wherein Public Keys serve as user address that is visible to all, while Private Keys act as secret counterparts, known only to the owner. This asymmetric encryption ascertains secure data transmission and transaction confirmation and thus corroborating the integrity and confidentiality of blockchain interactions.

17.2.1.14 Sharding

Refers to a scalability resolution that requires partitioning of the network into smaller, more manageable segments called shards (Mao & Golab, 2021). Each shard serves a subset of transactions, facilitating parallel processing and raising overall network efficiency. Sharding covers scalability challenges, permitting blockchain systems to deal with increased transaction throughput by disseminating the computational processing load across multiple smaller chains.

17.2.1.15 Smart contracts

Self-executing agreements (Mohanta et al., 2018) with predefined encoded rules on a blockchain which when activated by defined events or conditions automatically execute and implement the agreed-upon terms without the need for intermediaries. Smart contracts are written in specific programming (Wohrer & Zdun, 2020) languages designed for blockchain environments few of which include:

- **Solidity:** Widely used for Ethereum-based smart contracts and has syntax similar to JavaScript, making it easy for developers familiar with web development.
- **Vyper:** Also designed for Ethereum, Vyper is an alternative to Solidity, known for its simplicity and security focus.
- **Chaincode (Go):** Chaincode, used in Hyperledger Fabric, is often written in Go (Golang).
- **Rust (ink!):** Rust is deriving popularity for writing smart contracts, particularly for blockchain platforms like Polkadot and Kusama.
- **Move:** Developed by Facebook for the Libra blockchain (now Diem).
- **Michelson:** Used in Tezos, is a low-level stack-based language for smart contracts.

17.2.1.16 Tokenization

Tokenization in the blockchain context translates assets into digital tokens, making a confirmable and tradable identification on a blockchain. Nonfungible tokens (NFTs) are a prime example, uniquely representing digital or physical assets like art, music, or real estate. NFTs utilize blockchain's secure and transparent ledger to establish ownership and provenance, revolutionizing how we value and trade digital and real-world assets in decentralized ecosystems.

Fig. 17.2 shows a typical schema of how a smart contract deployment will facilitate a smooth, transparent and immutable HEI ecosystem

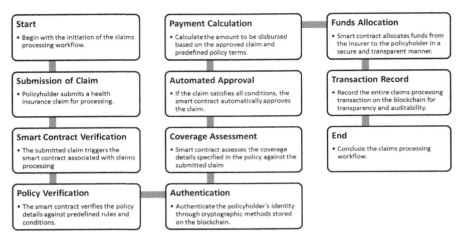

FIGURE 17.2   Smart contracts in claims processing.

17.3 Health insurance

HEI is a vital constituent of modern healthcare, allowing for financial protection against the high prices of medical treatment. HEI acts as a financial safety net, aiding individuals in meeting the financial demands of medical prices. Much like other insurance categories, HEI disperses the financial risk of healthcare expenses across a broad participant pool. By assessing the collective risk of health-associated expenditures and overall healthcare system prices within the insured group, insurance providers can institute a sustainable financial structure, typically supported by monthly premiums. This grouped or pooled funding authorizes the insurer to fulfill the healthcare benefits defined in the insurance agreement. The administration of these benefits is managed by a central entity, which can take the form of a government agency, private company, or non-profit organization.

As per the HEI Association of America, HEI is defined (Glossary of terms Terre Haute, 2024) as "coverage that provides for the payments of benefits as a result of sickness or injury. It includes insurance for losses from accident, medical expense, disability, or accidental death and dismemberment."

17.4 Challenges in traditional health insurance

Navigating the intricacies of conventional HEI divulges innumerable challenges (Trayush et al., 2021) that have long harassed the industry. From the maze of data security pertains to the cumbrous web of claims processing inefficiencies, each challenge casts a shadow on the unseamed provision of healthcare insurance coverage. Fallacious activities add another layer of complexness, jeopardizing the financial stability of insurers and eating away trust in the system. Furthermore, the permeant lack of transparency only escalates disconnect between stakeholders, exasperating the industry's opaqueness. Ahead in this section, we will analyze each challenge, providing a brief overview followed by ways on how BCT can associate to mitigate most.

- **Data Security and Privacy Concerns:** The storage and exchange of sensitive health information pose substantial privacy and security risks.
- **Ineffective Claims Processing:** The conventional claims processing system is often cumbrous, leading to retards in credits and administrative inefficiencies.
- **Fraudulent Activities:** HEI is susceptible to fallacious claims, costing the industry billions USD annually.
- **Lack of Transparency:** Opaqueness in insurance procedures leads to a lack of trust among stakeholders.
- **Lack of Interoperability:** HEI systems often clamber with interoperability, hampering seamless data exchange among several entities such as healthcare providers, insurers, and regulatory bodies. This division leads to inefficiencies, mistakes, and delays in processing claims.
- **Complex Regulatory Compliance:** Adherence to various and ever-evolving ordinances lays a substantial challenge. Navigating compliance necessities across different regions and jurisdictions lends complexness to HEI operations, calling for robust and adaptable systems.
- **Limited Accessibility and Affordability:** Traditional HEI models may not be easily reachable to all individuals, bestowing gaps in coverage. Affordability remains a concern, especially for those without employer-sponsored plans, lending certain demographics under-attended.
- **Ineffective Chronic Disease Management:** Current models often fall short in allowing for comprehensive solutions for chronic disease management. The lack of active and individualized approaches can lead to increased healthcare costs and contracted quality of life for individuals with chronic ailments.
- Inadequate Utilization of Data: While huge amounts of health data are rendered, traditional insurance models may not exploit this data efficaciously for analytics like risk assessment, preventive care, and personalized health schemes. This under utilization hinders the industry's ability to adjust to evolving healthcare needs.
- **Limited Consumer Engagement:** Engaging consumers in their healthcare journey is necessary for preventative attention and overall wellness. However, conventional HEI frameworks lack the tools and inducements needed to actively imply individuals in handling their health, resulting in missed opportunities for early treatment and cost savings.
- **High Administrative Costs:** A substantial portion of healthcare spending is exhausted by administrative chores, such as processing claims, affirming eligibility, and dealing patient records. This generally drives up the overall cost of insurance premiums and brings down the affordability of healthcare for consumers.
- **Rising Healthcare Costs:** The cost of healthcare services has been slowly but constantly increasing over the years, driven by factors such as advancements and niche progress in medical domain, ascending pharmaceutical prices, and senescence population. This has put a strain on traditional HEI models, as insurers struggle to keep up with the rising cost of care.

- **Limited Access to Quality Care:** Admittance to quality healthcare can deviate significantly depending on factors such as geo-location, socio-economic condition, and insurance coverage. In some areas, there may be a shortfall of healthcare professionals and providers or restricted access to specialised care. This can lead to inequalities in health effects and make it hard for individuals to receive the care they need.
- **Lack of Patient-Centric Approach:** Traditional HEI models often focus on cost containment and administrative efficiency, rather than prioritizing patient-centered care. This often leads to fragmented care, poor patient satisfaction, and sub-optimal health outcomes.
- **Inefficient Healthcare Delivery System:** The healthcare delivery system is often fragmentized and effete, with isolated containers of data, inadequate coordination of care, and limited use of technology. This results in duplicative testing, unnecessary referrals, recommendations, and time delays in treatment.
- **Limited Use of Technology:** The healthcare industry has been relatively slow to adopt technology, relative to other sectors. This limits the possibility for innovation, efficiency betterment's, improved patient engagement and overall facilitated patient care.

17.5 Analyzing health insurance challenges through a blockchain lens

In the intricate realm of HEI, a careful examination through the transformative lens of BCT unravels innumerable challenges (Arbabi et al., 2023) while elucidating potential avenues for revolutionary solutions. This section aims to shed light on the complexities surrounding HEI and how BCT with its unique attributes, holds the promise of addressing these challenges with innovation and efficiency. Fig. 17.3 shows a conventional methodology adopted in usual HEI processes.

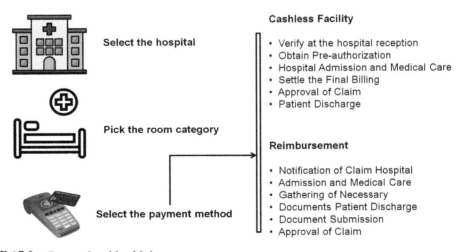

FIGURE 17.3   Conventional health insurance process.

17.5.1 Data security in health insurance: an underlying challenge

One of the cardinal challenges faced by the HEI industry centers on the security of sensitive health data. In conventional models, conserving the confidentiality and integrity of this information has been an intimidating task. Enter blockchain — a technology imbibed with cryptographic principles that could inspire new ways on how health data is managed and secured.

Blockchain's cryptographic foundations allow for an inviolable framework for protecting health information. By utilizing complex codes and algorithms, blockchain assures that health data stays tamper-proof and secure. The decentralized characteristic of BCT, wherein information is stored widespread across a network of computers, contributes an extra layer of protection against unauthorized access. In principle, blockchain becomes a digital fort, fortifying the confidentiality of health records and inculcating a trust in the overall system.

17.5.2 Streamlining claims processing: the need for efficiency

Claims processing has long been a chokepoint in the HEI work flow. The traditional systems often involve a complex web of paperwork and manual check processes, adding delays and administrative inefficiencies. BCT brings in a transformative solution through smart contracts.

Smart contracts (Abuhashim & Tan, 2020), a peculiar feature in few blockchain's, are self-executing contracts with predetermined rules. In the settings of HEI, these contracts can automatize and streamline the claims processing journey. Once the conditions specified in the contract are met, the contract deploys itself on the P2P network, negating the call for mediators and expediting the entire process. This not only quickens the speed of claims processing but also abbreviates the likeliness of errors and disputes, bringing up a more effective and transparent system. Fig. 17.4 shows one such schema of blockchain enabled HEI process.

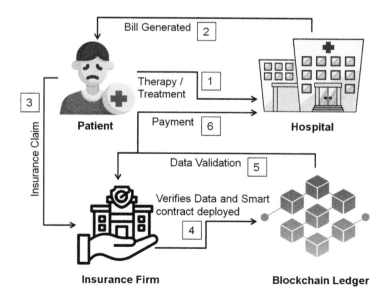

FIGURE 17.4 Blockchain enabled health insurance process.

17.5.3 Combating fallacious activities: a repeated menace

Fraudulent activities present a substantial threat to the financial stableness of HEI providers. From fabricated delusive claims to fraud, the current system is amenable to various forms of duperies. Blockchain's integral characteristics impart a formidable defense against such fraudulent activities.

Blockchain's transparency and immutability act as obstructers to fraudulent activities. Each transaction is indexed in a secure and unchangeable ledger accessible to all authorized participants. This makes a traceable and transparent trail of activities, making it exceedingly challenging for vicious actors to misrepresent the system without detection. The decentralized nature of blockchain, where no single entity holds control, further decreases the risk of insider fraud. In Fig. 17.5, a depiction of the strategic approach of traversing the HEI value chain by leveraging BCT and smart contracts, highlights the interconnected processes and advancements.

17.5.4 Blockchain's role in transforming health insurance

As we examine these challenges through the blockchain lens, a clear fact emerges — blockchain has the potency to redefine how we handle HEI. Imagine times ahead wherein health data is not just stored securely but is also easily accessible only when necessitated (Jain & Kumar, 2022).

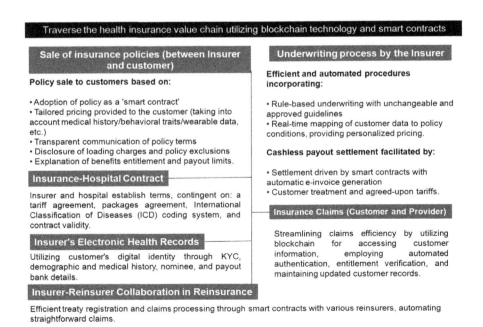

FIGURE 17.5   Traverse the health insurance value chain utilizing blockchain technology and smart contracts.

Consider a claims processing system that works seamlessly, without the usual conventional hurdles. Smart contracts on the blockchain make this possible by automating the verification and approval processes. The result is a smooth and efficient system that considerably reduces processing times, appropriating individuals to receive the care they need without inevitable delays.

17.6 Blockchain derivates for health insurance

This section will discuss few derivates of BCT which function on blockchain but extend peculiar functions other than the popular characteristics that have been discussed above. These majorly include:

- Cryptoeconomics (Iakovlev & Kruglova, 2021) and Incentives for HEI;
- NFTs (Rehman et al., 2021);
- IPFS (Zheng et al., 2019) for storage of Health records data.

17.6.1 Cryptoeconomics and incentives for health insurance

In HEI, the association of BCT brings in a paradigm shift, not only in terms of transparency and security but also through the emerging but well known concept of cryptoeconomics. This section delves into the intricate web of incentives that blockchain brings to the forefront, transforming the landscape of HEI.

17.6.1.1 Tokenomics: fostering participation and accountability

The introduction of cryptocurrency tokens within the HEI framework redefines the economic bonuses for all participants. Blockchain's tokenomics, driven by smart contracts, enables stakeholder being rewarded for positive behaviors and adherence to health protocols. Multiple healthcare companies are adopting cryptocurrency as a motivational tool to boost healthy habits and raise overall healthcare results. By utilizing the potential of BCT and cryptocurrency, these organizations are initiating innovative care delivery models, motivating patients to actively engage in their well-being. Listed below are ten healthcare companies utilizing cryptocurrency for incentivizing health-related participation.

- **Lympo:** Lympo (Changing the future of Blockchain & Sports (2022) Lympo. Available at, 2024) operates as a blockchain-centric platform, applying its proprietary cryptocurrency, LYM, to compensate users pursuing in fitness challenges and achieving health objectives. Through the utilization of fitness trackers, participants can consistently track their physical activities, subsequently earning LYM tokens upon the completion of challenges. These tokens, inherent to the Lympo blockchain ecosystem, serve as a means for users to buy a variety of goods and services.
- **Sweatcoin (SWC):** SWC is a mobile application (Fomenko, 2020) deployed on a blockchain, rendering users with its native cryptocurrency, SWC, as a reward for physical activity and exercises. The application utilizes step-tracking functional to translate users' physical movements into SWC tokens. These tokens are facilitated to be

exchanged for various rewards, including but not limited to fitness equipment, gift cards, and even cryptocurrencies such as Bitcoin and ethereum.

- **Healthcoin:** Healthcoin (Hanna et al., 2017) functions as a blockchain-centric platform, incentivizing users with its assigned cryptocurrency, HCN, for embracing health-conscious behaviors. Users collect HCN tokens by satisfying various health-related tasks, including timely medication adherence, supervising fitness activities, and having nutritive foods. The earned tokens hold usefulness within the Healthcoin ecosystem, enabling users to purchase healthcare products and services through their utilization.
- **Healthereum:** Healthereum functions (Healthereum, the blockchain platform for Modern Healthcare, 2024) as a blockchain-driven platform, unfolding patient's bonuses in the form of its blockchain crypto token, HEALTH, for active participation in their healthcare journey. Patients accumulate HEALTH tokens by undergoing various health-related tasks, which cover scheduling appointments, taking part in surveys, and binding to prescribed medication schedules. The earned tokens hold value inter Healthereum ecosystem while also easing and adjusting against payments for a range of healthcare products.
- **Doc.ai:** Doc.ai functions (Kashyap, 2021) as one unique blockchain-powered platform that employs artificial intelligence (AI) to serve patients in handling their health, incentivizing their involvement through its native cryptocurrency, NRN. Patients have the chance to cumulate NRN tokens by carrying out various health-related chores, including supervising fitness activities and putting up feedback on their care experiences. These earned tokens admit value within the Doc.ai ecosystem, serving as a means of payment for a range of healthcare products and services.

17.6.2 Nonfungible tokens for health insurance

Association of NFTs in HEI (Musamih et al., 2023) marks a crucial development in the application of BCT. NFTs refer to unique digital assets that can be verified on blockchain, and thus present innovational solutions and opportunities for remolding conventional paradigms within the HEI sector. Table 17.1 brings out key differences between NFTs and fungible tokens.

17.6.2.1 Immutable policy contracts

One of the important applications of NFTs in HEI dwells on the creation of immutable policy contracts. Each HEI policy can be mapped as a distinct NFT (Rai et al., 2023), providing an unalterable immutable record of the terms and conditions. This assures transparency and security, cutting down the risk of disputes or misinterpretations between insurers and policyholders. The smart contract deployments in NFTs also enable automatic fulfilling of policy terms, expediting claims processes and subduing administrative overheads.

17.6.2.2 Personalized health data ownership

In the times of data propelled healthcare, the possession and check of personal health data have become predominantly significant. NFTs can be utilized to authorize individuals with ownership of their health records. Each health record, indexed in an NFT token, becomes an immutable and decentralized representation of an individual's anamnesis.

TABLE 17.1 Nonfungible versus fungible tokens.

Feature	Nonfungible token	Fungible token
Uniformity	Nonuniform	Uniform
Interchangeability	Not interchangeable, each token is unique	Fully interchangeable, any token of the same type is identical
Divisibility	Undividable, only whole units can be transferred	Divisible, can be subdivided into smaller units
Scarceness	Can be artificially limited or kept restricted	Naturally abundant, often designed for large supply
Primary use cases	Ownership of digital or real-world assets, representation of unique identities, access rights, and fractional ownership	Currency, exchange of value, staking mechanisms, governance rights, utility within specific platforms
Technical standards	ERC-721, ERC-1155 (Ethereum), other blockchain-specific standards	ERC-20 (Ethereum), BEP-20 (Binance smart chain), TRC-20 (TRON), other fungible token standards
Applications	Art, collectibles, gaming items, music, real estate, event tickets, fractional ownership of assets	Cryptocurrency, payments, DeFi protocols, DAOs, supply chain management, fundraising
Value derivation	Subjective, based on uniqueness, rarity, utility, perceived value	Objective, derived from market demand and supply
Transaction costs	Typically higher due to increased complexity of nonstandard tokens	Typically lower due to simpler transaction structure
Regulation	Unclear currently and evolving, may be subject to securities or commodities regulations	More established regulatory framework, often treated as currencies or digital assets

This not only raises privacy but also grants patients to selectively share their health information with healthcare providers, researchers, or insurers, bringing up a more personalized control and secure data-sharing ecosystem.

17.6.2.3 Incentivizing healthy behaviors

NFTs can be used to make unique tokens that identify achievements in maintaining a healthy lifestyle. For example, accomplishing fitness goals, following medication schedules, or taking part in preventative health measures can be feted with exclusive health-related NFTs. These tokens not only serve as badges of honor but can also hold be used within the HEI ecosystem, granting individuals to earn incentives such as premium discounts rates, special packages or additional insurance coverage.

17.6.2.4 Transferability and portability

The fungibility of NFTs allows for a unseamed solution for policyholders who relocate or change insurance providers. HEI policies, identified as NFTs, can be easily reassigned from one individual to another or from one insurer to another without the need for elaborated and complex paperwork. This raises the portability and transfer of HEI, contributing to a more flexible and consumer-friendly industry.

17.6.2.5 Fraud prevention and authentication

NFTs lend an additional layer of security to HEI by playing role of unique identifiers. This aids in forbidding identity spoof and assures that only lawful policyholders have access to their benefits. Cryptography enabled backend of NFTs raises authentication processes, protecting sensitive health information from illegal or malicious access.

- Health records are screened from malicious and unauthorized access, with cryptographic hash functions strengthening data integrity.
- Riddance of a central authority brings down the risk of large-scale data breaches, instilling patient confidence and also security of data.
  Seamless Interoperability
- IPFS renders a standardized and ubiquitously accessible protocol for health records and data storage (Deshpande et al., 2023).
- Eases interoperability among different healthcare vendors for a consolidated view of a patient's medical history.
- Facilitates more informed decision-making by healthcare professionals and betters continuity of care.
  Patient-Controlled Data Sharing
- IPFS authorizes patients with control over own health records through proven multihashes and cryptographic keys.
- Patients can selectively share particular components of their health information with desired entities only as per choice.
- Granular control abides by patient liberty and streamlines the data-sharing process.
  Robust Disaster Recovery
- IPFS extends a robust disaster recovery solution for health records data.
- Decentralized and distributed nature assures data availability even in the face of natural disasters, cyberattacks, or system failures.

17.6.3 Navigating the blockchain landscape: healthcare organizations in action

This section discusses few organizations who have associated BCT in HEI.

BurstIQ: BurstIQ opens up secure and decentralized patient data management and provisions (Ricotta, 2023) a strengthened environment for storing and handling sensitive health data, including records, citizen social security numbers, and financial details. Also introduces a Web3-ready blockchain LifeGraph proposes new ways of data handling.

GuardTime: Ensuring the integrity of health data information can be a treacherous climb and Guardtime enabled (Bergstrom, 2024) on BCT offers to secure and streamline the path forward. Their solution engages peculiar time-stamped blockchain to validate each piece of information. From time-stamping documents to fixing pharmaceutical supply chains, its versatility has left its mark on various industries.

Chronicled: Chronicled leverages BCT (Pellicioti, 2023) to interrupt the nefarious trade in fake pharmaceuticals by optimizing pharmaceutical supply chain management. Its proprietary platform, MediLedger, takes on industry-wide inefficiencies head-on and furthers collaboration and alignment by automatizing error-prone processes, obviating chargeback challenges, and correcting pricing inconsistencies.

Robomed: The Robomed Network (Papapanagiotou, 2021) rides on BCT to forge a novel, patient-centric medical framework. Its core creation lies in a smart contract-driven network linking healthcare vendors and patients. Value, determined by target functioning metrics and patient satisfaction, is dynamically interwoven into the fabric of interactions through the network's native token. Robomed Network incorporates cutting-edge AI algorithms with BCTs secure infrastructure to offer seamless tele-consultations and better remote patient monitoring, paving the way for a more abreast and effective healthcare experience.

Avaneer Health: Avaneer Health (Hanson, 2023) uses BCT to build a public ledger, easing the smooth transmission of healthcare data. This comprehensive platform incorporates multiple tools and services to expedite development, including identity management, real-time data exchange, operability, and connectivity characteristics. It also offers a digital marketplace bringing up the launch and commercialization of healthcare solutions, connecting pioneers with the Avaneer Network participants. Furthermore, the platform offers up enterprise-ready tools for key management, log streaming, single sign-on, assuring compliance and security.

17.7 Blockchain technology challenges in health insurance

The indisputable potential of blockchain to remold the HEI sector is met with multiple and significant challenges that must be addressed to fully unlock its capabilities within the healthcare landscape. These have been discussed below:

Technological Immaturity:

- Applying BCT particularly within the complex healthcare ecosystem, is still in its infancy and needs due global support to actually derive benefits.
- Pertains over scalability, transactions per second speeds, energy consumption issues for consensus algorithms, make public blockchain's struggle to handle the required transaction volume for HEI.
- Private alternatives raise questions about decentralization and data governance. This basically refers to permissioned or private blockchain's where access to the nodes and participation is restricted to select nodes. These alternatives raise questions about decentralization and data governance for several reasons including centralized control, limited transparency, concerns about trust, potential for single points of failure, interoperability concerns, dependency on such consortium members.

Regulatory Uncertainty:

- The intemperately regularized nature of HEI, linked with the evolving legal framework for blockchain in healthcare, poses challenges (Steenmans et al., 2021).
- Abidance with rigorous and tight data privacy regulations like HIPAA and GDPR complicates implementation since BCT counters with GDPR/HIPAA's focus on

individual control. Consent management gets complex, wiping off data near impossible, and breach notifications get more difficult to comply with.

Interoperability Issues:

- Isolated databases and different proprietary software's in existing healthcare systems hamper seamless data exchange (Ren et al., 2023).
- Integrating blockchain demands interoperable solutions bridging the gap between legacy infrastructure and cutting-edge technology. To solve this, "side-chains" emerge as potential garage door openers where in side-chains act as bridges, allowing legacy systems to interact with the different blockchain tech without getting overwhelmed. Side chains extend additional space for high-volume transactions, keeping the primary blockchain running smoothly. However, this futurist solution isn't without its tolls. Setting it up assumes additional effort in configurations and existing architectures.
- Standardization of data formats and communication protocols is also much essential for smooth data flow across the healthcare ecosystem.

Lack of Trust and Adoption:

- Precaution within the healthcare industry, particularly amongst stakeholders handling and controlling sensitive health data, presents challenges to blockchain adoption.

Cost and Expertise:

- Substantial fiscal investments and specialized technical expertise are expected for carrying out and maintaining blockchain-based systems.
- Cost and complexness barriers may impede smaller insurance companies and healthcare service providers and vendors.
- Training professionals and staff on BCT usance adds another layer of complexity.

Cybersecurity Threats:

- Despite enhanced security features, blockchain is not immune to cyber attacks.
- Robust cyber security measures and continuous monitoring are necessary to protect sensitive health data from potential breaches.

Lack of Standardization:

- Absence of any global standards and protocols in BCT data formats peculiar to healthcare industry hampers interoperability and scalability. Although IEEE standards ere emerging and few peculiar to BCT are seen in Table 17.2 (Al-Dulaimi et al., 2023).
- Global collaborative efforts are essential for launching standardization and facilitating seamless data exchange among global blockchain's.

While the challenges laid by BCT in HEI are significant, collaborative efforts, inventions, and a united approach from industry stakeholders are deemed to subdue these hurdles. Dealing these challenges will set the way for a highly secured, transparent, and effective healthcare ecosystem powered by BCT.

17.8 Advanced extensions of blockchain in healthcare insurance

The healthcare insurance landscape today pivots on the edge of a transformative revolution, driven by the strong convergence of advanced BCT and niche innovations. The near future beckons with heightened meliorations through zero-knowledge proofs (ZKPs),

TABLE 17.2 Few global IEEE blockchain standards detail.

IEEE 2144.1-2020	**Framework of BCT based IoT data management**
IEEE 2146.1-2022	Approved draft standard for entity-based risk mutual assistance model through BCT
IEEE 2418.2-2020	Data format for BCT
IEEE 2418.7-2021	Use of BCT in supply chain finance
IEEE 2418.10-2022	BCT based digital asset management
IEEE 3205-2023	BCT interoperability data authentication and communication protocol
IEEE 3801-2022	BCT based electronic contracts
IEEE P2418.6	Framework of distributed ledger technology (DLT) use in healthcare and the life and social sciences (under development)
IEEE 2140.4-2023	IEEE standard for a custodian framework of cryptocurrency
IEEE 2140.5-2020	Distributed/decentralized exchange framework using DLT
IEEE 2142.1-2021	Recommended practice for e-invoice business using BCT

unchained scalability via sharding and sidechains, confidential data processing with homomorphic encryption(HE), and collaborative control unlocked by multisignature wallets. Smart contracts endued by oracles and external data integration are braced to automatize claims processing and reduce administrative burdens, while adherence to Health Level Seven (HL7) Fast Healthcare Interoperability Resources (FHIR) standards ascertains unseamed interoperability. Moreover, the possible fusion of AI and machine learning (ML) with BCT calls to usher in an era of predictive analytics, personalized care, and deter fake pharmaceuticals in supply chain, essentially re-defining healthcare insurance management. The following section discusses these in brief to get a gist of these possibilities.

17.8.1 Zero-knowledge proof for enhanced privacy

ZKPs play a cardinal role in bettering privacy (Pathak et al., 2021) within the context of HEI. In this innovative cryptographic technique, one party (the prover) can establish the legitimacy of certain information to another party (the verifier) without disclosing the existent details. In HEI, this interprets to a mighty mechanism for individuals to prove specific eligibility or medical conditions without revealing sensitive data. This not only maintains the confidentiality of an individual's health data but also increases trust between the insurer and the insured.

17.8.2 Sharding scalability solutions

Sharding (Vinodha et al., 2022) is a scalability solution that holds substantial assurance in dealing the scalability challenges within the HEI context. Sharding implies segmenting a database into smaller, more manageable parts called shards. In HEI, this could mean splitting up the huge datasets into smaller, autonomous subsets that can be processed in parallel. This approach makes possible parallel processing of transactions, thus significantly bettering the scalability of the system. Sharding ascertains that each shard functions independently, abbreviating the load on a single database and reducing constrictions during data retrieval.

17.8.3 Homomorphic encryption for confidentiality

Homomorphic encryption stands (Zhu et al., 2022) as another emerging cryptographic tool with sound significances for beefing up confidentiality in the HEI sector, peculiarly when integrated with BCT. This facilitates secure computation on encrypted health data, allowing for insurance companies to execute vital operations without the need to decrypt sensitive data. Within the domain of data analytics in HEI, homomorphic encryption assures the privacy of individual health records data during processes such as risk appraisal, fraudulence detection, and individualized policy pricing. The synergy with BCT appends an extra layer of security, as the encrypted health data can be stored on a distributed ledger, enhancing resiliency against malicious access and ensuring transparency. Thus the association of homomorphic encryption and BCT comes forth as a potent and indispensable strategy for ensuring confidentiality across various processes in the insurance lifecycle.

17.8.4 Multisignature wallets for enhanced authorization

Multisignature wallets along with BCT provide a potent solution for improving authorization and security in the HEI demesne. This innovational approach, which necessitates multiple private keys to authorize transactions, is particularly beneficial in dealing fiscal transactions which are central to HEI ecosystem. Multi-signature wallets add an additional layer of security by calling for consensus among multiple authorized individuals to finish transactions. This distributed approach extenuates the chances of fraudulent access, elevating accountability and transparency in financial dealings.

17.8.5 Health level seven fast healthcare interoperability resources standards and blockchain integration

HL7 constitutes a bunch of global standards (Bender & Sartipi, 2013) designed for the unseamed exchange of clinical and administrative healthcare data between multiple applications. Centering on the application layer, known as "layer 7" in the open systems interconnection (OSI) model, these standards are developed by HL7 International, a globally recognized standards establishment. The association of HL7 FHIR standards with BCT holds substantial potential for metamorphosing the HEI domain. When combined with BCT, HL7 FHIR can raise data integrity, security, and streamline multiple processes in the HEI context.

17.8.6 Quantum-resistant blockchain solutions

Quantum-resistant blockchain solutions (Dharani et al., 2023) are lately getting more popular in the HEI context. Once quantum computers accomplish sufficient hardware realizations to execute Shor's algorithm on a prominent scale, widely used asymmetric algorithms like RSA, ECDSA etc which are cardinal for digital signatures and message encryption, will no longer maintain their security. Quantum computers will have the potentiality to swiftly crack these algorithms, making them vulnerable. Likewise, Grover's algorithm that renders a quadratic advantage in mining blocks for peculiar consensus protocols like proof of work etc. While the quantum threat is not peculiar to HEI domain, it certainly effects into effecting decision of adopting conventional blockchains. While a lot of research is currently on to realize post quantum computing solutions, the realization of such advancements is expected to be a prolonged process.

17.8.7 Integration of artificial intelligence and machine learning with blockchain in health insurance

The integration of AI and machine learning with BCT in the HEI context implies a transformative synergism, offering multifarious benefits. By employing AI and ML algorithms for fake detection and prevention, HEI companies can improve the security of transactions and cut costs through the analysis of patterns and anomalies. Moreover, the personalized insuring capability of AI and ML, when integrated with blockchain, facilitates insurers to evaluate risks more precisely and tailor policies based on individual health profiles. This integration also promotes interoperability and secure data sharing across the HEI ecosystem, helping cooperative causes between insurers, healthcare providers, and regulators. Additionally, the predictive analytics rendered by AI and ML algorithms on health trends, employing historical data stored on the blockchain nodes, enable insurers to proactively deal possible health risks and better population health outcomes.

17.9 Conclusion: recap and future technical developments

In this chapter our exploration of HEI challenges through the lens of BCT brings out a transformative narrative with fundamental significances for the industry. The challenge of peculiar healthcare data security finds a robust solution in BCTs cryptographic framework, ascertaining the tamper-proof and confidential handling of confidential health information. This not only guards individual privacy but also demonstrates a foundation of trust necessary for the insurer-policyholder relationship. The conventionally sophisticated domain of claims processing finds a paradigm shift with the introduction of smart contracts enabled on BCT. Also fraudulent practices, a recurrent threat to the financial stability of health insurers, face a sturdy adversary in BCTs characteristic of transparency and immutability.

As we foresee this translated landscape, it becomes evident that BCT is not just a solution to isolated challenges but an accelerator for remolding the entire HEI ecosystem. It tenders a future vision where health data is secure, claims processing are fast, and fraudulent activities are a rarified exception.

However, the route ahead is not without challenges. The successful integration of BCT into HEI necessitates collaboration, education, scalability solutions, storage handling and regulatory adaptation. Stakeholders across the industry must link up to institute common global standards, ensuring interoperability and a unseamed transition to this forward-looking technology. Regulatory frameworks must evolve to admit the nuances of blockchain, offering clear guidelines to explore the changing landscape.

In this active interaction of technological innovation and industry evolution, the potential benefits are huge. A secure, effective, and trustable HEI ecosystem pivots on the horizon, impelled by the transformative capabilities of BCT. As we stand at the crossroads of tradition and innovation, adopting BCT in HEI facilitates not only a revolution in how we handle healthcare data but also takes a different approach of the very essence of trust and efficiency. The journey may be intriguing, but the terminus promises a future where HEI is not just a guarantee but a pharos of resiliency, transparency, and firm trust in the face of evolving healthcare landscapes.

References

Abuhashim, A., & Tan, C. C. (2020). Smart contract designs on blockchain applications. In *Proceedings - IEEE symposium on computers and communications*. Institute of Electrical and Electronics Engineers Inc., United States. Available from https://doi.org/10.1109/ISCC50000.2020.9219622, 9781728180861.

Alboaie, L., Alboaie, S., & Calancea, C. G. (2021). IEEE computer society romania optimal byzantine fault tolerance consensus algorithm for permissioned systems. In *Proceedings - RoEduNet IEEE international conference 2021*. Available from https://doi.org/10.1109/RoEduNet54112.2021.9638279 9781665413510, <http://ieeexplore.ieee.org/xpl/conferences.jsp>.

Al-Dulaimi, A., Dobre, O. A., I, C.-L., Arribas, I., Erbguth, J., Chuburkov, A., Tan, L. J. Y., & Jia, X. (2023). *Blockchain standards blockchains: Empowering technologies and industrial applications*. Wiley. Available from http://doi.org/10.1002/9781119781042.ch11.

Arbabi, M. S., Lal, C., Veeraragavan, N. R., Marijan, D., Nygard, J. F., & Vitenberg, R. (2023). A survey on blockchain for healthcare: Challenges, benefits, and future directions. *ieee communications surveys and tutorials*, 25(1). Available from https://doi.org/10.1109/COMST.2022.3224644, http://ieeexplore.ieee.org/xpl/RecentIssue.jsp?punumber = 9739.

Bender, D., & Sartipi, K. (2013). FHIR: An agile and RESTful approach to healthcare information exchange. In *Proceedings of CBMS 2013 - 26th IEEE international symposium on computer-based medical systems, Canada HL7* (pp. 326–331). Available from https://doi.org/10.1109/CBMS.2013.6627810.

Bergstrom, R. (2024). 2022 Guardtime health. Guardtime.

Changing the future of Blockchain & Sports (2022) Lympo. Available at (2024).

Deng, X., Li, K., Wang, Z., Li, J., & Luo, Z. (2022). A survey of blockchain consensus algorithms. In *Proceedings - 2022 international conference on blockchain technology and information security, ICBCTIS 2022* (pp. 188–192). Institute of Electrical and Electronics Engineers Inc., China. Available from https://doi.org/10.1109/ICBCTIS55569.2022.00050, <http://ieeexplore.ieee.org/xpl/mostRecentIssue.jsp?punumber = 9844748>, 9781665496919.

Deshpande, K.V., Patil, T., Nagare, S., Sarode, R., & Dhanke, A. (2023). MedNcrypt: A blockchain based decentralised health record storage system using IPFS. In *International conference on sustainable computing and smart systems, ICSCSS 2023 — proceedings* (pp. 1579–1587). Institute of Electrical and Electronics Engineers Inc., India. Available from https://doi.org/10.1109/ICSCSS57650.2023.10169706, <http://ieeexplore.ieee.org/xpl/mostRecentIssue.jsp?punumber = 10169129>, 9798350333602.

Dharani, D., Soorya, R., & Kumari, K.A. (2023). Quantum resistant cryptographic systems for blockchain network. In *3rd International conference on intelligent technologies, CONIT 2023*. Institute of Electrical and Electronics Engineers Inc., India. Available from https://doi.org/10.1109/CONIT59222.2023.10205646, <http://ieeexplore.ieee.org/xpl/mostRecentIssue.jsp?punumber = 10205372>, 9798350338607.

Fomenko (2020). Healthier planet. healthier, wealthier you.

Geekiyanage Don, J.S., Motalebi, F. (2021). Decentralization using blockchain health records management. In *International conference on green energy, computing and sustainable technology, GECOST 2021.* Institute of Electrical and Electronics Engineers Inc., Malaysia. <http://ieeexplore.ieee.org/xpl/mostRecentIssue.jsp?punumber = 9538520>, https://doi.org/10.1109/GECOST52368.2021.9538734, 9781665438650.

Hanna, E., Remuzat, C., Auquier, P., Dussart, C., & Toumi, M. (2017). Could healthcoin be a revolution in healthcare? *Value in Health, 20*(9), A672. Available from https://doi.org/10.1016/j.jval.2017.08.1648.

Hanson, S. (2023). Our vision for greater interoperability. *Avaneer,* 2023.

Healthereum, the blockchain platform for Modern Healthcare (2024). AMBCrypto. Available.

Iakovlev, A.I., & Kruglova, I.A. (2021). How the foundations of the crypto-economy methodology were formed. In *Proceedings - 2021 international conference engineering technologies and computer science, EnT 2021* (pp. 80–85). Institute of Electrical and Electronics Engineers Inc., Russian Federation. <http://ieeexplore.ieee.org/xpl/mostRecentIssue.jsp?punumber = 9622892> https://doi.org/10.1109/EnT52731.2021.00021, 9781665426749.

Jain, S., & Kumar, A. (2022) Role of Blockchain and Smart Contracts in Healthcare -Challenges and Benefits. In *Proceedings of 2022 IEEE international conference on current development in engineering and technology, CCET 2022.* Institute of Electrical and Electronics Engineers Inc., India. <http://ieeexplore.ieee.org/xpl/mostRecentIssue.jsp?punumber = 10079846> https://doi.org/10.1109/CCET56606.2022.10080211, 9781665454155.

Kashyap, N. (2021). Doc.ai case study google cloud.

Mao, C., & Golab, W. (2021). Sharding techniques in the era of blockchain. In *Proceedings of the IEEE symposium on reliable distributed systems.* IEEE Computer Society, Canada (pp. 343–344). https://doi.org/10.1109/SRDS53918.2021.00041, 9781665438193.

Misic, V.B., Misic, J., & Chang, X. (2019) On forks and fork characteristics in a bitcoin-like distribution network. In *Proceedings - 2019 2nd IEEE international conference on blockchain, Blockchain 2019* (pp. 212–219). Institute of Electrical and Electronics Engineers Inc., Canada. <http://ieeexplore.ieee.org/xpl/mostRecentIssue.jsp?punumber = 8938397> https://doi.org/10.1109/Blockchain.2019.00035, 9781728146935.

Mohanta, B.K., Panda, S.S., & Jena, D. (2018). An overview of smart contract and use cases in blockchain technology. In *9th international conference on computing, communication and networking technologies, ICCCNT 2018.* Institute of Electrical and Electronics Engineers Inc., India. <http://ieeexplore.ieee.org/xpl/mostRecentIssue.jsp?punumber = 8476666>, https://doi.org/10.1109/ICCCNT.2018.8494045, 9781538644300.

Musamih, A., Salah, K., Jayaraman, R., Yaqoob, I., Puthal, D., & Ellahham, S. (2023). NFTs in healthcare: Vision, opportunities, and challenges. *IEEE Consumer Electronics Magazine, 12*(4). Available from https://doi.org/10.1109/MCE.2022.3196480, https://www.ieee.org/membership-catalog/productdetail/showProductDetailPage.html?product = PER262-EPC.

Papapanagiotou, P. (2021). The robomed healthcare blockchain: Revolution or delusion?.

Pathak, A., Patil, T., Pawar, S., Raut, P., & Khairnar, S. (2021) Secure authentication using zero knowledge proof. In *Asian conference on innovation in technology, ASIANCON 2021.* Institute of Electrical and Electronics Engineers Inc., India. < http://ieeexplore.ieee.org/xpl/mostRecentIssue.jsp?punumber = 9544081 >, https://doi.org/10.1109/ASIANCON51346.2021.9544807, 9781728185835.

Pelliccioti, R. (2023).

Rai, S., Chaurasia, B.K., Gupta, R., & Verma, S. (2023). Blockchain-based NFT for healthcare system. In *Proceedings - 2023 12th IEEE International conference on communication systems and network technologies, CSNT 2023* (pp. 700–704). Institute of Electrical and Electronics Engineers Inc., India. < http://ieeexplore.ieee.org/xpl/mostRecentIssue.jsp?punumber = 10134573 >, https://doi.org/10.1109/CSNT57126.2023.10134632, 9781665462617.

Rehman, W., Zainab, H.E. I.J., & Bawany, N.Z. (2021). NFTS: Applications and challenges. In *22nd International Arab conference on information technology, ACIT 2021.* Institute of Electrical and Electronics Engineers Inc., Pakistan. < http://ieeexplore.ieee.org/xpl/mostRecentIssue.jsp?punumber = 9677036 >, https://doi.org/10.1109/ACIT53391.2021.9677260, 9781665419956.

Ren, K., Ho, N.-M., Loghin, D., Nguyen, T.-T., Ooi, B. C., Ta, Q.-T., & Zhu, F. (2023). Interoperability in blockchain: A survey. *IEEE Transactions on Knowledge and Data Engineering, 35*(12). Available from https://doi.org/10.1109/tkde.2023.3275220.

Ricotta, F. (2023) Technology, BurstIQ. Available at: https://burstiq.com/technology/ (Accessed: 26 January 2024).

Sadkhan, S.B., & Sadkhan, R.S.B. (2022). Analysis of different types of digital signature. In *8th IEC 2022 - international engineering conference: Towards engineering innovations and sustainability.* (pp. 241–246). Institute of

Electrical and Electronics Engineers Inc., Iraq. < http://ieeexplore.ieee.org/xpl/mostRecentIssue.jsp? punumber = 9807426 >, https://doi.org/10.1109/IEC54822.2022.9807502, 9781665478298.

Steenmans, K., Taylor, P., & Steenmans, I. (2021). Regulatory opportunities and challenges for blockchain adoption for circular economies. In *Proceedings - 2021 IEEE international conference on blockchain, blockchain 2021* (pp. 572–577). Institute of Electrical and Electronics Engineers Inc., United Kingdom. < http://ieeexplore.ieee.org/xpl/ mostRecentIssue.jsp?punumber = 9680465 >, https://doi.org/10.1109/Blockchain53845.2021.00086, 9781665417600.

Thuraisingham, B. (2020). Blockchain technologies and their applications in data science and cyber security. In *Proceedings - 2020 3rd international conference on smart blockchain, smartblock 2020* (pp. 1–4). Institute of Electrical and Electronics Engineers Inc., United States < http://ieeexplore.ieee.org/xpl/mostRecentIssue.jsp? punumber = 9415621 >, https://doi.org/10.1109/SmartBlock52591.2020.00008, 9780738113630.

Trayush, T., Bathla, R., Saini, S., & Shukla, V.K. (2021). IoT in healthcare: Challenges, benefits, applications, and opportunities. In *International conference on advance computing and innovative technologies in engineering, ICACITE 2021* (pp. 107–111). Institute of Electrical and Electronics Engineers Inc., India. < http://ieeexplore.ieee.org/xpl/ mostRecentIssue.jsp?punumber = 9404366 >, https://doi.org/10.1109/ICACITE51222.2021.9404583, 9781728177410.

Glossary of terms Terre Haute, Indiana (in), Union Health (2024). Available at: https://www.myunionhealth.org/ patients-and-visitors/for-patients/billing-and-insurance/glossary-of-terms (Accessed: 26 January 2024).

Vinodha, K., Jayashree, R., Kommineni, G., Tanna, M., & Prerna, G.P. (2022). Sharding in blockchain systems. In *Concepts and challenges. international conference on smart generation computing, communication and networking, SMART GENCON 2022.* Institute of Electrical and Electronics Engineers Inc., India. < http://ieeexplore.ieee. org/xpl/mostRecentIssue.jsp?punumber = 10083316 >, https://doi.org/10.1109/SMARTGENCON56628.2022, 10083582 9781665454995.

Wohrer, M., & Zdun, U. (2020). Domain specific language for smart contract development. In *IEEE international conference on blockchain and cryptocurrency, ICBC 2020* Institute of Electrical and Electronics Engineers Inc., Austria. < http://ieeexplore.ieee.org/xpl/mostRecentIssue.jsp?punumber = 9165689 >, https://doi.org/ 10.1109/ICBC48266.2020.9169399, 9781728166803.

Zheng, Q., Li, Y., Chen, P., & Dong, X. (2019). An innovative IPFS-based storage model for blockchain. In *Proceedings - 2018 IEEE/WIC/ACM international conference on web intelligence, WI 2018* (pp. 704–708). Institute of Electrical and Electronics Engineers Inc., China. < http://ieeexplore.ieee.org/xpl/mostRecentIssue.jsp? punumber = 8607139 >, doi: https://doi.org/10.1109/WI.2018.000-8, 9781538673256.

Zheng, Z., Xie, S., Dai, H., Chen, X., & Wang, H. (2017) An overview of blockchain technology: architecture, consensus, and future trends. In *Proceedings - 2017 IEEE 6th international congress on big data, bigdata congress 2017* (pp. 557–564). Institute of Electrical and Electronics Engineers Inc., China. https://doi.org/10.1109/ BigDataCongress.2017.85, 9781538619964.

Zhu, L., Song, S., Peng, S., Wang, W., Hu, S., & Lan, W. (2022). The blockchain and homomorphic encryption data sharing method in privacy-preserving computing. In *Proceedings - 2022 IEEE/ACIS 7th international conference on big data, cloud computing, and data science, BCD 2022* (pp. 84–87). Institute of Electrical and Electronics Engineers Inc., China. < http://ieeexplore.ieee.org/xpl/mostRecentIssue.jsp?punumber = 9900505 >, https:// doi.org/10.1109/BCD54882.2022.9900530, 9781665465823.

Blockchain for security and privacy in the smart healthcare

Hamed Taherdoost[1,2,3,4]

[1]Department of Arts, Communications and Social Sciences, University Canada West, Vancouver, BC, Canada [2]Research and Development Department, Hamta Business Corporation, Vancouver, BC, Canada [3]Q Minded | Quark Minded Technology Inc., Vancouver, BC, Canada [4]GUS Institute, Global University Systems, London, United Kingdom

18.1 Introduction

An innovative, technology-driven, patient-centered healthcare system, smart healthcare strives to enhance the standard of medical services. It comprises various critical elements, such as hospital, regional, and familial. Intelligent medical facilities utilize solutions based on information and communication technologies to improve both patient care and operational efficiency. This entails the utilization of diverse devices and networks to monitor patients remotely at the regional and family levels. This enables intelligent health analysis and facilitates prompt medical interventions (Tian et al., 2019).

The necessity to integrate healthcare providers and patients onto a unified platform for intelligent health surveillance has propelled the development of intelligent healthcare systems. The integration facilitates examining routine human health data, allowing physicians to render well-informed judgments even remotely operating. By implementing Internet of Things (IoT) technologies and establishing arbitrary limits for health measurements, intelligent healthcare systems can initiate critical medical interventions in response to these limits. This ultimately enhances patient outcomes and the quality of healthcare as a whole (Islam et al., 2020).

18.1.1 Role of technology in healthcare transformation

Technology is of the utmost importance in the healthcare industry's transformation, resulting in substantial enhancements to patient care, diagnosis, and the overall efficiency

Sensor Networks for Smart Hospitals
DOI: https://doi.org/10.1016/B978-0-443-36370-2.00019-0

of healthcare. Telemedicine and telehealth, which have revolutionized healthcare delivery by facilitating remote access to medical care, routine checkups, specialist consultations, and mental health support, are some of the most significant technological contributions to healthcare. Furthermore, implementing electronic health records (EHRs) has enhanced the efficiency of information sharing between clinics, clinicians, and patients, resulting in elevated standards of care accessibility and quality. In addition, using information and communication technology (ICT) and big data has enabled the correlation of health data, detection of risk factors, and suggestion of preventative measures; thus, these developments have improved patient outcomes and medical decision-making.

In the healthcare industry, digital transformation has evolved into a necessity for developing innovative solutions that enhance the patient experience and administration of care. The continuous digital revolution in healthcare, encompassing the implementation of wearable technology, virtual reality, and the IoT, has enhanced patient well-being and expanded the array of healthcare options available (Stoumpos et al., 2023). Further technological advancements are anticipated to result in additional innovations and enhancements to healthcare efficiency, patient care, and overall well-being. To remain at the vanguard of healthcare delivery and administration, healthcare providers and institutions must adopt these technological developments.

18.1.2 Importance of security and privacy in smart healthcare

Intelligent healthcare systems have significantly transformed the healthcare industry, which offers novel approaches to enhance patient care. However, one of the greatest challenges of intelligent healthcare systems is protecting the confidentiality and security of patients' health information (Rani et al., 2022). A substantial threat to patient privacy is posed when adversaries attempt to take patient information, deny system services, or upgrade patient data for financial gain (AbdulRaheem et al., 2022). The data obtained through monitoring devices may contain sensitive and personal information; thus, safeguarding the privacy and confidentiality of patient information emerges as a primary obstacle in intelligent healthcare systems (Vaiyapuri et al., 2021).

An additional obstacle arises from the extensive interconnectivity of intelligent healthcare systems with cutting-edge wearable technology, the IoT, and mobile internet. These networks facilitate the transmission of critical patient information and other significant medical records, thereby augmenting the vulnerability to data intrusions and cyber-attacks. Additionally, personal patient information and clinical documents are stored in preexisting databases that may be susceptible to cyber-attacks, increasing the risk of patient data theft.

Novel approaches are required to safeguard the confidentiality and integrity of patient information and mitigate the risks and difficulties associated with intelligent healthcare systems. The significance of adequate medical information security is expanding in tandem with the implementation of smart healthcare. Scholars and practitioners from academia and industry are investigating and exchanging methodologies, concepts, and strategies that center on privacy and information security solutions for smart healthcare.

Conventional approaches to safeguarding healthcare data, including encryption and firewalls, should be supplemented and fortified with cutting-edge technologies capable of adjusting to contemporary healthcare ecosystems' ever-changing and interdependent characteristics.

Blockchain technology has emerged as a highly promising and innovative solution for augmenting smart healthcare security and privacy. Its fundamental tenets of decentralization, transparency, and immutability present a significant departure from centralized models, endowing it with an intrinsic resistance to unauthorized access and manipulation. Blockchain technology substantially improves the resilience of healthcare systems against cyber threats by minimizing the risk of a single point of failure through the distribution of data across a network of nodes and the implementation of consensus mechanisms.

Furthermore, the necessity for novel resolutions transcends basic data protection and encompasses privacy-related issues. There is a growing demand among patients for enhanced authority regarding their confidential health information; consequently, novel strategies are necessary to empower individuals while upholding regulatory compliance. With its ability to enable secure and precise access control and its integration of cryptographic methods to safeguard privacy, blockchain is positioned as a revolutionary influencer in the quest for a smart healthcare environment that is more attentive to patient needs and concerns regarding privacy.

18.2 Blockchain in healthcare

Through enhanced privacy, security, and accessibility of patient data, blockchain technology may fundamentally transform the healthcare sector. Supply chain transparency, patient-centric EHRs, smart contracts for insurance and supply chain settlements, medical staff credential verification, and IoT security for remote monitoring are all applications of blockchain technology in healthcare. Medical record management, clinical trials, prescription drug traceability, and health insurance claims processing are additional prospective use cases. Utilizing blockchain networks allows healthcare organizations such as pharmacies, diagnostic laboratories, and hospitals to exchange and preserve patient data (Haleem et al., 2021; Moosavi & Taherdoost, 2024).

While reducing expenses, blockchain technology can solve some of the most significant problems in healthcare, including hospital cybersecurity and transparency, interoperability, and patient privacy. Implementing blockchain technology significantly reduces the likelihood of data breaches and enhances the personal security of network users. In addition to bolstering healthcare data defenses, managing the medicine supply chain, and facilitating the secure transmission of patient medical records, blockchain technology can also assist healthcare researchers in deciphering genetic code.

Nevertheless, several challenges must be overcome before blockchain technology's widespread implementation in the healthcare sector. These obstacles include achieving standardization, overcoming regulatory and legal barriers, and ensuring interoperability with existing systems. Notwithstanding these obstacles, blockchain technology possesses the capacity to enhance care quality and coordination in healthcare system management by facilitating secure data sharing across highly fragmented healthcare systems, contingent upon patient consent.

Blockchain technology provides numerous benefits about anonymity and security in the healthcare industry. The blockchain's decentralization, immutability, and transparency render it a feasible technological solution for enhancing the storage and exchange of healthcare data (Abu-elezz et al., 2020). Patient data management, including storing confidential information and health records (e.g., social security numbers), is among the most effective applications of blockchain technology in healthcare. Moreover, blockchain technology facilitates enhanced data security, secure management of EHRs, and supply chain transparency, thereby enhancing patient records management and ensuring data availability around the clock.

Blockchain technology's advantages in healthcare include enhanced data security, decreased medical errors, improved record administration, and increased efficiency in managing EHRs. The decentralized and secure blockchain technology platform empowers healthcare providers to handle and store patient data efficiently and securely, reducing costs and enhancing patient outcomes. In addition, blockchain can optimize clinical trials, reduce medical errors, and enhance invoicing management.

18.3 Security challenges in smart healthcare

Several security challenges confront intelligent healthcare and must be resolved to protect the privacy and safety of patients. The massive quantity of data perpetually collected from and about patients, which can be breached, duplicated, or altered by unauthorized parties via malicious attacks such as tag duplication, spoofing, radio frequency jamming, and cloud polling, is one of the greatest obstacles (Navaz et al., 2021). Healthcare organizations handle, manage, and transmit vast quantities of data to facilitate the provision of effective and appropriate care. However, their vulnerability to publicly disclosed information stems from inadequate security measures and a need for more technical support (Abouelmehdi et al., 2018). Smart home networks are susceptible to unauthorized access, and patient medical data is vulnerable to cyber security threats, compromising its safety, privacy, and security.

Moreover, the provision of erroneous and hazardous treatment recommendations can result from compromised data or algorithms. Potential targets within the healthcare industry comprise hospital servers, diagnostic equipment, wearable technology, wireless smart tablets, and medical devices (Gerke et al., 2020). To address these challenges, healthcare organizations need to implement healthcare data security solutions that safeguard patient information and privacy (Abouelmehdi et al., 2018). Fig. 18.1 depicts the steps in addressing security challenges in smart healthcare, emphasizing continuous improvement through a feedback loop.

18.3.1 Cybersecurity threats

The increasing popularity of intelligent healthcare systems can be attributed to their capacity to enhance patient care and accessibility. Nevertheless, implementing telehealth and technological advancements in healthcare raises security concerns, particularly cybersecurity. Unfortunately, the COVID-19 pandemic has facilitated the proliferation of privacy concerns and data intrusions within healthcare organizations. By 2021, cybercrime

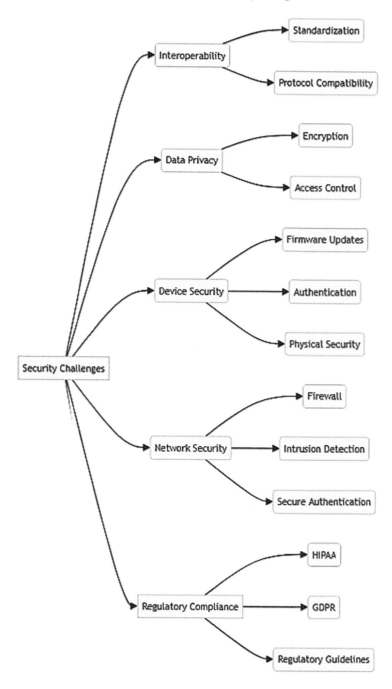

FIGURE 18.1 Security challenges in smart healthcare—workflow.

groups will have compromised over 40 million patient records. Adopting advanced technological applications in healthcare systems makes them susceptible to cyber threats that frequently surpass the benefits (Lieneck et al., n.d.).

A proposal has been made for a dynamic cybersecurity situational awareness framework for healthcare ICT infrastructures to mitigate the cybersecurity risks associated with smart healthcare. By providing a comprehensive view of the security posture of healthcare ICT infrastructures, the framework enables the implementation of proactive security measures. In addition, as a safeguard against cyber threats, vulnerability prediction for secure healthcare supply chain service delivery has been proposed (Silvestri et al., 2023).

18.3.2 Privacy concerns

In terms of service capacity, efficacy, and overall performance, the digitization of healthcare has produced substantial gains. Nonetheless, it has engendered apprehensions regarding the confidentiality and integrity of personal health information. According to research, the sensitive nature of private data collected by digital health technologies, such as mHealth apps and smart assistants, can cause users to be concerned about their privacy. The concerns above may impede implementing and utilizing these technologies, as individuals may be apprehensive about facing scrutiny, prejudice, or unauthorized access to their information. Moreover, implementing artificial intelligence (AI) in the healthcare sector introduces additional complexities to the privacy domain, resulting in privacy protection dilemmas that necessitate comprehensive legislation to tackle these obstacles (Paul et al., 2023; Schroeder et al., 2022; Wang, n.d.).

Numerous international legislative models, including the European Union's regulations and the Health Insurance Portability and Accountability Act (HIPAA) of the United States, have been considered regarding privacy protection in healthcare. The purpose of these models is to tackle the difficulties that arise from the integration of healthcare data into AI operations. They also underscore the importance of establishing strong privacy frameworks to protect individuals' sensitive health information. In addition, protecting privacy and security in contemporary healthcare systems, including potential assaults and extant defenses, has been the subject of extensive scholarly investigation. Given the dynamic advancements in healthcare technologies and the growing prevalence of EHRs, it is critical to establish robust privacy and security protocols to minimize the potential hazards of unauthorized access and data breaches (Newaz et al., 2021; Wang, no date).

Regarding IoT healthcare systems, security and privacy concerns remain of the utmost importance, including data integrity, device authentication, and confidentiality. Robust security measures are imperative in healthcare due to the interconnectedness of IoT devices, which threatens the confidentiality and integrity of sensitive health information. To tackle these concerns effectively, it is imperative to adopt a comprehensive strategy that integrates technical, regulatory, and ethical factors to establish a healthcare ecosystem that is both secure and upholds privacy (Sadek et al., 2022). The decision factors and critical stages associated with managing privacy concerns about healthcare data are depicted in Fig. 18.2.

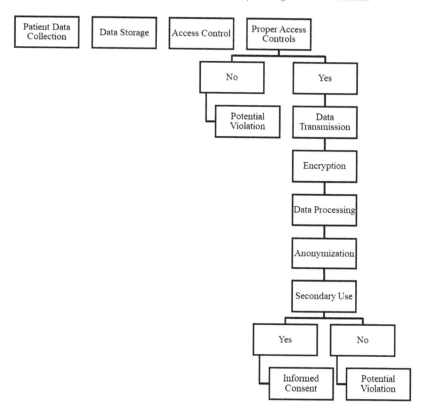

FIGURE 18.2 Privacy concerns in healthcare data flow.

18.3.2.1 *Patient data confidentiality*

Patient data confidentiality is an essential element of the healthcare industry, encompassing measures to safeguard individuals' health information against unauthorized disclosure or access. It is intrinsically linked to maintaining trust between healthcare providers and patients and protecting their privacy. The HIPAA is a significant legislation in the United States that safeguards patient privacy by permitting patients to lawfully acquire duplicates of their protected health information, which includes medical records, and by imposing stringent controls on the disclosure and utilization of this data (Tariq & Hackert, 2023).

Healthcare organizations and practitioners, which fall under the purview of HIPAA as covered entities, must comply with rigorous privacy and security protocols to protect patient information. This entails implementing suitable security protocols when collaborating with third-party contractors and purveyors and encrypting data transmitted over the Internet (Tariq & Hackert, 2023). Patient confidentiality is critical for establishing and sustaining trust between medical practitioners and patients. By fostering a sense of security in healthcare environments, patients are more inclined to divulge sensitive health data, ultimately contributing to enhanced health outcomes.

18.3.2.2 *Unauthorized access*

As a result of the usage of interconnected devices and the growing digitization of health-care data, unauthorized access is a major concern in intelligent healthcare. According to research, the most common types of attacks that result in healthcare data breaches are hacking and IT incidents; therefore, e-health data is extremely vulnerable to unauthorized access (Seh, n.d.). Enabled by the Internet, the digital ecosystem of healthcare tools poses formidable obstacles to protecting patient information's privacy and security, with risks such as unauthorized access to research results or patient data and compromise of sensitive data (Filkins et al., 2016). Unauthorized access to sensitive data, including medical images and personally identifiable information, presents significant security and privacy concerns within smart healthcare systems (Popoola et al., 2023; Yan et al., 2023).

Unauthorized access to smart healthcare has far-reaching consequences, given the heightened susceptibility of EHR data to cyber threats, wherein criminals exploit medical information for financial gain. Implementing EHR systems and the subsequent data processing give rise to numerous privacy concerns, particularly when unauthorized users gain data access (Tertulino et al., 2023). As a result, it is critical to ensure privacy and security in intelligent healthcare systems to prevent unauthorized access to and potential exploitation of sensitive patient data.

18.4 Blockchain solutions for smart healthcare security

Blockchain technology can transform the healthcare sector by delivering secure and efficient solutions for intelligent healthcare security. Between 2016 and 2021, one study by Saeed et al. (Saeed et al., 2022) conducted a systematic review of 53 articles concerning the application of blockchain technology in healthcare. According to the study, blockchain technology ensures nonalteration and manipulation of healthcare data, participant anonymity, preservation of patients' privacy, enhancement of drug supply chain management, and secure and rapid access to patient records in the healthcare blockchain. Nonetheless, the research also detected several areas for improvement in the existing body of knowledge, including ambiguous methodologies for selection and analysis tools.

A study by Shi et al. (2020) examined the security and privacy implications of blockchain approaches tailored for EHR systems through a systematic literature review. According to the study, blockchain-based EHR systems can provide secure and private storage of patient data and empower patients with control over their data via smart contracts. The study also identified research challenges and opportunities in this field.

18.4.1 Decentralized electronic health records

Implementing blockchain technology in the domain of intelligent healthcare is bringing about substantial changes to how EHRs are managed. EHRs have historically been stored in centralized databases, which has exposed them to the risk of security vulnerabilities and unauthorized access. Adopting blockchain-powered decentralized EHRs mitigates these concerns by instituting a more transparent and secure framework.

18.4.1.1 *Improving data integrity*

18.4.1.1.1 Immutability

Blockchain technology is distinguished by its immutability; in the context of intelligent healthcare, specifically EHRs, it serves as an indispensable protection for data integrity. The concept of immutability pertains to the intrinsic resistance that data on the blockchain possesses against modification or manipulation. This attribute is critical for guaranteeing the integrity of patient data, as every block in the blockchain comprises an individual cryptographic hash computed using the contents and hash of the preceding block. In addition to disrupting subsequent blocks, any attempt to modify data within a block would result in a hash change and render it nearly impossible to manipulate historical records undetected.

The improved integrity of data provided by immutability is critical within the framework of intelligent healthcare. Patient health records, treatment plans, and other vital data are preserved and maintained accurately due to the immutable quality of recorded information. This attribute is a strong deterrent against malevolent endeavors, including unauthorized modifications or tampering with data. An immutable foundation is established in the healthcare industry, where the precision of patient data is vital for making informed decisions; this ensures security and reliability.

Immutability serves the dual purpose of safeguarding against manipulation and furnishing healthcare systems with an auditable ledger of transactions, thereby fostering transparency and accountability. Ensuring this level of transparency is especially beneficial when preserving an unalterable and precise log of patient interactions, treatments, and outcomes. Ensuring the transparency and reliability of an ecosystem through the ability to trace each modification made to EHRs over time instils confidence in the smart healthcare paradigm among healthcare providers, patients, and other relevant stakeholders.

18.4.1.1.2 Transparent audit trail

Blockchain technology brings a transparent audit trail to intelligent healthcare systems, especially for EHR administration. The decentralized and distributed ledger that is a feature of blockchain technology makes this transparency possible by storing copies of the whole record on several network nodes. Every transaction—like updating patient information, for example—is time-stamped, giving an exact historical sequence of occurrences. Thanks to this feature, healthcare professionals may accurately track a patient's whole medical history, including diagnosis and treatments.

The usage of cryptographic hash algorithms further strengthens the audit trail's integrity. Because every block in the blockchain is connected to every other block by distinct hash values, data alteration attempts are detectable and nearly impossible. Furthermore, the ledger's public accessibility guarantees that network members—including patients and healthcare professionals—can independently confirm the accuracy and legitimacy of the data in the EHRs. A key component of blockchain technology is the consensus mechanism, which guarantees that all participants concur on a transaction's legitimacy before adding it to the ledger. This increases the audit trail's dependability and promotes accountability throughout the healthcare ecosystem.

This transparent audit trail builds stakeholders' confidence in smart healthcare by offering a clear and verifiable timeline of patient data. Patients may trust that the information in their medical history is accurate, and healthcare professionals gain from having a safe and responsible method for handling private patient data.

18.4.1.1.3 Consensus mechanism

The fundamental component of this process is decentralization, which distributes decision-making across nodes and reduces the risks connected to a central authority. Proof-of-work and Proof-of-Stake, commonly used consensus procedures, guarantee that participants provide computing power or stake collateral to validate transactions. These resource-intensive procedures connect members' incentives with preserving the blockchain's integrity while securing the network.

Byzantine fault tolerance (BFT), best illustrated by practical BFT, is a noteworthy consensus strategy. Nodes can still agree thanks to this technique, even in the case of malevolent or Byzantine nodes. Resilience to maladaptive behavior improves consensus process security and dependability, essential for preserving data integrity on the blockchain. Furthermore, the addition of smart contracts—self-executing contracts with programmed terms—automates and upholds transaction regulations, giving the consensus process additional transparency and dependability.

Selecting a suitable consensus method is critical for blockchain systems, particularly when data integrity is critical, such as smart healthcare. These systems' versatility enables adaptation according to scalability, energy efficiency, and security needs. The automation and enforcement of predetermined rules via smart contracts, which are integral to the consensus process, enhance the overall dependability and security of the blockchain.

18.4.1.1.4 Enhanced security measures

Blockchain uses advanced cryptographic techniques to protect data, creating linkages between blocks that are difficult to tamper with using cryptographic hashes. This guarantees the chain's integrity and renders historical record manipulation by attackers computationally impossible. Another important component of blockchain's improved security is its decentralized structure. Blockchain reduces susceptible single points of failure by spreading data among several nodes, protecting against deliberate assaults on centralized systems. Due to its reduced vulnerability to harmful intrusions, the decentralized design greatly strengthens the security of patient health data.

A key element of blockchain technology, consensus mechanisms enhance security by approving and verifying transactions before being added to the ledger. By establishing a secure updating system and preventing fraudulent operations, this distributed agreement guarantees that only legal transactions are documented. One of the most important security features of the blockchain is its immutability, which makes historical records immune to tampering. Adding data makes it a permanent link in the chain; to change it, all blocks that follow after it also need to change. This increases the overall integrity of patient health information. Additionally, operations are streamlined, and specified norms are enforced using smart contracts, automated and self-executing contracts with conditions put into code. This eliminates the need for intermediaries and improves the security and effectiveness of contractual agreements in healthcare settings.

Together, these improved security measures create a strong and reliable environment for handling private health information in the context of smart healthcare. With its combination of immutability, decentralization, consensus processes, cryptography, and smart contracts, blockchain offers a holistic solution for security issues, guaranteeing the privacy and accuracy of EHRs in the rapidly developing field of smart healthcare systems.

18.4.1.2 Ensuring access control

The potential of blockchain technology to improve EHR sharing systems' efficiency, security, and privacy has been acknowledged (Shuaib et al., 2022). Maintaining access control is essential in the context of decentralized EHRs to protect patient data security and privacy. There are worries regarding the ethical and safe processing of data access requests because outside parties frequently oversee traditional access control methods for EHR sharing. Access control techniques and blockchain technology may create a reliable and secure self-management system that gives users privacy protection and control over their data. In addition to facilitating safe and allowed data exchange between healthcare providers and other authorized users, this strategy tackles the problem of protecting data, whether it is in transit or at rest (Shi et al., 2020).

The patient becomes the true data owner in a blockchain-based EHR system, and access to their data is only permitted with their consent. A high degree of privacy and security is ensured by attribute authorities' ability to issue or withdraw attributes linked to patient data only with the patient's consent. To guarantee access to the EHR data, digital signatures, and encryption techniques are used, and patients need to give the information owner permission by using a decryption key. In addition to improving data security, this patient-centric approach gives people more authority over their health and medical records (Kiania et al., 2023).

Innovative solutions, including effective security measures and patient-controlled access schemes, are also used to solve access control in decentralized EHR systems. For example, patients can choose whether to share their data with other institutions by using a secure access control method that encrypts their Personal Medical Health Records and uses smart contracts to regulate access to their data. In addition to reducing the possibility of patient data leakage, this patient-centric access control paradigm gives patients the liberty to govern and provide access to their medical records (Yuan et al., 2023).

18.4.2 Secure interoperability

Secure interoperability is the smooth transfer of health data between various platforms and systems, guaranteeing that privacy and security are maintained while sharing information effectively. Achieving interoperability has become crucial as healthcare ecosystems grow more diverse and complicated. Blockchain technology provides creative answers to these problems and improves the safe sharing of medical records.

18.4.2.1 Standardization of data exchange

Standardizing data interchange is commonly known, and developing a single, universal, interoperable format for data transfer is difficult. The endeavor is complicated since

EHR systems created on the same platform are only sometimes interoperable (Reisman, 2017). The creation of regulatory frameworks and standards for EHR data has reinforced data interchange and secondary usage capacity. Although there has been tremendous progress, the advantages still need to be realized to the fullest extent anticipated, and there are still obstacles facing doctors because end users of EHRs limit the technology's ability to ease their workload and enhance patient care (Tsai et al., 2020).

Interoperability is made possible by standardized persistence and data modeling for EHRs. Standardized EHR data is stored in various database management systems, and research and development are still occurring to determine the state-of-the-art in this area (Gamal et al., 2021). By integrating different EHRs and pooling de-identified data from EHRs, initiatives like the Standardized Health Data and Research Exchange seek to advance a learning health system and offer a useful resource for research. The measures above enhance communication, cooperation, and data validation across healthcare institutions, propelling the progress of standardized health data interchange (Davis, no date).

The COVID-19 pandemic has further highlighted the significance of comprehensive health information exchanges and EHR interoperability. The US healthcare system's future depends on interoperability and comprehensive health information exchanges. Hence, policymakers are recommended to establish cooperative task forces and offer financial and commercial incentives to EHR suppliers to guarantee smooth data sharing across platforms. To access and use data in a meaningful and sustainable fashion, it is important to highlight the need for market and financial incentives for EHR suppliers to develop user-friendly health information exchanges and share data across platforms (Turbow et al., 2021). The current research and endeavors in this domain aim to tackle the obstacles and promote the standardization of data interchange within the Decentralized EHRs framework.

18.4.2.2 Cross-institutional communication

Blockchain technology can completely transform the healthcare industry by facilitating transparent and safe data sharing across various organizations. The systematic study by Agbo et al. (n.d.) highlights the difficulties with latency, interoperability, security, and privacy when using blockchain technology in the healthcare industry, underscoring the necessity of continuing research to support initiatives to resolve these difficulties. According to the study, open interoperability standards must be created to accept and fully implement blockchain in operational healthcare contexts. Hence, academics must concentrate on interoperability concerns and standards development (Agbo et al., n.d.).

Blockchain technology can be extremely helpful in smart healthcare security in guaranteeing the confidentiality and integrity of patient data across various organizations. A comprehensive literature analysis on blockchain and IoT highlights the potential advantages of blockchain implementation in healthcare, emphasizing its capacity to offer safe and decentralized data management, which is crucial for interinstitutional communication (Adere, 2022). Further highlighting the significance of blockchain in ensuring secure cross-institutional communication is an application-based analysis of the security of blockchain and AI-powered smart healthcare, which emphasizes the need for reliable and secure solutions for cross-institutional data sharing in the smart healthcare system (Alabdulatif et al., 2022).

18.4.2.3 Immutable audit trails

An immutable audit trail is a tamper-proof record of all transactions and events that cannot be changed or removed. On a blockchain, each data transaction is time-stamped and irreversible, producing a visible and trustworthy audit trail. Medical identity theft and other types of healthcare fraud may be avoided by ensuring that all medical data are correct, comprehensive, and secure through immutable audit trails.

Immutable audit trails in the healthcare sector can assist healthcare providers in adhering to laws like HIPAA. Using blockchain technology, healthcare companies may preserve the necessary records and show their dedication to data privacy and security. Data audit trails are crucial for compliance with healthcare regulations. Blockchain is a great tool for producing trustworthy audit trails because of its transparency and immutability.

Unchangeable audit trails are also advantageous for the banking sector. By using immutable audit trails, financial organizations may guarantee compliance with laws like antimoney laundering and know your customer. Additionally, when supported by immutable audit trails, transparent and accountable financial transactions can lower the risk of fraud and legal action.

Implementing immutable audit trails can be done in several ways. Using distributed ledger technology, like blockchain, is one popular strategy. The decentralized and distributed system known as blockchain has made data almost immutable possible by allowing for tamper-resilience. Blockchain provides an unchangeable historical record for accountability and traceability, occasionally combined with group signature cryptography (Shi et al., 2020).

18.4.2.4 Reduced redundancy and errors

Reduced redundancy in blockchain solutions for smart healthcare security can improve data management efficiency and patient care. Blockchain technology can reduce inefficiency, insecurity, disorganization, and duplicate records problems associated with traditional paper-based health records. Technologies and strategies for minimizing redundancy and errors in intelligent healthcare data management are summarized in Table 18.1.

By leveraging blockchain for EHRs, patients can have one-stop shopping access to their medical histories, reducing the redundancy and inefficiencies in the current healthcare data management systems. Applying blockchain technology in healthcare seeks to resolve problems, including security risks, medical mistakes, and redundant data. Blockchain technology integration with EHRs is viewed as a viable remedy for the inadequacies of EHRs about trust, equitable access, and efficient data management (Shen et al., 2022). Enhanced patient care, better patient outcomes, and decreased medical mistakes are among the main objectives of health information technology (Adere, 2022).

Lower redundancy in blockchain-based smart healthcare security systems can result in more effective data management and better patient care. The difficulties with traditional paper-based health records, such as inefficiencies, instability, disarray, and duplicate entries, may be lessened by blockchain technology. Patients may have one-stop shopping access to their medical records by utilizing blockchain for EHRs, reducing inefficiencies and redundancies in the present healthcare data management systems (Shen et al., 2022).

Blockchain technology can lower medical mistakes and enhance patient outcomes in the setting of errors. Blockchain technology is used in healthcare to improve patient care and

TABLE 18.1   Strategies for reducing redundancy and errors in smart healthcare data management.

Aspect	Technologies and tools	Implementation strategies
Reduced data redundancy	Database management systems (DBMS)	Data normalization and deduplication
	Cloud storage solutions	Centralized data repository
	Compression algorithms	Distributed databases
	Distributed ledger technologies (DLT)	Data compression algorithms
Error detection and correction	Cryptographic hash functions	Checksums and hash functions
	Error-correcting codes (ECC)	Error-detection codes
	Byzantine fault tolerance (BFT)	Consensus mechanisms
	Blockchain platforms	Blockchain technology
Automation in data handling	Automated validation tools	Automated data validation processes
	Machine learning frameworks	Machine learning algorithms
	Smart contract platforms	Smart contract implementation
Enhanced data quality	Data quality management tools	Establishment of data quality standards
	User interface (UI) design principles	User-friendly interfaces
	Data governance frameworks	Data governance policies and protocols

lower medical errors by improving data security, accessibility, and accuracy (Adere, 2022). To guarantee the successful mitigation of mistakes and security concerns, it is crucial to solve the issues of latency, interoperability, security, and privacy in connection to the application of blockchain technology in healthcare.

18.5 Privacy enhancement through blockchain

Healthcare providers may securely store and exchange sensitive health information, including EHRs and medical imaging data. The system uses smart contracts to guarantee that only those with permission may access the data. The blockchain's permissions-based architecture allowed for regulated data exchange without compromising privacy. Its effective data retrieval speeds demonstrated the framework's scalability for practical healthcare applications, even with rising data volumes (Ali, 2023).

Models to increase healthcare data security utilizing A structure known as DITrust Chain is proposed in the paper blockchain. The framework's goal is to enhance healthcare data availability, privacy, integrity, and trustworthiness (Kiania et al., 2023). The suggested approach integrates hybrid deep learning models and offers a strong basis for blockchain-powered healthcare systems. The research suggests a permissions-based blockchain framework for safe and scalable healthcare systems (Ali, 2023).

The report emphasizes the significance of exchanging data while protecting privacy in healthcare. The blockchain's permissions-based architecture allowed for regulated data exchange without compromising privacy (Ali, 2023).

A blockchain-based smart healthcare system employing IoMT devices for safe data exchange is proposed in the study chain: Blockchain-Based Healthcare Data Exchange with Enhanced Security and Privacy Location-Based-Authentication. The suggested solution employs symmetric and asymmetric keys to prevent unauthorized individuals from accessing sensitive information. By using location-based authentication, the system guarantees the legitimacy of the data source (Alruwaill et al., 2023).

18.5.1 Patient empowerment

A key component of healthcare is patient empowerment, which blockchain technology may improve. Thanks to blockchain technology, better health outcomes may result from giving individuals more control over their medical records and care. The benefits, difficulties, and constraints of blockchain technology in healthcare and EHR regarding patient empowerment were noted in a scoping assessment of blockchain-based frameworks for patient empowerment. Blockchain technology can give patients more control over the "selective" sharing of their medical records and increase their knowledge of their health (Anik et al., 2023).

Blockchain technology integrates several privacy-enhancing technologies to strengthen the security of sensitive patient data. Blockchain technology allows for the safe transmission and storage of healthcare data and patient control over who has access to it (Taherdoost, 2023). Several strategies to improve healthcare data security using blockchain technology were found in a comprehensive assessment of the literature on blockchain-based privacy and security in electronic health. These models include a DITrust Chain structure, a strategy for telecare of healthcare information utilizing blockchain, and enhanced access control and medical data sharing (Kiania et al., 2023).

Blockchain technology has been used in several research to propose frameworks and methods for the privacy-preserving usage of personal health data. For example, I-blockchain is an individual-centric paradigm for the privacy-preserving use of personal health data enabled by blockchain technology (Tandon et al., 2020). Healthchain is an additional blockchain-based medical data privacy protection system (Taherdoost, 2023). These frameworks and systems are designed to give patients more control over their medical information while protecting the confidentiality and security of sensitive patient data.

However, there are drawbacks and restrictions to using blockchain technology in the medical field. Scalability, mutual authentication, reliability, privacy, data integrity, and availability are a few of these. Furthermore, changing important medical data might harm medical prescriptions, illness identification, anomaly detection, and other areas. Therefore, these issues and constraints must be addressed to guarantee the effective application of blockchain technology in healthcare.

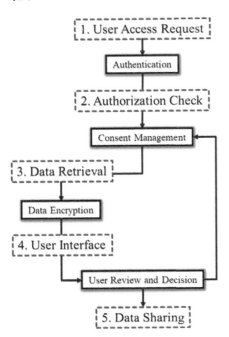

FIGURE 18.3 Managing personal health data access and control.

18.5.1.1 Control over personal health data

Blockchain technology has come to light as a potentially useful tool for improving the privacy and management of personal health data. Numerous uses, difficulties, and potential directions for privacy enhancement using blockchain technology have been covered in the literature. Blockchain provides a state-of-the-art method for integrating medical data, storing medical data, and conducting medical transactions (Taherdoost, 2023). It has been acknowledged that it can completely transform personal health records and provide a more patient-centered, safe, and effective healthcare system. Blockchain technology is used in medicine to provide decentralized identification solutions, secure data exchange, and patient consent management—all critical to bolstering data privacy and protecting patient information.

A secure, unchangeable record of a patient's medical history accessible to pharmacists, doctors, and patients is one of the main benefits of blockchain technology for the healthcare industry. This ensures that the data is current and correct. Furthermore, blockchain can solve the problem of patients needing more control over their health data by enabling people to take ownership of their health data and decide who has access to it. The transparency and tamper-proof nature of blockchain technology can greatly improve the privacy and security of personal health records.

Blockchain-based frameworks and models have been presented in several research papers to protect the privacy of individual health information. For example, a blockchain-based privacy-preserving smart healthcare architecture has been introduced (Taherdoost, 2023). Furthermore, a comprehensive analysis has looked at the state of affairs, design decisions, constraints, and potential future paths of blockchain-based personal health records, emphasizing the major benefits of blockchain in giving end users ownership, control, and access to data (Fang et al., 2021). The simplified procedure that allows users to manage and retrieve their health data safely is depicted in Fig. 18.3.

18.5.1.2 Consent management

Consent management has received much interest from academic researchers, especially regarding enhancing privacy with blockchain technology. It is being investigated if blockchain technology may help create consent management systems that are more user-centered, transparent, and safe. The potential of blockchain to streamline and secure the consent process, making it more transparent and user-friendly, is highlighted in a systematic evaluation of blockchain for consent management by Kakarlapudi and Mahmoud (n.d.). This is especially important when considering privacy rules and the requirement to guarantee adherence to data protection guidelines.

Dynamic consent management systems—which empower data subjects through decentralized data controllers and privacy-preserving strategies—are one area of particular interest. Dynamic consent management solutions that employ blockchain technology are thought to improve security and privacy assurances by enabling data subjects to control their consent to access their data dynamically. The privacy-first paradigm for dynamic consent management systems highlights the importance of privacy by design and the application of privacy-preserving strategies, including encryption, in blockchain-based consent management platforms (Khalid et al., 2023a).

Active assisted living blockchain-based consent management solutions are becoming increasingly popular in the healthcare industry. A blockchain-based permission management platform has been presented by research that gives consumers changeable power at the granular level and lets them manage consent for various data categories and timeframes. With a focus on active assisted living and IoT applications, this strategy seeks to solve the special consent management issues in the healthcare industry (Velmovitsky et al., 2020).

Additionally, the setting of biobanking and clinical data analytics about using blockchain technology in consent management systems is being investigated. Blockchain technology is thought to provide double-masked consent-driven data exchange, improving privacy and protection of sensitive medical data (Khalid et al., 2023b).

Consent and transparency privacy-preserving methods are becoming increasingly important in human-centered IoT applications. Blockchain technology creates privacy-preserving models in human-centered IoT contexts that provide verified and transparent consent management. This is especially crucial since IoT systems include billions of devices and are continually evolving, which raises privacy and data-gathering concerns (Rivadeneira et al., 2023). Table 18.2 concisely presents consent management components in smart healthcare, focusing on type, blockchain role, and future trends.

18.5.2 Anonymity and pseudonymity

Pseudonymy and anonymity are two key ideas for enhancing privacy using blockchain. The capacity to conceal a user's or transaction's identity is known as anonymity, whereas

TABLE 18.2   Consent management in smart healthcare: a blockchain perspective.

Component	Consent type	Blockchain role	Future trends
Informed consent	Explicit	Decentralized and immutable record	Smart contracts integration
Dynamic consent	Adjustable	Transparent ledger	Integration with wearables
Audit trails	Historical	Ensures accountability	Advanced analytics for consent patterns

using an alias or pseudonym to represent a user or transaction is known as pseudonymity. It is crucial to understand that pseudonymization is a technique that lessens the connection between a data collection and its original identity rather than an anonymization method (de Haro-Olmo et al., 2020).

The generalized blockchain problems of transaction linkability and associated address tracking are hurdles to ensuring blockchain privacy compliance in the digital world. Analysis attacks on wallet addresses, transaction currencies, and other relevant active attacks have plagued cryptocurrency. Even though Bitcoin has been around for more than 11 years, several attempts have been made to address these problems; nonetheless, it has been established that many of these solutions need to offer an adequate degree of anonymity (Bansod & Ragha, 2022; Amarasinghe et al., 2019).

One of the most important requirements for permissionless blockchain is privacy preservation. Peng et al. (2021) examined systems like Bitcoin's privacy and security features and discussed different risks to user privacy and transaction anonymity. Additionally, they suggested a set of rules for creating blockchain systems that protect privacy.

Cryptography is crucial to guarantee the anonymity of the entities involved in the blockchain. The degree of anonymization varies based on the cryptographic functions that are employed. Due to bandwidth constraints, the original blockchain topology presents a hurdle for utilizing blockchain in the IoT (de Haro-Olmo et al., 2020). The argument for data privacy to be recognized as a basic human right is becoming more and more compelling. It is clear from reading the most recent research that there are several holes in blockchain applications' privacy, safety, and security elements as they stand now.

18.6 Challenges and future directions

18.6.1 Remaining hurdles

Even with the potential of blockchain technology to augment security and privacy in intelligent healthcare systems, several obstacles and challenges persist. It is imperative to overcome these challenges to ensure the extensive implementation and smooth assimilation of blockchain technology within the healthcare industry.

Stringent compliance standards and regulations govern the healthcare sector to ensure data integrity and patient safety. Incorporating blockchain solutions necessitates adeptly navigating an intricate regulatory environment. The attainment of conformity with prevailing healthcare regulations, including the General Data Protection Regulation in the

European Union and the HIPAA in the United States, presents a substantial obstacle. It is imperative to guarantee that blockchain implementations conform to these regulations to utilize the technology in healthcare lawfully and ethically.

The technical challenges of scalability, interoperability, and energy efficiency persist in the ever-evolving landscape of blockchain technology. Intelligent healthcare systems produce enormous quantities of data that need to be securely processed and stored, frequently in real-time. Without jeopardizing decentralization or security, blockchain networks must progress to accommodate the scope and velocity demanded by healthcare applications. Furthermore, to achieve smooth integration, it is critical to have interoperability with preexisting healthcare IT infrastructure and standards. This necessitates the concerted cooperation of all stakeholders within the healthcare ecosystem.

Critical to the effective integration of blockchain technology into intelligent healthcare is the comprehension and adoption of the system by healthcare administrators, practitioners, and, above all else, patients. Convincing stakeholders of the advantages of blockchain technology, debunking misunderstandings, and establishing confidence are critical in surmounting opposition to change. Broad acceptance could be necessary for implementing blockchain solutions, compromising the overall efficacy of bolstering security and privacy in intelligent healthcare.

Blockchain solution implementation may necessitate substantial initial infrastructure, technology, and personnel training investments. Healthcare institutions, particularly those of a lesser scale operating with constrained resources, might need help allocating the requisite financial resources and specialized knowledge to implement blockchain technology. It is paramount to surmount financial limitations and establish the enduring value proposition of blockchain solutions to promote their extensive implementation in various healthcare environments.

Many healthcare organizations continue to depend on antiquated systems and procedures that may present challenges regarding seamless integration with blockchain technology. There is a significant challenge in transferring extant data to a blockchain-based system while ensuring that integrity and security are not compromised. It is critical to consider the coexistence of blockchain technology and legacy systems and to ensure a seamless transition to mitigate any potential disruptions to healthcare operations.

18.6.2 Emerging trends

The advancement of blockchain technology in the context of intelligent healthcare is currently undergoing substantial changes due to a succession of emergent trends that have the potential to revolutionize the sector. To begin with, there is increasing interest in integrating blockchain technology with other advanced systems, most notably AI and the IoT. In addition to serving as a secure ledger for IoT device data management, blockchain augments data analytics with AI algorithms. With this integration, healthcare services are anticipated to be more individualized and streamlined, reaffirming blockchain's pivotal position in the technological convergence that drives intelligent healthcare.

Standardization-oriented global collaboration is an additional crucial trend. In light of the imperative for regulatory compliance and interoperability, the healthcare sector actively promotes global collaboration to establish uniform protocols for integrating blockchain technology. These endeavors aim to establish universally applicable standards that guarantee the exchange of data securely and transparently, thereby cultivating confidence among all parties involved. Establishing standards is crucial to fully harness the capabilities of blockchain technology in the healthcare industry worldwide. It facilitates a cohesive strategy for tackling obstacles and guarantees the smooth incorporation of blockchain solutions.

Moreover, decentralization is becoming a prominent trend, specifically in the healthcare sector's identity administration realm. Blockchain provides a decentralized solution for identity management, enabling patients to administer their identities securely across many healthcare providers. This methodology allows individuals to regulate entry to their health records and judiciously distribute data. The concurrent investigation of advanced privacy methods, such as homomorphic encryption and zero-knowledge proofs, demonstrates a dedication to confronting the ever-changing landscape of privacy apprehensions. These advancements strive to achieve a harmonious equilibrium between the usefulness of data for analytical purposes and the necessity to uphold the privacy of confidential healthcare data. As these patterns develop, they collectively inaugurate a paradigm shift for blockchain technology in intelligent healthcare, fortifying security protocols and protecting patients' privacy in novel approaches.

18.7 Conclusion

Incorporating blockchain technology into the smart healthcare domain signifies a significant progression that has extensive ramifications concerning privacy and security. With the ongoing transformation of healthcare delivery by smart technologies, protecting patient data becomes an ever more critical imperative. Blockchain, which provides a secure framework for data administration and is distinguished by its decentralized and immutable architecture, arises as a potent remedy for the inherent difficulties in smart healthcare ecosystems.

In this chapter, we thoroughly examined the foundational principles of blockchain technology and its specific implementations in the healthcare sector, focusing on its pertinence to the intricate intricacies of smart healthcare. Blockchain technology is pivotal in strengthening security measures and safeguarding patient information, as evidenced by its impact on decentralized EHRs, secure interoperability, and standardized data exchange. The technology's capability to achieve a nuanced equilibrium between accessibility and confidentiality in the digital healthcare domain is further emphasized by patient empowerment mechanisms such as consent management and privacy enhancements like anonymity.

References

AbdulRaheem, M., Awotunde, J. B., Chakraborty, C., Adeniyi, E. A., Oladipo, I. D., & Bhoi, A. K. (2022). *Security and privacy concerns in smart healthcare system implementation of smart healthcare systems using AI, IoT, and Blockchain*. Nigeria: Elsevier. Available from https://doi.org/10.1016/B978-0-323-91916-6.00002-3, https://www.sciencedirect.com/book/9780323919166.

Abouelmehdi, K., Beni-Hessane, A., & Khaloufi, H. (2018). Big healthcare data: Preserving security and privacy. *Journal of Big Data*, 5(1). Available from https://doi.org/10.1186/s40537-017-0110-7, https://journalofbigdata.springeropen.com.

Abu-elezz, I., Hassan, A., Nazeemudeen, A., Househ, M., & Abd-alrazaq, A. (2020). The benefits and threats of blockchain technology in healthcare: A scoping review. *International Journal of Medical Informatics*, 142, 104246. Available from https://doi.org/10.1016/j.ijmedinf.2020.104246.

Adere, E. M. (2022). Blockchain in healthcare and IoT: A systematic literature review. (no date) *Array*.

Agbo, C. C., Mahmoud, Q. H., & Eklund, J. M. (n.d.) Blockchain technology in healthcare: A systematic review.

Alabdulatif, A., Khalil, I., & Saidur Rahman, M. (2022). Security of blockchain and AI-empowered smart healthcare: Application-based analysis. *Applied Sciences*, 12(21), 11039. Available from https://doi.org/10.3390/app122111039.

Ali, A. (2023). Blockchain-powered healthcare systems: Enhancing scalability and security with hybrid deep learning. (no date) *Sensors*.

Alruwaill, M. N., Mohanty, S. P., & Kougianos, E. (2023). hChain: Blockchain based healthcare data sharing with enhanced security and privacy location-based-authentication. In *Proceedings of the ACM great lakes symposium on VLSI, GLSVLSI*. Association for Computing Machinery, United States (pp. 97–102). https://doi.org/10.1145/3583781.3590255. 9798400701252.

Amarasinghe, N., Boyen, X., & McKague, M. (2019). A survey of anonymity of cryptocurrencies. In *ACM international conference proceeding series. Association for computing machinery*. Australia. http://portal.acm.org/ https://doi.org/10.1145/3290688.3290693. 9781450366038.

Anik, F. I., Sakib, N., Shahriar, H., Xie, Y., Nahiyan, H. A., & Ahamed, S. I. (2023). Unraveling a blockchain-based framework towards patient empowerment: A scoping review envisioning future smart health technologies. *Smart Health*, 29, 100401. Available from https://doi.org/10.1016/j.smhl.2023.100401.

Bansod, S. and Ragha, L. (no date) Challenges in making blockchain privacy compliant for the digital world: some measures. *Sādhanā*, 2022.

Davis, S. (n.d.) Standardized health data and research exchange (SHaRE): Promoting a learning health system. In *JAMIA open*.

Fang, H. S. A., Tan, T. H., Fang, Y., Tan, C., & Tan, C. J. M. (2021). Blockchain personal health records: Systematic review. *Journal of Medical Internet Research*, 23(4), e25094. Available from https://doi.org/10.2196/25094.

Filkins, B. L., Kim, J. Y., Roberts, B., Armstrong, W., Miller, M. A., Hultner, M. L., Castillo, A. P., Ducom, J. C., Topol, E. J., & Steinhubl, S. R. (2016). Privacy and security in the era of digital health: What should translational researchers know and do about it? *American Journal of Translational Research*, 8(3). Available from http://www.ajtr.org/files/ajtr0020863.pdf.

Gamal, A., Barakat, S., & Rezk, A. (2021). Standardized electronic health record data modeling and persistence: A comparative review. *Journal of Biomedical Informatics*, 114, 103670. Available from https://doi.org/10.1016/j.jbi.2020.103670.

Gerke, S., Minssen, T., & Cohen, G. (2020). *Ethical and legal challenges of artificial intelligence-driven healthcare artificial intelligence in healthcare*. United States: Elsevier. Available from https://doi.org/10.1016/B978-0-12-818438-7.00012-5, https://www.elsevier.com/books/artificial-intelligence-in-healthcare/bohr/978-0-12-818438-7.

Haleem, A., Javaid, M., Singh, R. P., Suman, R., & Rab, S. (2021). Blockchain technology applications in healthcare: An overview. *International Journal of Intelligent Networks*, 2. Available from https://doi.org/10.1016/j.ijin.2021.09.005.

de Haro-Olmo, F. J., Varela-Vaca, Á. J., & Álvarez-Bermejo, J. A. (2020). Blockchain from the perspective of privacy and anonymisation: A systematic literature review. *Sensors*, 20(24), 7171. Available from https://doi.org/10.3390/s20247171.

Islam, M. M., Rahaman, A., & Islam, M. R. (2020). Development of smart healthcare monitoring system in IoT environment. *SN Computer Science*, 1(3). Available from https://doi.org/10.1007/s42979-020-00195-y, https://www.springer.com/journal/42979.

Kakarlapudi, P. V., & Mahmoud, Q. H. (n.d.) *A systematic review of blockchain for consent management*.

Khalid, M. I., Ahmed, M., & Kim, J. (2023a). Enhancing data protection in dynamic consent management systems: Formalizing privacy and security definitions with differential privacy, decentralization, and zero-knowledge proofs. *Sensors*, 23(17). Available from https://doi.org/10.3390/s23177604, http://www.mdpi.com/journal/sensors.

Khalid, M. I., Ahmed, M., Helfert, M., & Kim, J. (2023b). Privacy-first paradigm for dynamic consent management systems: Empowering data subjects through decentralized data controllers and privacy-preserving techniques. *Electronics, 12*(24), 4973. Available from https://doi.org/10.3390/electronics12244973.

Kiania, K., Jameii, S. M., & Rahmani, A. M. (2023). Blockchain-based privacy and security preserving in electronic health: A systematic review. *Multimedia Tools and Applications, 82*(18). Available from https://doi.org/10.1007/s11042-023-14488-w, https://www.springer.com/journal/11042.

Lieneck, C., McLauchlan, M., & Phillips, S. (n.d.) Healthcare cybersecurity ethical concerns during the COVID-19 Global pandemic: A rapid review.

Moosavi, N., & Taherdoost, H. (2024). Blockchain technology, structure, and applications: A survey. Authorea preprints.

Navaz, A. N., Serhani, M. A., El Kassabi, H. T., Al-Qirim, N., & Ismail, H. (2021). Trends, technologies, and key challenges in smart and connected healthcare. *IEEE Access, 9*. Available from https://doi.org/10.1109/ACCESS.2021.3079217, http://ieeexplore.ieee.org/xpl/RecentIssue.jsp?punumber = 6287639.

Newaz, A. I., Sikder, A. K., Rahman, M. A., & Selcuk Uluagac, A. (2021). A survey on security and privacy issues in modern healthcare systems. *ACM Transactions on Computing for Healthcare, 2*(3). Available from https://doi.org/10.1145/3453176.

Paul, M., Maglaras, L., Ferrag, M. A., & Almomani, I. (2023). Digitization of healthcare sector: A study on privacy and security concerns. *ICT Express, 9*(4). Available from https://doi.org/10.1016/j.icte.2023.02.007.

Peng, L., Feng, W., Yan, Z., Li, Y., Zhou, X., & Shimizu, S. (2021). Privacy preservation in permissionless blockchain: A survey. *Digital Communications and Networks, 7*(3). Available from https://doi.org/10.1016/j.dcan.2020.05.008.

Popoola, O., Rodrigues, M., Marchang, J., Shenfield, A., Ikpehia, A., & Popoola, J. (2023). A critical literature review of security and privacy in smart home healthcare schemes adopting IoT & blockchain: Problems, challenges and solutions. *Blockchain: Research and Applications*, 100178. Available from https://doi.org/10.1016/j.bcra.2023.100178.

Rani, S., Rajagopal, M., Kumar, N., Hassan, S., & Shah, A. (2022). *Security and privacy issues in smart healthcare system using Internet of Things IoT-enabled smart healthcare systems, services and applications.* Wiley. Available from https://doi.org/10.1002/9781119816829.ch4.

Reisman, M. (2017). EHRs: The challenge of making electronic data usable and interoperable. *P and T, 42*(9). Available from https://www.ptcommunity.com/system/files/pdf/ptj4209572.pdf.

Rivadeneira, J. E., Jiménez, M. B., Marculescu, R., Rodrigues, A., Boavida, F., & Silva, J. S. (2023). A blockchain-based privacy-preserving model for consent and transparency human-centered Internet of Things. In *ACM international conference proceeding series association for computing machinery* (pp. 301–314). Portugal. <http://portal.acm.org/ https://doi.org/10.1145/3576842.3582379>. 9798400700378.

Sadek, I., Codjo, J., Rehman, S. U., & Abdulrazak, B. (2022). Security and privacy in the internet of things healthcare systems: Toward a robust solution in real-life deployment. *Computer Methods and Programs in Biomedicine Update, 2*, 100071. Available from https://doi.org/10.1016/j.cmpbup.2022.100071.

Saeed, H., Malik, H., Bashir, U., Ahmad, A., Riaz, S., Ilyas, M., Bukhari, W. A., Khan, M. I. A., & Vijayakumar, P. (2022). Blockchain technology in healthcare: A systematic review. *PLOS ONE, 17*(4), e0266462. Available from https://doi.org/10.1371/journal.pone.0266462.

Schroeder, T., Haug, M., & Gewald, H. (2022). Data privacy concerns using mhealth apps and smart speakers: Comparative interview study among mature adults. *JMIR Formative Research, 6*(6), e28025. Available from https://doi.org/10.2196/28025.

Seh, A. H. (n.d.) *Healthcare data breaches: Insights and implications.*

Shen, X., Jiang, C., Wen, Y., Li, C., & Lu, Q. (2022). A brief review on deep learning applications in genomic studies. *Frontiers in Systems Biology, 2*. Available from https://doi.org/10.3389/fsysb.2022.877717.

Shi, S., He, D., Li, L., Kumar, N., Khan, M. K., & Choo, K.-K. R. (2020). Applications of blockchain in ensuring the security and privacy of electronic health record systems: A survey. *Computers & Security, 97*, 101966. Available from https://doi.org/10.1016/j.cose.2020.101966.

Shuaib, K., Abdella, J., Sallabi, F., & Serhani, M. A. (2022). Secure decentralized electronic health records sharing system based on blockchains. *Journal of King Saud University - Computer and Information Sciences, 34*(8). Available from https://doi.org/10.1016/j.jksuci.2021.05.002.

Silvestri, S., Islam, S., Papastergiou, S., Tzagkarakis, C., & Ciampi, M. (2023). A machine learning approach for the NLP-based analysis of cyber threats and vulnerabilities of the healthcare ecosystem. *Sensors, 23*(2), 651. Available from https://doi.org/10.3390/s23020651.

Stoumpos, A. I., Kitsios, F., & Talias, M. A. (2023). Digital transformation in healthcare: Technology acceptance and its applications. *International Journal of Environmental Research and Public Health, 20*(4). Available from https://doi.org/10.3390/ijerph20043407, http://www.mdpi.com/journal/ijerph.

Taherdoost, H. (2023). Privacy and security of blockchain in healthcare: Applications, challenges, and future perspectives. (no date) *Science*.

Tandon, A., Dhir, A., Islam, A. K. M. N., & Mäntymäki, M. (2020). Blockchain in healthcare: A systematic literature review, synthesizing framework and future research agenda. *Computers in Industry, 122*, 103290. Available from https://doi.org/10.1016/j.compind.2020.103290.

Tariq, R. A., & Hackert, P. B. (2023). *Patient confidentiality. StatPearls*. Treasure Island (FL): StatPearls Publishing. Available from https://europepmc.org/article/nbk/nbk519540.

Tertulino, R., Antunes, N., & Morais, H. (2023). Privacy in electronic health records: A systematic mapping study. *Journal of Public Health*. Available from https://doi.org/10.1007/s10389-022-01795-z, Springer Science and Business Media LLC.

Tian, S., Yang, W., Grange, J. M. L., Wang, P., Huang, W., & Ye, Z. (2019). Smart healthcare: Making medical care more intelligent. *Global Health Journal, 3*(3). Available from https://doi.org/10.1016/j.glohj.2019.07.001.

Tsai, C. H., Eghdam, A., Davoody, N., Wright, G., Flowerday, S., & Koch, S. (2020). Effects of electronic health record implementation and barriers to adoption and use: A scoping review and qualitative analysis of the content. *Life, 10*(12), 327. Available from https://doi.org/10.3390/life10120327.

Turbow, S., Hollberg, J. R., & Ali, M. K. (2021). Electronic health record interoperability: How did we get here and how do we move forward? *JAMA Health Forum, 2*(3), E210253. Available from https://doi.org/10.1001/jamahealthforum.2021.0253, jamanetwork.com/journals/jama-health-forum.

Vaiyapuri, T., Binbusayyis, A., & Varadarajan, V. (2021). Security, privacy and trust in IoMT enabled smart healthcare system: A systematic review of current and future trends. *International Journal of Advanced Computer Science and Applications, 12*(2). Available from https://doi.org/10.14569/IJACSA.2021.0120291, http://thesai.org/Publications/Archives?code = IJACSA.

Velmovitsky, P. E., Miranda, P. A. D. S. E. S., Vaillancourt, H., Donovska, T., Teague, J., & Morita, P. P. (2020). A blockchain-based consent platform for active assisted living: Modeling study and conceptual framework. *Journal of Medical Internet Research, 22*(12), e20832. Available from https://doi.org/10.2196/20832.

Wang, C. (n.d.) Privacy protection in using artificial intelligence for healthcare: Chinese regulation in comparative perspective.

Yan, F., Li, N., Iliyasu, A. M., Salama, A. S., & Hirota, K. (2023). Insights into security and privacy issues in smart healthcare systems based on medical images. *Journal of Information Security and Applications, 78*, 103621. Available from https://doi.org/10.1016/j.jisa.2023.103621.

Yuan, W. X., Yan, B., Li, W., Hao, L. Y., & Yang, H. M. (2023). Blockchain-based medical health record access control scheme with efficient protection mechanism and patient control. *Multimedia Tools and Applications, 82*(11). Available from https://doi.org/10.1007/s11042-022-14023-3, https://www.springer.com/journal/11042.

Sensors and security considerations for emergency vehicles

Mohan Vandabona, Vithushan Gnanaraj, Malindu Attygala, Danish Kumar and Alireza Jolfaei

College of Science and Engineering, Flinders University, Tonsley, SA, Australia

19.1 Introduction

Emergency vehicles play an important role in protecting communities by responding to critical situations in a timely manner. In the current emergency services, the capabilities of emergency vehicles have significantly been augmented by technological advancements. There are different types of sensors which are integrated into emergency vehicles, facilitating efficiency, with enhanced safety and response capabilities. From location tracking systems to collision avoidance technologies, a sophisticated network is formed by these sensors that empowers emergency responders to navigate via dynamic environments while ensuring the emergency personnel and public safety. This study reviews diverse sensors employed in emergency vehicles. There are different types of emergency vehicles, such as fire truck, police vehicles, ambulances, and rescue vehicles.

Fire trucks are vital emergency response vehicles (ERVs) designed to combat various types of fires, including wildfires, and to transport firefighters and equipment to the scene of a blaze. Various types of fire trucks serve specific functions in fire extinguishing processes, including conventional fire trucks, fire engines, turntable ladder trucks, heavy rescue vehicles, Quints, A-wagons, and water tenders. Similarly, police vehicles are crucial in law enforcement operations, ranging from patrol vehicles, interceptors, and highway patrol vehicles to sport utility vehicles (SUVs). Equipped with essential gear such as weapons, medical supplies, and emergency identification lighting, police vehicles serve as indispensable tools for law enforcement officers, facilitating efficient responses to incidents and conducting patrols effectively. Ambulances play a critical role in providing emergency medical care, equipped with a range of medical devices and categorized based on their tasks, such as first responder ambulances, advanced life support (ALS) ambulances, and patient transport vehicles.

Sensor Networks for Smart Hospitals
DOI: https://doi.org/10.1016/B978-0-443-36370-2.00020-7

Ambulances come in various forms, including vans, buses, motorbikes, and helicopters, tailored to specific emergencies. Lastly, rescue vehicles, equipped with ropes and specialized gear, are deployed in hazardous scenarios to extricate individuals who are injured or trapped, particularly in natural disasters like earthquakes.

Since emergency vehicles appear in response to catastrophes and emergencies, they have mechanisms to address those situations effectively. The mechanisms employed by each vehicle can vary. These may include a Basic Life Support system, lighting, and sirens to indicate the vehicle's purpose, an ALS system, or an automatic external defibrillator for treating medical emergencies requiring immediate intervention. Additionally, firefighting equipment, a minimum of four first aid kits, mobility aids, and oxygen storage and dispensing systems, or onboard oxygen generating systems are among the components commonly found.

Mainly due to the critical operations nature, security audits in emergency vehicles are paramount which ensure that all systems, including navigation, communication, and data management, are optimally functioning to help reliable operations in emergency response. The integration of various technologies becomes increasingly complex as we strive to ensure compliance with strict standards and regulations. Moreover, the significance of robust security measures is further emphasized, particularly as emergency vehicles frequently operate within unpredictable and dynamic environments. Security audits play a crucial role in identifying vulnerabilities and weaknesses within systems, enabling timely remediation efforts to maintain the reliability and integrity of emergency services. The failure to conduct security audits typically leads to disruptions and compromises in public safety and emergency response operations.

The remainder of this chapter is as follows: Section 19.2 discusses the related works. Section 19.3 discusses the methodology and the challenges of finding the related research. Section 19.4 discusses sensors used in emergency vehicles. Section 19.5 discusses the integration of sensor technology in emergency operations. Section 19.6 discusses security considerations and challenges to the sensors. Security Threats are further discussed in Section 19.7. Finally, the last section concludes the chapter.

19.2 Related work

This section provides an overview of the recent literature on emergency vehicle failures and their security issues.

In Hsiao et al. (2018), the authors studied the causes of emergency vehicle crashes, and categorized risk factors into driver, task, vehicle, and environmental aspects. The authors discussed existing interventions and put forward research concepts to address knowledge gaps, with the ultimate goal of enhancing safety for both emergency responders and the public on the road.

In Humagain et al. (2020), the authors studied the growing use of unmanned aerial vehicle (UAV) across different industries, with a particular emphasis on safety and security applications. Humagain et al. identified the challenges associated with the UAV technology and highlighted the research directions with respect to the use of UAVs in timely and cost-effective delivery, especially in demanding environments.

In Alamdar et al. (2017), the authors investigated the utilization of multivendor sensor data in disaster management, focusing on flood response in Victoria, Australia. Through an empirical case study, it identifies technical barriers to interoperability and reveals mechanisms for integrating sensor data. The findings highlight the need for enhanced capabilities among stakeholders to effectively utilize sensor-derived disaster information.

In Sundar et al. (2014) study, an intelligent traffic control system is presented aimed at facilitating the smooth passage of emergency vehicles. Utilizing radio fequency identification (RFID) technology, each vehicle is equipped with a tag that communicates with readers strategically placed along the route. The system counts passing vehicles, assesses network congestion to adjust green light durations, and alerts authorities if a stolen vehicle is detected. Additionally, the system facilitates communication between ambulances and traffic controllers to prioritize their passage through intersections. Tested prototypes demonstrate successful functionality under various conditions in a wireless communication laboratory.

In Masini et al. (2018), the authors examined the development and potential impact of vehicle-to-everything (V2X) communications, focusing on short-range connectivity. Masini et al. discussed the technical and economic drivers behind V2X technology, including international mandates for onboard devices. Their analysis included various wireless access technologies, from IEEE 802.11p to Cellular-V2X and emerging options such as visible light communication and millimeter waves. Performance comparisons in urban scenarios highlight the complexity of predicting the future enabling technology, which may be influenced by international regulations.

In Kaurav et al. (2021), authors proposed an emergency vehicle routing solution where each vehicle connected to the Ethereum Blockchain integrated with Open Source Routing Machine (OSRM). Blockchain could enable secure information sharing among vehicles and the OSRM might provide the shortest trustworthy routes. The authors indicated that their approach might reduce the transit delay of the emergency vehicles while providing secured emergency healthcare services. In this direction, in Rajeshwari and Rajesh (2024), the authors proposed implementing blockchain for data transmission of road conditions between an ambulance and other registered vehicles via a roadside unit. Their proposed approach might eliminate the risk of receiving fake/bogus messages from other vehicles about road conditions.

19.3 Methodology

This section outlines the methods we used for the selection of resources from databases such as IEEE Xplore, ScienceDirect, and Google Scholar. We selected the articles written in English and chose the range of publication dates from 2014 to 2024, to ensure we identify the most recent research. The search terms included types, the role of sensor technology, sensors, security measures, and features in emergency vehicle operations. Only peer-reviewed articles with full-text and online availability were considered. The selection criteria are listed in Table 19.1.

The topic may not have a vast amount of dedicated research, making it challenging to find comprehensive articles. It was difficult to find a sufficient number of articles that comprehensively covered the subject matter. Focusing the research on a specific country

TABLE 19.1   Research paper selection criteria.

Selection criteria	Values/indicators
Research database	IEEE Xplore, ScienceDirect and Google Scholar
Type of publication	Academic journals only
Search terms	Role of sensor technology in emergency vehicle operations Sensor types in emergency vehicles Security in emergency vehicles
Search limits	Most recent Peer-reviewed articles
Language	Published in English
Availability	Full text online
Timeframes	From 2014 to 2024

limited the available literature further, as not all studies explicitly mention the country in their titles or keywords. All these resulted in a reduced pool of relevant articles and research papers. The interdisciplinary nature of the topic involves aspects of both sensor technology and security considerations. This can pose a challenge as relevant research may be dispersed across various disciplines such as engineering, security studies, transportation, etc. Finding a cohesive body of work that integrates these aspects may be challenging. In rapidly evolving fields like sensor technology, older research may not accurately reflect the current state of the field. Outdated information may not account for recent advancements, emerging technologies, or changes in security standards for emergency vehicles. Access to the full text of articles can be restricted due to paywalls or subscription requirements. This limitation can impede researchers from obtaining crucial information and insights from relevant studies. Important research findings might be presented in conference proceedings or exist in literature, which includes reports, theses, and other nontraditional publications. These sources may not always be indexed in standard databases, making them potentially overlooked in conventional searches.

19.4 Sensors used in emergency vehicles

Table 19.2 lists the sensors used for diagnostic purposes as well as ensuring safety within emergency vehicles. The list includes position sensors, chemical sensors, temperature sensors, and gas composition sensors, among others, crucial for diagnosing vehicle status and ensuring the safety of occupants and responders.

The table breaks down the diagnostic and safety sensors used in emergency vehicles. Diagnostic sensors are primarily used for monitoring vehicle performance and conditions that contain temperature sensors, position sensors, gas composition sensors, speed sensors, and pressure sensors among others. The Safety sensors ensure both occupant and vehicle safety during emergency operations that contain airbag sensors, micromechanical

TABLE 19.2 Diagnostic and safety sensors.

Diagnostic	Safety
Position sensor	Micro-mechanical oscillators
Chemical sensors	Speed sensors
Temperature sensors	Cameras
Gas composition sensors	Radars and laser beams
Pressure sensor	Inertial sensors
Airbag sensor	Ultrasonic sensors
	Proximity sensors
	Night vision sensors
	Haptic

TABLE 19.3 Category of sensors.

Traffic navigation sensors	Internal sensors
- Radars	- Gas composition sensor
- Camera	- Humidity sensors
- Ultra sonic	- Temperature sensors
- Proximity	- Position sensors
- Lidar (Almadani et al., 2015)	- Torque sensors
	- Image sensors
	- Rain sensors
	- Fogging prevention sensors
	- Distance sensors (Almadani et al., 2015)

Patient monitoring	Environment
- EEG/EMG/ECG sensors	- Pressure sensors
- Heart rate sensor	- Temperature sensors
- Thermometer	- Distance sensors
- Patient mirror	- Cameras weather conditions (Dodia et al., 2023)
- Defibrillator	
- Transport ventilators	
- Bag-Valve-Mask (BVM)	
- Suction unit	
- Oxygen supply units	
- Nebulizer	
- Haemo glucometer (HGT)	

oscillators, laser beams, cameras, radars, inertial sensors and ultrasonic sensors. Further, the list includes sensors such as night vision sensors, proximity sensors, and haptic feedback devices, which contribute to enhancing situational awareness and response capabilities in emergency situations.

An overview of different categories of sensors used in emergency vehicles is provided in Table 19.3. The first category, the traffic navigation sensors encompasses sensors like cameras, radars, proximity sensors, ultrasonic sensors, and Lidar, which monitor traffic conditions and ensure safe navigation. The second category, the internal sensors includes humidity sensors, temperature sensors, gas composition sensors, and others, which monitor the internal environment of the vehicle and ensure optimal functioning. The third category, patient monitoring includes sensors such as EEG/EMG/ECG sensors, thermometers, and heart rate sensors. Finally, the environment category comprises sensors like temperature sensors, pressure sensors, and cameras that monitor environmental conditions outside the vehicle, and aid in decision-making during emergency response operations (Table 19.4).

Ambulances are equipped with various safety features including emergency lighting, reflective striping, scene lighting, backup cameras, ABS, ESC, airbags, traffic signal preemption, occupant restraint systems, temperature control, vehicle monitoring systems, and antitheft devices. These features ensure efficient emergency responses and enhance safety for patients, medical personnel, and other road users. See Table 19.5 for further details.

19.5 The integration of sensor technology in emergency operations

In the dynamic landscape of Australian emergency vehicle operations, a significant shift is underway, marked by the integration of advanced sensor technologies Evaluating diverse sensors' effectiveness, their individual strengths and limitations are analyzed (Masoud & Belkasim, 2017). The deployment of purpose-specific sensors reflects a progressive transformation in emergency vehicle operations. These sensors, encompassing GPS for precise location tracking, advanced radar, Lidar systems, and cameras, have become integral components of emergency vehicle operations shaping their navigation capabilities, situational awareness, and risk assessment processes (Hargrave et al., 2020).

Global positioning system (GPS), as a foundational technology, provides precise location information critical for reducing response times and enhancing incident management. Advanced radar and Lidar systems significantly contribute to situational awareness, aiding in navigating complex urban environments with precision and safety. Advanced radar and Lidar systems contribute significantly to situational awareness enabling vehicles to navigate complex environments with precision and safety. Cameras play a pivotal role in risk assessment, offering visual information for informed decision-making in dynamic emergency scenarios (Ayesha & Komalavalli, 2024). This evolutionary process reflects the increasing sophistication of sensor technologies, reshaping the operational landscape of emergency vehicles.

Cameras, providing visual sensing capabilities, contribute to making informed decisions in dynamic emergency scenarios. The investigation conducted by Almadani et al. (2015) revealed that the integration of technological services into ERVs poses challenges in their design and construction. Despite the existence of international standards, research findings indicate shortcomings in ERVs, particularly in their alignment with the actual needs of end users. In the context of the mobile object bus integration research project, eight crucial focus areas were identified: emergency response preparedness, critical communication, real-time updates, ease of use in information and communication technology systems, optimization of power supply, resource availability, safety considerations, and sustainability (Wambura, 2020). The study adopted a grounded theory-based research approach to comprehensively understand the requirements of end users. Emergency vehicles, ranging from fire trucks and police vehicles to ambulances and rescue vehicles, employ a variety of sensors to enhance their operational capabilities (Wambura, 2020).

TABLE 19.4 Sensors and standards.

Sensor	Applied domain	Related ISO standards	Related IEEE standards
Temperature sensors	Ambient temperature in the ambulance during extreme weather conditions	ISO 80601-2-56:2017 - Medical electrical equipment—Part 2−56: Particular requirements for basic safety and essential performance of clinical thermometers for body temperature measurement	IEEE 11073-10408; Health informatics; Personal health device communication; Part 10408: Device specialization; Thermometer (Standards Australia Website, 2024)
Carbon monoxide (CO) sensors	Detecting leaks in the ambulance	IEEE 11073−10408; Health informatics; Personal health device communication; Part 10408: Device specialization; Thermometer	IEEE 484; Recommended Practice for Installation Design and Installation of Vented Lead-Acid Batteries for Stationary Applications
Oxygen concentration sensors	Monitoring oxygen levels	ISO 7767−1:2018; Anesthetic and respiratory equipment; Suction equipment; Part 1: Mains-powered suction equipment (Australian Government, 2024)	IEEE 11073−10441; Health informatics; Personal health device communication; Part 10441: Device specialization - Oxygen saturation monitor
Cardiac monitor/ defibrillator	Monitoring defibrillation capabilities	ISO 80601-2-44:2017;Medical electrical equipment; Part 2−44: Particular requirements for the basic safety and essential performance of X-ray equipment for computed tomography	IEEE 11073-10417; Health informatics; Personal health device communication; Part 10417: Device specialization; Cardiac monitor/defibrillator (Queensland Government, 2024)
Smoke and fire sensors	Detecting the presence of smoke or fire	ISO 7240−29:2017 - Fire detection and alarm systems - Part 29: Test methods for evaluating the performance of smoke detectors - Point detectors (no date).	IEEE 3004.8 - Standard for the Prevention of Fire and Dust Explosions from the Manufacturing, Processing, and Handling of Combustible Particulate Solids
Gas leak sensors	Detecting presence of gas	ISO 7165:2017 - Road vehicles; Equipment for lorry-mounted aerial working platforms; Safety requirements and testing	IEEE 484 - Recommended practice for installation; Design and installation of vented lead-acid; Batteries for stationary applications (Standards Australia Website, 2024)
Intrusion and security sensors	Alerting unauthorized access	ISO 21812−1:2019 - Intruder and hold-up alarm systems—Part 1: Systems	IEEE 802.11 - Wireless LAN medium access control (MAC) and Physical Layer (PHY) specifications
Shore power sensors	Detecting external power sources	ISO 6469−1:2009 - Electric road vehicles; Safety specifications; Part 1: On-board electrical energy storage systems (EESS)	IEEE 141 - Recommended Practice for Electric Power Distribution for Industrial Plants

(Continued)

TABLE 19.4   (Continued)

Sensor	Applied domain	Related ISO standards	Related IEEE standards
GPS and location sensors	Navigating, tracking, and communication	ISO 16494:2014 - Intelligent transport systems; Cooperative ITS; Use of GNSS/Inertial sensing (Standards Australia Website, 2024)	IEEE 802.11 - Wireless LAN Medium Access Control (MAC) and Physical Layer (PHY) specifications
Vehicle monitoring sensors	Monitoring vehicle conditions	ISO 14229−1:2020 - Road vehicles; Unified diagnostic services (UDS); Part 1: Specification and requirements	IEEE 1451 - Standard for a Smart Transducer Interface for Sensors and Actuators
Hydraulic lift and stretcher sensors	Operating during patient loading and unloading	ISO 10535:2011 - Hoists for the transfer of disabled persons - Requirements and test methods	IEEE 100 - IEEE Standard Dictionary of Electrical and Electronics Terms
GPS and communication systems	Transmitting patient data	ISO 14915:1999 - Software ergonomics for multimedia user interfaces	IEEE 802.11 - Wireless LAN Medium Access Control (MAC) and Physical Layer (PHY) specifications
Security and restraint sensors	Alerting patient security measures	ISO 10535:2011 - Hoists for the transfer of disabled persons - Requirements and test methods	IEEE 1149.1 - Standard Test Access Port and Boundary-Scan Architecture
ECG (electrocardiogram) sensor	Monitoring the electrical activity of heart	ISO 10993−1:2009- Biological evaluation of medical devices - Part 1: Evaluation and testing within a risk management process (Australian Government, 2024)	IEEE 11073−10101 - Health informatics - Point-of-care medical device communication Part 10101: Nomenclature
Pulse oximeter	Measuring oxygen saturation	ISO 80601−2-61:2017 - Medical electrical equipment; Part 2−61: Particular requirements for basic safety and essential performance of pulse oximeter equipment for medical use	IEEE 11073−10441 - Health informatics; Personal health device communication; Part 10441: Device specialization; Pulse oximeter
Blood pressure monitor	Measuring blood pressure	ISO 81060−2:2018 - Noninvasive sphygmomanometers; Part 2: Clinical investigation of automated measurement type (Australian Government, 2024)	IEEE 11073−10417 - Health informatics; Personal health device communication; Part 10417: Device specialization; Blood pressure monitor
Temperature sensor	Measuring body temperature	ISO 80601−2-56:2017 - Medical electrical equipment; Part 2−56: Particular requirements for basic safety and essential performance of clinical thermometers for body temperature measurement (Australian Government, 2024)	IEEE 11073−10408 - Health informatics; Personal health device communication; Part 10408: Device specialization; Thermometer

(Continued)

TABLE 19.4 (Continued)

Sensor	Applied domain	Related ISO standards	Related IEEE standards
Respiratory rate monitor	Measuring abnormal respiratory rates	ISO 80601−2-84:2021 - Medical electrical equipment; Part 2−84: Particular requirements for basic safety and essential performance of home healthcare environment ventilators	IEEE 11073−10408 - Health informatics; Personal health device communication; Part 10408: Device specialization; Respiratory rate monitor
Capnography sensor	Measuring patients end tidal carbon diocide levels	ISO 80601−2-55:2011 - Medical electrical equipment; Part 2−55: Particular requirements for the basic safety and essential performance of respiratory gas monitors (Australian Government, 2024)	IEEE 11073−10441 - Health informatics; Personal health device communication - Part 10441: Device specialization; Capnography monitor
Motion and position sensors	Detecting sudden movements	ISO 13482:2014 - Robots and robotic devices; Safety requirements for personal care robots	IEEE 1872 - Standard for wearable consumer electronic devices motion-based sleep measurement
Patient monitoring sensors	Monitoring vital signs	ISO 10993−1:2009 - Biological evaluation of medical devices; Part 1: Evaluation and testing within a risk management process	IEEE 11073−10101 - Health informatics; Point-of-care medical device communication Part 10101: Nomenclature (Australian Government, 2024)
Diagnostic sensors (position, chemical, temperature, gas composition, pressure, airbag)	Industry specific standards	ISO 26262 for automotive safety, is recommended.	
Pressure sensors	Safety standards	ISO 26262 for automotive (Australian Government, 2024)	IEC 61508 for industrial safety
Airbag sensors	Safety standards	ISO 26262 for functional safety and FMVSS regulations in the United States	
Position sensor	Safety standards	ISO 26262 for automotive applications or	IEC 61508 for industrial applications
Sensors for heart rate	Observing pertinent standards	ISO 13485 (Australian Government, 2024)	IEC 60601

Ambulances, as critical components of emergency medical services, showcase the integration of sensors for optimizing response efficiency and patient care. GPS technology ensures precise location tracking, facilitating swift responses to medical emergencies. Lidar and radar systems contribute to situational awareness, enabling ambulance drivers to navigate through challenging traffic conditions and complex urban environments with

TABLE 19.5 Vehicle Safety Features.

Emergency lighting and sirens	Ambulances are equipped with high-intensity emergency lighting systems, including strobe lights, LED bars, and flashing headlights. Sirens are used to alert other drivers and pedestrians to yield the right of way, allowing the ambulance to pass quickly and safely (Searson et al., 2015).
Reflective striping	Ambulance exteriors often have reflective striping or markings that enhance visibility, especially during low-light conditions. These markings make the ambulance more conspicuous to other motorists (Searson et al., 2015).
Scene lighting	Powerful scene lighting illuminates the area around the ambulance, enabling paramedics to work safely in low-light or nighttime situations. This lighting also helps in identifying hazards and obstacles.
Backup cameras	Ambulances are equipped with backup cameras that provide a clear view of the area behind the vehicle when reversing (Almadani et al., 2015). This feature helps prevent accidents and ensures the safety of personnel and patients.
Anti-lock braking system (ABS)	ABS is a safety feature that prevents wheel lockup during hard braking, helping the driver maintain control of the ambulance and reduce the risk of skidding.
Electronic stability control (ESC)	ESC systems help stabilize the ambulance during abrupt maneuvers or when driving on slippery roads. They can reduce the risk of rollovers or loss of control (Almadani et al., 2015).
Airbags	Ambulances are often equipped with airbags to protect the driver and front passenger in the event of a collision (Ayesha & Komalavalli, 2024).
Traffic signal preemption	Some ambulances have traffic signal preemption systems that can change traffic signals to green when the ambulance approaches, clearing the way and reducing response times.
Patient compartment safety	Safety features inside the patient compartment include securement devices for stretchers and seating to prevent patient movement during transport (Almadani et al., 2015). These features help ensure patient safety during transit.
Occupant restraint systems	Medical personnel in the patient compartment may have access to occupant restraint systems such as seatbelts or harnesses to secure themselves while attending to patients.
Temperature control	Ensuring a comfortable temperature inside the ambulance is vital for patient care. Ambulances are equipped with heating and air conditioning systems to maintain suitable conditions during transport (Ayesha & Komalavalli, 2024).
Vehicle monitoring systems	Some ambulances have vehicle monitoring systems that provide real-time data on vehicle performance and driver behavior. These systems help identify potential safety issues and promote safe driving practices.
Anti-theft devices	To prevent theft and unauthorized use, ambulances may have antitheft systems, including immobilizers and GPS tracking (Ayesha & Komalavalli, 2024).

enhanced safety (Hargrave et al., 2020). Cameras, integrated into ambulances, provide visual information for assessing the severity of injuries or medical conditions, aiding paramedics in making informed decisions for patient care. In conclusion, this comprehensive evaluation offers a nuanced understanding of the integration of sensor technology in emergency vehicle operations (Hargrave et al., 2020).

The historical evolution and the current state of sensor technology integration have been thoroughly examined, emphasizing the effectiveness of diverse sensors in enhancing navigation, situational awareness, and risk assessment. As technology continues to advance, future directions in the integration of sensor technologies in emergency vehicles should focus on continuous refinement and innovation (Pántya, 2023). This involves not only the development of more advanced sensor technologies but also strategic training programs for emergency personnel to effectively utilize these technologies. Additionally, ongoing research initiatives can explore novel applications of sensors, further expanding their capabilities in emergency scenarios.

19.6 Security considerations and challenges to the sensors

In emergency medical services, advanced safety technologies are at the forefront of ensuring the well-being of both responders and the public. Collision avoidance and automatic emergency braking systems are indispensable safeguards, providing a crucial layer of protection during critical phases of emergency response. The importance of emergency responses is needed when ambulances must navigate swiftly and safely through traffic to reach their destination.

The integration of advanced safety technologies, coupled with strategic visibility enhancements, forms a robust security framework for emergency vehicles, including ambulances (Dodia et al., 2023). This multifaceted approach not only mitigates the inherent risks of high-speed emergency operations but also ensures that these vehicles can navigate through diverse and challenging environments with the utmost safety and efficiency (Hsiao et al., 2018). As an integral part of security considerations, these measures collectively contribute to resilience, preparedness, and an elevated standard of safety within the domain of emergency medical services. A comprehensive exploration into historical incidents and real-world challenges reveals a spectrum of potential threats and risks encountered by emergency vehicles, with a specific focus on ambulances operating within the Australian landscape (Andrew & Robinson, 2019). This rigorous analysis encompasses scenarios where the safety of responders and patients may be compromised, ranging from traffic-related challenges to unforeseen obstacles in emergency response pathways. In the unique context of Australia, understanding the intricacies of the landscape and potential hazards is pivotal. This insight allows for the development of tailored security solutions that address the specific threats faced by emergency vehicles. Factors such as varied terrains, weather conditions, and traffic patterns play a significant role in shaping the risk landscape, emphasizing the need for proactive security measures.

In the realm of emergency medical services, an examination examination of risk management strategies reveals a multifaceted approach that encompasses both technological solutions and procedural methodologies. This dual perspective is crucial in ensuring a comprehensive and adaptive response to potential risks associated with emergency vehicles, particularly ambulances (Khirekar et al., 2023). Technological solutions form a critical component of risk management, with advancements such as collision avoidance systems, automatic emergency braking, and enhanced lighting contributing significantly to the overall safety of ambulances. The integration of these technologies aligns with the proactive mitigation of risks, addressing challenges posed by varied terrains, adverse weather conditions, and dynamic traffic scenarios unique to the Australian context (Hargrave et al., 2020).

Complementing technological interventions, procedural approaches are equally emphasized (Mohr et al., 2015). The establishment of a robust security framework is highlighted as essential, encompassing protocols designed for high-risk situations encountered during emergency operations. This framework serves as a guideline for responders, outlining best practices and standardized procedures to navigate challenges efficiently. A pivotal aspect of risk management involves real-time communication systems (Kopetz & Steiner, 2022). The integration of these systems enhances coordination among emergency vehicles, control centers, and relevant agencies. Seamless communication is identified as a proactive measure to address dynamic situations, ensuring swift responses and informed decision-making during emergencies.

19.7 Security threats

19.7.1 Unauthorized access

Data security and privacy could be breached when unauthorized access is granted during patient data collection by sensors or during data transmission. Ensuring robust encryption, access control measures, and authentication to safeguard sensitive information is a challenge. Also, implementing robust cybersecurity protocols, regular updates to address emerging threats, and ensuring secure communication channels is a complex task. Vehicular network security is about the mitigation of attacks on the communication networks connecting sensors.

In the scenario where a malicious actor gains unauthorized access to the vehicle's sensor network during data collection, there is a risk of intercepting sensitive patient health data as it is transmitted wirelessly to a central database. This unauthorized access could lead to the compromise of patient confidentiality and privacy, potentially putting individuals at risk. It highlights the critical importance of implementing robust security measures, such as encryption protocols and access controls, to safeguard sensitive data transmitted within the network. Additionally, regular security audits and monitoring can help detect and mitigate such security breaches promptly, ensuring the integrity and confidentiality of patient health information.

To counteract this threat, implementing robust encryption protocols like advanced encryption standard (AES) can be pivotal. By encrypting the data transmitted by sensors, even if intercepted, the data remains indecipherable to unauthorized parties. Furthermore, access control measures, such as authentication mechanisms (e.g., username/password or biometric authentication), can limit access exclusively to authorized personnel. Regular updates to the vehicle's software and security patches play a crucial role in addressing emerging vulnerabilities, thereby mitigating the risk of exploitation. These combined measures fortify the security of the sensor network, ensuring the protection of sensitive patient health data during transmission.

Indeed, a significant challenge in mitigating such threats lies in seamlessly integrating security measures into the vehicle's sensor network without compromising system performance or functionality. Balancing robust security with operational efficiency requires careful consideration of various factors, including resource constraints, communication protocols, and real-time processing requirements. Effective solutions involve adopting lightweight encryption algorithms, optimizing authentication processes, and implementing efficient access control mechanisms. Additionally, continuous monitoring and evaluation of the security measures are essential to ensure that they effectively protect against threats while maintaining the functionality and performance of the sensor network. Collaboration between security experts and system developers is vital to address these challenges and develop solutions that enhance security without hindering the operation of emergency vehicles.

19.7.2 Lack of authentication mechanism

Adhering to communication standards, implementing secure network protocols, and ensuring redundancy for reliable communication pose significant challenges. Integration challenges require security considerations, highlighting potential incompatibility issues between different sensor types, which can lead to system failures. Addressing these challenges involves standardizing communication protocols, ensuring seamless integration, and conducting thorough testing to identify and rectify integration issues.

Supply chain security introduces threats such as compromised components or sensors entering the supply chain, posing significant security risks. To tackle this challenge, implementing robust supply chain security measures, vetting suppliers, and ensuring the integrity of sensor components is imperative. These measures help mitigate the risk of compromised components infiltrating the supply chain and compromising the security of the system.

In an emergency vehicle's sensor network lacking authentication mechanisms, the potential for a malicious actor to gain unauthorized access is heightened, leading to risks of data tampering and system disruptions. To mitigate such risks, implementing robust authentication mechanisms is essential. Adhering to standards and ensuring redundancy further enhances security measures.

Challenges arise in seamlessly integrating authentication mechanisms across diverse systems within the sensor network. This integration process must balance security needs with operational efficiency to avoid hindering emergency response capabilities. Overcoming these challenges involves careful planning, rigorous testing, and collaboration between security experts and system developers.

By addressing these challenges and implementing effective authentication measures, emergency vehicle sensor networks can better protect against unauthorized access, data tampering, and system disruptions, ensuring the reliability and integrity of critical operations during emergencies.

To enhance security in the emergency vehicle's sensor network, implementing strong authentication mechanisms such as biometrics or cryptographic protocols is essential. Adhering to communication standards and deploying secure network protocols further fortifies the system against unauthorized access and data breaches. Ensuring redundancy with backup communication channels adds an extra layer of resilience to the network.

Mitigating supply chain security risks involves vetting suppliers and ensuring the integrity of components. However, challenges persist in seamlessly integrating authentication mechanisms across diverse systems without encountering compatibility issues. Maintaining redundancy while minimizing complexity is crucial for ensuring system reliability without compromising performance. Balancing security measures with operational efficiency and cost-effectiveness remains an ongoing challenge that requires careful consideration and strategic planning.

19.7.3 Lack of encryption mechanism: sending data in plaintext

Regulatory compliance is a paramount security consideration that faces threats such as noncompliance with safety standards and regulations, potentially leading to legal and operational challenges. Staying abreast of evolving regulations, conducting regular audits for compliance, and integrating necessary updates to meet regulatory requirements are ongoing challenges for organizations.

In an emergency vehicle's communication system lacking encryption, sensitive data transmitted in plaintext is vulnerable to interception by malicious actors, leading to potential breaches of data protection regulations and subsequent legal penalties and operational disruptions.

To mitigate such risks, implementing robust encryption mechanisms like Rivest–Shamir–Adleman (RSA) or general data protection regulation (GDPR) to secure data transmission is imperative. Adhering to data protection regulations such as GDPR or Health Insurance Portability and Accountability Act. (HIPAA) through regular audits and compliance assessments is essential. Integrating necessary updates to meet evolving regulatory requirements further strengthens the system's security posture.

However, challenges arise in effectively implementing encryption mechanisms across all communication channels without introducing compatibility issues or performance degradation. Additionally, staying updated on evolving regulations and integrating necessary updates to maintain compliance in a timely manner poses ongoing challenges. Balancing regulatory compliance with operational efficiency and cost-effectiveness remains crucial for operating in the emergency response sector.

19.7.4 Interoperability issues

Environmental factors indeed present significant security considerations, with adverse weather conditions potentially affecting sensor performance and leading to inaccurate readings. Designing sensors capable of functioning reliably in diverse environmental conditions, incorporating redundancy for critical sensors, and conducting regular maintenance to address wear and tear are essential challenges to overcome.

In an emergency vehicle's sensor network, interoperability issues between sensors can arise due to compatibility issues, resulting in inconsistent data collection and analysis. This compromises the vehicle's ability to accurately assess the surrounding environment and respond effectively to emergencies.

To address these challenges, implementing standardized communication protocols such as MQTT can facilitate seamless interoperability between sensors from different manufacturers. Thorough compatibility testing during the sensor integration phase helps identify and resolve interoperability issues. Middleware solutions can also be employed to translate data formats and protocols, ensuring smooth communication between heterogeneous sensor systems.

However, challenges persist in ensuring compatibility between sensors from different manufacturers, as they may use proprietary communication protocols or data formats. Additionally, maintaining compatibility as new sensors are added or upgraded over time presents an ongoing challenge. Balancing the need for interoperability with the complexity of sensor integration and system maintenance remains crucial for optimal performance in emergency response scenarios.

19.7.5 False data injection

False data injection poses a significant security consideration, with the potential for malicious actors to introduce false data into sensor inputs, leading to incorrect decisions by emergency systems. Implementing measures such as data integrity checks, anomaly detection algorithms, and secure communication protocols is critical to detect and prevent false data injection, albeit with challenges.

In a scenario where a malicious actor injects false data into an emergency vehicle's environmental sensors, signaling high levels of toxic gas, unnecessary emergency responses may be triggered. To mitigate this risk, data integrity checks, anomaly detection, and secure communication protocols are essential. However, challenges include distinguishing genuine data from false inputs without compromising system performance.

To address these challenges, implementing robust security measures such as data integrity checks, anomaly detection, and secure communication protocols like TLS is imperative. Cryptographic techniques can be utilized for data integrity, and tuning anomaly detection algorithms helps avoid false positives. Balancing these security measures with system performance requirements is crucial.

However, differentiating genuine data from false inputs without impacting system performance poses a challenge. Implementing robust security measures may require additional computational resources and could introduce latency, affecting real-time emergency response capabilities. Thus, striking a balance between security needs and operational efficiency is important in ensuring effective emergency response systems.

19.8 Discussion

Data Security and Privacy Concerns: Unauthorized access to patient data collected by sensors and potential data breaches during transmission pose significant challenges to the security and privacy of sensitive information. Robust encryption, access control measures, and authentication mechanisms are crucial to safeguard patient data from unauthorized access and ensure privacy compliance.

Cybersecurity Risk: Malicious attacks targeting sensor systems and potential hacking of communication channels represent major cybersecurity risks in vehicular networks. Implementing robust cybersecurity protocols, conducting regular updates to address vulnerabilities, and establishing secure communication channels are essential to mitigate the risk of cyberattacks and data breaches.

Vehicular Network Security: Attacks on communication networks connecting sensors pose a threat to the integrity and reliability of data transmission in emergency vehicles. Adhering to communication standards, implementing secure network protocols, and ensuring redundancy for reliable communication are necessary measures to protect against potential disruptions and maintain the integrity of vehicular networks.

Security Protocols: Implementing comprehensive security protocols, including end-to-end encryption, access controls, and multifactor authentication, is essential to ensure the security and privacy of data collected and transmitted by sensors in emergency vehicles. These measures help to prevent unauthorized access, mitigate the risk of data breaches, and ensure compliance with privacy regulations.

Regular Updates and Patch Management. Continuously updating systems to address emerging threats and vulnerabilities is crucial in mitigating cybersecurity risks in vehicular networks. Regular patch management and software updates help to strengthen security measures and protect against evolving cyber threats, ensuring the integrity and reliability of emergency response systems.

Redundancy and Fail-Safe Mechanisms: Incorporating redundant systems and fail-safe mechanisms is essential to ensure uninterrupted operation and resilience in emergency vehicles, even in the event of sensor failures or cyberattacks. Redundancy helps to mitigate the impact of system failures and cyber incidents, ensuring the reliability and effectiveness of emergency response operations.

19.9 Conclusion

In emergency vehicle operations, the integration of sensor technology plays a pivotal role in enhancing efficiency, safety, and response capabilities. However, along with the myriad benefits these sensors offer, they also bring forth a range of security challenges that must be addressed comprehensively.

By recognizing and addressing challenges such as data security and privacy concerns, cybersecurity risks, integration complexities, and regulatory compliance, emergency vehicle manufacturers and stakeholders can ensure that sensors are deployed and operated securely. Implementing robust security protocols, regular updates, redundancy measures, and supply chain transparency are crucial steps in mitigating risks and ensuring the integrity of sensor data.

Moreover, fostering a culture of continuous monitoring, threat intelligence utilization, and user awareness will further strengthen the security posture of emergency vehicles. By adopting a proactive approach to security, emergency services can not only mitigate risks but also enhance public trust and confidence in their capabilities.

Ultimately, the successful integration of sensor technology in emergency vehicles hinges upon a holistic security framework that addresses both technical and procedural aspects. By prioritizing security requirements and implementing appropriate solutions, emergency services can leverage the full potential of sensor technology to improve response efficiency, protect personnel and patients, and ultimately save lives. This chapter provided a summary of recent research and standards developed for the safety and operation of sensors used in emergency vehicles. These aspects are crucial to look into when conducting a thorough risk and security assessment.

References

Alamdar, F., Kalantari, M., & Rajabifard, A. (2017). Understanding the provision of multi-agency sensor information in disaster management: A case study on the Australian state of Victoria. *International journal of disaster risk reduction, 22*, 475–493.

Almadani, B., Bin-Yahya, M., & Shakshuki, E. M. (2015). E-AMBULANCE: real-time integration platform for heterogeneous medical telemetry system. *Procedia Computer Science, 63*, 400–407.

Andrew, W., & Robinson, T. (2019). https://www.intechopen.com/chapters/68207.

Australian Government Website. (2024). Vehicle Standard (Australian Design Rule 98/01 – Advanced Emergency Braking for Passenger Vehicles and Light Goods Vehicles) 2021. https://www.legislation.gov.au/F2021L01519/asmade/text.

Ayesha, A., & Komalavalli, C. (2024). Smart ambulance: A comprehensive IoT and cloud-based system integrating fingerprint sensor with medical sensors for real-time patient vital signs monitoring. *International Journal of Intelligent Systems and Applications in Engineering, 12*(2), 555–567.

Dodia, A., Kumar, S., Rani, R., Pippal, S. K., & Meduri, P. (2023). EVATL: A novel framework for emergency vehicle communication with adaptive traffic lights for smart cities. *IET Smart Cities, 5*(4). Available from https://doi.org/10.1049/smc2.12068, https://ietresearch.onlinelibrary.wiley.com/journal/26317680.

Hargrave, C., Munday, L., Kennedy, G., & de Kock, A. (2020). Mine machine radar sensor for emergency escape. *Resources, 9*(2), 16. Available from https://doi.org/10.3390/resources9020016.

Hsiao, H., Chang, J., & Simeonov, P. (2018). Preventing emergency vehicle crashes: Status and challenges of human factors issues. *Human Factors: The Journal of the Human Factors and Ergonomics Society, 60*(7). Available from https://doi.org/10.1177/0018720818786132.

Humagain, S., Sinha, R., Lai, E., & Ranjitkar, P. (2020). A systematic review of route optimisation and pre-emption methods for emergency vehicles. *Transport Reviews, 40*(1). Available from https://doi.org/10.1080/01441647.2019.1649319.

Kaurav, R. S., Rout, R. R., & Vemireddy, S. (2021). Blockchain for emergency vehicle routing in healthcare services: An integrated secure and trustworthy system. In *2021 International conference on communication systems & networks (COMSNETS)* (pp. 623–628). Bangalore, India. Available from https://doi.org/10.1109/COMSNETS51098.2021.9352903.

Khirekar, J., Badge, A., Bandre, G. R., & Shahu, S. (2023). Disaster preparedness in hospitals. *Cureus*. Available from https://doi.org/10.7759/cureus.50073.

Kopetz, H., & Steiner, W. (2022). *Real-time communication*. Springer Science and Business Media LLC. Available from http://doi.org/10.1007/978-3-031-11992-7_7.

Masini, B. M., Bazzi, A., & Zanella, A. (2018). A survey on the roadmap to mandate on board connectivity and enable V2V-based vehicular sensor networks. *Sensors, 18*(7), 2207.

Masoud, M., & Belkasim, S. (2017). WSN-EVP: A novel special purpose protocol for emergency vehicle preemption systems. *IEEE Transactions on Vehicular Technology, 67*(4), 3695–3700.

Mohr, D. C., Schueller, S. M., Riley, W. T., Brown, C. H., Cuijpers, P., Duan, N., Kwasny, M. J., Stiles-Shields, C., & Cheung, K. (2015). Trials of intervention principles: Evaluation methods for evolving behavioral intervention technologies. *Journal of Medical Internet Research, 17*(7). Available from https://doi.org/10.2196/jmir.4391, http://www.jmir.org/article/viewFile/jmir_v17i7e166/2.

Pántya, P. (2023). Special vehicles and equipment in fire operations used in different regions. *Academic and Applied Research in Military and Public Management Science, 22*(1). Available from https://doi.org/10.32565/aarms.2023.1.1.

Queensland Government website (2024). https://www.tmr.qld.gov.au/safety/road-safety/emergency-vehicle-priority.

Rajeshwari, R.M., & Rajesh, S. (2024). Improved data transmission technique for healthcare emergency vehicle using blockchain in VANET. *Blockchain for Healthcare 4.0* (pp. 278–290). CRC Press.

Searson, D., Ponte, G., Hutchinson, T., Anderson, R., & Lydon, M. (2015). Emerging vehicle safety technologies and their potential benefits: Discussion of expert opinions.

Standards Australia Website. (2024). Available from http://www.standards.org.au/.

Sundar, R., Hebbar, S., & Golla, V. (2014). Implementing intelligent traffic control system for congestion control, ambulance clearance, and stolen vehicle detection. *IEEE Sensors Journal, 15*(2), 1109–1113.

Wambura, F. M. (2020). Cost-efficient assessment of ambulance services for community critical care transport needs in Machakos County.

Swarm intelligence for Cancer Care 4.0/5.0

R. Gunasundari[1] and Rose Mary Mathew[2]

[1]Department of Computer Applications, Karpagam Academy of Higher Education, Coimbatore, Tamil Nadu, India [2]Department of Computer Applications, Federal Institute of Science and Technology, Ernakulam, Kerala, India

20.1 Introduction

In recent years, cancer care has undergone a profound transformation, marked by the integration of cutting-edge technologies. Among these advancements, swarm intelligence has emerged as a promising strategy, capitalizing on the collective behavior observed in decentralized, self-organized systems inspired by nature (Bitterman et al., 2020). This chapter delves into the application of swarm intelligence within the framework of Cancer Care 4.0/5.0, which prioritizes personalized, data-driven treatments and comprehensive patient care.

Cancer Care 4.0/5.0 signifies a new era in oncology characterized by the convergence of artificial intelligence, big data analytics, and precision medicine. Swarm intelligence, inspired by the cooperative behavior of social insect colonies, offers a unique approach to addressing the intricate challenges posed by cancer's complexity and heterogeneity (Saldanha et al., 2022). Swarm intelligence algorithms, such as ant colony optimization (ACO) and particle swarm optimization (PSO), are instrumental in navigating the multifaceted landscape of cancer treatment. By analyzing vast datasets (encompassing the medical sensor networks, Internet of Medical Things, electronic health record (EHR) genomic profiles, imaging scans, clinical histories, etc.), these algorithms optimize treatment strategies tailored to individual patient characteristics and preferences.

Moreover, swarm intelligence facilitates early detection and diagnosis through the synthesis of diverse data sources and the identification of subtle patterns indicative of early-stage disease. It also contributes to predictive modeling, enabling forecasts of disease progression, treatment response, and patient outcomes. However, the integration of swarm

Sensor Networks for Smart Hospitals
DOI: https://doi.org/10.1016/B978-0-443-36370-2.00021-9

intelligence into cancer care presents challenges (Kraus et al., 2021). These include data integration, algorithm transparency, ethical considerations, and validation in clinical settings. Addressing these hurdles is crucial for realizing the full potential of swarm intelligence and advancing the field of oncology towards personalized, effective treatments tailored to each patient's unique needs.

20.2 Swarm intelligence algorithms

Swarm intelligence algorithms represent a fascinating approach to problem-solving, inspired by the collective behavior of social organisms such as ants, bees, and birds. These algorithms mimic the decentralized, self-organized nature of natural swarms to tackle complex optimization tasks, decision-making processes, and pattern recognition challenges (Al-Tashi et al., 2023). By leveraging the collective intelligence of individual agents and their interactions within a swarm, these algorithms exhibit remarkable capabilities for finding optimal solutions in dynamic and uncertain environments. In recent years, swarm intelligence has gained significant attention across various fields, including optimization, robotics, finance, and healthcare, owing to its ability to address complex problems that traditional algorithms struggle to solve. This session explores the fundamental principles, key characteristics, and diverse applications of swarm intelligence algorithms, highlighting their potential to revolutionize problem-solving in the modern era.

20.2.1 Ant colony optimization

ACO is a metaheuristic algorithm inspired by the foraging behavior of ants. It mimics the way ants communicate and cooperate to find the shortest path between their nest and food sources. In ACO, artificial ants construct solutions to optimization problems by moving through a solution space and depositing pheromone trails along their paths (Dorigo et al., 2006). Ants preferentially follow paths with stronger pheromone concentrations, intensifying the paths leading to better solutions. Over time, the pheromone trails evaporate, allowing the algorithm to focus on exploring new solutions. Through this iterative process of solution construction and pheromone update, ACO effectively navigates the search space to find high-quality solutions to optimization problems.

ACO has been successfully applied to various optimization problems, including the traveling salesman problem, vehicle routing problem, and job scheduling. Its ability to exploit both local and global information, adapt to changing environments, and discover near-optimal solutions makes it a powerful tool for solving complex optimization problems inspired by the natural behavior of ants (Fahmi et al., 2020).

The ACO algorithm, inspired by the foraging behavior of ants, holds significant relevance in cancer care due to its ability to address the complex and dynamic nature of the disease. ACO operates on the principles of decentralized, self-organization, and collective intelligence, making it well-suited for optimizing treatment strategies, drug combinations, and therapeutic interventions tailored to individual patients. In cancer care, ACO algorithms excel at navigating the vast landscape of treatment options and identifying optimal solutions amidst the inherent heterogeneity of tumors and patient responses. By simulating the foraging behavior of ants laying pheromone trails to food sources, ACO can effectively explore the multidimensional space of cancer therapies, weighing factors such as efficacy, toxicity, and patient preferences to guide treatment decisions.

One of the primary applications of ACO in cancer care is treatment optimization. By analyzing patient-specific data, including genomic profiles, imaging scans, and clinical histories, ACO algorithms can generate personalized treatment plans that maximize therapeutic efficacy while minimizing adverse effects. This approach enables oncologists to tailor interventions to the unique characteristics of each patient's disease, optimizing outcomes and improving quality of life (Chopra & Arora, 2022). Additionally, ACO algorithms can facilitate the discovery of novel treatment combinations and therapeutic sequences by iteratively evaluating the efficacy of different regimens and adapting strategies based on real-time feedback. This dynamic optimization process mirrors the adaptive behavior of ant colonies, allowing for continuous refinement and improvement of treatment protocols over time.

Furthermore, ACO can aid in the identification of optimal pathways for drug delivery, radiation therapy, and surgical interventions, optimizing treatment delivery while minimizing damage to healthy tissues. By leveraging the collective intelligence of decentralized systems, ACO enhances the precision, efficiency, and effectiveness of cancer care, ultimately improving patient outcomes and advancing the field of oncology (Saldanha et al., 2022; Mbunge et al., 2021).

20.2.2 Particle swarm optimization

PSO is a population-based metaheuristic algorithm inspired by the social behavior of birds flocking or fish schooling. In PSO, a population of candidate solutions, called particles, moves through the search space to find the optimal solution (Gad, 2022). Each particle represents a potential solution to the optimization problem and maintains its position and velocity in the search space. The movement of particles is influenced by their own best-known position (personal best) and the best-known position of the entire swarm (global best) (Imran et al., 2013).

Particles adjust their velocity based on two main factors: personal experience (exploitation) and social influence (exploration). They are attracted towards the best-known solutions found by themselves and by the swarm. As the algorithm progresses, particles dynamically update their positions and velocities to explore the search space efficiently and converge towards the optimal solution (Rao & Yan, 2022). PSO's ability to balance exploration (searching diverse areas) and exploitation (refining promising areas) allows it to effectively solve various optimization problems.

PSO has been applied in a wide range of domains, including engineering design, robotics, data mining, and machine learning. Its simplicity, ease of implementation, and ability to find near-optimal solutions make it a popular choice for solving complex optimization problems inspired by social behavior. PSO algorithm, inspired by the collective behavior of bird flocks or fish schools, offers significant relevance in cancer care due to its capacity to optimize complex treatment strategies and enhance patient outcomes. PSO operates on principles of collaboration, iteration, and dynamic adaptation, making it well-suited for navigating the multifaceted landscape of cancer therapies and personalized medicine.

In cancer care, PSO algorithms excel at optimizing treatment parameters, including chemotherapy dosages, radiation therapy schedules, and drug combinations, to maximize therapeutic efficacy while minimizing adverse effects (Bitterman et al., 2020). By simulating the movement of particles in a multidimensional search space, PSO iteratively refines treatment plans based on patient-specific data, clinical preferences, and evolving disease dynamics.

One primary application of PSO in cancer care is treatment optimization. By analyzing diverse datasets encompassing genomic profiles, imaging scans, and treatment histories, PSO algorithms can identify optimal treatment regimens tailored to individual patient characteristics, optimizing outcomes, and enhancing quality of life. PSO's ability to balance competing objectives, such as tumor control and preservation of healthy tissues, enables oncologists to customize interventions that prioritize patient safety and long-term well-being.

Moreover, PSO algorithms facilitate the exploration of novel treatment strategies and therapeutic sequences by iteratively evaluating the efficacy of different approaches and adapting strategies based on real-time feedback. This dynamic optimization process mirrors the adaptive behavior of biological systems, allowing for continuous refinement and improvement of treatment protocols over time.

Furthermore, PSO can assist in the development of predictive models for disease progression, treatment response, and patient survival probabilities, by analyzing large-scale datasets and identifying prognostic factors indicative of clinical outcomes. By leveraging the collective intelligence of decentralized systems, PSO enhances the precision, efficiency, and effectiveness of cancer care, ultimately improving patient outcomes and advancing the field of oncology into the era of personalized medicine.

20.2.3 Swarm robotics

Swarm robotics is a field of robotics that involves the coordination of multiple autonomous robots, known as swarm robots or agents, to accomplish tasks collaboratively (Debie et al., 2023). Inspired by the collective behavior observed in natural systems such as ant colonies, bird flocks, and fish schools, swarm robotics aims to leverage decentralized control and local interactions to achieve complex objectives. In swarm robotics, individual robots typically have limited capabilities and intelligence, but collectively they exhibit emergent behaviors that enable them to adapt to dynamic environments, self-organize, and accomplish tasks beyond the capabilities of a single robot. The robots communicate and coordinate with each other through local interactions, such as sharing information about their position, velocity, and environment.

Swarm robotics has applications in various domains, including search and rescue operations, environmental monitoring, exploration of hazardous environments, construction, agriculture, and healthcare. By working together, swarm robots can perform tasks more efficiently, robustly, and adaptively than individual robots or centralized systems (Schranz et al., 2020). The key advantages of swarm robotics include scalability, fault tolerance, flexibility, and robustness to environmental changes. However, challenges such as coordination, communication, resource allocation, and task allocation need to be addressed to realize the full potential of swarm robotics in real-world applications. Overall, swarm robotics offers a promising approach to solving complex tasks in a wide range of domains by leveraging the power of collective intelligence and decentralized control.

Swarm robotics, which involves the coordination of multiple autonomous robotic agents to perform tasks, holds significant relevance in cancer care due to its potential to revolutionize diagnostics, treatment delivery, and surgical interventions. By harnessing the collective intelligence and decentralized nature of swarm systems, swarm robotics offers innovative solutions to address the complexities and challenges of cancer treatment. One of the primary applications of swarm robotics in cancer care is targeted drug delivery. By deploying swarms of miniature robots equipped with sensors and actuators, physicians can precisely navigate through the intricate vasculature and microenvironments of tumors to deliver therapeutic payloads directly to cancerous cells. This targeted approach minimizes systemic toxicity and enhances the efficacy of chemotherapy, immunotherapy, and gene therapy, while reducing side effects on healthy tissues.

Swarm robotics also facilitates minimally invasive surgeries and interventional procedures in cancer care. By coordinating the movements of multiple robotic agents with high precision and dexterity, surgeons can perform complex tasks such as tumor resections, lymph node dissections, and organ-preserving surgeries with greater accuracy and efficiency (Mbunge et al., 2021). Swarm robots can access hard-to-reach areas within the body, navigate through tight spaces, and collaborate seamlessly to achieve surgical objectives while minimizing trauma and recovery time for patients. Furthermore, swarm robotics enables real-time monitoring and imaging of tumors during procedures, enhancing intraoperative visualization and decision-making. By integrating imaging modalities such as ultrasound, fluorescence imaging, and magnetic resonance imaging (MRI) into robotic platforms, surgeons can obtain comprehensive, three-dimensional views of tumor morphology and tissue characteristics, facilitating more precise localization and delineation of cancerous lesions.

Additionally, swarm robotics can revolutionize cancer diagnostics by enabling high-throughput screening and analysis of tissue samples for early detection and characterization of tumors. By automating processes such as biopsy collection, histopathological analysis, and molecular profiling, swarm robots can accelerate the diagnostic workflow, improve diagnostic accuracy, and enable timely interventions for patients. It offers transformative opportunities to enhance the precision, efficiency, and effectiveness of cancer care by enabling targeted drug delivery, minimally invasive surgeries, intraoperative imaging, and high-throughput diagnostics. By harnessing the collective intelligence and capabilities of robotic swarms, physicians can deliver personalized, cutting-edge treatments that improve patient outcomes and redefine the standard of care in oncology.

20.3 Applications of swarm intelligence in cancer care

In recent years, the integration of advanced technologies has revolutionized the field of cancer care, paving the way for personalized, data-driven approaches to diagnosis, treatment, and patient management. Among these innovations, swarm intelligence has emerged as a promising paradigm, drawing inspiration from the collective behavior of decentralized systems in nature. This session explores the diverse applications of swarm intelligence in

Cancer Care 4.0/5.0, where the emphasis lies on tailoring treatments to individual patient characteristics, optimizing therapeutic strategies, and enhancing patient outcomes. From treatment optimization and predictive modeling to decision support systems and early detection, swarm intelligence offers innovative solutions to address the complexities and challenges of cancer care, marking a significant advancement towards precision medicine and holistic patient-centered care in oncology.

20.3.1 Treatment optimization

One of the most promising applications of swarm intelligence in cancer care is treatment optimization. Cancer is a highly heterogeneous disease, characterized by diverse tumor types, genetic mutations, and patient responses to therapy. Traditional treatment approaches often rely on standardized protocols that may not fully account for the individual variability and complexity of each patient's disease. Swarm intelligence algorithms offer a novel approach to navigating this complexity by leveraging the collective intelligence of decentralized systems to optimize treatment strategies tailored to the unique characteristics of each patient.

Swarm intelligence algorithms, such as ACO and PSO, excel at exploring the vast landscape of treatment options and identifying optimal solutions amidst the inherent uncertainty and variability of cancer. By analyzing patient-specific data, including genomic profiles, imaging scans, and clinical histories, these algorithms can generate personalized treatment plans that maximize therapeutic efficacy while minimizing adverse effects. This approach enables oncologists to tailor interventions to the unique characteristics of each patient's disease, optimizing outcomes and improving quality of life.

One key advantage of swarm intelligence in treatment optimization is its ability to balance competing objectives, such as tumor control and preservation of healthy tissues. By iteratively evaluating the efficacy of different treatment regimens and adapting strategies based on real-time feedback, swarm intelligence algorithms can dynamically optimize treatment plans to achieve the best possible outcomes for patients. This dynamic optimization process mirrors the adaptive behavior of biological systems, allowing for continuous refinement and improvement of treatment protocols over time.

Furthermore, swarm intelligence algorithms can facilitate the discovery of novel treatment combinations and therapeutic sequences that may not be apparent through traditional trial-and-error approaches. By exploring the synergies between different therapies and identifying optimal pathways for drug delivery, radiation therapy, and surgical interventions, swarm intelligence algorithms can enhance the effectiveness of cancer treatments and improve patient outcomes.

This treatment optimization is a key application of swarm intelligence in cancer care, offering personalized, data-driven approaches to navigate the complexity and heterogeneity of the disease. By leveraging the collective intelligence of decentralized systems, swarm intelligence algorithms empower oncologists to deliver more effective, tailored treatments that maximize therapeutic efficacy while minimizing adverse effects, ultimately improving outcomes and quality of life for cancer patients.

20.3.2 Early detection and diagnosis

Early detection and diagnosis play a crucial role in improving cancer outcomes by enabling timely intervention and treatment initiation. Swarm intelligence offers innovative approaches to enhance early detection and diagnosis through the integration of diverse data sources and the identification of subtle patterns indicative of early-stage disease. Swarm intelligence algorithms, such as ACO and PSO, excel at analyzing large-scale datasets encompassing patient demographics, medical histories, imaging scans, and biomarker profiles to identify individuals at high risk of developing cancer. By leveraging the collective intelligence of decentralized systems, these algorithms can detect subtle deviations from normal physiological patterns and identify early warning signs of cancer, enabling proactive screening and surveillance strategies.

One key advantage of swarm intelligence in early detection and diagnosis is its ability to integrate diverse data sources and identify complex relationships between different variables. By analyzing patterns of gene expression, protein biomarkers, and imaging features, swarm intelligence algorithms can identify signatures indicative of early-stage disease and distinguish between benign and malignant lesions with high accuracy.

Furthermore, swarm intelligence algorithms can facilitate the development of predictive models for cancer risk assessment, enabling healthcare providers to stratify individuals based on their likelihood of developing specific cancer types. By incorporating factors such as age, family history, lifestyle behaviors, and genetic predisposition, these models can identify high-risk populations for targeted screening and preventive interventions, ultimately reducing cancer morbidity and mortality.

In addition to risk assessment, swarm intelligence algorithms can enhance the sensitivity and specificity of cancer screening tests by optimizing the interpretation of imaging studies, laboratory tests, and diagnostic procedures. By analyzing subtle features that may be missed by human observers, these algorithms can improve the detection of early-stage tumors and facilitate prompt referral for further evaluation and treatment. The early detection and diagnosis are critical components of effective cancer care, and swarm intelligence offers innovative approaches to enhance these processes through the integration of diverse data sources and the identification of subtle patterns indicative of early-stage disease. By leveraging the collective intelligence of decentralized systems, swarm intelligence algorithms empower healthcare providers to identify individuals at high risk of developing cancer, improve the sensitivity and specificity of screening tests, and facilitate timely intervention and treatment initiation, ultimately improving outcomes for cancer patients.

20.3.3 Predictive modeling

Predictive modeling plays a crucial role in cancer care by forecasting disease progression, treatment response, and patient outcomes based on diverse clinical and biological factors. Swarm intelligence offers innovative approaches to predictive modeling through the integration of large-scale datasets, the identification of complex relationships between variables, and the development of robust prognostic models. Swarm intelligence algorithms, such as ACO and PSO, excel at analyzing heterogeneous data sources, including genomic profiles, imaging scans, clinical histories, and treatment outcomes, to identify predictive biomarkers and develop prognostic models. By leveraging the collective intelligence of decentralized systems, these algorithms can identify subtle patterns and interactions between variables that may not be apparent through traditional statistical methods, enabling more accurate predictions of disease outcomes.

One key advantage of swarm intelligence in predictive modeling is its ability to handle high-dimensional data and complex interactions between variables. By exploring the multidimensional space of potential predictors and outcomes, swarm intelligence algorithms can identify nonlinear relationships and synergies between different factors, improving the accuracy and robustness of predictive models. Furthermore, swarm intelligence algorithms can facilitate the development of personalized prognostic models that account for individual variability and heterogeneity in cancer patients. By analyzing patient-specific data, such as genetic mutations, tumor characteristics, and treatment responses, these algorithms can tailor predictions to the unique characteristics of each patient's disease, enabling more precise risk stratification and treatment decision-making.

In addition to predicting disease outcomes, swarm intelligence algorithms can also optimize treatment strategies and identify optimal pathways for intervention based on predicted outcomes. By simulating different treatment scenarios and evaluating their impact on predicted outcomes, these algorithms can guide clinicians in selecting the most effective and personalized treatment options for individual patients, ultimately improving patient outcomes and quality of life (Saldanha et al., 2022). This predictive modeling is a critical component of cancer care, and swarm intelligence offers innovative approaches to developing accurate, robust, and personalized prognostic models (Papachristou et al., 2023). By leveraging the collective intelligence of decentralized systems, swarm intelligence algorithms empower clinicians to predict disease progression, treatment response, and patient outcomes with greater accuracy and precision, ultimately improving decision-making and patient care in oncology.

20.4 Challenges

While the potential of swarm intelligence in cancer care is promising, several challenges must be addressed to realize its full impact and integration into clinical practice.

20.4.1 Data integration and standardization

One of the primary challenges in applying swarm intelligence to cancer care is the integration and standardization of heterogeneous data sources. Cancer data are often dispersed across different healthcare systems, institutions, and databases, making it challenging to access, aggregate, and analyze. Standardizing data formats, terminologies, and protocols is essential to ensure interoperability and facilitate seamless data exchange for swarm intelligence algorithms.

20.4.2 Algorithm transparency and interpretability

Swarm intelligence algorithms, such as ACO and PSO, operate as black-box models, making it difficult to interpret their decision-making processes and understand the rationale behind their recommendations. Ensuring algorithm transparency and interpretability is critical to gaining trust and acceptance from healthcare providers and patients, as well as regulatory authorities, who require explanations for algorithmic decisions to ensure patient safety and accountability.

20.4.3 Ethical and regulatory considerations

The use of swarm intelligence in cancer care raises ethical and regulatory considerations related to patient privacy, data security, informed consent, and algorithmic bias. Protecting patient confidentiality and ensuring data security are paramount to safeguarding sensitive health information from unauthorized access or misuse. Additionally, addressing algorithmic bias and ensuring fairness and equity in algorithmic decision-making is essential to mitigate potential disparities in patient outcomes and access to care.

20.4.4 Clinical validation and adoption

Despite promising results in research settings, swarm intelligence algorithms must undergo rigorous clinical validation to demonstrate their efficacy, safety, and clinical utility before widespread adoption in clinical practice. Conducting prospective clinical trials, real-world studies, and comparative effectiveness research is essential to evaluate the performance of swarm intelligence algorithms in real-world settings, validate their predictive accuracy, and assess their impact on patient outcomes and healthcare delivery.

20.4.5 Integration with existing systems and workflows

Integrating swarm intelligence algorithms into existing clinical systems and workflows poses technical and logistical challenges. Ensuring seamless interoperability with EHRs, clinical decision support systems, and other healthcare IT infrastructure is essential to facilitate the adoption and integration of swarm intelligence into routine clinical practice without disrupting existing workflows or imposing additional burdens on healthcare providers.

20.5 Conclusion

In this chapter, the applications of swarm intelligence in cancer care hold immense promise for transforming the landscape of oncology and improving patient outcomes. From treatment optimization to early detection and diagnosis, predictive modeling, decision support systems, and beyond, swarm intelligence offers innovative approaches to address the complex challenges of cancer treatment and management. By leveraging the collective intelligence of decentralized systems, swarm intelligence algorithms empower healthcare providers to personalize care, optimize treatment strategies, and make more informed, evidence-based decisions tailored to the unique characteristics of each patient's disease.

However, several challenges must be addressed to realize the full potential of swarm intelligence in cancer care. Data integration, algorithm transparency, ethical and regulatory considerations, clinical validation, and integration with existing systems and workflows are critical areas that require attention and collaboration from interdisciplinary teams of researchers, clinicians, policymakers, and industry stakeholders. Overcoming these challenges will be essential to harnessing the transformative power of swarm intelligence and ensuring its successful integration into routine clinical practice.

Looking to the future, emerging trends and future directions in swarm intelligence offer exciting opportunities to drive transformative advancements in cancer care. Integration with emerging technologies, explainable AI and interpretability, ethical and regulatory frameworks, clinical validation, and patient-centered care are key areas of focus that will shape the future of swarm intelligence in oncology (Saraswat et al., 2022). Moving forward, continued research, innovation, and investment in swarm intelligence technologies, coupled with robust clinical validation and implementation efforts, will be essential to realizing the vision of personalized, data-driven cancer care. By working together to address these challenges and seize the opportunities offered by swarm intelligence, we can revolutionize cancer care, improve patient outcomes, and advance the field of oncology into the era of precision medicine and personalized care.

Acknowledgments

My acknowledgments to all the dear and near ones who helped me to complete the article.

References

Al-Tashi, Q., Saad, M. B., Sheshadri, A., Wu, C. C., Chang, J. Y., Al-Lazikani, B., Gibbons, C., Vokes, N. I., Zhang, J., Lee, J. J., Heymach, J. V., Jaffray, D., Mirjalili, S., & Wu, J. (2023). SwarmDeepSurv: Swarm intelligence advances deep survival network for prognostic radiomics signatures in four solid cancers. *Patterns, 4*(8)100777. Available from https://doi.org/10.1016/j.patter.2023.100777.

Bitterman, D. S., Aerts, H. J. W. L., & Mak, R. H. (2020). Approaching autonomy in medical artificial intelligence. *The Lancet Digital Health, 2*(9), e447. Available from https://doi.org/10.1016/S2589-7500(20)30187-4, https://www.sciencedirect.com/journal/the-lancet-digital-health.

Chopra, D., & Arora, P. (2022). Swarm intelligence in data science: Challenges, opportunities and applications. *Procedia Computer Science, 215*, 104–111. Available from https://doi.org/10.1016/j.procs.2022.12.012, http://www.sciencedirect.com/science/journal/18770509.

Debie, E., Kasmarik, K., & Garratt, M. (2023). Swarm robotics: A survey from a multi-tasking perspective. *ACM Computing Surveys, 56*(2). Available from https://doi.org/10.1145/3611652, http://dl.acm.org/citation.cfm?id = J204.

Dorigo, M., Birattari, M., & Stützle, T. (2006). Ant colony optimization artificial ants as a computational intelligence technique. *IEEE Computational Intelligence Magazine, 1*(4). Available from https://doi.org/10.1109/CI-M.2006.248054.

Fahmi, H., Zarlis, M., Nababan, E. B., & Sihombing, P. (2020). Ant Colony Optimization (ACO) Algorithm for Determining The Nearest Route Search in Distribution of Light Food Production. *Journal of Physics: Conference Series, 1566*(1)012045. Available from https://doi.org/10.1088/1742-6596/1566/1/012045.

Gad, A. G. (2022). Particle Swarm Optimization Algorithm and Its Applications: A Systematic Review. *Archives of Computational Methods in Engineering*, 29(5). Available from https://doi.org/10.1007/s11831-021-09694-4, https://www.springer.com/journal/11831.

Imran, M., Hashim, R., & Khalid, N. E. A. (2013). An overview of particle swarm optimization variants. *Procedia Engineering*, 53, 491–496. Available from https://doi.org/10.1016/j.proeng.2013.02.063, http://www.sciencedirect.com/science/journal/18777058.

Kraus, S., Schiavone, F., Pluzhnikova, A., & Invernizzi, A. C. (2021). Digital transformation in healthcare: Analyzing the current state-of-research. *Journal of Business Research*, 123. Available from https://doi.org/10.1016/j.jbusres.2020.10.030, http://www.elsevier.com/locate/jbusres.

Mbunge, E., Muchemwa, B., Jiyane, S., & Batani, J. (2021). Sensors and healthcare 5.0: transformative shift in virtual care through emerging digital health technologies. *Global Health Journal*, 5(4). Available from https://doi.org/10.1016/j.glohj.2021.11.008, https://www.sciencedirect.com/journal/global-health-journal.

Papachristou, N., Kotronoulas, G., Dikaios, N., Allison, S. J., Eleftherochorinou, H., Rai, T., Kunz, H., Barnaghi, P., Miaskowski, C., & Bamidis, P. D. (2023). Digital transformation of cancer care in the era of big data, artificial intelligence and data-driven interventions: Navigating the field. *Seminars in Oncology Nursing*, 39(3)151433. Available from https://doi.org/10.1016/j.soncn.2023.151433.

Rao, X., & Yan, X. (2022). Particle swarm optimization algorithm based on information sharing in Industry 4.0. *Wireless Communications and Mobile Computing*, 2022. Available from https://doi.org/10.1155/2022/4328185, https://www.hindawi.com/journals/wcmc/.

Saldanha, O. L., Quirke, P., West, N. P., James, J. A., Loughrey, M. B., Grabsch, H. I., Salto-Tellez, M., Alwers, E., Cifci, D., Ghaffari Laleh, N., Seibel, T., Gray, R., Hutchins, G. G. A., Brenner, H., van Treeck, M., Yuan, T., Brinker, T. J., Chang-Claude, J., Khader, F., ... Kather, J. N. (2022). Swarm learning for decentralized artificial intelligence in cancer histopathology. *Nature Medicine*, 28(6). Available from https://doi.org/10.1038/s41591-022-01768-5.

Saraswat, D., Bhattacharya, P., Verma, A., Prasad, V. K., Tanwar, S., Sharma, G., Bokoro, P. N., & Sharma, R. (2022). Explainable AI for healthcare 5.0: Opportunities and challenges. *IEEE Access*, 10. Available from https://doi.org/10.1109/ACCESS.2022.3197671, http://ieeexplore.ieee.org/xpl/RecentIssue.jsp?punumber = 6287639.

Schranz, M., Umlauft, M., Sende, M., & Elmenreich, W. (2020). Swarm robotic behaviors and current applications. *Frontiers in Robotics and AI*, 7. Available from https://doi.org/10.3389/frobt.2020.00036, journal.frontiersin.org/journal/robotics-and-ai.

Exploring human-based digital twins in healthcare: a scoping review

Nilmini Wickramasinghe and Nalika Ulapane

La Trobe University, Bundoora, VIC, Australia

21.1 Introduction

Digital twins are commonly defined as digital replicas of physical-world entities capable of simulating the characteristics of their real-world counterparts through data transfer (Mihai et al., 2022). Digital twins have sparked transformative innovations across numerous industries, notably influencing product design and smart manufacturing (Ciano et al., 2021). In recent years, the healthcare sector has increasingly embraced the potential of digital twins and the applications have ranged to fields such as genomics (Björnsson et al., 2020), aged care (Liu et al., 2019), cancer care (Singh et al., 2021) and dementia (Wickramasinghe et al., 2022a, 2022b). The adaptability of digital twins allows for effortless visualization, reasoning, experimentation, and forecasting of specific aspects within the physical realm, offering an efficient, safe, and cost-effective approach (Singh et al., 2021). The significance of digital twins in addressing key challenges in healthcare has been recognized over time. As such, researchers have started proposing ways to leverage this concept to enhance precision and personalization of care (Wickramasinghe et al., 2023), marking a pivotal exploration into the intersection of digital twin technology and healthcare innovation.

This chapter provides an overview of the expansive landscape of digital twin applications within healthcare, with a particular emphasis on the pivotal role of simulating and forecasting human physiological conditions through digital twins. Digital twins that can simulate and forecast human physiological conditions are termed "human-based digital twins" in this chapter. As we embark on a comprehensive exploration of this domain, this paper presents a scoping review that scrutinizes relevant works published until late 2023. Our review focuses on summarizing the existing literature, delineating the strengths, weaknesses, opportunities, and threats associated with human-based digital twins in healthcare applications. By addressing these key aspects, we aspire to contribute to the understanding of the potential impact of human-based digital twins in healthcare. This

Sensor Networks for Smart Hospitals
DOI: https://doi.org/10.1016/B978-0-443-36370-2.00022-0

chapter's overarching objective is to respond to the research question: "How may human-based digital twins be useful for healthcare?" Through this inquiry, we aim to provide valuable insights and foster further discourse on the transformative possibilities that human-based digital twins offer to the healthcare sector.

21.2 Methodology

Scopus, a comprehensive academic database spanning various disciplines, served as the primary source for this scoping review. The search was meticulously conducted between October 20 and October 25, 2023, with a specific focus on identifying papers related to digital twins in healthcare. The search strategy employed the following keyword string: ("digital twin" OR "digital twins") AND ("sensor" OR "sensors") AND ("healthcare" OR "health care"). These keywords were strategically applied to the titles, abstracts, and keywords of reported items, aiming to pinpoint literature highly pertinent to our targeted theme.

The culmination of this search on October 25, 2023, yielded a curated list of 70 items, meticulously chosen as a representative sample encapsulating the essence of digital twins in healthcare. Subsequently, the identified items underwent a thorough screening of titles and abstracts to discern relevance to our research focus. The screening process employed specific criteria, encompassing the inclusion of items discussing digital twins in support of particular healthcare delivery tasks and the exclusion of those not centering on "specific healthcare tasks" or neglecting the concept of digital twins.

During the screening phase, a few papers related to pharmaceutical production processes surfaced. While pharmaceuticals are undeniably relevant to healthcare, the decision was made to exclude papers on pharmaceutical production processes, deeming them more aligned with sectors such as manufacturing and product quality control. This strategic exclusion aimed to maintain a concentrated focus on healthcare delivery within clinician/patient encounters, ensuring that the review remains pertinent to the intended scope.

Following the abstract review process, 33 items were excluded for various reasons, including their lack of relevance to healthcare, articles lacking a specific healthcare application focus (e.g., survey or review papers, or guest editorials), overviews of conference proceedings and books, emphasis on biopharma or other pharmaceutical sectors, and inaccessibility of the full text. Consequently, 37 items were selected to undergo a comprehensive full-text review.

During the full-text review, we identified 20 items aligning with our targeted focus on human-based digital twins simulating human physiological conditions. Subsequently, we proceeded to distil key information from these 20 items, elucidating their healthcare context, the specific physiological element of the human body simulated by the digital twin, and the intended purpose for which the digital twin was utilized.

21.3 Results

Table 21.1 presents the summarization of the 20 items taken for full-text review.

TABLE 21.1 Summary of human-based digital twins found through this scoping review.

Research item	Healthcare context	Physiological element simulated by digital twin	Intended purpose for which the digital twin (DT) has been used
Alcaraz et al. (2019)	Rehabilitation care	Lower body joint angles	The DT is intended to simulate lower body joint angles, facilitate gait analysis for rehabilitation, enable precise gait assessment, enhance the wearability of sensor systems, and reduce physical errors in measurements.
Conte Alcaraz et al. (2021)	Rehabilitation care	Lower limb joint angles	The DT is intended to model and simulate lower limb joint angles' gait kinematics through neural networks to enable accurate gait assessment for rehabilitation and thereby enhance the wearability of sensor systems by reducing the necessary number of sensors.
Meraghni et al. (2021)	Breast cancer	Breast skin temperature	The DT is intended to facilitate personalized breast cancer detection by employing a simulated bio-heat model of breast skin temperature, enabling consideration of individual behaviors and factors influencing breast skin temperature for enhanced accuracy.
Xie et al. (2021)	Patient assessment and monitoring	Patient's health status	The DT is intended to facilitate the evaluation of the health status of patients by integrating diverse data sources and delivering feedback, offering personalized care through extensive patient assessment and monitoring that incorporates real-time data and medical history.
Al-Naime et al. (2022)	Perioperative rehabilitation (i.e., Prehabilitation)	Preoperative patients' movement	The DT is intended to enable continuous monitoring and providing personalized recommendations and alerts based on patient movement data to facilitate flexible and supervised as well as unsupervised prehabilitation support.
Cara Mihai et al. (2022)	Clinical decision support	Patient's health status	The DT is intended to facilitate clinical decision-making by employing digital twins of patients, leveraging sensor data and AI to provide efficient access to medical services, assist family doctors, and aid medical experts in making informed decisions.
Gupta et al. (2022)	Patient lifestyle monitoring for personalized care	Patient's lifestyle and state of mind	The DT is intended to assist in anticipating future lifestyle and mental states of people to optimize treatment decisions for personalized healthcare, enhancing health tracking and fostering healthier lifestyles.

(Continued)

TABLE 21.1 (Continued)

Research item	Healthcare context	Physiological element simulated by digital twin	Intended purpose for which the digital twin (DT) has been used
Khan et al. (2022)	Care at home	Patient in a care-home environment	The DT is intended to facilitate patient monitoring, disease diagnosis, fall detection, and breathing abnormality analysis to enhance patient care and recovery by enabling early diagnosis, reducing complications and accidents, and aiding in the recovery process.
Aluvalu et al. (2023)	Emergency room services	The patients— patient's health conditions and histories	The DT is intended to enhance ER treatment and patient risk assessment by facilitating quicker, more informed treatment decisions, ultimately reducing ER stays and improving patient risk evaluation.
Avanzato et al. (2023)	Cardiovascular disease	Patient's heart	The DT is intended to enhance patient care by improving patient-doctor relationships, expediting treatment, and reducing medical costs through AI-based analysis of ECG signals to support interpreting and managing cardiac pathologies.
Geoffrey Chase et al. (2023)	Intensive care unit (ICU) care	Patients—patient physiology and conditions	The DT is intended to enhance care and productivity by tailoring care through real-time monitoring using patient-specific models, improving outcomes, improving personalization, improving efficiency, and reducing costs.
Dias De Oliveira et al. (2023)	Emotion Modeling	Human behavior and emotions	The DT is intended to model human behavior and emotions, and thereby enable visualization and analytics for personalized healthcare, and also to enable early disease detection and lifestyle optimization.
Fahim et al. (2023)	Aged care—elderly behavior monitoring	Elderly individuals' activities at home	The DT is intended to enable unobtrusive monitoring, assessment of daily tasks, and identification of emergency risks to support elderly care by monitoring daily activities of elders.
Gazerani (2023)	Migraine care	Patients' condition for migraine care	The DT is intended to enable the collection of diverse data to generate actionable insights on patient health conditions and responses to therapy, and thereby facilitate personalized treatment and cost reduction, and also contribute to patient-centric care and optimization of migraine treatment while minimizing long-term healthcare costs.

Reference	Application	Description
Haleem et al. (2023)	Personalized care—patient-specific care plans, medication optimization, and chronic illness management	Patients—health conditions, behaviors, and treatment responses
		The DT is intended to utilize patient data to forecast surgery outcomes, recommend medications, and aid in chronic illness management, contributing to enhanced care and precise treatment through tailored treatment plans, alerts for prescriptions, dietary adjustments, and predictive healthcare.
Khan et al. (2023)	Patient monitoring and clinical decision support	Patient's biological properties and characteristics
		The DT is intended to utilize WiFi CSI, signal processing, and machine learning to monitor and classify patient respiration, supporting clinical decision-making by enabling unobtrusive monitoring, accurate estimation of breaths per minute, and optimal patient classification for healthcare decisions.
Moztarzadeh et al. (2023)	Dentistry—cervical vertebral maturation (CVM)	CVM—development stage of cervical vertebrae relevant to dental surgery
		The DT is intended for the implementation of MobileNetV2 for dental diagnostics without additional sensors with the aim of automating the diagnosis, leading to enhanced efficiency, cost reduction, and improved diagnostics in dental treatment through deep learning-based automated processes.
Qu et al. (2023a)	Aged care—monitoring seniors living alone or in nursing homes using IoT and DT technologies	Individual seniors—seniors' activities and health status
		The DT is intended to mirror seniors' activities in a virtual community in the Metaverse to enable real-time monitoring and alert generation for potential risks while protecting seniors through instant alerting when anomalies like falls are detected without compromising privacy.
Vats et al. (2023)	Cardiovascular disease prediction and clinical decision support	Patient—human digital twin
		The DT is intended to enable prediction and assisting in diagnosis of cardiovascular diseases and thereby enable early disease prediction, diagnosis assistance, improved patient care, and extended life expectancy.
Winter and Chico (2023)	Cardiovascular diseases	Patients—patient physiology and health status
		The DT is intended to facilitate personalized healthcare through enhanced disease prevention, personalized simulation of disease scenarios, and thereby enable tailored medical interventions for cardiovascular conditions.

21.4 Discussion on human-based digital twins

This review highlights the diverse applications of human-based digital twins in healthcare, particularly focusing on chronic conditions, habilitative therapy, and patient monitoring. Several chronic conditions, such as breast cancer, heart conditions, migraines, and dental surgery, have been addressed through digital twins utilizing predictive analytics and clinical decision support (Avanzato et al., 2023; Gazerani, 2023; Meraghni et al., 2021; Moztarzadeh et al., 2023; Vats et al., 2023; Winter & Chico, 2023). For instance, the digital twin of a patient's heart aids in interpreting and managing cardiac pathologies through AI-based analysis of ECG signals (Avanzato et al., 2023). This aligns with the broader trend of leveraging digital twins to tackle chronic conditions (Singh et al., 2021; Wickramasinghe et al., 2022a, 2022b).

Sensors play a pivotal role in these digital twins, with smart and wearable sensors being predominant. Examples include skin temperature sensors for breast cancer detection (Meraghni et al., 2021), various biomedical sensors for heart conditions (Avanzato et al., 2023; Vats et al., 2023; Winter & Chico, 2023), and wearable sensors for migraine care (Gazerani, 2023). Traditional sensors, like imaging for CVM assessment in dental surgery, are also occasionally used (Moztarzadeh et al., 2023). Additionally, human-generated data, such as patient journals for migraine care, supplements sensor data (Gazerani, 2023). The integration of human-generated data emphasizes that sensing and data collection for digital twins in healthcare extend beyond mere devices, embodying a "human plus device" approach.

Habilitative therapy, specifically rehabilitation and prehabilitation care, emerges as another prominent domain. Wearables, inertial measurement units, accelerometers, and gyroscopes are employed to collect kinematic data for digital twins in these therapeutic contexts (Al-Naime et al., 2022; Alcaraz et al., 2019; Conte Alcaraz et al., 2021). These digital twins support rehabilitation by monitoring, simulating, and visually representing human kinematics. Objectives such as minimizing the number of sensors worn by patients, enhancing the precision of gait assessment, and offering personalized recommendations underscore the therapeutic potential of these digital twins (Alcaraz et al., 2019; Conte Alcaraz et al., 2021; Al-Naime et al., 2022).

The remainder of the works primarily emphasizes patient monitoring, encompassing hospital settings (e.g., intensive care) and living environments (e.g., aged-care settings) (Geoffrey Chase et al., 2023; Fahim et al., 2023). Employing various sensors, including wearables and unobtrusive sensors, these digital twins aim to monitor patients in real-time for efficient detection of acute events or anomalies like illness or falls.

Crucially, all discussed human-based digital twins demonstrate compatibility with the Internet of Things (IoT). This compatibility is vital for facilitating seamless data transfer from the physical world to the virtual realm of digital twins.

In summary, the overarching objective of human-based digital twins in healthcare is to provide precise, personalized, and timely care to patients, resulting in economic benefits, clinical advancements, increased patient satisfaction, and positive societal outcomes

(Wickramasinghe et al., 2021). This scoping review underscores the multifaceted applications of digital twins across diverse healthcare domains, positioning them as transformative tools in the pursuit of enhanced healthcare delivery.

21.5 Strengths, weaknesses, opportunities, threats, enablers and barriers

It became clear from this review, that the emergence of human-based digital twins has promise to reshape the landscape of healthcare, offering transformative solutions to address diverse challenges ranging from chronic conditions to habilitative therapy to patient monitoring, and more. This technological paradigm leverages advanced data analytics, artificial intelligence, and sensor technologies to create and enable the use of human-based digital twins that can simulate human physiological conditions, and thereby enabling precise, personalized, and timely healthcare interventions. As we delve further into the applications and implications of human-based digital twins in healthcare, this section provides analysis of the strengths, weaknesses, opportunities, threats, as well as enablers and barriers that shape the utilization and potential widescale adoption human-based digital twins in healthcare. This discussion aims to provide insights into the multifaceted nature of digital twins, shedding light on their capabilities, limitations, and the intricate dynamics surrounding their integration into contemporary healthcare ecosystems.

21.5.1 Strengths of human-based digital twins in healthcare

Diverse Applications: Human-based digital twins demonstrate versatility in addressing various healthcare challenges, including chronic conditions, habilitative therapy, and patient monitoring, showcasing their adaptability to different contexts (Mihai et al., 2022; Alcaraz et al., 2019; Conte Alcaraz et al., 2021; Meraghni et al., 2021; Xie et al., 2021; Al-Naime et al., 2022; Cara; Gupta et al., 2022; Khan et al., 2022; Aluvalu et al., 2023; Avanzato et al., 2023; Geoffrey Chase et al., 2023; Dias De Oliveira et al., 2023; Fahim et al., 2023; Haleem et al., 2023; Khan et al., 2023; Moztarzadeh et al., 2023; Qu et al., 2023b; Vats et al., 2023; Winter & Chico, 2023).

Predictive Analytics: The integration of predictive analytics and AI in digital twins enables proactive healthcare interventions, aiding in the early detection, diagnosis, and management of chronic conditions (Avanzato et al., 2023; Haleem et al., 2023).

Wearable Sensors: The utilization of smart and wearable sensors facilitates real-time monitoring, data collection, and personalized care, contributing to more effective and patient-centric healthcare solutions (Meraghni et al., 2021; Avanzato et al., 2023; Vats et al., 2023).

IoT Compatibility: All discussed digital twins demonstrate compatibility with the IoT, ensuring seamless data transfer between the physical and virtual realms, which is crucial for effective healthcare applications.

Enhanced Efficiency: By leveraging technology, digital twins have the potential to reduce errors, increase precision, expedite treatment decisions, and ultimately enhance healthcare delivery (Aluvalu et al., 2023; Avanzato et al., 2023; Geoffrey Chase et al., 2023; Winter & Chico, 2023).

21.5.2 Weaknesses of human-based digital twins in healthcare

Sensor Dependence: The reliance on sensors, especially wearables, may introduce challenges related to user compliance, sensor accuracy, and potential discomfort, impacting the overall effectiveness of digital twin applications.

Data Privacy Concerns: The collection of diverse data, including sensitive patient information, raises privacy concerns. Balancing data utilization for healthcare benefits while ensuring patient privacy remains a challenge (Qu et al., 2023b).

Integration Complexity (Challenges with Interoperability): Implementing digital twins in healthcare requires seamless integration with existing systems, electronic health records, and healthcare workflows, posing challenges in terms of interoperability and system compatibility (Xie et al., 2021).

21.5.3 Opportunities in human-based digital twins in healthcare

Personalized Healthcare: Digital twins offer the opportunity to tailor healthcare interventions based on individual patient data, providing more personalized and effective treatments (Khan et al., 2023).

Efficient Disease Management: The integration of digital twins with predictive analytics creates opportunities for more efficient disease management, early diagnosis, and timely interventions, potentially reducing healthcare costs and improving patient outcomes (Haleem et al., 2023).

Enhanced Patient Engagement: Digital twins can empower patients by involving them in their healthcare journey, fostering engagement, and encouraging proactive health management (Gupta et al., 2022).

21.5.4 Threats to/in human-based digital twins in healthcare

Security Risks: The interconnected nature of digital twins and their reliance on IoT expose them to cybersecurity threats, including data breaches and unauthorized access, posing risks to patient confidentiality and system integrity (Qu et al., 2023b).

Resistance to Technology (or Resistance to Adoption): Healthcare professionals and patients may exhibit resistance to adopting and trusting digital twin technologies, particularly due to concerns related to reliability, data accuracy, and unfamiliarity with AI-driven healthcare solutions (Xie et al., 2021).

21.5.5 Enablers to human-based digital twins in healthcare

Technological Advancements: Advances in AI, machine learning, and computing power are all enablers to realizing fast and effective digital twins in data rich healthcare environments (Singh et al., 2021).

Interdisciplinary Collaboration: Collaborations between healthcare professionals, technologists, and researchers can enhance the development and implementation of digital twin technologies, ensuring they align with healthcare needs (Singh et al., 2021; Alcaraz et al., 2019; Conte Alcaraz et al., 2021).

21.5.6 Barriers to human-based digital twins in healthcare

Limited Standardization: The lack of standardized protocols for digital twin development and integration hinders widespread adoption, as it complicates interoperability and data sharing across different healthcare systems (Singh et al., 2021; Xie et al., 2021).

Cost Implications: The initial investment and ongoing costs associated with implementing digital twins, including sensor deployment and maintenance, may present barriers, particularly for resource-constrained healthcare settings (Gupta et al., 2022; Winter & Chico, 2023).

21.6 Discussion

Based on our above review of the literature, we contend that the use of human-based digital twins in the area of cancer care is very compelling. Cancer treatments are complex and require the processing of multispectral data in a rapid fashion. Moreover, time is very significant in order to have the best possible clinical outcomes. Cancer care is also expensive and has many unpleasant side effects. From the patient's perspective, the need is to have the best treatment possible that minimizes unpleasant side effects, maximizes the probability of successful outcomes and enables quality of life to be maintained. From the clinician's perspective, the need is to have support to extract pertinent information and germane knowledge at the point of care to enable optimal clinical decision-making to occur for the presenting patient. This in turn will ensure the best clinical outcomes. From the regulator and payer perspective, the need is to ensure the most correct treatment is the one chosen to minimize waste and unnecessary treatments that will not provide good clinical outcomes. While the perspective may differ from the three key parties; patient, clinician and payer/regulator, the goals are aligned in so much as all desire the best treatment to be chosen expeditiously. To do this, have precision and personalization as well as be able to make an assessment about the progression of the cancer, we contend this is only possible with human-based digital twins.

Our proposed approach is illustrated in Fig. 21.1.

As can be seen in Fig. 21.1A, the construction of the digital model is provided based on patient record, genetic information and lab/radiology test results. Then in Fig. 21.1B the constructed digital model is compared with past records to find a similar matching cohort. In Fig. 21.1C, the chosen cohort is then used to train the model and develop the digital

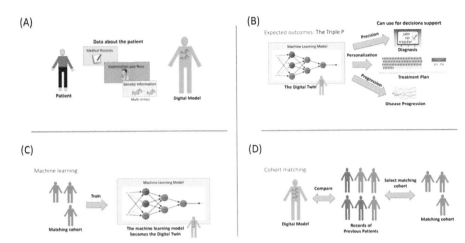

FIGURE 21.1 (A) Digital model based on patient record, genetic information and lab/radiology test results. (B) Digital model is compared with past records to find a similar matching cohort. (C) The chosen cohort is then used to train the model and develop the digital twin. (D) Digital twin is used to predict critical issues about the cancer.

twin. Finally, in 1d, the digital twin is used to predict critical issues about the cancer and which treatment is likely to be best for the presenting patient, it includes personalization and can assist with understanding the progression of the presenting patient's cancer.

21.7 Conclusion

In conclusion, the performed scoping review delved into the dynamic landscape of human-based digital twins in healthcare, exploring their applications, methodologies, and technological frameworks. The reviewed literature underscored the versatility of digital twins, addressing various healthcare challenges, from chronic conditions to habilitative therapy and patient monitoring. The strengths of human-based digital twins are evident in their diverse applications, predictive analytics capabilities, utilization of wearable sensors, IoT compatibility, and potential for enhanced efficiency in the healthcare system. However, challenges arise, including sensor dependence, data privacy concerns, integration complexities, and also regulatory challenges along with human reluctance for technology adoption. Opportunities lie in personalized healthcare, efficient disease management, and enhanced patient engagement, while threats include security risks and resistance to technology adoption. Enablers such as technological advancements and interdisciplinary collaboration propel the field forward, yet barriers like limited standardization and cost implications persist. The analysis in this chapter illuminates the multifaceted nature of human-based digital twins, providing valuable insights for researchers, healthcare professionals, and policymakers. From this we have proffered a model for digital twins, their construction and use for cancer care. As digital twins continue to evolve, the synthesis of existing knowledge in this chapter serves as a foundation for future research endeavors, guiding the healthcare industry toward harnessing the full potential of digital twins for improved patient outcomes and healthcare system optimization specifically in the area of better cancer care but is also applicable to other disease and their respective treatments.

References

Alcaraz, J. C., Moghaddamnia, S., Fuhrwerk, M., & Peissig, J. (2019). Efficiency of the memory polynomial model in realizing digital twins for gait assessment. In *27th European Signal Processing Conference (EUSIPCO)* (pp. 1-5). IEEE.

Al-Naime, K., Al-Anbuky, A., & Mawston, G. (2022). IoT based pre-operative prehabilitation program monitoring model: Implementation and preliminary evaluation. In *4th International Conference on Biomedical Engineering (IBIOMED)* (pp. 24-29). IEEE.

Aluvalu, R., Mudrakola, S., Kaladevi, A. C., Sandhya, M. V. S., & Bhat, C. R. (2023). The novel emergency hospital services for patients using digital twins. *Microprocessors and Microsystems, 98*, 104794.

Avanzato, R., Beritelli, F., Lombardo, A., & Ricci, C. (2023). Heart DT: Monitoring and preventing cardiac pathologies using AI and IoT sensors. *Future Internet, 15*(7), 223.

Björnsson, B., Borrebaeck, C., Elander, N., Gasslander, T., Gawel, D. R., Gustafsson, M., Jörnsten, R., Lee, E. J., Li, X., Lilja, S., Martínez-Enguita, D., Matussek, A., Sandström, P., Schäfer, S., Stenmarker, M., Sun, X. F., Sysoev, O., Zhang, H., & Benson, M. (2020). Digital twins to personalize medicine. *Genome Medicine, 12*(1). Available from https://doi.org/10.1186/s13073-019-0701-3, https://genomemedicine.biomedcentral.com.

Ciano, M. P., Pozzi, R., Rossi, T., & Strozzi, F. (2021). Digital twin-enabled smart industrial systems: A bibliometric review. *International Journal of Computer Integrated Manufacturing, 34*(7-8). Available from https://doi.org/10.1080/0951192X.2020.1852600, http://www.tandfonline.com/loi/tcim20.

Conte Alcaraz, J., Moghaddamnia, S., & Peissig, J. (2021). Efficiency of deep neural networks for joint angle modeling in digital gait assessment. *EURASIP Journal on Advances in Signal Processing, 2021*(1), 10.

Dias De Oliveira, C., Khanshan, A., & Van Gorp, P. (2023). Exploring the feasibility of data-driven emotion modeling for human digital twins. In *Proceedings of the 16th International Conference on PErvasive Technologies Related to Assistive Environments* (pp. 568-573).

Fahim, M., Sharma, V., Hunter, R., & Duong, T. Q. (2023). Healthy aging: A deep meta-class sequence model to integrate intelligence in digital twin. *IEEE Journal of Translational Engineering in Health and Medicine, 11*, 330−340.

Gazerani, P. (2023). Intelligent digital twins for personalized migraine care. *Journal of Personalized Medicine, 13*(8), 1255.

Geoffrey Chase, J., Zhou, C., Knopp, J. L., Moeller, K., Benyo, B., Desaive, T., . . . Chiew, Y. S. (2023). Digital twins and automation of care in the intensive care unit. *Cyber−Physical−Human Systems: Fundamentals and Applications*, 457−489.

Gupta, D., Kayode, O., Bhatt, S., Gupta, M., & Tosun, A. S. (2022). Hierarchical federated learning based anomaly detection using digital twins for smart healthcare. In *2021 IEEE 7th international conference on collaboration and internet computing (CIC)* (pp. 16-25). IEEE.

Haleem, A., Javaid, M., Singh, R. P., & Suman, R. (2023). Exploring the revolution in healthcare systems through the applications of digital twin technology. *Biomedical Technology, 4*, 28−38.

Khan, S., Alzaabi, A., Iqbal, Z., Ratnarajah, T., & Arslan, T. (2023). A Novel Digital Twin (DT) model based on WiFi CSI, Signal Processing and Machine Learning for patient respiration monitoring and decision-support. *IEEE Access*.

Khan, S., Arslan, T., & Ratnarajah, T. (2022). Digital twin perspective of fourth industrial and healthcare revolution. *Ieee Access, 10*, 25732−25754.

Liu, Y., Zhang, L., Yang, Y., Zhou, L., Ren, L., Wang, F., Liu, R., Pang, Z., & Deen, M. J. (2019). A novel cloud-based framework for the elderly healthcare services using digital twin. *IEEE Access, 7*. Available from https://doi.org/10.1109/ACCESS.2019.2909828, http://ieeexplore.ieee.org/xpl/RecentIssue.jsp?punumber = 6287639.

Meraghni, S., Benaggoune, K., Al Masry, Z., Terrissa, L. S., Devalland, C., & Zerhouni, N. (2021). Towards digital twins driven breast cancer detection. In *Intelligent Computing: Proceedings of the 2021 Computing Conference*, Volume 3 (pp. 87-99). Springer International Publishing.

Mihai, S., Yaqoob, M., Hung, D. V., Davis, W., Towakel, P., Raza, M., Karamanoglu, M., Barn, B., Shetve, D., Prasad, R. V., Venkataraman, H., Trestian, R., & Nguyen, H. X. (2022). Digital twins: A survey on enabling technologies, challenges, trends and future prospects. *IEEE Communications Surveys and Tutorials, 24*(4). Available from https://doi.org/10.1109/COMST.2022.3208773, http://ieeexplore.ieee.org/xpl/RecentIssue.jsp?punumber = 9739.

Moztarzadeh, O., Jamshidi, M., Sargolzaei, S., Keikhaee, F., Jamshidi, A., Shadroo, S., & Hauer, L. (2023). Metaverse and medical diagnosis: A blockchain-based digital twinning approach based on MobileNetV2 algorithm for cervical vertebral maturation. *Diagnostics*, *13*(8), 1485.

Qu, Q., Sun, H., and Chen, Y. (2023a). Light-weight real-time senior safety monitoring using digital twins." In *Proceedings of the 8th ACM/IEEE Conference on Internet of Things Design and Implementation.*

Qu, Z., Li, Y., Liu, B., Gupta, D., & Tiwari, P. (2023b). Dtqfl: A digital twin-assisted quantum federated learning algorithm for intelligent diagnosis in 5G mobile network. *IEEE journal of biomedical and health informatics.*

Singh, M., Fuenmayor, E., Hinchy, E. P., Qiao, Y., Murray, N., & Devine, D. (2021). Digital twin: Origin to future. *Applied System Innovation*, *4*(2). Available from https://doi.org/10.3390/asi4020036, https://www.mdpi.com/2571-5577/4/2/36/pdf.

Vats, T., Singh, S. K., Kumar, S., Gupta, B. B., Gill, S. S., Arya, V., & Alhalabi, W. (2023). Explainable context-aware IoT framework using human digital twin for healthcare. *Multimedia Tools and Applications*, 1−25.

Winter, P. D., & Chico, T. J. (2023). Using the non-adoption, abandonment, scale-up, spread, and sustainability (NASSS) framework to identify barriers and facilitators for the implementation of digital twins in cardiovascular medicine. *Sensors*, *23*(14), 6333.

Wickramasinghe, N., Jayaraman, P. P., Forkan, A. R. M., Ulapane, N., Kaul, R., Vaughan, S., & Zelcer, J. (2021). A vision for leveraging the concept of digital twins to support the provision of personalized cancer care. *IEEE Internet Computing*, *26*(5), 17−24.

Wickramasinghe, N., Ulapane, N., Andargoli, A., Ossai, C., Shuakat, N., Nguyen, T., & Zelcer, J. (2022a). Digital twins to enable better precision and personalized dementia care. *JAMIA open*, *5*(3), ooac072.

Wickramasinghe, N., Ulapane, N., Andargoli, A., Shuakat, N., Nguyen, T., Zelcer, J., & Vaughan, S. (2023). Digital twin of patient in clinical workflow. *Proceedings of the Royal Society of Victoria*, *135*(2). Available from https://doi.org/10.1071/RS23013, https://www.publish.csiro.au/RS/pdf/RS23013.

Wickramasinghe, N., Ulapane, N., Nguyen, T. A., Andargoli, A., Ossai, C., Shuakat, N., & Zelcer, J. (2022b). Towards discovering digital twins of dementia patients: Matching the phases of cognitive decline. *Alzheimer's & Dementia*, *18*, e066336.

Xie, S., Zhu, S., & Dai, J. (2021). Feasibility study of intelligent healthcare based on digital twin and data mining. In *2021 International Conference on Computer Information Science and Artificial Intelligence (CISAI)* (pp. 906-911). IEEE.

Cloud security for smart sensor network

Satyavathi Divadari

People's Education Society University, Bangalore, Karnataka, India

22.1 Introduction

This session explores the evolution of smart sensor technology from standalone devices to interconnected networks, driving innovations across industries such as healthcare, environmental monitoring, and industrial automation. It will have the learnings about the pivotal milestones, technological advancements, and future prospects shaping the landscape of smart sensor networks in the 21st century.

22.1.1 Evolution of smart sensor networks

Originally heralded by Business Week ("21 Ideas for the 21st Century," 1999) as one of the 21 most important technologies for the 21st century, smart sensor technology was characterized by the deployment of inexpensive, intelligent devices equipped with multiple sensors. These devices are interconnected through wireless links and the Internet, creating vast opportunities for instrumenting and controlling homes, cities, and the environment.

The origins of smart sensor networks can be traced back to the early developments in sensor technology. Initially, sensors were standalone devices with limited capabilities, designed for specific applications such as temperature or pressure monitoring. The first milestone in the evolution occurred as researchers and engineers began exploring ways to interconnect these sensors, forming the foundation for collaborative data collection.

Networked microsensors offer unprecedented capabilities for a wide range of applications. In the defense arena, they contribute to new capabilities in reconnaissance, surveillance, and tactical applications. The applications of sensor networks span military sensing, physical security, air traffic control, traffic surveillance, video surveillance, industrial automation, distributed robotics, environmental monitoring, and building and structures monitoring.

Sensor Networks for Smart Hospitals
DOI: https://doi.org/10.1016/B978-0-443-36370-2.00023-2

Smart sensor networks have undergone a remarkable evolution, driven by technological advancements and the growing demand for real-time data collection and analysis across various domains.

Table 22.1 provides a brief summary of the evolution of sensor technologies.

22.2 Smart sensor networks and their applications

22.2.1 Overview of smart sensors and their applications in various industries

Smart sensor networks represent a sophisticated ecosystem of interconnected sensor nodes designed to collaboratively collect, process, and transmit data in real-time. This section provides a comprehensive overview of the diverse applications of smart sensor networks.

Driven by a relentless pursuit of innovation and the quest for more connected, intelligent, and efficient systems, Internet of Things (IoT)/smart sensor networks are getting implemented in diverse domains. The versatility is showcased through their applications across a spectrum of industries. Environmental applications leverage sensor networks for real-time data collection, contributing to climate studies and disaster management. In healthcare, for instance, smart sensor networks enable continuous patient monitoring and facilitate early disease detection. Additionally, in industrial settings, these networks optimize processes through predictive maintenance and data-driven decision-making.

Table 22.2 provides a brief summary of the key applications of smart sensor network in Industry 4.0 (Attaran, 2023; Buratti et al., 2009; Chong & Kumar, 2003; Dodda, 2016; Khan & Abbasi, 2016; Sun & Li, 2021).

22.2.2 Smart sensor applications in smart healthcare

The IoT has the potential to transform healthcare by enabling smart healthcare solutions that enhance patient care, improve efficiency, and reduce costs.

Table 22.3 Summarizes several IoT use cases for smart healthcare in the context of IoT ("The Application of Internet of Things in Healthcare: A Systematic Literature Review and Classification," 2019; Kashani et al., 2021; Tunc et al., 2021).

22.3 Security challenges in cloud-integrated smart sensor networks

22.3.1 Smart sensor integration with cloud computing

The integration of smart sensor networks with cloud computing introduces a dynamic dimension to data management and analysis. Cloud platforms offer scalable infrastructure, allowing seamless integration of sensor data and providing a centralized hub for processing and storage. This section will delve into the motivations and benefits of integrating smart sensor networks with cloud computing, emphasizing the potential for improved accessibility,

TABLE 22.1 Evolution of technology capabilities.

Time period	Technology capabilities
Early developments (early 2000s):	
Standalone devices	Sensors were standalone devices with limited capabilities, designed for specific applications such as temperature or pressure monitoring. Researchers and engineers began exploring ways to interconnect these sensors, forming the foundation for collaborative data collection.
Integration with wireless technologies (mid-2000s):	
Wireless connectivity	The shift from wired to wireless connectivity marked a transformative moment, enabling the deployment of sensor nodes in distributed and remote environments. This advancement facilitate the creation of dynamic and flexible networks capable of adapting to diverse scenarios.
Advancements in energy efficiency (late 2000s—early 2010s):	
Low power and energy-efficient sensors	Technological developments, including low-power processors, energy-efficient communication protocols, and advancements in battery technologies, extended the operational lifetime of sensor nodes. This breakthrough was essential for the widespread adoption of sensor networks in applications where continuous, long-term monitoring is crucial.
Emergence of IoT paradigm (mid-2010s):	
Internet connection	This integration brought about a new era where sensors became interconnected nodes within a vast network, capable of seamlessly communicating with each other and with cloud platforms. The IoT paradigm facilitated the generation of massive datasets and laid the groundwork for real-time monitoring and control across industries.
Cloud integration (late 2010s):	
Cloud computing and edge computing	The integration of smart sensor networks with cloud computing and edge computing technologies represents a recent and influential development. Cloud integration enables scalable storage, processing power, and data accessibility, while edge computing brings computation closer to the data source, reducing latency and enhancing real-time decision-making capabilities. These integrations have further expanded the potential applications and scalability of smart sensor networks.
Artificial intelligence (AI) and machine learning (ML) integration (late 2010s):	
AL/ML infusion into smart sensors	The infusion of artificial intelligence (AI) and machine learning (ML) into smart sensor networks has ushered in a new era of intelligent and adaptive systems. ML algorithms enable smart sensors to learn and adapt based on data patterns, enhancing their ability to detect anomalies, predict events, and optimize performance. This development has significantly improved the efficiency and autonomy of smart sensor networks.
Current landscape and future prospects (2020s):	
Smart compute for Industry 4.0	In the contemporary landscape, smart sensor networks are integral to a wide array of applications, including healthcare, environmental monitoring, industrial automation, and smart cities. As we look to the future, ongoing research and development will likely focus on addressing security challenges, improving energy efficiency, and exploring novel sensor technologies. With the sensor miniaturization and energy harvesting, sensor network deployment is rapidly accelerating with the availability of 5G networks and steady growth of Industry 4.0.

TABLE 22.2 Smart sensor networks using Internet of Things (IoT) in Industry 4.0.

Industry application	Functionalities
Aerospace and aviation	IoT assists in enhancing safety and security in the aerospace and aviation industry. Addresses the threat of suspected unapproved parts (SUPs) using RFID tags. Sensors on aircraft provide data for maintenance, planning, troubleshooting, and energy reduction.
Smart cities, homes, and buildings	IoT optimizes traffic control systems, power grids, and vehicle parking in smart cities. Smart homes and buildings leverage IoT for resource optimization, energy efficiency, and carbon reduction.
Automotive industry	RFID technology in the automotive industry improves logistics, production, and quality control. IoT technologies support real-time locating systems (RTLSs) for vehicle tracking and testing.
Environmental monitoring	IoT aids in environmental conservation, including applications like forest fire detection and pollution monitoring. Wireless sensor networks with IoT technologies are used for monitoring environmental parameters.
Logistics applications	IoT supports goods monitoring, improper storage detection, and tracking of goods in logistics. Large-scale operations and standard tagging solutions are among the challenges in this domain.
Food traceability	IoT enables efficient supply chain management through product recall solutions. Smart animal farming enhances productivity and quality of animal products through continuous monitoring.
Media coverage	IoT infrastructure captures multimedia footage for media coverage. Wireless multimedia sensor networks, in conjunction with IoT, contribute to these applications.
Smart water monitoring	IoT applications include monitoring water quality and distribution statistics using pressure and flow sensors. Challenges involve continuous monitoring, processing, and communication of sensed data in real-time.
Vehicle insurance	Insurance premiums can be reduced with IoT technologies that monitor vehicle parameters. Classical wireless sensor networks (WSNs) with IoT technologies can be used for vehicle monitoring.
Material recycling	IoT and WSNs support optimal recycling processes, including the collection and processing of recyclable material. RFID technology aids in identifying electronic products for efficient recycling.
Home automation	IoT technologies are applied in domestic and commercial buildings for safety, sustainability, and appliance control. Classical WSNs are utilized with IoT technologies to achieve these objectives.
Agricultural applications	Smart agriculture focuses on soil and environmental monitoring to maximize yield and ensure product quality. Challenges include operations in harsh environments and lack of proper infrastructure.

collaboration, and resource optimization. Additionally, it will introduce the primary focus of the chapter – addressing the security challenges inherent in this integration to ensure the integrity and confidentiality of the data transmitted and stored in the cloud.

Sensor Networks for Smart Hospitals

TABLE 22.3 Internet of Things applications in smart healthcare.

Smart healthcare feature	Usage description of the Internet of Things
Remote patient monitoring:	
Wearable devices	IoT-enabled wearables can continuously monitor vital signs such as heart rate, blood pressure, and activity levels. This data can be transmitted to healthcare providers in real-time, allowing for proactive intervention and remote patient management.
Implantable devices	Implantable IoT devices, like pacemakers or glucose monitors, can send data to healthcare providers, enabling them to monitor patients with chronic conditions without the need for frequent in-person visits.
Smart medication management:	
IoT-enabled pill dispensers	These devices can remind patients to take their medications, dispense the correct dosage at scheduled times, and alert healthcare providers if doses are missed.
Smart inhalers	Inhalers equipped with IoT technology can track medication usage, provide usage reminders, and transmit data to healthcare providers for analysis.
Telehealth and virtual consultations:	
IoT in telemedicine equipment	Connected medical devices, such as digital stethoscopes, otoscopes, and cameras, enable healthcare professionals to conduct remote examinations and consultations.
Home monitoring systems	IoT devices at home can facilitate virtual monitoring of patients recovering from surgeries or managing chronic illnesses, reducing the need for hospital readmissions
Health and wellness tracking:	
IoT fitness trackers	Beyond medical applications, fitness trackers and smartwatches can collect data on physical activity, sleep patterns, and stress levels, providing a holistic view of a person's health.
Smart scales and blood pressure monitors:	These devices can transmit data to healthcare providers, enabling them to monitor and intervene in case of abnormalities.
Hospital asset tracking:	
IoT tags and sensors	Hospitals can use IoT to track the location of medical equipment, optimize asset utilization, and reduce the time spent searching for critical devices.
Environmental monitoring in healthcare facilities:	
IoT sensors for air quality:	Monitoring air quality, temperature, and humidity in healthcare facilities can help prevent the spread of infections and create a healthier environment for patients and staff.
Emergency response systems	
IoT-enabled panic buttons	Hospital staff and patients can use connected devices to quickly alert emergency responders in case of emergencies or security threats.
Supply chain management	
IoT for medication and equipment tracking:	IoT can be used to monitor the supply chain, ensuring that medications and medical equipment are stored under proper conditions and are readily available when needed.

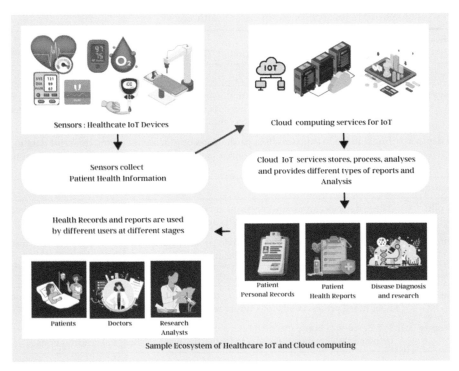

FIGURE 22.1   Sample ecosystem of healthcare smart sensors (Internet of Things) and cloud computing.

The ecosystem contains healthcare sensors, cloud IoT services, different stakeholders, and personal healthcare information. We will discuss each of those elements in the next sections.

Fig. 22.1 indicates a sample ecosystem of healthcare smart sensors (IoT) and cloud computing (Al-Joboury & Hemiary, 2018).

22.3.1.1 Healthcare sensors (Internet of Things/operational technology)

Healthcare sensors and devices play critical roles in modern healthcare, enabling clinicians to diagnose medical conditions, monitor patient health status, and deliver timely and effective medical interventions.

Some of the key healthcare sensors are as follows:

Magnetic resonance imaging (MRI) machines: Used for noninvasive imaging of the body's internal structures, MRI machines utilize strong magnetic fields and radio waves to generate detailed images. They are commonly employed in diagnosing various medical conditions such as tumors, injuries, and neurological disorders.

Intravenous (IV) pumps: These devices are used to administer fluids, medications, or nutrients directly into a patient's bloodstream via IV infusion. IV pumps ensure accurate dosing and controlled delivery rates, critical for patients requiring precise fluid or medication management.

Heart monitors: Heart monitors, including electrocardiogram monitors, continuously monitor a patient's heart activity, detecting abnormalities in heart rate, rhythm, and electrical conduction. They are essential in diagnosing and monitoring cardiovascular conditions such as arrhythmias, heart attacks, and heart failure.

Glucometers: Glucometers are portable devices used to measure blood glucose levels, commonly utilized by individuals with diabetes to monitor and manage their blood sugar levels. They provide quick and convenient blood glucose measurements, enabling timely adjustments to insulin doses or dietary interventions.

Ultrasound machines: Ultrasound machines use high-frequency sound waves to produce real-time images of internal body structures, such as organs, tissues, and blood vessels. They are widely used for diagnostic purposes, including prenatal imaging, assessing abdominal pain, and guiding minimally invasive procedures.

Patient monitors: Patient monitors are multiparameter monitoring devices that track vital signs such as heart rate, blood pressure, oxygen saturation, and respiratory rate. They provide continuous monitoring of a patient's physiological parameters in various healthcare settings, including intensive care units, operating rooms, and general wards.

Medicine dispensers: These devices automate the dispensing of medications, ensuring accurate dosing and timely administration of medications to patients. Medicine dispensers can range from simple pill organizers to sophisticated automated medication dispensing systems used in hospitals and long-term care facilities.

Picture archiving and communication system (PAC) servers: PACS servers store, retrieve, and distribute medical images such as X-rays, CT scans, and MRIs digitally. They facilitate efficient image management, interpretation, and sharing among healthcare providers, improving diagnostic accuracy and patient care.

Radiography systems: Radiography systems, including X-ray machines and computed radiography systems, produce images of the body's internal structures using ionizing radiation. They are commonly used for diagnosing fractures, detecting abnormalities in the chest or abdomen, and monitoring disease progression.

Digital imaging and communications in medicine (DICOM) workstations: DICOM () workstations are specialized computers equipped with software for viewing, interpreting, and analyzing medical images in DICOM format. They are used by radiologists, clinicians, and other healthcare professionals to visualize and interpret diagnostic imaging studies, facilitating accurate diagnosis and treatment planning.

These sensors and devices play critical roles in modern healthcare, enabling clinicians to diagnose medical conditions, monitor patient health status, and deliver timely and effective medical interventions.

22.3.1.2 *Cloud Internet of Things services*

Cloud IoT services that store, process, analyze, and provide different types of reports and analysis" refer to cloud-based platforms specifically designed to manage data collected from IoT devices. Here's a more detailed explanation:

1. **Storage:** These services offer scalable and reliable storage solutions for the vast amounts of data generated by IoT devices. Cloud storage allows for flexible scaling to accommodate growing data volumes without the need for extensive infrastructure management. Data can

be stored in various formats and structures, including databases, data lakes, or object storage, depending on the specific requirements of the application.

2. **Processing:** Cloud IoT services provide capabilities for processing incoming data in real-time or batch processing modes. Real-time processing enables immediate analysis and response to incoming data streams, while batch processing allows for more comprehensive analysis over historical data sets. Processing tasks may include data normalization, aggregation, filtering, and enrichment to prepare the data for analysis.

3. **Analysis:** Once the data is processed, cloud IoT services offer a range of analytical tools and techniques to derive insights and actionable intelligence. This can include descriptive analytics to summarize the data, predictive analytics to forecast future trends or outcomes, and prescriptive analytics to recommend actions based on the analysis. Advanced analytics techniques such as machine learning (ML) and artificial intelligence (AI) may also be employed to uncover patterns, correlations, and anomalies in the data.

4. **Reports and analysis:** Cloud IoT services enable the generation of various types of reports and analyses based on processed data. These reports can range from simple visualizations and dashboards that provide real-time insights into key performance indicators, to more sophisticated analytics reports that delve deeper into specific trends, patterns, or anomalies detected in the data. Reports can be customized to meet the needs of different stakeholders, such as executives, analysts, or field engineers, and can be accessed via web interfaces, mobile applications, or integrated into existing business intelligence tools.

Overall, cloud IoT services play a crucial role in enabling organizations to harness the full potential of IoT data by providing scalable, flexible, and powerful platforms for storing, processing, analyzing, and reporting on IoT data streams. By leveraging these services, organizations can gain valuable insights into their operations, optimize processes, and drive informed decision-making.

22.3.1.3 *Sensitive information*

Sensitive information in healthcare encompasses a wide range of data that is considered confidential and requires protection to ensure patient privacy, confidentiality, and security. Here's a discussion on some key categories of sensitive information in healthcare:

Patient health reports:

- Patient health reports include medical records, clinical notes, test results, imaging studies, and treatment histories documenting a patient's health status and care received.
- This information is highly sensitive as it contains details about a patient's medical conditions, diagnoses, treatments, medications, and responses to therapy.
- Access to patient health reports must be restricted to authorized healthcare professionals involved in the patient's care, and strict confidentiality measures should be in place to prevent unauthorized access or disclosure.

Disease diagnosis and research:

- Disease diagnosis and research data encompass information related to the diagnosis, treatment, and management of diseases and medical conditions.

- This data may include laboratory test results, genetic information, pathology reports, and research findings related to disease etiology, progression, and treatment outcomes.
- Protecting the confidentiality of disease diagnosis and research data is crucial to safeguard patient privacy, prevent discrimination, and maintain the integrity of research studies.

Patient personal records:

- Patient personal records include demographic information, contact details, insurance information, and other identifying data associated with an individual's healthcare records.
- This information is sensitive as it can be used to identify and track individual patients, posing risks to privacy and security if accessed or disclosed without authorization.
- Healthcare organizations must implement robust security measures to protect patient personal records from unauthorized access, identity theft, and fraud.

Other sensitive information:

- Other categories of sensitive information in healthcare may include mental health records, substance abuse treatment records, HIV/AIDS status, reproductive health information, and sensitive family medical histories.
- Protecting the confidentiality of this information is essential to respect patient autonomy, preserve patient-provider trust, and comply with legal and ethical obligations to safeguard patient privacy.
- Healthcare professionals and organizations must adhere to privacy regulations such as the Health Insurance Portability and Accountability Act (HIPAA) in the United States or the General Data Protection Regulation (GDPR) in the European Union to ensure the proper handling and protection of sensitive healthcare information.

In summary, sensitive information in healthcare encompasses various types of data related to patient health, diagnosis, treatment, and personal information. Safeguarding this information is critical to maintaining patient privacy, confidentiality, and trust in the healthcare system. Healthcare organizations must implement robust security measures, privacy policies, and compliance frameworks to protect sensitive healthcare information from unauthorized access, use, or disclosure.

22.3.1.4 Stakeholders

Different stakeholders utilize healthcare information for various purposes, each with its own set of needs, responsibilities, and ethical considerations. Here's a discussion on how patients, doctors, and research analysts utilize healthcare information:

Patients:

- Patients are primary stakeholders in healthcare and have a vested interest in their own health information.
- They use healthcare information to understand their medical conditions, treatment options, and prognosis.
- Patients rely on healthcare information to make informed decisions about their health, including treatment preferences, lifestyle modifications, and preventive measures.

- Access to their own healthcare information empowers patients to actively participate in their care, communicate effectively with healthcare providers, and advocate for their health needs.
- Patients may also share their healthcare information with family members, caregivers, or other healthcare professionals involved in their care to ensure coordinated and comprehensive treatment.

Doctors:

- Healthcare providers, including doctors, nurses, and allied health professionals, rely on healthcare information to deliver quality care to their patients.
- Doctors use patient health records, medical histories, diagnostic test results, and treatment plans to assess patients' health status, make accurate diagnoses, and develop personalized care plans.
- Access to comprehensive and up-to-date healthcare information enables doctors to monitor patients' progress, adjust treatment regimens, and coordinate care across multiple healthcare settings.
- Doctors also use healthcare information for communication and collaboration with other members of the healthcare team, including specialists, consultants, and support staff.
- Electronic health record (EHR) systems and health information exchange (HIE) platforms facilitate efficient access to patient information, streamline clinical workflows, and enhance care coordination and continuity.

Research analysts:

- Research analysts, including scientists, epidemiologists, and public health researchers, utilize healthcare information to advance medical knowledge, improve patient outcomes, and inform healthcare policies and practices.
- They analyze large datasets of healthcare information, such as EHRs, clinical trial data, population health data, and disease registries, to identify trends, patterns, and associations related to diseases, treatments, and healthcare delivery.
- Research analysts use healthcare information to conduct epidemiological studies, clinical trials, outcomes research, health services research, and translational research to generate evidence-based insights and recommendations.
- Access to diverse and comprehensive healthcare information is essential for research analysts to address pressing public health challenges, develop innovative interventions, and evaluate the effectiveness and safety of healthcare interventions.
- Research analysts must adhere to ethical and regulatory standards for the responsible conduct of research, including patient privacy, data security, informed consent, and research integrity.

In summary, patients, doctors, and research analysts are key stakeholders in healthcare who utilize healthcare information for various purposes, including clinical care, patient empowerment, and medical research. Collaborative efforts among these stakeholders are essential to promote patient-centered care, advance medical knowledge, and improve healthcare outcomes for individuals and populations.

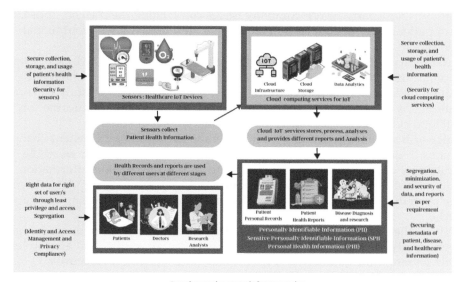

Sample security controls for processing
Healthcare IoT using Cloud computing

FIGURE 22.2 Security controls for processing healthcare Internet of Things using cloud computing.

Fig. 22.2 indicates the security controls needed to protect healthcare information and patient's privacy rights.

22.3.1.5 Challenges in protecting sensitive information

Here are some brief lists of the challenges in protecting patient information (Abouelmehdi et al., 2018; Gupta & Dutta, 2021; Jabeen et al., 2021; Jahan et al., 2018)

- **Ransomware attacks:** This refers to the malicious software that encrypts the data or systems of the victims and demands a ransom for their decryption. Ransomware attacks can target healthcare organizations and compromise their patient information, as well as disrupt their operations and services.
- **Improper data handling:** This refers to the careless or negligent handling of patient information, such as storing, transmitting, or disposing of it without proper security measures or protocols. Improper data handling can expose patient information to unauthorized access, theft, or loss.
- **Uncertainties in health research data:** This refers to the ethical and legal dilemmas that arise from the use of patient information for health research purposes, such as clinical trials, epidemiological studies, or genomic analysis. Uncertainties in health research data can stem from the lack of clear consent, transparency, or accountability from the data subjects, providers, or users.
- **Third-party health company issues:** This refers to the potential risks and liabilities that arise from the involvement of third-party health companies, such as insurers, pharmaceuticals, or vendors, in the collection, processing, or sharing of patient

information. Third-party health company issues can include the misuse, abuse, or breach of patient information, as well as the violation of privacy or contractual obligations.

- **Poor internet hygiene and data security practices:** This refers to the lack of awareness, education, or training on the best practices and standards for securing patient information online, such as using strong passwords, encryption, or antivirus software. Poor internet hygiene and data security practices can make patient information vulnerable to cyberattacks, phishing, or malware.
- **Dynamics of healthcare technology:** This refers to the rapid and constant changes and innovations in healthcare technology, such as EHRs, telemedicine, or wearable devices, that create new opportunities and challenges for protecting patient information. The dynamics of healthcare technology can require the adaptation and update of security policies, procedures, and systems, as well as compliance with emerging regulations and standards.
- **Ineffective cybersecurity implementation:** This refers to the failure or inadequacy of the cybersecurity measures, such as firewalls, backups, or audits, that are implemented to protect patient information from cyber threats. Ineffective cybersecurity implementation can result from the lack of resources, expertise, or coordination among healthcare organizations and their stakeholders.
- **HIPAA compliance:** This refers to the adherence to the requirements and standards of the HIPAA of 1996, which is a US federal law that protects the privacy and security of health information. HIPAA compliance can involve the implementation of administrative, technical, and physical safeguards, as well as the provision of notices, training, and audits.
- **Hospital security:** This refers to the protection of the physical and digital assets, such as equipment, devices, or networks, that are used to store, process, or transmit patient information within the hospital premises. Hospital security can involve the installation of locks, cameras, or alarms, as well as the enforcement of access control, authentication, or authorization.
- **Noncompliance with regulatory standards:** This refers to the violation or disregard of the regulatory standards or frameworks that govern the protection of patient information, such as the GDPR in the European Union, or the ISO/IEC 27001 in the international context. Noncompliance with regulatory standards can result in legal sanctions, fines, or penalties, as well as reputational damage or loss of trust.

Fig. 22.3 indicates major challenges in protecting the patient information.

22.3.1.6 Challenges in protecting healthcare smart sensors (Internet of Things/OT devices)

- **Data protection:** Smart sensors collect, process, and transmit sensitive health data, which need to be secured from unauthorized access, modification, or leakage. Data encryption, authentication, and access control are some of the techniques to ensure data protection.
- **Supporting interfaces:** Smart sensors interact with various interfaces, such as mobile devices, cloud platforms, and medical systems. These interfaces need to be compatible

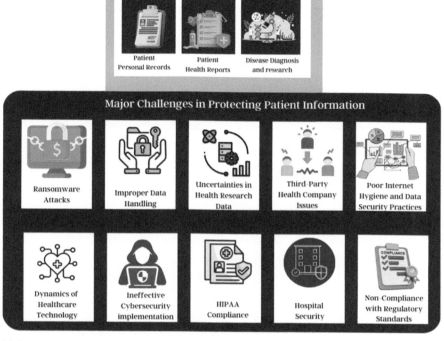

FIGURE 22.3 Major challenges in protecting patient information.

and secure, as they can be potential entry points for cyberattacks. Security standards, protocols, and audits are some of the methods to ensure supporting interface security.

- **IT networking:** Smart sensors rely on wireless networks to communicate and exchange data. These networks need to be reliable, scalable, and resilient, as they can be vulnerable to interference, congestion, or jamming. Network segmentation, monitoring, and optimization are some of the strategies to ensure IT networking security.
- **Forgotten IoT devices:** Smart sensors can be easily misplaced, lost, or stolen, as they are often portable and wearable. These devices need to be tracked, managed, and updated, as they can contain valuable data or access credentials. Device inventory, remote control, and wipeout are some of the solutions to ensure forgotten IoT devices security.
- **Password protection:** Smart sensors often use default or weak passwords, which can be easily guessed or cracked by hackers. These devices need to use strong and unique passwords, which can be changed regularly and stored securely. Password managers, multifactor authentication (MFA), and biometrics are some of the tools to ensure password protection.
- **Skills gaps:** Smart sensors require specialized skills and knowledge to design, deploy, and maintain them securely. Healthcare professionals and staff need to be trained and educated on the best practices and standards of smart sensor security. Cybersecurity awareness, certification, and training are some of the ways to ensure skills gaps security.

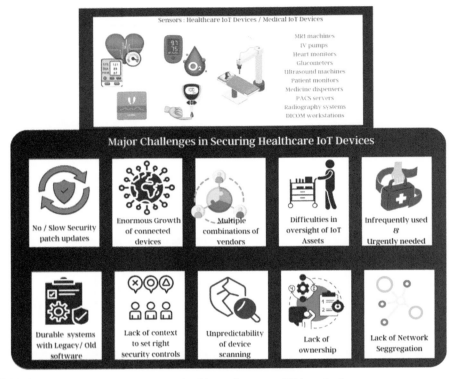

FIGURE 22.4   Major challenges in securing healthcare Internet of Things devices.

- **Regular updates:** Smart sensors need to be updated frequently to fix bugs, patch vulnerabilities, and improve performance. However, updates can be challenging due to device compatibility, availability, or cost issues. Update management, testing, and verification are some of the steps to ensure regular updates security.

Fig. 22.4 indicates major challenges in securing healthcare IoT devices (Formica & Schena, 2021; Masood et al., 2018).

22.3.1.7 Challenges in protecting and securing cloud computing infrastructure and associated services

- **Security misconfigurations:** This refers to the incorrect or incomplete settings of cloud resources, such as storage buckets, databases, servers, or applications, that expose them to unauthorized access or misuse. Security misconfigurations can result from human errors, lack of best practices, or insufficient automation and monitoring.
- **Weak control plane and exposure:** This refers to the vulnerability of the cloud management interface or console, which allows users to configure, monitor, and operate cloud resources. A weak control plane can be compromised by attackers who can

exploit weak passwords, phishing, or brute force attacks to gain access to the cloud environment and perform malicious actions. A weak control plane can also be exposed by misconfigurations, such as allowing public access or using default credentials.

- **Growth of data breaches:** This refers to the increasing frequency and severity of data breaches in the cloud, where sensitive or confidential data is accessed, copied, modified, or deleted by unauthorized parties. Data breaches can occur due to various reasons, such as cyberattacks, insider threats, human errors, or misconfigurations. Data breaches can have serious consequences for the affected organizations and individuals, such as financial losses, reputational damage, legal liabilities, or regulatory penalties.
- Insufficient identity, credential, access & key management: This refers to the inadequate or ineffective management of the identities, credentials, access rights, and encryption keys of the cloud users, administrators, and applications. Insufficient identity, credential, access, and key management can lead to unauthorized or excessive access to cloud resources, data leakage, or data tampering.
- **Lack of cloud security architecture and strategy:** This refers to the absence or deficiency of a coherent and comprehensive cloud security architecture and strategy that aligns with the business objectives, risk appetite, and compliance requirements of the organization. A lack of cloud security architecture and strategy can result in inconsistent, ineffective, or inefficient security controls, policies, and processes across the cloud environment.
- **Lack of visibility:** This refers to the difficulty or inability of the cloud users, administrators, or security teams to monitor, audit, or analyze the cloud activities, events, or data. A lack of visibility can result from the complexity, dynamism, or heterogeneity of the cloud environment, as well as the limitations or gaps of the cloud service providers' tools or services. A lack of visibility can hamper the detection, prevention, or response to cloud security incidents, as well as the compliance or governance of the cloud environment.
- **Account hijacking:** This refers to the unauthorized takeover of a cloud user's or administrator's account, which can be used to access, manipulate, or destroy cloud resources, data, or applications. Account hijacking can occur due to various methods, such as phishing, malware, credential theft, or social engineering. Account hijacking can have serious impacts on cloud security, availability, or performance, as well as the reputation or trust of the cloud user or provider.
- **Insecure interfaces and application programming interfaces (APIs):** This refers to the vulnerability of the cloud interfaces and APIs that enable the interaction, integration, or automation of cloud resources, data, or applications. Insecure interfaces and APIs can be exploited by attackers who can intercept, modify, or inject malicious data or commands, or bypass the security controls or policies. Insecure interfaces and APIs can result from poor design, development, or testing, as well as misconfigurations, or lack of encryption or authentication.
- **Abuse and nefarious use of cloud:** This refers to the malicious or illegal use of cloud resources, data, or applications by unauthorized or unethical parties. Abuse and nefarious use of the cloud can include various activities, such as launching cyberattacks, hosting malicious content, mining cryptocurrencies, or conducting fraud or espionage. Abuse and nefarious use of the cloud can affect the cloud's security, availability, or performance, as well as the reputation or trust of the cloud user or provider.

- **Metastructure and applistructure failures:** This refers to the failure or disruption of the cloud metastructure and applistructure, which are the layers of abstraction that enable the cloud services and applications. The metastructure consists of the cloud management interface, orchestration, and automation tools, while the applistructure consists of the cloud APIs, microservices, and containers. Metastructure and applistructure failures can result from various causes, such as cyberattacks, human errors, misconfigurations, or technical glitches. Metastructure and applistructure failures can affect the cloud security, availability, or performance, as well as the functionality or reliability of the cloud services and applications.
- **Cloud computing services for IoT:** This refers to the use of cloud computing services to enable, support, or enhance the IoT, which is the network of physical devices, sensors, or actuators that collect, process, or exchange data over the Internet. Cloud computing services for IoT can provide various benefits, such as scalability, flexibility, efficiency, or analytics. However, they can also introduce various challenges, such as data privacy, security, interoperability, or governance.

Fig. 22.5 indicates major challenges in securing cloud computing (Chaudhary, 2020; Cloud Security Alliance, 2020).

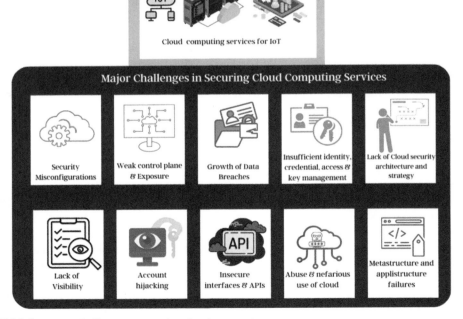

FIGURE 22.5   Major challenges in securing cloud computing.

22.4 Security controls needed for the ecosystem

22.4.1 Securing sensors

Securing healthcare sensor devices is crucial to safeguard patient privacy, prevent unauthorized access to sensitive health data, and mitigate the risk of cyber threats.

Here are several security controls and best practices to protect healthcare sensor devices: (Challenges and opportunities in IoT healthcare systems: a systematic review, 2020; IoT health devices: Exploring security risks in the connected landscape, 2023; Sharma et al., 2019)

- **Encryption:** Implement end-to-end encryption to secure data transmission between healthcare sensors and backend systems. Encrypting data ensures that it remains confidential and protected from interception or tampering by unauthorized parties.
- **Authentication and access control:** Utilize strong authentication mechanisms, such as biometric authentication, MFA, or digital certificates, to verify the identity of users accessing healthcare sensor devices and data. Implement access controls to limit access privileges based on user roles and responsibilities, ensuring that only authorized individuals can interact with the devices and access sensitive information.
- **Secure communication protocols:** Use secure communication protocols, such as transport layer security (TLS) or secure sockets layer, to establish secure connections between healthcare sensor devices and backend systems. These protocols encrypt data during transmission and authenticate the identity of the communicating parties, preventing eavesdropping and man-in-the-middle attacks.
- **Device authentication and authorization:** Implement device authentication mechanisms to verify the identity and integrity of healthcare sensor devices before allowing them to connect to the network or access sensitive data. Utilize device certificates, unique identifiers, or cryptographic keys to authenticate devices and enforce access controls based on device identity.
- **Network segmentation and isolation:** Segment healthcare sensor devices into separate network zones or virtual local area networks to isolate them from other network resources and minimize the impact of security breaches or compromises. Implement firewalls, intrusion detection/prevention systems (IDS/IPS), and network access controls to monitor and control traffic to and from healthcare sensor devices.
- **Secure firmware and software updates:** Regularly update the firmware and software of healthcare sensor devices to patch known vulnerabilities and address security weaknesses. Use secure update mechanisms, such as code signing and secure boot, to ensure the integrity and authenticity of firmware and software updates and prevent unauthorized modifications.
- **Physical security measures:** Implement physical security controls to protect healthcare sensor devices from theft, tampering, or unauthorized access. Secure devices in locked cabinets or enclosures, utilize tamper-evident seals or sensors and implement alarm systems or surveillance cameras to monitor physical access to sensitive areas.
- **Security monitoring and incident response:** Deploy security monitoring tools and systems to detect and respond to security incidents, anomalies, or suspicious activities involving

healthcare sensor devices. Monitor device logs, network traffic, and user activities for signs of unauthorized access, data breaches, or malicious behavior, and establish incident response procedures to mitigate risks and minimize the impact of security incidents.

By implementing these security controls and best practices, healthcare organizations can enhance the security posture of sensor devices, protect patient health data, and maintain compliance with regulatory requirements such as the HIPAA and the GDPR.

22.4.2 Security for cloud computing services

Securing cloud computing infrastructure and associated components is crucial to protecting data, ensuring system integrity, and mitigating potential cybersecurity threats.

Here are several security controls and best practices for securing cloud computing infrastructure: (Al-Joboury & Hemiary, 2018; Divadari et al., 2023; Guezguez et al., 2018)

Identity and access management (IAM):

- Implement robust IAM controls to manage user identities, roles, and permissions across cloud environments. Utilize techniques such as role-based access control (RBAC) to enforce least privilege principles and restrict access to sensitive resources based on user roles and responsibilities.
- Utilize strong authentication mechanisms, such as MFA and identity federation, to verify the identity of users and control access to cloud resources.

Network security:

- Implement network segmentation and isolation to separate different tiers of infrastructure and control traffic flow between them. Utilize virtual private clouds, subnets, and security groups to enforce network boundaries and restrict communication between resources.
- Utilize firewalls, IDS/IPS, and network monitoring tools to detect and respond to suspicious activities, anomalies, or potential security breaches within cloud environments.

Data encryption:

- Encrypt data at rest and in transit to protect sensitive information from unauthorized access or interception. Utilize encryption techniques such as TLS for secure communication between components and encryption algorithms such as advanced encryption standard (AES) for encrypting data stored in databases or object storage.
- Utilize key management services to manage encryption keys securely and ensure the integrity and confidentiality of encrypted data.

Security patching and updates:

- Regularly update and patch cloud infrastructure components, including operating systems, hypervisors, virtual machines, and container images, to address known vulnerabilities and security weaknesses. Utilize automated patch management tools and processes to ensure timely deployment of security updates and minimize exposure to emerging threats.

Logging and monitoring:

- Deploy security monitoring and logging solutions to capture, analyze, and correlate security events and activities within cloud environments. Monitor system logs, network traffic, and user activities for signs of unauthorized access, data breaches, or malicious behavior.
- Implement centralized logging and log management platforms to aggregate and retain logs from multiple sources, enabling proactive threat detection, incident response, and forensic analysis.

Configuration management:

- Establish and enforce configuration management policies and procedures to ensure consistency and compliance across cloud infrastructure components. Utilize configuration management tools to automate the provisioning, configuration, and management of resources, reducing the risk of misconfigurations and vulnerabilities.
- Implement configuration baselines, standards, and benchmarks based on industry best practices and security frameworks such as the Center for Internet Security benchmarks or the National Institute of Standards and Technology (NIST) guidelines.

Incident response and disaster recovery:

- Develop and document incident response plans and procedures to detect, respond to, and recover from security incidents and data breaches effectively. Establish communication channels, escalation paths, and coordination mechanisms to facilitate timely incident response and resolution.
- Implement backup and disaster recovery strategies to ensure the availability and integrity of critical data and infrastructure components. Utilize backup solutions, replication technologies, and failover mechanisms to minimize downtime and data loss in the event of system failures or disasters.

By implementing these security controls and best practices, organizations can enhance the security posture of cloud computing infrastructure, protect sensitive data, and mitigate the risks associated with cloud deployments. Additionally, organizations should stay informed about emerging threats and security trends and continuously reassess and update their security strategies to address evolving cybersecurity challenges.

22.4.3 Securing metadata of patient, disease, and healthcare information

Securing metadata associated with patient, disease, and healthcare information is essential to protect the confidentiality, integrity, and privacy of sensitive healthcare data. Metadata often contains valuable insights and identifiers that, if compromised, could lead to privacy breaches or unauthorized access.

Here are several security measures and best practices for securing metadata in healthcare (Abouelmehdi et al., 2018; Bibri et al., 2023; Divadari et al., 2023; Gupta & Dutta, 2021; Jabeen et al., 2021; Jahan et al., 2018; Masood et al., 2018):

Encryption:

- Encrypt metadata stored in databases, repositories, or transmitted over networks to prevent unauthorized access or interception. Utilize strong encryption algorithms and key management practices to ensure the confidentiality and integrity of metadata.

Access controls:

- Implement access controls to restrict access to metadata based on user roles, responsibilities, and least privilege principles. Utilize RBAC or attribute-based access control (ABAC) mechanisms to enforce granular access controls and limit access to metadata to authorized users only.

Data minimization:

- Minimize the collection, storage, and retention of metadata to reduce the risk of exposure and misuse. Only collect and retain metadata that is necessary for legitimate purposes, and implement data minimization policies and procedures to ensure that metadata is not retained longer than necessary.

Anonymization and pseudonymization:

- Anonymize or pseudonymize metadata to remove or obfuscate personally identifiable information (PII) and protected health information. Utilize anonymization techniques such as data masking, tokenization, or hashing to protect patient identities and enhance privacy while retaining the utility of metadata for analysis and research purposes.

Audit logging and monitoring:

- Implement audit logging and monitoring mechanisms to track access to metadata, detect unauthorized activities, and investigate security incidents or data breaches. Monitor metadata access logs, user activities, and system events for signs of suspicious behavior or unauthorized access attempts.

Data governance and compliance:

- Establish data governance policies, procedures, and standards to govern the collection, use, and sharing of metadata in compliance with regulatory requirements such as the HIPAA or the GDPR.
- Conduct regular risk assessments and compliance audits to assess the security posture of metadata management practices and ensure adherence to privacy and security regulations.

Secure data sharing and collaboration:

- Implement secure data sharing and collaboration mechanisms to facilitate the exchange of metadata with authorized stakeholders while maintaining data privacy and confidentiality. Utilize encryption, access controls, and secure communication protocols to protect metadata during transit and sharing.

Employee training and awareness:

- Provide training and awareness programs to educate employees about the importance of securing metadata, the risks associated with unauthorized access or disclosure, and best practices for protecting sensitive healthcare data. Ensure that employees understand their roles and responsibilities in safeguarding metadata and maintaining patient privacy.
- By implementing these security measures and best practices, healthcare organizations can enhance the security posture of metadata associated with patient, disease, and healthcare information, protect patient privacy, and comply with regulatory requirements. Additionally, organizations should regularly review and update their security policies and procedures to address emerging threats and ensure ongoing protection of sensitive healthcare data.

22.4.4 Identity and access management

Different users access health information at different stages. Examples, patients, doctors, and research analysts. Unauthorized access to smart sensor networks poses a significant threat, potentially leading to data manipulation, theft, or malicious disruption of network functionality. Vulnerabilities may allow unauthorized entities to gain access to sensitive data or compromise the integrity of the sensor network.

Here we discuss briefly the controls for managing access at a granular level in smart healthcare environments (Jahan et al., 2018; Tanwar et al., 2020):

RBAC: Utilize RBAC to assign permissions and privileges to users based on their roles, responsibilities, and organizational hierarchy. Define roles such as patient, doctor, nurse, administrator, and research analyst, and associate specific permissions with each role to limit access to relevant data and resources. For example, patients may have access to their own medical records, doctors may have access to patient records within their care, and research analysts may have access to anonymized aggregated data for research purposes.

ABAC: Implement ABAC to make access control decisions based on attributes such as user attributes (e.g., department, job title), resource attributes (e.g., sensitivity level, location), and environmental attributes (e.g., time of access, device used). ABAC enables fine-grained access control by dynamically evaluating multiple attributes to determine access rights. For example, access to specific patient records may be granted based on the patient's assigned doctor or department, or the researcher's area of expertise.

Least privilege principle: Adhere to the principle of least privilege, ensuring that users are granted only the minimum level of access permissions necessary to perform their job functions. Patients should have access only to their own medical records, doctors should have access to patient records within their specialty or care team, and research analysts should have access to aggregated datasets relevant to their research projects.

Data segregation and isolation: Segregate and isolate data based on sensitivity levels, user roles, or organizational units to prevent unauthorized access or leakage of sensitive information. For example, patient medical records may be stored in separate databases or partitions based on patient identifiers, and access may be restricted based on patient-provider relationships or treatment teams.

MFA: Require users, including patients, doctors, and research analysts, to authenticate using multiple factors (e.g., passwords, biometrics, smart cards) to access sensitive data or critical systems. MFA adds an additional layer of security beyond traditional username/password authentication, reducing the risk of unauthorized access due to compromised credentials.

Audit logging and monitoring: Implement audit logging and monitoring mechanisms to track user activities, access attempts, and changes to sensitive data or access controls. Monitor access logs in real-time and generate audit trails to detect and investigate suspicious behavior or security incidents across all user groups.

Data masking and redaction: Employ data masking and redaction techniques to anonymize or obfuscate sensitive information in user interfaces, reports, or logs. Masking or redacting sensitive data ensures that users only see the information they are authorized to access while protecting sensitive data from unauthorized disclosure.

Access reviews and recertification: Conduct regular access reviews and recertification processes to validate user permissions, roles, and access rights for all user groups. Review user access privileges periodically to ensure that they align with current job responsibilities, patient-provider relationships, and research projects. Remove or adjust access rights for users who no longer require them.

User training and awareness: Provide training and awareness programs to educate users about access control policies, procedures, and best practices. Ensure that users, including patients, doctors, and research analysts, understand their responsibilities for protecting sensitive data and adhering to access control policies to maintain the security and confidentiality of smart healthcare systems.

By integrating these controls with the specific needs and roles of patients, doctors, and research analysts, healthcare organizations can effectively manage access at a granular level in smart healthcare environments, ensuring that sensitive data is protected, and access is restricted to authorized individuals based on their roles and responsibilities. Additionally, organizations should regularly assess and update access control policies and procedures to address evolving threats and compliance requirements across all user groups.

22.4.5 Data privacy and regulations

Data privacy emerges as a paramount concern in the context of cloud-integrated smart sensor networks. It is important to safeguard sensitive information collected by sensors, considering factors such as data encryption, anonymization techniques, and secure data transmission. Exploitation might lead to implications of compromised data privacy and consequences for individuals' and organizations' compliance with privacy regulations and standards.

A Brief summary of the regulations (Challenges and opportunities in IoT healthcare systems: a systematic review, 2020; HITRUST and HIPAA Safe Harbor, 2021; IoT Health Devices: Exploring Security Risks in the Connected Landscape, 2023; Mirza et al., 2021; Tunc et al., 2021):

- **HITRUST framework on US healthcare laws:** This is a comprehensive and scalable framework that integrates various standards and regulations relevant to the healthcare industry, such as HIPAA, HITECH, GDPR, PCI-DSS, ISO 27001, and NIST. It provides a common set of security and privacy controls, assessment methods, and certification processes for healthcare organizations and their business associates.
- **HIPAA:** This is a US federal law that establishes requirements for the protection and privacy of health information, such as medical records, diagnoses, and treatments. It applies to covered entities, such as health plans, healthcare providers, and healthcare clearinghouses, and their business associates, such as vendors and contractors.
- **The Health Information Technology for Economic & Clinical Health (HITECH) Act:** This is a US federal law that promotes the adoption and meaningful use of health information technology, such as EHRs and health information exchanges. It also strengthens the enforcement of HIPAA rules and introduces new breach notification requirements for health information.
- **GDPR:** This is a European Union regulation that sets principles and rules for the protection of personal data of natural persons in the EU and the European Economic Area. It applies to data controllers and processors, such as organizations and individuals, that collect, process, or transfer personal data of EU residents, regardless of their location. It also grants data subjects, such as patients and consumers, certain rights over their personal data, such as the right to access, rectify, erase, and port their data.
- **The payment card industry data security standards (PCI-DSS):** This is a set of standards and best practices for ensuring the security of payment card data, such as credit card numbers, expiration dates, and security codes. It applies to merchants, service providers, and other entities that store, process, or transmit payment card data. It also requires regular audits and assessments to verify compliance.
- **Quality system regulation (QSR):** This is a US federal regulation that requires medical device manufacturers to establish and maintain a quality system that ensures the safety and effectiveness of their products. It covers various aspects of the design, development, production, distribution, installation, and servicing of medical devices. It also requires medical device manufacturers to comply with the FDA's cybersecurity guidance for premarket and postmarket management of medical device cybersecurity.
- **ISO/IEC 27001:** This is an international standard that specifies the requirements for establishing, implementing, maintaining, and improving an information security management system. It helps organizations manage the security of their information assets, such as financial data, intellectual property, employee information, and customer information. It also provides a framework for conducting risk assessments, implementing security controls, and conducting audits and reviews.
- **NIST framework for improving critical infrastructure cybersecurity:** This is a voluntary framework that provides a common language and approach for managing

cybersecurity risks for critical infrastructure sectors, such as healthcare, energy, and transportation. It consists of three components: the Framework Core, which identifies the key cybersecurity functions, categories, and subcategories; the framework implementation tiers, which describe the degree of rigor and sophistication of cybersecurity practices; and the Framework Profiles, which align the framework core elements with the business objectives and risk appetite of the organization.

22.5 Machine learning and artificial intelligence in security

The incorporation of ML and AI in the security framework of cloud-integrated smart sensor networks represents a paradigm shift, enabling proactive threat detection, sophisticated mitigation strategies, and enhanced overall resilience. (Ahmed et al., 2021; Ullah et al., 2020).

22.5.1 Role in threat detection

ML algorithms have demonstrated significant efficacy in identifying patterns indicative of potential security threats. This subsection explores the role of ML in threat detection within smart sensor networks. Topics include anomaly detection algorithms, behavior analysis, and the utilization of historical data to train models for recognizing irregularities. Case studies illustrating instances where ML has successfully detected and thwarted security threats will provide tangible examples of its application.

22.5.2 Advanced mitigation strategies

Beyond detection, ML and AI contribute to the development of advanced mitigation strategies that adapt in real-time to evolving threats. This section delves into the application of ML for dynamic threat response, automated incident response systems, and the integration of AI-driven decision-making processes. Additionally, it examines the use of reinforcement learning for creating adaptive security measures that learn and adjust based on ongoing network activities and emerging threat landscapes.

22.5.3 Enhancing resilience

Resilience in the face of cyber threats is a crucial aspect of a secure smart sensor network. This subsection explores how ML and AI technologies contribute to enhancing the overall resilience of these networks. Topics include predictive maintenance using AI, self-healing capabilities, and the ability to dynamically reconfigure security parameters in response to detected vulnerabilities. Real-world examples will showcase instances where ML and AI have played a pivotal role in bolstering the resilience of smart sensor networks against various cyber threats.

By examining the multifaceted role of ML and AI in threat detection, mitigation, and resilience enhancement, this section aims to underscore the transformative impact these technologies can have on the security posture of cloud-integrated smart sensor networks.

22.6 Conclusion

The conclusion of the chapter synthesizes the key findings and outlines future directions for research and development in the realm of cloud-integrated smart sensor network security.

22.7 Future directions for research and development

As the field of cloud-integrated smart sensor network security continues to evolve, this section outlines potential avenues for future research and development. It explores emerging technologies, methodologies, and areas where further innovation is needed to address evolving security challenges. Topics for future exploration may include advancements in encryption algorithms, novel authentication methods suitable for resource-constrained environments, and the integration of blockchain technology for enhanced data integrity and traceability. Additionally, research can be conducted in the context of regulatory frameworks, user education, and the development of standardized security practices for healthcare sensors and cloud computing.

AI disclosure

During the preparation of this work the author(s) used AutoPilot in order to get the language correction and fine-tuning for lexical purposes. After using this tool/service, the author(s) reviewed and edited the content as needed and take(s) full responsibility for the content of the publication.

References

21 ideas for the 21st century. (1999). *Business Week*, pp. 78–167.

Abouelmehdi, K., Beni-Hessane, A., & Khaloufi, H. (2018). Big healthcare data: Preserving security and privacy. *Journal of Big Data*, 5(1). Available from https://doi.org/10.1186/s40537-017-0110-7, https://journalofbigdata. springeropen.com.

Ahmed, S., Hossain, M. F., Kaiser, M. S., Noor, M. B. T., Mahmud, M., & Chakraborty, C. (2021). Artificial intelligence and machine learning for ensuring security in smart cities. *Advanced Sciences and Technologies for Security Applications*. Bangladesh: Springer. Available from https://link.springer.com/bookseries/5540, 10.1007/978-3-030-72139-8_2.

Al-Joboury, I. M., & Hemiary, E. H. (2018). Internet of Things architecture based cloud for healthcare. *Iraqi Journal of Information & Communications Technology*, 1(1). Available from https://doi.org/10.31987/ijict.1.1.7.

Attaran, M. (2023). The impact of 5G on the evolution of intelligent automation and industry digitization. *Journal of Ambient Intelligence and Humanized Computing*, 14(5). Available from https://doi.org/10.1007/s12652-020-02521-x.

Bibri, S. E., Alexandre, A., Sharifi, A., & Krogstie, J. (2023). Environmentally sustainable smart cities and their converging AI, IoT, and big data technologies and solutions: An integrated approach to an extensive literature review. *Energy Informatics*, 6(1). Available from https://doi.org/10.1186/s42162-023-00259-2, https://www. springer.com/journal/42162.

Buratti, C., Conti, A., Dardari, D., & Verdone, R. (2009). An overview on wireless sensor networks technology and evolution. *Sensors, 9*(9). Available from https://doi.org/10.3390/s90906869.

Challenges and opportunities in IoT healthcare systems: a systematic review. (2020). *SN Applied Sciences, 2*(1), 139. < https://doi.org/10.1007/s42452-019-1925-y >.

Chaudhary, A. (2020). *Cloud Security Challenges in 2020, cloudsecurityalliance.org.* Alliance, CSA: Publisher: Cloud Security. Available from https://cloudsecurityalliance.org/blog/2020/02/18/cloud-security-challenges-in-2020.

Chong, C. Y., & Kumar, S. P. (2003). Sensor networks: Evolution, opportunities, and challenges. *Proceedings of the IEEE, 91*(8), 1247–1256. Available from https://doi.org/10.1109/JPROC.2003.814918.

Cloud Security Alliance. (2020). Top threats to cloud computing: Egregious eleven. < https://cloudsecurityalliance.org/download/artifacts/top-threats-to-cloud-computing-egregious-eleven >.

Divadari, S., Surya Prasad, J., & Honnavalli, P. (2023). Managing data protection and privacy on cloud. *Lecture Notes in Networks and Systems, 540*, 383–396. Available from https://doi.org/10.1007/978-981-19-6088-8_33, https://www.springer.com/series/15179.

Dodda, R. (2016). The evolution of Internet of Things (IoT) and its impact on existing technology. *International Journal of Science Technology & Engineering, 2*(07), 2016.

Formica, D., & Schena, E. (2021). Smart sensors for healthcare and medical applications. *Sensors (Switzerland), 21* (2). Available from https://doi.org/10.3390/s21020543, https://www.mdpi.com/1424-8220/21/2/543/pdf.

Guezguez, M. J., Rekhis, S., & Boudriga, N. (2018). A sensor cloud for the provision of secure and QoS-aware healthcare services. *Arabian Journal for Science and Engineering, 43*(12). Available from https://doi.org/10.1007/s13369-017-2954-8, https://link.springer.com/journal/13369.

Gupta, N., & Dutta, A. (2021). A study on data protection and privacy issues in healthcare data. Springer Science and Business Media LLC. Available from https://doi.org/10.1007/978-981-16-5207-3_25.

HITRUST and HIPAA Safe Harbor. (2021). < https://hitrustalliance.net/content/uploads/HITRUST-and-HIPAA-Safe-Harbor.pdf >, (accessed 02.21).

IoT health devices: Exploring security risks in the connected landscape (2023). *MDPI, 4*(2), 150–182. Available from https://doi.org/10.3390/iot4020009.

Jabeen, T., Ashraf, H., & Ullah, A. (2021). A survey on healthcare data security in wireless body area networks. *Journal of Ambient Intelligence and Humanized Computing, 12*(10), 9841–9854. Available from https://doi.org/10.1007/s12652-020-02728-y.

Jahan, S., Chowdhury, M., Islam, R., & Gao, J. (2018). Security and privacy protection for eHealth data. *Communications in Computer and Information Science, 878*, 197–205. Available from https://doi.org/10.1007/978-3-319-94421-0_16, http://www.springer.com/series/7899.

Kashani, M. H., et al. (2021). A systematic review of IoT in healthcare: Applications, techniques, and trends. *Journal of Network and Computer Applications, 192*103164. Available from https://doi.org/10.1016/j.jnca.2021.103164.

Khan, Z. A., & Abbasi, U. (2016). Evolution of wireless sensor networks toward Internet of Things. *Emerging communication technologies based on wireless sensor networks: Current research and future applications.* Saudi Arabia: CRC Press. Available from https://www.crcpress.com/Emerging-Communication-Technologies-Based-on-Wireless-Sensor-Networks-Current/Rehmani-Pathan/p/book/9781498724852.

Masood, I., Wang, Y., Daud, A., Aljohani, N. R., & Dawood, H. (2018). Towards smart healthcare: Patient data privacy and security in sensor-cloud infrastructure. *Wireless Communications and Mobile Computing, 2018*. Available from https://doi.org/10.1155/2018/2143897.

Mirza, M. A., Mahboob, R. M. M., Jahangir, H., Khawar, M., & Imam, M. (2021). Security issues of IoT in healthcare sector: A systematic review. Springer Science and Business Media LLC. Available from https://doi.org/10.1007/978-981-16-5301-8_50.

Sharma, N., Shamkuwar, M., & Singh, I. (2019). The history, present and future with IoT. *Intelligent Systems Reference Library, 154*. Available from https://doi.org/10.1007/978-3-030-04203-5_3, http://www.springer.com/series/8578?detailsPage = titles.

Sun, Y., & Li, S. (2021). A systematic review of the research framework and evolution of smart homes based on the Internet of Things. *Telecommunication Systems, 77*(3). Available from https://doi.org/10.1007/s11235-021-00787-w, http://www.kluweronline.com/issn/1018-4864.

Tanwar, S., Tyagi, S., & Kumar, N. (2020). Security and privacy of electronic healthcare records: Concepts, paradigms and solutions. *Security and Privacy of Electronic Healthcare Records.* India: Institution of Engineering and Technology. Available from https://doi.org/10.1049/PBHE020E, https://digital-library.theiet.org/content/books/he/pbhe020e.

The application of internet of things in healthcare: A systematic literature review and classification. (2019). *University Access Information Society, 18*, 837−869. <https://doi.org/10.1007/s10209-018-0618-4>.

Tunc, M. A., Gures, E., & Shayea, I. (2021). A survey on IoT smart healthcare: Emerging technologies, applications, challenges, and future trends. *arxiv., 2109*(02042), 15. Available from https://doi.org/10.48550/arXiv.2109.02042, arXiv:2109.02042 [cs.IT]: Arxiv.

Ullah, Z., Al-Turjman, F., Mostarda, L., & Gagliardi, R. (2020). Applications of artificial intelligence and machine learning in smart cities. *Computer Communications, 154*. Available from https://doi.org/10.1016/j.comcom.2020.02.069.

Applications of fog computing for smart sensor network

Mostafa Haghi Kashani[1] and Sepideh Bazzaz Abkenar[2]

[1]Department of Computer Engineering, Shahr-e-Qods Branch, Islamic Azad University, Tehran, Iran [2]Department of Computer Engineering, Science and Research Branch, Islamic Azad University, Tehran, Iran

23.1 Introduction

The development of science and technology, as well as their usage in medical applications, have a direct impact on humankind's progress. Healthcare IT systems have been around for decades, gathering, analyzing, and regulating patient situations, as well as making decisions concerning diagnoses (Roy et al., 2018). Furthermore, there are still too few medical resources available. Few medical professionals collaborate in one concentrated area, like an urban medical center to provide outstanding medical treatment. Geographical limitations lead to a significant imbalance in the system, which makes it challenging for patients in rural areas to receive timely, reliable, and accurate health services (Gostin, 2011). The mentioned problem can be resolved with the help of smart sensors like body sensor networks (BSNs). Small-sized smart sensors that can be employed inside, outside, or on the body for tracking health have recently been made possible by developments in embedded technology, electronics, and wireless networks (Sahoo et al., 2016).

The advancement of the BSN makes it possible to efficiently and continuously gather medical data from patients in rural areas (Xu et al., 2019). On the other hand, keeping the patient in their home is one of the most effective ways to treat disease and speed up recovery (Pushpan & Velusamy, 2019). Sensors in an electronic health (e-health) record system continuously monitor a person's health by employing a variety of advanced biosensors, offering benefits such as decreasing medical error, lessening hospital staff workload, enhancing patient comfort, making decisions regarding abnormality of human wellness, offering high accuracy of essential data at a reasonable price, and decreasing the complexity of healthcare data analysis (Hasan et al., 2019; Nikravan, 2011). The sensors are placed on a person's body to enable continuous monitoring in natural surroundings, with records

Sensor Networks for Smart Hospitals
DOI: https://doi.org/10.1016/B978-0-443-36370-2.00024-4

kept on a medical server or in the cloud for easy access by physicians. Traditional cloud computing using data centers is not appropriate for future massive healthcare Internet of Things (IoT) services due to latency and rapid broadband connections (Zhou et al., 2019).

Numerous real-time requirements of mobile edge nodes, like geographic location, cannot be met by standard cloud computing. Thus, fog computing was created by Cisco in 2012 to overcome each of the abovementioned technological barriers. Fog computing has a hierarchical architecture including cloud, fog, and user device layers, where the user device layer contains IoT devices and sensors. The standard cloud architecture concept evolved to the network's edge when fog computing technology complemented cloud computing architecture (Zhao et al., 2019). Additionally, fog computing broadens cloud-based services to the network edge to reduce latency by spatially dispersing IoT application pieces (Zhou et al., 2023), and it facilitates device movement (Bonomi et al., 2012) in medical applications as they develop more resilient (Liang et al., 2022). The idea of "health fog" (Ahmad et al., 2016) guarantees reduced latency for e-health in case of medical issues.

This chapter aims to investigate fog computing applications for smart sensors associated with smart hospitals based on recent research findings. This chapter coincides with the possible classification of the approaches of fog computing for smart sensors. It also highlights the applied evaluation factors, algorithms, and tools. The development of fog computing in the IoT framework in the healthcare system resulted in dramatic improvements in the medical industry. It assisted medical professionals to improve patient satisfaction and manage patient care more quickly and efficiently. The IoT-based healthcare system still faces difficulties due to the current constraints, resulting in the need for additional research and improvement in the future. In view of this, the chapter also seeks to highlight the critical research avenues, present constraints, and significant challenges in fog computingapplications for smart sensors.

The remainder of this chapter is organized as follows. In Section 23.2, the research questions, the paper selection procedure, and the study methodology are stated. Section 23.3 offers a classification and an in-depth analysis of the selected articles, highlighting their benefits and drawbacks. The findings analysis, unsolved issues, and future directions are included in Sections 23.4 and 23.5, respectively. Finally, Section 23.6 includes an explanation of the conclusion.

23.2 Research methodology

Numerous studies on fog computing, smart sensors, their applications, and difficulties have been carried out by researchers. We first identify the concerns and requirements that drive this chapter's motivation to complete a thorough examination of this era. Finding the answers to the questions makes it possible to identify any gaps in the subject, which can assist researchers in developing novel perspectives and concepts. This chapter also aims to define, categorize, compare, and provide a possible classification for the approaches of fog computing for smart sensors. To achieve this goal, the following research questions were also determined:

- **RQ₁:** What is the possible classification of the approaches of fog computing for smart sensors?
- **RQ₂:** What are the applied evaluation factors, algorithms, and tools in fog computing applications for smart sensors?

- **RQ₃:** What are the current research gaps and challenges related to fog computing applications for smart sensors?

Then, from 2019 to 2023, we conducted an online search for articles on this topic employing Google Scholar as the primary search engine and reputable scientific publishers like Springer, IEEE, ScienceDirect, SAGE, Taylor & Francis, Wiley, Emerald, ACM, Inderscience, and Hindawi according to titles and keywords. The following search terms were used:

(hospital OR hospitals OR health OR e-health OR patient OR patients) AND
(fog OR edge) AND
(sensor OR sensors OR wearable)

Additionally, nonpeer-reviewed, non-English articles, theses, review papers, short papers, and book chapters were excluded to retrieve the most relevant publications. Afterward, the articles' abstracts and conclusions were investigated. Following a thorough review of the full texts of all the articles, 28 papers that could adequately address our research concerns and disclose the procedures and difficulties were selected for further in-depth investigation.

After extracting and choosing the papers, we suggest a classification of the approaches of fog computing for smart sensors in Section 23.3. The observations are finally recorded, the data is analyzed, compared, and visualized to come up with the responses to the defined questions, and the explanation of the final results is provided.

We present analytic and statistical research on them after outlining the available approaches, their key concepts, benefits, and drawbacks. This evaluation also outlines the motivations behind defining the list of significant and unresolved challenges and issues, as well as the key areas where further studies can enhance the approaches employed in the papers.

23.3 A classification of the approaches of fog computing for smart sensors

This section presents a classification of the approaches of fog computing for smart sensors. Fig. 23.1 displays the suggested classification in which the studied papers are

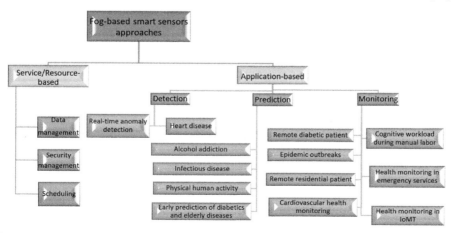

FIGURE 23.1 Classification of the approaches of fog computing for smart sensors.

classified into two main categories, namely service/resource-based and application-based, which are defined in Sections 23.3.1 and 23.3.2, The service/resource-based category consists of data management, security management, and scheduling. The application-based category consists of detection, prediction, and monitoring strategies.

23.3.1 Service/resource-based category

The service/resource-based category includes data management, security management, and scheduling. These approaches are explained in Sections 23.3.1.1—23.3.1.3.

23.3.1.1 Data management strategies

Monitoring systems use effective methods for analyzing and responding rapidly to the enormous amount of real-time data gathered daily via sensors and biosensors. Solutions to minimize data loss and methods to handle noisy data are needed to deal with this massive volume of data. Even with fog computing's quick processing speed, real-time processing for inpatient care requires a low-latency solution. Thus, various data management strategies are offered, wherein the optimal fog node inside the fog layer is selected to minimize the transfer of useless data. Data management strategies enable the most effective handling of patient data with the least amount of delay or data loss. The articles containing data management strategies are reviewed in this section, and the merits and demerits are discussed in Table 23.1.

Sarkar et al. (2022) developed an intelligent health architecture to determine the suitable fog node and minimize unnecessary data transmission of health sensors. They introduced the fog ranking service and fog probing service to aid in selecting the most effective fog node. Comparative performance analysis showed that i-Health outperformed existing methods by reducing the time required to analyze critical patient data. They did not, however, utilize deep learning algorithms to enhance the efficiency of i-Health. Similarly, Aiswarya et al. (2022) suggested a three-tiered fog computing architecture to solve the current cloud and IoT latency issues within the healthcare domain. The authors decreased network latency by enhancing traditional cloud computing techniques combined with fusing fuzzy logic and reinforcement learning.

23.3.1.2 Security management strategies

Hacking may be used to access, compromise, or change patient data. Thus, the main issues in fog computing that need to be considered are security, privacy, and user

TABLE 23.1 Reviewing and comparing data management strategy.

Category		Ref.	Advantage(s)	Disadvantage(s)
Service/ resource-based	Data management	Sarkar et al. (2022)	Low transmission delay	Not applying deep learning algorithms such as CNN and recurrent neural network (RNN) to improve the performance of i-health.
		Aiswarya et al. (2022)	Low network latency	Low security of private health data Not considering the agility of distributed nodes

anonymity. Security management solutions utilizing blockchain technology or other techniques have been adopted by many researchers to address issues such as malicious nodes or unauthorized access attempts to valuable patient data. Furthermore, within the security management domain, some authentication approaches have been developed to avoid unauthorized access to medical data. This section reviews the papers which include security management strategies, and the merits and demerits are discussed in Table 23.2.

Since IoT devices could be exposed to hacking owing to the absence of authentication and encryption policies, presenting severe risks to consumers, Mani et al. (2022) addressed the problem by offering a three-tiered architecture based on edge computing, fog computing, and blockchain for enhancing the securing and supporting transactions in the IoT. The fog computing nodes in a three-tiered architecture were connected to medical sensor nodes. They were employed to verify and identify healthcare IoT devices using fog computing technology, analytical models, and a signature encryption (SE) algorithm. The assessment results showed that fog computing -based blockchain achieved more effectiveness in recognizing malicious nodes concerning packet error rate, reliability, and throughput. However, the scalability limitations of blockchain were not investigated in relation to the SE algorithm.

Likewise, regarding the significant difficulties of key exchange and authentication that must be taken into account in fog computing, (Huang et al, 2023) suggested a three-layer mutual authentication key establishment architecture—sensor layer, fog layer, and cloud layer—according to elliptic curve cryptography. The fog nodes were assigned to authenticating the device and distributing the established session key, hence reducing the computational burden on the cloud server, once mutual authentication had taken place. The suggested protocol was much safer than the previous techniques, and the scheme was robust enough to endure multiple attacks. The proposed system, on the other hand, could be set up to establish reliable and safe data transmission, which may enhance healthcare services.

Similarly, Gokulakrishnan et al. (2023) presented a smart maliciously roaming person detection system for hospital surfaces that employs cognitive dimensionality reduction and the Hilbert Spectrum. The data was collected through a sensor-enabled camera. The

TABLE 23.2 Reviewing and comparing security management strategy.

Category		Ref.	Advantage(s)	Disadvantage(s)
Service/ resource-based	Security management	Mani et al. (2022)	High detection accuracy High reliability Minimizing packet error Low execution time Minimizing the percentage of malicious nodes	Low scalability Not analyzing the complexity of the system
		Huang, Chen and Wang (2023)	Reducing communication costs High security Maintaining user anonymity and untraceability Reducing computational load	Not evaluating F-measure Low security Not stable data transmission
		Gokulakrishnan et al. (2023)	High accuracy High specificity High sensitivity	High response time

Hilbert spectrum is a statistical tool for differentiating between moving signals. Cognitive dimensionality reduction, a type of unsupervised machine learning technique, assisted in reducing the amount of features in a dataset.

23.3.1.3 Scheduling strategies

These days, the Internet of Medical Things (IoMT)-enabled medical equipment automatically and continually conveys the gathered health data, enabling healthcare practitioners to monitor health problems and make behavioral adjustments in real-time. IoMT and healthcare services require rapid reaction, especially when sending emergency notifications to doctors. To give patients continuous real-time reactions and minimal latency, some researchers use scheduling methods to design health monitoring systems. In this regard, researchers use load balancing and work offloading between fog nodes to reduce reaction time. While cooperation among fog nodes is valuable, load balancing is essential. Since offloading all tasks to a master node may result in delays, cautious scheduling is required. Collaboration and response time can be increased with a well-balanced task plan in the fog layer. Furthermore, sophisticated methods, including scheduling and application partitioning, are essential for managing IoT resources and separating workflow between local and remote execution, resulting in benefits of energy consumption, performance, and cost. This section reviews the papers involving scheduling strategies, and the merits and demerits are discussed in Table 23.3.

Amudha and Murali (2021) proposed an intelligent proactive routing algorithm for area networks to mitigate latency and optimize battery life. They also used deep learning-based adaptive distance-energy features to achieve energy efficiency in routing and scheduling. Their suggested approach contained four steps, including data collection—collecting of sensor data, data cleaning for the removal of undesired and noisy data, model training for creating a neural network model employing machine learning algorithms, testing—applying a real-time data collection for testing, and deployment—deploying the deep learning model in real-time to monitor elderly patients at home or in a hospital. The presented algorithm demonstrated high accuracy; however, the evaluation was limited to indoor environments.

TABLE 23.3 Reviewing and comparing scheduling strategy.

Category		Ref.	Advantage(s)	Disadvantage(s)
Service/ resource-based	Scheduling	Amudha and Murali (2021)	High accuracy	Not applying security algorithms to prevent attacks
		Lakhan et al. (2022)	Low cost Low energy consumption	Low security Not considering dynamic environments with complex mobility features Not evaluating F-measure
		Alotaibi and Baroudi (2022)	Reducing task response (low latency and delay)	Not evaluating F-measure Not implementing the presented approach on a real testbed
		Xu et al. (2019)	High accuracy Low latency High reliability	Not evaluating F-measure Low scalability

Further investigation in real-time and outdoor scenarios was recommended for more precise findings. Furthermore, incorporating trusted safety algorithms in the fog gateway could enhance security.

Similarly, Lakhan et al. (2022) developed an algorithm called DNNECTS to improve mobile workflow scheduling and offloading processes. The algorithm included three sections: application partitioning, task sequencing, and scheduling. They used sensor data as input and evaluated the gathered information using a deep neural networks (DNNs) algorithm to filter out irrelevant and noisy data. The objective was to optimize partitioning and reliability. Experimental findings demonstrated that the proposed techniques surpassed current approaches in a dynamic setting concerning cost and energy consumption. However, the study did not consider a dynamic circumstance with sophisticated mobility features.

Likewise, Alotaibi and Baroudi (2022) employed an ant colony optimization approach to balance the load of sensors sent to the fog nodes by employing a fog master. The fog node handled some of the incoming load before offloading it to the fog master for tasks whose likelihood was above a predetermined threshold. Based on the fog master's input, the threshold will be modified and updated. Even when there are more end customers, the suggested work achieved superior results in minimizing the delay.

Regarding the limited and imbalanced medical resources, Xu et al. (2019) used wearable sensors to offer rural areas an opportunity for real-time and high-quality healthcare facilities. First, they concentrated on developing a semantic-based and edge-intelligent e-health service to lessen delays for patients in various locations. Secondly, they proposed a fog AI collaborative analysis system to integrate medical insights and balance the computational load. Moreover, to identify geographic variations in illness risks, they developed a specialized fog e-health system. The simulation findings proved the effectiveness of the proposed system, which guarantees high accuracy and low latency while employing minimal resources.

23.3.2 Application-based strategy

The application-based category includes detection, prediction, and monitoring. These approaches are explained in Sections 23.3.2.1–23.3.2.3.

23.3.2.1 Detection strategies

Several techniques and algorithms are used in detection strategies to look for possible anomalies in data streams that are captured by sensors. Finding unusual abnormalities in data streams helps identify risks and makes it possible to enhance early treatment. Medical services, particularly in rural areas with BSNs, demand not only reduced latency but also high-quality services. To anticipate and recognize emergencies, the system needs to identify any anomalies nearly instantly. Hence, reducing data loss and processing data in real-time online are significant problems in this strategy, as wearables sensors handle the massive volumes of data streams created in a real medical scenario. Internet of things and fog computing integrated with real-time human activity analysis and detection in intelligent controlled environments. This section reviews the papers that provide detection strategies, and the merits and demerits are discussed in Table 23.4.

Greco et al. (2019) suggested a four-layer architecture proposed for an IoMT scenario. The architecture utilized wearable sensors to detect and respond to problems quickly. The HTM algorithm was used to detect anomalies in data streams, and semantic technologies helped differentiate between emergencies and regular biological changes. The modularity of the architecture made it simple to expand and modify. However, a more robust physical framework was needed in real-world scenarios while other anomaly detection systems were not implemented or tested. Additionally, applying noninvasive wearable sensors for the elderly and those with dementia was not considered.

Decisions were conveyed to the individuals immediately by Lavanya et al. (2023), which conducted preprocessing and deep learning-based evaluation in the edge computing layer. Employing heart rate variation features and physiological parameters, the authors built a model using deep learning to estimate strokes. The suggested edge computing with wearable sensors approach was superior to current smart healthcare-based methods concerning accuracy, execution speed, latency, and power consumption. Additionally, cloud servers were used to store individual healthcare data for later analysis.

Likewise, Phukan et al. (2022) conducted research on human activity recognition (HAR) employing convolutional neural networks (CNNs) architecture. They investigated the impact of different factors, such as activation function, filter size, and number of layers on the optimal HAR approach. Previous studies did not focus on selecting the ideal activation function, filter size and number, but the researchers found that choosing the appropriate

TABLE 23.4 Reviewing and comparing detection strategy.

Category	Ref.	Advantage(s)	Disadvantage(s)
Application- Detection based	Greco, Ritrovato and Xhafa (2019)	Modularity capability	Not evaluating other anomaly detection algorithms on the proposed architecture Not applying noninvasive wearable sensors for elderly and dementia patients
	Lavanya et al. (2023)	High accuracy High execution speed Low latency Low power consumption High sensitivity High specificity	Not evaluating F-measure
	Phukan et al. (2022)	High accuracy Low latency	Not evaluating F-measure Not evaluating AUROC
	Ray and Dash (2022)	High capability of anomaly detection	Low scalability Not focusing on the multivariate time series dataset covering multiple health sensor raw values
	Xhaferra and Cina (n.d.)	High accuracy High scalability	Not evaluating the proposed approach in real-world scenarios, such as hospitals or clinics that apply fog and IoT devices

combination of these factors can improve efficiency. The study also found that selecting the suitable segment duration and size leads to recognizing objects more accurately while requiring less processing time. The optimal CNN-based approaches for HAR were put into practice with constrained resources to show their accuracy and real-time effectiveness with reasonable latency.

Similarly, Ray and Dash (2022) developed the IoTSAnom architecture for detecting covariate shifts in univariate time series pulse rate data. They demonstrated the effectiveness of probability, shift detection, and time-series seasonal decomposition in anomaly detection. The presented algorithm showed significant time consumption. They also did not concentrate on multivariate time series datasets that include raw values of health sensors.

Moreover, for early heart attack prevention, Xhaferra and Cina (n.d.) suggested a fog-based healthcare architecture based on DNN to classify heart patients into high-risk and low-risk categories. The findings demonstrated that the proposed model performed better than traditional methods and offered a higher degree of accuracy when classifying patients into high-risk and low-risk groups. Nevertheless, the scientists did not employ a hybrid model that combines multiple ML approaches to enhance diagnosis. Additionally, they did not adapt the framework to take advantage of sensor devices and fog computing in the real hospital environment.

23.3.2.2 Prediction strategies

Some of the suggested health systems in the examined papers utilize wearable sensors to identify patients in a prediction model and predict healthcare data. Prediction models have been trained with the data gathered from health monitoring devices to identify underlying trends, forecast needs, and provide individualized care. Since sensor parameters could differ across various subjects or even the same individual, prediction systems should employ approaches that are stable and robust enough to deal with noisy sensor data. Moreover, timely prediction of infectious diseases and decision-making depends on the design of a smart healthcare prediction system. The articles using prediction strategies are studied in this section, and Table 23.5 discusses the advantages and disadvantages.

Uddin (2019) proposed a multimodal activity prediction framework based on wearable sensors for an edge device. The system's input data were collected by various wearable healthcare sensors, including electrocardiography, magnetometer, accelerometer, and gyroscope sensors. The features were then trained in a recurrent neural network (RNN) to predict activities. On a publicly available standard dataset, namely MHEALTH (Banos et al., 2014, 2015), the system was compared with conventional methods. The experiment results showed that the suggested approach surpasses other traditional techniques.

Furthermore, Gupta et al. (2023) suggested a smart healthcare system that combines sensor layer and edge computing concepts with a prediction model based on CNN. Edge computing allowed for efficient resource accessibility and low response times through local edge servers connected to IoT devices. The CNN model was utilized to analyze the health data collected by these IoT devices. The purpose of edge devices was to provide timely health forecast reports to physicians and patients via the edge servers. The results demonstrated high accuracy, precision, and recall, highlighting the effectiveness of the

TABLE 23.5   Reviewing and comparing prediction strategy.

Category		Ref.	Advantage(s)	Disadvantage(s)
Application-based	Prediction	Uddin (2019)	Fast consumption High accuracy High robustness	Not evaluating the presented system on varied datasets Low scalability
		Gupta et al. (2023)	High accuracy High precision High recall Low processing time Low classification cost	Low scalability
		Doulani, Adhikari and Hazra (2023)	High accuracy Low training time	Low privacy of healthcare data Low F-measure
		Dhillon et al. (2022)	High precision High specificity Low response time	Low scalability Not tested on other datasets

suggested mechanism. The proposed mechanism, however, required less processing time and incured lower classification costs, especially in large datasets.

Moreover, Doulani et al. (2023) created an artificial intelligence (AI)-based healthcare prototype with biosensors in edge networks to remotely track and analyze health parameters to minimize connectivity between infected patients and physicians. The simulation findings showed the proposed model's efficiency over the current ML models regarding accuracy. However, developed ML models could be implemented in edge networks to improve decision-making and increase medical data privacy.

Similarly, Dhillon et al. (2022) offered IoTPulse, an IoT-based health information solution. The system employed machine learning in the framework of fog computing to identify alcohol addiction. Different machine learning models were utilized to predict alcohol addiction. IoTPulse was evaluated using a baseline technique called smartwatch sensor data-based prediction system in a real-world FogBus environment to examine the efficiency of QoS metrics such as energy, latency, response time, and bandwidth on the network. Additional medical fields, including diabetes, cancer, and hepatitis, can benefit from the prediction capabilities of IoTPulse and provide services to related patients.

23.3.2.3 Monitoring strategies

A significant portion of research uses fog computing in their health monitoring systems. The health monitoring systems that are offered use a variety of sensors and biosensors to gather information about human vitals and health. The medical staff and physicians can then view this data as it has been transferred to the fog storage. Remote health monitoring (RHM) allows people to be diagnosed and followed up outside of a hospital, usually at home, to monitor their health and track alterations in medical problems over time that may need treatment and medical attention. So, in situations like remote locations with limited access to healthcare or aging populations with a scarcity of medical professionals and hospital facilities, remote patient monitoring has become more crucial. In the case of infectious disorders, it also lowers the danger of exposure to and transmission of the disease by avoiding unneeded hospital stays and visits. Continuous patient monitoring and health tracking improve patient quality of life while reducing hospital stays and expenditures and enabling early sickness detection. Table 23.6 discusses the benefits and drawbacks of the papers with monitoring strategies that are addressed in this section.

TABLE 23.6 Reviewing and comparing monitoring strategy.

Category		Ref.	Advantage(s)	Disadvantage(s)
Application-based	Monitoring	Masinelli et al. (2020)	Improve energy consumption	Similar accuracy to the state-of-art
		Pavithra et al. (2023)	High accuracy	Not analyzing the proposed model for multiple disease prediction with more security
		Singh and Chatterjee (2023)	High security High accuracy Low cost Low latency	Not having an access control mechanism in the proposed framework
		Ilyas et al. (2022)	Low network latency Low network utilization	Low security Not considering privacy approaches such as blockchain Not considering patient and medical practitioner mobility aspects
		Karunanithy and Velusamy (2022)	Reduce packet loss and retransmission of data Mitigate overflow Minimize latency High scalability	Not evaluating F-measure
		Yan et al. (2022)	Reduce response latency Low energy consumption Optimizing the load balance between edge server	Not adapting traffic in different regions and changes in traffic caused by city construction
		Dieye et al. (2022)	High reliability High performance High availability	Not evaluating the fault tolerance of the proposed framework
		Suggala et al. (2022)	Short transmission latency High accuracy High precision High F-measure High recall	Low scalability Not evaluated on a real dataset
		Gopinath et al. (n.d.)	Low latency Low energy usage High security Low network usage	High data transmission time
		Talha et al. (n.d.)	High accuracy High scalability Low energy consumption	High response time

Masinelli et al. (2020) offered a low-power multimodal machine learning system for self-awareness and activity monitoring systems that permit the framework to monitor itself in connection with the environmen. The proposed system managed its resources more efficiently by activating only when necessary to achieve the intended reliability. They extended the edge wearable sensors' battery life to keep track of multimodal workload and health. The proposed ML approach recognized cognitive workload during physical activity with similar accuracy compared to the state-of-the-art. They enhanced the energy consumption to 27.6% by accepting the idea of self-awareness, along with less than 6% performance loss.

Likewise, Pavithra et al. (2023) proposed a multitier secured architecture and an optimized deep recurrent neural network (O-DRNN) model for processing patient data collected from sensors. The data was transmitted to an edge computing healthcare server, processed, and saved in the cloud using a security model. The particle swarm optimization algorithm was employed to preprocess the data and choose the best features. Bayesian optimization was applied to improve diagnosis by optimizing the O-DRNN algorithm hyperparameters. The architecture provided superior results in accuracy and encryption delays compared to other existing models for safely processing remote data transfer in edge computing. The authors, however, did not conduct a more secure analysis of several disease predictions.

Similarly, Singh and Chatterjee (2023) provided a secure edge of things framework for monitoring health in real time while protecting the privacy and security of medical records. This research focused on clustering approaches to analyze sensor data to find abnormalities and attribute-based encryption for safe access and bio-signal data security. The performance results demonstrated an increase in abnormal data detection accuracy. However, the efficiency may be enhanced by using blockchain technology or by adding additional edge devices at the edge layer to increase security and restrict access procedures.

Likewise, Ilyas et al. (2022) proposed a bidirectional method to improve real-time data transmission in health monitoring systems. The device layer, which consisted of wearable IoT sensors and end-user devices, was one of the three layers of the architecture; the fog layer included an intelligent element for making dynamic decisions to increase fog efficiency; and the cloud layer provided end users with services by having the capacity to process, store, and retrieve data. Their architecture consisted of three layers, including the device layer, the fog layer, and the cloud layer. The system optimized fog node selection and load balancing while improving network usage and latency. However, the researchers did not consider blockchain approaches for the security of health monitoring data. Furthermore, neither patient nor physician mobility was investigated in this research.

Moreover, Karunanithy and Velusamy (2022) developed the ant colony algorithm for adjusting the network's global state, resulting in revealing the shortest probable routing path within the source and BS. Furthermore, minimum edge-shared vertex path selection (MEVPS) was designed to identify the optimal path with the least interference and collision. In the MEVPS, a body controller was utilized to gather data from the biosensor, analyze it, and categorize it to either be sent to the base station or rejected based on standard values. Furthermore, MEVPS was designed to identify the optimal path with the least interference and collision.

Similarly, Yan et al. (2022) suggested a technique for continuous health monitoring by applying the IoMT and employing fuzzy C-means clustering to divide health monitoring units. Likewise, Dieye et al. (2022) suggested a fog-based RHM system and utilized a reinforcement learning and enhanced differential evolution-based technique to allocate tasks to remote sensors linked to patients. The simulation results showed that it performed more reliably than the latter. However, they did not examine the advantages of different fault tolerance techniques.

In another study, Suggala et al. (2022) offered a method for continuously tracking, evaluating, and identifying the illness spread by mosquitoes. The proposed system utilized sensors to gather pertinent user data, which was then used to identify diseases spread by mosquitoes. Furthermore, the system employed the temporal social network analysis to estimate the probability of disease outbreaks, assess afflicted users, and transmit low-latency awareness messages to initiate preventive steps. The technology successfully stopped epidemics and attained great accuracy. The authors did not, however, test the proposed method by applying a real dataset.

Likewise, Gopinath et al. (n.d.) presented the RHM framework to handle common issues with healthcare systems, including response delays, latency, and security. Body and camera sensors were used by the system for diagnosis to increase efficiency, privacy, and accuracy. This research led to the creation of an intelligent medical infrastructure that was reliable and secure. Furthermore, Talha et al. (n.d.) suggested an IoMT-based cardiac health monitoring system that applies machine learning algorithms to detect anomalies in vital signs. The system aimed to identify abnormal human crucial signs in real-time by integrating ML classification algorithms with IoMT-enabled biosensors and edge intelligence. The authors found that Random Forest provided high accuracy, however, further work was needed to apply wearable sensor vests for testing and monitoring cardiovascular health and assess the effectiveness of deploying the ML model on an edge device.

23.4 Analysis of results

Considering the guidelines outlined in Section 23.2, we examine the reviewed papers in this section. Section 23.3 provides a summary of the papers that have been studied. Additionally, a comparison of them is provided in this section by responding to the previously stated research questions:

RQ₁: What is the possible classification of the approaches of fog computing for smart sensors?

Considering RQ_1, according to the papers that are reviewed in Sections 23.3, the approaches applied in fog computing for smart sensors are classified into two primary categories, namely service/resource-based and application-based. The service/resource-based category consists of data management, security management, and scheduling, while the application-based category consists of detection, prediction, and monitoring strategies. Fig. 23.2 illustrates that the majority of research is carried out employing monitoring strategies at 36%, while detection strategies have 18%. Scheduling and prediction strategies have been applied in 14% of the applied approaches of fog

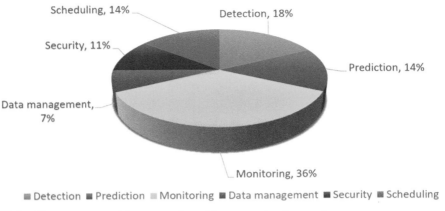

FIGURE 23.2   The percentage of the approaches of fog computing for smart sensors.

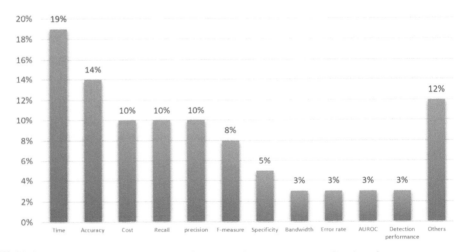

FIGURE 23.3   The percentage of evaluation factors for fog computing applications for smart sensors.

computing each. Security and data management strategies have been used at 11% and 7%, respectively.

RQ₂: What are the applied evaluation factors, algorithms, and tools in fog computing applications for smart sensors?

Based on RQ₂, researchers have employed various evaluation factors. According to Fig. 23.3, time accounts for the largest percentage of evaluation factors (19%). Accuracy comes next with 14%. Cost, precision, and recall have been applied to evaluated presented approaches 10% each. Fig. 23.3 indicates that most of the approaches made attempts to reduce response time and enhance accuracy, precision, and recall while lowering cost.

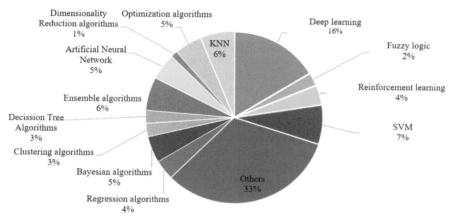

FIGURE 23.4 The percentage of applied algorithms in fog computing applications for smart sensors.

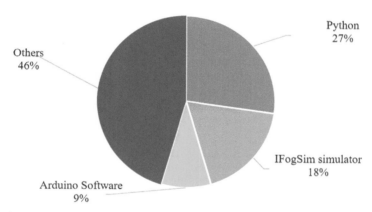

FIGURE 23.5 The percentage of evaluation tools in fog computing applications for smart sensors.

As shown in Fig. 23.4, deep learning, SVM, KNN, and ensemble algorithms are the most applied approaches and classifiers in the studied papers.

Considering RQ$_2$, Fig. 23.5 shows the statistical demonstration of the percentage of tools in the examined papers. Python has 27% of usage, and IFogSim simulator and Arduino software have 18% and 9%, respectively.

23.5 Open issues

By analyzing the reviewed papers, several research obstacles need to be removed for the applications of sensors and nanosensor networks to benefit fog-based healthcare systems. Thus, considering RQ$_3$, this section discusses the challenges in detail.

RQ$_3$: What are the current research gaps and challenges related to fog computing applications for smart sensors?

- **Scalability:** One critical aspect of the healthcare system is scalability. It refers to the system's potential to meet evolving requirements and adjust to larger-scale shifts in the future. While some nodes or devices guarantee the validity of the offered approaches, most fog computing solutions for healthcare are validated in small-scale contexts in the studied papers. This considers an extensive user base and a decision-making methodology that may aid public health professionals in identifying patterns in the spreading of diseases. It appears to be a challenge that the recommended methods were primarily applied in restricted situations. These studies do not come close to meeting the real needs of a large medical community, even if some of them employ extensive patient populations.

- **Privacy:** Although fog-based healthcare devices in smart and nanosensor networks improve patient quality of life and give new sources of earnings for healthcare providers, there are significant privacy concerns about patient data that will become more serious in increasing adoption (Gopinath et al., n.d.). Preventing unwanted access to patients' and service providers' private information is known as privacy. Additionally, as the number of IoT devices for healthcare rises, these devices are developed and expanded using data gathered from sensors and nanosensor networks. The enormous volumes of data being sent and preserved also make them more vulnerable (Huang et al., 2023). Thus, privacy remains a highly challenging open issue in terms of lowering the possibility of sensitive data being compromised and enhancing data security (Suggala et al. 2022), such as a person's habits, sleeping patterns, locations, and medical histories during time.

- **Blockchain:** Blockchain is an alternative that might be connected to the fog-based environment of future studies. The blockchain is the most effective technology for the healthcare system as it makes it possible to securely maintain and analyze vast volumes of health data and keeps it from being altered or deleted (Mani et al., 2022). Furthermore, patient-permission-based authorization techniques are required as patients acquire and possess their medical data. In addition, it is an unchangeable, unambiguous consensus and long-lasting protocol that uses distributed and peer-to-peer communication to overcome the requirement for centralized authority (Dhillon et al., 2022). Therefore, it is intended to support the current fog-based environment in acting independently and transparently while handling the requests of decentralized end users. As a result, blockchain may be a promising future option. In fact, this subject has not gotten much academic attention.

- **Mobility:** Mobility is another important factor that has received less attention in the healthcare system. The capacity for patients and medical professionals to utilize network assistance for connecting to the gateway at any time and from any location is known as mobility in healthcare systems (Ilyas et al., 2022). Mobility is also required to improve service quality, give full access to information regardless of location, and make the network fault-tolerant (Lakhan et al., 2022). As healthcare provisioning is so essential, a mobility protocol needs to be dependable to reduce packet loss, end-to-end delays, and network failures in any scenario. As such, mobility presents a compelling research issue.

- **Real testbed environment:** While only a small portion of the examined investigations were carried out in real testbeds, the approaches suggested in the studies should be implemented in real contexts. All of the suggested strategies need to be implemented in real testbeds to determine whether or not they can create an appropriate healthcare system. Implementing a proper testbed is still a significant challenge.

23.6 Conclusion

The goal of this chapter was to analyze and present a technical classification for the approaches of fog computing for smart sensors in smart hospitals. The offered classification is categorized into two main categories, namely service/resource-based and application-based. The service/resource-based category consists of data management, security management, and scheduling, while the application-based category consists of detection, prediction, and monitoring strategies. According to RQ_1, the majority of researches are carried out by monitoring strategies with 36%, while detection strategies have 18%. The lowest percentage was related to security and data management strategies by 11% and 7%, respectively. Additionally, the purpose of this paper is to examine the evaluation parameters, advantages, disadvantages, and used tools of the selected papers. Considering RQ_2, the highest percentage of evaluation parameters is related to time, with 19%. Accuracy comes next with 14%. As shown in Fig. 23.4, deep learning, SVM, KNN, and ensemble algorithms are the most applied approaches and classifiers in the studied papers. Based on the statistical percentage of the applied tools, Python has 27% of usage, while the IFogSim simulator has 18%. Finally, to answer RQ_3, we described challenges and future trends in detail to highlight existing research gaps.

References

Ahmad, M., Amin, M. B., Hussain, S., Kang, B. H., Cheong, T., & Lee, S. (2016). Health fog: A novel framework for health and wellness applications. *Journal of Supercomputing*, 72(10). Available from https://doi.org/10.1007/s11227-016-1634-x, http://www.springerlink.com/content/0920-8542.

Aiswarya, S., Ramesh, K., Sasikumar, S., Sheema, D., & Prabha, B. (2022). Internet of Health Things: A Fog computing Paradigm. In *6th International conference on trends in electronics and informatics, ICOEI 2022 — Proceedings* (pp. 598–604). Institute of Electrical and Electronics Engineers Inc., India. <http://ieeexplore.ieee.org/xpl/mostRecentIssue.jsp?punumber = 9776594>, https://doi.org/10.1109/ICOEI53556.2022.9776777, 9781665483285.

Alotaibi, B. K., & Baroudi, U. (2022). Offload and schedule tasks in health environment using ant colony optimization at fog master. In *International wireless communications and mobile computing, IWCMC 2022* (pp. 469–474). Institute of Electrical and Electronics Engineers Inc. Saudi Arabia. <http://ieeexplore.ieee.org/xpl/mostRecentIssue.jsp?punumber = 9823957>, https://doi.org/10.1109/IWCMC55113.2022.9825020, 9781665467490.

Amudha, S., & Murali, M. (2021). Deep learning based energy efficient novel scheduling algorithms for body-fog-cloud in smart hospital. *Journal of Ambient Intelligence and Humanized Computing*, 12(7). Available from https://doi.org/10.1007/s12652-020-02421-0.

Banos, O., Garcia, R., Holgado-Terriza, J. A., Damas, M., Pomares, H., Rojas, I., Saez, A., & Villalonga, C. (2014). mHealthDroid: A novel framework for agile development of mobile health applications. *Lecture notes in computer science (including subseries lecture notes in artificial intelligence and lecture notes in bioinformatics)*, 8868. Available from https://doi.org/10.1007/978-3-319-13105-4_14, https://www.springer.com/series/558.

Banos, O., et al. (2015). Design, implementation and validation of a novel open framework for agile development of mobile health applications. *BioMedical Engineering OnLine*, 14(Suppl 2). Available from https://doi.org/10.1186/1475-925X-14-S2-S6, Springer Nature.

Bonomi, F., Milito, R., Zhu, J., & Addepalli, S. (2012). Fog computing and its role in the Internet of Things. In *MCC'12 - Proceedings of the 1st ACM mobile cloud computing workshop* (pp.13–15) United States. Available from https://doi.org/10.1145/2342509.2342513.

Dhillon, A., Singh, A., Vohra, H., Ellis, C., Varghese, B., & Gill, S. S. (2022). IoTPulse: machine learning-based enterprise health information system to predict alcohol addiction in Punjab (India) using IoT and fog computing. *Enterprise Information Systems*, 16(7). Available from https://doi.org/10.1080/17517575.2020.1820583, http://www.tandf.co.uk/journals/titles/17517575.asp.

Dieye, M., Mseddi, A., Jaafar, W., & Elbiaze, H. (2022). Towards reliable remote health monitoring in fog computing networks. *IEEE Transactions on Network and Service Management, 19*(3). Available from https://doi.org/10.1109/TNSM.2022.3194806, http://www.ieee.org/products/onlinepubs/news/0806_01.html.

Doulani, K., Adhikari, M., & Hazra, A. (2023). Edge-based smart health monitoring device for infectious disease prediction using biosensors. *IEEE Sensors Journal, 23*(17). Available from https://doi.org/10.1109/JSEN.2023.3296897, http://ieeexplore.ieee.org/xpl/RecentIssue.jsp?punumber = 7361.

Gokulakrishnan, S., Jarwar, M. A., Ali, M. H., Kamruzzaman, M. M., Meenakshisundaram, I., Jaber, M. M., & Kumar, R. L. (2023). Maliciously roaming person's detection around hospital surface using intelligent cloud-edge based federated learning. *Journal of Combinatorial Optimization, 45*(1). Available from https://doi.org/10.1007/s10878-022-00939-x.

Gopinath, A., Singh, Y. P., & Narawade, N. S. (n.d.). Design of fog based remote health monitoring system. In *2022 IEEE 7th International conference for convergence in technology (I2CT)* (pp. 1–7). IEEE.

Gostin, L. O. (2011). Health worker shortages and global justice, *Health worker shortages and global justice. Millbank memorial fund.*

Greco, L., Ritrovato, P., & Xhafa, F. (2019). An edge-stream computing infrastructure for real-time analysis of wearable sensors data. *Future Generation Computer Systems, 93*. Available from https://doi.org/10.1016/j.future.2018.10.058.

Gupta, P., Chouhan, A. V., Wajeed, M. A., Tiwari, S., Bist, A. S., & Puri, S. C. (2023). Prediction of health monitoring with deep learning using edge computing. *Measurement: Sensors, 25*. Available from https://doi.org/10.1016/j.measen.2022.100604, http://www.journals.elsevier.com/measurement-sensors.

Hasan, K., Biswas, K., Ahmed, K., Nafi, N. S., & Islam, M. S. (2019). A comprehensive review of wireless body area network. *Journal of Network and Computer Applications, 143*. Available from https://doi.org/10.1016/j.jnca.2019.06.016, http://www.elsevier.com/inca/publications/store/6/2/2/8/9/3/index.htt.

Huang, Y. T., Chen, T. S., & Wang, S. D. (2023). Authenticated key agreement scheme for fog computing in a health-care environment. *IEEE Access, 11*. Available from https://doi.org/10.1109/ACCESS.2023.3275017, http://ieeexplore.ieee.org/xpl/RecentIssue.jsp?punumber = 6287639.

Ilyas, A., Alatawi, M. N., Hamid, Y., Mahfooz, S., Zada, I., Gohar, N., & Shah, M. A. (2022). Software architecture for pervasive critical health monitoring system using fog computing. *Journal of Cloud Computing, 11*(1). Available from https://doi.org/10.1186/s13677-022-00371-w, https://journalofcloudcomputing.springeropen.com.

Karunanithy, K., & Velusamy, B. (2022). Edge device based efficient data collection in smart health monitoring system using wireless body area network. *Biomedical Signal Processing and Control, 72*, 103280. Available from https://doi.org/10.1016/j.bspc.2021.103280.

Lakhan, A., Mastoi, Q. U. A., Elhoseny, M., Memon, M. S., & Mohammed, M. A. (2022). Deep neural network-based application partitioning and scheduling for hospitals and medical enterprises using IoT assisted mobile fog cloud. *Enterprise Information Systems, 16*(7). Available from https://doi.org/10.1080/17517575.2021.1883122, http://www.tandf.co.uk/journals/titles/17517575.asp.

Lavanya, R., Vidyabharathi, D., Kumar, S. S., Mali, M., Arunkumar, M., Aravinth, S. S., Zainlabuddin, M., Jose Triny, K., Sathyendra Bhat, J., Tesfayohanis, M., & Venkatesan, C. (2023). Wearable sensor-based edge computing framework for cardiac arrhythmia detection and acute stroke prediction. *Journal of Sensors, 2023*. Available from https://doi.org/10.1155/2023/3082870.

Liang, W., Hu, Y., Zhou, X., Pan, Y., & Wang, K. I. K. (2022). Variational few-shot learning for microservice-oriented intrusion detection in distributed industrial IoT. *IEEE Transactions on Industrial Informatics, 18*(8). Available from https://doi.org/10.1109/TII.2021.3116085, http://ieeexplore.ieee.org/xpl/RecentIssue.jsp?punumber = 9424.

Mani, V., Ghonge, M. M., Chaitanya, N. K., Pal, O., Sharma, M., Mohan, S., & Ahmadian, A. (2022). A new blockchain and fog computing model for blood pressure medical sensor data storage. *Computers and Electrical Engineering, 102*, 108202. Available from https://doi.org/10.1016/j.compeleceng.2022.108202.

Masinelli, G., Forooghifar, F., Arza, A., Atienza, D., & Aminifar, A. (2020). Self-aware machine learning for multimodal workload monitoring during manual labor on edge wearable sensors. *IEEE Design and Test, 37*(5). Available from https://doi.org/10.1109/MDAT.2020.2977070, http://ieeexplore.ieee.org/xpl/RecentIssue.jsp?punumber = 6221038.

Nikravan, M., et al. (2011). An intelligent energy efficient QoS-routing scheme for WSN. *International Journal of Advanced Engineering Sciences and Technologies, 8*(1).

Pavithra, D., Nidhya, R., Shanthi, S., & Priya, P. (2023). A secured and optimized deep recurrent neural network (DRNN) scheme for remote health monitoring system with edge computing. *Automatika, 64*(3). Available from https://doi.org/10.1080/00051144.2023.2195218.

Phukan, N., Mohine, S., Mondal, A., Manikandan, M. S., & Pachori, R. B. (2022). Convolutional neural network-based human activity recognition for edge fitness and context-aware health monitoring devices. *IEEE Sensors Journal, 22*(22). Available from https://doi.org/10.1109/JSEN.2022.3206916, http://ieeexplore.ieee.org/xpl/RecentIssue.jsp?punumber = 7361.

Pushpan, S., & Velusamy, B. (2019). Fuzzy-based dynamic time slot allocation for wireless body area networks. *Sensors, 19*(9), 2112. Available from https://doi.org/10.3390/s19092112.

Ray, P. P., & Dash, D. (2022). IoT-edge anomaly detection for covariate shifted and point time series health data. *Journal of King Saud University—Computer and Information Sciences, 34*(10). Available from https://doi.org/10.1016/j.jksuci.2021.11.014, http://www.journals.elsevier.com/journal-of-king-saud-university-computer-and-information-sciences/.

Roy, A., Roy, C., Misra, S., Rahulamathavan, Y. & Rajarajan, M. (2018). CARE: Criticality-aware data transmission in CPS-based healthcare systems. In *IEEE International conference on communications workshops, ICC workshops 2018—Proceedings* (pp. 1−6). Institute of Electrical and Electronics Engineers Inc., India. <http://ieeexplore.ieee.org/xpl/mostRecentIssue.jsp?punumber = 8400291>, Available from https://doi.org/10.1109/ICCW.2018.8403540, 9781538643280.

Sahoo, P. K., Mohapatra, S. K., & Wu, S. L. (2016). Analyzing healthcare big data with prediction for future health condition. *IEEE Access, 4*. Available from https://doi.org/10.1109/ACCESS.2016.2647619, http://ieeexplore.ieee.org/xpl/RecentIssue.jsp?punumber = 6287639.

Sarkar, J. L., V, R., Majumder, A., Pati, B., Panigrahi, C. R., Wang, W., Qureshi, N. M. F., Su, C., & Dev, K. (2022). I-health: SDN-based fog architecture for IIoT applications in healthcare. *IEEE/ACM Transactions on Computational Biology and Bioinformatics*. Available from https://doi.org/10.1109/TCBB.2022.3193918, http://ieeexplore.ieee.org/xpl/RecentIssue.jsp?punumber = 8857.

Singh, A., & Chatterjee, K. (2023). Edge computing based secure health monitoring framework for electronic healthcare system. *Cluster Computing, 26*(2). Available from https://doi.org/10.1007/s10586-022-03717-w, https://www.springer.com/journal/10586.

Suggala, R. K., Krishna, M. V., & Swain, S. K. (2022). Health monitoring jeopardy prophylaxis model based on machine learning in fog computing. *Transactions on Emerging Telecommunications Technologies, 33*(7). Available from https://doi.org/10.1002/ett.4497, http://onlinelibrary.wiley.com/journal/10.1002/(ISSN)2161-3915.

Talha, M., Mumtaz, R., & Rafay, A. (n.d.) Paving the way to cardiovascular health monitoring using Internet of Medical Things and Edge-AI. In *2022 2nd international conference on digital futures and transformative technologies (ICoDT2)* (pp. 1−6). IEEE.

Uddin, M. Z. (2019). A wearable sensor-based activity prediction system to facilitate edge computing in smart healthcare system. *Journal of Parallel and Distributed Computing, 123*. Available from https://doi.org/10.1016/j.jpdc.2018.08.010, http://www.elsevier.com/inca/publications/store/6/2/2/8/9/5/index.htt.

Xhaferra, E., & Cina, E. (n.d.). A fog-health architecture for early alarming system of heart attack: A deep neural network-based approach. In *2022 International interdisciplinary conference on mathematics, engineering and science (MESIICON)* (pp. 1−6). IEEE.

Xu, C., Dong, M., Ota, K., Li, J., Yang, W., & Wu, J. (2019). SCEH: Smart customized e-health framework for countryside using edge AI and body sensor networks. In *Proceedings - IEEE global communications conference, GLOBECOM*, China. <https://ieeexplore.ieee.org/xpl/conhome/1000308/all-proceedings>, Available from https://doi.org/10.1109/GLOBECOM38437.2019.9014057, 25766813.

Yan, H., Bilal, M., Xu, X., & Vimal, S. (2022). Edge server deployment for health monitoring with reinforcement learning in Internet of Medical Things. *IEEE Transactions on Computational Social Systems*. Available from https://doi.org/10.1109/TCSS.2022.3161996, http://ieeexplore.ieee.org/servlet/opac?punumber = 6570650.

Zhao, Y., Wang, W., Li, Y., Colman Meixner, C., Tornatore, M., & Zhang, J. (2019). Edge computing and networking: A survey on infrastructures and applications. *IEEE Access, 7*. Available from https://doi.org/10.1109/ACCESS.2019.2927538, http://ieeexplore.ieee.org/xpl/RecentIssue.jsp?punumber = 6287639.

Zhou, X., Hu, Y., Wu, J., Liang, W., Ma, J., & Jin, Q. (2023). Distribution bias aware collaborative generative adversarial network for imbalanced deep learning in industrial IoT. *IEEE Transactions on Industrial Informatics, 19*(1). Available from https://doi.org/10.1109/TII.2022.3170149, http://ieeexplore.ieee.org/xpl/RecentIssue.jsp?punumber = 9424.

Zhou, X., Liang, W., Wang, K. I. K., & Shimizu, S. (2019). Multi-modality behavioral influence analysis for personalized recommendations in health social media environment. *IEEE Transactions on Computational Social Systems, 6*(5). Available from https://doi.org/10.1109/TCSS.2019.2918285, http://ieeexplore.ieee.org/servlet/opac?punumber = 6570650.

24

Quantum computing for smart healthcare

Padmapriya Velupillai Meikandan, Paramita Basak Upama,
Masud Rabbani, Md Martuza Ahamad and
Sheikh Iqbal Ahamed

Ubicomp Lab, Department of Computer Science, Marquette University, Milwaukee,
Wisconsin, United States

24.1 Mission

To further the implementation of quantum-based nanosensors for improved mental health monitoring. We hope to get the word out about this groundbreaking technology and its transformative role in healthcare. (1) *Promoting Quantum-Based Nanosensors*: To promote the understanding and use of quantum-based nanosensors for better mental health monitoring. We aim to spread the word on the capability that nanosensors, which are based on using quantum materials and semiconductor technology, have amongst the population about how this cutting-edge technology can revolutionize how we do healthcare. (2) *Advancing Precision Mental Health Monitoring*: The second objective of this chapter is to apply quantum nanosensors to advance the field of precision mental health monitoring. Our goal is to specifically invest in research and development exploring the use of nanosensors to track and analyze psychological and neurochemical markers associated with mental health conditions. (3) *Enhancing Data Security*: It is committed to improving data security and privacy. In doing so, we will ensure the data discussed in the chapter is confidential and as secure as possible. We will guarantee that data transferred within the chapter is done through encrypted ports and that files that contain data are password-encrypted as well. Ethical data handling is something that the chapter will do as well. This means we only ask the questions, get the data, and retain the data we need. All the remaining data will be destroyed. (4) *Enabling Healthcare Providers*: To enable healthcare providers with information and tools to employ quantum-based nanosensors in their practice effectively. Offer resources, training, and support to allow healthcare professionals to

Sensor Networks for Smart Hospitals
DOI: https://doi.org/10.1016/B978-0-443-36370-2.00025-6

use this technology to provide more precise and personalized mental health interventions. (5) *Pioneering a New Era in Mental Health Care*: In line with our goal of pioneering a new mental healthcare era, Quantum Nano Vision seeks to promote the integration of Quantum-based Nanosenor in Care Hospitals. The objective of Pioneering a New Era in the mental healthcare area is to provide insights, case studies, and guiding technical assistance for the broader adoption of transformative technology by patients suffering from conditions relating to their mental health.

24.2 Introduction

Quantum Nanosensors based on the principles of quantum mechanics seem poised to revolutionize mental fitness tracking within the ambit of smart hospitals. Within the United States, a rising necessity for improved mental fitness interventions is recognized, and conventional monitoring methods seem to struggle with the intricacies of many physiological and neurochemical markers tied to stress, anxiety, depression, and postpartum depression (Donohoe et al., 2016; Wang et al., 2012). To respond to this growing necessity, this paper will explore the transformative capability of quantum-based total nanosensors to accurately track these markers and fundamentally alter the mental fitness care landscape through unheard accuracy, real-time monitoring, and early intervention (Javaid et al., 2021; Purohit et al., 2020). The confidential nature of the mental fitness information accumulated on the nanoscale stage mandates a complete technique for facts security and consistency at every level of its lifecycle—from collection to evaluation and storage. In this context, the encryption and deidentification of affected person-stage facts emerge as crucial additives, ensuring the data's most straightforward analytical value and compliance with legal and ethical norms (Purohit et al., 2020). Quantum nanosensors operating inside smart hospitals necessitate a paradigm shift within the recognition and education of experts in this area. The importance of training and education in healthcare cannot be underestimated. Continuous training and education are necessary to raise awareness among healthcare professionals about the security and privacy concerns of using quantum-based nanosensors (Ahirwar & Khan, n.d; Bozal-Palabiyik et al., 2019; Donohoe et al., 2016; Knudsen et al., 2013).

Embedding security considerations in the inception of database projects will be extremely critical, paving the way for the practical and robust use of quantum nanosensors. This method addresses on-the-spot facts and security-demanding situations and anticipates future tendencies, especially in quantum computing (QC) (Wang et al., 2012). With the evolution of QC, the focus highlights the need for strong encryption standards, which can withstand future quantum attacks, protecting the integrity and confidentiality of patient-sensitive mental health information (Knudsen et al., 2013).

The intention of this essay goes way beyond the mere explanation of quantum nanosensors. The objective here is to expand the knowledge and familiarity of this revolutionary generation to be utilized in the healthcare sector. This observation tends to furnish healthcare providers with the skills and know-how to easily bridge the quantum nanosensor technology into their practice through three approaches: gaining accuracy in monitoring mental healthcare, enhancing the security of health-related information, and finally, giving early education to the users

(Li et al., 2020; Sengupta & Srivastava, 2021; Wei et al., 2023). The closing intention is to pioneer new technology in intellectual healthcare characterized by surely personalized, accurate, and timely interventions, aligning with the escalating call for transformative healthcare answers inside the United States (Gupta et al., 2023a; Pathak et al., 2021).

24.3 Related works

QC is now a cutting-edge technology for analyzing complex data with higher accuracy and speedup than classical computing (Stanford Encyclopedia of, 2024). In 1984, this technology was first applied to different "cryptography protocols" where quantum key distribution (QKD) was developed by QC, which enhanced the security information (Wikipedia, 2024). This novel method has been spanned in many areas, including healthcare data analysis and security. Research has been finished to increase superior imaging strategies, decorate diagnostic accuracy, and optimize remedy protocols with safety through QC. In the healthcare system, QC can improve scientific photo analysis, offer quicker medical predictive equipment, and offer novel strategies for intellectual health monitoring. However, QC faces challenges in the healthcare system, such as technological infancy, requiring sophisticated hardware and substantial expertise. A hybrid method with QC and classical algorithms can leverage the current challenges and bridge the gaps between QC and classical medical science. This study will briefly describe the challenges and solutions to intelligent health, especially mental health monitoring.

24.3.1 Quantum computing on medical images

QC has revolutionized clinical pictures by introducing advanced quantum-inspired algorithms for processing complicated scientific pictures appropriately with unparalleled speed and dependable results. This emerging generation can appreciably enhance diagnostic methods, permitting healthcare professionals to identify and deal with illnesses more efficaciously than before. For instance, quantum system studying (Quantum Machine Learning, QML) is now a famous technique in medical picture analysis, with improvements in parameter optimization, execution performance, and mistakes in price discount execution (Wei et al., 2023). In quantum image analysis, the reconstruction of clinical images may be expedited by using quantum mechanical strategies for amassing imaging information, introducing a singular approach that drastically quickens the procedure (Kiani et al., 2020). QC has also been deployed for classifying COVID-19 from Computed Tomography (CT) images, which improved the diagnosis of COVID-19 patients by image analysis (Sengupta & Srivastava, 2021). Quantum-inspired algorithms can speed up medical image analysis like human tissues (Altmann et al., 2018). Medical image analysis by 3D reconstruction using quantum algorithms is very innovative (Li et al., 2020). This method is used and effective for poor resolution of medical images where traditional machine learning algorithms show insignificant accuracy. QC is also practical in the ophthalmological area, for example, classifying diabetic retinopathy by analyzing eye images (Padha & Sahoo, 2024).

24.3.2 Quantum computing on mental health monitoring

QC is emerging as a transformative tool for human mental health monitoring by analyzing complex neurological data and enhancing predictive models. This integration in mental health research already opens a potential path in mental health monitoring by revolutionizing diagnosis, treatment planning, and developing models. Quantum-inspired long short-term memory networks (Quantum-LSTM) are helpful as a self-supervised contrastive learning approach to monitor mental health continuously (Wang et al., 2012). QC can be leveraged with deep learning for scoring projective psychological tests effectively and reducing the high personnel costs for the projective psychological test (Knudsen et al., 2013). QC can also analyze immune psychiatry and neuroquantology data for understanding psychiatric disorders (Demirkan & Smart, 2013).

24.3.3 Quantum computing on healthcare data security

Data security is crucial to today's intelligent healthcare solutions (El Azzaoui et al., 2022). Millions of data, like diagnostic images, electronic health records, radiology, laboratory findings, mental health counseling reports, treatment plans, DNA profiles, etc., are created every second. Classical computers use cryptographic techniques, creating keys to secure those data, but a quantum computer can break those codes easily. So, it is threatening for those purposes. So, blockchain and quantum terminal machines (Kaushik & Kumar, 2022) are solutions. Quantum blockchain technology can potentially ensure the confidentiality, availability, and integrity of stored data (Wang et al., 2022). Quantum blockchain technology can improve quantum critical distribution solutions and introduce secure quantum signature technology (Gupta et al., 2023b).

24.3.4 Quantum computing on COVID-19

The authors already found the flaws of current medical technologies, and it also reveals the need for research in healthcare during the COVID-19 pandemic. Traditional computing was insufficient for new drug discovery, treatment plans, vaccination priorities, and many other factors (Pathak et al., 2021). Because the people were so scared and frustrated, the policy made it necessary to find fast solutions. So, only QC can deliver timely outcomes through its ability to process the Coronavirus compound at an exceptionally high rate of computation (Sengupta & Srivastava, 2021). The use of QC in COVID-19 research is analyzing disease prognosis using CT scan images (Kairon & Bhattacharyya, 2020), outbreak prediction using quantum neural network (Chengoden et al., 2023), measuring the effects of lockdown (Maheshwari et al., 2022), etc. It earnestly wishes that, like past worldwide pandemics, this one may be transient due to advancements in science and technology, such as QC.

24.4 Security and privacy of data

An emerging technology that can significantly impact patient care is using quantum sensors in hospitals as intelligent mental healthcare systems that provide real-time surveillance, infrastructure maintenance, and personalized intervention as required. Thus, maintaining patients' trust and fulfilling regulatory constraints necessitate that data security and privacy are integral to this system. This chapter is intended to dive into the particular security challenges faced by quantum sensors, utilized by hospitals as part of intelligent mental healthcare solutions, and the countermeasures by which to ensure the protection of data (Li et al., 2022).

The quantum cryptography protocol guarantees secure communication in the future of network technology and treatment. This protocol ensures the security of data transmission. It also guarantees the protection of healthcare treatment while doctors exchange patients' data and treatment information in a telemedicine wired and wireless network. The existing security protocols in mental healthcare, like conventional encryption protocols, have limitations in quantum attacks regarding future development in QC. But today and in the future, the data integrity and confidentiality of patient-sensitive mental health data appear to be a nightmare in an extensive data-collecting and data-storing environment. And other encryption algorithms will also be broken with the development of QC. All communities pay attention to mental healthcare data collecting with extensive obtaining with the IoT and Ubicomp computing (Aujla et al., 2019; Fernández-Caramés, 2020).

24.4.1 Security challenges in hospital-based smart mental healthcare

There are many possibilities for smart technologies in mental healthcare for hospitals. These new implementations come with many new advantages but also new security breaches. Some benefits are real-time data on people to improve care, real-time location tracking to improve care, and faster disease detection and treatment methods. On the other hand, the widespread adoption and detection analysis of QC in smart healthcare provides greater abilities but poses a whole other list of security measures because quantum technologies are quite different in nature.

24.4.1.1 Security challenges in healthcare

Some security breaches include data integrity, insider threats, and device security. They are explained in more detail in the chapter.

24.4.1.1.1 Data integrity

The heart of the issue is to ensure that mental health data collected via quantum sensors and computer sensors remains intact and trustworthy. This chapter explores cryptographic approaches that help mitigate tampering risks and aid in data verification and nonrepudiation.

24.4.1.1.2 Insider threats

An internal threat to data in the hospital environment can take many forms. This chapter examines proactive approaches healthcare organizations can take to mitigate insider threats properly, including strict access control policies, organizational data partitioning, proper data handling, monitoring all access control incidents and logs, and using security event correlation applications.

24.4.1.1.3 Device security

Quantum sensors are ultimately physical devices susceptible to tampering, unauthorized access, trunk theft, malicious probing/deviations to the physical device, and mass dissemination of compromised devices.

24.4.1.2 Encryption and authentication protocols

(a) **Secure Communication:** Disquisition is the implantation of secure communication protocols to defend the data transmitted between quantum sensors and hospital information systems by embodying encryption algorithms and specific channels.

(b) **Two-Step Authentication:** Two-step authentication methods enhance access control to verify that only authorized personnel can communicate, and access generated mental health data via quantum sensors.

24.4.1.3 Regulatory compliance

The healthcare industry is vastly different from other industries in that they face challenges that they must overcome, especially keeping their patient's data safe.

24.4.1.4 Continuous monitoring and auditing

To maintain a proactive security posture, it is essential to continuously monitor and audit access and interactions with quantum sensor data. This section discusses implementing monitoring tools and audit trails to detect and respond to real-time security incidents.

24.4.1.5 Patient consent and transparency

Informed consent is a primary ethical consideration in this area, and possible strategies could include entities being more open with patients about how they are dealing with their data, getting the patient to be in control of their data - which does not happen today. This becomes very important when quantum sensors become integral to intelligent mental healthcare in hospitals.

24.4.2 Mitigation strategies

24.4.2.1 Quantum-resistant cryptography

This includes developing and using asymmetric cryptographic algorithms resistant to quantum computer attacks.

24.4.2.2 Privacy-preserving technologies

Differential privacy and secure multi-party computation are implemented to mask individual mental health data.

The process of quantum cryptography consists of several key technical aspects, such as QKD, quantum encryption, and quantum-resistant cryptography. QKD allows two people to produce a shared random secret key known only to them, which can then be used to cipher and decipher messages. A predator can't ascertain the key to quantum data, which can neither be set nor altered when observed, so the information is safe from predators.

Quantum cryptography is a prime example of quantum sensing. It can be employed to create highly secure means of communication. For instance, quantum cryptography can safeguard individuals' health information during transfer. Quantum cryptography uses the concepts found in quantum mechanics to provide absolute knowledge to both sender and receiver that the information has been received and that the content of the information has not been altered during transmission. Quantum cryptography can boost the security and privacy of sensitive health data. Hence, innovative hospital and healthcare setups will profit from technology by protecting patient information from threats not only of today but also the ones that might emerge out of the future advancements in QC and align very well with the mandatory need to protect Personal health information and keep the integrity of intelligent healthcare data in an ever-distributed and data-rich healthcare scenario.

The potential application of quantum sensing in mental healthcare can be supported by leveraging quantum-resistant encryption protocols and privacy-enhancing technologies. Quantum sensing, coupled with robust security measures, has the potential to enhance the confidentiality and integrity of mental healthcare data, thereby contributing to improved patient privacy and data security. By integrating quantum-resistant encryption and privacy-preserving technologies, the protection and confidentiality of mental healthcare data can be strengthened, laying the foundation for the responsibility and secure utilization of quantum sensing in this critical domain.

Indeed, security and privacy need to be ensured. For this kind of setting, mental healthcare within a hospital, what is required can be robust protocols of encryption, authentication, and monitoring, along with regulatory compliance providing a corresponding environment that can result in a secure and trustworthy environment that does not breach security and privacy of patients while enjoying on the quantum potential for the improvements of mental healthcare (Abd El-Latif et al., 2018; Aujla et al., 2019; Chengoden et al., 2023; Fernández-Caramés, 2020; Kairon & Bhattacharyya, 2020; Li et al., 2022; Maheshwari et al., 2022).

24.5 Future direction

According to the sections above, quantum nanosensors are emerging as an up-and-coming tool for several sensitive tasks in healthcare and related fields nowadays (Ahirwar & Khan, n.d; Bozal-Palabiyik et al., 2019; Donohoe et al., 2016; Javaid et al., 2021; Knudsen et al., 2013; Purohit et al., 2020; Wang et al., 2012). However, few works have been published and implemented in mental health with a quantum nanosensor. The above discussions mentioned the potential of quantum nanosensors to be vastly used in this field only if data security and other related concerns are guaranteed beforehand. They can be utilized for early diagnosis and precise detection of several diseases in the future. The current advancements in quantum technology may soon lead us to more robust quantum nanosensors, which can have improved sensitivity and enhanced performance. Then, they can bring much-needed improvements in mental health, related datasets, and applications. In the light of this discussion, the following future directions can be proposed in the field of mental healthcare using quantum nanosensors:

1. **Faster and precise diagnosis of diseases:** Quantum nanosensors are proven to have the potential to provide accurate diagnosis results and more insights of data for faster analysis of several mental diseases, which are currently not in use. Implementing such technology will lead us toward more successful interventions and advanced treatment plans.
2. **Personalized medicine and treatment design:** The goal of precision medicine and personalized treatment plans is to look into the needs of each individual and develop a better understanding of diseases and treatments for future generations. Quantum nanosensors can help us with that goal while maintaining data security.
3. **Applications of QC algorithms:** With the advancement of QC in recent years, there are prospects to utilize quantum algorithms with quantum nanosensors for digging deep into vast and sensitive mental health datasets.
4. **Integration with wearable devices:** Wearable technologies are currently in trend for physical health monitoring purposes and can show potential for future noninvasive mental health marker monitoring.

24.6 Discussion

This chapter presents quantum-based nanosensors as a game-changer tool for customized mental healthcare services at smart hospitals. The chapter highlights the significance of data encryption protocols, considering the most critical aspect of securing patients' data and protecting it against quantum hacking on conventional encryption. The security side of quantum sensors is fulfilled from various prospects, including data integrity, device vulnerabilities, and insider threats. Proposed mitigation techniques evolved to align with quantum-resistant cryptography and privacy-preserving details, confining confidentiality. Early disease detection and powering precision medicine can be worth mentioning. Future promises by quantum computers will positively impact the mental healthcare system from a research perspective driven by QC algorithms. QC for smart healthcare is like a vast ocean full of opportunities, but data confidentiality from threats is the basic need of any intelligent system.

24.7 Conclusion

This e-book chapter explores the transformative potential of quantum nanosensors in reshaping intellectual healthcare. Faced with a significant call delivery within the United States, quantum nanosensors emerge as a groundbreaking option to reveal stress, tension, depression, and postpartum melancholy with unparalleled precision. The overarching challenge is to advance the implementation of those sensors, promoting the information of their utility in precision mental health tracking, improving information safety, enabling healthcare companies, and pioneering a new generation in intellectual fitness care.

This chapter's main idea is to emphasize that smart hospitals are not an exception to other connected devices, which are equally endangered regarding security and privacy. To apply quantum nanosensors in smart hospitals' Internet of Things (IoT) healthcare, security, and privacy, researchers are required in advance. Quantum cryptography protocols, especially QKD, are critical to secure data transmission in the quantum era. Security challenges in smart mental healthcare are fully elaborated, stressing the requirement of encryption and authentication protocols to tackle issues like data integrity, insider threats, and device security.

Regulatory compliance, continual monitoring, and audits are stressed to maintain a proactive safety position. Patient consent and transparency are moral imperatives to establish, discuss, and empower patients to control their data. The chapter concludes by sketching future directions, envisioning faster and more accurate disease diagnosis, personalized medicines, integration with wearable devices, and implementation of QC algorithms. This heralds a quantum revolution in mental healthcare, promising a future of intelligent, personalized, and secure interventions that prioritize patients' mental health.

References

Abd El-Latif, A. A., Abd-El-Atty, B., & Talha, M. (2018). Robust encryption of quantum medical images. *IEEE Access, 6*, 1073–1081.

Ahirwar, R., & Khan, N. (n.d.). Smart wireless nanosensor systems for human healthcare. In *Nanosensors for futuristic smart and intelligent healthcare systems*.

Altmann, Y., et al. (2018). Quantum-inspired computational imaging. *Science (New York, N.Y.), 361*, 6403 eaat2298.

Aujla, G. S., Chaudhary, R., Kaur, K., Garg, S., Kumar, N., & Ranjan, R. (2019). SAFE: SDN-assisted framework for edge–cloud interplay in secure healthcare ecosystem. *IEEE Transactions on Industrial Informatics, 15*(1), 469–480.

El Azzaoui, A., Sharma, P. K., & Park, J. H. (2022). Blockchain-based delegated quantum cloud architecture for medical big data security. *Journal of Network and Computer Applications, 198*, 103304.

Bozal-Palabiyik, B., Uslu, B., & Marrazza, G. (2019). Chapter 11 - Nanosensors in biomarker detection. *New Developments in Nanosensors for Pharmaceutical Analysis*, 327–380.

Chengoden, R., et al. (2023). Metaverse for healthcare: A survey on potential applications, challenges, and future directions. *IEEE Access, 11*, 12765–12795.

Demirkan, H., & Smart, A. (2013). Healthcare systems framework. *IT Professional, 15*(5), 38–45.

Donohoe, M., Balasubramaniam, S., Jennings, B., & Jornet, J. M. (2016). Powering in-body nanosensors with ultrasounds. *IEEE Transactions on Nanotechnology, 15*(2), 151–154.

Fernández-Caramés, T. M. (2020). From pre-quantum to post-quantum IoT security: A survey on quantum-resistant cryptosystems for the internet of things. *IEEE Internet of Things Journal, 7*(7), 6457–6480.

Gupta, S., Modgil, S., Bhatt, P. C., Chiappetta Jabbour, C. J., & Kamble, S. (2023a). Quantum computing led innovation for achieving a more sustainable COVID-19 healthcare industry: Technovation, *120*, 102544.

Gupta, S., Modgil, S., Bhatt, P. C., Chiappetta Jabbour, C. J., & Kamble, S. (2023b). Quantum computing led innovation for achieving a more sustainable COVID-19 healthcare industry. *Technovation, 120*, 102544.

Javaid, M., Haleem, A., Singh, R. P., Rab, S., & Suman, R. (2021). Exploring the potential of nanosensors: A brief overview. *Sensors International, 2*.

Kairon, P., & Bhattacharyya, S. (2020). Covid-19 outbreak prediction using quantum neural networks. *Intelligence Enabled Research*, 113–123.

Kaushik, K., & Kumar, A. (2022). Demystifying quantum blockchain for healthcare. *Security and Privacy, 6*(3).

Kiani, Toussi, B., Villanyi, A., & Lloyd, S. (2020). Quantum medical imaging algorithms. arXiv preprint arXiv:2004.02036.

Knudsen, B. R., Jepsen, M. L., & Ho, Y.-P. (2013). Nanosensors for futuristic smart and intelligent healthcare systems. *Expert Review of Molecular Diagnostics, 13*(4), 367–375.

Li, C., et al. (2022). Efficient medical big data management with keyword-searchable encryption in healthchain. *IEEE Systems Journal, 16*(4), 5521–5532.

Li, X., Sui, J., & Wang, Y. (2020). Three-dimensional reconstruction of fuzzy medical images using quantum algorithm. *IEEE Access, 8*, 218279–218288.

Maheshwari, D., Garcia-Zapirain, B., & Sierra-Sosa, D. (2022). Quantum machine learning applications in the biomedical domain: A systematic review, in. *IEEE Access, 10*, 80463–80484.

Padha, A., & Sahoo, A. (2024). QCLR: Quantum-LSTM contrastive learning framework for continuous mental health monitoring. *Expert Systems with Applications, 238*121921.

Pathak, N., Misra, N. K., Bhoi, B. K., & Kumar, S. (2021). Concept and algorithm of quantum computing during the COVID-19 pandemic. *In Smart Systems: Innovations in Computing*, 523–535.

Purohit, B., Vernekar, P. R., Shetti, N. P., & Chandra, P. (2020). Biosensor nanoengineering: Design, operation, and implementation for. *Sensors International, 1*.

Sengupta, K., & Srivastava, P. R. (2021). Quantum algorithm for quicker clinical prognostic analysis: An application and experimental study using CT scan images of COVID-19 patients. *BMC Medical Informatics and Decision Making, 21*, 11–14.

Stanford Encyclopedia of. (2024). *Philosophy.* < https://plato.stanford.edu/entries/qt-quantcomp/ > .

Wang, W., Yu, Y., & Du, L. (2022). Quantum blockchain based on asymmetric quantum encryption and a stake vote consensus algorithm. *Scientific Reports, 12*, 8606.

Wang, W. U., Chen, C., Lin, K.-H., Fang, Y., & Lieber, C. M. (2012). Label-free detection of small-molecule–protein interactions by using nanowire nanosensors. *Proceedings of the National Academy of Sciences of the United States of America (PNAS), 109*(2), 005.

Wei, L., et al. (2023). Quantum machine learning in medical image analysis: A survey. *Neurocomputing, 525*, 42–53.

Wikipedia. (2024). *Quantum_Computing,* < https://en.wikipedia.org/wiki/Quantum_computing#:~:text = In/20a/201984/20paper/2C/20Charles,able/20to/20break/20RSA/20encryption > .

Knowledge graph-based reasoning in medical healthcare scenarios for IoT applications

Jialong Liu[1], Zhiwu Liang[1], Chong Mu[2], Lizong Zhang[3] and Anthony S. Atkins[4]

[1]Shenzhen Institute for Advanced Study, University of Electronic Science and Technology of China, Shenzhen, Guangdong, P.R. China [2]School of Information and Software Engineering, University of Electronic Science and Technology of China, Chengdu, Sichuan, P.R. China [3]School of Computer Science and Engineering, University of Electronic Science and Technology of China, Chengdu, Sichuan, P.R. China [4]School of Digital, Technology, Innovation and Business (DTIB), Staffordshire University, Stoke on Trent, Staffordshire, United Kingdom

25.1 Introduction

The emergence of the Internet of Things (IoT) marks the third wave in the evolution of the global information industry. (Jianjun & Jin, 2011) IoT has undergone continuous development over the past two decades. Currently, applications of the IoT are ubiquitous, evident in technologies such as Smart cars and intelligent home heating systems etc., where the underlying IoT infrastructure plays a pivotal role. The idea behind the IoT involves employing information sensing devices, including but not limited to infrared sensors, global positioning systems, laser scanners, and radio-frequency identification (RFID). These devices adhere to prescribed protocols, establishing a connection between physical objects and the Internet, thereby facilitating the exchange of information and communication. This connectivity facilitates smart identification, positioning, tracking, and administration of objects within the network.

Understanding IoT marks only the beginning; it is equally crucial to comprehend how IoT operates or, in other words, how it achieves intelligence. To illustrate this concept, consider the scenario of purchasing a Smart air conditioner system. Following professional installation, the initial step involves powering the device. Subsequently, following the instructions or scanning the QR code on the air conditioner, download the corresponding app or open a designated mini program. The primary objective is to connect the device to the network. Once accomplished, users gain the ability to remotely control the air conditioner, adjusting settings such as temperature and scheduling automatic shutdowns, thereby exemplifying the practical implementation of IoT intelligence.

From this description, an insight into the workings of the IoT becomes apparent. However, within this framework, three pivotal layers merit considerable attention: which are the three foundational layers of IoT (Yang, 2023)—namely, the perception layer, network layer, and application layer.

The perception layer, analogous to our sensory organs, aids in measuring various aspects of things and events, such as an object's temperature, air quality index, or even odor. This layer primarily relies on sensor technology and maybe the use RFID techniques.

The network layer serves the purpose of data transmission, facilitating the transfer of information collected by the Perception Layer to the Application Layer.

The application layer, akin to a computer's central processing unit, classifies, assesses, and responds to the received data, making informed actions or decisions. For instance, consider a voice-activated light bulb that illuminates upon detecting sound. To better depict the functionalities of these layers, Fig. 25.1 illustrates the workflow of these three layers.

In a hospital setting, aside from patient care, medical experimentation holds significant importance. Clinical trials, in particular, have been a focal point of attention. With substantial financial investments from both national governments and authorities, coupled with the collaborative efforts of researchers, clinical trials have yielded numerous outcomes. However, this progress has also given rise to some managerial challenges.

For instance, at a medical clinical trial center in China, deficiencies in drug distribution and clinical trial management (Zhang et al., 2017) have been identified. According to the

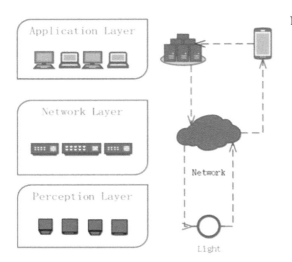

FIGURE 25.1   Three layers in Internet of Things.

regulations governing medical experiments, participants are supposed to bring the empty packaging of the previously administered drug to receive the next dosage. Unfortunately, the reality is that only a minority of individuals fulfill this obligation. The occurrence of such instances indicates managerial shortcomings, necessitating measures for improvements in the process.

Another example pertains to on-site medical experiments with homeopathic treatment (Ostermann et al., 2023). Typically, participants are required to stay at the experimental center for several months, adhering to specific dietary items. Due to the extended duration and restricted diet, and some of the participants may be inclined to violate the guidelines by leaving the experimental area to obtain additional dietary items. The emergence of such behavior underscores the need to enhance supervision and management of participant conduct to ensure the smooth progression of experiments.

These issues primarily stem from a lack of real-time information regarding participant locations, drug inventory, and drug distribution records at the experimental center. The utilization of IoT technology proves instrumental in addressing this challenge. This chapter introduces a knowledge graph (KG)-based IoT model tailored for medical scenarios. Leveraging IoT technology for data acquisition, the model employs a temporal KG for inference, providing decision support to enhance the overall management of medical experiments.

KGs possess superior capabilities in expressing node concepts and relationship structures. In recent years, they have experienced robust development and widespread application in various machine learning, deep learning, and large-scale models. Notable applications include recommendation systems (Jianjun & Jin, 2011), information retrieval (Castano et al., 2024), question-answering systems (Lang et al., 2022), and more. Time knowledge graphs (TKGs), an extension of KG, introduce a temporal attribute, allowing knowledge to evolve over time. The temporal attribute is manifested as a timestamp, transforming the graph from using triplets as basic units to quadruplets with timestamps as basic units.

For example, data representing the action "Patient Jack took Medication B at 3:30:21 PM on October 10, 2023" can be expressed in TKG as (Patient Jack, took, Medication B, 20231010153021). By incorporating such information, TKG can perform reasoning, providing hospitals with a more detailed understanding of patients. It can also assist or remind patients of their next medication pickup time. This extrapolation process is akin to forecasting in international relations (Wang et al., 2023b), financial analysis (Mu et al., 2023), and other practical applications, offering crucial and valuable information. In recent years, TKG has garnered widespread attention for its potential across various domains.

Due to the current training datasets for KGs being primarily composed of generic datasets such as WordNet (Omar & Al-Shaar, 2023), YAGO (Zhong et al., 2022), and Google KG (Sheth et al., 2019), which contain vast amounts of knowledge but lack specificity for certain application scenarios, and propose leveraging IoT technology in the medical field, specifically utilizing RFID technology to gather data. By organizing and integrating this data with existing datasets, a dedicated dataset tailored for a specific application scenario can be established.

Fixed knowledge bases may not always adapt well to the environments in which they are deployed. This model addresses this challenge by recognizing and embracing the intricate and dynamic nature of the real-world environment identifying relevant knowledge elements and adapting the local knowledge base from evaluations of past decisions. To reduce the granularity of the knowledge base, unlike other localized decision support systems, the model's decision process is not locally confined. Thus, the local knowledge possesses a fundamental decision unit, leading to more accurate decision outcomes.

This model can be applied in medical fields, providing intelligent guidance such as medication dispensing reminders, inventory management, and issuing warnings when drug trial protocols are violated. The overall process of our suggested model is illustrated in Fig. 25.2.

The subsequent sections of this chapter are structured as follows: an overview of relevant research; then a discussion of the methodology of the proposed model, followed by a summary of the approach and prospects for future applications and improvements.

25.2 Related work

A KG is a data structure designed to encapsulate relationships between diverse entities and their attributes (Ji et al., 2021). These models amalgamate data from disparate sources, encompassing both structured and unstructured data, and have been extensively researched to bolster an array of applications including search engines (Wang et al., 2019), recommendation systems (Zhou et al., 2020), and question- answering systems (Kan et al., 2021). In the healthcare domain, KGs play a pivotal role in furnishing an interpretable representation of medical concepts. They facilitate effective decision management in healthcare, augment clinical research efforts, and enhance the outcomes of healthcare services (Chandak et al., 2023).

KGs typically derive their foundation from the intricate landscape of complex medical systems, including electronic health records, medical literature, clinical guidelines, and patient-generated data (Rajkomar et al., 2018). Nevertheless, these data resources frequently exhibit heterogeneity and dispersion, posing challenges in their efficient integration and analysis. Diversity in data may lead to partial or conflicting depictions within KGs, limiting their effectiveness for subsequent healthcare functions. Moreover, the prevalent utilization of domain-specific KGs might restrict the scope and detail of knowledge

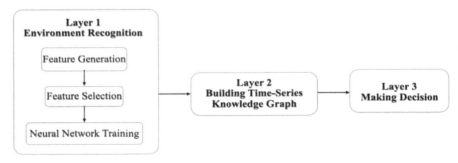

FIGURE 25.2   Three layers structures of TKG-based Internet of Things model. *TKG,* Time-series knowledge graph.

acquisition across various levels, impeding the recognition of correlations and connections among medical concepts from diverse domains.

Comprehensive and fine-grained healthcare KGs hold the potential to transform healthcare across diverse domains and at various levels (Santos et al., 2022). On a microscientific level, KGs can assist researchers in uncovering novel phenotypic and genotypic correlations, providing insights into the underlying mechanisms of diseases, and thereby enabling more precise and effective treatments. At the clinical care level, KGs can be leveraged to develop clinical decision support systems that provide clinicians with relevant information, improving clinical workflows and patient outcomes (Eberhardt et al., 2012). In this chapter, a proposed TKG model based on IoT data, which can be applied to various tasks in the healthcare domain is outlined.

25.3 Model

25.3.1 Environment recognition

To address management and decision-making issues in the healthcare domain, a proposed technical framework based on the IoT technology and a TKG is outlined. This framework emphasizes the structure of the system, the flow of data, and the relationships between each component. It integrates a knowledge-based system that utilizes TKG technology for automating the scheduling and processing of unforeseen events, such as event handling functionality.

The framework consists of three levels, each describing the data flow and functionalities as follows. The first level is the *environment recognition layer*, which uses sensors and other technologies to identify the environment. A neural network processes the environmental data, generating a matrix reflecting information about each node's environment. This matrix is used as a baseline for selecting knowledge elements from a predefined knowledge base, providing the foundation for subsequent inference and decision-making. The second level is the *knowledge management layer*, which constructs a TKG for nodes in the healthcare scenario and related medical knowledge to fulfill specific requirements. The third level is the *inference decision layer*, which, based on the environmental data obtained in the first level, performs inference and decision-making within the KG constructed in the second level. It provides decisions tailored to the current environment to improve clinical workflows and patient outcomes.

The decision support model comprises three main components: environment recognition, knowledge fusion, and decision formulation. The first step is environment recognition, which detects the environment using sensors such as RFID, motion sensors, barcode readers, etc., providing the foundation for environment identification. An artificial neural network generates a matrix reflecting the environmental information of nodes, serving as a baseline for selecting knowledge elements from a predefined knowledge base.

Given that neural networks are commonly used for classification and pattern recognition (Cao, Xia, et al., 2024), a neural network was chosen to be in the environment recognition layer. Considering the dynamic and complex nature of real healthcare scenarios, the neural network output is a matrix describing environmental information. This matrix includes possible domains or contextual aspects, providing a more accurate basis for decision results than specifying a single environment type. The construction of the neural network in the environment recognition layer involves three steps: feature generation, feature selection, and model training.

Feature Generation is the first step in building the neural network. The number of features should be neither too many nor too few to balance model training efficiency. Too many features may lead to an excessive training workload and a bulky model with suboptimal performance, while too few features may result in the omission of critical information. Consequently, feature generation typically involves two steps: first, identifying as many features as possible to ensure the inclusion of all key aspects, and then subsequently reducing the number of features to a manageable quantity.

Feature selection varies depending on the specific application scenario and focuses on selecting objects in the application scenario, including object parameters and statistical information for all objects. In healthcare applications, the selected features may include participant positions, drug inventory, drug distribution records, etc. Recognition techniques using widely applied wireless communication technologies in the IoT are employed to obtain relevant feature data. Features and their time-domain and frequency-domain formats from the radio domain, such as received signal strength indication, can be used for environment recognition. The flow of feature selection is shown in Fig. 25.3.

The number of original features may surpass one hundred, rendering it inefficient for network training or environment recognition purposes. A tight network method was used, to consider the impact of individual features and their combined effects on network performance, to filter effective features. This reduces the number of features to a reasonable quantity, enhancing network efficiency. The tight network method (Biazar et al., 2024) ranks all features based on their impact on network performance and sequentially adds features to an empty set according to their ranking. Each time a feature is added, the network's accuracy on the current set is tested to determine whether to accept the feature. The feature selection process is illustrated in Fig. 25.3.

The neural network structure used by the model consists of a hidden layer, with the input being the selected features and the output being a matrix serving as the result of environment recognition. This matrix's elements describe the degree of confidence in the predetermined environmental condition types. The training employs the back-propagation algorithm.

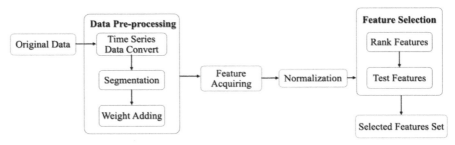

FIGURE 25.3 Feature selection.

25.3.2 Time-series knowledge graph reasoning

In the second layer, TKG was employed for knowledge selection, fusion, and extraction. Simultaneously, the proposed model exhibits commendable interpretability during the inference process, allowing a discernible understanding of the results through the information conveyed by each output path. This section will elaborate extensively on the procedural aspects of our TKG in handling data. Naturally, the discussion will unfold in accordance with both preliminary knowledge and the data processing facilitated by TKG.

25.3.2.1 Preliminary knowledge

Before delving into the exposition of the second layer, it is imperative to establish a foundational understanding of temporal knowledge graphs (TKG). This preliminary knowledge will facilitate a more profound comprehension of the subsequent processes.

25.3.2.1.1 Temporal knowledge graphs

A temporal knowledge graph can be articulated as $Graph = (Entity, Predicates, Time)$ where Entity and Predicates denote the sets of entities and relations, respectively (Mu et al., 2023). Time represents a collection of timestamps corresponding to relevant facts. In essence, a temporal knowledge graph comprises these three components. In a KG, each node represents a piece of data denoted by F representing a set of facts. Each fact can be expressed as a quadruple (e_i, p, e_j, t) where in the KG, e is an element in the set of entities, p is an element in the set of edges, and each node is composed of an entity and its corresponding timestamp. Relations P represents directed edges in the graph, connecting two entities within the KG.

25.3.2.1.2 Subgraph inference

A subgraph is constructed using the same strategy as the xERTE (Han et al., 2020) model to visualize the inference process. Within the subgraph G_{inf}, each node is represented as an entity-timestamp pair $v_i = (e_i, t_i)$, as illustrated in Fig. 25.4.

25.3.2.2 Time-series knowledge graph reasoning

The second layer serves as the knowledge management layer, predominantly employing a temporal knowledge graph approach to construct the knowledge structure. The subgraph is equivalent to the local knowledge base, and a node's determination is made through sequential construction and inference on the local knowledge base. The model structure, as depicted in Fig. 25.5, comprises four main components: (1) the neighbor

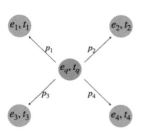

FIGURE 25.4   An example of an inference subgraph.

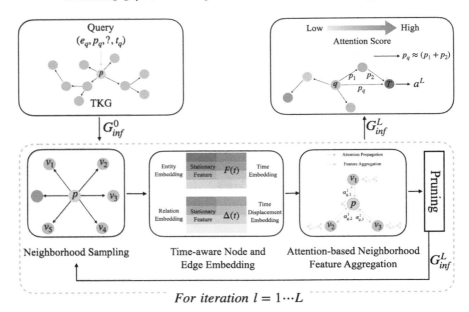

FIGURE 25.5   The architecture of Time-aware relation representation (TiAR).

adoption module, (2) the module for temporal node and edge embeddings, (3) the attention-based neighbor feature aggregation module, and (4) the subgraph pruning module (Mu et al., 2023).

Given the information of a query node, the establishment of a local knowledge base involves combining the predefined knowledge base. The initial step is to construct the node v_q for the first local knowledge base.

During an iteration, the graph expands the inference subgraph by sampling the preneighbors of the first node v_q through the neighbor adoption module. As the preneighbors are added to the subgraph, the edges between the two nodes are labeled as p_k, indicating the directed edge from v_q to v_j (neighbor node). Next, the embedding module is utilized to generate temporal features for nodes and edges. It is crucial to note that these temporal features are independent of the query.

Subsequently, the attention-based neighbor feature aggregation module computes the temporal feature attention scores for each edge. Then, the aggregation module propagates information within the subgraph based on these attention scores, generating temporal features for nodes and edges.

To mitigate the proliferation of the inference subgraph, the pruning module trims edges with lower attention scores, thereby reducing the overall number of edges.

During each iteration, information from nodes at a distance of one hop from the query node is sampled as neighboring nodes. After L iterations, a subgraph is generated consisting of neighbor nodes reached through L hops from the query node. In the final graph, the entity with the highest score in the inference subgraph is regarded as the query object. Furthermore, the subgraph can be viewed as a visual representation of the inference results.

With the above description, there is a certain understanding of the temporal knowledge graph techniques employed in the knowledge management layer. The next, section will delve into each process of graph data processing.

25.3.2.2.1 Neighbor sampling

During the inference process, it is necessary to sample information from all neighboring nodes adjacent to the query node. The color depth in the graph represents the magnitude of the correlation between neighboring nodes and the query node, expressed through attention scores.

However, as the iteration progresses, the number of nodes in the subgraph tends to grow exponentially, leading to subgraph explosion. Therefore, in the sampling process, a subset of nodes with higher attention scores within each hop distance is selected as neighboring nodes. This helps reduce the complexity of sampling. Additionally, if there is more than one predicate between neighboring nodes, at least one predicate needs to be sampled to represent the relationship between nodes.

It is important to note that bias is inevitable during the sampling process. To mitigate these influences of biases, sampling events closer to the current timestamp are used, as events that occurred earlier have a diminished impact on the current node (Mu et al., 2023). This strategy was generally employed as xERTE (Han et al., 2020), modeling bias through the use of a linear function.

25.3.2.2.2 Temporal node and edge embeddings

Its primary function lies in generating temporal features for nodes and edges when processing them. In a temporal knowledge graph, the presence of timestamps results in the relationships between entities changing over time as temporal dynamics come into play. Consequently, relationships between entities also continuously change over time.

In this module, a static approach was employed to generate features for entities and relationships in the graph. These features are represented by $\bar{e}_i \in R^{d_e}, \bar{p}_i \in R^{d_e}$, denoting embeddings for entities and relationships, respectively. R^{d_e} represents the size of the static features. To obtain these time-sensitive features, we utilize an encoding method (Goel et al., 2020) to generate time embeddings. This can be formulated as (Mu et al., 2023):

$$F(\tau) = \sqrt{\frac{1}{d}}[\cos(w_1\tau + d), \ldots, \cos(w_d\tau + d)] \in R^{d_\tau} \tag{25.1}$$

where R^{d_τ} represents the embeddings of time information. The representation of the generated node embedding is as follows (Mu et al., 2023):

$$e_i = \left[\bar{e}_i \| F(\tau)\right] \in R^{d_e + d_\tau} \tag{25.2}$$

Different relationships exhibit varying degrees of temporal sensitivity. However, conventional approaches tend to embed time directly into entity encoding during the construction of temporal knowledge graphs (TKGs), often overlooking this crucial aspect. To capture the temporal sensitivity features of relationships effectively, it becomes imperative to concurrently assimilate both the semantic information of relationships and the temporal difference information between the query timestamp and the timestamp associated with each fact. Specifically, the embedding of time-aware relationships (predicates) is defined as follows (Mu et al., 2023):

$$p_i = W_{\lambda(\Delta(\tau))}\left(\left[\overline{p}_I \| |\Delta(\tau)|\right]\right) \in R^{d_e + d_\tau} \tag{25.3}$$

where $\Delta(\tau) = F(\tau) - F(\tau_q)$ is represented as the magnitude of temporal differences. The variable W_λ is a learnable parameter that signifies the specific weight assigned to the magnitude of temporal differences for each relationship, taking into account their respective significance.

25.3.2.2.3 Aggregation of neighbor features based on attention

After the sampling phase, the relational reasoning process occurs within the inference subgraph. Within a KG, the diversity among neighbors signifies varying degrees of importance, underscoring the importance of capturing correlations between relationships.

In this process, two primary operations are predominantly executed: (1) adjustment of attention distribution pertaining to sampled edges, reflecting the semantic relevance strength between the query relationship and the newly sampled edges; (2) updating the latent representations of newly sampled nodes and relationships.

In this module, the input comprises embeddings of nodes and relationships present in the inference subgraph, while the output consists of a new set of hidden node and relationship representations. This is primarily achieved by computing an attention score for each relationship relative to the query (Mu et al., 2023).

To fine-tune the attention distribution, it was postulated that the tail entity within the present factual context serves as the target entity. The computed attention scores, coupled with pertinent query data, are deployed to evaluate the edge attention among individual nodes within the subgraph and their neighboring counterparts. Consequently, by incorporating the tail entity, the query forms a complete triple. This process facilitates the computation of edge attention scores, capturing the relevance of each node in the subgraph to the query. Described as (Mu et al., 2023):

$$e^l_{uv}(q, p_k) = Leaky\,Re\,LU\left(W^l_{p_k}(h^{l-1}_v \| p^{l-1}_k \| h^{l-1}_u) \cdot W^l_q(h^{l-1}_{e_q} \| p^{l-1}_q \| h^{l-1}_u)\right) \tag{25.4}$$

represents the attention score of the edge (v, p_k, u). Where p^{l-1}_k, p^{l-1}_q corresponds to the relationship embedding in the $(l-1)^{th}$ iteration. In the $(l-1)^{th}$ iteration, x and y represent the hidden layer representations of node v and query node q, respectively. In the initial iteration, weight initialization is performed using a linear function,

$$h^0_v = W_v e_i + b_v, \quad p^0_i = W_p p_i + b_p \tag{25.5}$$

where W^l_{pk}, W^l_q are two weight matrices.

Subsequently, the softmax function is employed to normalize attention scores, following the formula:

$$\alpha^l_{uv}(q, p_k) = \frac{\exp(e^l_{uv}(q, p_k))}{\sum_{i \in \widehat{N}} \sum_{p_j \in p_{iv}} \exp(e^l_{iv}(q, p_j))} \tag{25.6}$$

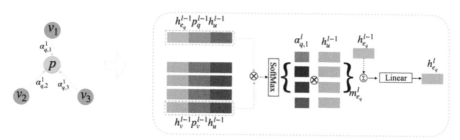

FIGURE 25.6 Aggregation process applied for node feature representations remains consistent.

There may exist multiple relationships between node and its neighbors, where p_j represents the set of relationships.

After obtaining attention scores, the model proceeds with localized aggregation of representations. The aggregation process of node features is depicted in Fig. 25.6, utilizing graph neural networks (GNNs) (Velickovic et al., 2017) to compute node representations. This mainly involves graph dependencies between nodes. The detailed description is as follows (Mu et al., 2023):

$$\tilde{m}_v^l = AGGRECATE(\{h_i^{l-1} : i \in \widehat{N_v}\}, h_v^{l-1}, p_j \in P_{iv}), \tag{25.7}$$

$$h_v^l = COMBINE(h_v^{l-1}, \tilde{m}_v^l) \tag{25.8}$$

In this module particularly, exclusively facilitates the transmission of messages from a node to its immediate neighbors, precluding the incorporation of future information. In the feature aggregation process for the inference subgraph, the module employs normalized scores of relevant edges to perform weighted aggregation on previous neighborhood representations. This process can be expressed in the following form:

$$\tilde{m}_v^l = \sum_{i \in \widehat{N_v}} \sum_{p_j \in P_{iv}} \alpha_{iv}^l(q, p_j) W_p^l h_i^{l-1} \tag{25.9}$$

where W_p^l denotes the transformation matrix for information propagation on the relationship p during the lth iteration. As a regularization method, a shared mechanism is employed in each layer's transformation matrix. In the lth iteration process, α_{iv}^l represents the attention connecting node i and v, while $\tilde{m}_v^l$ denotes the aggregated neighbor representations of node v in the lth iteration. Following this, the LeakyReLU activation function in the model's MLP generates a new hidden representation for node v by computing the aggregated neighborhood representation and the hidden representation of the lth node, as illustrated as follows (Mu et al., 2023):

$$h_v^l = MLP(W_h^l(\gamma h_v^{l-1} + (1 - \gamma)\tilde{m}_v^l) + b_h^l), \tag{25.10}$$

$$p_k^l = MLP(W_h^l(\gamma p_k^{l-1}) + b_h^l), \tag{25.11}$$

where γ is a hyperparameter. It is noteworthy that the layer updating relationship.

To empower the model in discerning the node most likely to be the target node, a similar strategy was employed to compute attention for each node (Mu et al., 2023), as delineated by the following equation:

$$a_v^l(q) = \sum_{i \in \widehat{N_v}} \sum_{p_j \in P_{iv}} \alpha_{iv}^l a_i^{l-1}(q),$$

(25.12)

where $a_v^l(q)$ represents the attention score of node v regarding query q in the lth iteration process. The propagation process is illustrated in Fig. 25.7.

25.3.2.2.4 Subgraph pruning

Introducing contribution scores allows for the identification of facts that are particularly significant during the inference process. This operation is typically executed subsequent to the acquisition of attention scores for both nodes and edges. The precise procedure is delineated as follows:

$$c_{uv}(p_k) = \alpha_{uv}^l(q, p_k) a_v^l(q)$$

(25.13)

where p_k represents the relationship between node v and neighbor node u. To reduce computational complexity, during each iteration of the inference process, only the top L edges with the highest attention scores are retained.

Finally, the result of the inference is obtained by selecting the entity with the highest score. Attention scores for nodes containing the same entity are aggregated using a summation function. If a specific entity is absent from the subgraph, its attention score is regarded as 0. The function is defined as follows (Mu et al., 2023):

$$a_{ei}^L(n) = sum(a_V^l(n))$$

where $v(e) = e_i$.

25.3.2.2.5 Path constraints

The aforementioned inference process relies solely on GNNs to learn feature conditions on neighbor nodes and relationships. However, this inference method has limitations: as it does not focus on the semantic interaction information of paths in the subgraph, it may compromise interpretability. However, some studies (Yang et al., 2014) have observed that in the recursive reasoning process of a->b->c, b can be viewed as representing the relationship connecting a and c. Therefore, it assumes that in a path, with the head node and the remaining part as the body nodes in the path, if these nodes are semantically similar, they are deemed trustworthy.

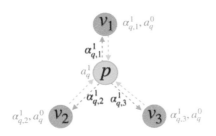

FIGURE 25.7   Propagation process of node attention.

Based on this intuition, constraints are enforced to enhance the search for target node path features, aiming to improve the model's capabilities in subgraph exploration and reasoning. To illustrate this approach, consider the following path:

$$p_2(z, x) \wedge p_1(y, z) \to p_0(x, y) \tag{25.14}$$

Typically, once a query and a set of predicates are known, it is necessary to establish a set of constraints. When these constraints are satisfied, the inference path is considered correct; otherwise, it is deemed incorrect. It is important to note that there may be more than one path between nodes, and this is also within the comparison between the aggregation process of paths and constraints illustrated in the following Fig. 25.8. Constraints can be defined in the following form:

$$P_{e_q, e_i} \approx \sum_{P_j \in Path(x,y)} \sum_{k \in P_j} c_{uv}(p_k) p_k^L \tag{25.15}$$

where P_{e_q, e_i} represents the path from the query entity to the answer entity, and $c_{vu}(p_k)$ is the contribution score of the relationship. It is worth noting that, besides this function, tasks of aggregation can also be accomplished using techniques such as Gated Recurrent Unit (GRU), CNN, and others. However, this substitution would concurrently increase the model's parameter count and complexity, which needs to be explored in future work.

25.3.2.2.6 Loss functions

The objective is to perform reasoning using temporal knowledge graphs (TKGs). Accordingly, the obtained node is partitioned allowing data into training, testing, and validation sets based on timestamp values. The task is defined as a multiclass classification problem, consistent with the formulation introduced by xERTE (Han et al., 2020). The cross-entropy loss function is employed and is defined as follows:

$$L_1 = -\frac{1}{|Q|} \sum_{q \in Q} \frac{1}{|\varepsilon_{\inf}(q)|} \sum_{ei \in \varepsilon_{\inf(q)}} (y_{ei,q} \log(\widehat{y}_{ei,q}) + (1 - y_{ei,q})\log(1 - \widehat{y}_{ei,q})) \tag{25.16}$$

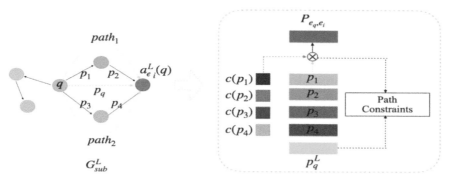

FIGURE 25.8 The left side of the figure depicts the subgraph generated by the final iteration. The right side of the figure illustrates the aggregation process used for the path features work (Mu et al., 2023).

Here, $\varepsilon_{\text{inf}}(q)$ is the set of entities in the KG, and the binary label $y_{ei,q}$ is used to indicate whether the entity e_i can answer the query q.

In the path constraint, we introduce the cosine function as the loss function,

$$L_2 = (P_{e_q,e_i}, p_q^L) = 1 - \frac{P_{eq,ei} \cdot p_q^L}{||P_{eq,ei}|| \cdot ||p_q^L||} \tag{25.17}$$

where p_q^L represents the features from the last iteration of querying predicates. The model's loss function consists of two components as follows:

$$L = L_1 + L_2(P_{eq,ei}, p_q^L) \tag{25.18}$$

25.3.2.2.7 Computational complexity analysis

In this section, a computational complexity analysis was employed for the proposed model. Assuming that during the sampling process, each node samples at most E edges, and N is the number of nodes in the subgraph. In each iteration, the computational complexity of the sampling process is $O(NE)$, where each node visits E edges. In the aggregation module, the computational complexity for calculating d-dimensional features is determined by $O(d^2 * N) + O(d * N)$. Finally, the primary function of the path constraint module is to compute the summation of path features, with a computational complexity of $O(pd)$, where p denotes the number of paths in the subgraph. Consequently, when the number of iterations is known as L, the model's complexity can be expressed as follows:

$$O((E * N + d^2 * E + d * N) * L + d * P).$$

When the total number of nodes in the graph is significantly greater than the number of nodes in the subgraph, the model's complexity will be relatively lower than that of the entire graph model. Complexity can be mitigated by reducing the number of sampled edges (E) or by decreasing the number of nodes within the subgraph (Mu et al., 2023). However, this may result in a performance decline in downstream tasks. In addition, the feature aggregation module determines the spatial complexity of the Time-aware relation representation (TiAR) model since the feature matrix for each node requires storage space. Calculations with relatively lower space complexity, such as edge sampling or path feature computation processes, can be disregarded. Moreover, employing a weighted aggregation approach for computing path features can reduce the model's complexity while concurrently decreasing the number of parameters.

25.3.2.3 Decision-making

In the second layer, the information acquired which is needed for decision-making, including node-specific details and path information. Simultaneously, each node serves as a local knowledge base, represented as a subgraph. In contrast to (Zhang et al., 2017), the knowledge processing workflow was streamlined by employing a temporal knowledge graph (TKG) for operations such as knowledge selection and fusion. This approach enhances interpretability, as each inference process is associated with specific paths, allowing for a clear understanding of the directionality of each path in relation to the decision-making process.

In this layer, the task is decision-making, which occurs at the node level rather than globally, distinguishing it from other models that make decisions at a global scale. While this model incorporates a global decision unit, it serves merely as an adaptive process. It is noteworthy that, in contrast to the adaptive process in (Zhang et al., 2017), the model handles the adaptive process in the second layer. Through subgraph pruning and iterative updates, the adaptive process continually adjusts the weights and quantities of neighboring nodes, achieving adaptability. This approach reduces computational costs while enhancing efficiency.

The proposed knowledge representation method in the model adheres to the format of data in KGs, making it suitable for the management of applications relevant to human activities. The expert system is responsible for the decision-making process, and automation is realized through a time-driven architecture: rules are employed to determine when events occur. Once an event is confirmed, the decision-making process is initiated based on the established facts.

25.4 Conclusion

The principal aim of the chapter is to propose a novel model for a KG-based IoT system within the healthcare domain, with the overarching goal of furnishing more support for practical IoT applications. The model integrates four primary methodologies: sensor and RFID technology for data acquisition and environment identification, a temporal knowledge graph for knowledge processing and inference culminating in decision-making, and a decision model providing support for IoT applications. These methodologies collectively facilitate adaptive functionality for knowledge employed in decision-making processes. The process involves utilizing the results of environmental recognition as criteria to select multiple predictive knowledge bases. Subsequently, the knowledge processing module in the temporal knowledge graph is employed. This entails establishing a local knowledge base through the neighbor sampling module, and embedding temporal representations for nodes and edges using the temporal node and edge embedding module. Knowledge fusion is achieved through an attention-based neighbor feature aggregation module. Subsequently, the subgraph pruning module is utilized to trim edges with lower attention, reducing their quantity and averting an explosion of the local knowledge base. Moreover, acknowledging the complexity and dynamics of the real world, adjustments are made to the weights and quantities of nodes in the subgraph during each iteration, further refining the local knowledge base.

While the model finds application in medical scenarios, it represents just one facet. The model can be extended to numerous decision-supporting scenarios, such as question-and-answer systems, intelligent customer service aiding in decision-making, or chatbots capable of offering professional guidance. Notably, the output structure of the model is interpretable, providing insights into the specific reasoning process behind decisions. This transparency allows for the identification and correction of erroneous decisions. This feature can guide future research endeavors by offering valuable insights.

References

Biazar, S. M., Shehadeh, H. A., Ghorbani, M. A., Golmohammadi, G., & Saha, A. (2024). Soil temperature forecasting using a hybrid artificial neural network in Florida subtropical grazinglands agro-ecosystems. *Scientific Reports, 14*(1), 1535.

Cao, Y., Xia, H., Tan, X., Shi, C., Ma, Y., Meng, D., ... Jin, Y. (2024). Intratumoural microbiota: a new frontier in cancer development and therapy. *Signal Transduction and Targeted Therapy, 9*(1), 15.

Castano, S., et al. (2024). Enforcing legal information extraction through context-aware techniques: The ASKE approach. *Computer Law & Security Review, 52*105903.

Chandak, P., Huang, K., & Zitnik, M. (2023). Building a knowledge graph to enable precision medicine. *Scientific Data, 10*(1), 67.

Eberhardt, J., Bilchik, A., & Stojadinovic, A. (2012). Clinical decision support systems: potential with pitfalls. *Journal of Surgical Oncology, 105*(5), 502–510.

Goel, R., Kazemi, S.M., Brubaker, M., & Poupart, P. (2020, April). Diachronic embedding for temporal knowledge graph completion. In *Proceedings of the AAAI conference on artificial intelligence* (Vol. 34, No. 04, pp. 3988–3995).

Han, Z., Chen, P., Ma, Y., & Tresp, V. (2020, October). Explainable subgraph reasoning for forecasting on temporal knowledge graphs. In *International conference on learning representations*.

Ji, S., Pan, S., Cambria, E., Marttinen, P., & Philip, S. Y. (2021). A survey on knowledge graphs: Representation, acquisition, and applications. *IEEE transactions on neural networks and learning systems, 33*(2), 494–514.

Jianjun, H. A. O., & Jin, L. I. (2011). Determination of threshold for energy detection in cognitive radio sensor networks. *China Communications, 8*(1), 14–19.

Kan, X., Cui, H., & Yang, C. (2021). Zero-shot scene graph relation prediction through commonsense knowledge integration. In *Machine learning and knowledge discovery in databases. Research track: European conference, ECML PKDD 2021, Proceedings, Part II* (Vol. 21, pp. 466–482), Bilbao, Spain, September 13–17, 2021. Springer International Publishing.

Lang, Q., Liu, X., & Jia, W. (2022). AFS graph: multidimensional axiomatic fuzzy set knowledge graph for open-domain question answering. In *IEEE Transactions on neural networks and learning systems*.

Mu, C., Zhang, L., Ma, Y., & Tian, L. (2023). Temporal knowledge subgraph inference based on time-aware relation representation. *Applied Intelligence, 53*(20), 24237–24252.

Omar, K., & Al-Shaar, M. (2023, May). Method for Arabic text summarization using statistical features and word2vector approach. In *Proceedings of the 2023 9th international conference on computer technology applications* (pp. 258-262).

Ostermann, T., Burkart, J., De Jaegere, S., Raak, C., & Simoens, S. (2023). Overview and quality assessment of health economic evaluations for homeopathic therapy: An updated systematic review. *Expert Review of Pharmacoeconomics & Outcomes Research*, 1–26.

Rajkomar, A., Oren, E., Chen, K., Dai, A. M., Hajaj, N., Hardt, M., ... Dean, J. (2018). Scalable and accurate deep learning with electronic health records. *NPJ Digital Medicine, 1*(1), 18.

Santos, A., Colaço, A. R., Nielsen, A. B., Niu, L., Strauss, M., Geyer, P. E., ... Mann, M. (2022). A knowledge graph to interpret clinical proteomics data. *Nature Biotechnology, 40*(5), 692–702.

Sheth, A., Padhee, S., & Gyrard, A. (2019). Knowledge graphs and knowledge networks: the story in brief. *IEEE Internet Computing, 23*(4), 67–75.

Velickovic, P., Cucurull, G., Casanova, A., Romero, A., Lio, P., & Bengio, Y. (2017). Graph attention networks. *Stat, 1050*(20), 10–48550.

Wang, J., Yan, Y., & Zhao, G. (2023). Self-evolving reasoning for task-user relationships in mobile crowdsensing via the autonomic knowledge graph. *Artificial Intelligence Review, 56*(Suppl 3), 3789–3819.

Wang, P., Jiang, H., Xu, J., & Zhang, Q. (2019). Knowledge graph construction and applications for web search and beyond. *Data Intelligence, 1*(4), 333–349.

Yang, B., Yih, W. T., He, X., Gao, J., & Deng, L. (2014). Embedding entities and relations for learning and inference in knowledge bases. *arXiv preprint arXiv, 1412*, 6575.

Yang, H. (2023). Research and implementation of intelligent monitoring and evaluation system for farm animals breeding environment. *Automatic Control and Computer Sciences, 57*(4), 355–363.

Zhang, L., Alharbe, N. R., & Atkins, A. S. (2017). A self-adaptive distributed decision support model for Internet of Things applications. *Transactions of the Institute of Measurement and Control, 39*(4), 404–419.

Zhong, M., Zheng, Y., Xue, G., & Liu, M. (2022). Reliable keyword query interpretation on summary graphs. *IEEE Transactions on Knowledge and Data Engineering, 35*(5), 5187–5202.

Zhou, S., Dai, X., Chen, H., Zhang, W., Ren, K., Tang, R., ... Yu, Y. (2020, July). Interactive recommender system via knowledge graph-enhanced reinforcement learning. In *Proceedings of the 43rd international ACM SIGIR conference on research and development in information retrieval* (pp. 179–188).

MedSync: blockchain-driven electronic health record on cloud

C.M. Nalayini, Shruthi Arunkumar and K.S. Jaishree

Department of Information Technology, Velammal Engineering College, Surapet, Chennai, Tamil Nadu, India

26.1 Introduction

26.1.1 Background

Thus, the forms of electronic health records (EHRs) storage have been changed over a period of time. Initially in healthcare informatics, humans managed EHR data using somewhat antiquated procedures that relied heavily on manual labor and lacked the sophistication and security precautions available today. In modern healthcare, the use of cutting-edge storage solutions has been gradually embraced on the record of technological development, while centralized databases and server-based architectures still hold sway. The applicability of these methods is reasonable, yet their security, integrity, and data access have been discussed.

Today's EHR environment employs a multiplicity of data storage platforms and technologies. Healthcare professionals have researched several alternatives, from cloud-based systems to on-premise servers, for the purpose of digital health records catering to the increased demand. This paper scrutinizes various uses of cloud computing for the healthcare sector with a focus on the benefits such as information accessibility, operational efficiency and far-reaching for the physicians. This issue focuses on interoperability issues, security concerns, privacy issues, and data ownership. The intercloud transition will allow for improving patient safety, provide cost-effective storage solutions and create favorable conditions for data analysis and research. To enable a successful roll-out, concretion of the infrastructure, observance of regulations, and removal of organizational barriers shall be of paramount importance. We can easily achieve interoperability among different systems with SNOMED and ICD-10. Thinking about everything as a whole, cloud computing opens up a huge prospect for the healthcare sector yet it is necessary to handle security, privacy,

Sensor Networks for Smart Hospitals
DOI: https://doi.org/10.1016/B978-0-443-36370-2.00027-X

and legal compliance in an imprecise way (Singh et al., 2022). To ensure security and transactions with the exponentially increasing health records, an encapsulated architecture is developed which combines blockchain functionality into cloud platforms and also solves security and privacy issues. Cloud service providers have facilitated managing of the Blockchain as a Service (BaaS), which is friendly to a healthcare organization. Privacy and Security issues have not been erased though, and there is still insufficiency of confidence in the cloud service providers. However, it is also worth noting that by using AI to boost the privacy of data, scalability, and the level of accuracy in diagnosis, the IBcC architecture has a vast potential to transform the healthcare system completely (Ismail et al., 2021). To come up with a solution that will take care of the limitations of the current system and the need for innovative solutions, it is important to know the history of this development.

EHRs are primarily stored in a number of ways based on various types of electronic technologies and databases in today's healthcare. Numerous health organizations deploy centralized database systems and those systems allow for the rational running of patient records. Electronic medical records (EMRs) systems are widely used by healthcare providers; there are stand-alone systems and systems which are incorporated into centralized databases. Interoperability is supported by the adoption of health information exchange technologies, which enable different healthcare providers to share their EHRs safely. Cloud-based solutions are so appealing to users thanks to the cloud scalability and accessibility of distant servers. This approach offers economic and effective storage, resulting in its increasing popularity. Vendor-specific EHR systems, which are provided by specialized vendors and possess features adapted to the healthcare sector, are heavily implemented. Two important standards, HL7 and FHIR should be applied to ensure the smooth sharing of health information between different systems. Among the two security techniques, encryption and access controls are the essential ones which secure data from privacy breaches and stop anyone from unauthorized access. The changes taking place in the health system requirements and technical innovations lead to a continuous evolution of the landscape of EHR storage.

To deal with a security and confidentiality problem of healthcare systems EHR sharing, the paper gives a solution secure and robust healthcare-based blockchain. Under attribute-based encryption, it ensures the confidential transfer of patient data obtained by wearable devices from a centralized system for processing. Blockchain lowers latency, increases the speed of system running and success rate in comparison with traditional methods, and provides anonymity by creating unique blocks for each record. This means not only the patients, insurance brokers, and medical professionals, but also facilitates the exchange of data by simplifying its encoding (Mubarakali, 2020).

26.1.2 Problem statement

Looking at the present stage of EHR systems' data storage, the current strategy has crucial limitations and has problems for the healthcare system. Security flaws in centralized storage systems are often among the things that are most worrisome. These systems can be easily forged, illegally accessed or their data can be tampered with, which may compromise the integrity and confidentiality of patients' data. Additionally, whether data of the EHRs is true is raised due to the lack of the method of tamper proof from the conventional storage techniques.

Accessibility issues of the type caused by the slowness of the current storage approach make the problems even worse. The faulty communication and teamwork among medical practitioners handicaps the proper flow of information among them, and it may impinge on patient care. Centralized data repositories are also a privacy concern, as the probability of data leak among organizations or government agencies would occur. Also, the data could be used legally at any time, which may cause problems later on. This is important as they need to be looked into to guarantee the security of EHR data.

26.1.3 Objectives

The growing problem of the present EHR data storage seems to have a solution implemented with the technologies of blockchain and cloud serving together. Blockchain would be the greatest support for healthcare data since that is basically the technology that allows you to believe that your data are intact and cannot be changed. The integrity of data in EHR can be ensured by decentralizing storage and utilizing cryptographic methods, which stem the associated risks of centralized systems.

Blockchain technology has now been enriched by cloud computing thereby making the EHR data much more accessible, scalable, and flexible. Overall, healthcare systems run smoothly when data from different servers become easy to gather and access. The employment of cloud technology to keep blockchain-based eHealth records is intended to increase data security, preserve data integrity, and make sure that authorized parties can share and cooperate on treatment-related issues easily. This novel approach seeks to better the present EHR storage limitations thus developing a healthcare system that is patient-centered, safer and more effective.

Through the patient-centered study, the system that utilizes blockchain technology, as well as enhanced privacy, is recommended. The user data remains in user-centric EHR settings thanks to permissioned blockchain blocks where this information is stored. The system utilizes elliptic curve cryptography (ECC) to guarantee that information is securely encrypted and pseudonymous, which, in turn, obstructs the passage of unauthorized persons. Analyzing smart contract financial viability and data processing rules is a very important process in understanding how the system protects patient privacy well (Al Omar et al., 2019).

26.2 Literature review on blockchain-based electronic health record systems

In the MedChain model, a decentralized network was established to connect healthcare providers with major providers and minor providers like super peers and edge peers. The system is a Certificate Authority that we can trust, a directory service for organizing medical data and a blockchain service. The architecture of the system includes blockchain servers, directory servers, and healthcare databases as well. MedChain guarantees privacy and makes users willing to adopt the platform by feeding on the same data instead of shifting it. ECC is used for security; the necessary components are encryption keys, roles, and health records (Shen et al., 2019). The authors underline the way blockchain-based EHR systems enrich interoperability and guarantee privacy protection for patients while analyzing many of these technical systems. It describes solutions such as Healthcare Blockchain System, Ancile, MedRec, and OmniPHR that use blockchain and smart contracts to implement and maintain privacy and security. Nevertheless, a lack of confidence between medical workers and patients, disparities in access and energy needs and blockchain inefficiencies are also discussed. The proposed solutions are as follows: the legal frameworks and privacy differences as the means for resolving these challenges. Finally, when implementing blockchain into EHRs, a collaborative effort is necessary to deliver a successful working of the system, ethnic parity and trust in the appropriate use of healthcare data (Han et al., 2022). In this study, a blockchain-based solution for efficient and secure cloud storage of EHRs is presented: We propose to further develop the current version of our TAC-EHR. Employing a blockchain technology and its decentralized structure offers tamper-proofing and resolves issues related to data security and integrity. EHRs are acyclic into Ethereum blockchain transactions and the InterPlanetary File System (IPFS) for scalability and accessibility. Security arrangement makes illegal surgeons and service providers in cloud computing unable to work together to compromise the functionality, integrity, confidentiality, and availability of EHRs. In addition, it improves the overall security and effectiveness of the management of EHRs by making use of a key-agreement system with password protection for safe communication (Ramesh et al., 2023). An elastic cybersecurity strategy for cloud-based EHR management is given in the paper. EHRs have an authentication and verification support system in place to protect some of the attacks and retain their validity. The security features of the EMCE encryption algorithm proposed are achieved through early scrambling and diffusion. The TL-CH de-duplication method is beneficial as it helps in reducing the collision as well as false negative rates during the recognition of duplicate data chunks. By performance evaluation and security proof, one can see that the method is better than the former in terms of computation time, storage capacity and verification delay, but the system resists any attack. Eventually, this plan ensures auditable online health record storage with integrity control, confidentiality, and authentication features (Benil & Jasper, 2023). This research puts the blockchain and decentralized storage as the innovative way of sharing the mobile cloud EHR service. In doing so, there are some main contributions like the user access control framework that manages data access, smart contracts-based data access control mechanisms, and data sharing protocol. Usability testing of an Android application and measurements of performance on AWS serves as the initial evidence that the proposed paradigm is practical and effective. The article features a comparative assessment and security analysis to show that it comes with improved security relative to existing methods of sharing EHRs. In addition, it offers an introduction to blockchain principles as well as system design objectives (Nguyen et al., 2019). The focus of this article is the concept of "Healthcare 4.0" where in the healthcare sector digitization and data processing technologies are experiencing rapid development. It talks about paper-based and digital medical record transition and stresses its importance for the fast and efficient sharing and disseminating of medical data. Data security, integrity and privacy concerns are largely discussed, emphasizing the need for a strong data management framework. Through the document, the function of blockchain systems in the context of medical data sharing and storage is discussed, especially the issue of a dissemination model and the immutability of the system. It presents a holistic evaluation of blockchain-based security options and identifies future directions for the research community to expand the knowledge base on Healthcare 4.0 (Mahajan et al., 2023). This article suggests a blockchain-based EHR solution integrated with

Aadhaar, an Indian Unique Patient Identifier (UPI). The issue thematizes the shortcomings of the existing EHR systems and it points out interoperability and standardization as the key drivers of health systems. The design proposed encompasses these issues through the use of blockchain technology that offers traceability, immutability, decentralization and heightened security. The framework using Aadhaar as UPI aims to build a people-driven standardized, interoperable and unified EHR system to connect the whole of India (Singh et al., 2023). In this paper, we develop a blockchain technology that drives an EHR system which is cloud-based, using the IPFS technology and the Ethereum blockchain network. The structure of the given architecture is a combination of the Blockchain Handshake protocol, which is a cloud-based EHR management system, and data storage services. The system has users (admin, doctors and patients) who can connect with it through the prevailing dashboards. Steps in the process are writing up medical records, putting them on IPFS, and using the transaction IDs to securely retrieve them. Physicians provide a review and update of patient records, and system administrators ensure the software runs smoothly. Patients are allowed to access their information and make any change within the proposed architecture in such a way that data is kept confidential and there is safe access to their data (Nishi et al., 2022). The paper informs on the role of cloud networks in the interchange of data among providers and in protecting and securing the platforms where personal health records (PHR), EHRs, and EMRs are stored. It also draws attention to the security risks connected with that data, medical and puts forward blockchain as a possible answer to this puzzle. Blockchain technology offers a decentralized consensus, data integrity, and patients' ownership over data, thus improving its security and the possibility of certifying the genesis and immutability of any medical information. On the other hand blockchain technology requires to carefully analyze the costs, compatibilities and the regulatory policies (Esposito et al., 2018). The study presents a cloudless platform on blockchain as a potential remedy for e-health systems that outsource to the cloud due to security and privacy concerns. Its use of pairing-based cryptography to produce tamper-proof data has since then been linked to blockchain transactions, it provides another means that ensures the security of electronic health data (EHRs). In addition, secure payment protocols apply smart contracts that facilitate trustful real-time interaction between patients and hospitals as well as the cloud service provider (CSPs). The performance review shows that the system works efficiently and security analysis proves that the system has the resistiveness to different attacks (Zhang et al., 2022). The paper gives a description on the creation of the EHR system by means of blockchain using the Hyperledger Fabric and Composer tools. The system involves four main parties: administrators, clinicians/doctors, patients and labs. The patients and the patients only update data for those who have been permitted to do so; while laboratories and physicians can only update the information. Administrators configure the network and control the encryption. Medical records are the assets in the network and any operation concerning their creation, access, and modification constitutes a transaction (118 words). Hyperledger Fabric consists of plug-and-play components, and Composer makes it easier to develop smart contracts. Some of these phases include data collection, node deployment, networking, establishment of recordkeeping, transaction creation, and node allocation (Sharma & Balamurugan, 2020). Blockchain application is examined in the study to resolve data privacy and security issues in healthcare. The spotlight is placed on how vital the protection of the patient's privacy is, even if wearable IoT devices and the use of predictive modeling improve healthcare outcomes. The proposed framework makes use of blockchain for secure utilization and analysis of the information; it also ensures the acquittal from the shortcomings of the tra-ditional system and wider safety of the personal medical data (Sharma et al., 2020). This research offers a cloud approach employing keyless signature infrastructure and blockchain technology for the purpose of enhancing security, integrity, and authentication of health elec-tronic records. It uses Health Level Seven (HL7) International Healthcare Standards Organization criteria and Fast Healthcare Interoperability Resources (FHIR) standards to bring the system level to cybersecurity attacks and maintain confidentiality. The evaluation's results indicate that the integration of blockchain technologies with healthcare data management is efficient, and the results show significant performance increases with regard to time and cost reduction over more conventional approaches (Nagasubramanian et al., 2020). This study pro-poses an architecture based on the software as a service (SaaS) that uses the software as a ser-vice model for the purpose of the security of EHRs and prescriptions. the solution is based on the combination of cloud storage, a not only SQL (NoSQL) database and blockchain technolo-gies supplying data integrity, authentication, and confidentiality. Licensed doctors can do this activity using the system's graphical front end as well as the Python web server. The patients' data is anonymized and stored in a NoSQL database and an Ethereum private network where the smart contracts are executed. Data is uploaded to a local storage instance that guarantees professional data protection rules. Research by the performance shows that transactions can be executed successfully. However, the scalability is made possible by the Proof-of-Work of Ethereum (Ruggeri et al., 2020). The article aims at highlighting the impact of Information Technology on the health sector by pointing out the urgency for digitization of the data to overcome the information glut and enhance the quality of medical care. It is the emphasis on advantages of cloud computing which makes it feasible and inexpensive to counter these pro-blems. The paper presents the cloud-based service delivery system in healthcare and the case study on the service that is being implemented (John & Shenoy, 2014). In this study, we sys-tematically compare and analyze the best blockchain research works related to healthcare published between 2008 and 2019. After stringent criteria and a rigorous screening process, 33 articles were included. Judgment: Moderate Extent of filtering and screening of the review method is monitored by CASP Systematic Review Checklist. The data was extracted from the articles in respect to who's who, contributions, the health goals of adopting blockchain tech-nology, real-world uses, blockchain components, and use of smart contracts. Among the most outstanding contributions of blockchain to the health sector are the areas of data sharing, sup-ply chains, auditing, health records management, and identity management (Hölbl et al., 2018). This article systematically examines blockchain research in the healthcare sector, focus-ing on new technological paths and approaches that evolved from 2008 to 2019. A total of 33 publications met the inclusion criteria after accepting only the most rigorous standards and carefully screening the articles. The review stage of the intervention was moderated by CASP Systematic Review Checklist. A mix of the publication's data included the main information, the contribution, the objectives to introduce blockchain technology into healthcare, the avail-ability of real-life applications, components of blockchains, and smart contracts. Probably, the most noteworthy improvements that blockchain has enabled in healthcare are the areas it is used for exchange of data, supply chain management, audit trails, health record management and access control (Mayer et al., 2020). The recent evolution of remote medical services and the necessity of EHR sharing motivates this study to develop an EHR system sharing and integration in healthcare clouds. Thus, the system will use cloud computing technology to make it possible for remote access to medical information and services. This further emphasizes the importance of solid security methods as it indicates the threats to privacy and security that come up when using or administering this kind of the EHRs in these environments (Chen et al., 2012). In this work, CHISTAR, an approach that leverages clouds to achieve interoperability within EHRs systems, is presented. To reach semantic interoperability, CHISTAR use a generic design model that combines an archetype model and a model of reference for data aspects of clinics. This solves the problems affordability, data quality, and data interoperability standards. The system takes the design of cloud components as its architecture which has flexible links and allows synchronous intercommunication. This work describes the overall architecture of CHISTAR with focus on semantic interoperability, data integration and security through regard (Bahga & Madisetti, 2013). The presented structure utilizes the features of endogenous cryptography such as IBE, ABE, and IBS to provide a secure architecture for EHR systems. Data integrity and traceability is ensured through blockchain technology. The system effectively offers access control, data integrity, and confidentiality, in addition to authentication for medical records. We propose to develop a healthcare insurance demonstration application that combines all security prerequisites into one cryptography system (Wang & Song, 2018). This chapter delves into privacy protection and data integrity in the framework of cloud-assisted eHealth service, where criminal doctors who cooperate with cloud servers can pollute the EHRs of patients who are outsourced. The current programs do not have a mechanism that ensures authenticity and accuracy of medical records, when physicians customized and outsourced their own personal health records. The proposed TP-EHR solution is designed in such a way that it supports distributed verification and tampers-the-proofing of transactions through the use of the blockchain technology to record EHR transactions without the need to rely on reliable third parties. An approach of password-based key agreement method preserves the communication channel between the physician and patient and improves the security of password guessing attacks. The effectiveness of TP-EHR is demonstrated by the performance tests and in terms of security the system is able to hold its end even in the face of threat of any collusion (Cao et al., 2019). The paper looks closely at the increased popularity of the cloud-based electronic health systems, known as eHealth Systems, in the healthcare sector. It spotlights the advantages of these systems in that they can assist to archive and handle EHRs. Yet, cloud services have security and privacy issues as they are centralized and face difficulties in fine-grained data sharing. The article recommends Blockchain Consortium in Energy Systems (BCES), a blockchain-based eHealth system that has been designed for easy revision of transaction logs, flexible access restrictions, and the safety of EHR data. BCES can guard its assets against multiple threats using blockchain features. Proof of concept and performance tests are used to verify reliability and efficiency (Huang et al., 2021). EHR storage in cloud environments is the main theme for this study, specifically regarding the availability, confidentiality, and integrity of such storage. It proposes the effectiveness of EHR transactions management and information security and integrity by using a deletable consortium blockchain, also known as "DS-Chain." What's more, there is the suggestion of a multicloud storage approach which can increase scalability and resilience against single points of failure (Mishra et al., 2022). This report draws attention to the use of EHRs in healthcare systems but it is also important to note its challenges in regard to patient privacy and security. It unfolds problems like detecting frauds, fake medicines and the vulnerability issues associated with wearable sensors and Internet of Things (IoT). Based on the study, the medical industry could adopt the blockchain technology which could over time develop both the security and privacy more. It performs a detailed analysis of the existing Blockchain-based techniques which are classified as being their positive sides, negative sides, and research orientations (Cao et al., 2020). These findings are of importance to healthcare systems as they confirm the added value and usefulness of EHRs, but they also caution about the issues of patient privacy and security. It covers areas such as fraud detection, fake medicines and cybersecurity in that of smart sensors and the IoT. Modern medicine can be protected legally and eliminate security and privacy concerns by using blockchain technology (according to the study). It gives a comprehensive analysis of the current Blockchain-based methods, highlighting their reasons, benefits, limitations, and guidance on their future research (Murala et al., 2023). This study supports the exploration of the usage of blockchain technology widely in healthcare through employing a different approach based on the existing research in this regard. However, the review now is systematizing literature reviews and mapping research which is different from previous reviews that only used the specific case study approach. It examines employment of blockchain in healthcare to identify strong and weak points and to define a course for future actions. Further, the assessment of the 65 chosen publications state the technical tools, approach, and ideas, and that which can be an opportunity for the future research. It's interesting that it gives attention to more modern contexts and trends, showing the quickly growing number of healthcare blockchain studies. The paper ends with a technical summary, research methodologies, results, discussion, and more importantly, some suggestions on the need for further research (Agbo et al., 2019). Particular blockchain strategies aimed at handling patient-centric protocols, record management, and healthcare data exchange are very well represented and assessed in this study. Many of them take advantage of blockchain technology's immutability, decentralization, and cryptographic security to fix the data integrity, interoperability, and access control problems that arise in healthcare systems. The existing systems apply various consensus models, smart contracts and cryptographic methods to ensure secure data transmission, patient privacy as well as the Health Insurance Portability and Accountability Act (HIPAA) regulatory compliance. But there are challenges such as scalability, implementation, and efficiency in the area, and it necessitates more research and development in the blockchain solutions in healthcare (Zubaydi et al., 2019). The piece looks at the rising security requirement of EHRs as growth in cyber threats escalates. It draws out the significance of the use of blockchain technology in the setting up of a central repository for health data collection. We suggest a holistic architecture that integrates sensors, databases, the IoT, and computational capacity to address the security and privacy issues of EHR which are superior to the security and privacy of traditional healthcare systems with the goal of lowering the cybersecurity risks in the healthcare sector (Quasim et al., 2020). The study offers a new hybrid approach based on the blockchain technology to secure COVID-19 induced data storage pitfalls of healthcare information. Patient safety is ensured by the integration of distributed and centralized blockchain functions, which provide the interoperability between different medical facilities and equipment. It develops information privacy through the access to patients, hospitals, and third parties data by the help of Ethereum-based smart contracts that manage the access. The cost of deployment is the only disadvantage that sees its competitors appear superior in interoperability, scalability, and data ownership. Prospective goals pursue to put into practice the hybrid approach to take the manner of health data security to a superior degree (Verma et al., 2022).

26.3 Methodology

Fig. 26.1 Methodology Flowchart

26.3.1 Storing electronic health record data in blockchain

The medical data storage technique of EHRs is now conducted on a distributed ledger of blockchain systems. Blockchain technology ensures secure data storage and sharing on a distributed and tamper-proof open ledger by authorized parties. Regardless of whether these should be public, private or consortium blockchains, the choice of the right blockchain architecture is crucial to securely storing the EHRs. A type of solution for a blockchain that has a trade-off balance between data control and decentralization is also a hybrid solution. Adequate consideration should be given to the nature of the data structure to be used in the EHR records technology that is to be stored and retrieved in the block chain to ensure secure access to the patients' information. Patient-sensitive data is secured and available only authorized people through the use of techniques for cryptography such as asymmetric cryptography. On the one hand, smart contracts maintain access permissions and on the other hand, they guarantee compliance with Data sharing agreements. Patients might delegate who may view their EHR and under what conditions by merging consent processes into the smart contracts. It creates more privacy and also complies with laws such as the General Data Protection Regulation (GDPR) and HIPAA.

Interoperability standards such as HL7 FHIR are instrumental in the provision of an uninterrupted data flow and efficient communication between different healthcare systems. Using established protocols, the healthcare providers can have access to EHR data kept in the blockchain without shifting from the platforms to one another, thus improving the delivery of healthcare services and coordination. Scalability problems related to the use of blockchain technology need to be addressed so as to store millions of EHR data on a daily basis. The throughput and performance of the blockchain network are highly improved with the use of strategies such as sharding, sidechains, or layer 2 solutions that deliver fast access to the patient's data. Applying blockchain technology transparency, appropriate audit trails and provenance of EHR data become an option.

Like a forensic audit, each ledger in the blockchain has a generated timestamp and cryptographic linkage, this provides a tamper-proof history of data access and modifications. The use of the blockchain as a storage medium for EHR requires very much adherence to local data protection laws and regulatory frameworks like the GDPR and HIPAA. Privacy protection consists of using differential privacy or zero-knowledge proofs in practice. These technologies allow to ensure the privacy of patients while complying with legal requirements. The blockchain infrastructure needs to routinely be inspected and managed to locate and eliminate any possible security breakdowns or sluggishness. The blockchain system can be trusted since the EHR data is safe from the illegal passing through and modification of privacy data by proactive legal provisions as well as automatic monitoring systems.

The main objective of the proposed framework is the creation of a scalable, robust, and secure private and personalized blockchain-based EHR system. Seen are its three core modules namely the User Layer, Blockchain Layer and System Implementation. Patients—including doctors, nurses and office personnel—interact with the system and access features relative to

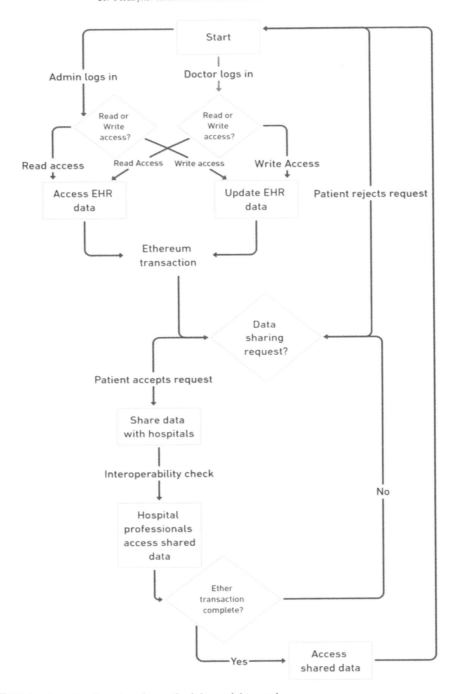

FIGURE 26.1   Show the flowchart for methodology of this work.

their functions by using a DApp browser. The blockchain layer of our protocol uses Ethereum blockchain for transactions, P2P communication and rules to the government systems. How the data can be added, modified, deleted, or viewed, depending on which person has access to it, is one of the most important issues. The OpenZeppelin library is a supporting component in system implementation that allows the deployment of secure contracts. Ethereum is also implemented as well as our team of virtual characters uses smart contracts with role-defining and recordkeeping (Shahnaz et al., 2019). The paper presents a cloud-assisted blockchain system, which overcomes data security problems, privacy preservation, and interoperability issues in exchange for EHRs. The tactic combines searchable encryption and proxy re-encryption to maintain confidentiality. EHR ciphertext is kept safe via cloud storage and only the keyword cipher for search queries is stored on the consortium blockchain The crucial elements are the consensus mechanism, the format of data, and the idea of the network. The consensus algorithm acts as a "proof of authority." This policy assures the confidentiality of patient information and security of EHR interchange (Wang et al., 2019). This paper deals with the development, design, and components of the MedCloud system, a cloud computing platform developed to handle various services that run on healthcare applications. MedCloud, unlike traditional software, has achieved a quality of applicability; you can access simultaneously multiple applications through its web interface. The system is divided into three main layers: the storage of data, administration of servers, and application layers, besides a client interface. The storage layer employs both distributed file systems and NoSQL databases in order to optimally process and store medical data. The control layer follows the master-slave topology for the master-slave control layer, while the application layer deals with user services such as authentication, authorization, and service requests. Service Request Processing acts as another topic discussed alongside Application Deployment (Sobhy et al., 2012).

26.3.2 Cloud hosting implementation

Cloud hosting, the most practical solution for meeting the scalability, accessibility and reliability parameters for healthcare data storage and management, is at the heart of implementing blockchain-based EHR systems. Choosing the right provider and infrastructure configuration is vital to ensuring that the blockchain network uses up the minimum computing resources and is extensible as much as possible. Thereby, high availability and failover against hardware failures or network outages are enabled by redundancy and failover techniques inside the cloud infrastructure.

The recovery plans from disasters reduce the possibility of data loss and downtime during an emergency by conducting data backups, the recovery point objective (RPOs) and recovery time objective (RTOs) practice on a regular basis. Good security practices that can stop cyberattacks, illegal access, and compromise of essential EHR data are important to keep in the cloud. There is a swift increase in credit scores of individual borrowers, which has an overall positive impact on the credit health of the economy.

In order to safeguard user satisfaction and ensure quick access to EHR data, it is essential that the performance of chains that are deployed in the cloud be optimized. With the use of content delivery networks, caching mechanisms, and scalable storage solutions, both healthcare providers and patients can share data with a faster delivery time and reduced latency thus benefiting from the same. Hosting EHR data in the cloud calls for compliance with industry standards specific to its field and laws on compliance, such as HIPAA and GDPR. It is up to the providers of healthcare to take extra measures and develop the necessary protections to ensure compliance throughout the whole lifecycle of data, in spite of giving certifications and assurances to the cloud service providers.

Optimizing resource utilization, using cost-effective pricing plans, and monitoring usage to prevent skyrocketing surprises are what cloud hosting cost management is all about. Healthcare companies will be able to take advantage of the cloud to scale better by dedicating meticulous effort towards enabling cloud spending transparency and accountability, such as cost allocation and budgeting. The cloud is required to continuously check blockchain infrastructure in order to ensure that all technical issues, vulnerabilities or infringements are identified and eliminated. Reliability as well as resilience of the EHR system are maintained by proactive optimization and troubleshooting that can be enabled by the log analysis, performance tuning approaches and the monitoring tools.

This chapter focuses on blockchain, as well cloud computing, and how blockchain technologies can provide security for cloud applications. Even though it is becoming more popular day by day, cloud computing security is still a challenge. Blockchain is considered as one of the solutions by people in this regard because of its uncorrupted operation and data privacy protection attributes. While smooth running of the integration between blockchain and cloud computing might be an effect of the impeachment. The chapter is analyzing security implications in the systems and blockchain can be used as part of data security in the cloud using concepts that are advanced from the academic literature and research areas (Alromaihi et al., 2022).

26.4 System architecture

Fig. 26.2 presents the system architecture for the health data storage and sharing system. Application layer:

- **Domain Name System (DNS):** Allows people to get to websites and services with names that can be read by humans using the DNS which translates domain names into IP addresses.
- **Simple Mail Transfer Protocol:** In charge of communication between servers via a messaging system, such as an email, is facilitated.
- **Hypertext Transfer Protocol:** protocol that lets browsers from the web and servers of the web communicate with each other, by sending each buffer of hypertext documents, or pages of websites between clients and servers.
- **File Transfer Protocol:** A protocol that enables the transfer between a client and a server. Moreover, it enables users to launch and manage internet functions in terms of uploading, downloading, and moving files.

Presentation layer:

- **Access Control:** It is responsible for that a single user only has permission to access only permitted resources or perform certain tasks and that depends on the user authentication credentials and permissions predefined by the system administrator.
- **Authentication:** Verifies who is entering the system or who has control over the system, using login credentials such as passwords, security tokens or usernames.

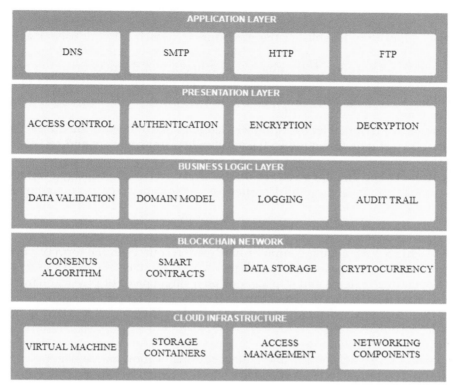

FIGURE 26.2 System architecture.

- **Encryption:** Employs cryptographic methods for performing encryption that turns plaintext data into ciphertext, hence providing protection to data or information security.
- **Decryption:** Transfers to intelligible and decryptable plaintext from the encrypted text, making it possible for authorized users to utilize it.

Business logic layer:

- **Data Validation:** Ensures the incoming data satisfies previously setup thresholds and limits or constraints, thereby protecting data integrity and averting mistakes and inconsistencies.
- **Domain Model:** It is the abstraction and representation of relationships, behavior, and conceptual entities found in a business domain; it provides a structure for items and business activities.
- **Logging:** Performs the job of keeping an archive of system behavior by registering system events, activities, and errors for purposes of monitoring, auditing, and troubleshooting.
- **Audit Trail:** It has the capability of ensuring accountability, compliance, and forensic analysis by recording and storing an organized historical record of system operations which includes data access, alterations, and user actions.

Blockchain network:

- **Consensus Algorithm:** Establishes the procedure by which network users reach a consensus relevant to accepting the new block of the transactions for the blockchain and validating the information's truthfulness and reliability of the network.
- **Smart Contracts:** Self-executing contracts are coded into the blockchain and the terms and conditions are programmed with logic and rules making it difficult to mess with and enforce between the two parties.
- **Data Storage:** An immutable, decentralized ledger is used to store the transaction data and other types of data to guarantee the auditability, transparency and resistance to change the data.
- **Cryptocurrency:** The digital currencies that take advantage of blockchain technology to send secure, not-controlled-by-third-parties transactions between peers, removing the need for banks as a middleman.

Cloud infrastructure:

- **Virtual Machine:** Virtualizing computer hardware resources in the form of virtual machines with the exact mimicry of their real-world counterparts allows users to run multiple operating systems and applications on a single piece of physical hardware.
- **Storage Containers:** Software items that are lightweight and portable which add together the programs and their dependencies for handling and deploying in diverse settings are resources.
- **Access Management:** guarantees the secure use of the cloud resources through identity management, user rights control, and suitable authentication mechanisms.
- **Networking Components:** Network constructs like virtual networks, load balancers, firewalls, and virtual private clouds that connect and talk to other cloud services.

The proposed design for the health data storage and sharing system has three roles: the Users, the Users' Key Keepers, and the Client. Each app development is complementary with its appropriate one for every position. The User App assembles, encrypts, and compresses health data created by wearable devices. It not only submits the data to cloud storage but it also attaches the identifying labels. Key Keepers act as a depository for decryption keys that are released upon transaction validation. Via the Customer App, customers explore and buy datasets, and the blockchain logs the reception of such transactions. The five elements of our technical solution are data encryption, cloud storage integration, data validation, verification of blockchain transactions and the application of a token-based incentive program. It involves acquiring data and verifying it, constructing transactions, approving them, unscrambling them, and issuing rewards based on their results (Zheng et al., 2018). The paper presents a protected protocol for cloud-aided EHR systems, and the system is developed based on the Hyperledger Fabric. Authorized users have the capacity to outsource EHRs, all data entered is done as blockchain transactions. It consists of six stages: registration, authentication, contracts, smart contract uploading, storing EHRs, retrieving EHRs, and uploading log transactions. Before registration, the network organizations configure the network and distribute systems assignments. Both the medical center and the patient undergo separate procedures of key agreement and registration for obtaining security. This authorization procedure enables safe communication through session key negotiation. Contracts are uploaded to a distributed ledger which is the blockchain, storage and request phases are the next steps with all of these actions aiming at keeping the privacy and integrity of the electronic health information (Kim et al., 2020).

26.5 Implementation

Fig. 26.3 is the schematic implementation design. Bringing our concept to life is a complex process which includes several vital stages, such as two hospitals, patients access rights as read-only, hospitals with read-and-write ability, and then connecting them all to the blockchain network on the cloud using a web interface. Within each hospital, there's a blockchain node that helps data move in a safe, transparent manner while also securing, and protecting its integrity. Smart contracts are applied to grant access permissions, permit healthcare professionals with the read-access to patients' (Controlled) EHRs while retaining the patients' control over their data. On the flip side, such organizations are able to rethink the position of and rights within the network and thereupon be able to access and write patient data. The web-based user interface simplifies the data processing procedures, improves collaboration between healthcare parties, and gives healthcare professionals a simple way of interacting and accessing the blockchain-based EHR system. The cloud hosting which we use ensures

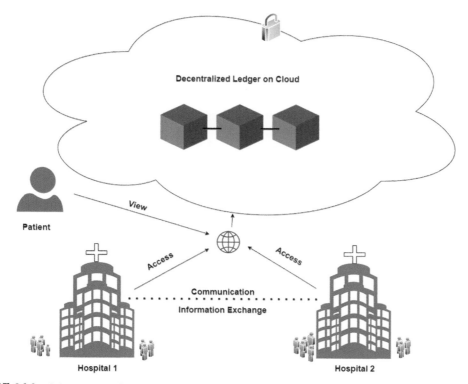

FIGURE 26.3 Schematic implementation design.

security, scalability, and availability of our infrastructure along with strict compliance to regulations and privacy requirements. This allows for easy retrieval of critical patient detail Taking into account, the above discussed implementation allows healthcare establishments to get benefits using electronic health information on the blockchain-enabled cloud platform, improve delivery of medical services, enhance interoperability, and solve privacy issues.

This study introduces a blockchain-inspired system that includes a smart contract implementation for centralized and secure management of EHRs. It addresses security issues of healthcare facilities through blockchain cryptography features exploited for protection of EHRs from hackers. The solution utilizes the proof-of-stake (POS) consensus algorithm with SHA-256 for data integrity and ECDSA for verification which provides a secure environment for the cloud-based sharing of EHRs. Implantation is upon storing sensor data on cloud computing whose security is high. Audits proclaim satisfactory security levels. Moreover, the article describes a unique decentralized system that protects, manages, and efficiently transfers health data in a safe and secure manner (Amanat et al., 2022; Nalayini, Jeevaakatiravan, et al., 2023; Nalayini, Katiravan, et al., 2023).

Cloud infrastructure:

- The blockchain network is delineated on the cloud hosting platform such as Google Cloud Platform, Azure, or AWS respectively. This implies that the system can be dependable, scalable and highly available.
- Cloud infrastructure which encompasses virtual computers, storage services, and networking features is where the blockchain network development and operation gets support from.

Blockchain network:

- IBM gives a solution for EHR sharing and healthcare record interoperability through cloud healthcare infrastructure as nodes of the blockchain network, which produces immutable, decentralized ledger for EHR storage.
- It doesn't matter whether the architecture of the blockchain is permissioned (private or consortium) or permissionless (public), nodes can be designed in line with that selection.
- In the blockchain, smart contracts are employed to manage patient consent processes, data sharing agreements, and access conditions.

Web interface for patients:

- This web interface is secure and by using fingerprint recognition or patient credentials such as password or username, they can check in.
- Patients can access their EHR records, decide how many access settings to allow and reply to the sent requests for data access from doctors after signing in.

Hospital interfaces:

- Some APIs will facilitate hospitals to exchange and map up with the blockchain network.
- Staff in designated roles at each hospital can request and obtain access to patient data after access is granted through individual user accounts.

Request and consent workflow:

- Requesting data is done through the system by a healthcare professional coming from Hospital 1 who is in need of retrieving the electronic health information from Hospital 2.

- The request consists of specifying facts on the identity of the patient why access is needed and the particular data that is needed.
- By means of the user interface, the patient is notified about the request and she or he can accept or refuse the request.
- Hospital 1 will have temporary access to the requested EHR data if it receives patient consent and a smart contract provides access control logic.

Data exchange and encryption:

- Provided that the enabling consent is obtained from the patient, hospitals 1 and 2 exchange encrypted EHRs through a blockchain network.
- Asymmetric cryptography is among the encryption techniques that seek to ensure that sensitive data will not be easily intercepted either during the transmission or storage phase.
- Decryption will arise, and accessibility will be possible just for the respected healthcare professionals, only in case we have proper access credentials.

26.6 Results and discussion

Our objectives that utilize blockchain technology in integration with cloud computing have helped to handle crucial areas of data security, accessibility, privacy concerns, interoperability and scalability in the management of EHRs. Notably, the distributed and immutable characteristics of the blockchain ensure data security and impenetrable tampering, preventing the patient data from being compromised or tampered with by anyone or anything from outside. An auditable and traceable public record of every single transaction or data entry, secured by cryptographically linking each transaction to the earlier block is created. This strict security mechanism preserves patient confidentiality, and data integrity by reducing the probability of wanted attacks or data change. Second, our technology improves data exchange and accessibility improve greatly. With blockchain functionalization as cloud platforms, healthcare workers will be able to securely share and to exchange EHRs in real-time as they need it, across multiple organizational and geographic locations. Through patient permissions built into the blockchain, individuals can maintain control over their health information since it is encrypted and therefore can only be accessed and shared with known and verified parties. Additionally, our privacy concerns have been addressed and solved through blockchain-based and EHR systems. The medical records of patients need to be encrypted and access is only granted to authorized medical personnel in accordance with strict privacy laws such as HIPAA. However, we go further: we make sure that we are compliant with the privacy rules. Bringing a uniform architecture for data sharing among multiple health systems also enhances interoperability. As the blockchain is transparent to assess and interoperable, it is easy to be integrated into the current infrastructure, which may lead to stakeholder engagement in healthcare and improvement of care coordination. Our solution ensures scalability through provided scalability features to handle the rising EHR data share. Healthcare firms may overcome demand changes by the use of cloud services which can scale dynamically. This is to maintain access to a patient's vital information while getting optimum thought for resource consumption.

26.7 Comparative analysis

Table 26.1 shows the comparison of traditional EHR systems and our MEDSYNC, whereas Table 26.2 is the figurative assessment of EHR systems. Fig. 26.4 shows the key metrics of traditional EHR systems and our MedSync.

TABLE 26.1   Comparison of traditional electronic health records systems and MedSync.

Aspect	Traditional EHR	MedSync (our work)
Data security	centralized storage which makes data vulnerable to security breaches with varying degrees of protection.	Cryptography is one of the useful techniques is used by the decentralized storage systems to ensure data integrity and immutability.
Access control	Roles and their related rights are often abused in role-based access control designs though they are commonly applied.	One of the ways smart contracts can lower the possibility of unwanted access is that they transparently and securely enforce access control restrictions.
Data interoperability	Fragmentation at the point of limited communication between different EHR systems and data silos.	The advanced interoperability resulting from protocols and data formats standardization, therefore means data transfer between different systems is made easier.
Patient consent management	Consent management could be manual and lacking transparency.	Consent management complying with open and traceable blockchain features, ensures data's patron leasing.
Data integrity and auditability	the immutability and lack of transparency in the data pose a threat to the public.	but blockchain, an immutable, traceable system of recordkeeping that provides a verifiable audit trail of each transaction.
Scalability	the scalability problems or specifically the scalability issues that arise from the increasing data volumes, users and demand.	The cloud-based architecture can scale resources in an efficient way, according to their demand.
Reliability and availability	Hardware malfunctions, maintenance, and system outages can all have an impact on reliability.	High availability and dependability because of cloud hosting's redundancy and decentralized architecture.
Regulatory compliance	Regulations such as GDPR, and HIPAA may require a lot of hiring of employees or purchasing of specialized technology to comply with.	Improved adherence to legal mandates by means of transparent and auditable blockchain data management.
Data ownership and control	Option of data monetization by the third-party and restriction of data ownership ownership control.	mitigated threats of data abuse or misuse, and enhanced user's transparency and self-sufficiency over their data.
Cost efficiency	Software upgrades, data management, and infrastructure maintenance, though costly, need to be done in the long run.	Possibility of cost reductions through decreased middlemen, improved processes, and optimal cloud resource usage.

EHR, Electronic health records.

TABLE 26.2 Figurative assessment of electronic health records systems.

Aspect	Traditional EHR	MedSync
Accuracy	85	95
Efficiency	70	90
Interoperability	62	89
Ease of access	75	91
Reliability	90	95

EHR, Electronic health records.

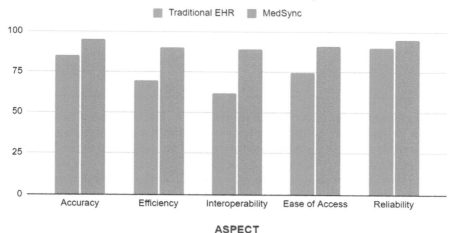

FIGURE 26.4 Key metrics of traditional electronic health records system and MedSync. *EHR*, Electronic health records.

26.8 Conclusion

Blockchain technology has been integrated into the systems for storing EHR through blockchain and cloud infrastructure, thus achieving notable progress in the transformation of healthcare data management. Through the implementation of HIM, improvements have been realized in some of the top areas of healthcare information management and this validates our firm commitment to quality patient care and safety of the PHI. Prior to this, blockchain technology provided unequaled data security and tamper-proofing features on user data. The blockchain's decentralized and unalterable nature makes the patient records to be kept safe and difficult even for an unauthorized party to access; keeping medical records safe, secure, and incorruptible. Furthermore, a steady and secure platform for healthcare providers accessing patient data with the express agreement is the added advantage we took to improve the easiness and fairness of the system. By overcoming corporate silos and geographical constraints, leveraging cloud hosting has made it possible to access vital patient data with ease, promoting collaboration and improving the quality of care. As a concluding factor to this issue, the strict encryption and access control features of the blockchain network have enhanced privacy protections. Patients get all the rights, authorized parties can access their Private Information if granted by the patient at different levels, and privacy laws and HIPAA are also maintained. Interoperability—a problem of healthcare data management for a long-time—has been efficiently addressed by the blockchain thanks to its transparency and high-level interoperability. This is because it is simple to integrate with current systems and provides a universal platform for data exchange across different stakeholders. Scalability has been achieved finally via cloud infrastructure exploiting the elastic features, ensuring the system can easily meet the growing amount of EHR data without a drop in performance level or resource efficiency. Finally, our new paradigm of the blockchain storing EHRs and their being stored in the cloud is a departure from the old way of how healthcare data management is done. It is going to raise the quality of patient care, make data available, address confidentiality issues, enhance data exchange in cross-organizational platforms, support large-scale projects, and safeguard privacy of data.

26.9 Future works

The EHR blockchain-cloud project will have two main directions in the future to ensure that it will continue to operate at its optimal performance and meet the dynamic requirements of the healthcare industry. Accepting the universal unified common interoperability standards similar to be compatible with each healthcare facility would promote the connectivity of healthcare data across different facilities and pave the way towards a more collaborative healthcare environment. FHIR is one example. Moreover, a multilevel approach may be used to enhance user access control. The scope of the system's penetration transcends in terms of payment when applied to Ethereum-based transactions. In addition to these, securing the authenticity of verification through multifactor authentication or biometrics would also provide a great improvement in preventing unauthorized healthcare workers from compromising the privacy of patients. For privacy, the Project could work using the latest cryptography. There are a number of approaches that would allow secure computations on encrypted medical information whilst maintaining the protection of privacy throughout all stages of processing including homomorphic encryption or zero-knowledge proofs. This action is in line with the primary goal of the project of providing appropriate security to sensitive health details as much as possible. Follow-up efforts to maintain the relevance and effectiveness of this approach and EHR evolution in the dynamic medical sector largely depend on the strong partnership with medical stakeholders, staying abreast of new technologies, and considering the changing data privacy issues.

References

Agbo, C. C., Mahmoud, Q. H., & Eklund, J. M. (2019). *Blockchain technology in healthcare: a systematic review*. *Healthcare* (7, p. 56). MDPI, April.
Al Omar, A., Bhuiyan, M. Z. A., Basu, A., Kiyomoto, S., & Rahman, M. S. (2019). Privacy-friendly platform for healthcare data in cloud based on blockchain environment. *Future Generation Computer Systems*, *95*, 511–521.

Alromaihi, N., Ismail, Y., & Elmedany, W. (2022 October). Literature review of blockchain-based cloud computing: Data security issues and challenges. In *2022 International conference on data analytics for business and industry (ICDABI)* (pp. 484-492). IEEE.

Amanat, A., Rizwan, M., Maple, C., Zikria, Y. B., Almadhor, A. S., & Kim, S. W. (2022). Blockchain and cloud computing-based secure electronic healthcare records storage and sharing. *Frontiers in Public Health, 10*, 938707.

Bahga, A., & Madisetti, V. K. (2013). A cloud-based approach for interoperable electronic health records (EHRs). *IEEE Journal of Biomedical and Health Informatics, 17*(5), 894–906.

Benil, T., & Jasper, J. (2023). Blockchain based secure medical data outsourcing with data deduplication in cloud environment. *Computer Communications, 209*, 1–13.

Cao, S., Zhang, G., Liu, P., Zhang, X., & Neri, F. (2019). Cloud-assisted secure eHealth systems for tamper-proofing EHR via blockchain. *Information Sciences, 485*, 427–440.

Cao, S., Zhang, X., & Xu, R. (2020). Toward secure storage in cloud-based ehealth systems: A blockchain-assisted approach. *IEEE Network, 34*(2), 64–70.

Chen, Y. Y., Lu, J. C., & Jan, J. K. (2012). A secure EHR system based on hybrid clouds. *Journal of Medical Systems, 36*, 3375–3384.

Esposito, C., De Santis, A., Tortora, G., Chang, H., & Choo, K. K. R. (2018). Blockchain: A panacea for healthcare cloud-based data security and privacy? *IEEE Cloud Computing, 5*(1), 31–37.

Han, Y., Zhang, Y., & Vermund, S. H. (2022). Blockchain technology for electronic health records. *International Journal of Environmental Research and Public Health, 19*(23), 15577.

Huang, H., Sun, X., Xiao, F., Zhu, P., & Wang, W. (2021). Blockchain-based eHealth system for auditable EHRs manipulation in cloud environments. *Journal of Parallel and Distributed Computing, 148*, 46–57.

Hölbl, M., Kompara, M., Kamišalić, A., & Nemec Zlatolas, L. (2018). A systematic review of the use of blockchain in healthcare. *Symmetry, 10*(10), 470.

Ismail, L., Materwala, H., & Hennebelle, A. (2021). A scoping review of integrated blockchain-cloud (BcC) architecture for healthcare: Applications, challenges and solutions. *Sensors, 21*(11), 3753.

John, N., & Shenoy, S. (2014, September). Health cloud-healthcare as a service (HaaS). In *2014 International conference on advances in computing, communications and informatics (ICACCI)* (pp. 1963–1966). IEEE.

Kim, M., Yu, S., Lee, J., Park, Y., & Park, Y. (2020). Design of secure protocol for cloud-assisted electronic health record system using blockchain. *Sensors, 20*(10), 2913.

Mahajan, H. B., Rashid, A. S., Junnarkar, A. A., Uke, N., Deshpande, S. D., Futane, P. R., Alkhayyat, A., & Alhayani, B. (2023). Integration of Healthcare 4.0 and blockchain into secure cloud-based electronic health records systems. *Applied Nanoscience, 13*(3), 2329.

Mayer, A. H., da Costa, C. A., & Righi, R. D. R. (2020). Electronic health records in a blockchain: A systematic review. *Health Informatics Journal, 26*(2), 1273–1288.

Mishra, R., Ramesh, D., Edla, D. R., & Qi, L. (2022). DS-Chain: A secure and auditable multi-cloud assisted EHR storage model on efficient deletable blockchain. *Journal of Industrial Information Integration, 26*, 100315.

Mubarakali, A. (2020). Healthcare services monitoring in cloud using secure and robust healthcare-based blockchain (SRHB) approach. *Mobile Networks and Applications, 25*, 1330–1337.

Murala, D. K., Panda, S. K., & Sahoo, S. K. (2023). *Securing electronic health record system in cloud environment using blockchain technology. Recent advances in blockchain technology: Real-world applications* (pp. 89–116). Cham: Springer International Publishing.

Nagasubramanian, G., Sakthivel, R. K., Patan, R., Gandomi, A. H., Sankayya, M., & Balusamy, B. (2020). Securing e-health records using keyless signature infrastructure blockchain technology in the cloud. *Neural Computing and Applications, 32*, 639–647.

Nalayini, C. M., Jeevaakatiravan., Vimala Imogen, P., & Sahana, J. M. (2023). A study on digital signature in blockchain technology. *ICAIS*, 398–403. Available from 10.1109/ICAIS56108.2023.10073680.

Nalayini, C. M., Katiravan, J., & Sathya, V. (2023). Available from 10.4018/978-1-6684-8666-5.ch009 June *Intrusion detection in cyber physical systems using multichain, malware analysis and intrusion detection in cyber-physical systems*. IGI Global Platform.

Nguyen, D. C., Pathirana, P. N., Ding, M., & Seneviratne, A. (2019). Blockchain for secure ehrs sharing of mobile cloud based e-health systems. *IEEE access, 7*, 66792–66806.

Nishi, F. K., Shams-E-Mofiz, M., Khan, M. M., Alsufyani, A., Bourouis, S., Gupta, P., & Saini, D. K. (2022). Electronic healthcare data record security using blockchain and smart contract. *Journal of Sensors, 2022*, 1–22.

Quasim, M.T., Radwan, A.A.E., Alshmrani, G.M.M., & Meraj, M., (2020, October). A blockchain framework for secure electronic health records in healthcare industry. In *2020 International conference on smart technologies in computing, electrical and electronics (ICSTCEE)* (pp. 605–609). IEEE.

Ramesh, D., Mishra, R., Atrey, P. K., Edla, D. R., Misra, S., & Qi, L. (2023). Blockchain based efficient tamper-proof EHR storage for decentralized cloud-assisted storage. *Alexandria Engineering Journal, 68*, 205–226.

Ruggeri, A., Fazio, M., Celesti, A., & Villari, M. (2020). Blockchain-based healthcare workflows in federated hospital clouds. In *Service-oriented and cloud computing: 8th IFIP WG 2.14 European conference, ESOCC 2020, Heraklion, Crete, Greece, September 28–30, 2020, Proceedings 8* (pp. 113–121). Springer International Publishing.

Shahnaz, A., Qamar, U., & Khalid, A. (2019). Using blockchain for electronic health records. *IEEE access, 7*, 147782–147795.

Sharma, S., Mishra, A., & Singhai, D. (2020). April. Secure cloud storage architecture for digital medical record in cloud environment using blockchain. In *Proceedings of the international conference on innovative computing & communications (ICICC)*.

Sharma, Y., & Balamurugan, B. (2020). Preserving the privacy of electronic health records using blockchain. *Procedia Computer Science, 173*, 171–180.

Shen, B., Guo, J., & Yang, Y. (2019). MedChain: Efficient healthcare data sharing via blockchain. *Applied sciences, 9* (6), 1207.

Singh, S., Pankaj, B., Nagarajan, K., Singh, N. P., & Bala, V. (2022). Blockchain with cloud for handling healthcare data: A privacy-friendly platform. *Materials Today: Proceedings, 62*, 5021–5026.

Singh, S., Rakhra, M., Malik, A., & Singh, D. (2023, January). Blockchain-based EHR system for Indian healthcare industry using Aadhar. In *2023 International conference on intelligent and innovative technologies in computing, electrical and electronics (IITCEE)* (pp. 997–1001). IEEE.

Sobhy, D., El-Sonbaty, Y., & Abou Elnasr, M. (2012, December). MedCloud: Healthcare cloud computing system. In *2012 International conference for internet technology and secured transactions* (pp. 161–166). IEEE.

Verma, D.K., Tyagi, R.K., & Chakraverti, A.K. (2022). Secure data sharing of electronic health record (EHR) on the cloud using blockchain in Covid-19 scenario. In *Proceedings of trends in electronics and health informatics: TEHI 2021* (pp. 165–175). Singapore: Springer Nature Singapore.

Wang, H., & Song, Y. (2018). Secure cloud-based EHR system using attribute-based cryptosystem and blockchain. *Journal of Medical Systems, 42*(8), 152.

Wang, Y., Zhang, A., Zhang, P., & Wang, H. (2019). Cloud-assisted EHR sharing with security and privacy preservation via consortium blockchain. *Ieee Access, 7*, 136704–136719.

Zhang, G., Yang, Z., & Liu, W. (2022). Blockchain-based privacy preserving e-health system for healthcare data in cloud. *Computer Networks, 203*108586.

Zheng, X., Mukkamala, R.R., Vatrapu, R., & Ordieres-Mere, J. (2018). September. Blockchain-based personal health data sharing system using cloud storage. In *2018 IEEE 20th International conference on e-health networking, applications and services (Healthcom)* (pp. 1–6). IEEE.

Zubaydi, H. D., Chong, Y. W., Ko, K., Hanshi, S. M., & Karuppayah, S. (2019). A review on the role of blockchain technology in the healthcare domain. *Electronics, 8*(6), 679.

Innovative artificial intelligence tools: exploring the future of healthcare through IBM Watson's potential applications

Kimia Norouzi[1], Alireza Ghodsi[1], Pendar Argani[1], Pedram Amiri Andi[1] and Hossein Hassani[2]

[1]Faculty of Dentistry, Tehran Medical Sciences, Islamic Azad University, Tehran, Iran
[2]Research Institute of Energy Management and Planning (RIEMP), University of Tehran, Tehran, Iran

27.1 Introduction

The growing prominence of artificial intelligence (AI) and its wide-ranging applications as a breakthrough technology in the fields of information technology and computer science has captured the attention of experts in several fields in recent years. Dentistry is no exception to this rule. Both virtual (software) and physical (robotic) AI have made significant advances in this field (Shan et al., 2021). Among them are dental implant robots, endo microrobots, VEL SCOPE (used to detect oral and dental cancers) (Hassani et al., 2021), radiography diagnostic software, and treatment output analysis. To some extent, these examples can save dentists and students time and money, and even assist in correcting potential mistakes (Hassani et al., 2021; Chen et al., 2020).

It is important to acknowledge, however, that despite these achievements, AI in dentistry is still evolving, and ongoing efforts are dedicated to developing more efficient and accurate solutions. efforts to provide more efficient tools with higher accuracy are constantly being made (Schwendicke et al., 2020).

Among the powerful AI systems deployed in various sectors such as finance, healthcare, transportation, and customer service, International Business Machines Corporation

Sensor Networks for Smart Hospitals
DOI: https://doi.org/10.1016/B978-0-443-36370-2.00028-1

(IBM)'s Watson stands out. Developed by IBM, Watson is an advanced cognitive and problem-solving supercomputer capable of processing natural language, analyzing it, and employing the derived insights to uncover hidden answers and patterns within vast amounts of data. This enables informed decision-making that is relevant to the context (Russo-Spena et al., 2019). The multipurpose capabilities of IBM Watson make it highly beneficial across diverse fields, offering a wide array of services including Discovery, Personality insights, Tone analyzer, Visual recognition, and various other applications (Russo-Spena et al., 2019). One such area where Watson has garnered considerable attention is the healthcare industry.

Since its introduction in 2011, Watson has been the focal point for leading healthcare companies, numerous projects related to diagnosis and medical treatment planning have been carried out, These projects encompass diverse areas such as cancer detection and treatment, as well as women's health (Lee & Kim, 2016; Zou et al., 2020). Dentistry, as a specialized branch of healthcare, also holds promise for AI integration (Hassani et al., 2023). While current articles on IBM Watson in healthcare are fairly consistent, dentistry remains a relatively unexplored field.

In an effort to address this gap, we conducted a comprehensive search using the Google Scholar database, employing the keywords "IBM Watson" AND "dentistry" OR "dental" to identify relevant research literature. Through a meticulous manual screening process, irrelevant materials were excluded, and the results revealed a limited number of studies that primarily focused on IBM Watson applications in dentistry rather than the broader healthcare context. Some examples include the analysis of dental images (Yu, 2016), restorative dentistry (Derchi et al., 2020), treatment planning in dental implants (Roongruangsilp & Khongkhunthian, 2021), and limited studies on oral and dental cancers (Tranby et al., 2022). These few instances indicate the scarcity of research conducted in the field of dentistry regarding these topics. Moreover, as AI is a new concept in dental practice, dentists still lack comprehensive familiarity with these technologies. Therefore, increasing awareness among dental professionals about this technology is essential for a better understanding and utilization of these advancements to enhance their specialized field.

the present manuscript endeavors to concentrate on the application of IBM Watson in dentistry and offer a timely conceptual exploration of its potential uses. Not only does this chapter reflect upon the scarcity of previous studies, but it also presents a summary of additional potential applications, drawing from the intersecting needs of dentistry and our ongoing research in AI (AI), IBM Watson, and other pertinent technological advancements. These applications are systematically organized according to various dental practice operations, facilitating easy reference for dental professionals. Furthermore, it is anticipated that this conceptual framework will continue to evolve and expand, attracting greater attention to dentistry and inspiring further collaborative research endeavors.

For the convenience of interested readers and dental professionals, the contributions of this study can be summarized as follows:

- This chapter contributes to the existing body of knowledge on IBM Watson, dentistry, and healthcare by providing a perspective on the application of IBM Watson in dentistry, raising awareness of IBM Watson technology among dental professionals since the field has been under-researched despite its wealth of data and potential benefits.

- This chapter outlines a visionary approach to implementing IBM Watson in dentistry, elucidating its role in various dental practice operations, thus enabling dental professionals to easily explore applications relevant to their specific areas of interest.
- In addition, this chapter identifies and discusses the challenges associated with implementing IBM Watson in dentistry, offering insights into future research directions within the field of IBM Watson in dentistry.

The subsequent sections of this chapter are organized as follows: Section 27.2 elucidates the theoretical background, including a concise explanation of IBM Watson and a general explanation of how it functions; Section 27.3 discusses the role and applications of Watson in the healthcare system. Section 27.4 presents a conceptual framework outlining potential applications of IBM Watson technology in dentistry; Section 27.5 delves into the detailed analysis of different Watson services and their individual impacts on dentistry. existing challenges and concerns are deliberated in Section 27.6; finally, the last section concludes by summarizing the key findings and suggesting avenues for future research.

27.2 Theoretical background and how IBM Watson works

In simple terms, Watson is a type of AI system. Through AI, machines gain knowledge, adjust to evolving information, and enhance their decision-making abilities (Duan et al., 2019). Machine learning (ML), which is a division of AI, involves computer algorithms that analyze data and determine intelligent choices based on what it has learned (Aggarwal et al., 2022). Watson employs a ML technique known as deep learning. Deep learning uses algorithms to create an artificial neural network. This enables Watson to continuously learn while working and improve its quality and accuracy. This ability allows Watson to learn from a variety of data sources, such as images, videos, and recordings, even if they are not well-organized (LeCun et al., 2015). Furthermore, by breaking down sentences and analyzing their concepts and relationships, Watson can figure out the meaning and intention behind messages; this enables it to understand human language more effectively through deep learning. Understanding the specific language and terminology used in different healthcare fields is also crucial for Watson. It would normally take a long time to complete this process since it requires a lot of extra data and computing capability. It is thanks to a technique referred to as transfer learning, however, that Watson is capable of performing these tasks at an incredibly fast pace. With transfer learning, Watson does not have to learn everything from square one (Hsu et al., 2022), as it builds off from what it already knows, as for a faster learning process, prior knowledge can be provided.

Watson's transfer learning functions in a three-layered AI model. The first layer contains general knowledge, such as information available in regular web search engines for AI (Wilhelm & Ziegler, 2021). In a dental setting, for example, this layer provides Watson with the ability to gather foundational knowledge about various diseases. The second layer is specifically designed for particular industries, custom-built to each company's needs. This layer equips Watson to comprehend industry-specific terms, crucial for its application in dentistry. The third layer represents individualized learning, where Watson adapts itself to the unique requirements of the organization it serves (Wilhelm & Ziegler,

2021). By incorporating the company's data and expertise, the model captures specific risk characteristics and policy pricing strategies relevant to the specific company. Employing transfer learning results in a reduction in operating costs. It does so by learning quickly from smaller datasets while safeguarding the privacy of its information. Unlike many other AI systems, which often use data to build general ML models profiting all users, Watson's three-layer model ensures each company's data security and confidentiality.

27.3 The role of IBM Watson in the healthcare sector

Exploring AI uses in healthcare and hospital settings stands as a vital realm of progress. The integration of AI technologies like ML into smart healthcare is imperative, driven by the unique complexities of delivering healthcare (Klumpp et al., 2021). The healthcare industry today faces problems like soaring expenses, deteriorating care quality, less productivity, and also the care providers and payers aka hospitals and labs' interactions with insurance companies and patients seem to be increasing, all of which seem to cause more confusion (Bigus et al., 2011). Data-driven medical research was revolutionized with IBM Watson's advent. A growing public fascination with the potential perks of employing cutting-edge digital technologies that could enhance both community health and the level of patient care was sparked. IBM's vision encompassed the transformation of technology through the creation of an AI supercomputer, Watson, endowed with the capacity to uncover and evaluate solutions in unstructured data, as well as structured data; setting Watson apart from conventional systems operating only within structured data paradigms (Lee & Yoon, 2021; Prateek et al., 2021). IBM offers cognitive analytical tools that extract insights from diverse healthcare data. The tools fall into two categories: one driven by knowledge, extracting insights from trusted sources like academic papers and guidelines etc., and the other driven by data, identifying patterns in real-world information, including images and text from electronic health records. These categories of decision support can be combined to offer valuable insights into healthcare choices (Kohn et al., 2014). Watson's ability to gain knowledge from user interactions is a core competency applicable to healthcare. With each interaction, Watson's performance and comprehension are elevated to new heights, leading to remarkably precise and pertinent guidance. In healthcare, this cyclical learning process is crucial (Neill, 2013). IBM Watson has transitioned from its initial role in entertainment to making a significant contribution to healthcare, mainly in healthcare facilities like hospitals (Neill, 2013). The preeminent AI application within the healthcare sector is IBM's "Watson for Oncology" (WFO) distinguished as the world's pioneer medical AI, this groundbreaking platform operates in the cloud and is tailored for inputting patient data related to cancer (Lee & Yoon, 2021). Medical professionals benefit from its capability to formulate treatment approaches grounded in a wealth of prior clinical cases. A notable partnership with Memorial Sloan Kettering Cancer Center exemplifies this influence. This collaboration uses Watson's capabilities to offer IBM WFO that stands as a clinical decision support tool, purposefully crafted to guide physicians in making individualized diagnostics and treatment plans customized to each type of cancer (Neill, 2013; Hamilton et al., 2019). Accordingly, in situations involving rectal cancer, Watson's treatment alignment with doctors stood at 85%, compared to a lesser 17.8% agreement rate observed for lung cancer. This discrepancy highlights the impact of cancer type on the conclusions drawn. it is to be considered that the variation in Watson's agreement across various cancer types underscores the importance of ongoing enhancement and broadening of the data in use (Lee & Yoon, 2021). Moreover, IBM Watson's impact on healthcare stretches past cancer treatment; Outlined below are a few instances;

- Continuous health information and patient-physician connections are used in diabetes care to anticipate patient results (Raj et al., 2015).
- Regarding women's health, Watson's capacity becomes evident in tackling recurrent miscarriages. Watson could possibly improve patient outcomes by considering patient profiles, and genetic factors and merging treatment approaches (Shader, 2016).
- There is currently work being done by IBM research on a novel radiologist cognitive assistant known as the Medical Sieve. This advanced system employs image-guided algorithms to sift through crucial clinical data that physicians require for patient diagnosis and treatment planning (Kohn et al., 2014).

In summary, IBM Watson dramatically transforms healthcare. Combining vast medical records, processing natural language, aiding in decision-making, and optimizing through user input, it's become an indispensable tool for healthcare providers, offering insightful guidance for evidence-based care (Neill, 2013). Watson's function is not to give direct prescriptions but to propose evidence-driven theories for decision-makers to ponder. Its primary role involves offering decision assistance rather than independently making decisions (Kohn et al., 2014). in fact, the primary objective of developing Watson was not centered on mimicking the remarkable capacities of the human brain, according to David Ferricci. Instead, the focus rested on establishing a system with the capability to engage users in "natural language," albeit not fully adhering to human patterns (Prateek et al., 2021).

Moreover, advances in technology and increased access to information are reshaping healthcare structures, and altering the interaction between healthcare professionals and patients. This shift converts the medical approach from one directed solely by professionals to a collaborative effort involving patients. This transition aligns with the growing trend of patient-centered care, as patients contribute substantial information along with regular medical procedures. The concept of a capable and well-informed patient gains prominence, actively engaged in decision-making and care, aided by decision support implements and smart home systems. These systems, illustrated by scenarios like sensor-equipped mirrors connected to doctors, fall sensors installed in carpets, or any smart wearable devices, enable real-time data utilization and emergency detection in smart cities, as if the patient needs drive aid dispatch or hospital selection. However, collecting patient data, especially in hospitals, strains nursing staff. Intelligent devices with voice recognition alleviate this, leveraging AI and thorough data analysis to enhance emergency care amidst the challenge of dwindling skilled personnel in an aging society (Hassani et al., 2023; Kohn et al., 2014; Ghazal et al., 2021).

27.4 IBM Watson in dentistry and its practical implications

AI has been increasingly utilized in the medical field, with IBM Watson emerging as a prominent AI system supporting clinical decision-making (Chen et al., 2016). However, the application of AI in dentistry, particularly IBM Watson, requires validation of its clinical accuracy across diverse dental cases and imaging modalities, considering the challenges in standardizing dental radiology (Chen et al., 2016; Thornhill et al., 2018). This validation is crucial for IBM Watson to play a significant role in making diagnostic recommendations (Chen et al., 2016).

IBM Watson has demonstrated potential in various aspects of dentistry, including clinical decision support. Its cognitive computing abilities enable the analysis of extensive patient data, such as medical histories, radiographic images, and treatment outcomes, assisting dental professionals in making informed clinical decisions (Chen et al., 2016; Fiehn et al., 2020). It improves diagnostic accuracy, treatment planning, and prognostic evaluations (Chen et al., 2016).

In addition to diagnostic support, IBM Watson shows promise in treatment planning and resource optimization. Integrating evidence-based dentistry guidelines and patient-specific factors, aids in developing personalized and optimized treatment plans, reducing resource overutilization (Chen et al., 2016; Fiehn et al., 2020).

IBM Watson's natural language processing (NLP) capabilities enhance patient outcomes and education. It provides information on oral health, preventive care, and treatment options, empowering patients to actively participate in their oral healthcare management (Chen et al., 2016; Fiehn et al., 2020).

The utilization of IBM Watson in dentistry extends to analyzing data on dental emergencies, treatment procedures, and patient visits. Such analyses offer insights into the frequency of dental emergencies, the need for definitive treatment, and the potential for effective triage using teledental services (Fiehn et al., 2020).

The opioid crisis has raised concerns in dentistry, and IBM Watson has been employed to analyze opioid prescription patterns. Studies demonstrate consistent decreases in opioid prescription rates, emphasizing the potential of AI systems like IBM Watson to optimize pain management and address responsible prescribing practices (Okunev et al., 2021).

Early detection and preventive care are critical in reducing the disease burden in dentistry. IBM Watson's capabilities in analyzing patient data and identifying risk factors contribute to enhancing oral health screenings, improving treatment outcomes, and minimizing the need for restorative procedures (McGivern et al., 2021).

The practical implications of implementing IBM Watson in dentistry encompass improved clinical decision-making, enhanced diagnostic accuracy, and cost-efficiency through resource optimization (Okunev et al., 2022). However, ethical and legal considerations must be addressed to ensure responsible and transparent use of AI systems, including IBM Watson, in dental practice (Okunev et al., 2022).

In conclusion, IBM Watson holds promising opportunities for enhancing clinical decision-making, improving diagnostics, and optimizing patient care in dentistry. Validating its clinical accuracy, addressing ethical and legal concerns, and conducting further research is vital to harnessing the full potential of AI in dentistry and ensuring its seamless integration into clinical practice (Okunev et al., 2022; Okunseri et al., 2023).

27.5 Introduction to Watson services

IBM has pioneered Watson, an AI equipped with advanced Application Programming Interfaces (APIs), specialized tools, and Software-as-a-service applications tailored explicitly for enterprise-level usage. This makes Watson exceptionally adept at managing intricate tasks while seamlessly integrating into the very platforms professionals rely on daily.

Within the expansive Watson AI portfolio, an array of services, tools, and APIs are at your disposal. Through Watson Assistant, crafting chatbots and virtual assistants for mobile devices, messaging platforms, and even robots becomes effortlessly achievable. Watson Discovery leverages a cloud-native insight engine to unearth invaluable insights, track trends, and identify service patterns within data. Watson Studio provides a streamlined environment to build, train, deploy, and manage AI models, while also facilitating data analysis and preparation.

With Watson ML, the creation, training, and deployment of ML and deep learning models are accessible using your own data. Furthermore, Watson Visual Recognition empowers you to swiftly and precisely tag, classify, and train visual content through ML techniques. Encouraging collaboration and the transformation of data and AI into a reliable enterprise asset, Watson Knowledge Catalog introduces dynamic data policies and their enforcement.

For those seeking domain-specific applications, Watson Knowledge Studio enables you to teach Watson the nuances of your industry's language. This customizes models to identify domain-specific entities and relationships. Addressing the health of AI, Watson OpenScale provides insights and recommendations to enhance outcomes while orchestrating tasks to rectify performance, accuracy, and fairness issues.

Lastly, Watson Compare and Comply streamlines contract workflows, optimizing time, accuracy, and governance in the realm of contract management. In essence, IBM's Watson presents an extensive suite of AI solutions that cater to the most intricate of business needs.

27.5.1 Watson Assistant

IBM Watson Assistant is an AI-driven platform that enables meaningful engagement in natural language conversations. It has the ability to understand, learn, and respond to various user queries, providing valuable and personalized responses. Its sophisticated language processing capability is not limited to basic responses; it can be customized and trained to respond in a contextually appropriate manner based on the type of inquiry and the conversation history. It can also integrate with a variety of platforms and applications, such as websites, mobile apps, and messaging systems, enhancing its accessibility and functionality.

The deployment of Watson Assistant in the field of dentistry offers several benefits. First and foremost, it can be used as a round-the-clock customer service representative. Dental practices can use Watson Assistant to handle patient inquiries, provide information about dental procedures, dental hygiene, and preventive care, and even clarify doubts about prescribed treatments. This improves the patient experience by providing them with a readily available source of information while freeing up valuable time for dental professionals.

Secondly, Watson Assistant can aid in efficient appointment scheduling. Integrated with the dental practice's appointment system, Watson Assistant can automate the process of setting, rescheduling, or canceling appointments based on patient requests. This not only simplifies the process for patients, allowing them to manage their appointments at their convenience but also reduces administrative workloads in the dental office.

The AI platform can also function as a tool for dental staff, providing quick access to relevant information. Whether it's assisting with procedure guidelines, information about dental tools, or even pulling up patient records, Watson Assistant can significantly improve the operational efficiency of a dental clinic.

Furthermore, Watson Assistant can contribute to patient triaging and preliminary assessment. Programmed to ask targeted questions about a patient's symptoms, Watson Assistant can provide a preliminary analysis of potential dental issues. While not a substitute for professional diagnosis, it offers a valuable starting point that informs further clinical evaluation.

IBM Watson Assistant can greatly benefit the field of dentistry by enhancing patient engagement, streamlining administrative tasks, and supporting staff in their roles, thereby enabling dental professionals to focus more on delivering excellent patient care.

27.5.2 Watson Discovery

IBM Watson Discovery is an advanced cloud-native insight engine that enables organizations to find value in complex and unstructured data. It uses advanced data ingestion, ML, and NLP capabilities to help businesses discover patterns and valuable insights in their data. Watson Discovery can read, understand and interpret a multitude of data formats and sources, including PDFs, Word documents, webpages, and more. The application of Watson Discovery in the field of dentistry can have significant implications. Dentists and researchers can use Watson Discovery to sift through large volumes of research articles, clinical studies, patient records, and other unstructured data to identify important patterns, trends, and insights (Strickland, 2019). For instance, it could help uncover new research on the effectiveness of certain treatments, the side effects of specific medications, or the links between oral health and other medical conditions.

The tool could also be leveraged to improve patient care and outcomes. By analyzing patient records and histories, Watson Discovery can provide personalized treatment recommendations and identify potential risk factors or health concerns. These capabilities can enable a more personalized approach to dental care, improving patient satisfaction and health outcomes.

In terms of professional development and knowledge sharing, Watson Discovery can be a powerful tool for dental professionals. It can be used to stay up-to-date with the latest research and advances in the field of dentistry, ensuring that dental professionals can continue to provide the best possible care to their patients. This kind of continuous learning is key in an ever-evolving field like healthcare.

Additionally, Watson Discovery can assist in regulatory compliance. By scanning and analyzing policy documents and guidelines, the system can highlight areas of concern and help dental practices remain compliant with industry regulations and standards. In this way, Watson Discovery can reduce the risk of non-compliance and help dental practices focus on what they do best - caring for their patients' oral health. Overall, IBM Watson Discovery is a powerful tool that can support dentistry in various ways, from enhancing patient care to promoting professional development and ensuring regulatory compliance.

27.5.3 Watson's natural language understanding

IBM Watson's natural language understanding (NLU) is a powerful AI service specifically designed to analyze textual data, making sense of the human language's nuances and complexities. It employs the principles of ML, NLP, and cognitive computing to analyze text for themes, sentiments, categories, keywords, and semantic roles, effectively enabling machines to interpret human language in its natural and unstructured form (Kumar et al., 2022).

Within the sphere of dentistry, the utility of Watson's NLU service cannot be overstated. A large portion of dental health data, from electronic dental records to patient feedback, is unstructured. Watson's NLU service holds the capacity to process this data, distilling relevant information and interpreting the semantic relationships within the data. It can identify associations between specific dental symptoms and conditions, providing crucial insights that can inform clinical decision-making and shape preventive strategies in dental healthcare. Moreover, Watson's NLU service can play a pivotal role in enhancing patient engagement and communication. By utilizing sentiment analysis, it can assess patients' attitudes and emotions based on their communication, allowing dental care providers to better understand patients' perspectives and tailor their approaches accordingly. Watson's NLU can also translate complex dental jargon into everyday language, enhancing patient understanding and communication, and thereby improving the overall patient experience. On the research front, Watson's NLU service can serve as an invaluable tool for exploring vast amounts of scientific literature and identifying emerging trends and novel insights. This could drive groundbreaking research in dental health, contributing to the development of more effective treatments and preventive strategies. By aiding in the synthesis of systematic reviews, meta-analysis, and evidence-based guidelines, Watson's NLU can greatly enhance the reliability and efficiency of dental research, thus contributing significantly to the advancement of dental science.

27.5.4 Watson Knowledge Studio

Watson Knowledge Studio is an advanced cloud-based application that allows experts to teach Watson how to interpret specific terms, phrases, and concepts within a particular domain or industry. This is achieved through a process known as 'ML annotation', where subject matter experts label and connect various concepts in text documents to train Watson to understand their relationships and meanings. This knowledge is then utilized by other Watson services like NLU and Discovery to enhance their understanding and analysis of similar texts. In the context of dentistry, Watson Knowledge Studio can be used to train Watson to understand the unique terminology and relationships used within the field. Dentistry encompasses a wide range of specialized terms and complex relationships among conditions, treatments, and anatomy. By annotating dental literature, research papers, and case studies in the Watson Knowledge Studio, Watson can be trained to understand these terms and their interrelations, allowing it to accurately interpret and analyze dental texts. One possible application is in the analysis of dental literature and research. By training Watson on the nuances of dental research language, researchers could use Watson's services to quickly and accurately analyze vast amounts of dental literature, helping to identify trends, compare studies, and extract valuable insights. This could significantly reduce the time spent on literature reviews and increase the pace of research in the field of dentistry. Watson Knowledge Studio could also be instrumental in the development of intelligent virtual assistants for dental practices. By teaching Watson the language of dentistry, virtual assistants could accurately interpret and respond to patient inquiries about complex dental conditions and treatments, providing valuable information and reducing the administrative burden on dental staff. IBM Watson Knowledge Studio offers immense potential for enhancing the understanding and application of AI in the field of dentistry. By empowering Watson to comprehend the specialized language and complex relationships inherent in dental practice and research, it could enable more effective use of AI for a variety of dental applications.

27.5.5 Watson OpenScale

IBM Watson OpenScale is a platform designed to help organizations automate, manage, and optimize AI models in real-time. Watson OpenScale provides transparency into how AI models make decisions, can detect and mitigate algorithmic bias, and tracks model performance over time. This solution supports models built with a variety of ML frameworks and can be deployed in any environment, including IBM Cloud, other clouds, or on-premises systems.

Within the field of dentistry, Watson OpenScale could be used to manage and optimize AI models developed to support various aspects of dental care. For instance, models used for predicting oral diseases, personalizing treatment plans, or optimizing clinic operations can be monitored and adjusted as needed using Watson OpenScale. The platform can track the accuracy and fairness of these models over time, ensuring they continue to function effectively and ethically.

Watson OpenScale's ability to detect and mitigate bias is particularly beneficial in dentistry, given the critical importance of fairness in healthcare outcomes. For example, an AI model might be used to triage patients based on the urgency of their condition. If the model is biased—perhaps due to unbalanced training data—it might incorrectly prioritize some patients over others. With Watson OpenScale, these biases can be detected and mitigated, ensuring equitable treatment for all patients.

The platform's capability to provide transparency in decision-making is also vital in a healthcare setting. Dentists and patients alike need to trust AI models and understand how they reach their decisions, especially when these decisions impact patient care. Watson OpenScale's explainability feature can help demystify AI model decisions, fostering trust among practitioners and patients and promoting the adoption of AI in dental practices.

Furthermore, Watson OpenScale helps ensure the performance of AI models in real-world scenarios. As more dental practices adopt AI technologies, it's critical that these models deliver accurate and reliable results. Through continuous monitoring and management, Watson OpenScale can help ensure these AI tools remain effective, even as conditions change or new data becomes available. In this way, Watson OpenScale supports the sustainable and responsible use of AI in dentistry, ultimately helping to improve patient care and outcomes.

27.5.6 Watson Visual Recognition

IBM Watson Visual Recognition is a powerful AI service that uses deep learning algorithms to analyze images for scenes, objects, faces, colors, food, and explicit content. This innovative technology can even be trained to recognize and classify specific visual content by creating and training a custom model. The service's capabilities extend beyond simple image analysis, providing detailed insights and understanding into the visual content (Kumar et al., 2022).

In the realm of dentistry, Watson Visual Recognition can be instrumental in analyzing and interpreting dental imagery, such as X-rays, CT scans, and intraoral photographs. Traditionally, these images are evaluated by dental professionals to diagnose oral health conditions, determine treatment plans, and monitor progress. Watson's visual recognition capabilities can augment this process by providing automated, consistent, and potentially more accurate assessments.

For instance, Watson Visual Recognition could be trained to identify dental caries, periodontal disease, or oral cancer in dental X-rays and other imagery. Not only could this help dentists in identifying these conditions, but it could also potentially detect them in their early stages, enabling timely intervention and treatment. This is particularly valuable given that early detection is crucial to successful treatment outcomes, especially in cases of oral cancer.

Additionally, Watson Visual Recognition could be used to streamline routine dental tasks such as charting. Traditionally, dental charting, which involves recording the condition of a patient's teeth and gums, is a manual and time-consuming process. However, by using Watson's Visual Recognition, dental images can be automatically analyzed and relevant findings could be directly mapped to a dental chart, saving time and reducing the likelihood of human error.

Lastly, the use of AI-based visual recognition in dentistry could lead to more personalized patient care. By analyzing a patient's dental imagery over time, Watson Visual Recognition could help in tracking changes, predicting potential issues, and customizing treatment plans. As such, Watson Visual Recognition is poised to play a significant role in transforming the dental field, providing dentists with powerful tools for diagnosis, treatment planning, and patient care.

27.5.7 Watson knowledge catalog

The IBM Watson knowledge catalog (WKC) is a cloud-based solution that assists in organizing and making sense of complex data, providing a reliable and consistent way of managing data assets and AI models, It conceals its ML and cataloging capabilities beneath a user-friendly workspace that is organized based on different roles (Goetz, 2018). As part of the IBM Cloud Pak for Data, the catalog can help businesses and professionals across various industries to improve their data governance, accelerate data science, and achieve compliance. A vital component of WKC is its data quality and profiling tools which provide transparency into data, support effective governance and enhance data discovery, ensuring that users work with the best data possible.

In the field of dentistry, the application of the Watson Knowledge Catalog can revolutionize the way practitioners access, understand, and use their patient data. By integrating all relevant patient data into the catalog, dental practitioners can better visualize and analyze their patient's health history, treatment progress, and potential risk factors. This can support more personalized treatment plans and improve patient care outcomes.

A key advantage of WKC in dentistry is its ability to streamline compliance efforts. Dentists deal with a wealth of sensitive patient information and are subject to stringent data protection regulations. WKC's robust data governance features can help dental practices manage consent, maintain data privacy, and ensure compliance with standards such as the Health Insurance Portability and Accountability Act and the General Data Protection Regulation.

The WKC also assists in predictive analysis, a feature that can be particularly useful in the dental field. The catalog can analyze numerous data points, identify patterns, and predict dental health trends. For instance, it could predict the likelihood of a patient developing periodontal disease based on a combination of genetic, behavioral, and environmental factors. This capability enables dental professionals to take preventive measures and deliver more proactive care.

Lastly, WKC promotes collaboration and knowledge sharing among dental professionals. Dentists, hygienists, and dental researchers can access and contribute to a shared pool of resources, such as best practice guidelines, research findings, and patient cases. This supports the development of a learning healthcare system within dentistry, where data is continuously used to learn and improve patient care. In summary, the WKC can be a powerful tool in advancing data-driven dentistry, ensuring compliance, and enhancing patient outcomes.

27.5.8 Watson Compare and Comply

IBM Watson Compare and Comply is a powerful AI tool designed to analyze and understand legal and business documents, turning unstructured data into structured, actionable information. Using advanced features such as element classification, table understanding, and comparison, it can extract critical information, identify anomalies, and compare multiple documents for discrepancies.

In the realm of dentistry, Watson Compare and Comply can be utilized in several ways. One major application lies in contract and policy management. Dental practices often deal with numerous agreements such as employee contracts, vendor contracts, and insurance agreements. Watson Compare and Comply can help to manage these documents more effectively by extracting key information, such as contract terms, obligations, and expiration dates, making it easier for dental practices to track and manage their contractual commitments.

Another application of Compare and Comply is in regulatory compliance. Dental practices are subject to various regulations and guidelines pertaining to areas such as patient privacy, sterilization procedures, and waste management. Watson Compare and Comply can analyze these regulatory documents, extract the key requirements, and highlight any changes or updates, helping dental practices stay on top of their compliance obligations.

Additionally, Watson Compare and Comply can assist in managing patient consent forms. Before undergoing any dental procedure, patients are required to sign consent forms that detail the nature of the procedure and its associated risks. The AI tool can help dental practices manage these consent forms more efficiently, highlighting key information such as patient consent and any special considerations or conditions.

In terms of financial management, Watson Compare and Comply can be employed to review and analyze billing and insurance documents. Extracting relevant data, it can help ensure that services are billed correctly and that insurance claims are accurately processed, reducing financial errors and discrepancies.

In summary, Watson Compare and Comply can greatly contribute to improving the efficiency of dental practices. By automating the review and management of various documents, the AI tool can save time, reduce errors, and help dental practices focus on their primary goal — providing quality dental care to their patients.

27.6 Challenges

When discussing the intervention of AI in our businesses, especially in the field of healthcare, dealing with patients, there are always concerns such as patient data security, privacy preservation and trust, data accuracy (Hassani et al., 2023) and other ethical considerations; yet if these technologies are to be used in the treatment process, clear guidelines must be established for all parties involved (Li et al., 2022).

IBM Watson struggles in the healthcare industry due to its limitations in computer intelligence compared to human problem-solving and decision-making. In spite of advancements in AI technologies, computers still heavily rely on human programming, making it extremely challenging to replicate human intelligence (Wagle, 2013). This limitation hinders Watson's ability to understand complex medical scenarios and provide accurate recommendations.

Regulatory hurdles further impede the implementation of AI systems in healthcare. Current regulations lack standardized protocols to assess the safety and effectiveness of AI technologies, leading to uncertainty and hindering widespread adoption. Additionally, data exchange presents a significant challenge as AI systems require ongoing adjustment with data from clinical studies. However, the healthcare industry faces obstacles in stimulating data sharing, limiting the availability of up-to-date information to improve AI systems (Jiang et al., 2017). Medical science relies on a physician's simultaneous use of cognitive skills, creativity, and insight, as well as individual judgment and even intuitive decisions and major breakthroughs often result from the expertise of healthcare professionals, In addition to these, one cannot deny the impact of human empathy on the healthcare professionals efficacy. as well. coupling the cognitive and intuitive capabilities of human doctors with AI solutions remains a critical challenge for IBM Watson in healthcare (Schilling, 2017). Medical diagnosis is a far more intricate task compared to answering Jeopardy questions. besides Institutions and healthcare professionals utilize medical terminology in diverse forms, so despite the diligent work of software engineers, IBM Watson still falls short in handling medical language with the same level of proficiency as humans (Schmidt, 2017). The failed partnership between IBM Watson Health and The University of Texas MD Anderson Cancer Center exemplifies the resistance to digital transformation in healthcare. The project initially demonstrated Watson's potential in formulating cancer treatment plans but faced technical issues, lack of concentration, and outdated information (Schilling, 2017). Despite all the concerns mentioned above, the question is how long will healthcare providers' resistance to the adaption of AI services in their work, may have them survive in the current competitive, fiercely evolving business world.

27.7 Conclusion

In conclusion, AI's rapid advancement in healthcare highlights IBM Watson as a potent AI system applicable to this sector. Despite its broad adoption in various medical fields, IBM Watson's potential in dentistry remains largely untapped. Overcoming challenges and building trust are crucial to unlocking its capabilities for enhancing dental care. Collaborative efforts between AI systems and healthcare experts promise more efficient patient care, with transformative effects on the broader healthcare industry. AI integration in smart healthcare reshapes patient-provider interactions, empowering informed decisions through AI-driven tools and smart home systems. However, implementing AI requires validation, ethical considerations, and further research. IBM Watson stands out as a leading AI system, utilizing cognitive capabilities to process natural language and extract insights from data. This enables informed decision-making tailored to specific contexts. This versatile system has applications in various fields, including healthcare. Watson employs deep and transfer learning, continuously adapting to industry-specific languages while ensuring data security. Its applications extend to healthcare and dentistry, empowering enterprises with services from chatbots to data analysis. In essence, IBM Watson's journey in healthcare and dentistry underscores AI's transformative potential. Overcoming challenges, fostering collaboration, and building trust between AI systems and professionals heralding an exciting era in efficient and impactful patient care.

References

Aggarwal, K., Mijwil, M. M., Al-Mistarehi, A.-H., Alomari, S., Gök, M., Alaabdin, A. M. Z., et al. (2022). Has the future started? The current growth of artificial intelligence, machine learning, and deep learning. *Iraqi Journal for Computer Science and Mathematics, 3*(1), 115−123.

Bigus, J. P., Campbell, M., Carmeli, B., Cefkin, M., Chang, H., Chen-Ritzo, C.-H., et al. (2011). Information technology for healthcare transformation. *IBM Journal of Research and Development, 55*(5), 6: 1-6: 14.

Chen, Y., Argentinis, J. E., & Weber, G. (2016). IBM Watson: How cognitive computing can be applied to big data challenges in life sciences research. *Clinical Therapeutics, 38*(4), 688−701.

Chen, Y.-w, Stanley, K., & Att, W. (2020). Artificial intelligence in dentistry: Current applications and future perspectives. *Quintessence International, 51*(3), 248−257.

Derchi, G., Visentin, M., Marchio, V., Lardani, L., Barone, A., Prenassi, M., et al. (2020). Application of IBM Watson to support literature reviews: A preliminary experience in restorative dentistry. *Studies in Health Technology and Informatics, 270*, 1201−1202.

Duan, Y., Edwards, J. S., & Dwivedi, Y. K. (2019). Artificial intelligence for decision making in the era of Big Data−evolution, challenges and research agenda. *International Journal of Information Management, 48*, 63−71.

Fiehn, R., Okunev, I., Bayham, M., Barefoot, S., & Tranby, E. P. (2020). Emergency and urgent dental visits among Medicaid enrollees from 2013 to 2017. *BMC Oral Health, 20*(1), 1−7.

Ghazal, T. M., Hasan, M. K., Alshurideh, M. T., Alzoubi, H. M., Ahmad, M., Akbar, S. S., et al. (2021). IoT for smart cities: Machine learning approaches in smart healthcare—A review. *Future Internet, 13*(8), 218.

Goetz, M. (2018). Leaders C. The Forrester Wave™: Machine learning data catalogs, Q2 2018. Forrester Research, Consortium Report.

Hamilton, J. G., Genoff Garzon, M., Westerman, J. S., Shuk, E., Hay, J. L., Walters, C., et al. (2019). A tool, not a crutch": Patient perspectives about IBM Watson for oncology trained by Memorial Sloan Kettering. *Journal of Oncology Practice, 15*(4), e277–e288.

Hassani, H., Amiri Andi, P., Ghodsi, A., Norouzi, K., Komendantova, N., & Unger, S. (2021). Shaping the future of smart dentistry: From artificial intelligence (AI) to intelligence augmentation (IA). *IoT, 2*(3), 510–523.

Hassani, H., Norouzi, K., Ghodsi, A., & Huang, X. (2023). Revolutionary dentistry through blockchain technology. *Big Data and Cognitive Computing, 7*(1), 9.

Hsu, T.-H., Wang, Z.-H., & See, A. R. (2022). A cloud-edge-smart IoT architecture for speeding up the deployment of neural network models with transfer learning techniques. *Electronics, 11*(14), 2255.

Jiang, F., Jiang, Y., Zhi, H., Dong, Y., Li, H., Ma, S., et al. (2017). Artificial intelligence in healthcare: Past, present and future. *Stroke and Vascular Neurology, 2*(4).

Klumpp, M., Hintze, M., Immonen, M., Ródenas-Rigla, F., Pilati, F., Aparicio-Martínez, F., et al. (2021). Artificial intelligence for hospital health care: Application cases and answers to challenges in European hospitals, editors *Healthcare*.

Kohn, M. S., Sun, J., Knoop, S., Shabo, A., Carmeli, B., Sow, D., et al. (2014). IBM's health analytics and clinical decision support. *Yearbook of Medical Informatics, 23*(01), 154–162.

Kumar, A., Tejaswini, P., Nayak, O., Kujur, A. D., Gupta, R., Rajanand, A., et al. (2022). A survey on IBM Watson and its services, editors *Journal of Physics: Conference Series*.

LeCun, Y., Bengio, Y., & Hinton, G. (2015). Deep learning. *Nature, 521*(7553), 436–444.

Lee, D., & Yoon, S. N. (2021). Application of artificial intelligence-based technologies in the healthcare industry: Opportunities and challenges. *International Journal of Environmental Research and Public Health, 18*(1), 271.

Lee, K. Y., & Kim, J. (2016). Artificial intelligence technology trends and IBM Watson references in the medical field. *Korean Medical Education Review, 18*(2), 51–57.

Li, F., Ruijs, N., & Lu, Y. (2022). Ethics & AI: A systematic review on ethical concerns and related strategies for designing with AI in healthcare. *AI, 4*(1), 28–53.

McGivern, S., Ahmed, I., Beymer, M. R., Okunev, I., Tranby, E. P., Frantsve-Hawley, J., et al. (2021). Association between first oral examination characteristics and dental treatment needs in privately insured children: A claims data analysis. *The Journal of the American Dental Association, 152*(11), 936–942, e1.

Neill, D. B. (2013). Using artificial intelligence to improve hospital inpatient care. *IEEE Intelligent Systems, 28*(2), 92–95.

Okunev, I., Frantsve-Hawley, J., & Tranby, E. (2021). Trends in national opioid prescribing for dental procedures among patients enrolled in Medicaid. *The Journal of the American Dental Association, 152*(8), 622–630, e3.

Okunev, I., Tranby, E. P., Jacob, M., Diep, V. K., Kelly, A., Heaton, L. J., et al. (2022). The impact of underutilization of preventive dental care by adult Medicaid participants. *Journal of Public Health Dentistry, 82*(1), 88–98.

Okunseri, C., Frantsve-Hawley, J., Thakkar-Samtani, M., Okunev, I., Heaton, L. J., & Tranby, E. P. (2023). Estimation of oral disease burden from claims and self-reported data. *Journal of Public Health Dentistry, 83*(1), 51–59.

Prateek, M., Singh, T., Choudhury, T., Pandey, H.M., & Nhu, N.G. (2021). *Proceedings of International Conference on Machine Intelligence and Data Science Applications: MIDAS 2020*. Springer.

Raj, P., Raman, A., Nagaraj, D., Duggirala, S., Raj, P., Raman, A., et al. (2015). Big data analytics for healthcare. *High-Performance Big-Data Analytics: Computing Systems and Approaches*, 391–424.

Roongruangsilp, P., & Khongkhunthian, P. (2021). The learning curve of artificial intelligence for dental implant treatment planning: a descriptive study. *Applied Sciences, 11*(21), 10159.

Russo-Spena, T., Mele, C., & Marzullo, M. (2019). Practising value innovation through artificial intelligence: The IBM Watson case. *Journal of Creating Value, 5*(1), 11–24.

Schilling, R. B. (2017). What hospitals can learn from IBM Watson health's challenges. *Application Radiology, 46*(9), 8.

Schmidt, C. M. D. (2017). *Anderson breaks with IBM Watson, raising questions about artificial intelligence in oncology*. Oxford University Press.

Schwendicke, F., Samek, W., & Krois, J. (2020). Artificial intelligence in dentistry: chances and challenges. *Journal of Dental Research, 99*(7), 769–774.

Shader, R. I. (2016). Some reflections on IBM Watson and on women's health. *Clinical Therapeutics, 38*(1), 1–2.

Shan, T., Tay, F., & Gu, L. (2021). Application of artificial intelligence in dentistry. *Journal of Dental Research, 100* (3), 232–244.

Strickland, E. (2019). IBM Watson, heal thyself: How IBM overpromised and underdelivered on AI health care. *IEEE Spectrum, 56*(4), 24–31.

Thornhill, M. H., Gibson, T. B., Cutler, E., Dayer, M. J., Chu, V. H., Lockhart, P. B., et al. (2018). Antibiotic prophylaxis and incidence of endocarditis before and after the 2007 AHA recommendations. *Journal of the American College of Cardiology, 72*(20), 2443–2454.

Tranby, E. P., Heaton, L. J., Tomar, S. L., Kelly, A. L., Fager, G. L., Backley, M., et al. (2022). Oral cancer prevalence, mortality, and costs in Medicaid and commercial insurance claims data. *Cancer Epidemiology, Biomarkers & Prevention, 31*(9), 1849–1857.

Wagle, K. (2013). IBM Watson: Revolutionizing healthcare? *Young Scientists Journal, 6*(13), 17.

Wilhelm, A., & Ziegler, W. (eds.) (2021). Extending semantic context analysis using machine learning services to process unstructured data. In *SHS web of conferences*. EDP Sciences.

Yu, Y.-J. (2016). Machine learning for dental image analysis. *arXiv preprint arXiv*.

Zou, F.-w, Tang, Y.-f, Liu, C.-y, Ma, J.-a, & Hu, C.-h (2020). Concordance study between IBM Watson for oncology and real clinical practice for cervical cancer patients in China: A retrospective analysis. *Frontiers in Genetics, 11*, 200.

Multiple digital patient check-in through blockchain and medical sensor network

Bao Le, Vikram Puri, Nhu Gia Nguyen and Chung Van Le

School of Computer Science, Duy Tan University, Da Nang, Vietnam

28.1 Introduction

In recent years, the healthcare sector has witnessed notable advancements, resulting in a profound and revolutionary influence on the industry. The aforementioned improvements have facilitated the delivery of improved healthcare services to individuals, consequently making a positive impact on their holistic welfare (El Khatib et al., 2022). Technological breakthroughs have brought about substantial changes in the healthcare industry, leading to a shift in focus from conventional medical techniques to the integration of cutting-edge instruments like magnetic resonance imaging scanners and telemedicine services. In addition, wearable devices provide additional support in the monitoring of patients' real-time activities (Wu et al., 2022). The healthcare sector has experienced significant developments due to the emergence of the digital revolution, which has served as a main accelerator. Presently, there exists an emerging inclination towards the implementation of digital patient check-in systems (DPCSs) within medical facilities owing to the numerous benefits they offer to healthcare practitioners and patients alike. The examined ecosystem provides autonomous services that encompass the entirety of the patient registration and check-in process through electronic means, thereby diminishing the reliance on paper-based documentation and traditional ways of data entry. The utilization of digital patient systems inside medical environments has a number of noteworthy benefits.

Sensor Networks for Smart Hospitals
DOI: https://doi.org/10.1016/B978-0-443-36370-2.00029-3

28.1.1 Data accuracy

The implementation of a DPCS serves to guarantee the accuracy of patient information and important data while also facilitating real-time collection. By doing so, this system effectively mitigates errors in data and contributes to the improvement of healthcare quality (Samha et al., 2022).

28.1.2 Efficient system

Digital patient check-in procedures can shorten wait times and enhance patient experiences by automating certain processes (Lawton et al., 2023).

28.1.3 Enhance patient engagement

The DPCS offers easy-to-use services that eliminate barriers between technology and patients, hence improving the platform for involvement by patients (Barony Sanchez et al., 2022).

28.1.4 Reduce cost

The use of digital check-in systems has resulted in the elimination of paper-based requirements and traditional methods of patient data entry. This technological advancement has shown to be beneficial in reducing costs associated with administrative activities.

Currently, the majority of patient check-in solutions rely on cloud-based ecosystems. While the healthcare industry widely adopts these systems, it is imperative to acknowledge and solve certain challenges associated with their implementation. These concerns encompass security, patient privacy, usability, and limitations in data storage capacity. Furthermore, the issue of single-point failure inside the healthcare ecosystem. The implementation of blockchain technology has the potential to address the aforementioned challenges and offer an improved solution for the multipatient check-in system (Maathavan & Venkatraman, 2022).

28.2 Background

This section provides a concise overview of the existing knowledge regarding the advantages and disadvantages of DPCSs. It also presents a brief introduction to blockchain technology and explores its potential application in conjunction with sensor technology (Heponiemi et al., 2022).

28.2.1 Digital patient check-in systems—merits and demerits

The DPCS has seen significant advancements, resulting in a range of advantages and disadvantages in practical application (see Fig. 28.1). The system possesses several commendable attributes.

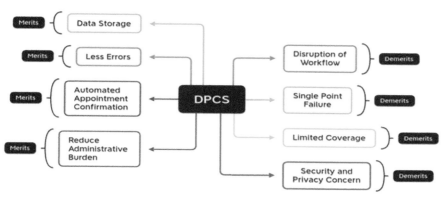

FIGURE 28.1   Merits and demerits of a digital patient check-in system.

28.2.1.1 *Automated appointment confirmation*

DPCS has the capability to autonomously verify the patient's appointment, hence mitigating the need for medical personnel to engage in telephonic communication or dispatch reminders to patients.

28.2.1.2 *Reduce administrative burden*

DPCS has the potential to mitigate administrative burdens inside medical facilities.

28.2.1.3 *Less errors*

The use of DPCS has the potential to mitigate or eradicate errors commonly seen in electronic health records, electronic physician prescriptions, and the identification of patient processes.

28.2.1.4 *Data storage*

DPCS is widely acknowledged for its several advantages compared to manual data record-keeping. These advantages encompass reduced waiting time, enhanced system efficiency, improved data security, and the generation of comprehensive and detailed reports, surpassing the capabilities of manual recording approaches.

Despite the DPCS's advantages, there are several limitations (Odeh et al., 2022), including the following:

28.2.1.4.1 Disruption of workflow

DPCS have the drawback of temporarily decreasing efficiency for medical workers and healthcare professionals by interfering with operations.

28.2.1.4.2 Single-point failure issue

Cloud-enabled DPCS may encounter the challenge of a single-point failure, resulting in the deletion of patient data and system downtime until it is reinitiated.

28.2.1.4.3 Limited coverage

Although Medicare offers coverage for virtual check-ins, it should be noted that not every insurer offers the same coverage for this service.

28.2.1.4.4 Security and privacy concern

Medical professionals who desire enhanced privacy safeguards and data security for telehealth services, particularly when utilizing video communication solutions, may consider engaging technology suppliers to facilitate these services.

28.2.2 Overview of blockchain technology and medical sensor network

Blockchain technology is characterized by its decentralized nature and immutability, which facilitates the tracking and recording of transactions inside an intranet environment (Lim et al., 2021). The data stored within the blockchain network is in a digitized format. The distinguishing characteristic of a blockchain network is its ability to instill confidence in participants without relying on intermediaries, as it guarantees the integrity and reliability of recorded data. Data is collected within the blockchain network through the assembly of blocks, which are subsequently linked together to establish chains. The current structure of the system distinguishes it from centralized databases. The blockchain is a contemporary technology that is characterized by its high level of security and ongoing development (Haleem et al., 2021). The possibilities of blockchain technology expand beyond the realm of cryptocurrencies and find applications in other sectors such as healthcare, government administration, agriculture, and tourism.

Medical sensor networks are a component of wireless sensor networks that are employed in medical facilities for the purpose of monitoring current information pertaining to patients' vitals and overall health conditions. This type of network comprises wearable and portable devices capable of gathering information about patients, which is then transmitted to a centralized surveillance system for subsequent analysis (Muzammal et al., 2020). The primary advantages of a medical sensor network lie in its ability to promptly offer assistance upon detecting any form of patient anomaly.

The integration of blockchain technology with medical sensors serves to augment the levels of confidentiality and privacy pertaining to patient data. The integration of blockchain technology with sensor networks offers several significant advantages (Godawatte et al., 2022; Taherdoost, 2023). Firstly, the implementation of a secure access and authentication system for multiple patient data across many stakeholders is crucial (see Fig. 28.2). This ensures the protection of data from any unauthorized modification, maintains data integrity, and establishes accountability. Additionally, the incorporation of decentralization within the network is of utmost importance as it mitigates the risk of a single-point failure.

28.2.3 Applicability of blockchain and sensors for multipatient check-in

The integration of blockchain technology with sensors can be utilized for the purpose of facilitating multipatient check-in (Khezr et al., 2019). Table 28.1 represents the applicability of the integral approach of blockchain and sensors in multipatient check-in systems.

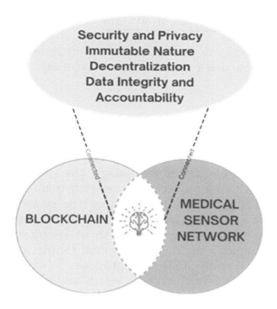

FIGURE 28.2 Fusion of the blockchain with medical sensor network.

TABLE 28.1 Integrating sensors and blockchain for multipatient check-in.

Service	Usage
Patient unique identity (PUID) Identification system	**Sensors:** Camera recognizes the patient's face and recognizes its ID. **Blockchain:** Provide decentralized and encrypted ledger to store the patient data.
Autonomous multi check-in system	**Sensors:** RFID, bluetooth, NFC could recognize the patient by its PUID. **Blockchain:** All transactions through these sensors recorded in the ledger which are immutable in nature.
Payment processing	**Sensors:** Biometric or RFID sensor embedded with payment account and insurance card.**Blockchain:** Smart contract deployed to deduct the money as per the insurance policy.
Tracking medical partitioner team	**Sensors:** The main purpose of the medical practitioner team is to track the movement of teams and enhance the coordination between the team members.**Blockchain:** Smart contract helps to alert the team regarding patient activities and maintain the record of every activity with high security.
Reduce waiting time for patients	**Sensors:** Sensors possess the capability to effectively monitor patient flows and wait periods, establish communication with patient lineups through blockchain-based data, and optimize patient channeling in order to mitigate the occurrence of blockages.**Blockchain:** It is used to collect and store in the ledger and take action through the use of Blockchain technology.
Tracking of medical equipment	**Sensors:** Sensors have the potential to track medical supplies in order to optimize the process of registration and clearance. **Blockchain:** It records all data for auditing purposes.

28.3 Blockchain-enabled multipatient check-in system

This section discusses the current solutions available for multipatient check-in systems utilizing blockchain technology, as well as the private and public blockchain solutions for such systems.

28.3.1 Review of existing blockchain solutions for patient check-in

In recent years, a number of academic works have emerged that examine the implementation and impact of patient check-in systems utilizing blockchain technology. The authors of the study (Naresh et al., 2021) presented a proposition for a decentralized system aimed at managing electronic health records while ensuring privacy preservation. The system consists of four unique layers, specifically the data gathering layer, access and authentication layer, communication layer, and storage layer. The integration of smart contracts in tandem with the elliptic curve encryption methodology augments the overall security of the system. In the current study, the authors (Rajput et al., 2021) have proposed a health management framework that leverages blockchain technology to offer a secure and robust solution for implementation within specified rules. The aforementioned policies span the areas of access and authentication control, as well as auditing. The application of smart contracts is integrated into the proposed system for electronic health records, as outlined in the reference (Celladurai et al., 2021). The main objective of the smart contract is to streamline the process of patient registration and develop a secure network login system. Additionally, its objective is to produce digital documentation of the individual receiving medical care, guaranteeing the safe and protected storage of this information inside the healthcare system. Furthermore, the contractual agreement incorporates a provision for the modification of licenses, specifically in situations of urgency. In addition, it facilitates patients' ability to get care in their own homes. In their publication, the authors (Sonkamble et al., 2023) have presented a proposal for a decentralized health management system that leverages blockchain technology. The primary objective of this system is to address many issues, such as safeguarding data privacy, ensuring control over access, and enhancing security measures. This paper introduces a new methodology for password authentication by incorporating key exchange techniques and applying them via smart contracts.

Furthermore, the research investigates the utilization of InterPlanetary File System (IPFS) as a means of storing data. Numerous analyses and research studies have also explored the use of blockchain technology in enhancing the security of electronic health data and protecting patient privacy. This study (Kiania et al., 2023) presents a systematic literature evaluation with the objective of examining existing scholarly articles that discuss the application of blockchain technology in the context of electronic health systems. The main aims of this investigation were to assess the efficacy of blockchain technology in safeguarding patient data and enhancing patient confidentiality. In order to discover and present future opportunities and study areas for fellow scholars, a comprehensive analysis was conducted on a total of 51 publications. Similarly, the importance of blockchain technology in the context of electronic health records has been underscored in scholarly works

TABLE 28.2 Analysis of related work regarding multipatient check-in.

Study	Blockchain	Medical sensor network	Authentication system	Smart contract	Decentralized storage	Review
Naresh et al. (2021)	✓	✗	✓	✓	✗	✗
Rajput et al. (2021)	✓	✗	✓	✓	✗	✗
Celladurai et al. (2021)	✓	✗	✓	✓	✗	✗
Sonkamble et al. (2023)	✓	✗	✓	✓	✓	✗
Kiania et al. (2023)	✓	✗	✗	✗	✗	✓
Wang et al. (2021)	✓	✓	✓	–	✗	✗
Yu and Park (2022)	✓	✓	✓	–	✗	✗

(Al Mamun et al., 2022; Fang et al., 2021; Mahajan, 2022). The lightweight authentication mechanism developed by the authors in reference (Wang et al., 2021) was specifically built for wireless medical sensor networks. This protocol integrates the application of blockchain technology and physically unclonable features. Furthermore, the use of a fuzzy extractor technique is utilized for the processing of the biometric data. As stated in the referenced source Yu and Park (2022), the lightweight protocol examined by Wang et al. (2021) demonstrates susceptibility to various attacks and does not include mutual authentication capabilities (Table 28.2).

28.3.2 Role of permissioned and permissionless for multipatient ecosystem

This section discusses the function of several blockchain system kinds in the multipatient setting.

28.3.2.1 Permissionless blockchain for multipatient system

28.3.2.1.1 Open access

In the context of a permissionless blockchain system, those seeking to participate as patients are required to satisfy specific criteria in order to gain access to the network. The presence of a third party is not necessary for the authorization or cancellation of a patient's check-in. This facilitates unrestricted patient access (Corradini et al., 2023).

28.3.2.1.2 Pseudonymous identities

In the permissionless blockchain, patients' generated hash addresses can be used instead of their actual identities. This serves to protect the patient's confidentiality.

28.3.2.1.3 Proof-of-work applicability

Consensus is commonly obtained through the utilization of either Power-of-Work (PoW) mining or claiming mechanisms. The network's security is achieved by employing cryptoeconomics mechanisms instead of relying just on access controls.

28.3.2.1.4 No central authority

One of the primary advantages of utilizing a public blockchain is the absence of a centralized authority governing access management systems, resulting in enhanced privacy and increased resilience to regulation.

28.3.2.1.5 Performance

The utilization of public blockchain technology presents several issues, including elevated latency and CPU utilization. Additionally, the level of accountability is diminished due to the pseudonymous nature of participants.

28.3.2.2 Permissioned blockchain for multipatient check-in

28.3.2.2.1 Permission required

Within the framework of a permissioned blockchain, it is necessary for patients to obtain an invitation and subsequent authorization from the hospital in order to participate (Kuo & Shieh, 2020). The network is overseen by medical professionals or healthcare institutions.

28.3.2.2.2 Traditional method

In order to attain scalability inside the blockchain network, consensus mechanisms may opt to employ conventional algorithms instead of relying just on mining preferences.

28.3.2.2.3 No pseudonymous

The exposure of patient privacy within a private blockchain network allows for identification. The aforementioned data possesses utility for academics and medical experts in the context of conducting study. Furthermore, it has the potential to be utilized in monitoring the advancement of patients and their therapeutic interventions. The blockchain technology ensures the secure storage of any data, safeguarding it against unauthorized access.

28.3.2.2.4 Less privacy

One of the primary concerns associated with private blockchain technology is the diminished level of patient privacy, along with the increased control exerted by central bodies. Private blockchains also exhibit limited scalability compared to public blockchains, hence posing challenges in effectively managing substantial volumes of data. Moreover, the maintenance of private blockchains might incur significant costs and pose heightened challenges in terms of security.

28.3.2.2.5 Flexibility

The primary advantage of utilizing a private blockchain is the ability to optimize system efficiency by fine-tuning parameters. Additionally, it facilitates adherence to healthcare rules pertaining to multipatient check-in and enables the utilization of identity procedures.

28.3.3 Privacy protection techniques for the multipatient blockchain system

The maintenance of patient confidentiality holds significant significance inside a healthcare blockchain system that incorporates a multitude of patient records. The implementation of a permissioned blockchain, as opposed to a public blockchain, can effectively restrict access and writing permissions exclusively to authorized parties, such as healthcare practitioners. To safeguard the confidentiality of patient data, a viable approach involves assigning pseudonymous IDs to patients, which can afterwards be associated with their genuine identifiers external to the blockchain. To bolster security protocols, it is feasible to utilize encryption methodologies to protect vital patient information before incorporating it into the blockchain. Furthermore, the decrypted information might be subject to exclusive access restrictions, limited only to individuals or institutions with proper authorization. Zero-knowledge proofs facilitate the validation of access rights while retaining the secrecy of the underlying information. Categorizing data according to its sensitivity level is advantageous as it enables the distinction between public data, which exhibits a lower level of sensitivity, and restricted data, which is characterized by a higher degree of sensitivity. The incorporation of private channels and the use of whitelisting practices provide improved means for exercising authority over the dissemination of data. Patient-mediated access controls, which pertain to the process of patients granting authorization for data access, function as a mechanism to protect privacy boundaries from potential violations. By implementing suitable privacy protocols, blockchain technologies possess the capacity to securely store records belonging to several patients. This system enables the secure transmission of patient data, ensuring that only authorized personnel have access to the information. In addition, blockchain systems provide a transparent ledger documenting the identities of individuals who have interacted with the data, along with the associated timestamps of their interactions. Fig. 28.3 represents the privacy protection for multipatient check-in.

28.4 Challenges to combine blockchain with medical sensors in multipatient check-in systems

The integration of blockchain technology and medical sensor networks in the patient check-in system has significantly transformed the healthcare business. However, there are certain issues that still need to be addressed (see Fig. 28.3). These challenges include the following.

28.4.1 Network scalability

A significant amount of data is created within the healthcare ecosystem through diverse patient check-in systems. The existing platforms, specifically Bitcoin and Ethereum, possess intrinsic constraints in their ability to conduct transactions (Ali et al., 2023).

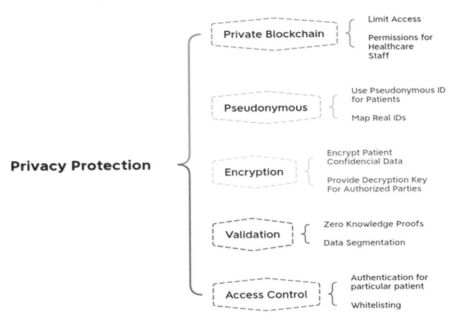

FIGURE 28.3   Privacy protection for multipatient check-in.

The management of substantial quantities of patient data within the network poses a complex and demanding scenario. In order to address these challenges, certain forms of distributed ledger technology, such as directed acyclic graphs, have the potential to offer a solution.

28.4.2 Security and privacy on patient data

Ensuring the protection of patients' medical data is of paramount significance owing to its very sensitive and confidential characteristics, hence requiring the adoption of strong measures to guarantee privacy and security (Abu-Elezz et al., 2020). When encryption techniques and access control mechanisms are not in place, systems are consistently vulnerable to exploitation by malevolent actors. Healthcare providers ought to allocate substantial resources towards implementing cutting-edge security measures to protect patient data. Furthermore, it is crucial for firms to consistently evaluate and modify their security processes in alignment with changing demands or possible vulnerabilities. In addition, it is crucial for healthcare providers to establish a well-defined protocol in order to efficiently handle occurrences of data breaches and other privacy-related issues.

28.4.3 Energy consumption of ecosystem

Permissioned blockchains, such as Bitcoin and Ethereum, employ a consensus process called PoW, which requires a significant amount of energy consumption (Alofi et al., 2022).

The limited energy storage capacity of portable medical devices presents a significant obstacle to their successful integration into a network. To address this concern, one potential approach for minimizing the energy consumption connected with the device is to examine the deployment of proof of stake.

28.4.4 Infrastructure cost

The integration of sensors with a blockchain infrastructure might lead to significant financial costs associated with its construction and maintenance. It is imperative to consider the expenses associated with sensors, network charges, storage prices, and other related expenditures. Engaging in proactive strategic planning is of utmost importance to ensure the availability of essential resources for these expenditures (Pereira et al., 2019). Furthermore, it is imperative to prioritize the security and dependability of the infrastructure. To optimize system performance, it is imperative to conduct routine maintenance and testing procedures. The cost could potentially undergo a substantial escalation in instances where a considerable quantity of patients concurrently establish connections.

28.4.5 Healthcare regulations

The convergence of blockchain technology and medical sensor networks gives rise to a multitude of legal and regulatory inquiries, including those pertaining to health data privacy legislation and the requisite clinical authorizations (Shuaib et al., 2021). It is imperative to ensure that ecosystems are accountable and reliable, devoid of any system mistakes or security breaches. Blockchain networks possess the inherent capacity to transcend geographical boundaries. Nevertheless, it is a prevailing practice for governing bodies to enforce restrictions on the storage and transfer of healthcare data across international borders. Healthcare providers are obligated to uphold the practice of retaining medical records for an extended period of time. Exclusively depending on blockchain technology for the storage of records may not entirely adhere to regulations for the preservation of comprehensive medical histories.

28.4.6 Need of skilled experts

In order to effectively manage healthcare services and the blockchain network, it is vital to have an individual with a high level of expertise who can complete the necessary responsibilities in this domain (Kassab et al., 2021). Healthcare personnel, encompassing medical practitioners, nurses, and medical researchers, sometimes demonstrate a limited understanding of blockchain technology and its consequential implications. Individuals may struggle to fully grasp the diverse range of options or limitations that are present. Similarly, it is frequently noted that developers who specialize in blockchain technology often exhibit a restricted comprehension of the complexities linked to healthcare procedures, the particular privacy prerequisites of medical data, and the regulatory structure that governs the healthcare sector (Fig. 28.4).

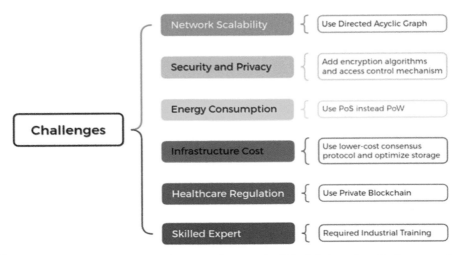

FIGURE 28.4 Challenges and solution of integrated approach of blockchain and medical sensor network.

28.5 Conclusion

The potential of blockchain technology to significantly transform and enhance the medical sensor network is substantial. The utilization of blockchain technology presents the possibility of achieving decentralization within the domain of medical sensor nodes. Moreover, it facilitates the secure dissemination and authentication of health data acquired from wearable devices and medical sensors using encryption techniques. This technology permits the concurrent registration of several patients within the ecosystem and provides their access to real-time patient data, while also assuring the highest level of security and confidentiality for the data. Moreover, it additionally enables the construction of provenance for sensor data and a ledger that is immutable, capable of recording every transaction carried out within the network. This measure facilitates the reduction of data tampering, eradication of errors, and identification of detrimental data. The incorporation of blockchain technology into the medical sensor network functions as a safeguard against potential security breaches or unwanted disturbances inside the network. The objective of this study is to provide a comprehensive analysis of the benefits and drawbacks associated with the implementation of blockchain technology inside medical sensor networks. In summary, blockchain exhibits considerable promise as a foundational technology for establishing trustworthy and decentralized networks that can facilitate the functioning of medical Internet of Things (IoT) and telehealth applications.

References

Abu-Elezz, I., Hassan, A., Nazeemudeen, A., Househ, M., & Abd-Alrazaq, A. (2020). The benefits and threats of blockchain technology in healthcare: A scoping review. *International Journal of Medical Informatics, 142,* 104246.

Al Mamun, A., Azam, S., & Gritti, C. (2022). Blockchain-based electronic health records management: A comprehensive review and future research direction. *IEEE Access, 10,* 5768–5789.

Ali, A., Ali, H., Saeed, A., AhmedKhan, A., Tin, T. T., Assam, M., & Mohamed, H. G. (2023). Blockchain-powered healthcare systems: Enhancing scalability and security with hybrid deep learning. *Sensors, 23*(18), 7740.

Alofi, A., Bokhari, M. A., Bahsoon, R., & Hendley, R. (2022). Optimizing the energy consumption of blockchain-based systems using evolutionary algorithms: A new problem formulation. *IEEE Transactions on Sustainable Computing, 7*(4), 910−922.

Barony Sanchez, R. H., Bergeron-Drolet, L. A., Sasseville, M., & Gagnon, M. P. (2022). Engaging patients and citizens in digital health technology development through the virtual space. *Frontiers in Medical Technology, 4,* 958571.

Celladurai, M. U., Pandian, S., & Ramasamy, K. (2021). A blockchain based patient centric electronic health record storage and integrity management for e-health systems. *Health Policy and Technology, 10*(4), 100513.

Corradini, F., Marcelletti, A., Morichetta, A., Polini, A., Re, B., & Tiezzi, F. (2023). A flexible approach to multi-party business process execution on blockchain. *Future Generation Computer Systems, 147,* 219−234.

El Khatib, M., Hamidi, S., Al Ameeri, I., Al Zaabi, H., & Al Marqab, R. (2022). Digital disruption and big data in healthcare-opportunities and challenges. *ClinicoEconomics and Outcomes Research,* 563−574.

Fang, H. S. A., Tan, T. H., Tan, Y. F. C., & Tan, C. J. M. (2021). Blockchain personal health records: Systematic review. *Journal of Medical Internet Research, 23*(4), e25094.

Godawatte, K., Branch, P., & But, J. (2022). Use of blockchain in health sensor networks to secure information integrity and accountability. *Procedia Computer Science, 210,* 124−132.

Haleem, A., Javaid, M., Singh, R. P., Suman, R., & Rab, S. (2021). Blockchain technology applications in healthcare: An overview. *International Journal of Intelligent Networks, 2,* 130−139, vol.

Heponiemi, T., Kaihlanen, A. M., Kouvonen, A., Leemann, L., Taipale, S., & Gluschkoff, K. (2022). The role of age and digital competence on the use of online health and social care services: A cross-sectional population-based survey. *Digital health, 8,* 20552076221074485.

Kassab, M., Destefanis, G., DeFranco, J., & Pranav, P. (2021, May). Blockchain-engineers wanted: An empirical analysis on required skills, education and experience. In *2021 IEEE/ACM 4th International workshop on emerging trends in software engineering for blockchain (WETSEB)* (pp. 49−55). IEEE.

Khezr, S., Moniruzzaman, M., Yassine, A., & Benlamri, R. (2019). Blockchain technology in healthcare: A comprehensive review and directions for future research. *Applied Sciences, 9*(9), 1736.

Kiania, K., Jameii, S. M., & Rahmani, A. M. (2023). Blockchain-based privacy and security preserving in electronic health: A systematic review. *Multimedia Tools and Applications,* 1−27.

Kuo, Y. J. J., & Shieh, J. C. (2020). Cross-domain design of blockchain smart contract for library and healthcare privacy. *Proceedings of the 4th international conference on medical and health informatics,* 122−126.

Lawton, S., Mallen, C., Muller, S., Wathall, S., & Helliwell, T. (2023). Investigating the usefulness of automated check-in data collection in general practice (AC DC study): A multicentre, cross-sectional study in England. *BMJ Open, 13*(1), e062389.

Lim, M. K., Li, Y., Wang, C., & Tseng, M.-L. (2021). A literature review of blockchain technology applications in supply chains: A comprehensive analysis of themes, methodologies and industries. *Computers & Industrial Engineering, 154,* 107133, vol.

Maathavan, K. S. K., & Venkatraman, S. (2022). A secure encrypted classified electronic healthcare data for public cloud environment. *Intelligent Automation & Soft Computing, 32*(2).

Mahajan, H. B. (2022). Emergence of healthcare 4.0 and blockchain into secure cloud-based electronic health records systems: solutions, challenges, and future roadmap. *Wireless Personal Communications, 126*(3), 2425−2446.

Muzammal, M., Talat, R., Sodhro, A. H., & Pirbhulal, S. (2020). A multi-sensor data fusion enabled ensemble approach for medical data from body sensor networks. *Information Fusion, 53,* 155−164.

Naresh, V. S., Reddi, S., & Allavarpu, V. D. (2021). Blockchain-based patient centric health care communication system. *International Journal of Communication Systems, 34*(7), e4749.

Odeh, A., Keshta, I., & Al-Haija, Q. A. (2022). Analysis of blockchain in the healthcare sector: Application and issues. *Symmetry, 14*(9), 1760.

Pereira, J., Tavalaei, M. M., & Ozalp, H. (2019). Blockchain-based platforms: Decentralized infrastructures and its boundary conditions. *Technological Forecasting and Social Change, 146,* 94−102.

Rajput, A. R., Li, Q., & Ahvanooey, M. T. (2021). A blockchain-based secret-data sharing framework for personal health records in emergency condition. *Healthcare, 9*(2), 206, MDPI.

Samha, A. K., Alrashdi, A. M., & Alshammri, G. H. (2022). The influencing factors of digital health passport adoption and acceptance during COVID-19 in Saudi Arabia. *Digital Health, 8*, 20552076221142668.

Shuaib, M., Alam, S., Alam, M. S., & Nasir, M. S. (2021). Compliance with HIPAA and GDPR in blockchain-based electronic health record. *Materials Today: Proceedings.*

Sonkamble, R. G., Bongale, A. M., Phansalkar, S., Sharma, A., & Rajput, S. (2023). Secure data transmission of electronic health records using blockchain technology. *Electronics, 12*(4), 1015.

Taherdoost, H. (2023). Blockchain-based Internet of Medical Things. *Applied Sciences, 13*(3), 1287.

Wang, W., Chen, Q., Yin, Z., Srivastava, G., Gadekallu, T. R., Alsolami, F., & Su, C. (2021). Blockchain and PUF-based lightweight authentication protocol for wireless medical sensor networks. *IEEE Internet of Things Journal,* *9*(11), 8883−8891.

Wu, C. T., Wang, S. M., Su, Y. E., Hsieh, T. T., Chen, P. C., Cheng, Y. C., & Lai, F. (2022). A precision health service for chronic diseases: development and cohort study using wearable device, machine learning, and deep learning. *IEEE Journal of Translational Engineering in Health and Medicine, 10*, 1−14.

Yu, S., & Park, Y. (2022). A robust authentication protocol for wireless medical sensor networks using blockchain and physically unclonable functions. *IEEE Internet of Things Journal, 9*(20), 20214−20228.

Integration of digital twin and blockchain for smart hospitals

Hossein Hassani[1] and Steve MacFeely[2]

[1]Research Institute of Energy Management and Planning (RIEMP), University of Tehran, Tehran, Iran [2]World Health Organization (WHO), Geneva, Switzerland

29.1 Introduction

The advent of digital twins represents a paradigm shift in how industries leverage data for optimization, prediction, and insight (Hassani et al., 2022b). Originating from the fields of aerospace and manufacturing, the concept of a digital twin—a dynamic, digital replica of physical entities or systems—has rapidly gained traction across various sectors (Hassani et al., 2022a). Among these, healthcare stands out as a particularly promising domain for the application of digital twins, given its complex systems, diverse patient needs, and the critical importance of precision and efficiency (Armeni et al., 2022; Corral-Acero et al., 2020; Haleem et al., 2023; Schwartz et al., 2020; Sun et al., 2022, 2023; Tao & Qi, 2019; Voigt et al., 2021).

Digital twins in healthcare simulate the physical and biological attributes of patients, medical devices, or healthcare environments, enabling a sandbox of sorts for innovation, analysis, and improvement (Venkatesh et al., 2022; Kamel Boulos & Zhang, 2021; Volkov et al., 2021). This chapter delves into the emergence of digital twins, tracing their evolution from a novel technological concept to a cornerstone of modern healthcare strategy. It highlights how digital twins, powered by advancements in computing, data analytics, and artificial intelligence, are being used to revolutionize patient care, from personalized treatment plans to the optimization of smart hospital operations.

The core objectives of this chapter are multifaceted. Firstly, it aims to provide a comprehensive overview of how digital twins are being applied within the healthcare sector, illuminating their role in enhancing patient outcomes, streamlining operations, and facilitating medical research. Secondly, the chapter seeks to assess the benefits of these applications, including improved accuracy in diagnosis, enhanced treatment efficacy, and increased operational efficiency. Lastly, it addresses the challenges and limitations of

Sensor Networks for Smart Hospitals
DOI: https://doi.org/10.1016/B978-0-443-36370-2.00030-X

implementing digital twins in healthcare, such as data privacy concerns, the need for standardization, and the technological and financial barriers to adoption.

This chapter is designed to cover a broad spectrum of topics related to digital twins in healthcare. It encompasses a range of patient populations, from neonatalto geriatric, with a particular focus on how digital twins can be tailored to meet the diverse needs of these groups. Various healthcare settings are considered, including acute care hospitals, long-term care facilities, and outpatient clinics, to provide a comprehensive view of potential applications. Moreover, the report examines the integration of digital twins with other emerging technologies, such as wearable health devices and the Internet of Medical Things, to explore how they can collectively enhance patient care and healthcare delivery.

By navigating through these areas, this chapter aims to furnish healthcare professionals, policymakers, and technology developers with insights into the transformative potential of digital twins in healthcare, offering a roadmap for harnessing these innovations to foster a more efficient, effective, and personalized healthcare ecosystem.

29.2 Understanding digital twins

Digital twins are at the forefront of technological innovation, serving as a bridge between the physical and digital worlds (Elkefi & Asan, 2022). In healthcare, this concept takes on a profound significance, offering unprecedented opportunities for enhancing patient care and operational efficiency (Hassani et al., 2022b). This section delves into the definition and concept of digital twins, their historical development, the essential components that constitute a digital twin in healthcare, and the key technologies that enable their implementation.

29.2.1 Definition and concept

A digital twin is a dynamic digital representation of a physical object, system, or process. It mirrors the real-world entity in a virtual space, enabling real-time monitoring, simulation, and analysis (Abernethy, 2022; Hassani et al., 2022a). In healthcare, digital twins can represent individual patients, organs, healthcare facilities, or broader health systems (Allen et al., 2021). These virtual models are characterized by their ability to integrate vast amounts of data, adapt to changes over time, and predict future states (Tao & Qi, 2019). By simulating different scenarios and interventions, digital twins allow healthcare providers to make informed decisions, personalize treatments, and optimize resources (Voigt et al., 2021).

29.2.2 Historical development

The concept of digital twins originated in the early 2000s within the aerospace industry, with NASA's Apollo program being a precursor to its development (Hassani et al., 2022a). Early applications focused on improving the design, manufacturing, and maintenance of complex systems. Over time, the use of digital twins expanded into various sectors, including automotive, energy, and infrastructure. The healthcare industry began to explore digital twins relatively recently, recognizing their potential to transform patient care, medical research, and health system management (Elkefi & Asan, 2022; Schwartz et al., 2020; Venkatesh et al., 2022).

29.2.3 Components of a digital twin

The construction of a digital twin in healthcare involves several key components:

Data Acquisition: The foundation of a digital twin is data. In healthcare, this includes patient medical records, sensor data from medical devices, and broader health system data. Effective data acquisition systems are critical for capturing real-time and historical data accurately (Sun et al., 2022).

Modeling: The data is then used to create models that represent the physical counterparts. These models can range from simple representations to complex simulations of biological processes or health system dynamics (Haleem et al., 2023).

Simulation: With the model in place, digital twins can simulate various scenarios, treatments, or interventions, predicting their outcomes based on the data. This capability is invaluable for treatment planning, disease management, and health system optimization (Tao & Qi, 2019).

Feedback Loops: Digital twins are not static; they continuously evolve based on new data. Feedback loops allow for the adjustment of models in response to changes in the physical counterpart or outcomes of simulated interventions, ensuring the twin remains an accurate reflection over time (Armeni et al., 2022).

29.2.4 Technology enablers

Several key technologies underpin the development and implementation of digital twins in healthcare (Hassani et al., 2022a):

- **Internet of Things (IoT):** IoT devices play a crucial role in data acquisition, providing real-time monitoring of patient health and operational data from healthcare facilities.
- **Artificial Intelligence (AI) and Machine Learning (ML):** AI and ML algorithms analyze the vast amounts of data collected, identifying patterns, predicting outcomes, and optimizing simulations.
- **Cloud Computing:** The cloud offers the computational power and storage capacity necessary to handle the large datasets and complex processing required for digital twins.
- **Data Analytics:** Advanced data analytics techniques are employed to interpret the data, enabling healthcare providers to gain insights and make evidence-based decisions.

Together, these components and technologies facilitate the creation of digital twins in healthcare, offering a powerful tool for advancing patient care and healthcare management. By leveraging digital twins, the healthcare industry can move toward a more predictive and personalized approach, improving outcomes and efficiency at every level.

29.3 Digital twins in healthcare

The integration of digital twins into healthcare signifies a monumental shift toward more personalized, predictive, and efficient healthcare delivery and clinical research. This transformative technology has the potential to redefine patient care, smart hospital management, and medical device development (Abernethy, 2022; Corral-Acero et al., 2020; Kamel Boulos & Zhang, 2021; Sun et al., 2022, 2023; Tao & Qi, 2019; Venkatesh et al., 2022; Volkov et al., 2021).

29.3.1 Overview

Digital twins in healthcare offer a comprehensive and nuanced view of patient health, hospital operations, and the lifecycle of medical devices. By simulating real-world scenarios in a controlled digital environment, healthcare providers can anticipate outcomes, optimize processes, and make informed decisions. The potential of digital twins extends from individualized patient care to system-wide operational enhancements, setting the stage for a revolution in healthcare delivery and clinical research (Voigt et al., 2021).

29.3.2 Current applications

29.3.2.1 Patient-specific models

Digital twins create detailed and dynamic patient-specific models that reflect the unique physiology and health status of individuals (Corral-Acero et al., 2020). These models allow for precise diagnosis, personalized treatment planning, and accurate prediction of treatment outcomes. By analyzing how a patient's digital twin responds to various interventions, healthcare providers can tailor treatments to the individual, potentially improving efficacy and reducing side effects.

29.3.2.2 Smart hospital operations

In the realm of smart hospital operations, digital twins serve as a powerful tool for enhancing efficiency, resource allocation, and patient flow. By simulating the complex ecosystem of a healthcare facility, administrators can identify bottlenecks, optimize workflows, and predict the impact of changes in resource distribution. This not only improves patient care but also enhances the working environment for healthcare professionals (Volkov et al., 2021).

29.3.2.3 Medical device design and simulation

Digital twins revolutionize medical device design by enabling virtual prototyping, testing, and validation (Schwartz et al., 2020). This approach reduces the need for physical prototypes, accelerates the development process, and enhances safety by identifying potential issues before devices are used in clinical settings (Venkatesh et al., 2022). Moreover, it allows for the simulation of device performance across a wide range of patient conditions, ensuring adaptability and efficacy.

29.3.3 Benefits and challenges

29.3.3.1 Improving patient outcomes

The personalized insights provided by digital twins facilitate more effective and efficient healthcare, leading to improved patient outcomes. By understanding patient-specific responses to treatments, healthcare providers can avoid trial-and-error approaches, reducing the time and cost associated with finding the right treatment plan (Corral-Acero et al., 2020; Sun et al., 2022; Sun et al., 2023).

29.3.3.2 Operational efficiency

Digital twins offer a strategic advantage in optimizing healthcare operations, from resource management to patient scheduling. This efficiency not only reduces healthcare costs but also enhances patient satisfaction by minimizing wait times and improving the quality of care (Armeni et al., 2022).

29.3.3.3 Data integration challenges

Despite their potential, digital twins face significant challenges in integrating data from diverse sources. Creating a cohesive digital twin requires harmonizing data across various formats, systems, and standards, posing a substantial hurdle to effective implementation (Hassani et al., 2022a).

29.3.3.4 Privacy and security concerns

The extensive data collection and processing inherent in digital twins raise critical questions about privacy and security. Ensuring the confidentiality and integrity of patient data is paramount, necessitating robust data protection measures and ethical considerations in the deployment of digital twins. This is particularly important as Digital Twin requires unit-level records (Hassani et al., 2022a).

In summary, while digital twins in healthcare promise to enhance patient care and operational efficiency, realizing their full potential requires overcoming significant challenges in data integration, privacy, and security. As the healthcare sector navigates these obstacles, the adoption of digital twins stands to significantly impact clinical outcomes and the future of healthcare delivery.

29.4 The role of official data

The construction and operation of digital twins in healthcare rely heavily on the foundation of high-quality data. This section explores the critical importance of accurate and reliable data, the sources from which this data can be drawn, the governance and standards that ensure its integrity, and the challenges faced in its collection and management (Hassani et al., 2022a).

29.4.1 Importance of accurate and reliable data

Accurate and reliable data forms the backbone of digital twins, enabling them to function as true replicas of their physical counterparts. High-quality data ensures that digital twins can provide precise simulations, predictions, and insights, which are essential for personalized patient care, operational efficiency, and the safe design of medical devices. Without trustworthy data, the decisions made based on digital twins could lead to ineffective treatments, operational inefficiencies, or even harm to patients.

29.4.2 Sources of healthcare data

Healthcare data can be derived from a variety of sources, each contributing valuable information for the creation of comprehensive digital twins (Hassani et al., 2022b):

- **Electronic Health Records (EHRs):** Contain detailed patient medical histories, treatment plans, and outcomes.
- **Medical Imaging Databases:** Offer insights into the anatomical and physiological conditions of patients.
- **Wearable Devices and Remote Monitoring Tools:** Provide real-time data on patient health metrics.
- **Pharmaceutical and Research Databases:** Include data from clinical trials and medication effectiveness studies.
- **Public Health Records:** Offer broader insights into population health trends and determinants.

Integrating data from these diverse sources allows for the development of digital twins that are as detailed and accurate as possible.

29.4.3 Data governance and standards

Effective data governance and adherence to standards are paramount in ensuring the quality, privacy, and security of the data used in digital twins (Hassani & MacFeely, 2023). Data governance policies must address data accuracy, accessibility, consistency, and compliance with regulations such as the General Data Protection Regulation (GDPR) or Health Insurance Portability and Accountability Act (HIPAA). Standards, both technical and ethical, ensure that data is interoperable across different systems and that digital twins are built and used responsibly (Hassani & MacFeely, 2023). These frameworks are critical for maintaining patient trust and for the sustainable implementation of digital twins in healthcare.

29.4.4 Challenges in data collection and management

Collecting, storing, and managing healthcare data for digital twins presents several practical challenges:

- **Data Volume and Complexity:** The sheer amount of data, along with its complexity, requires robust data management systems and advanced analytical tools.
- **Interoperability and data sharing:** Data from different sources often comes in varied formats, making interoperability and data sharing a significant technical hurdle.
- **Privacy and Security:** Ensuring the confidentiality and integrity of sensitive health data while allowing for its productive use in digital twins is a delicate balance.
- **Data Bias and Quality:** Data collected from disparate sources can introduce biases or may be of inconsistent quality, affecting the reliability of digital twins.

Addressing these challenges requires a coordinated effort among healthcare providers, technology developers, and regulatory bodies to ensure that digital twins are built on a foundation of reliable, secure, and ethically gathered data. As the healthcare industry continues to evolve toward more data-driven approaches, the role of high-quality data in the development and application of digital twins will only grow in importance, necessitating ongoing attention to these critical issues.

29.5 Case studies

The transformative potential of digital twins in healthcare is best illustrated through real-world examples. This section explores successful implementations across various healthcare settings, highlighting the impact on patient care, operational efficiency, and medical innovation. Additionally, it distills key lessons learned and best practices to guide future digital twin projects (Corral-Acero et al., 2020; Haleem et al., 2023; Schwartz et al., 2020; Sun et al., 2022, 2023; Tao & Qi, 2019; Venkatesh et al., 2022; Voigt et al., 2021).

29.5.1 Successful implementations of digital twins in healthcare

29.5.1.1 Personalized treatment plans for chronic conditions

- **Overview:** Digital twins revolutionize the management of chronic diseases such as diabetes and cardiovascular disorders by merging continuous monitoring data from wearable devices with patients' EHRs. These personalized digital twins are crafted to simulate and forecast individual reactions to varying treatment plans.
- **Outcome:** This method facilitates tailored medication regimens and lifestyle advice, markedly elevating patient outcomes through decreased hospital readmissions and improved quality of life.

29.5.1.2 Optimization of smart hospital operations

- **Overview:** Digital twins are deployed to emulate the operations of hospital emergency departments. By integrating real-time data on patient arrivals, staff availability, and resource utilization, the model pinpoints bottlenecks and enhances patient flow.
- **Outcome:** Adjustments informed by the digital twin simulations lead to a 20% decrease in patient waiting times and a more equitable distribution of workload among healthcare staff.

29.5.1.3 *Virtual prototyping for medical devices*

- **Overview:** Digital twins are utilized for the design, testing, and validation of a novel heart valve. The digital twin assesses the device's performance across a broad spectrum of physiological conditions before the manufacturing of any physical prototypes.
- **Outcome:** This approach not only shortens the development timeline of the device but also guarantees its safety and efficacy while minimizing the costs associated with clinical trials.

29.5.2 Lessons learned and best practices

- **Integrating Multidisciplinary Expertise:** Successful digital twin projects combined expertise from healthcare professionals, data scientists, and engineers, ensuring that the models were medically relevant, technically sound, and operationally feasible.
- **Ensuring Data Quality and Privacy:** High-quality, secure data was foundational. Implementations that prioritized data integrity and patient privacy built trust and ensured compliance with regulatory standards.
- **Iterative Development and Feedback Loops:** Projects that adopted an iterative approach, incorporating feedback from end-users and continuously refining the digital twin models, were more successful in achieving their objectives.
- **Scalability and Flexibility:** Designing digital twins with scalability in mind allowed for their application across different patient populations and healthcare settings, maximizing their impact.
- **Stakeholder Engagement:** Engaging all stakeholders, including patients, healthcare providers, and administrators, from the early stages of development was crucial for the alignment of goals, expectations, and outcomes.

These case studies demonstrate the diverse applications and benefits of digital twins in healthcare, providing valuable insights for future projects. By adhering to best practices such as interdisciplinary collaboration, rigorous data management, and stakeholder engagement, the healthcare industry can continue to harness the power of digital twins to improve patient care and operational efficiency.

29.6 Future trends and directions

The horizon for digital twins in healthcare is expanding rapidly, driven by technological advancements and a shift toward more personalized, predictive medicine. This section explores the potential impacts of emerging technologies on digital twins, their role in advancing predictive analytics and personalized medicine, and the benefits and challenges of integrating digital twins with other cutting-edge technologies (Armeni et al., 2022; Hassani et al., 2022a; Hassani & MacFeely, 2023; Sun et al., 2022; Venkatesh et al., 2022).

29.6.1 Advancements in technologies and their implications

- **Quantum Computing:** Quantum computing promises to revolutionize the processing power available for complex simulations, potentially allowing digital twins to model biological processes and treatment outcomes with unprecedented accuracy and speed. This could lead to breakthroughs in understanding disease mechanisms and developing new treatments.

- **Blockchain:** Blockchain technology offers a secure, decentralized platform for sharing healthcare data, which could enhance the collaboration between healthcare providers and patients in managing digital twins. It ensures data integrity, transparency, and security, crucial for sensitive health information.

The integration of these technologies with digital twins could address some of the current limitations in computational capabilities and data security, opening new avenues for research and application in healthcare.

29.6.2 Predictive analytics and personalized medicine

Digital twins stand at the forefront of a paradigm shift toward personalized medicine, leveraging predictive analytics to tailor healthcare to individual patients. By simulating the impact of various treatment options on a patient's digital twin, healthcare providers can predict outcomes more accurately, leading to more effective and personalized treatment plans. This approach not only improves patient care but also optimizes resource allocation by focusing on interventions that are most likely to succeed.

29.6.3 Integration with other emerging technologies

The synergy between digital twins and other emerging technologies such as AI, IoT, and blockchain holds tremendous potential:

AI and ML: AI algorithms can analyze the vast datasets generated by digital twins, identifying patterns and insights that humans may overlook. This can enhance the predictive accuracy of digital twins, making them even more effective tools for personalized medicine.

IoT: IoT devices provide real-time data that feeds digital twins, enabling them to reflect the current state of the patient or healthcare system accurately. The integration of IoT with digital twins facilitates continuous monitoring and adjustment of treatment plans, ensuring they remain optimal as conditions change.

Blockchain: When integrated with blockchain, digital twins benefit from enhanced data security and privacy, facilitating the safe sharing of healthcare data. This can improve collaboration and data accuracy across different stakeholders in the healthcare ecosystem.

However, integrating these technologies also presents challenges, including the need for standardized data formats, concerns over data privacy and security, and the complexity of managing and analyzing large-scale, multisource datasets. Addressing these challenges requires a collaborative effort from technology developers, healthcare providers, and regulatory bodies.

29.7 Regulatory and ethical considerations

The integration of digital twins into healthcare raises significant regulatory and ethical considerations. Ensuring the responsible use of digital twins involves navigating complex regulatory landscapes and addressing ethical concerns related to patient consent, data privacy, and potential biases. This section delves into the regulatory frameworks governing digital twins in healthcare and explores the ethical implications of their use (Hassani & MacFeely, 2023).

29.7.1 Regulatory frameworks governing digital twins in healthcare

Regulatory frameworks for digital twins in healthcare are evolving to address the unique challenges posed by this technology. These frameworks aim to ensure that digital twins are developed, implemented, and used in a manner that is safe, effective, and respectful of patient rights. Key aspects of these regulatory frameworks include the following:

- **Data Protection and Privacy:** Regulations such as the GDPR in the European Union and the HIPAA in the United States set stringent requirements for handling personal health information. These regulations mandate the secure collection, storage, and sharing of data, ensuring patient privacy is protected.
- **Medical Device Regulations:** In some contexts, digital twins used for diagnostic or therapeutic purposes may be classified as medical devices, subjecting them to regulatory scrutiny similar to that for traditional medical devices. This includes demonstrating safety, efficacy, and quality through rigorous testing and validation processes.
- **Interoperability Standards:** To facilitate the integration of digital twins with existing healthcare systems and ensure the reliability of their simulations, regulatory bodies are increasingly focusing on interoperability standards. This ensures that digital twins can effectively communicate with EHRs, medical devices, and other healthcare technologies.

29.7.2 Ethical implications and patient consent

The use of digital twins in healthcare also raises important ethical considerations:

- **Patient Consent:** Obtaining informed consent from patients is crucial, especially when their data is used to create and operate digital twins. Patients must be fully informed about how their data will be used, the benefits and risks associated with digital twins, and their rights to withdraw consent at any time.
- **Data Privacy:** Protecting the privacy of the data used to create and update digital twins is paramount. Ethical practices must ensure that patient data is anonymized where possible and securely protected against unauthorized access.
- **Potential Biases:** Digital twins rely on data that may reflect existing biases in healthcare delivery and outcomes. Ethical considerations must include efforts to identify and mitigate biases in digital twin models to prevent perpetuating or exacerbating disparities in healthcare.

- **Transparency and Accountability:** There must be transparency in how digital twins are used in patient care and decision-making processes, with clear lines of accountability for the outcomes of decisions informed by digital twin simulations.

29.8 Recommendations for policymakers and healthcare providers

The successful integration of digital twins into healthcare hinges on enhancing data quality, fostering innovation in a safe and privacy-conscious manner, and building public trust through transparency and engagement. This section outlines strategic recommendations for policymakers and healthcare providers to navigate these challenges effectively.

29.8.1 Enhancing data quality and accessibility

- **Standardization of Data Formats:** Policymakers should work toward establishing and adopting standards for data formats and interoperability across healthcare systems. This facilitates the seamless exchange and integration of data from diverse sources, crucial for creating accurate digital twins.
- **Investment in Data Infrastructure:** Healthcare providers and governments should invest in robust data infrastructure, including secure cloud storage and advanced data analytics platforms, to ensure the high-quality management and analysis of health data.
- **Promoting Data Sharing Initiatives:** Encourage the development of secure data-sharing frameworks and protocols that respect patient privacy while making anonymized data available for research and development in digital twins.

29.8.2 Fostering innovation while ensuring patient safety

- **Regulatory Sandboxes:** Establish regulatory sandboxes that allow innovators to test new digital twin technologies in a controlled environment. This approach can accelerate the development of promising technologies while ensuring patient safety and data privacy are not compromised.
- **Clear Guidelines for Digital Twin Development:** Policymakers should provide clear guidelines and best practices for the development and implementation of digital twins, including requirements for validation, testing, and clinical trials where applicable.
- **Cross-Sector Partnerships:** Encourage partnerships between healthcare organizations, technology companies, and academic institutions to pool resources, share knowledge, and drive innovation in digital twins, while ensuring ethical standards and patient safety are maintained.

29.8.3 Building public trust through transparency and engagement

- **Transparent Communication:** Healthcare providers and developers of digital twins should prioritize clear, transparent communication about how digital twins are used, the benefits they offer, and the measures in place to protect patient data and privacy.

- **Patient and Public Involvement:** Involve patients and the public in the development and deployment processes of digital twins through advisory panels, public consultations, and educational campaigns. This engagement helps ensure the technology meets the needs and concerns of those it is intended to serve.
- **Ethical Oversight:** Establish ethical oversight committees to evaluate the use of digital twins in healthcare, focusing on issues such as consent, equity, and the impact on patient care. These committees can provide guidance and build public confidence in digital twin technologies.

29.9 Conclusion

29.9.1 Summary of key findings

This report has explored the transformative potential of digital twins in healthcare, detailing their definition, development, applications, and the critical role of data. Key findings include:

- **Digital Twins in Healthcare:** Digital twins offer a groundbreaking approach to personalized medicine, operational efficiency, and medical device development by creating dynamic, virtual representations of patients, processes, or devices.
- **Importance of Data and Data Governance:** The effectiveness of digital twins heavily relies on the quality and accessibility of data. Accurate, reliable, and comprehensive data sets are foundational for building effective digital twins. Robust data governance will be a prerequisite.
- **Technological Enablers:** Emerging technologies like AI, IoT, blockchain, and quantum computing are vital for the development and implementation of digital twins, offering enhanced capabilities for simulation, analysis, and security.
- **Regulatory and Ethical Considerations:** The adoption of digital twins faces challenges related to data privacy, security, and ethical use, necessitating clear regulatory frameworks and ethical guidelines.
- **Innovation and Public Trust:** Fostering innovation while ensuring patient safety, and building public trust through transparency and engagement with stakeholders, are essential for the successful integration of digital twins in healthcare.

29.9.2 Final thoughts

The journey toward integrating digital twins into healthcare is at a critical juncture. The potential for digital twins to revolutionize patient care, enhance operational efficiency, and accelerate medical research is immense. However, realizing this potential requires a coordinated effort across the healthcare ecosystem.

Policymakers are called upon to develop and update regulatory frameworks that facilitate innovation while protecting patient privacy and ensuring data security. Investing in infrastructure and standards for data quality and interoperability will be key to enabling the effective use of digital twins.

Healthcare Providers have an opportunity to embrace the adoption of digital twins, integrating them into clinical practice and operational strategies. This involves investing in technology, training staff, and participating in research and development efforts.

Researchers and Technology Developers are encouraged to continue advancing the capabilities of digital twins, addressing technical challenges, and exploring new applications. Collaboration with healthcare professionals and adherence to ethical guidelines will be crucial for their success.

All Stakeholders should engage in open dialog, fostering an environment of transparency and trust. Public engagement and ethical considerations must be at the forefront of the digital twin revolution in healthcare.

References

Abernethy, A. et al. (2022). The promise of digital health: then, now, and the future. *NAM Perspect.* doi:10.31478/202206e.

Allen, A., Siefkas, A., Pellegrini, E., Burdick, H., Barnes, G., Calvert, J., Mao, Q., & Das, R. (2021). A digital twins machine learning model for forecasting disease progression in stroke patients. *Applied Sciences, 11*(12), 5576. Available from https://doi.org/10.3390/app11125576.

Armeni, P., Polat, I., De Rossi, L. M., Diaferia, L., Meregalli, S., & Gatti, A. (2022). Digital twins in healthcare: Is It the beginning of a new era of evidence-based medicine? A critical review. *Journal of Personalized Medicine, 12* (8), 1255. Available from https://doi.org/10.3390/jpm12081255.

Corral-Acero, J., Margara, F., Marciniak, M., Rodero, C., Loncaric, F., Feng, Y., Gilbert, A., Fernandes, J. F., Bukhari, H. A., Wajdan, A., Martinez, M. V., Santos, M. S., Shamohammdi, M., Luo, H., Westphal, P., Leeson, P., DiAchille, P., Gurev, V., Mayr, M., . . . Lamata, P. (2020). The 'digital twin' to enable the vision of precision cardiology. *European Heart Journal, 41*(48). Available from https://doi.org/10.1093/eurheartj/ehaa159.

Elkefi, S., & Asan, O. (2022). Digital twins for managing health care systems: Rapid literature review. *Journal of Medical Internet Research, 24*(8), e37641. Available from https://doi.org/10.2196/37641.

Haleem, A., Javaid, M., Pratap Singh, R., & Suman, R. (2023). Exploring the revolution in healthcare systems through the applications of digital twin technology. *Biomedical Technology, 4*. Available from https://doi.org/10.1016/j.bmt.2023.02.001.

Hassani, H., Huang, X., & MacFeely, S. (2022a). Enabling digital twins to support the UN SDGs. *Big Data and Cognitive Computing, 6*(4). Available from https://doi.org/10.3390/bdcc6040115.

Hassani, H., Huang, X., & MacFeely, S. (2022b). Impactful digital twin in the healthcare revolution. *Big Data and Cognitive Computing, 6*(3). Available from https://doi.org/10.3390/bdcc6030083.

Hassani, H., & MacFeely, S. (2023). Driving excellence in official statistics: Unleashing the potential of comprehensive digital data governance. *Big Data and Cognitive Computing, 7*(3), 134. Available from https://doi.org/10.3390/bdcc7030134.

Kamel Boulos, M. N., & Zhang, P. (2021). Digital twins: From personalised medicine to precision public health. *Journal of Personalized Medicine, 11*(8), 745. Available from https://doi.org/10.3390/jpm11080745.

Schwartz, S. M., Wildenhaus, K., Bucher, A., & Byrd, B. (2020). Digital twins and the emerging science of self: Implications for digital health experience design and "small" data. *Frontiers in Computer Science, 2*. Available from https://doi.org/10.3389/fcomp.2020.00031.

Sun, T., He, X., & Li, Z. (2023). Digital twin in healthcare: Recent updates and challenges. *Digital Health, 9*. Available from https://doi.org/10.1177/20552076221149651, 205520762211496.

Sun, T., He, X., Song, X., Shu, L., & Li, Z. (2022). The digital twin in medicine: A key to the future of healthcare? *Frontiers in Medicine, 9*. Available from https://doi.org/10.3389/fmed.2022.907066.

Tao, F., & Qi, Q. (2019). Make more digital twins. *Nature, 573*(7775). Available from https://doi.org/10.1038/d41586-019-02849-1.

Venkatesh, K. P., Raza, M. M., & Kvedar, J. C. (2022). Health digital twins as tools for precision medicine: Considerations for computation, implementation, and regulation. *NPJ Digital Medicine, 5*(1). Available from https://doi.org/10.1038/s41746-022-00694-7, https://www.nature.com/npjdigitalmed/.

Voigt, I., Inojosa, H., Dillenseger, A., Haase, R., Akgün, K., & Ziemssen, T. (2021). Digital twins for multiple sclerosis. *Frontiers in Immunology, 12*. Available from https://doi.org/10.3389/fimmu.2021.669811.

Volkov, I., Radchenko, G., & Tchernykh, A. (2021). Digital twins, internet of things and mobile medicine: A review of current platforms to support smart healthcare. *Programming and Computer Software, 47*(8). Available from https://doi.org/10.1134/s0361768821080284.

Challenges of sensor network in smart hospitals

Sepideh Bazzaz Abkenar[1] and Mostafa Haghi Kashani[2]

[1]Department of Computer Engineering, Science and Research Branch, Islamic Azad University, Tehran, Iran [2]Department of Computer Engineering, Shahr-e-Qods Branch, Islamic Azad University, Tehran, Iran

30.1 Introduction

The healthcare sector is developing rapidly in both technology and services, especially in rural regions where such issues as growing elderly populations, shortage of medical experts, and scarcity of hospital facilities are common. Biosensor-based remote monitoring can be beneficial in these situations because it enables isolated patients, maybe at home, to have their vital signs monitored (Bariya et al., 2018). With the aid of healthcare systems, this strategy lowers expenses, improves patient quality of life, and enables physicians to monitor patients remotely without the need for clinical assistance. Precise remote monitoring and decision-making prevent infections in physicians and other healthcare professionals (Etemadi et al., 2023; Malasinghe et al., 2019).

There are additional benefits to remote patient monitoring, including early sickness diagnosis, continuous and remote patient monitoring, shorter hospital stays, and decreased mortality. Numerous medical research have been carried out to monitor patient health factors and control the spread of illness (Bariya et al., 2018). Health sector research aims to monitor patient health using portable devices installed with biosensors or wearable sensors (Adhikari et al., 2023). Wearable/portable devices have massive potential for enhancing digital health by giving patients access to real-time monitoring and diagnostic capabilities (Tu et al., 2020). The creation of wearable sensors to assess physiological and biochemical indicators has advanced significantly.

Wearable devices or sensors can be attached to clothes, mounted on the skin, or implanted devices. These technologies provide an appealing option for both consumers and medical professionals by delivering a practical and affordable way to monitor

DOI: https://doi.org/10.1016/B978-0-443-36370-2.00031-1

different physiological signs. The increasing use of wearable sensors offers a remarkable potential to combine personal health data with tailored solutions (Mirjalali et al., 2022). Sensing components are frequently coupled with wireless data transmission systems and energy storage devices to gather data and send it to computers or smartphones for processing (Nikravan et al., 2011). This allows for the continuous monitoring of a person's vital signs. By providing real-time monitoring of biomarkers, smart and customized healthcare technologies have changed the early detection and evaluation of disease states and concurrently enabled therapy with promising medicines (Dias & Cunha, 2018). Biomarkers give vital information regarding our health status (Chung et al., 2019).

Based on current research findings, this chapter explores the issues of sensor networks within smart hospitals. This chapter represents the potential classification of sensor network issues in e-health. It also emphasizes the tools, algorithms, and the evaluation factors. The design and implementation of a remote tracking system raises several problems, such as the processing methods employed, the secure data connection, and the sensors utilized. This chapter covers the underlying issues and outstanding challenges that providers and medical centers must face to optimize sensor network performance in smart hospitals, make accurate decisions, and enhance patient care.

The remainder sections of the chapter are structured as follows. The research's methodology, article selection process, and research questions are outlined in Section 30.2. Section 30.3 overviews the reviewed studies, highlighting their main ideas, tools, and applied algorithms. Sections 30.4 and 30.5 provide the findings analysis, open issues, and future directions, respectively. Finally, Section 30.6 concludes with an explanation of the result.

30.2 Research methodology

Researchers have conducted a great deal of study on sensors in healthcare. To perform a comprehensive analysis, we first clarify the requirements and issues that motivate this chapter (Abkenar et al., 2020; Haghi Kashani et al., 2021). Answering research questions enables one to determine gaps in this subject, which may help researchers provide innovative viewpoints and solutions. Additionally, the primary objective of this chapter is the potential classification of sensor network challenges in smart hospitals. The following research questions were also established to fulfill this objective:

RQ_1: What are the evaluation factors applied in sensor networks in smart hospitals?
RQ_2: What are the algorithms and tools applied in sensor networks in smart hospitals?
RQ_3: What is the possible classification of sensor network challenges in smart hospitals?

After that, we utilized Google Scholar as our main search engine and respected scientific publishers like Springer, IEEE, ScienceDirect, SAGE, Taylor & Francis, Wiley, Emerald, ACM, Inderscience, and Hindawi based on titles and keyword phrases to search for online articles between 2013 and 2023 on this subject. The subsequent search phrases were applied:

(biosensors OR biosensor OR sensors OR sensor OR wearable) AND
(health OR e-health OR hospital OR hospitals)

Furthermore, we eliminated nonpeer-reviewed, non-English articles, theses, review papers, short papers, and book chapters to extract the most significant publications. The abstracts and conclusions of the articles were then examined. After a comprehensive analysis of all the articles' full texts, 20 publications that could properly answer our study questions and reveal the methods and challenges were chosen for a deeper investigation. We conduct analytical and statistical studies after assessing the presented approaches, including their essential concepts, advantages, and limitations. This evaluation also outlines the explanation for choosing the most significant open issues, challenges, and the primary areas where further study might enhance the approaches employed in the research. Further, in Section 30.5, we propose a classification of sensor network challenges in smart hospitals based on the reviewed articles.

30.3 Overview of reviewed studies

A structured taxonomy of the challenges of sensor networks in smart hospitals was defined in Section 30.5, as well as a detailed description of each classification. In this section, we study the existing articles based on the presented taxonomy in Section 30.5. Furthermore, Table 30.1 provides an overview of the main ideas, applied tools, and algorithms along with the suggested classification.

A wearable 3D accelerometer sensor was applied to automatically measure the stress levels of nurses by Sakib and Pervez (2023). This study provided beneficial information on nurses' mental health that was gathered using a wearable accelerometer sensor. Numerous popular machine learning (ML) approaches demonstrated efficiency in discovering stress. Specifically, the support vector machine (SVM) technique achieved the most accurate classification. The SVM model's average accuracy was 80.4%, while the classification average F-measure was 80.2%. Further investigation into the automated stress detection process using accelerometer sensors shows considerable potential in several important domains. First, new datasets and physiological data such as heart rate, electroencephalogram (EEG) signals, and photoplethysmography sensor data could be integrated for greater effectiveness. Moreover, adding audio or video recordings to the research is a valuable avenue. Secondly, this presents a chance to investigate and use more effective feature extraction techniques.

Xu and Zhu (2023) proposed an algorithm for improving technical human motion posture and health estimation, including applying nano biosensors and deep learning. The methodology comprised the utilization of angular velocity and nano biological acceleration sensors to record motion posture and medical data. Following fusion processing, blood pressure and heart rhythm were identified, coordinate systems were converted, and a physiological information recognition unit recognized physiological information. A deformable convolutional neural network (CNN), part of the deep learning model, was developed for posture estimation. The algorithm's accuracy in determining and approximating human posture for identity identification and sports performance analysis was shown by experimental outcomes. More studies are necessary to eliminate interfering noise and enhance results, as the method does not include a de-noising technique for nanobiosensor data.

Similarly, Alshurafa et al. (2014) developed an approach to guarantee the authenticity and consistency of sensor data utilizing ML and classification approaches. This approach improved the accuracy of remote physical activity tracking by distinguishing between

TABLE 30.1 An overview of the reviewed studies.

Category	Ref.	Main idea	Tools	Applied algorithms
Data challenges	Sakib and Pervez (2023)	Presenting an automated stress level detection system by applying wearable 3D accelerometer sensors	MATLAB®	K-nearest neighbor classifiers (K-NN), neural networks (NN), support vector machines (SVMs), naive bayes (NB), discriminant analysis (DA), decision trees (DT), ensemble classifier
Reliability and accuracy	Xu and Zhu (2023)	Applying nanobiosensor to acquire human motion posture estimation	Not mentioned	CNN
	Alshurafa et al. (2014)	Proposing classification methods and algorithms to address the cheating issue in remote health monitoring systems	Not mentioned	Random forest
Real-world dataset availability	Hassantabar et al. (2022)	Applying wearable sensors and ANN to detect mental disorder	Python	Deep neural network
	Nagwanshi et al. (2022)	Monitoring children's health using wearable sensors integrated with IoT and EEG data processing	MATLAB	Adaptive wavelet transform, neural network, genetic algorithm
Data management and analytics	Kumar and Dhulipala (2020)	Data management on IoT-enabled wearable sensor platform using fuzzy allocation model	Not mentioned	Fuzzy-based allocation algorithm
User acceptance and decision-making	Ebada et al. (2020)	Predicting health status from real-time analysis obtained via biosensors with cloud-based machine learning	Apache spark, power BI, NOSQL, Python, Microsoft Azure	SVM

	Reference	Description	Tools	Methods
Context awareness and data fusion	Janidarmian et al. (2017)	Applying wearable sensors in a health application for multiobjective hierarchical classification	Not mentioned	Genetic evolutionary algorithm, ensemble classifier composed of DT, DA, KNN, SVM, NB, and neural networks (NNs)
Customized and patient-oriented medical care	Yin and Jha (2017)	Offering a disease diagnosis system applying ensemble machine learning and wearable medical sensors	Weka, Python	NB, bayes network, SVM, KNN, best-first DT, J48, decision table, multilayer perceptron, stacker, adaBoost (Booster), DECORATE (Voter), bagger, random tree, random forest
Preventive medical care and analytic prediction	Selvakarthi et al. (2023)	Presenting a waste separation system with Iot-integrated sensor technologies to prevent the spread of illness	MySQL, MATLAB	Deep learning algorithms, gray level co-occurrence (GLCM)
	Wu et al. (2021)	Providing a hospital-associated infection prevention system via an autonomous hand hygiene tracking sensor	MySQL, Python	Not mentioned
Deployment challenges — Wearable and implantable sensors	Alghamdi (2023)	Proposing a deep learning approach utilizing wearable sensors and recurrent neural networks to track athletes' health	MATLAB	CNN, regression method
Interoperability	Doulani et al. (2023)	Proposing a health monitoring prototype to predict infectious disease by applying three different biosensors	Python	MLP, NN, one-class SVM, logistic regression, DT, random forest, XGBoost

(Continued)

TABLE 30.1 (Continued)

Category	Ref.	Main idea	Tools	Applied algorithms
Technical challenges	Mousavi et al. (2020)	Investigating the ideal placement and quantity of sensors for a hospital operating room	MATLAB	Monte Carlo
Power management and energy efficiency	Al-khafajiy et al. (2019)	Designing an elderly remote health monitoring system through wearable sensors to prevent hospitalization	Arduino Software	Not mentioned
	Chen et al. (2015)	Suggesting an adaptable sensor data segment selection approach for wearable health care services to efficiently transmit the sensing data and increase the health care services' overall lifetime	Not mentioned	Bayesian network
Scalability	Umapathi et al. (2021)	Proposing a scalable patient health monitoring system based on predictive data regression technique, biosensor, and carbon nanotube	Not mentioned	Regression, principle component analysis (PCA)
Protection and ethical challenges Security	Zendehdel et al. (2022)	Introducing an automated security approach to find vulnerabilities in wearable BLE-enabled e-health devices	Python	Not mentioned
Privacy-preserving challenges	Amoon et al. (2020)	Developing an artificial intelligence-based heuristic health management system to enhance patient privacy preserving in real-time datasets	MATLAB	Swarm optimization algorithm, spiral optimization algorithm
	Yang et al. (2020)	Using wearable sensors and a differential privacy algorithm as part of a privacy-preserving system for tracking students' physical health	Python	Differential privacy

legitimate physical activity and cheating or routine tasks. With a receiver-operating characteristic curve (ROC) area under the curve (AUC) of 99%, it attained a high accuracy rate of 90%. In addition, they developed a classification-based method with a ROC curve (AUC) of 94% and an average accuracy of 90% that recognized cheating in physical activities by learning individual activity routines. Their work assisted in distinguishing between legitimate physical activity and deceptive activity for the women's heart health project.

To diagnose schizoaffective, major depressive, and bipolar illnesses, Hassantabar et al. (2022) developed MHDeep, a framework employing effective deep neural networks models and commercial wearable medical sensors (WMSs). Eight types of data, including physiological signals, mobility patterns, and environmental factors, were used by MHDeep from sensors in smartwatches and smartphones. The framework processed participant data streams directly, avoiding the need for manual feature engineering. A module for creating synthetic data augmented real data to help with DNN model pretraining due to insufficient data. Throughout the training phase, the grow-and-prune DNN synthesis technique was used to learn both architecture and weights. A customized questionnaire can be added to the data categories in the future to improve MHDeep's functionality. Moreover, including features from different WMSs, such as blood pressure, may enhance model performance.

Likewise, Nagwanshi et al. (2022) presented an augmenting decomposition technique that combines the "adaptive wavelet transform" and the "versatile inspiring wavelet transform" to analyze the frequency of electroencephalography (EEG). They utilized wearable sensors on children to gather information from many sources sent over the Internet of Things (IoT). The suggested method was assessed using two EEG datasets: one recorded in a shielded environment and the other in a nonshielded one. The outcomes revealed the training method's effectiveness and helped identify the children's brain activity. MATLAB was used to evaluate the system's performance, considering factors such as F-measure, recall, accuracy, precision, and filtering response. Even with such high precision, the accuracy and F-measure still require refinement.

Moreover, Kumar and Dhulipala (2020) suggested an improved health monitoring system based on the heuristic hybrid time slot fuzzy-allocation algorithm. This algorithm enhanced health monitoring using an IoT-enabled wearable sensor platform. Fog computing was employed in this platform as it made timely communication possible and was suitable and reliable in life-critical applications. The authors emphasized optimizing network performance using a low-cost energy approach for data packet routing. With the introduction of dynamic slot assignment, network latency was decreased, and channel usage grew, which made it beneficial for managing heavy data loads during emergencies. The authors did not, however, address the significance of looking into the safety and privacy of IoT medical data using encryption techniques and procedures.

In another study, Ebada et al. (2020) presented a system intended for utilization in the IoT environment that can manage large amounts of heterogeneous data. The proposed system processed streaming data from medical wearables, performed analysis, and employed Apache Spark to store the findings. To eliminate redundant features, the suggested architecture included preprocess and process stages. Adaptive SVM classifiers and hybrid feature selection were used to ensure accurate classification. The next phase of the proposed work would be to offer a cloud-based platform that supports any illness dataset along with a set of predetermined factors for the disease categorization procedure. The suggested system will be implemented using deep learning methods to achieve high F-measure in the future.

Furthermore, Janidarmian et al. (2017) proposed a multiclassification approach that addresses classification problems' two opposing key objectives: accuracy and sensitivity. Alternative metrics are fundamentally needed to assess classifiers, as standard measures like overall accuracy may not be sufficient. This research tackled a model selection challenge by developing a tree-based hierarchical model using an ensemble of six distinct classifiers. Within the suggested methodology, a multiobjective optimization attempted to optimize the sensitivity of the multiclass issue in addition to taking classification accuracy into account. The recommended approach to create a wearable remote monitoring device was evaluated on nine distinct classes of breathing-related illnesses. The proposed model correctly categorized the respiratory patterns of ten participants with an accuracy of 99.25% and a sensitivity of 97.78%.

(Yin and Jha (2017) introduced a hierarchical health decision support system that integrates health-related data from WMSs with computer-based clinical decision support systems (CDSSs) to diagnose diseases. A disease diagnostic module in the multitiered system enabled individual illness tracking, starting with a WMS tier enabled by ML algorithms. Six illness diagnostic modules concentrating on four ICD-10-CM disease categories were used to show the system's feasibility. Additionally, the WMS tier demonstrated remarkable diagnosis accuracy for several illnesses. Nevertheless, developing a distinct illness signature for other conditions, such as psychological diagnoses, remains a challenging issue.

To reduce the spread of diseases in hospitals due to improper hospital waste segregation and to limit the impact caused by incorrect disposal of trash, Selvakarthi et al. (2023) introduced an automated waste detection framework utilizing deep learning algorithms and image processing approaches. The framework employed a large dataset of images to train algorithms and establish predictive patterns for object detection and classification. The applied algorithms successfully classified waste medical materials into six categories, providing an automated method to segregate waste and prevent the spread of diseases. By employing sensors and an automated classification system using image processing, the framework efficiently and accurately separated medical waste, reducing the need for manual labor and mitigating the risk of spreading diseases throughout hospitals.

Moreover, An autonomous technology was launched by Wu et al. (2021) to track hand hygiene and decrease hospital-acquired infections (HAIs). The presented system employed intelligent hand sanitizer dispensers that can track and identify users' handwashing habits using wearable ID cards. For short- and long-range communication, wireless networks, Bluetooth low energy (BLE), and long-range (LoRa) were used to transfer data, including time, position, and frequency of hand hygiene. Real-time feedback was supplied, and data was preprocessed through edge computing on routers and IoT gateways. The collected data was kept and analyzed on a cloud server to improve hospital hand hygiene compliance. Experimental results demonstrated over 88% accuracy; further advancements will try to improve tracking accuracy by utilizing sophisticated indoor BLE localization approaches. The solution highlighted using the LoRa protocol for network simplicity, enhanced coverage, and resolving security and privacy concerns. It merged proximity sensors and BLE modules into a whole product for large-scale hospital experimentation.

Alghamdi (2023) presented an approach to football player health prediction by leveraging wearable technologies and recurrent neural networks. The proposed approach applied wearable sensors for tracking athlete conditioning while monitoring players' health in real-time. Recurrent neural networks were used to analyze time-step data and produce deep features, subsequently employed for health prediction. Numerous experiments validated the approach's efficacy, allowing the coaching staff and medical personnel to customize training regimens and treatment schedules according to player health information. The study highlighted the significance of performing a comprehensive health analysis prior to creating efficient training plans. With an accuracy rate of 81%, the simulation findings showed the suggested method's practicality and dependability. The algorithm's effectiveness was highlighted by comparing it to techniques employed in earlier investigations, demonstrating its extensive recognition and dependability.

Furthermore, Doulani et al. (2023) developed an artificial intelligence (AI)-based healthcare prototype using biosensors in edge networks to monitor and assess health data remotely to lessen the interaction between infected patients and doctors. When the recommended model was compared to the current ML models, the outcomes indicated that it was more accurate. However, ML models might be used in edge networks to enhance decision-making and protect the privacy of medical data.

Mousavi et al. (2020) optimized the quantity and positioning of sensors in a hospital operating room (OR) to minimize the detection time for possible contamination, prioritizing patient safety. They presented three approaches: Monte Carlo simulation models, decomposition methodology, and an integer programming method. The algorithms proved highly effective when applied to real OR data, emphasizing the importance of sensor placement around the patient beds and OR entrance because of the vast volume of individual mobility in these places. Random sensor placement yielded undesirable outcomes, highlighting the significant influence of optimal sensor placement on detection time, affecting health and energy consumption. The study proved highly effective in placing sensors around patient beds and the OR entrance due to substantial human mobility. However, no further restrictions were applied to influence the ideal location in any particular way; the selection was made purely based on the features of the problem itself.

The smart healthcare monitoring system (SW-SHMS) was developed by Al-khafajiy et al. (2019) to overcome the issues of home-based healthcare monitoring and minimize hospitalization. SW-SHMS gathered physiological data from patients via wearable sensors and transmited it to the cloud for analysis. Any observed concerns were immediately sent to the patient's doctors via a hospital platform. Simulation results indicated that the system performed more efficiently with very little packet loss and low latency. However, the presented approach did not employ AI or ML algorithms to predict severe illnesses in the early phases. Moreover, fog computing nodes might be added to the network architecture. By processing data at the network's edge, these nodes eliminated the need to transmit data to the cloud at vast distances. By running within the local network, fog computing not only decreased the transfer of data in the cloud but also allowed for better healthcare choices.

Moreover, maximizing sensing frequency and data transfer between devices was the main emphasis of the approach presented by Chen et al. (2015) for wearable healthcare services segmenting sensor data. They employed the concepts of correlation coefficient and bayesian networks for both energy savings and continuous advancement in the body sensor network. The proposed technique was successful in properly conveying sensing data and increasing the effectiveness of healthcare services. With minimal power consumption, the system could learn continuously and only went into complete operation during an emergency. Achieving a balance between energy savings and efficient healthcare delivery was made possible by modifying the sensor frequency, which decreased transmission frequency and avoided excessive power usage.

Umapathi et al. (2021) presented the predictive data regression technique (PDRT) for employing carbon nanotube biosensors in health monitoring. The technology helps patients by allowing them to communicate with doctors remotely, seek consultations, and schedule follow-up appointments. Clinical telemedicine was enabled by PDRT through the integration of information technology and wireless sensor networks. Their studies aimed to create a real-time data processing and transmission heartbeat sensor network. Despite this, the technology achieved high accuracy at 94.6% and real-time data transfer for healthcare services. Future enhancements could connect mobile patient systems to doctors and use wireless body area networks to improve surveillance systems. In another study, Zendehdel et al. (2022) provided a framework for evaluating the security of three commercial BLE-enabled applications. The suggested framework covered data analysis, attack execution, vulnerability scanning, and fingerprinting to discover man-in-the-middle and denial-of-service attacks. This framework may be modified for various protocols and used for certification or the design of wearable personal gadgets.

Amoon et al. (2020) developed a heuristic health management system based on AI. This solution aimed to improve the privacy of patient data in hospital environments by utilizing IoT devices. Positive results from the experiment included high precision and low error rates. However, encryption techniques were not used to improve security, although AI approaches were employed to assess data quality. Similarly, researchers are pretty worried about students' physical health. Smart wearable gadgets are a common method of tracking fitness levels. These gadgets do, however, entail the potential for privacy breaches. In this respect, Yang et al. (2020) proposed a differential privacy-based algorithm and a privacy-preserving framework specifically designed for smart wearables to tackle this issue. They utilized a shielding condition to disseminate data selectively, lowering the likelihood that attackers could compromise their privacy. Their algorithm surpassed typical methods in maintaining privacy when they applied approximate entropy to evaluate their approach's confidentiality level.

30.4 Discussion

We investigate the papers in this section after considering the principles given in Section 30.2. An overview of the articles that have been examined is given in Section 30.3. Furthermore, a comparison between them is presented in this section by addressing the research questions that were previously mentioned:

RQ_1: What are the evaluation factors applied in sensor networks in smart hospitals?

Different assessment variables have been utilized by researchers based on RQ_1. The highest percentage of evaluation factors (22%) is accounted for accuracy, as seen in

Fig. 30.1. Time comes next with 11%. Precision and F-measure were applied to evaluate the presented approaches at 9% each. Fig. 30.1 indicates that most approaches attempted to reduce response time and enhance accuracy, precision, and F-measure.

RQ₂: What are the algorithms and tools applied in sensor networks in smart hospitals?

As shown in Fig. 30.2, the majority of classifiers and techniques employed in the articles under review are ensemble algorithms and deep learning.

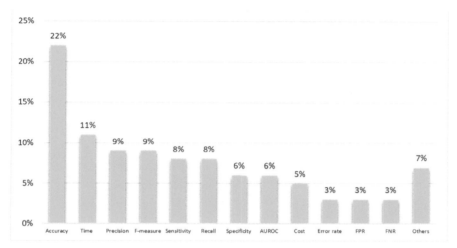

FIGURE 30.1   The percentage of evaluation factors for sensor networks in smart hospitals.

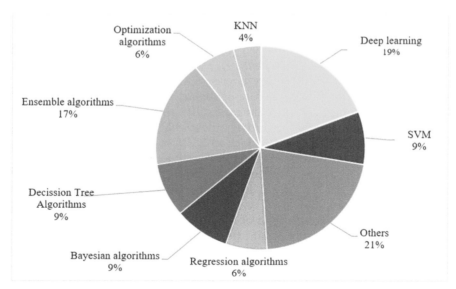

FIGURE 30.2   The percentage of applied algorithms for sensor networks in smart hospitals.

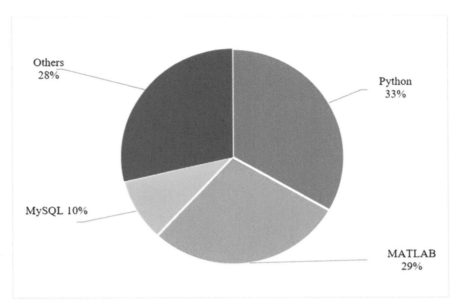

FIGURE 30.3   The percentage of evaluation tools for sensor networks in smart hospitals.

Concerning RQ_2, the statistical illustration of the proportion of tools in the reviewed studies is presented in Fig. 30.3. Python accounts for 33% of all usage, while MATLAB and MySQL have 29% and 10%, respectively.

30.5 Open challenges

Many advantages are provided by sensor networks in smart hospitals, including automated tasks, capturing data for analysis, and real-time monitoring. Nevertheless, their proper implementation necessitates addressing several unresolved concerns and obstacles that come with them. To improve the state-of-the-art sensor networks and achieve their full capability in smart hospitals, academics, healthcare providers, technology vendors, and researchers must work together to address these challenges and open issues.

Considering the guidelines outlined in Section 30.2, we examine the reviewed papers in Section 30.3. Additionally, a discussion of them is provided in Section 30.4 by responding to the previously stated research questions. Considering RQ_3, according to the examined papers addressed in Section 30.3, the challenges of sensor networks in smart hospitals are illustrated in this section.

RQ_3: What is the possible classification of sensor network challenges in smart hospitals?

Fig. 30.4 displays the suggested classification in which the studied papers are classified into five main categories: data challenges, user acceptance and decision-making, deployment challenges, technical challenges, and protection and ethical challenges. It is difficult to classify the relevant issues due to the extensive and diverse research on sensor networks within smart hospitals; other taxonomies may also be possible.

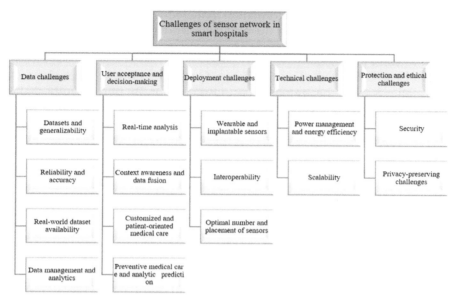

FIGURE 30.4 Challenges of sensor network in smart hospitals.

The data challenges are categorized as datasets and generalizability, reliability and accuracy, real-world dataset availability, and data management and analytics. The user acceptance and decision-making category consist of real-time analysis, context-awareness and data fusion, customized and patient-oriented medical care, and preventive medical care and analytic prediction. The deployment challenges deal with wearable and implantable sensors, interoperability, and optimal number and placement of sensors. The technical challenges are divided into power management and energy efficiency, and scalability. Finally, the protection and ethical challenges include security and privacy-preserving challenges.

According to the articles analyzed, several research constraints must be overcome to benefit sensor networks in smart hospitals. Regarding RQ$_3$, the investigated challenges are thoroughly discussed as follows:

- **Datasets and generalizability:** Due to physiological features, medical backgrounds, and behavioral patterns, models constructed from data of a patient or community could not generalize well to other populations. Furthermore, obtaining medical data, particularly from patients suffering from uncommon illnesses or disorders, can be difficult due to privacy issues, ethical constraints, and data access limitations. So, training robust models can be challenging, and generalizability may be limited due to small and imbalanced datasets or even short sampling periods that may not adequately reflect the complexity and diversity of clinical circumstances. Although some of this issue has been discussed in a few studies (Sakib & Pervez, 2023), it is essential that algorithms be resilient across various patient groups for reliable and unbiased treatment.
- **Reliability and accuracy:** Sensor networks must offer reliable data to support critical healthcare decisions. Problems including signal interference, sensor drift, and

inaccurate data might make the information gathered less reliable and could result in the wrong diagnosis or subsequent therapy. In addition, it is critical to guarantee the validity and correctness of data obtained by monitoring patients' physical activities remotely for health purposes.

The main issue concentrated on by Alshurafa et al. (2014) was proposing techniques to prevent patients from cheating on an activity monitor. By purposefully shaking the activity monitor gadget to maximize their physical activity points, patients might participate in "self-inflicted" cheating. Providing the activity sensor to a friend or someone else to wear and participate in physical activity on their behalf is another type of cheating known as "impersonator" cheating. Despite developing an extensive range of systems, tools, and methods for monitoring activities, the challenge of avoiding manipulating patient activity sensors remains largely unaddressed.

In addition, Xu and Zhu (2023) utilized nano biosensors to collect human body estimation data. Efficient and portable data collection is one of the features of nano biosensors. Despite the relatively high accuracy of the health data collected by the nano biosensor, the findings of health estimation are nonetheless impacted by varying degrees of noise in the data. As a result, further study should be done on this topic in the future to address how noise affects the prediction findings.

- **Real-world dataset availability:** All proposed techniques must be tested in real-world datasets to evaluate whether they can produce a suitable healthcare system. Sensitive and private information about patient's health and medical histories is frequently contained in sensor data in smart hospitals. However, healthcare restrictions like health insurance portability and accountability act (HIPAA) make it challenging to obtain real-world datasets. Due to the complexities of the human brain, Nagwanshi et al. (2022) gathered the EEG data, which contains a variety of brain wave patterns associated with everyday activities, including sleeping, reading, and watching movies.

  The scientists used EEG data from wearable sensors to present a frequency analysis method utilizing versatile inspiring wavelet transform and adaptive wavelet transform. The approach was evaluated on datasets from shielded and noisy circumstances, showing its resilience and helping discover particular brain activity in the participants. In some studies, however, synthetic data was produced based on mathematical models. Hassantabar et al. (2022) focused on creating synthetic data from the same distribution as the original data to address the shortage of large real datasets. As a result, developing a suitable testbed tends to be quite challenging.

- **Data management and analytics:** Massive volumes of data are generated by sensor networks and real-time applications used in hospitals for healthcare monitoring. These data must be processed, assessed, and utilized immediately. As a result, there is an increased requirement for robust communication systems that assure energy effectiveness. Data may be incomplete and unprocessed for end users due to excessive data transfer, network congestion, and delay caused by a considerable volume of data. These factors also increase the number of hops between the IoT and cloud servers.

  Consequently, medical centers must invest in advanced data management infrastructure and analysis technologies to generate relevant insights from sensor data and assist healthcare practitioners in making well-informed choices. In other words, the primary obstacles to real-time monitoring using wearable sensor networks aided by the

IoT include lower reaction time, declined reliability, and higher energy consumption. Dynamic time slot allotment was utilized instead of fixed slot allocations by Kumar and Dhulipala (2020) to overcome these limitations, while data management remains a significant challenge.

- **Real-time analysis:** Improving patient outcomes and operational performance requires the capacity to rapidly analyze sensor data and give healthcare practitioners timely decision assistance. Data collection, processing, and storage are significant challenges that real-time processing solutions encounter, especially when handling large quantities. The data storage system must support large volumes of data, and processing operations must be carried out in a way that doesn't disrupt the incoming pipeline. Reacting quickly to the data—for example, by sending out warnings or displaying it on a dashboard in real-time or almost real-time—is an additional challenge. Although improving the real-time processing of sensor data has been the subject of a few articles (Ebada et al., 2020), the problem remains an open issue. The continuing research effort is on enhancing low-latency analytics algorithms and decision support systems designed for handling massive amounts of sensor data at high speeds.
- **Context awareness and data fusion:** Sensor networks provide heterogeneous data streams from several sources, such as wearable technology, surrounding sensors, and patient monitoring equipment. By integrating cutting-edge sensor technology and multi-objective hierarchical classification techniques, Janidarmian et al. (2017) were able to transform low-level sensor data into rich contextual information for real-world scenarios. The effective fusion and analysis of disparate data streams to derive valuable insights and context-aware information remains an outstanding open issue.
- **Customized and patient-oriented medical care:** By gathering individual health data in real-time and adapting treatment plans to each patient's specific requirements and preferences, sensor networks will make it possible to provide individualized and personalized care. Patients will be encouraged to manage their medical care actively, and their health conditions will be improved through personalized tracking, feedback, and interventions. Preventable medical mistakes rank as the third most significant cause of mortality, highlighting the tremendous hurdles facing the US healthcare system despite its enormous budget. CDSSs that depend on computers have enhanced treatments, although they are only available in medical centers and hospitals. Patient data that is regularly collected by WMSs is not utilized by CDSSs.

  WMSs can capture continuous patient data. Unlike prior work, which mainly focused on hardware and procedures rather than successfully exploiting this data, Yin and Jha (2017) demonstrated that physiological data gathered from WMSs may provide considerable illness classification accuracy. For each of the roughly 69,000 disorders, HDSS could not create a unique disease signature. However, the approach described by Yin and Jha (2017) encouraged healthcare organizations and academics to capture data from WMSs for more complex illnesses like mental diagnosis. Thus, as more models were added to HDSS, the system is anticipated to become increasingly valuable for individualized diagnosis and therapy.
- **Preventive medical care and analytic prediction:** Predictive analytical models that use sensor data, AI, and ML algorithms will be able to predict undesirable scenarios, patterns of diseases, and trends in medical treatments. By detecting high-risk

individuals, improving therapies, and lowering rates of hospitalizations, these models will assist in prevention operations. A prototype for automatic hand hygiene monitoring integrating IoT technologies was presented by Wu et al. (2021). It was used in medical facilities to track procedures for hand hygiene and more effectively reduce hospital-associated infections (HAIs).

Another research examined the substantial issue of dangerous medical waste created by hospitals and the health threats connected with manual segmentation. It brought attention to a study that utilizes deep learning to identify different kinds of medical waste to lower health concerns. To lessen the effects of improper disposal, Selvakarthi et al. (2023) presented an automated trash identification system to improve waste management procedures and prevent the spread of infections within hospitals. To increase patient surveillance and continual evaluation of symptoms for various indicators of illnesses, several contemporary digital and predictive techniques remain a significant concern.

- **Wearable and implantable sensors:** The network of hardware components, software programs, and Internet-connected medical equipment that link healthcare IT is known as the Internet of Medical Things or IoMT. This IoMT ecosystem enables real-time patient monitoring, remote healthcare services, and personalized treatment. The development of wearable technology and implanted sensors has made it possible to continuously monitor patients both inside and outside of hospitals, providing information on their activity levels, treatment compliance, and overall health. A few researchers attempted to utilize this technology. Wearable health monitoring technology was used by Alghamdi (2023) to collect information on athletes' physical conditions. The IoT-integrated wearable sensors was added to an already-existing sports health monitoring system. The authors gathered and evaluated data in real-time by utilizing neural networks and wearable sensor capabilities. Future advancements in wearable and implanted sensor technology are expected to contribute to a more significant role for wearable devices in healthcare applications as well as medical treatment.

- **Interoperability:** It may be challenging to smoothly integrate disparate sensors from different manufacturers into a single network since they may employ specific protocols or standards. The development of interoperable sensor technologies and the promotion of data sharing among healthcare institutions will be facilitated by standardized data formats, protocol standards, and compatibility frameworks. Three distinct kinds of biosensors are used in the portable healthcare prototype that was designed by Doulani et al. (2023) to monitor the symptoms of an infected patient for further processing and data analytics. For efficient data exchange and analysis, guaranteeing interoperability between sensors and the medical center's systems is vital, but this is still an issue that must be fully solved.

- **Optimal number and placement of sensors:** Placing sensors strategically within a hospital to achieve full coverage while minimizing expenses and detection time is a significant optimization challenge. Having additional sensors tends to reduce the time it takes to detect abnormalities, although only a few studies (Mousavi et al., 2020) have addressed the issue. The placement procedure must, however, carefully consider several factors, including patient privacy, sensor range, and environmental circumstances.

- **Power management and energy efficiency:** There is an urgent need to decrease healthcare costs while improving service quality due to the rising aging population, the emergence of sensors and biosensors, and wearable technology. Many hospital sensors are powered by batteries, requiring frequent maintenance and replacement. Extending battery life and reducing operating costs necessitate implementing efficient power management solutions, such as low-power sensor designs, energy harvesting techniques, and optimal data transfer scheduling. The learning mechanism suggested by Chen et al. (2015) decreased the amount of power used in long-term care. In addition, intending to provide a practical and cost-effective system for remote patient monitoring, Al-khafajiy et al. (2019) presented the SW-SHMS architecture. The proposed framework functioned well in terms of gathering and organizing data, and it gives priority to issues that impact costs.

  The two main factors affecting costs are the software's functionality and the hardware's quality, which are crucial system components. The entire installation cost is determined by the scale of the system (such as the total amount of gateways, sensors, data centers, and sensor varieties), the number of platforms in the system, and the software's functionality, performance, and security features. On the other hand, installation charges are one-time costs that vary depending on the system's needs. Long-term expenses must include maintenance and data-related expenditures, especially those linked to data management and storage. Enhancing healthcare cost-effectiveness, computer power, and energy efficiency for existing medical institutions remains a significant issue.

- **Scalability:** The architecture of the sensor network must be extensible to support growing numbers of sensors and increasing coverage parts as medical centers develop and grow. Scalability is an essential component of the medical system. It relates to the system's capacity to accommodate emerging requirements and make adjustments for significant modifications in future studies. Umapathi et al. (2021) provided a scalable clinical telemedicine by utilizing wireless sensor networks and communication methods. It highlighted recent developments in environmental tracking together with the unsupervised execution of current applications, system integration, and technical as well as medical support for large-scale implementations. Designing a scalable and adaptable infrastructure from the beginning might help medical centers avoid costly upgrades and interruptions in the future.

- **Security:** Even if technology is advancing and enriching our lives on a daily basis, security and safety issues are becoming more and more crucial, particularly in the healthcare context. Medical gadgets are generally still vulnerable to cyberattacks because of their simple designs and inadequate security measures. Even more seriously compromised is the security of wearable medical devices (Zendehdel et al., 2022). In this respect, a semi-automated system was developed by Zendehdel et al. (2022) to detect vulnerabilities in wearable health monitoring devices. Creating suitable processes to develop reliable and safe devices for patients and users is crucial. Thus, closer cooperation between manufacturers, security researchers, and physicians is necessary to keep a balance between security and design goals, which is still an open issue.

- **Privacy-preserving challenges:** As sensor networks acquire more sensitive medical data, privacy-preserving solutions like differential privacy and encryption approaches will become widespread. Such innovations will allow for safe and secure data sharing while adhering to healthcare laws and safeguarding patient privacy. Additionally, there are strict regulations for the management and confidentiality of patient data set out by healthcare rules and standards, like the general data protection regulation in Europe and the HIPAA in the United States. To enhance patient data privacy preservation, a heuristic health management system based on AI was designed by Amoon et al. (2020). Nevertheless, security was not ensured by the encryption mechanisms. In another study, Yang et al. (2020) suggested a framework for protecting privacy to stop smart wearables that track teens' physical fitness from leaking personal information. Therefore, to reduce the risk of data breaches and illegal access, ongoing research is required to create robust encryption algorithms, access control systems, and privacy-preserving procedures.

30.6 Conclusion

In a smart hospital, sensor networks are essential for tracking multiple features of patient health, equipment status, and environmental factors. These networks create massive amounts of data that may be utilized for real-time monitoring, detection, analytics prediction, and enhanced treatment of patients. However, interacting with this data comes with several challenges. This chapter aimed to analyze and present a classification for the challenges of sensor networks in smart hospitals. The offered classification is categorized into five main categories: data challenges, user acceptance and decision-making, deployment challenges, technical challenges, and protection and ethical challenges.

The data challenges are categorized as datasets and generalizability, reliability and accuracy, real-world dataset availability, and data management and analytics. The user acceptance and decision-making category consists of real-time analysis, context-awareness and data fusion, customized and patient-oriented medical care, and preventive medical care and analytic prediction. The deployment challenges deal with wearable and implantable sensors, interoperability, and optimal number and placement of sensors. The technical challenges are divided into power management, energy efficiency, and scalability. Finally, the protection and ethical challenges include security and privacy-preserving challenges.

According to RQ_1, accuracy accounts for the most significant percentage of evaluation factors, at 22%. Time is ranked second with 11%. With regard to RQ_2, in the reviewed papers, deep learning and ensemble algorithms are the most often used classifiers and techniques. Python has a 33% utilization rate compared to 29% for MATLAB based on the statistical proportion of tools used. Finally, in response to RQ_3, we detailed the obstacles and potential challenges to identify existing research gaps. A multidisciplinary strategy incorporating expertise within cybersecurity, data science, sensor technology, and medical informatics is required to tackle these obstacles.

References

Abkenar, S. B., Kashani, M. H., Akbari, M., & Mahdipour, E. (2020). Twitter spam detection: A systematic review. *arXiv, Iran arXiv*. Available from https://arxiv.org.10.48550/arxiv.2011.14754.

Adhikari, M., Hazra, A., & Nandy, S. (2023). Deep transfer learning for communicable disease detection and recommendation in edge networks. *IEEE/ACM Transactions on Computational Biology and Bioinformatics, 20*(4). Available from https://doi.org/10.1109/TCBB.2022.3180393, http://ieeexplore.ieee.org/xpl/RecentIssue.jsp?punumber = 8857.

Alghamdi, W. Y. (2023). A novel deep learning method for predicting athletes' health using wearable sensors and recurrent neural networks. *Decision Analytics Journal, 7*100213. Available from https://doi.org/10.1016/j.dajour.2023.100213.

Al-khafajiy, M., Baker, T., Chalmers, C., Asim, M., Kolivand, H., Fahim, M., & Waraich, A. (2019). Remote health monitoring of elderly through wearable sensors. *Multimedia Tools and Applications, 78*(17). Available from https://doi.org/10.1007/s11042-018-7134-7, https://link.springer.com/journal/11042.

Alshurafa, N., Eastwood, J.A., Pourhomayoun, M., Nyamathi, S., Bao, L., Mortazavi, B., & Sarrafzadeh. M. (2014). Anti-cheating: Detecting self-inflicted and impersonator cheaters for remote health monitoring systems with wearable sensors. In *Proceedings - 11th International Conference on Wearable and Implantable Body Sensor Networks, BSN 2014* (pp. 92–97). IEEE Computer Society, United States. Available from https://doi.org/10.1109/BSN.2014.38, 9781479949328.

Amoon, M., Altameem, T., & Altameem, A. (2020). Internet of things sensor assisted security and quality analysis for health care data sets using artificial intelligent based heuristic health management system. *Measurement, 161*107861. Available from https://doi.org/10.1016/j.measurement.2020.107861.

Bariya, M., Nyein, H. Y. Y., & Javey, A. (2018). Wearable sweat sensors. *Nature Electronics, 1*(3). Available from https://doi.org/10.1038/s41928-018-0043-y, https://www.nature.com/natelectron/.

Chen, S. Y., Lai, C. F., Hwang, R. H., Lai, Y. H., & Wang, M. S. (2015). An adaptive sensor data segments selection method for wearable health care services. *Journal of Medical Systems, 39*(12). Available from https://doi.org/10.1007/s10916-015-0343-y, http://www.wkap.nl/journalhome.htm/0148-5598.

Chung, M., Fortunato, G., & Radacsi, N. (2019). Wearable flexible sweat sensors for healthcare monitoring: A review. *Journal of The Royal Society Interface, 16*(159)20190217. Available from https://doi.org/10.1098/rsif.2019.0217.

Dias, D., & Cunha, J. P. S. (2018). Wearable health devices—Vital sign monitoring, systems and technologies. *Sensors, 18.*

Doulani, K., Adhikari, M., & Hazra, A. (2023). Edge-based smart health monitoring device for infectious disease prediction using biosensors. *IEEE Sensors Journal, 23*(17). Available from https://doi.org/10.1109/JSEN.2023.3296897, http://ieeexplore.ieee.org/xpl/RecentIssue.jsp?punumber = 7361.

Ebada, A.I., Abdelrazek, S., & Elhenawy. I. (2020). Applying cloud based machine learning on biosensors streaming data for health status prediction. In *11th International Conference on Information, Intelligence, Systems and Applications, IISA 2020.* Institute of Electrical and Electronics Engineers Inc., Germany. <http://ieeexplore.ieee.org/xpl/mostRecentIssue.jsp?punumber = 9284145>, doi:10.1109/IISA50023.2020.9284349, 9781665422284.

Etemadi, M., Abkenar, S. B., Ahmadzadeh, A., Kashani, M. H., Asghari, P., Akbari, M., & Mahdipour, E. (2023). A systematic review of healthcare recommender systems: Open issues, challenges, and techniques. *Expert Systems with Applications, 213*118823. Available from https://doi.org/10.1016/j.eswa.2022.118823.

Haghi Kashani, M., Madanipour, M., Nikravan, M., Asghari, P., & Mahdipour, E. (2021). A systematic review of IoT in healthcare: Applications, techniques, and trends. *Journal of Network and Computer Applications, 192*103164. Available from https://doi.org/10.1016/j.jnca.2021.103164.

Hassantabar, S., Zhang, J., Yin, H., & Jha, N. K. (2022). MHDeep: Mental health disorder detection system based on wearable sensors and artificial neural networks. *ACM Transactions on Embedded Computing Systems, 21*(6). Available from https://doi.org/10.1145/3527170, http://dl.acm.org/citation.cfm?id = J840.

Janidarmian, M., Roshan Fekr, A., Radecka, K., & Zilic, Z. (2017). Multi-objective hierarchical classification using wearable sensors in a health application. *IEEE Sensors Journal, 17*(5). Available from https://doi.org/10.1109/JSEN.2016.2645511, http://ieeexplore.ieee.org/xpl/RecentIssue.jsp?punumber = 7361.

Kumar, M.S., & Dhulipala, V.S. (2020). *Fuzzy allocation model for health care data management on IoT assisted wearable sensor platform.*

Malasinghe, L. P., Ramzan, N., & Dahal, K. (2019). Remote patient monitoring: A comprehensive study. *Journal of Ambient Intelligence and Humanized Computing, 10*(1). Available from https://doi.org/10.1007/s12652-017-0598-x, http://www.springer.com/engineering/journal/12652.

Mirjalali, S., Peng, S., Fang, Z., Wang, C. H., & Wu, S. (2022). Wearable sensors for remote health monitoring: Potential applications for early diagnosis of Covid-19. *Advanced Materials Technologies, 7*(1). Available from https://doi.org/10.1002/admt.202100545, http://onlinelibrary.wiley.com/journal/10.1002/(ISSN)2365-709X.

Mousavi, E., Khademi, A., & Taaffe, K. (2020). Optimal sensor placement in a hospital operating room. *IISE Transactions on Healthcare Systems Engineering*. Available from https://doi.org/10.1080/24725579.2020.1790698, http://www.tandfonline.com/loi/uhse20.

Nagwanshi, K. K., Noonia, A., Tiwari, S., Doohan, N. V., Kumawat, V., Ahanger, T. A., & Amoatey, E. T. (2022). Wearable sensors with Internet of Things (IoT) and vocabulary-based acoustic signal processing for monitoring children's health. *Computational Intelligence and Neuroscience*, 2022. Available from https://doi.org/10.1155/2022/9737511, http://www.hindawi.com/journals/cin.

Nikravan, M., Jameii, S. M., & Kashani, M. H. (2011). An intelligent energy efficient QoS-routing scheme for WSN. *International Journal of advanced Engineering sciences and Technologies*, 8, 2011.

Sakib, M., & Pervez, S.S. (2023). Automated stress level detection for hospital nurses: A single triaxial wearable accelerometer sensor system approach. In *2023 20th International Conference on Electrical Engineering, Computing Science and Automatic Control, CCE 2023*. Institute of Electrical and Electronics Engineers Inc., Bangladesh. <http://ieeexplore.ieee.org/xpl/mostRecentIssue.jsp?punumber = 10332458>, Available from https://doi.org/10.1109/CCE60043.2023.10332832, 9798350306767.

Selvakarthi, D., Sivabalaselvamani, D., Wafiq, M.A., Aruna, G., & Gokulnath. M. (2023). An IoT integrated sensor technologies for the enhancement of hospital waste segregation and management. In *International Conference on Innovative Data Communication Technologies and Application, ICIDCA 2023 − Proceedings* (pp. 797−804). Institute of Electrical and Electronics Engineers Inc., India. <http://ieeexplore.ieee.org/xpl/mostRecentIssue.jsp?punumber = 10099475>, Available from https://doi.org/10.1109/ICIDCA56705.2023.10099836, 9798350397208.

Tu, J., Torrente-Rodríguez, R. M., Wang, M., & Gao, W. (2020). The era of digital health: A review of portable and wearable affinity biosensors. *Advanced Functional Materials*, 30(29). Available from https://doi.org/10.1002/adfm.201906713, http://onlinelibrary.wiley.com/journal/10.1002/(ISSN)1616-3028.

Umapathi, K., Vanitha, V., Anbarasu, L., Zivkovic, M., Bacanin, N., & Antonijevic, M. (2021). Predictive data regression technique based carbon nanotube biosensor for efficient patient health monitoring system. *Journal of Ambient Intelligence and Humanized Computing*. Available from https://doi.org/10.1007/s12652-021-03063-6, http://www.springer.com/engineering/journal/12652.

Wu, F., Wu, T., Zarate, D. C., Morfuni, R., Kerley, B., Hinds, J., Taniar, D., Armstrong, M., & Yuce, M. R. (2021). An autonomous hand hygiene tracking sensor system for prevention of hospital associated infections. *IEEE Sensors Journal*, 21(13). Available from https://doi.org/10.1109/JSEN.2020.3041331, http://ieeexplore.ieee.org/xpl/RecentIssue.jsp?punumber = 7361.

Xu, W., & Zhu, Z. (2023). Estimation for human motion posture and health using improved deep learning and nano biosensor. *International Journal of Computational Intelligence Systems*, 16(1). Available from https://doi.org/10.1007/s44196-023-00239-0, https://www.springer.com/journal/44196.

Yang, M., Guo, J., & Bai, L. (2020). A data privacy-preserving method for students' physical health monitoring by using smart wearable devices. In *Proceedings - IEEE 18th International Conference on Dependable, Autonomic and Secure Computing, IEEE 18th International Conference on Pervasive Intelligence and Computing, IEEE 6th International Conference on Cloud and Big Data Computing and IEEE 5th Cyber Science and Technology Congress, DASC/PiCom/CBDCom/CyberSciTech 2020* (pp. 29−34). Institute of Electrical and Electronics Engineers Inc., China. <http://ieeexplore.ieee.org/xpl/mostRecentIssue.jsp?punumber = 9251108>, Available from https://doi.org/10.1109/DASC-PCom-CBDCom-CyberSciTech49142.2020.00021, 9781728166094.

Yin, H., & Jha, N. K. (2017). A health decision support system for disease diagnosis based on wearable medical sensors and machine learning ensembles. *IEEE Transactions on Multi-Scale Computing Systems*, 3(4). Available from https://doi.org/10.1109/TMSCS.2017.2710194, https://www.ieee.org/membership-catalog/productdetail/showProductDetailPage.html?product = PER474-ELE&utm_source = Mainsite_CSE&utm_medium = CSE_Promotion&utm_campaign = Catalog_Promotion-PER474.

Zendehdel, G. A., Kaur, R., Chopra, I., Stakhanova, N., & Scheme, E. (2022). Automated security assessment framework for wearable BLE-enabled health monitoring devices. *ACM Transactions on Internet Technology*, 22 (1). Available from https://doi.org/10.1145/3448649, http://dl.acm.org/citation.cfm?id = J780.

Index

Note: Page numbers followed by "*f*" and "*t*" refer to figures and tables, respectively.

Printed and bound by CPI Group (UK) Ltd, Croydon, CR0 4YY

13/06/2025

01900651-0018